STENDHAL

STENDHAL was born Marie-Henri Beyle in Grenoble in 1783. He spent much of his lifetime in Italy and in 1800 he followed Napoleon's armies to Italy where he was a member of the French Ministry of War under Napoleon. In 1802 he returned to Paris to study and eventually obtained a place in the Commissariat. He served as an officer in Napoleon's army for eight years, taking part in many campaigns, including the retreat from Moscow. In 1814, with the fall of Napoleon, he retired to Milan, returning in 1821 to Paris where his first major work, *On Love,* was published in 1822. In 1831 he was appointed consul at Civita-Vecchia. He spent his remaining years either in Italy or Paris and died in Paris in 1842.

Stendhal's writings published during his lifetime include biographies of Haydn and Rossini, a history of Italian painting, *Armance* (1827), *Walks in Rome* (1829, *The Red and the Black* (1830), and *The Charterhouse of Parma* (1839). *Memoirs of Egotism* (1832), *The Life of Henri Brulard* (1835), *Lucien Leuwen* (1834), and *Lamiel* (1840) were not published until interest in Stendhal was revived during the 1880's and 1890's.

The Private Diaries of
STENDHAL

(MARIE-HENRI BEYLE)

Edited and Translated by
Robert Sage

The Norton Library
W · W · NORTON & COMPANY · INC ·
NEW YORK

FIRST PUBLISHED IN THE NORTON LIBRARY 1962

By arrangement with Doubleday and Company, Inc.

W. W. Norton & Company, Inc. is also the publisher of
The Norton Anthology of English Literature, edited by M. H.
Abrams, Robert M. Adams, David Daiches, E. Talbot Donaldson,
George H. Ford, Samuel Holt Monk, and Hallett Smith; *The Ameri-
can Tradition in Literature,* edited by Sculley Bradley, Richmond
Croom Beatty, and E. Hudson Long; *World Masterpieces,* edited
by Maynard Mack, Kenneth Douglas, Howard E. Hugo, Bernard
M. W. Knox, John C. McGalliard, P. M. Pasinetti, and René Wellek;
and other fine anthologies.

Printed in the United States of America

Contents

Introduction

Nosce te ipsum.

THE ERRATIC genius of Henri Beyle, dissipating itself in false starts and abrupt terminations, essaying all forms of literary expression before belatedly stumbling on the one to which it was best suited, was composed of as many conflicting forces as the period in which he lived.

Born in 1783, he belonged to that artistically unproductive generation which began life during the last years of the *ancien régime,* passed its childhood amid the turbulent events of the French Revolution, and came of age in the Napoleonic epoch, only to spend its energy in action, die on the battlefield, or be bribed into silence by a job-giving emperor who was well aware of what literature had done to the Bourbons. Beyle, an isolated figure, was almost the only French writer of talent who remained faithful to his vocation through the Revolution, the Consulate and Empire, the Bourbon Restoration, and the Monarchy of July.

That he was able to maintain his equilibrium while buffeted by the shifting winds of a stormy transition was due in large measure to the fact that the conflict without was equaled, even surpassed, by the conflict within. For Beyle was one of those rare beings who possessed a philosopher's lucid intellect coupled with a poet's delicate sensibility. In theory a cynical "seducer of women," a Valmont of the *ancien régime,* he was in practice as shy and soulful a wooer as any descendant of Mme. de Staël could have desired. As a youth he could derive equal stimulation from the dry logic of Helvétius and the exuberant sentimentality of Rousseau. Thus he stood, in inclination as in birth, midway between the cold classicism of the eighteenth century and the feverish romanticism of the early nineteenth. His inner conflict gave him points of contact with the two extremes of the transition, but, too passionate to be satisfied with the one and too intelligent to be taken in by the other, he could never entirely adapt himself to his age, could never subscribe to the doctrines of a single party. Among his contemporaries, the older men looked on him as too advanced, the younger men as too old-fashioned, the general public as incomprehensible and eccentric.

Almost certainly he would have found the twentieth century more congenial than his own, for, among so many contradictions, there was one fundamental constant that made his spirit altogether modern. It was his unflagging gusto for what he called *the knowledge of the human heart* and what we today should call psychology. Since become a more or less exact science, it was then merely a vague philosophical concept, common enough coin with the pre-revolutionary writers, but largely withdrawn from circulation with the decline of creative thought during the Napoleonic epoch and the rise of romanticism in the years that followed it. And his appeal to the modern reader rather than to the one of his day is to be explained by the fact that, at a time when others were attaining popularity through florid descriptions of puppets moving before unreal settings, he continued to write in his unadorned style about the passions and mores he had painstakingly studied in the life around him. He was justified in hoping to be read in 1935. The passage of a century has rubbed little of the freshness off his works, while the mighty ones who preceded and immediately succeeded him, Chateaubriand and Mme. de Staël, Lamartine and Victor Hugo, even to some extent Balzac, already seem to be speaking the language of another world.

Beyle determined early in life to become an "observer of the human heart," and, his profession once chosen, set out methodically to perfect himself in it. Studying the works of the great writers and witnessing the plays of the leading dramatists was one way to acquire knowledge of the human heart. To read history and memoirs was another. To observe real people in action and to compare the mores of the present with those of the past was an even better means. Withal, it was imperative to be constantly in society, to talk to men and make love to women. But the most trustworthy of all ways to know the human heart was through honest and relentless self-analysis, for only by experiencing a thing personally could one be absolutely sure that it was authentic. The rest was guesswork, valuable but unproven and unprovable. Did not the "divine" Shakespeare himself, the greatest observer of the human heart that ever lived, say, "Thou canst not speak of what thou dost not feel"?

Here, then, we have the basic reason why Beyle kept his diaries, and kept them with surprising regularity for fourteen years while scores of other projects, entered upon with warm enthusiasm, were quickly discarded from discouragement or loss of interest. *"Nosce te ipsum,* know thyself," he wrote. "My means is this diary . . . It aims at being a mathematical and rigid report on my manner of being, neither too favorable nor too unfavorable, but stating purely and severely what I believe to have taken place . . . It is a written part of my intimate consciousness."

By chronicling his sensations, thoughts, opinions, and actions from day to day, in varying moods and under the varying circumstances of life, he hoped to end up by possessing precious data on the mechanism of that strange animal, man. The extreme "egotism" with which he has sometimes been reproached was in reality only a means to an end, for, as he later said, "egotism, *provided it be sincere,* is one way of portraying the human heart."

For Beyle, the most subjective and unliterary of literary men, as he was one of the most imaginative and least inventive, the diaries offered an ideal form of self-expression. He had a positive mania for "putting black on white": thinking and writing were almost synonymous. Immediately a thought came to his mind, the impulse was to jot it down somewhere, anywhere, on the margin of a book or manuscript if one were within reach, in the dust on the furniture if it were not; there were even occasions when he scratched notes on his bedroom slippers, his suspenders, or across the crystal of his watch. Throughout his youth the diaries served as the principal recipient for this torrent of egotism. Everything went into them: the most intimate details of his love affairs; his impressions—largely unfavorable—of plays, books, and his fellow men; his own rare triumphs and frequent blunders; his experiences in the army, as a functionary and *dandy* of the Empire; amid the suave *dolce far niente* of Italy; his medical prescriptions and his amatory theories; his dreams and disgusts; his reflections on the manners and morals of his century; his everlasting pursuit of elusive womanhood; his extravagant ambitions and his humiliating setbacks—all the thousand and one things that held his attention a minute or a decade during the period when his destiny, like that of France, was linked to the fortunes of Napoleon. He writes of his intimate being with the disconcerting candor and informality of a man thinking aloud. He holds nothing back: why should he? He himself is his only audience.

From this results the unique quality of his diaries. The published records of most other diarists have been written after the fresh enthusiasm, the trials and errors, the intellectual curiosity of youth have passed. The style of these men was already formed; they knew life and usually they had an eye on a possible future reader. Under such circumstances, omissions, reticences, embellishments, a concern with the manner of presentation, a deliberate placing of accent are inevitable. Nothing of the kind is to be found in Beyle's diaries, which were written with total lack of self-consciousness during his impressionable years, without any thought of eventual publication, solely in an earnest effort to know the human heart by knowing himself. Even he, honest egotist that he was, never attained the same degree of naked sincerity in his other writings, most of which—whether they be classified as fiction, essays, criticism, travel, or autobiography—are little more than a disguised continuation of his youthful diary, but no longer destined for himself alone.

Seeking knowledge of the human heart represented to him a way of setting out on the *chasse au bonheur,* the pursuit of happiness, and this, in the Beylistic code, was sufficient justification for any act. But, too utilitarian to be content with knowledge that did not serve a practical purpose, he had an underlying reason for acquainting himself with the hidden springs of human conduct: it was his ambition to become not only a "seducer of women" but also "the successor of Molière," to be a writer of comedies in verse, to exhibit the nobleness and ridicule of mankind on the stage. "I've had the good fortune to have made up my mind very young," he congratulated himself. "From earliest childhood, as far back as I can remember, I've wanted to be a comic poet. All the operations of my body, mind, and soul have taken place with this end in view."

His passionate desire to become a great "dramatic-bard," which has been missed or little stressed by many of his biographers, should be apparent to even the most casual reader of the diaries. In the first pages we find him as a young sub-lieutenant in Italy rushing off to the theater as soon as he reaches a new town, exploring the shelves of the local bookseller for plays he has not read, scribbling dramatic notes, diligently scouting about for Italian plays that might be adapted in French. Later, in Paris, we see him going night after night to the pit of the Théâtre Français, severely criticizing plays and actors, filling his notebooks with theories of dramaturgy, reflecting on the rules of comedy, trying to expand Hobbes's definition of laughter. We see him struggling with the refractory Alexandrines of his own *The Two Men* and working for years over the plot of his ambitious but never-finished *Letellier.* We see him in optimistic moments drawing up lists of his future plays and calculating the probable fortune he will make from them, in moments of discouragement anxiously searching for the ages of the leading comic poets when their first plays were produced. We see him copying and analyzing the jokes told by his friends to discover why they are funny, studying the manners and morals of his century in order to choose the phases best lending themselves to ridicule, again in the theater, this time with an open copy of the play on his knees to check the places where the audience laughs and to find out why. He obsequiously cultivates the acquaintance of rhymesters and third-rate playwrights; he is flattered to go backstage and shyly talk with the people of the theater; two of the three mistresses who figure in the diaries are actresses. And the late Paul Valéry of the Académie Française, could write in all seriousness, "It is difficult to understand why Stendhal did not devote himself to the theater, for which everything destined him"!

If Stendhal let some of the best years of his life go by without writing for publication, if he turned to the novel only when he was well over forty, it was precisely because he had persisted in the illusion that he was destined for the theater. In his thirties and early forties he wrote a handful of books about the things that interested him—music, painting, travel, love, literature. But these he regarded as merely stopgaps: he was still waiting for that tardy "moment of genius" which would permit him to appear in what he believed were his true colors, those of a comic poet. The truth, which he stubbornly refused to admit for so many years, was that nothing qualified him for the theater. Totally lacking in a poetic sense, he spent hours tying together twelve syllables that formed a stiff, prosaic, and sometimes incorrect Alexandrine. He had none of the inventiveness and dexterity required for comic situations. And, never capable of submitting to the discipline of form, he was hopelessly cramped and ill at ease when fenced in by the rigid technique of the still classical stage. An excellent dramatic critic and theorist he was, as his diary and notes attest, but the many unfinished plays he has left are conclusive proof that the theater was not his destiny.

It would be futile to speculate on what Stendhal might have accomplished had be concentrated his efforts from the outset on becoming a novelist. The French novel in the days of his youth had not yet come into its own; the taste of the *ancien régime* was still dominant, and, for a budding author as imbued as he was with "the love of glory," the theater was the natural outlet for artistic expression. When the day finally came for him to discover that the novel was better suited than the theater to both his own talent and the taste of the new generation, the observations of the human heart recorded in his diaries served him just as well for the medium in which he was to succeed as for that in which he had failed.

These diaries also served to form his highly individual style, a subject with which, contrary to widespread belief, he was concerned all his life. But instead of worrying about rhythm, word values, well-rounded periods, and other literary niceties, he sought to be natural, simple, and truthful, to combine concision with piquancy, to hold the reader's interest by sprightliness, pithiness, and quick transitions. Three sentences written in his youth sum up his creed:

"A man may be said to possess a style if, upon coming across a phrase in a newspaper, you can say that it is written by him."

"Style should be like a transparent varnish . . . ; it should spread completely over the colors, make them brighter, but not alter them."

"My style will have a character all its own by scoffing a bit at everyone; it will be apt and concise, and won't put the reader to sleep."

This style, which so admirably fitted Beyle's individuality and which the diaries show in the making, is not the smoothest reading in the world. It is broken up; the sentences are divided into short, direct statements separated, more or less arbitrarily, by commas, semicolons, or colons; the structure is frequently slipshod; the same word may be repeated a half dozen times in as many lines; now and then a passage of lyric beauty appears in the midst of carelessly worded trivialities. At all times, however, it has the charm of being as natural and spontaneous as conversation. Rapid and stripped of all excess wordage, yet possessing a flexibility that permits an abrupt ending as readily as the addition of afterthoughts, it is an ideal vehicle for a man whose mind moves faster than his pen, and who feels so intensely what he is saying that he has no time to reflect on how he is going to say it.

Always intent on communicating sensations and imparting information, Beyle likewise paid little attention to form and proportion. Yet by a curious accident this diary, written piecemeal over a fourteen-year period of his capricious life, possesses more form than most of the books he wrote for publication. It has a definite beginning, middle, and end; it has unity and infinite variety; it is quite capable of standing by itself as a work of literature.

Roughly speaking, the diary is the pendant and sequel of *Vie de Henry Brulard,* for it starts at almost the exact point where the unfinished autobiography leaves off. There is, however, a vast difference between the two books: *Henry Brulard* is a synthesis, written in the last years of his life, far from the events, after the perspective had been altered by the passage of time: the diary is an analysis, written on the spot, when the events and reactions are still fresh. The Henry Brulard who joyfully reaches the Italian wonderland in the closing pages of the autobiography is not the Henri Beyle who composes the first pages of his diary a few months later. The one is the creation of an elderly man's fond memory; the other is the reality. Both the man and the boy are trying to tell the truth, but only the latter approximately succeeds. And his honest and intimate record of the years when he was seeking to know his complex self forms an invaluable document for those who today share his conviction that the best way of all to go forth on "the pursuit of happiness" is to study the human heart.

A BOOK as spirited as the diaries of Henri Beyle should, in my opinion, be edited for the general reader rather than for the specialist. Consequently, I have reduced to a minimum the notes and references that abound in the French editions. I have not been able, however, to keep them out of the book altogether. Since Beyle wrote his diaries only for himself, he continually speaks of people and events without bothering to introduce them, and he sometimes treats of a minor episode lengthily while failing to make any mention of a major one. In order that the reader may be familiar with the circumstances of the author's life without being repeatedly interrupted by footnotes, I have divided the diaries into thirteen parts, prefacing each with a narrative outline aimed at providing the background necessary for a full appreciation of the text.

I have been as sparing as possible of footnotes, confining them for the most part to some of the commentaries Beyle himself wrote on the margins of his diaries. In the detailed index at the end will be found biographical data on the principal persons mentioned.

Such words as "soul," "passions," "tender," and "sublime," which are only employed rarely and with caution by modern writers in English, I have preserved, for more familiar substitutes would have distorted Beyle's thought and manner of expression. I have filled certain gaps of the diaries proper with short autobiographical extracts from the author's voluminous correspondence—otherwise, it would have been necessary to pass over in silence such essential portions as his strange courtship of Victorine Mounier and nearly the whole of his experiences with Napoleon's army in Russia. (Incidentally, to get the complete picture of this period of his life, one would have to read not only the diaries but the two volumes of his *Pensées,* the first volume of his *Mélanges Intimes,* the first four volumes of his *Correspondance,* the three volumes of his *Théâtre,* the second volume of his *Mélanges de Littérature,* the four volumes of *Lettres à Stendhal,* and, of course, *Vie de Henry Brulard.*)

As the diaries are filled with initials, I have, in each case where the identity is not doubtful, placed the full name with no indication that it is not spelled out in the original—thus, where Beyle writes M. D., I have substituted M. Daru, instead of M. D[aru], as the French editors have done.

The complete text of Beyle's diaries—taking up nearly two thousand pages in the five-volume Martineau edition—contains considerable matter (as the interminable discussions of forgotten plays and books) that is of minor interest to the English-speaking reader of today. As this translation is for the general reader rather than the student, such passages have been omitted—as have the scattered fragments written after the 1801–14 period. I have respected the delightfully incorrect English with which Beyle peppered his diaries, apparently in the naïve belief that this would baffle a possible eavesdropper, but his youthful frankness of expression has obliged me in a few instances to modify his terms or resort to the unsatisfactory makeshift of dashes. As for the translation itself, my aim has been at all times to make it as informal and swift as the original.

The *Journal de Stendhal* was first published by Casimir Stryienski and François de Nion in the very incomplete and defective Charpentier edition of 1888. Further portions appeared in 1911 in Paul Arbelet's excellent *Journal d'Italie,* published by Calmann-Levy. Only in 1923 did the complete text, edited and annotated by Henry Debraye and Louis Royer, begin appearing in the Champion edition, but the last of the five Champion volumes was not published until eleven years later. In 1937, Henri Martineau, who has scrutinized every word in the jumble of Stendhalian manuscripts (many of them illegibly written) in the Grenoble library and elsewhere, issued the diaries in a slightly different and fuller form in his monumental Divan edition of Stendhal's complete works. This version, with some corrections and additions, has recently appeared in the Pléiade india-paper volume devoted to Stendhal's autobiographical writings.

In the preparation of the present translation, the French texts of both the Debraye-Royer and the Martineau editions have been used, preference being given to the latter, which is more recent and more reliable. I have likewise had recourse to the texts and abundant notes of the entire seventy-five volumes of the Divan (Martineau) edition and the twoscore volumes of the uncompleted Champion edition, to the editors of which I hereby make grateful acknowledgment. As for the many other works consulted, particular mention should be made of those by the late Paul Arbelet and especially by M. Martineau, who has devoted his life to the study of Stendhal, and whose impressive knowledge of the subject in its most minute details is distilled into his two-volume biography, *Le Coeur de Stendhal,* which appeared after this translation was completed.

The *Notice* of Romain Colomb and the two essays of Prosper Mérimée will always remain essential source works, but, unless balanced by the reading of later and more thorough researches, they are hopelessly misleading. The same may be said of Arthur Chuquet's *Stendhal-Beyle,* which is a rare example of erudition led astray by prejudice. There are countless other books on Stendhal in French, English, and German, but everything important they have to say—and much, much more—is to be found (minus their errors) in the numerous writings of Henri Martineau, certainly one of the most faithful, conscientious, and meticulous biographers since Boswell.

Robert Sage

Paris

NOTE

The passages of his diaries
that Beyle wrote in English
are printed in small capitals.

The Private Diaries of Stendhal

"The Aurora of Life"

THESE diaries open with the brief jottings, immature, frequently naïve, sometimes unexpectedly perspicacious, of an alert provincial boy of eighteen years who already knows his mind and who, coming abruptly into contact with real life for the first time, sets out solemnly to keep a day-by-day record of his actions, observations and sensations.

"The aurora of my life," Henri Beyle afterward called the period from June 1800 to December 1801, when he was wandering through Milan and the little towns of Lombardy and Piedmont with the soldiers of the First Consul's army. It was both his first taste of freedom and the beginning of his lifelong passion for Italy. New and strange and wonderful for this ardent, inexperienced lad were Italian women, Italian nature, Italian music and Italian *dolce far niente*. To the end they remained the most desirable things in life, just as the months spent in their midst remained the most enchanting memory of his youth. Nearly twoscore years later, when he wrote *La Chartreuse de Parme* at the full maturity of his wayward genius, he turned back with the sentimental fondness of an old lover to his recollections of Bonaparte's invasion of 1800 to describe that of 1796, which he had not witnessed.

It was by one of those mere chances which trace the path of a career that he crossed the St. Bernard and the luxuriant plains of Lombardy at the impressionable age of seventeen years and five months as a supernumerary in a French army of 40,000 men. He had but recently emerged from a lonely, frustrated childhood, saddened by the premature death of his dearly loved mother and passed with books and daydreams among gloomy adults in his native Grenoble.[1] After graduating from the local school with the highest honors in mathematics, he had started out for Paris, ostensibly to enter the Ecole Polytechnique, but with the secret

[1] The complex story of his childhood is told by Stendhal in his *Vie de Henry Brulard*.

resolution to set himself up as "a seducer of women" and "the successor of Molière." He did neither. In the capital, where he arrived on the morrow of General Bonaparte's coup d'état at Saint-Cloud, he floundered pitifully, fell ill and was at length rescued by some cousins, the Daru family, who were to act willy-nilly as his benefactors throughout the Consulate and Empire.

His particular protector was the eldest son of the family, Pierre Daru, brilliant, pompous, possessed of a cold driving force that was to win him honor after honor in the Empire and to make him Napoleon's right-hand man. In all their fifteen years of association, neither he nor Beyle had the slightest sympathy for the other. The mighty Pierre was aloofly and severely kind to a relative whom he considered a scatterbrained youth, while Beyle was sullenly respectful toward a cousin who was in a position to gain him favors but whose affected and pedantic character he loathed. At the outset of their relations it was merely to relieve his family of a troublesome problem that Pierre, little realizing what he had let himself in for, found Beyle work at the War Office and, a few months later, allowed him to follow the army to Italy.

On that sunny June morning in 1800 when Beyle, uniformless and jobless, blithely rode into Milan, the city was passing through an animated, colorful and slightly hysterical period of its history. At twilight, Milanese society gathered on the Corso di Porta Orientale, formerly a Spanish rampart, which commanded a magnificent view over the surrounding countryside. Here, following an old Italian custom, the women, accompanied by their cavalier servants, would drive the length of the Corso, then draw up for an hour of gossip before continuing to the cafés for their ices. The same society was to be found in the evening at the Teatro della Scala. In the loges of the aristocratic second tier, each owned and furnished by a prominent family and passed down from generation to generation, husbands, cavalier servants and unattached bachelors joined the women to while away a few hours talking, munching ices, gambling and making love.

After the opera came the dances—often fancy-dress balls—at which, through the soft summer nights, the scantily clad beauties of the pleasure-loving capital waltzed and flirted alike with their townsmen and their foreign conquerors.

These arrogant warriors from the Transalpine were everywhere. They made their way toward the carriages of the prettiest women, insolently pushing aside the local aspirants and unfortunate cavalier servants. A bit later the staccato tones of French drowned out the thick Milanese accent in the Caffè dei Servi. At night the streets were clamorous with carousing soldiers, and the taverns resounded with their brawls. The officers came unasked to the loges of the Scala, invaded the parties and balls, appropriated the mistresses of the civilians. The army was enjoying itself boisterously, and, in the military tradition, took its pleasures where they were to be found. Noblewomen, actresses, bourgeois housewives, shopkeepers' daughters, prostitutes—the soldiers loved them all.

In this whole frivolous, army-occupied, tumultuous city, Henri Beyle was perhaps the only French youth who had no amorous victories to boast about when the soldiers met for their ices at the Caffè dei Servi. Fresh from the gloomy atmosphere of Grenoble, too bashful, too proud, too fastidious, too grotesquely bookish and romantic to become a vulgar intruder or promiscuous philanderer like the others, he wistfully witnessed the colorful spectacle of Milan from the sidelines, regarding it as something infinitely desirable but utterly unattainable.

Although merely an onlooker, he was conscious from the very first of a serene happiness at being in the congenial atmosphere of Lombardy. He experienced moments of strange exaltation: walking through the streets, he had the impression of finding the materialization of his childhood dreamworld; he was enthralled by this exciting new life that surged about him; the mists descending over the Corso and the warm summer rains beating down on the verdure gave him "delightful sensations." His love for Milan was one of the first of his great loves and it was the most enduring—he even requested that the words, "Arrigo Beyle, Milanese," be placed on his tombstone.

His sensations were especially poignant in the great auditorium of the Scala, where the vivacious and sensual melodies of eighteenth-century operas mingled with the low murmur of voices and the subtle odor of perfume floating down from the loges. Here, while the elegant Milanese were assembling in their loges, Beyle, shabbily dressed, found a place in the plebeian pit. Being unable to participate in any of the charming nonsense that went on above him, he could only look on enviously and, when the curtain went up, devote his entire attention to the opera. This was an original reason for going to the Scala in 1800; but the opera was a magnificent compensation for his disappointments. Ignorant of all the arts, literature excepted, he was carried away by this spirited music, so irresistible, so easy to understand. A decade later he wrote in his diary, "This theater has had a great influence on my character. If ever I amuse myself by describing how my character was formed by the events of my youth, the Teatro della Scala will be in the front rank."

Pierre Daru at length arranged for Beyle to do clerical work under Claude Petiet, who had been appointed Governor of Lombardy with the title of Minister Extraordinary. Given lodgings in the Casa Bovara, which also served as the French Embassy, Beyle spent the rest of the year in the very center of Milanese life. The Embassy windows looked out on the Corso di Porta Orientale, and in the evenings the city's society gathered at the Casa Bovara for the dinners and balls given by the Governor. But all this brilliance was of no avail to the obscure clerk named Beyle. "Being nothing in Milan at the home of Monsieur and Madame Petiet," he wrote later, "and already having too much pride to make any advances, I passed my days in an excessive tenderness full of melancholy."

On the headquarters staff he had several good friends, who formed a rough-and-ready band, flippant, coarse in manner and bawdy in conversation. The most important was the "incomparable" Martial Daru, Pierre's philandering younger brother, who was now diligently seeking new conquests on the happy hunting grounds of Milan. Principal among the others were handsome Edouard Cardon, a friend of the Darus and now aide-de-camp to Carnot; Alexandre and Augustin Petiet, sons of the Minister; Augustin Marignier and Henri Mazeau, respectively distinguished and vulgar, and Louis Joinville, an indulgent commissary and assistant to Pierre Daru.

Firmly convinced of his own superiority, Beyle nevertheless sincerely envied the swagger of his army comrades, their vulgar boisterousness and, above all, their facile triumphs in amour. "I saw Joinville, Mazeau . . . and others succeed," he said. "I saw them do things I felt I could do better; they were happy, had mistresses. I didn't budge. I was waiting for some romantic accident, like the breakdown of a carriage, etc., so that fate might reveal my heart to some sensitive soul."

At length a "sensitive soul"—or so the daydreaming Beyle believed—did appear, in the form of Angiola Pietragrua (whom he calls Angela or Angelina), the mistress of Louis Joinville, who was not her first lover nor by any means her last. She was the wife of a minor civil servant and the daughter of shopkeepers. Although the mother of a six-year-old son, she was only in her twenty-fourth year. She was a majestic brunette with a magnificent body, sharply delineated features, ardent dark eyes and sensual, expressive lips. Accompanying her undeniable charm, there was an indecorous heartiness and an easy familiarity which for an objective observer might have suggested vulgarity. But the smitten Beyle saw only her "grace filled with voluptuousness," and he "loved her beyond all expression." For him she became the personification of Italy: he confessed that he loved the Italian language because her memory was associated with it, that he had an unreasonable affection for every object in Milan because it belonged to the city in which she lived. He never entirely recovered from his love for this "sublime wench." It took him fifteen years to see her as she was—a frivolous and deceitful woman, a "wench" without the "sublime."

Realizing that there was not the least chance of possessing her at present, his thoughts gamboled off into the future. "Not being able to be loved by Signora Pietragrua, who was loved by Louis, in the millions of castles in Spain that I built for her I pictured myself returning one day as a colonel or having some promotion superior to that of being one of M. Daru's employees, kissing her and bursting into tears." A naïve dream, to be sure, Angela being what she was: strangely enough, it happened to be one of the few that came true.

But eleven years were to elapse before that occurred. In the interval many other things were in store for him. One of the most unfortunate, in fact, can be dated from this period. Although details are lacking, it is reasonable to suppose that, no "sensitive souls" being readily accessible, Beyle ended up by following the soldiers to the city's brothels. In any case, he contracted the venereal disease which, apparently inadequately treated, cast a deep shadow over his early Italian adventures and plagued him periodically the rest of his life.

Thus it is that, when his diary opens in the spring of 1801, ten months after his arrival, it reveals him morosely occupied with febrifuges, purgatives and emetics; now and then he has recourse to leeches, those inevitable old cure-alls; his fevers and vomitings are recorded with depressing scrupulosity. There is little evidence of the "excessive happiness" he experienced in Italy to be found in the first pages of his diary: for that, one must look in his letters to his beloved little sister Pauline, and especially his notes and books of later life.

In September 1800, Pierre Daru had obtained him a provisional sub-lieutenancy on some vague merit officially described as "good conduct and talents." A month later this erstwhile functionary who had never served as a common soldier had his commission confirmed. He was now given the resplendent uniform of a dragoon officer—gilt helmet with dappled fur and flowing plume of horsehair, green jacket with scarlet trimmings, leather breeches, high riding boots. After lingering on in Milan another two months, he belatedly joined the 6th Dragoons near Brescia, where eighteen cavalry divisions were concentrated in the expectation of new fighting with the Austrians.

Life with the Dragoons was not to his liking, and he was only too happy to be sent back in December on a nebulous "mission" to Milan, where he strolled on the Corso, dreamed in the Scala and timidly courted Angelina while his regiment, finally seeing action, crossed the Mincio and saved the army's right wing after a furious combat. Beyle received a certificate stating that he had "distinguished himself" at Mincio—but the certificate was made out four years later by an indulgent general to aid him in finding a job.

This general was a paternal Jacobin named Claude Michaud, who, upon Beyle's assurance that Pierre Daru would be delighted, took the young sub-lieutenant as his aide-de-camp. Beyle had at last found an army post that appealed to him: he began to regard himself as "an art lover attached to the army for the purpose of looking on, but destined to write comedies like Molière." Henceforth he was to devote as much time as possible to literature and as little as possible to military duties.

Being the general's aide-de-camp was very pleasant indeed. He visited the little towns of northern Italy and reveled in the beauties of the countryside; now and then he made a trip to Milan; on no occasion did his work seriously interfere with his life as a dilettante.

This state of affairs came to an end at the close of the summer of 1801, when Daru, nettled at Beyle's having left his regiment, ordered him to return at once and prove to his comrades that "he was flattered to serve like them and with them." Overwhelmed by this blow, Beyle stayed on with the easygoing Michaud as long as he could, and then reported to his regiment at Bra, where he again plunged into his studies.

His fever persisted and his boredom increased. Glumly he set out to track down the source of happiness. "The best resolution to make," he wrote his sister, "is to try to adapt ourselves to our situation and to derive the greatest possible fund of happiness from it. That's the only genuine philosophy." Excellent counsel, but he himself made no attempt to apply it. The truth was that Beyle's enthusiasms, like those of all passionate men, were as short-lived as they were intense: he had already had enough of life in the army, and he was even tiring of Italy.

Moreover, his health was really bad; besides his fever, he was suffering from the results of fording an icy stream. The doctor detected "some symptoms of nostalgia and melancholy," the leeches were again applied, the colonel, worried, spoke of a furlough. Righteously Beyle replied that, sick or well, it was his duty to remain with his regiment. It was no more than a feeble flicker of heroism. The next day he asked for a leave; a week later he was fuming because it had not been granted; in another fortnight he was on his way to Grenoble. The first Italian adventure was over.

1801   Lombardy

Milan, 28 Germinal, Year IX [April 18, 1801].—I'm undertaking to write the history of my life day by day. I don't know whether I'll have the fortitude to carry out this plan, which I already started in Paris. There's a mistake in French already; there will be a lot more, because I'm making it a rule not to stand on ceremony and never to erase. If I have the courage to do so, I'll go back to 2 Ventôse [February 21], the day I left Milan to rejoin Lieutenant General Michaud in Verona.

28 Germinal.—On the slope outside the castle, I saw the maneuvers of the cavalry and mounted artillery of the second Polish Legion, coming from the Army of the Rhine to proceed, so they say, to Florence, where they'll be established in the pay of the new Grand Duke; some thirty of the best officers have left because of that. The cavalry, in blue coats and crimson piping, armed with hussars' sabers and spears with little tricolored banners, wheeled about several times very adroitly. Generals Moncey, Davout and Michaud attended in full-dress uniform.

29 Germinal [April 19].—Minister Petiet received an extraordinary post from Paris announcing that Paul I had been found dead in his bed on March 20. It's expected that this death will bring about great changes.

I've just been to the ball at Angélique's. Gibory told Ferdinand that he's discarded Signora Martin. I think I saw her going up as I was coming down.

10 Floréal [April 30].—I'm still in Milan. The 6th Dragoons passed on their way to Piedmont, where Lieutenant General Delmas is in command of the soldiery under the orders of General Jourdan, who has a viceroy's authority. Today there was a big celebration on the castle square in honor of peace. They laid the cornerstone of the *Foro Bonaparte*. In the evening, a paltry little fireworks display. A rather tiresome lyric show at the big theater and a ball where respectable women danced.

11 Floréal [May 1].—I'm leaving for Bergamo tomorrow. Martial is going to Florence, Marignier to Bologna. M. Daru has drawn up a voluminous draft resolution on the organization of the army in peacetime. The First Consul was pleased with it and invited him to come to Malmaison to discuss it. There's much war talk. Moreau has received the order to remain with his army, and Augereau to return at once to his. Adjutant Commander Mathys, who came from Bergamo the ninth for the celebration, returned this afternoon. Since I've stopped thinking of Signora Martin, now Saladini, I've read a great deal of La Harpe. I've read Volumes I, II, III, IV, V, VI, VII and VIII of his *Lycée*. I reflected deeply on the dramatic art as I reread the verses of *Selmours*.[1] They didn't seem to me as bad as when I was writing them. I want to learn how to compose them, as it would be better if *Les Quiproquos*[2] were in verse.

12 Floréal [May 2].—The Italians have found the secret of denaturing Regnard's *Le Légataire Universel*. I didn't stay for the second play, but went to play lotto at the café of the Porta Orientale. The road from Milan to Bergamo is superb and in the most beautiful land in the world.

[1] A play Beyle had written—or rather, copied—from a story by Florian.
[2] Another of his childhood plays.

At Canonica, a village twenty miles from Milan and ten from Bergamo, situated on the Adda, there's one of the most beautiful views possible. The one from the town of Bergamo is less attractive and infinitely more extensive. From the Casa Terzi, where General Michaud is staying, the Apennines, twenty-five leagues away, can be seen quite clearly. The details can be made out very well with a twenty-inch Ramsden spyglass which the general has. There are two theaters here, a splendid one in the Borgo, which is the part of the town situated on the plain, the other, built of wood, in the square of the old town. We go to the latter every night, as it's quite near the place where we're staying. The other is a half hour away. Signora Nota has the reputation of being the prettiest woman in town, and really she's not bad; they say she has an income of 60,000 livres; she has a *cavaliere servente,* a fine-looking man who spends a great deal on her; she's consequently unattackable. We might —— two countesses who are staying near us, but they are twenty-eight or thirty years old and have a dirty look which is repellent.

19 Floréal [*May 9*].—For dinner, the general had Citizen Foy, the future general, chief of the 5th Regiment of Light Artillery, adjutant commander of the 9th Light Cavalry Regiment. He's a young military man, small in stature and large in promise, full of ambition and attainments. The others, generally speaking, are jealous of him, although they do him justice. Besides, he has defects of character—a spirit of contradiction and a pronounced arrogance. He stole a carriage at Bergamo.

I took a fencing master about the 18th.

I raced through the seventh volume of Voltaire's works, the twenty-first of the *Mémoires Secrets de la République des Lettres, La Description du Palais-Royal,* and *La Cabane Mystérieuse,* which I brought with me from Milan. I have been greatly bored by the lack of books. The chief lent us the Abbé Coyer's *Voyage en Italie.* A worthless book. I read a few of Mallet du Pan's *Mercures Britanniques.*

The 21st, they gave Federici's *Avventuriere Notturno,* a play that might be done in French; there's nothing here but *Il Teatro Moderno Applaudito,* a set of forty or forty-five volumes. If it hasn't already been done in France, a nice semi-drama could be made of it.

The 22nd, the general gave a luncheon for Adjutant Commander Delord, employed by General Moncey, whom he addresses in the second person singular. General Moncey is under forty-five. Dalbon and Combe have stolen 100,000 écus. Delord is a very amiable man, genuine good breeding. He came here to see Mme. ——, his mistress, with whom he's been living for three months. They say she's made him spend 200 louis. He's still in mufti.

General Franceschi, who left the staff two weeks ago, is a poltroon. He's rumored to have made two or three millions through contemptible extortions and through having eighty or a hundred commands in Corsica, which he handed out to the highest bidders.

23 Floréal [May 13].—Alpy, Farine and Picoteau came to see General Michaud. I had fever tonight.

25 Floréal [May 15].—They left about two hours ago. Alpy was crying; the general showed quite a bit of emotion. The general was anxious because of his departure. The general said to Alpy, "I'm very fond of that little Beyle, he's full of spirit. I'd like to get him his aide-de-camp's commission, but he's too outspoken, too trenchant."

Alpy left me his mare for 100 écus. I gave him 183 lire from my pay for Vendémiaire and Germinal. I made out an IOU for the remaining 127 lire, which he took reluctantly. I've got about 90 lire left.

27 Floréal [May 17].—A dose of quinine greatly reduced my fever. The players gave *La Prevenzione Paternella* today. A priest accuses his brother of all sorts of crimes; a general, whose daughter the other is to marry, believing himself to be betrayed, has him sentenced to death. The villain is discovered, and all ends well.

28 Floréal [May 18].—Foy took over the command of Bergamo; he has an inflammation in one testicle.

I had a very strong attack of fever last night; I have a mind to ask the general for permission to go to Milan for a day to consult M. Gonel.

They gave *Epicharide e Nerone,* not a bad tragedy, here last night.

29 Floréal [May 19].—My servant arrived from Milan with my two horses. Couldn't a play be written with the title, *La Soldatomanie* or *La Manie du Militaire?*

1 Prairial [May 21].—My daily fever continues. I went to Milan to consult M. Gonel.

Inspector Félix continues to give proof of his pettiness of mind. He wrote an improper letter to Marignier, who told him off. Mmes. Petiet and Dumourey returned the 3rd from the Lago di Garda. Amid a host of smutty stories, which entertained the ladies and their daughters, Mazeau, whom they had gone to tease in his bed, slipped off his nightshirt and, taking a flambeau, came in to see them in that state. The daughters were present and didn't object. Sommariva, who was there, courted Mme. Dumourey throughout. I don't know whether he —— her, as Mazeau advised him to right in front of her.

Martial is courting Signora Monti, with whom he's smitten; he'd already made considerable progress by the time I left.

7 Prairial [*May 27*].—I took twenty-five grains of ipecacuanha and one of antimonic tartar, which only made me vomit once, and feebly.

I'm reading Caesar's *Campaigns,* commented—badly, in my opinion —by Davon. Antonio, the bookseller on the square of the upper town, lent me the first volume of Goldoni's comedies.

10 Prairial [*May 30*].—Martial sent me a letter that Colonel Le Baron wrote him, with the order to rejoin attached to it. I answered Martial, begging him to write M. Daru, and I wrote Colonel Le Baron that I'd join the regiment at Savigliano, in Piedmont, as soon as my health permitted. The two papers signed by Le Baron are joined herewith.

Their wording overwhelmed me for a minute. I haven't anyone to advise me, no friend, I'm weakened by my long spell of fever; yet I'm full of determination, convinced that through audacity and perseverance I shall end up by being General Michaud's aide-de-camp. Then I'll owe this success, like all the others, to myself alone.

Tomorrow I've decided to take a medicine similar to that which I vomited six days ago.

17 Prairial [*June 6*].—The medicine succeeded fairly well; I seem to have less fever. I shaved myself. I'm starting in again on my saber lessons tomorrow. I wrote a short letter yesterday to M. Daru. I'm halfway through my translation of *Les Amours de Zéline et Lindor.*

18 Prairial [*June 7*].—After my fencing lesson, I went all the way around the range of hills back of Bergamo. The countryside is superb and has delightful aspects. I covered nine or ten miles in about three hours, all the time at a walking pace.

20 Prairial [*June 9*].—I started yesterday taking two drams of quinine. The fever persists, although it's weak. I started today to take clarinet lessons from the band leader of the 91st. He doesn't look to me as though he were worth much.

23 Prairial [*June 12*].—Finished the translation of *Zéline et Lindor* at one o'clock in the morning. My fever continues, although slight; I plan to purge myself tomorrow. I dismissed my clarinet teacher, who wasn't any good.

The Italian Army no longer exists. The troops stationed in the Cisalpine will be under the command of a lieutenant general, six division generals and twelve brigade generals. These troops will consist of sixteen half brigades, twelve cavalry regiments, one regiment of foot artillery, two mounted, etc., etc. The generals are to be chosen by General Moncey.

Antonio, the bookseller, wouldn't lend me the second volume of Goldoni; the Abbé Raggi lent me *Siroe* and *Catone in Utica,* two operas by Metastasio.

27 and 28 Prairial [*June 16 and 17*].—I've been on several long horseback rides with General Michaud. The country around Bergamo is really the loveliest I've ever seen. The woods on the hills back of Bergamo are the most delightful imaginable. They're nearly all laid out in hunting grounds, with a hunting lodge.

At the French Theater on the fifth of Floréal, they gave *Phédor et Waldamir,* a five-act tragedy by Ducis, as cold as the climate in which the action takes place, and that's so cold it brings the heroine to the gates of death.

It seems that *Atala,* a Christian novel by Chateaubriand, criticized by André Morellet, has finally been put in its place as an unusual but mediocre work. I haven't read it.

28.—General Brunet came to see General Michaud with his aide-de-camp. He's a thief, vain, stupid, and gossipy; his aide-de-camp is gossipy without any feeling for propriety and probably has the pox; Mathys had them to dinner.

3 Messidor [June 22].—Left my fencing and clarinet masters, paid five lire eight sous to the first and fourteen lire to the second.

After much hesitation, caused by Durzy writing the general that General Gazan wasn't due to leave Brescia till the 11th, we finally departed the 5th upon receiving the news that General Gazan had left Brescia the 4th in order to take over the command of the 5th Division in Romagna. We arrived at Brescia after seven hours on the road, Casa Avogadro, where Brune, the general-in-chief, was lodged in Nivôse. The general went to Cremona the next morning with Durzy; he returned the following day. We reached the Casa Contrera on the 13th.

13 Messidor [July 2].—Took an Italian master. My fever continues.

18 Messidor [July 7].—I went to Cremona; I returned 20 Messidor. Cremona is a rather big town where you perish from heat and boredom.

23 Messidor [July 12].—They played a good comedy by Albergati entitled *Il Sagio Amico,* which, translated just as it is, would have a success in France. There's a brothel on the stage.

They played *Ariodant;* it seems to me a fine tragedy might be composed on this subject.

I've been having slight attacks of fever every night at eleven o'clock.

Let us put the present to good use, for our minutes are numbered. The hour I've spent fretting has nonetheless brought me that much nearer death. Let us work, for work is the father of pleasure, but let us never fret. Let us reflect sanely before deciding on our course; once our decision is taken, we ought never to change our minds. With a steadfast heart, anything can be attained. Give us talent; the day will come when I'll regret the time I've wasted.

A major source of consolation is the fact that you can't simultaneously be an expert in everything. You formulate an elevated idea of yourself by observing your superiority in a certain line, your mind is stimulated by this reflection, you compare yourself to those who are inferior to you, you develop a feeling of superiority to them; then you are mortified to see that they are more successful than you in some other line that often is the principal subject of their attention. It would be too cruel for the same man to have every kind of superiority; I even wonder if the apparent happiness he'd get from this wouldn't quickly fade into boredom. It's essential, however, to try to attain this superiority, because, though never absolute, it does exist, more or less, and usually is the source of success; moreover, it gives a feeling of assurance that is almost always the decisive factor in success.

I believe, for instance, that one of these days I'll do something in the theatrical line. The draft of *Selmours,* of *Le Ménage à la Mode,* of *Les Quiproquos,* the ideas of *L'Aventurier Nocturne,* the tragedies of *Le Soldat Croisé Revenant chez ses Parents* and *Ariodant*[1] seem to justify this confidence. My mind, which is constantly occupied, always drives me to seek instruction which may justify my hopes. As soon as there is an opportunity to improve myself and have a good time, I need to remind myself that I must acquire worldly experience to be able to choose my pleasures. After that, how can I be surprised to be awkward with women, not to succeed with them and to shine in society only when the argument gets heated or the conversation turns on the multitude of characters or passions that form my continual subject of study?

28 Messidor [*July 17*].—Received official notice of the confirmation of my rank of sub-lieutenant in the 6th Regiment.

You must be very distrustful; mankind in general merits it; but never let your mistrustfulness be noticed.

6 Thermidor [*July 25*].—General Michaud offered to give me permission to return to France.

10 Thermidor [*July 29*].—A great torchlight fete in honor of the patriots who were imprisoned at Carrara. Concert, illumination by day and ball. I heard a castrato who was rather good.

12 Thermidor [*July 31*].—It looks as though the air of Brescia is making the French forget the gallantry which has always been one of their distinguishing marks. Adjutant Commander Cacault kicked up a terrible row with Mme. Carrara [Michaud]. Quesnel has just kicked up another with Signora Calini, at whose home he is staying. He made a move as if to jump out the window. A minute later, she came into his room at the head of her obliging Cisalpines and servants to attack him, she hurled a cane at Quesnel's head; very solemnly, he hurled it back at

[1] Titles of plays he had written or was planning to write.

her and sent her packing with great dignity. Martinengo, the municipal officer, Percheron's host, took it upon himself to oust Quesnel.

13 Thermidor [August 1].—"The negligent man becomes attached neither to things nor persons, but derives enjoyment from all, takes the best of what is within reach, without envying a higher rank or worrying about less desirable positions: to please him, provide him with every means of pleasing, and, since he lacks the strength for either friendship or hatred, you can be nothing more than agreeable or indifferent to him."

Adèle de Sénange [novel by Mme. de Souza]

Such principles can never be mine: they're diametrically opposed to everything I am. But I believe I'd be far happier if I came slightly closer to them. I'd please people less, but I'd be more generally appreciated, and that's worth more. Besides, as soon as I fell in love, my character would take the upper hand in short order.

Like many others, I'm embarrassed when it comes to —— a respectable woman for the first time. Here's a very simple method. While she's lying down, you start kissing her lightly, you titillate her, etc., she begins to like it. Still, through force of habit, she keeps on defending herself. Then, without her realizing what you're up to, you should put your left forearm on her throat, beneath her chin, as if you were going to strangle her. Her first movement will be to raise her hand in defense. Meanwhile, you take your —— between the index and middle finger of your right hand, holding them both taut, and quietly place it in the ——. If you go about the business calmly, you can't fail. It's important to cover up the decisive movement of the left forearm by whimpering. Percheron confided this method to me, he's an expert at it.

18 Thermidor [August 6].—I received a letter from Le Baron informing me that I've been transferred from the 6th Company to the 4th, under the orders of Debelle. The 4th is at Bra, opposite Cherasco, Department of Tanaro.

Everything is beginning to resemble the hubbub of a country fair. The opera starts on the 20th.

20 Thermidor [August 8].—Brescia is quite a pretty town of medium size situated at the foot of a little mountain. It is sheltered from the north wind by its fort, situated on a ridge of the mountain. The town, which is practically round, is 600 toises in diameter. The people go walking on the Milan highway, which is nothing but a treeless road.

The families in Brescia are very large. The Martinengos have seven or eight big houses, and the Gambaras three or four. The prettiest woman in town is Signora Calini. Signora Martinengo is quite a beautiful woman.

25 *Thermidor* [*August 13*].—Even the man with the best mind is change-able; he goes through periods of animation, but they don't last. If he is wise, when they're over he'll say little, write nothing and won't attempt to exercise his imagination (his most strenuous efforts would produce nothing more than memories) or to make an effect through brilliant sallies (he'd only be awkward). He should make his dress, behavior and speech conform to the state in which he feels himself to be. That day, he should go to see the men and women of his acquaintance who he knows like calm and regularity. Most important of all, he should avoid his rivals. They would make him forget his good resolutions, and then it would be a simple matter for them to make him ridiculous.

2 *Fructidor* [*August 20*].—In order to be instructive, a trip ought to be a sort of critique of the various things you encounter. When I arrived in Italy, I wasn't familiar with France; therefore, my voyage can only be useful when I am familiar with France or some other country, and am thus able to make comparisons.

I'll nearly always be mistaken if I think that a man has only a single character.

25 *Fructidor* [*September 12*].—Joinville, Marignier, Mazeau, Augustin Petiet, Signora Grua [Angelina Pietragrua], La Gaforini, Grua, Giletti, etc. went through here on their way to Venice. I'd have gone along with them if there had been room in one of the three carriages.

Second Notebook

Memoirs to Serve for the History of My Life

1st Complementary Day, Year IX [*September 18, 1801*].—I left Brescia for Bra at half-past five this morning on horseback with my servant, my horses carrying the luggage. Dined at Chiari and slept in . . . , a miser-able hamlet where I was very uncomfortable. Had an inflammatory fever.

2nd Complementary Day [*September 19*].—I left my dismal inn at eight o'clock. Went to Cassano for dinner; there I rented a *sediolo* which cost fifteen lire and took me to Milan in two hours. It's fully six leagues from Cassano to Milan, and nineteen from Brescia.

3rd Complementary Day [*September 20*].—Saw M. Gonel, surgeon and friend of General Michaud.

4th Complementary Day [*September 21*].—I've made a number of pur-chases. I cashed a letter of exchange for 600 lire, which, together with the 312 lire I received at Brescia from Allier, the paymaster, makes 912 lire.

5th Complementary Day [*September 22*].—Paid Joinville the 102 lire that Ferdinand lent me. Bought a pair of stable trousers which cost 54 lire. Had my helmet fixed, which cost 8 lire. Bought some steel spurs for 6 lire, and 33 lire worth of officer's stripes; an English grammar, 3 lire; three and a quarter brasses of cloth at 36 lire a brasse = 135 lire; a brasse of white cashmere, 14 lire 10 sous; buttons, 16 lire 10 sous; paid the tailor 30 lire. Those are the expenditures I remember; together with the 102 lire, they make 402 lire. On the 4th Complementary Day, I had 1,000 lire; subtract 402, remains 598.

1 Vendémiaire, Year X [*September 23, 1801*].—Minister Petiet gave a grand ball in the Palace of the Consulta. In the morning, there were maneuvers at the Foro Bonaparte before General Murat and his entire staff. The 12th Dragoons paraded very badly. Foy, as commander of the city, led the maneuvers.

In the evening, the theater was lit up as brightly as in daytime; there was a free performance and afterward a masked ball. At midnight, the crowd was so large that it was impossible to get in; I moved forward three steps in half an hour. There weren't any fireworks at the Foro.

4 Vendémiaire [*September 26*].—I left the Albergo del Falcone at half-past four on the front seat of a *vettura*. The *vetturino* drove me and my luggage to Tortona for twenty-nine lire. My servant followed with the horses.

We reached Pavia at noon. I found a bookseller there who had the latest publications, but at triple the price of Paris.

We continued on our way. At two o'clock, we crossed the Ticino on a covered bridge. Five miles from there, we crossed the Po on a pontoon bridge lengthened by a ferry; we walked over the former bed of the river. We finally arrived at Voghera at eight o'clock after greatly fearing an attack.

5 Vendémiaire [*September 27*].—We left Voghera at half-past four this morning. From Voghera to Tortona, the road is beautiful; you have a view of the mountains nearly all the way. Travelers are often attacked on this road.

I reached Tortona at seven o'clock. This town lies at the bottom of a hill which used to be a very strong fortress—now entirely razed. I encountered some Dragoons of the 8th who were on furlough from Calabria, where their regiment is. They told me that there was an epidemic there. They'd stayed a whole month in a carriage, in order to get from Calabria to Voghera. I saw them again at Asti. At noon, I left Tortona on horseback; for seven lire, I hired an ass, which carried my portmanteaus to Alessandria. Coming out of Tortona, the road is barely cut through; you cross the Staffora. This district is always full of brigands because it's easy for them to escape to the mountains. Three leagues from Tortona, I saw the famous battlefield of Marengo; several shattered trees and numerous bones of man and horse are still there. I passed by it fifteen months and fifteen days after 25 Prairial, the day of the battle. I saw a column erected this year on the first anniversary; it's piddling. Before arriving in Alessandria, I crossed the Bormida, quite a large stream; I entered Alessandria and put up at the Albergo d'Atalia, where they fleeced me roundly. Alessandria is the principal town of this department, which is under the command of General Spital, former chief of staff of the left wing; they say he makes as much as 1,200 Piedmont francs a day through smuggling in grain from Liguria. That's all arranged between the prefect and him.

6 Vendémiaire [September 28].—I left Alessandria at six o'clock; a *vetturino* took me to Asti for twelve lire. I arrived in the evening at the Lion d'Or, where I had to pay very dear. A *vetturino* took me from Asti to Bra for a gold louis.

7 Vendémiaire [September 12].—I reached Bra at six in the evening. I put up at La Bonne Femme. I immediately went to see Commander Remy, commanding officer of the 3rd and 4th squadrons, which are together at Bra. Citizen Debelle, my captain, was out hunting. I arranged to take my meals with Commander Remy, Debelle, Jobert, Moutonnet, Hautmonté, Cachelot and the contractor.

8 Vendémiaire [September 30].—I put up at the home of the physician Fazzolio, an old miser.

10 Vendémiaire [October 2].—I went hunting with Captain Debelle. While very hot, I waded across an arm of the Stura, which gave me flatulent colic and horrible pains for a week. I took decoctions of quinine and a few grains of opium, which cured me. At present, I only feel pain resulting from the pox and the mercury.

1 Brumaire [October 23].—Chief Remy received an order to take the 3rd and 4th squadrons to Fossano on the 3rd. I'll leave Bra with pleasure, because this little town has nothing in its favor except its charming position. We haven't any society and there's only one billiard table.

3 Brumaire [October 25].—We left Bra at eight this morning. We arrived at Fossano at one. I went to see Mme. la Comtesse Dijon, Garavac's mistress, who's a woman of great intelligence.

4 Brumaire [October 26].—We left at eight o'clock for Saluzzo, where we arrived at two. I was terribly tired.

5 Brumaire [October 27].—I had a fever and was very depressed. I sent for M. Depetas, an excellent physician of this town, who made me vomit. I was bled three times, in addition to the ten leeches which were applied the 3rd. Finally, after much sweating, I got up 16 Brumaire and was well.

18 Brumaire [November 9].—The bell of the Commune of Saluzzo rang in honor of 18 Brumaire[1] and the peace with England.

The town of Saluzzo is situated half on the slopes of a hill and half on the level ground at the bottom of the hill. The nobles live near the castle on the hill, while the bourgeois and all the business places are below. Nearly all the shops are beneath the arcades which are at the left of the square as you arrive, and which are very animated. The ramp from the lower town to the section above is very steep. There are streets that twist and turn and go uphill quite gradually; there are also little passageways with steps made of big stone blocks which are absolutely perpendicular.

18 Frimaire [December 9].—Still sick or convalescent. I was bled twice more. I'm finally feeling better. I've been staying in the lower town at the home of Citizen Chiesa since the 6th. There's a likelihood of my going to spend a month in Grenoble.

This morning while I was reading Bitaubé's translation of the *Odyssey,* it occurred to me that Penelope was a superb subject for a tragedy. The great advantage is that you can present characters who are already known to the audience—Ulysses, Telemachus, Penelope; among the suitors, all that could be desired, the impetuous Antinous, the prudent Eurymachus, the faithful Eumaeus and Eurycleia, Ulysses' nurse.

19 Frimaire [December 10].—I'm still tormented by illness. I'll get out tomorrow.

To inspire in a woman a high opinion of one's learning is a sure means of gaining one's end. Heroes have intervals of fear, poltroons moments of bravery, and virtuous women moments of weakness. It's a great art to be capable of discerning and benefiting from these moments.

Nearly all life's misfortunes come from our false notions about the things that befall us. To know mankind thoroughly and to judge events sanely is consequently a great stride toward happiness.

21 Frimaire [December 12].—According to a long conversation I've just had with M. Depetas, whom I believe to be an excellent physician, it looks as though my habitual malady is boredom. A lot of exercise, a lot of work and the avoidance of solitude will cure me. I believe I'd do well to be very active all my life. M. Depetas told me I had some symptoms of nostalgia and melancholy.

29 Frimaire [December 20].—I have fever every night. I'm waiting impatiently for my sick leave. Faure wrote me today that, since 1 Fri-

[1]The anniversary of the day Napoleon seized power.

maire, he's been working twelve hours a day with a banker in the Rue Taitbout.

I was born January 23, 1783, in Grenoble, Rue Vieux-Jésuites. I left for Paris 8 Brumaire, Year VIII. I arrived there the 19th of the same month. I left 17 Floréal, after a stay of five months and twenty-eight days. I arrived in Geneva the 28th of the same month. I left 3 Prairial for Milan. I was made a sub-lieutenant 1 Vendémiaire, Year IX, and assigned to the 6th Dragoons 1 Brumaire. I became General Michaud's aide-de-camp 12 Prairial, Year IX, and I left him at Brescia to rejoin the corps on the First Complementary Day of the same year. I arrived at Bra, where was stationed the 4th Company, in which I am a sub-lieutenant, 7 Vendémiaire, Year X.

Love in Theory and Practice

HENRI BEYLE, with customary disregard for military authority, took it upon himself to stretch his month's furlough into three. Only in April 1802 did he leave Grenoble—not to rejoin his regiment, but to set out for Paris. He later explained his change of plans in various ways: he fled to the capital in pursuit of a woman he loved, was one; he was bored with his army companions and wanted to live in Paris "as a philosopher," was another.

The latter idea seems to have been uppermost in his mind upon his arrival, for a few hours later he was busy drawing up a program for study and meditation. But this was soon forgotten, since, if he had fallen "in love with glory"—the glory of Molière—he had fallen even more in love with love.

During his stay in Grenoble, he had glimpsed a girl of exactly his own age by the name of Victorine Mounier, the elder daughter of a family which has its paragraph in the history of France. Her father, Jean-Joseph Mounier, a former protégé of Beyle's grandfather, had risen from a humble drapery clerk to a judge in the Grenoble law courts. Active in the agitation that led up to the French Revolution, he was elected secretary of the assembly of the three estates at Vizille in 1788, and moved the vote of protest that was sent to the King. As deputy to the States General at Versailles the following year, he was largely responsible for the Tennis Court Oath, which pledged the deputies of the Third Estate not to disband until a constitution was granted.

At this point, Mounier, who was no Jacobin, began to realize that events were rushing ahead of him at a dizzy rate. Having done his part in unleashing the Revolution, he hastily withdrew and fled with his family first to Switzerland, then to Germany. He founded a school at Weimar for the sons of exiled noblemen, but, with the advent of Napoleon, he gave up teaching to return to Grenoble, where he arrived a few weeks before Beyle.

The latter, during his stay, apparently encountered the Mouniers only casually. He was not very sure what Victorine looked like, but no matter: with an imagination such as his, intangibility was an asset, reality a liability. She immediately assumed the form of the ideal mistress he had been dreaming about since early childhood: she possessed, or so it seemed, a noble character, an admirable melancholy, and, best of all, an "understanding soul." Beyond that, Victorine remained for him "a name, a pair of eyes, a personality." Several years later he wrote, "I loved her dearly and I saw her seven times in my life." Such was the shadowy creature who haunted his imagination for a decade and who, he said, "was the cause of my abandoning a military career and fleeing to Paris."

Whether by coincidence or not, Beyle actually did reach the capital on the heels of the Mounier family. Once there, he had the disagreeable surprise of learning that M. Mounier had been appointed by Bonaparte as Prefect of the Ille-et-Vilaine Department, and was to take over his duties a month later. Little hope seemed left that rainy May morning when, hiding in a doorway of the Rue Montmartre, he watched Victorine climb into the stagecoach and drive off for Rennes.

But Beyle was not yet ready to admit defeat. If he had simulated a hearty friendship for Victorine's brother during those four weeks in Paris, it was solely in order to make him promise to write frequently. A pitiful resource of a desperate lover, for neither he nor young Mounier had any illusions about their fondness for each other. Indeed, Claude-Edouard-Philippe Mounier was the very type of individual that Beyle hated the most. Ambitious, calculating, devoid of spontaneity and passion, he was a model social opportunist and superior functionary, handsome, gracious, and empty. "He's the coldest man I know," was Beyle's description of him.

While Beyle, driven by passion and caprice, was leading an irregular life of false starts and abrupt terminations, Edouard was steadily advancing along the road that led to a brilliant social and administrative career. Friend and rival of literary celebrities, companion of nobility, favorite of kings and emperors, he passed easily from distinction to distinction. At the age of twenty-six he was already Baron Mounier, secretary and protégé of Napoleon. The second restoration saw him under the protection of the Duc de Richelieu, head of the royal police, officer of the Legion of Honor, and Peer of France. And this was the man through whom the harum-scarum Henri Beyle hoped to reach the heart of the melancholy Victorine!

When three weeks had passed with no letter from Edouard, Beyle resigned himself to making the first move. Here begins an extraordinary one-way correspondence, the key to which is to be found among Beyle's notes: "Mirabeau wrote letters to Sophie which had to pass before the eyes of M. Lenoir, giving them the appearance of being written for M. Lenoir as much as for Sophie . . . The art of writing to two persons . . ."

The curious products of this experiment in "the art of writing to two persons" form the major part of the section which follows, and their inclusion is justified, I believe, by the fact that, since there is little in the way of a diary for 1802 and 1803, they are an invaluable commentary on his life at this period. It is hardly necessary to add that the flattering picture they build up is almost entirely fiction. The less brilliant truth we can glimpse from the scraps of his diary and from other sources, which tell of his struggle to learn Shakespeare's language from an Irish friar, of his resignation from the army, of his "battle" (flirtation) with the difficult Adèle Rebuffel and her facile mother, and especially of the months spent at the end of 1802 studying philosophy and the drama in an attic room across from the Louvre.

Here he lived "as solitary and as mad as a Spaniard, a thousand leagues from real life." Always excessive, he "flooded" himself with coffee, thus tautening his nerves for the benefit of his "genius" but to the serious detriment of his health, and plunged into an orgy of heterogeneous reading. Still under the influence of his mathematical triumphs at school, he naïvely tried to reduce the art of writing comedies to an algebraic formula. Doggedly, he sought, as he was to seek for many years, the open sesame to greatness.

It seemed to him at the time that the password lay in *La Pharsale,* a grandiose composition in twelve cantos which was to be "the first epic written about the Romans." With youthful optimism he intended to include all time and all subjects in this heroic masterpiece, making it "a vast encyclopedia of beauties," as perfectly proportioned as St. Peter's in Rome! Among other things, it was to be built around the time-honored conflict of love and duty, and to glorify Caesar—the same Caesar who, in his republican fervor of the following years, he was to hate above all men.

Even in this puerile concoction, there was a glimmer of Stendhal, for he was already intent on finding the "maximum" of passion in races and individuals. "There has been a people for each passion," he noted, "and, during this people's existence, there has been a period when this passion has manifested itself the most clearly and intensely. I must place such of my heroes as are motivated by this passion among the people most thoroughly imbued with it, at the time of its most powerful manifestation. I must study this passion in the monuments of this people: its poetry, history, sculpture, painting, etc." The impulse to write epics about the

Romans fortunately did not last very long, but this preoccupation with the passions was the work of his entire life.

In his garret he dreamed by the hour. When he looked up from his books, the majestic colonnade of the old Louvre opposite his window met his eye and inspired him with visions of glory. "Every evening," he wrote his sister, "I see the sun, the moon and all the stars go down behind those galleries which have witnessed the *grand siècle*. I imagine I see the shades of the Grand Condé, of Louis XIV, of Corneille, of Pascal concealed behind those great columns looking down on the passage of the men who are their descendants, and promising the wretches a sanctuary in their midst." And he never doubted that he too was destined to be gathered up into the midst of those seventeenth-century masters. "I must go entirely out of my century," he wrote in his notebook, "and consider myself to be beneath the eyes of the great men of the century of Louis XIV. I must always work for the twentieth century."

Thus, in the few months covered by the following pages, we can catch a glimpse of Stendhal as he was all his life—occupied above all else with literature and love. He failed dismally in both, for he was still a bit of a provincial bumpkin. But his time was not completely wasted: in the uncertain groundwork he had laid, there were a few firm spots on which he could build in the eventful next few years.

1802-4   Grenoble—Paris—Grenoble

Grenoble. Today, 18 Pluviose [February 7].—Alphonse Périer came to see me in my room in the Grande-Rue at five o'clock and stayed till nine. Félix Faure came over at six and also stayed till nine. We talked about Shakespeare and banking. Alphonse read Thompson's poem beginning, "BUT HAPPY, etc."

He told me he went to mass at the Eglise Saint-André, which was reopened today. Mmes. Marion and de Viennois, who took up the collection, asked for him by name; he only had an écu of three livres and a twelve-sol piece. He put in the three livres, and went home to get some more money. There's a character trait for you. The way he told about it was remarkable. You could see his shame at putting in only three livres at first, and then the pleasure he experienced at putting in six livres.

He told us he didn't attach any value to possessing a woman, that what he could understand the least was why a man should want to keep a woman. Faure has an unresponsive character and no mistake.

At Lyon, as he was returning from England, Alphonse met a lawyer of thirty-three (a very lively imagination but very little education) who, while he was in Lyon, purchased an alum factory in the South of France without seeing it and merely after looking over the plans and inventories.

Alphonse said to him, "But aren't you afraid of being fleeced?" "You surprise me," said the Englishman. "You're the sixteenth person who's asked me the same thing. Is there, then, so little honesty in France?"

And Périer told us that really he had found more honesty in England. He told us that he'd felt a tightening of the heart upon arriving in England and seeing that everything was completely different. Ignorance of the language undoubtedly contributed much to this fact.

Almost the only thing played in England is Shakespeare. The plays prized the most highly are *Othello* (*Ocello*), *Hamlet* and *Richard III*. The English are particularly fond of *Richard III*: 1. because the subject is national, 2. because there's a lot of pomp in it.

The national spirit is far stronger in England than in France.

13 Ventôse [*March 4*].—At seven o'clock in the evening, she[1] was practicing a symphony by Haydn which she was to play the same evening at Mme. Périer's.

I arrived in Grenoble on . . . Nivôse, Year X.

I had a fairly good time up to 13 Nivôse. I danced in several social circles and at the Redoubt.

15 Germinal [*April 5*].—I left on horseback at seven in the morning for Les Echelles. I had thirty-four louis, four of which were from my grandfather; I arrived at Les Echelles. I left on the . . . for Lyon in the stage-coach.

I arrived in Paris 25 Germinal [April 15];[2] I came in a Gouge cabriolet, a bracket seat cost me forty-eight livres.

There's one thing quite simple—if you're going to accomplish something, you've got to work, and work with a fresh mind. The proper time for that appears to be in the morning. I think I'll be able to go to bed at ten o'clock, at the conclusion of the performance at the theater. In that case, I can get up at six o'clock and I'll have four hours of good work from six to ten. I don't know whether that's the time

[1]Possibly Victorine Mounier, with whom Beyle was in love.

[2]All his life Beyle got his dates mixed up. Many times in the diaries he let several days go by without writing and then went back and gave the entries the proper dates—only to forget immediately and write of events that took place later than the date of the entry. Thus, in this case, he made the entry April 15 or later, although he dated it the fifth.

of day when you're most fit, but I fully realize that it's the only part of the day when I can work more or less uninterruptedly. I could live near the Tuileries and rouse myself every morning by taking a half hour's walk. One reads very badly in bed, and there's nothing worse than to read badly. This time badly employed is wasted the next day. When I don't care to go to the theater, I can use the time between five and six o'clock for a walk, and from six to ten for work.

I began taking English lessons 13 Floréal. Stopped after three days. Began again 1 Prairial with Dowtram.

She left 25 Floréal for Rennes.

Letter to Edouard Mounier, Paris, 17 Prairial, Year X [June 6, 1802].— So that's what the promises of friends are worth! When you left, you swore you'd write me; you'd let me hear from you the day after you reached Rennes. The days have passed, nearly a month has gone by, and the newspapers are the only things that have let me know you are still alive.

I realize that your time has been taken up; you've seen new places, made new acquaintances, acquired new friends. Is that any reason to neglect the old ones? As for me, I see inconstancy daily, but I'm not yet capable of understanding it. In friendship, as in love, once two people have seen each other, once their souls have communed, is it possible for them to change? But I'm ready to forgive you on condition that you write soon and often.

Since your departure, all Paris has flocked to [Beaumarchais's] *Le Mariage de Figaro;* all the elegant women whose beauty or adventures are celebrated went to show off their charms, and I must confess that I found the show in the loges far more interesting than the one on the stage. I was highly dissatisfied with Dugazon, who turned the witty Figaro into a dull buffoon. Fleury, as Almaviva, and Mlle. Contat, as the countess, performed in a way that was mediocre enough, but on the other hand Mlle. Mars interpreted the role of the page Chérubin divinely. I've never seen anything as moving as the young man at the feet of the countess he worships, taking leave of her to depart with the army; on both sides, those restrained sentiments which they dare not avow, their eyes which understand each other so well, though their lips dare not speak. What picture could be more natural and at the same time more interesting!

. . . I am trying to isolate myself as much as possible; I'm working hard on my English, and reading Virgil and Jean-Jacques [Rousseau] over and over again. I expect to get rid of my uniform before long, and to be able to settle down in Paris. Not that this city appeals to me more than another; but, as it's not possible to be where I'd like to spend my life, this is the one that provides me with the best means of continuing my education.

Perhaps the day will come when I can live in the only land where happiness exists for me; in the meantime, dear friend, write me often; kind hearts are so rare that they can't draw too close together.

Transmit, I beg you, the homage of my respect to Monsieur your father, as well as to Mlle. Victorine.

HAPPINESS AND FRIENDSHIP,

H. B.

Letter to Edouard Mounier, Paris, 16 Messidor, Year X [July 5, 1802].— I only received your letter today, my dear Edouard, upon returning from Fontainebleau, where I spent several days hunting and talking with my general [Michaud]. He was set on taking me back as his aide-de-camp and having me appointed a lieutenant; for my part, I was determined to hand in my resignation, and the day before yesterday I did so. Thus, I became a free citizen again on 12 Messidor.[1]

What kind of an idea do you have of our letters anyway, my dear Mounier? Are we writing each other for the purpose of exercising our wit or in order to communicate frankly what we feel? Write me from your heart and I'll never fail to be satisfied. It's in vain that you may joke about my passing loves; you, just like the next one, Monsieur Philosopher, will be the first to be swept off your feet by women who are frivolous and ardent. With a bit of coquetry, one of them will have an easy time convincing you that you worship her and that she loves you a little. You'll be madly in love for a couple of months, you'll think you've found the only woman on earth who's capable of making you happy. But you'll soon find out that she has done the same thing to a score of others that she has done to you. You'll curse her, you'll be furious at yourself. A bit later, you'll find a lovable woman with an entirely different character, the only woman of her kind; this one is as reserved and gentle as the other was lively and brilliant. Sure of victory, she doesn't take the initiative but leaves it up to you to make the advances, and greets you with apparent coolness which a tender look quickly contradicts. You're enraptured, you're the happiest of men; this time you've made no mistake. Alas, a fortnight later you discover her playing the same role with some other man!

Soon wearied of this commerce of deception, you will get used to looking on women as merely charming children with whom it's permissible to trifle but to whom one should never become attached. When this happens, you'll become what's called debonair. You'll make

[1] Another example of Beyle's extremely vague concept of dates.

light of everything, you'll be enterprising, you'll court all the pretty women you meet and they'll find you delightful.

But all of a sudden you'll come across a woman in whose presence all your assurance will vanish; you'll try to speak to her and the words will expire on your lips; you'll try to be amiable and you'll only be able to utter commonplaces. Then, believe me, my dear Mounier, if absence only makes your heart grow fonder, if the things you like most become dull and boring, it's in vain that you may struggle to resist; you're in love and in love for life.

Remember that you pledged me complete candor; you needn't fear my severity.

Non ignara mali, miseris succerrere disco.

You see that I've taken your advice and am reading the *Aeneid* from time to time.

I find your Friday gatherings splendid; I can see Mlle. Victorine from here doing the honors of the house, and you, Signor Prefettino, distributing puns right and left; I regret only one thing—not to be one of the general's aides-de-camp for whom you have such a hospitable welcome.

Tell me what's going on and being said, in a word tell me whether they're good fellows, and above all ANSWER FAST TO YOUR EVERLASTING FRIEND.

H. B.

Thermidor [*July–August*].—I'm in love with Adèle; she shows her preference for me in a thousand ways. She gave me a lock of hair.

6 Fructidor [*August 24*].—Big luncheon. She told me at two o'clock in the embrasure of the window in the salon that she'd been in love with Cardon for a long time. I asked for her friendship.

7 Fructidor [*August 25*].—I answered Cardon. I went to Mme. Rebuffel's at seven o'clock, Mme. Le Brun and M. and Mme. Mure were there. They left at nine o'clock. I stayed till a quarter past eleven. I put on a very sad look. I held forth on my violent character. During the last hour, I had a conversation of double meanings with Adèle and Mme. Rebuffel. The latter gave me a date for half-past one the next day. I wrote to Adèle on a volume of Fl., *"Brama assai, poco spera, nulle chiede"*—wish for much, hope for little, ask for nothing.

8 Fructidor [*August 26*].—Three times and, snuffing the candle, I encountered Adèle. I kissed her as I left at a quarter to four.

9 Fructidor [*August 27*].—I saw Mme. Rebuffel at seven o'clock in the evening. I found M. Rebuffel there, and he greeted me with the greatest kindness. He went out, I went to bed with R. [Mme. Rebuffel].

Adèle returned at eleven o'clock. She treated me with the most natural indifference.

10 Fructidor [August 28].—We went to the Bois de Boulogne in beautiful weather. I returned. Adèle treated me with charming familiarity, at the same time telling me she was thinking of Arras.[1] I believe Mme. Rebuffel was a little suspicious and told her not to let herself be kissed.

11 Fructidor [August 29].—Sunday. They were to go to M. Guastalla's. I went with F. to Versailles. Charming fireworks, set off from the top of the Marlborough Tower. The Petit Trianon, a delightful garden.

12 Fructidor [August 30].—I had a two-hour tête-à-tête with M. Rebuffel. I saw Adèle a moment. I was rather gay. She told me she didn't want to read any more novels. I'm convinced that her mother's suspicions are aroused.

21 Fructidor [September 8].—I went there in the morning. I feigned extreme coolness. In the evening, I found M. and Mme. Mure. Tender interest. She told me she was writing novels, that Mme. Rebuffel liked me. I went with the latter to Frascati where I remained till midnight.

22 Fructidor [September 9].—I had a date at seven in the evening.

23 Fructidor [September 10].—I feigned complete indifference. Adèle teased me in a thousand ways. I scoffed at all that.

26 Fructidor [September 13].—Adèle treated me as she did when I thought she loved me.

27 Fructidor [September 14].—I told her what I think: that she's always play-acting. She promised to tell me the truth. I went out a moment with Mme. Rebuffel. When we came back, we found her almost asleep; she told us she'd just passed the happiest half hour of her life.

28 Fructidor [September 15].—She dined at Isidore's. I went to see the mother at eight o'clock. The story of Fanny. Adèle came back at half-past ten. She shook hands with me. I reproached her for liking the country.

29 Fructidor [September 16].—Nothing decisive on my part. She didn't shake hands with me. They're leaving for the country tomorrow and will stay there till Wednesday.

My pay for six months at 95 livres a month is due me. Joinville has the papers.

I owe Faure	104	livres
For my watch	72	"
To Alpy	144	"
To Douenne, tailor	60	"
Total	380	livres

[1] Edouard Cardon was in the town of Arras.

Letter to Edouard Mounier, Paris, 1st Complementary Day, X [September 18, 1802].—I haven't written you for two months, my dear Edouard, because I was plunged in somber melancholy and I didn't want to say anything about it to my freinds. But they tell me your father has fallen out with your bishop. Give me the fullest details about this, I beg you. The cause of philosophy defended by the greatest of my fellow citizens makes my blood boil.

Adieu, my dear friend. Be so kind as to convey my respects to Mlle. Victorine. Aren't you coming to Paris this winter?

H. B.

Notes in the diaries at the end of 1802.—I wrote her [Adèle] 7 Vendémiaire and she rejected my letter. I gave her another 25 Vendémiaire. At present, 20 Brumaire, we have practically fallen out.

Cardon told me he had sought her out because she looked like a mistress with whom he used to be in love.

I took lessons from Dowtram for only one month; on 16 Messidor, I took M. Jeky, an Irish Franciscan recommended to me by Théophile Barrois and with whom I'm very well satisfied.

I've been working exclusively on English since 20 Vendémiaire, and will continue until 1 Frimaire, when I intend to take a Greek teacher.

On 13 Vendémiaire, I started riding horseback at the Provence riding school. I paid seven louis for three months.

On 3 Vendémiaire, I received 860 francs from Messrs. Doyen for my allowance until Fructidor.

I handed in my resignation at the beginning of Fructidor.

Faure and I roomed until 3 Frimaire [November 24] at the home of Mme. Bonnemain, Rue Neuve des Augustins, No. 736.

I have been —— Mme. R. since the beginning of Fructidor.

Effective 1 Brumaire, my father gave me a credit of 150 livres with Messrs. Périer. I had asked him for 234, and he'll have to give me that amount because I need it.

My regiment is still at Savigliano.

Mante is here, learning banking with Messrs. Périer.

Letter to Edouard Mounier, Paris, 21 Nivôse, XI [January 11, 1803].—What was there to say to you, my dear Edouard, during six months of my life given over to utter folly? At last I've known the passion that my ardent youth desired with such ardor. But now that pleasant gallantry has replaced somber love, after being laughed at so much by my friends, I can laugh at it with you. Yes, my friend, I was in love, and in love in a strange manner, with a young lady whom I had no more than glimpsed and who only rewarded the deepest love with her contempt. But all that is over at last: I no longer have the time to dream; I dance nearly every day. In my capacity of a madcap, I confided myself to the keeping of my friends, who could find no better way of curing me than to make me fall in love. Accordingly, I became smitten with the very pretty wife of a banker; I danced with her several times; I got myself introduced into her circle. I've just sent her my fifth letter; she sent back three unread, she tore up the first; according to the rules, she ought to read the fifth, and reply to the sixth or seventh.[1] Six months ago, she married the brilliant equipage and the two millions of a simpleton who's silly enough to be jealous of her—jealous of a Parisian woman! He's picked the right time for it; I'll have some fun yet with that lout! The day before yesterday, he put on a priceless comedy in front of me! Malli had given me her handkerchief to take care of for her; she left much earlier than she had planned, with the result that Mr. Husband came to look for me during a quadrille I was dancing at the other end of the hall in order to ask for his wife's *belongings*. He was so ridiculously serious while running this pretty errand that everyone burst out laughing; I'm still laughing as I write you about it. Last night he had the sulks, and, when I said I was delighted to see swords and embroidered coats coming back in style, he put on a judicious look and said it was but one excuse more for addlepates to disturb society.

Everyone is congratulating me on my rapid progress. I'm Mme. B.'s first lover; she's turned down far better men than me. That's what I keep telling myself in an effort to be proud, but the truth is that these pleasures of self-esteem are very, very short-lived. I experience a moment of enjoyment when, leaning on the arm of her chair, I make her smile, or twist up her handkerchief into a little man; but, when I try to take pride in the thought of how different my successes of this year are from those of last, I fall to dreaming. I recall the charming smile of her whom I still love in spite of myself. I feel tears coming to my eyes at the thought that I'll never see her again—but here I am relapsing into my old vagaries; I'm a great fool, as you'll agree. And yet, after all, what has this girl done to deserve so much love? She'd smile at me one day in order to have the pleasure of fleeing from me the next. She's never let me say a word to her. I wrote to her only once, and she rejected my letter with scorn; in fine, of this love, which was so violent, the only token I still possess is a scrap of a glove. You'll agree, dear Mounier, that my friends are right and that, for a Dragoon officer, I'm playing a fine role indeed. If only she had shown some love for me—but the cruel girl has always taken pleasure in plaguing

[1] This is what happened when Julien Sorel courted Mme. de Fervaques in *Le Rouge et le Noir*.

me. No, she's nothing but a coquette, and therefore I put her out of my thoughts forever, and, were I to see her this very moment, I'd be as indifferent to her as she was to me when my love was the most intense.

But forgive me, my friend. I'm wearying you with my follies—it's the last time, I feel that I'm forgetting her. Am I not going to have the pleasure of seeing you this winter? Come for a little while to see our Paris now that it's at its most brilliant. I'm sure that, philosopher though you may be, it will appeal to you more than in the spring. In any case, I hope we'll be able to go grape-gathering together in our Dauphiné. Come along, my dear Mounier, compare the gay peasants of our valley with your Bretons. Isn't Mlle. Victorine planning to come too? In any case, give her my regards, and believe in the ENDLESS FRIENDSHIP OF

H. B.

Letter to Chérubin Beyle, Paris, 12 Ventôse, XI [March 3, 1803].—It's impossible, my dear papa, to be more grieved than I am to have given you cause for displeasure. I beg you to believe that it was entirely by inadvertence, and I assure you that I haven't a single feeling or thought which could offend you the least in the world.

I am thoroughly aware of all I owe you, and in my heart I give thanks to you daily for permitting me to devote to my instruction a period employed by most young men in acquiring a fortune. This benefit is all the more valuable to me since, once this age is past, it's impossible to make up for it, and a man's whole life is but the development of the qualities he has acquired in his youth.

I don't understand how I could have made a mistake in my accounts for Fructidor to the extent of overlooking the sum of 100 francs in my expenses. Yet it's certain that, outside of a few books, I've acquired nothing since I've been in Paris. With the exception of my two masters, each of whom costs me 40 sous a lesson, I've had no pleasure outside the theater. I never go anywhere but in the pit, which costs 44 sous here. Besides, this pleasure has the essential advantage of improving my pronunciation and curing me of my Allobrogian locutions. Even if I had not been fond of Faure for a long time, our habitual financial state would have forced us to become friends. One or the other of us is nearly always without money, so we help each other while waiting for the first of the month. I wish, moreover, that you had someone here to watch my conduct; you'd see that I lead a well-ordered life and that I pass a large part of my time in reading. I prefer by far the company of great men to that of the shriveled souls I meet everywhere. As this taste becomes a habit, I soon forget the pleasures that are out of my reach.

Letter to Edouard Mounier, Paris, 27 Ventôse, XI [March 18, 1803].—Do you realize that you're behaving very badly, my dear Mounier? I write you superb letters, four-page letters, and you let three months go by without showing any sign of life. That's shocking; if you're not dead, I can't excuse you. A stay of more than six months in Paris would be necessary to restore your former character. Give me some details of the carnival at Rennes. I've been enjoying myself here like a god. If you were here, I'd procure you the finest acquaintances in the world. Every Thursday, I go to a house where Mme. Récamier is present; there's music; the mothers play cards, their daughters little games, and we nearly always end up by dancing. On Fridays, I go to the Marais to a social circle of the *ancien régime,* where I'm called M. de Beyle. There's much talk of the religion of our fathers, and, after taking refreshment, the charming Abbé Delille recites verse for us. Saturday, the best of all my evenings, we go to M. Dupuy's where there are savants of all colors, languages and countries. Mlle. Duchesnois frequently comes there with her master, Legouvé! *Greek* is spoken there, do you realize what that means? If you were present, you would take the center of the stage. Really, I don't understand how you can live in Rennes. Your credit is good, come to Paris. Get a job here and you won't have any regret at leaving your Bretons.

Is it true that you're coming to Grenoble in the autumn? That would be splendid. I'm going to incredible trouble three times a week to learn the gavotte so I'll be able to make some pretty little girl of our COUNTRY show off. Will you be a witness of my successes? This pleasant hope would make me redouble my efforts.

Come, my dear Edouard, bestir yourself and write me a couple of pages of gossip. A thousand respects to your father, as well as to your sisters—and a reply, I beg of you.

FRIENDSHIP AND HAPPINESS

H. B.

Letter to Edouard Mounier, Paris, 5 Germinal, XI [March 26, 1803].—Apparently you're going to stay in Rennes forever. That's all very well for you, since you're enjoying yourself there, but you must agree that it's hard on your friends. Aren't you at least coming to gather grapes from the charming vines of the valley? I implore you solemnly and with all appropriate melancholy, I implore you by memories of yore, by the long hours spent in the shadow of those lofty crags crowned by white clouds, by that love of one's birthplace which makes a gentle smile of tenderness stray over the lips . . . My friend, forgive me, I no longer know where I am or how to finish my sentence. As you realize, *Delphine* has made all the pretty women infatuated with the Ossianic style, and I, wretch that I am, sweat blood and water trying to put a little melancholy in the letter or two of sentiment that I'm obliged to write daily.

You mention my B. . . . I left her in the lurch a couple of months ago, and, what's more, I left her without having possessed her. A niece whose husband is a slave owner in Santo Domingo was visiting her. In turn, I set out to make her my slave, but she's putting up a superb resistance: she's aided by her aunt, who's furious and makes me lose all the opportunities to get the thing over with. I'm so annoyed that perhaps I'll end up by having the aunt in order to get at the niece. What astonishes me most of all is that the little thing loves me. She writes me letters which, in spite of the mistakes in spelling, are quite tender; she kisses me with all her heart when I give her a chance, but *niente più*. Devil take me, I'm beginning to believe in platonic love. In love as in war all is not success, you see, my dear Edouard. I've decided to take the ladies to the ball in a couple of hours; I want to get it over with, because it makes me mad to realize that I'm being upset by a little flirt of twenty . . .

H. B.

Letter to Chérubin Beyle, Paris, 11 Floréal, Year XI [May 1, 1803].—I'm going to speak of money matters again, but I hope it will be the last time.

Of the 240 fr. that you were kind enough to send me two months ago, I used 100 to pay Faure and 36 to buy a hat. I drew up my accounts yesterday, and this is how I stand. I owe Douenne 125 fr.—97 of which I have already told you about, and 28 for two vests he made for me and for mending my frock coat. I owe 37 to my restaurateur and 132 to M. Paquin, my landlord.

Besides that, Alpy, one of my former comrades, an aide-de-camp of General Michaud, reminded me that I still owe him 6 louis for the balance of the price of the mare he sold me at Bergamo. I thought he'd been more than paid by the three months' salary, coming to 265 fr., that I thought he'd received for me, but he told me that, as I didn't have my certificate of aide-de-camp from the Minister at the time, they wouldn't pay me, and he left my papers with Joinville. Besides, he told me he wasn't in a hurry and would wait as long as I wanted.

General Michaud, who's going to leave for his inspection and who wanted to re-engage me and who constantly overwhelms me with kindness, invited me to spend six days with him at Belleville and Fontainebleau. Instead of six days, I stayed eight; I was obliged to take a cabriolet to go to Fontainebleau, and the trip came to more than 58 fr. I arrived back yesterday, and this morning I've just received a nice invitation from M. Micou, who asked me to spend next week at Clamart, where the Abbé Delille is going to be. I can see that, if I stay here, all my acquaintances, especially Mme. Nardon, will oblige me to visit them in the country, and, once arrived, to stay on. My expenses this summer will be heavy, and probably more so this winter. Consequently, I'd prefer, if the idea seems to you a good one, to go to Claix in order to save money for five months. While there, I'll spend absolutely nothing and thus I'll be able to go out in society next winter.

I couldn't ask to be more satisfied with my acquaintances of this winter; leaving for the country, everyone showed the keenest desire to entertain me next winter, and I've already been invited to three balls a week. The only thing that could keep me here now when all my friends have left is my dancing master, but I feel that I wouldn't make much progress and that I'd be on the road more often than in Paris, and it would be better to avoid the risk of going bankrupt than to be worried for two days because of the need of asking for money. I thirst for the country, and I feel that it would be impossible to resist Mme. Nardon, who has invited me to her place every Sunday. On that day, she gathers her winter circle about her. This circle, which is composed of a score of intelligent men, all of them outstanding in their way, and seven or eight women, has shown me much kindness, and I couldn't stay away two Sundays in succession without something appearing to be amiss, and I wouldn't want this to be the case for anything in the world. All these reasons are concerned only with my Parisian friends; you know the ones that call me back to the midst of a cherished family I haven't seen for a year.

I have almost no expenses before leaving: a pair of boots, 36 fr.; a brace of pistols, 48—that's what is necessary, together with two or three pairs of nankeen trousers. To this, I might add a score of volumes that will be very helpful in my work at Claix.

Besides that, I owe two months of lessons to Father Jeky and two louis to Faure—I had to borrow them to go to Fontainebleau; not wishing to accompany General Michaud on his tour of inspection, I couldn't very well refuse to spend eight days with him. Moreover, I greatly desired to meet General Moreau, and he came to spend a couple of days with us.[1]

[1] On the back of his draft of this letter, which of course is almost entirely a pleasant fiction, Beyle wrote:

"Paris, 11 Floréal, I wrote that I owe: Douenne 125, Faure 48, M. Paquin 132, Alpy 144, the restaurateur 38, M. Jeky 48 = 534. — Plus boots 36, round hat 30, pistols 50 = 650. — And 240 for the trip. Total: 890 francs.

"Actual debts: Jeky 96, Paquin 200, Douenne 130, watch 72, Deschamps 24, boots 36, hat 24, bookbinder 12. — Needed to pay all that, 600 francs."

9 Prairial, XI [May 29, 1803].—I'm going to write *Les Deux Hommes,* the
subject of *Le Philosophe* expanded.

> After that, *Hamlet.*
> Then a rest of three years.
> Perhaps afterward:
> *Le Courtisan,* a lofty and fine subject.

Le Séducteur and *Le Séducteur Amoureux,* fine subjects which I
shall leave aside as incapable of enduring more than two hundred
years.

TRAGEDIES

Hamlet, tragedy in five acts and in verse. Start with that.

Othello ou le Jaloux.

Constantin, the subject of Don Garcia, having Julia and perhaps her
father appear.

Transport to the French stage Sophocles's *Oedipus,* this tragedy with
all its pomp and the choruses sung would produce a great effect at the
Opéra.

POEMS

Le Paradis Perdu, in four cantos. (This project seems to me excellent
as a preparation for the Φ [*La Pharsale*].)

The fall of the Roman Republic and the establishment of the Empire
by Caesar.

The poetics of Boileau are dull, Horace's are much more that of a
poet. Write some myself when I am fifty years old. Put in them all the
warmth of the subject, which is the art of stirring people. My *Ode à la
Gloire* will be but an episode in them. Put in them only things that are
new.

WORKS IN PROSE

History of Bonaparte.

History of the French Revolution.

History of the great men who lived during the French Revolution.

I should begin these three works at the age of thirty-five, fifteen years
from now.

From Beyle's notes, 14 Prairial, Year XI [June 3, 1803].—At four o'clock,
I received a letter from Victorine.

Letter to Edouard Mounier, Paris, 16 Prairial, XI [June 5, 1803].—I only
received your letter of 9 Pluviôse a week ago, my dear Mounier. Never
was a reprimand more appropriate; I was fed up with two women who
have been clinging to me for the past three months. My father has been

urging me for a long time to go to see him; he complained of being abandoned by his son. Upon my word, your reprimand decided me. I'm leaving, I'm going to end my sojourn in agreeable Paris, delighted with the truly fine things to be found there, but thoroughly disgusted with what's called polite society. Besides, it's time to think things over. I'm twenty years old, I must formulate principles on many things and try to lead a less agitated life than in the past! Were I not afraid that you'd make fun of me, I'd tell you that, like a ship without a pilot, I've drifted at the mercy of all the passions that, one after the other, have buffeted me. There remains but one, and it takes possession of me heart and soul; all the others have vanished, leaving me the most consummate contempt for the things I formerly desired intensely. You'll no longer doubt my wisdom when you know that, since evil is good for something, one of the illustrious ladies I worship and who pays me the honor of being jealous of me wanted to set me up here by giving me the post of sub-lieutenant in the Consul's light infantry guard. It was tempting, you'll agree. Admire my wisdom: I refused.

After this sublime character trait, I'm counting on your esteem for the rest of my life, and consequently on your opinion. No flattery; tell me frankly your opinion, and be assured that I'll do the same thing for you if I'm able to discover some defect in you.

Adieu, I plan to stay four months in Grenoble. I'm expecting a letter from Rennes; the minute I receive it, I'll rush to your cherished land.

Write me, I beg you; at Grenoble, to Henri Beyle, Henri spelled out to avoid any error. How agreeable it would be if you came to Grenoble this autumn to dance with the young ladies and tell them nice bad things!

Letter to Edouard Mounier, Grenoble, 9 Messidor, XI [June 28, 1803].— You're an abominable man, I swear; it's impossible to get along with you; you're always right. You banter me about what you call my good luck with women, but there are no more good fortunes in this world. Any man who boasts of that kind of success is afflicted with the fatuity of which you accuse me, for he prizes something he doesn't possess . . .

Farewell, come along to Grenoble; we'll ramble through the mountains, we'll have fun, we'll go hunting; as for myself, I'm going out to roam among the cliffs like the hapless Cardenio. The truth is that the region enchants me and is in harmony with what is left of the romantic in my soul; if a Julie d'Estange were really still in existence, I feel that a person would die of love for her among these lofty mountains and beneath this magic sky.

There he is back in magic again; I'm always slipping back into the ridiculous. Youth, poor thing, is unfortunate indeed, love without peace of mind or peace of mind without love. As far as you are concerned, I believe you have peace of mind; tell me about that, and get into the habit of writing long letters; with you, I recover from the boredom that weighs down on me in a town where I'd die of pleasure if all its inhabitants were present.

H. B.

Letter to Edouard Mounier, Claix, 12 Thermidor, XI [July 31, 1803].—All well and good, when you're lonely there's nothing so delightful as to receive a letter which, in the first place, is interesting, and, in the second place, gives you the rare pleasure of finding fault in your turn. I'm surprised that you, a man of wit and education, the son of a man worthy of making his country's laws, should scandalize a soldier who has never known anything more than Clairaut's algebra and the cavalry maneuvers. Do you mean to tell me that it's less criminal to be the hundredth lover of a married woman than the first! For my part, I'd prefer to bring about my damnation through accurate reasoning. It seems to me that a law is only binding—and consequently its violation only a crime—when it guarantees the thing for which it was made. The law of fidelity in marriage guarantees you a faithful wife, a companion, a lifelong friend and children of whom we are presumably the fathers —in fine, a happiness that, in my opinion, is far superior to the fleeting pleasure we find in the arms of a light woman. But this law no longer exists outside of books, and such a thing as a faithful spouse is no longer to be found even in novels. Moreover, it's quite obvious that the Frenchman of today, not being occupied in the *forum,* is driven to adultery by the very nature of his government.

What is there left for the sensitive and honorable man to do when he has the misfortune to be disillusioned to this extent? Is he to marry, only to have the sorrow of seeing the debauchery of his wife and the ghastly misfortune of not daring to show his own sadness? Or is he to hope that his wife will have sufficient virtue to struggle against all the effort of her century's morals? And, in the latter case, the certainty of the danger's immensity would make him suspicious, and when suspicion appears happiness is far away.

Provided you endow this sensitive man with enough intellectual power to reason this way when he is self-possessed, but not enough to master both the trend of his century and all the impetuosity of his passions, what will he become in a storm, since he is suspicious even in a calm?

I'll own up, my dear Edouard, that, plagued by these reflections, which I have only settled within the past few days, I have been led along by hazard until now. I hoped to find a woman who was capable of experiencing love in a better fashion than that. I believed all of them to be sensitive, and I have seen but sensuality and vanity. I've come to regret having built up a chimera which I have been trying to find for the past five years. I try to exert all my reason to drive it away, but it always comes back. I gave it a name, a pair of eyes, a personality; I see it incessantly. I speak to it sometimes, but it doesn't reply, and, like a child who has kissed a doll, I weep because it doesn't return my kisses. I realize now that only great things are capable of diverting me from this frightful state of constantly longing for a being who doesn't exist, or who, existing, unhappily doesn't return my love. Since it isn't within the power of love such as I conceived it to bring me happiness, I began some time ago to be in love with glory; I long to follow in the footsteps of that generation of great men who, after building up the Revolution, were destroyed by their own work. Not yet having reached this goal, I am participating in the factions of Rome, not being able to do anything more; and in my heart I foster the immortal hope of one day imitating the great men whom, for the moment, I can do no more than admire.

But I am being carried away; my best friends say, *"You're crazy."* You yourself laugh at this nonsense. All I ask of you is to do your laughing alone.

There's nothing new in Grenoble. The women talk of virtue and take the consecrated wafer, but they behave just the same as anywhere else. Now and then, their husbands notice it. And what happens then? They become smitten with them and love them more than ever.

You see by the above, my dear Mounier, that hermits are gossips; make me believe you are a hermit, otherwise I'll no longer dare to scratch out four pages to you. I beg you to give my respects to your whole family.

H. B.

Letter to Edouard Mounier, Grenoble, 20 Vendémiaire, XII [October 13, 1803].—Don't you intend ever to write me again, my dear friend? You have no idea of how highly I value a word from you. Do you look on me merely as a friend of the regiment? Do you consider that what happens to you doesn't interest me? If that's the case, I'm quite different from you, and my heart is in Rennes oftener than you imagine. Write me in great detail.

Aren't you going to rush on a flatboat with the Consul TO HEAR SHAKESPEARE'S DIVINE LANGUAGE IN HIS COUNTRY? Were I in your place, I'd be wild, not out of ambition, but to see one of the finest periods in modern history.

After the most beautiful autumn imaginable, we're having weather worthy of Ossian for our vintage—exciting rainstorms and winds whistling through the high mountains; on the morrow, the Alps covered with snow, and pure, chill air that bids to the hunt. I find that all these revolutions, in the great works of nature as in the hearts of men, are alike—sublime from afar and depressing indeed from anear. Farewell, my dear Mounier, look on me as one of your best friends.

H. B.

Letter to Edouard Mounier, Claix, 23 Frimaire, XII [December 15, 1803]. —It may be, my dear friend, that you will no longer recognize the voice that is speaking to you. It's a long time indeed since I've written, but don't attribute my silence to negligence. I was ashamed to let my friends see the dreams of a madman; these dreams must have bored you no end in my previous letters. Still, I can't resign myself to going on without having some news from you and telling you how fond I am of you. I've passed my time during the past three months in extreme solitude. The contrast pleased me after coming from Paris, where there was so much for the mind and so little for the heart. The strange thing is that my sensibility has caused me to be regarded by my family as insensitive. They imagined that it must have been because I was bored in their company that I spent the day hunting, and their suspicions increased when they noticed that I went to read in an abandoned cottage. I believe that's the best place to read *La Nouvelle Héloïse,* and this novel consequently never appeared to me so charming. While there, I also reread several letters I had received from friends, and especially one of which I have only a copy, but which remains very close to my heart in spite of that. It seemed to me that, in the present order of society, lofty souls must nearly always be unhappy, and all the more so because they scorn the obstacle standing in the way of their felicity. For instance, wouldn't it be the severest test that this kind of soul could encounter if its most cherished desires were blocked by money considerations and by the respect due the wishes of a man whose opinion it holds in contempt? I don't know whether you will understand, but, if you comprehend what is stopping me, I should be justified in your eyes and you should reply to me.

These ideas and the sadness inspired by them have brought me around to reading works dealing with the laws which are at the bottom of customs and morals. Therefore, I read *Le Contrat Social* and *L'Esprit des Lois.* The first work delighted me, except when it said that 600,000 Romans could cast their vote with full knowledge of what they were voting for. The second, which I read twice, appeared to me far beneath its reputation. What good does it do me to know the spirit of a bad law? It teaches me to make out a certificate, and nothing else. Isn't it more worth while to speak of the laws which, accepting men as they are, attempt to procure the greatest possible amount of happiness for them? Such a book, written as Montesquieu was capable of writing it, might have anticipated the Revolution.

I finally read a book that seemed to me strange indeed—superb in some parts, contemptible in others, and quite discouraging throughout. It was Helvétius's *De l'Esprit*. In the first part, this book so carried me away that, for a few days, it made me entertain some doubts concerning friendship and love. I ended up by seeing that Helvétius, never having experienced the tender sentiments, was, in accordance with his own principles, incapable of describing them. How could he explain that unknown disturbance which seizes a person at the first sight of another, and that eternal constancy which love, once kindled, fosters hopelessly? He doesn't believe in this constancy, of which I've heard so many examples cited; do you believe in it yourself? Do you believe in that incomprehensible force of love which, amid a thousand trivial phrases, enables a lover to distinguish the one that is written for him, and that, causing him to give ear to the almost imperceptible voice that is raised above the others and that he alone can hear, tells him the torments of the person who loves him, and reminds him that he is the only one from whom consolation may come?

It seems to me that Helvétius is incapable of explaining these feelings and a thousand others like them. I wish for many reasons that you had read this work, which seems to me to be really extraordinary. If you have read it, I beg you to tell me at length how you feel about it.

Give me abundant details on your manner of living and your future plans. Wouldn't you like to have your father a senator and to live in Paris? If the government is ever going to know him, it ought to do so by this time.

Farewell, my dear friend; were I not afraid of appearing ridiculous to you, I'd venture to ask you if, in reading this letter, you feel the gentle emotion which inspired it. Whether or not our hearts have been fortunate enough to commune, believe me when I say that my feelings will never change. I'd say more, but I'm afraid of giving myself away. If you have understood me, you'll reply, and when I write again I'll be able to tell you all.

You must confess, my dear Edouard, that the above sentences are almost unintelligible. Coming back to earth, I want to tell you that I'll be in Grenoble a week from now and probably in Paris at the beginning of spring. Aren't we ever going to have the pleasure of seeing each other again? There are so many means. But, in the meantime, write us often, that's up to you alone; I'll have plenty of addresses if I have one. To the devil with your enigmas!

Adieu, my friend, don't burn my letter and three days after you receive it, its meaning will become clear, or I'll give up. With all my heart, farewell.

H. B.

Letter to Edouard Mounier, Grenoble, Pluviôse, XII [February, 1804].—
A thousand excuses, my good friend, for my long delay in answering your letter. For the past month, I've been in the thick of what are called the pleasures of the carnival. I danced until six o'clock this morning; I got up at four in order to tell you at least some of the things your letter made me experience, for it's impossible to tell you all of them.

For the past month, my life has been given over to every dissipation possible. I was trying to forget my emotions. Here, as everywhere else, I've found much selfishness and no soul. I prefer the passions, with all their tumults, to the chilly insensibility into which I've seen plunged the fortunate ones around here. These passions make me unhappy today, but perhaps at another time they'll make me happy; besides, what road am I to take to escape their power? Isn't a single moment of their happiness worth all the pleasures that might be given by self-esteem?

What is the world to me?
Its pomp, its pleasures, and its nonsense all?

There couldn't be a better time to see Grenoble at its most brilliant. There's a ridotto every Wednesday. They start at seven o'clock, there's supper at midnight, and dancing goes on till six in the morning.

You see, my dear Mounier, what my life has been for the past month: I've stayed up till the small hours six days a week, and I've taken a little trip in the country.

As I'm thoroughly convinced of your friendship, I'm following the trend of my thoughts and replying to your letter. You have guessed my secret, but have a wrong idea of me: I have little esteem for men because I have seen very few who are worthy of esteem. I have even less esteem for women because I have seen almost all of them behave badly; yet I still believe in the virtue of both. This belief is the cause of my greatest happiness; without it I should have had no friends, I should have had no mistresses. You believe me *gallant,* and as far as you are concerned my name stands for a stupid animal. I too thoroughly realize what the ridiculous is ever to be so myself in the full sense of the word. I may have had a few conceited spells, like every young man; I may have been foppish, because it was the fashion to be like that and I thought I was attracting attention; but all my arrogance vanished as soon as I looked at my predecessors and those who will succeed me. In a word, you will be entirely undeceived regarding my fatuity when you learn that, having had the opportunity at any time of seeing the woman I loved, I never said that simple word, "I love you," and I have every reason to believe she never noticed me, or that, if she did notice me for a moment, she has forgotten me completely. You see, that's quite different from believing yourself loved. I have thought sometimes of going to her and saying, "Do you want me for a husband?" But, apart from the fact that the proposal would have been absurd coming from me, and that—as you say quite rightly—I should have been refused, I don't believe I am qualified to make her happy; I am still too impulsive to be a good husband, and I'd blow out my brains if I believed she might think, "I would have been happier with another."

When I left him for the first time six years ago, my father made me promise that I wouldn't get married before the age of thirty.

In truth, the only ambition I had was for her; consequently, what reason would I have for taking up a profession, and in what profession could I start? I am thoroughly disgusted with women. Never again will one of them be my mistress, and those possessed in cold blood bore me. I place little value on the esteem of a private circle of acquaintances, because I've seen that you are sure of obtaining it as long as you flatter all the members. I'll have an income of three or four thousand livres, that's enough to live on. Were I to be ruined, I could become a professor of mathematics after a year of work. Why, then, should I go out in society, flattering by word and deed all the influential men I might meet?

I feel that I should keenly love glory were I to succeed in getting over another love. There is military glory, literary glory, the glory of the orators in the Republics. I have renounced the first because you have to abase yourself too much before reaching the lowest posts, and it's only when you get that far that your actions may be noticed. I'm not a savant, therefore I mustn't think of the second. Remains the third career, in which character may partially replace talent. And it's only in rare circumstances that the people have any need of you, and you may die calumniated, and so many persons without talent have appeared in the field that an extremely great genius is needed if you are going to be protected from ridicule. Such are the obstacles.

Give me your opinion on this matter, my dear Mounier, frankly, sincerely and without being afraid to talk to me sensibly. For the moment, I cast myself with a pure heart into the stream of events. I shall try to acquire some talent, I shall dwell alone with my soul and my books, and I shall wait for the wind to fill my sails before starting out.

I well realize that, in a moment of good sense, I might take a job, but I don't feel that I have enough perseverance to follow it through, and one must avoid appearing changeable.

There's where I've arrived, my dear Edouard, I expect to be in Paris in thirty or forty days. Once there, I'll study politics and political economy, a science which appears to me to be the basis of the other in a century in which everything can be bought. Give me all the details of your future voyage, and above all write me your advice. Good night, if you aren't already asleep.

H. B.

Letter to Edouard Mounier, Geneva, 8 Germinal, XII [March 29, 1804].— I'm going to Paris. I don't need to tell you that one of the greatest pleasures I anticipate in that city is the one of embracing you. We're no longer held up by trifles, which accounts for my not quibbling with you because you haven't written for three months. The pleasures of the Grenoble carnival formed a society of young men which only lacked you to assemble everyone I like and esteem in this region. You know nearly all of them, except perhaps Félix Faure and Ribon; the others are Mallein, Alphonse Périer and Diday. One day I told Alphonse and Mallein that I'd like to go to Paris by way of Geneva. Immediately, they looked at each other, we arranged our trip and left 29 Ventôse to come to Geneva to spend a couple of days. We passed through Les Echelles, where we were put up by my uncle, through Chambéry, where we stayed twenty-four hours, and we finally arrived in Geneva. We had planned to stay here only two days; we have already been here three, and, if I listened to my heart, I'd stay six months.

What struck us most on our arrival was the beauty of the women and girls, and that curious and admirable custom of letting the girls go everywhere alone, the touching candor of their behavior, revealing souls that don't even know what coquetry is, and that are so sensitive to love. I would appear to you to be crazy were I to tell you all my thoughts on this subject; I'm trying to restrain myself, and I see that I'm writing sentences that are unintelligible. I despair of finding women like these elsewhere; I was seeking to get over a chimerical hope; picture my delight upon finding Geneva even better than I had imagined. First of all, my dear friend, I have never felt this candor so thoroughly; it's the only thing that can't be imitated by coquetry, this pure joy of a soul that has nothing to hide. The soul that dissembles can't be gay: it has a satirical gaiety that repulses, it has none of the pure joy of youth. What a difference between the women I'm leaving and those I'll find in Paris! For once, they're going to call me the Philosopher.

I'm tearing myself away from here—but much as Telemachus tore himself away from Calypso's island. Mallein has already gone back to Grenoble. Périer is leaving tomorrow; I'll have to be getting along too, but it won't be without the hope of seeing my dear Geneva again.

Farewell, my dear Edouard, tell me all you know about Geneva.

Send your letter to Henri B. . . . in care of M. Crozet, student at the Ponts et Chaussées, Hôtel de Nice et de Modène, Rue Jacob, Faubourg Saint-Germain.

FARE YOU WELL.

H. B.

A Molière in the Making

THE long period of solitude had come to an end by the time that Henri Beyle, but lately turned twenty-one and bursting with confidence in his own dramatic genius, returned to Paris in April 1804. For the first time in his life he was to find a little circle of friends whose interests were the same as his. Bookish, impulsive and bashful he still was, but daily contact with his fellows acted as a brake on his romantic imagination, relieved the mental strain of incessant reading and writing, and served as an introduction to the world of reality with which, until then, he had but a nodding acquaintance.

The closest of his friends during the following months was his old schoolmate, Fortuné Mante. Beyle's elder by two years, a graduate of the Ecole Polytechnique and at present studying banking, Mante was for some time considered by his enthusiastic comrade as "a rare man indeed" —although slightly lacking in warmth and spontaneity.

The second on the list was little Louis Crozet, ugly and pock-marked, who, five years earlier, had shared first honors with Beyle in mathematics. He had gone to the Ecole Polytechnique at the same time as Mante and was now completing his engineering studies at the Ecole des Ponts et Chaussées. The youngest of the trio of Grenoble youths, he was to remain Beyle's friend through life—although it was some time before their association in Paris ripened into close friendship.

At bottom the two were remarkably alike. Both possessed that rare combination of a lucid intelligence, strong passions and a boundless imagination; both, equipped with a somewhat bookish idealism, took life seriously and had a mania for classifying its phenomena. In Crozet, Beyle found the first man who shared his curiosity about the human heart, who placed his entire faith in logical analysis, who made a religion of concrete facts. Side by side they read, studied, made notes and composed character studies of their acquaintances—Crozet even wrote portions of Beyle's diary.

In all his life Beyle never doubted that he was vastly superior to the common run of humankind, but during his youth he was seldom sure of himself in the presence of other people. Association with his friends soon made it obvious that he had a tendency to be ponderous; that, bashful and overdesirous to please, he was erratic and frequently offended by monopolizing the conversation. He resolved to exercise more self-control, merely to say what came into his head, to be "simple, natural and sincere."

He attempted to put his difficult resolution into effect with Mante, Crozet and his other friends, a mixed band of some twenty youths who divided their time between studying and sowing a modest crop of wild oats. Martial Daru—Beyle's model as a society man and "seducer of women"—was still on good terms with him, although the rest of the Daru family remained chilly after his resignation from the army. In addition, there was Louis de Barral, whose allowance always evaporated promptly in the gambling halls of the Palais-Royal; tiny Camille Basset, the scatter-brained chum of Barral and roommate of Crozet; Joseph Rey, a grave philosopher, and Dalban, an embryo Corneille. A sprinkling of third-rate dramatists, would-be poets and indefinite hangers-on at the Théâtre Français were respectfully cultivated by all these youths, for if they had one thing in common it was their infatuation with everything theatrical.

With his friends or alone, Beyle nightly took his place in the queue outside the pit entrance of the Français and patiently submitted to two hours of heat or cold, rain or snow, before the doors finally opened and the wild scramble for seats began. Squeezed in on a hard bench between clerks and delivery boys, this fastidious little aristocrat regarded the play with a critical eye, afterward returning to his room to analyze it and write out his impressions. Nor was he easily satisfied: no author was too great and no actor too famous to escape his severe judgments—the only exception was Mlle. Mars, whom he invariably found "divine," "an angel," "ever more perfect."

Dramaturgy, the pit, theatrical gossip, and shop talk—such was the stuff of which, in 1804, Beyle's daily life was made. All that lacked was admission to the land of mystery and make-believe that lay beyond the stage door. It was Crozet who at length opened this door and took him behind the scenes to meet Mlle. Duchesnois.

At the moment the tall, gawky, ignorant and incredibly ugly actress known as Mlle. Duchesnois was the center of a controversy that impassioned all Paris. After making a promising debut at the Français in the major role of Phaedra, the actress, whose talent outweighed her lack of beauty, had run up against the opposition of a powerful group that was pushing a comely but ungifted fifteen-year-old named George Weymar

(Mlle. George) for the same role. Mlle. Duchesnois had the backing of the tumultuous pit, but Mlle. George's powerful support included her coach, Mlle. Raucourt, a veteran of the Français; Geoffroy, the pedantic but influential critic of the *Journal des Débats,* and no less a personage than Bonaparte, then First Consul, whose interest was not merely platonic.

The quarrel between the rival partisans of the two actresses forms a long and lively chapter in the history of the period. Many references to it are scattered through Stendhal's works, and the following pages make some amusing revelations of his earnest but clumsy attempts to become Mlle. Duchesnois's defender. His only reward, unhappily, was a rebuff so stinging that he temporarily lost interest in the Français backstage and returned to his studies. After all, there was no time to be lost in equipping himself to be a character analyst and writer of comedies, in proving to the world that he possessed genius.

Genius, he was convinced, was no divine afflatus: it was, rather, the result of endless application, meditation, planning. "I believe," he wrote gravely, "that genius, in whatever category it may be, is only a large dose of good sense; and good sense is acquired by working; that is, by observing and reflecting on one's observations." From 1802 to 1805 he observed and reflected a great deal, and if he never became a "comic poet" or a "nineteenth-century Molière," he did succeed during those four years in laying the groundwork of his entire philosophy and learning the method which gave the peculiar merit to his later writings. In a passage that might serve as his epitaph, he wrote at this time, "I endeavor to discern the truth and to describe it in the most poignant manner possible. Working thus, I shall not go out of style, nor will my glory fade."

From the outset he had taken Shakespeare as his model: it was to read Shakespeare's plays in the original that he was struggling with English as it was to see them played that he later went to London. The French classical dramatists appealed only to the intellect, while in the "romantic" Shakespeare he had the pleasure of seeing human nature as he really felt it to be.

Although the first two books Beyle was to publish were to be respectively on music and painting, these two arts were among the few cultural subjects that played little part in his "real education"—as he later referred to this period. He rarely went to the Opéra, and the only work of this kind that appears to have aroused his enthusiasm was Cimarosa's *Il Matrimonio Segreto,* which, from the first time he heard it upon his arrival in Italy as a soldier, ran through his life like a theme song. The Louvre was bursting with art treasures that Bonaparte had plundered in Italy, but when Beyle strolled through the galleries his only reflection was that he should enlighten himself "by frequently comparing poetry and painting."

His early mathematical and philosophical training, on the other hand, composed the very basis of his program. "Outside geometry, there's but a single manner of reasoning, that of facts," was his belief, forecasting the Stendhal of later years, with his insatiable appetite for "little true facts" and "the juice of facts." Indeed, facts were the fuel of observation-analysis-judgment, that magical truth-detecting triad of Destutt de Tracy's *Idéologie,* which was soon to become his Bible. It was only through the cognizance and analysis of facts that one could reach the WHY of things.

Beyle's chief purpose, of course, was to apply this apparatus to the soul and mind of men: he would observe each, collect all possible data on their action and interaction, subject this data to rational analysis, and end up by coming into possession of the all-important formula that explained human nature. It was the study of his entire life, but during the years 1803–5 he drew up a detailed classification, based in large part on Hobbes and Helvétius, which he later modified but little.

At this period he believed that, having squeezed the facts out of the human mechanism, classified them and mastered their basic WHY, he would be able to begin the somewhat complicated but magnificently logical process of composing his comedies in verse. First of all, he would draw up a list of the various levels of contemporary society, decide which were the characteristic absurdities of each level and select the ones best suited to his purpose. That done, he would outline characters having "the finest soul together with the best mind" to personify the qualities he wished to present, placing beside each a list of all the virtues and vices, and choosing those that were appropriate.

The rest would be easy. All he would have to do would be to invent three or four sets of lines, melt this multiple dialogue down into a single succession of nicely balanced Alexandrines, polish his verses until they took on the warmth of "the language of passion," make a few corrections —and presto, a philosophic comedy would have been created! "This is the whole of art," he exulted. *"Sic itur ad astra."*

Underlying all his projects were the twin passions: the love of glory and the love of virtue. His virtue, which naturally had nothing to do with chastity, was merely "that which is useful to the public." As a fervent republican, he intended to be useful to his fellow men by defending the sacred cause of Liberty and destroying Tyranny's hateful yoke. In his obsession with virtue, Beyle saw Napoleon not as the glorious figure he afterward, on occasion, depicted him, but as a modern Caesar, a tyrant who had throttled the revolutionary republic and was robbing his country of liberty. If Caesar-Bonaparte was the incarnation of vice, the "divine" Marcus Junius Brutus, Caesar's slayer, the hero who "for his country's sake killed the man he loved," was Beyle's model of inflexible republican virtue.

But he contemplated nothing as sanguinary as the overthrow of the government or the assassination of Bonaparte. His ambition was to become immortal through the more subtle means of creating comedies which would fire the public with the passion for liberty, at the same time annihilating tyranny with the deadly weapon of ridicule.

There remained only to discover a rule for making his comedies comic, and his authors remained discouragingly silent on the subject of laughter. Only Cailhava, in his *Art de la Comédie,* touched lightly on the matter, quoting Addison, who in turn quoted Hobbes: "The Passion of Laughter is nothing else but a sudden Glory arising from some sudden Conception of some Eminency in our selves by Comparison with the Infirmity of others, or of our own formerly: For Men laugh at the Follies of themselves past, when they come suddenly into Remembrance, except they bring with them any Present Dishonour."

For lack of a better definition, he adopted this one, but he doggedly tried to improve on it. He copied the jokes he heard, classified them, sought to ascertain why they were funny. The subject haunted him: for twenty years he was intermittently occupied with it, but in his many essays on laughter he invariably returned to the point of departure— which he sometimes credited to Hobbes and sometimes passed off as his own.

The year before, he managed laboriously to put together his first comedy, *Les Deux Hommes,* or *The Two Men* (he usually wrote the title in English). It was inspired by Rousseau's *Emile* and Barbieri's painting, *The Reconciliation,* and composed according to Alfieri's principles of *sceneggiatura.* Othello served as the model of passion, Tartufe as that of hypocrisy, while Rousseau's Julie d'Estange, Fielding's Tom Jones and Mme. de Staël's Delphine played the roles of incidental guides. The tone was taken from Molière's "masterpiece of good manners," *Les Amants Magnifiques.* This motley assemblage had been called together to aid Beyle in being useful to his countrymen. He intended to pit the modern republican-philosophical system of education against the antiquated monarchistic-religious system. "This," he assured himself, "is perhaps the greatest idea that has ever underlain a comedy."

In composing the play, he servilely followed those tyrannical rules of classicism he was later to find so ridiculous. His plot was puerile and unoriginal, his dialogue stilted, his characters unreal personifications of abstract ideas who suddenly appeared when they were due to speak and unceremoniously disappeared when their presence was no longer required. In a word, his comedy was clumsy, naïve—and not in the least comic.

Limping along under its burden of philosophy and youthful idealism, *The Two Men* also announces the reason its author never succeeded as a dramatist. "I have drafted more than twenty plays," he confessed years later. "Always too many details and too profound, too little intelligible for the thick-witted public"—all of which was true, although too much of the blame is perhaps put on the public.

Another reason for his failure was that the task of converting his prose version into verse was too herculean for him. Totally lacking in a feeling for poetry, he went through heroic efforts to hammer out two or three Alexandrines in a day, and the result was flat and often incorrect.

Many another project was started and dropped during the summer of 1804, and to add to his discouragement his pecuniary woes began. His father had promised him an allowance of 240 francs a month and additional money for clothes, but this amount was soon reduced to 200 francs with no extras. At the time, even the latter sum was by no means negligible, but for a youth who patronized the theater and bookstalls as regularly as Beyle it was obviously inadequate. By May he was attempting—with disastrous results—to increase it in the gaming rooms of the Palais-Royal; by June he was borrowing from Mante, Barral and Rey; by July he owed his landlady, porter and tailor, and by August his only pair of shoes had holes, he was further in debt for his room and board, had pawned his watch and was unable to pay the doctor.

This did not prevent him from thinking of going to Rennes and trying to see Victorine as she was "taking a walk at nightfall." He appears to have gone as far as borrowing 1,244 francs 13 sous, his diary, letters and voluminous notes inexplicably stop from 3 to 30 Vendémiaire (September 27 to October 22), and a marginal note thirty years later refers to "a little voyage incognito" to Rennes, but there is no definite evidence that he ever actually carried out his romantic plan.

Meanwhile he conceived the idea of undertaking a second comedy, to be called Le Bon Parti. His aim this time was to ridicule those who would like to see France in the clutches of despotism. He rather wished he could employ Bonaparte himself as the principal victim, but this, of course, was out of the question; moreover, he reflected, the First Consul was not a good subject for comedy, "being very odious and very little ridiculous." But, if he could not use Bonaparte, there was nothing to stop him from using Bonaparte's "lackey," Geoffroy.

He fortified himself with "lots of coffee" and, with "the greatest enthusiasm," set to work. The play might well give him from 2,000 to 6,000 francs for spending money, and he estimated optimistically that it could be written in ten days. Ten days! Under its various titles of l'Intérieur d'un Journal, Le Bon Parti, Quelle Horreur! ou l'Ami du Despotisme Pervertisseur de l'Opinion Publique, L'Eteignoir, La Cheminée de Marbre and Letellier (his favorite title), he was to work intermittently on this play for nearly thirty years—and never to finish it.

As the end of 1804 approached, Beyle began to realize that he had failed all along the line. "My productions stink," he muttered when he read over his plays; his financial state was desperate; he had had no love affair and had been unable to benefit from Victorine's arrival in Paris; even his love of virtue was weakening and he felt that the time to be a republican had passed. But, with all this, he had made a capital discovery, although a disheartening one; namely, that he knew very little about life after all, that what he had mistaken for reality was only the visionary world of Jean-Jacques Rousseau, in which he had lived ever since the nights when, as a child, he had locked himself up in his room and shed tears over the adventures of Julie d'Estange in *La Nouvelle Héloïse*.

He now made the resolution: "I must try to undo the prejudices that J.-J. Rousseau has given me, and he has given me plenty . . . I must seek *mankind in mankind and no longer in books*." Already a year earlier, in a moment of lucidity, he had suspected the truth and written: "I'm over twenty years old; if I don't launch myself out into society, if I don't seek to become acquainted with mankind through experience, *I'm lost*. I only know mankind through books; there are some passions I've never encountered elsewhere. How am I to depict them? My pictures would only be copies of copies. All my science, or at least a great part of it, consists of prejudices. If all the authors I've read had agreed among themselves to invent a nonexistent passion, I'd believe in it." Finally, in December 1804, he determined to rely less on books, to put Rousseau behind him and to immerse himself in life. "Before everything else," he said, "it's necessary that the poet should have experienced an immense number of emotions, from the strongest—the terror of seeing a ghost—to the mildest—the murmur of a faint breeze among the leaves."

1804 Paris

Journal of My Third Voyage to Paris

18 Germinal [*April 8*].—I arrived in fine, although rather cold, weather, at sunset, at half-past six, Sunday, 18 Germinal, Year XII.

I left my traveling companions, and got off at M. Paquin's with M. Salmon, a highly sensitive and very learned man. We went to the Français, where, from the gallery of the third tier of loges, we saw *Le Vieux Célibataire* and *Le Mariage Secret,* a detestable play. I saw Mante there.

19 Germinal [April 9].—I find myself more reasonable than I was during my last stay, and consequently I'll be happier. I owe that to the experience acquired at Grenoble, where I saw mankind in man instead of in books; my distinction OF HEART AND UNDERSTANDING will be useful to me, EVEN AS A BARD.

Visit from good Father Jeky. I went to Crozet's twice. I went to the museum with M. Salmon; dinner at Muron's, from there to the boulevard and finally to *Agamemnon* and *Sganarelle*. I wasn't at all satisfied with Talma and Mlle. Duchesnois. My distinction (between soul and mind) made me see a number of things I oughtn't to have seen in these two plays. I'll soon be able to solve the problem: What is humor?

M. Salmon, whose opinion has great weight with me, considered, as I did, that Cassandra produces a good effect in *Agamemnon:* when I read the play, possibly being led astray by Alfieri's principles, I judged her otherwise. Here, as elsewhere, I must consequently look closely.

20 Germinal [April 10].—Crozet came to see me and we looked for a room.

21 Germinal [April 11].—M. Salmon believes that Helvétius spoke the truth and what Kant says is very subtle but true. We went together to the first performance of *La Fausse Honte*. From the third act on, I was half asleep; the play dragged along to the end amid hisses and applause. The author was named, but there was so much noise that Baptiste the Younger couldn't make himself heard. I've found the audience I'd like FOR THE TWO MEN. I must never sacrifice energy of expression for a vague good breeding. Every character has a word for his idea; any other word, any other means of expression, is wrong.

23 Germinal [April 13].—Saw Dalban in the Rue Jacques, No. 139. He told me that he encloses his thought in twelve syllables the same as he takes strides of two feet and a half, that nothing is easier once the habit is acquired.

24 Germinal [April 14].—M. Salmon and I have just been to see *Le Jaloux sans Amour* and *La Gageure Imprévue,* a show that put me to sleep, although Fleury and Contat played their parts very well; Contat never really speaks to my heart. Imbert's *Jaloux* is as ordinary as a play could be; the *Gageure* is written in a bourgeois style.

I gossiped with Mante this morning, from there to the Prefecture of Police, from there to the Panthéon, where I read Vauvenargues, with whom I'm very well satisfied. I find that I'm more reasonable than I was last year; coffee used to make me continually frantic; I have more good sense now, but maybe I'm more mediocre.

I talked with M. Salmon about his system concerning women; I urged him to publish it. He said no, but I believe he has made up his mind and the book is possibly already written. He holds that the

Italian woman is the primitive woman; by modifying her in various ways, you get the French woman, the German woman, etc. He believes only in the virtues of temperament. He believes that woman's whole character consists of *an insatiable desire to please,* and that it's consequently impossible to overpraise them. He's seen miracles wrought by praise. A woman said of a man whose face was almost hideous, "What a monster! He's an eyesore." The monster praised her, succeeded in pleasing her and ended by sleeping with her.

He believes that men are more sensitive than women, that a man or a woman always puts feeling into the first love affair. I feel that he's made me bolder with A. [Adèle Rebuffel].

25 *Germinal* [*April 15*].—I gave a luncheon for Dalban, Rey and Mante at the Café Valois. Rey, the philosopher, proposes to establish a system whereby he'll prove that individual happiness is always linked to general happiness. Good luck to him. Wants to write several comedies in conformity with this system. Appears to me to have little feeling at the age of twenty-five.

Dalban has much in common with Jean-Jacques [Rousseau] in the matter of conceit and distrust. They kept me till half-past twelve and bored me no little. They haven't any tact—however, I often lack it myself. I'm ashamed to praise a person to his face: I must get over this dismal idea.

It won't seem to me that I'm back in Paris until I've seen Adèle and her family. I must be sure to remember that I can win her back by combining amiability with an outward appearance of indifference. To achieve that, I must employ much naturalness, praise and banter.

26 *Germinal* [*April 16*].—Crozet came to see me; a noble simplicity served me well.

Il Bugiardo, by Goldoni, appeared to me full of naturalness and gave me an idea for a little opera while waiting for my trunk.

Didon and *Les Trois Sultanes.* The theater interests me far less this year than last; it almost bores me. Mlle. Duchesnois as Dido appeared to me far too affected. I saw all the flaws of the play, which appeared to me unnatural throughout. I perhaps owe my fervent feeling for natural beauty to my reading of the natural Shakespeare. Perhaps our actors will please me more when I get used to their affectation.

Crozet is going to introduce me to Mlle. Duchesnois any day now.

27 *Germinal* [*April 17*].—On getting up, I went to the Jardin des Plantes with M. Salmon. He believes that the professors of Paris are consummate quacks and worthless as professors, although very good as writers. An Italian savant said to M. Salmon, *"Tutti i Francesi sono gentili fuor che i letterati."* The people of other countries complain a lot of their arrogance.

In M. Salmon I see a profoundly sensitive soul, so much so that he can't even countenance the description of a depraved character. He hasn't any use for Molière and is very fond of Collin: he points out with pleasure that M. Evrard is the only depraved character he depicts. His is a soul, quite perceptible to an artist, that's prevented by too much sensibility from judging accurately.

I'm impatient for my trunk to arrive so I can get down to work, I'm tired of being obscure.

29 *Germinal* [*April 19*].—Tonight, under the name of Junius, I wrote a reply to the article of the 27th in which Geoffroy abuses Mlle. Duchesnois.

M. Salmon left for Utrecht at five o'clock this morning. I took board with Mme. Gruel for 51 francs.

I had a very erroneous idea of the word friend. I was looking for a single friend,

Mais qu'il fût tout pour moi, comme moi tout pour lui.

Mankind isn't perfect enough for that. I must be content with seeing scattered among all my friends the qualities I should wish to be contained in a single friend. Besides, I can't have too many acquaintances; in Paris I have: Mante, TRUE FRIEND; Crozet, Jacquinet, M. P. Daru, Martial Daru, M. Daru THE FATHER, M. Debord, Boissat, Cardon, TRUE FRIEND, Prunelle, Rey, Dalban, La Roche, Dard, L. Barral.

Nothing is easier than to be on good terms with a man you see only once a month.

30 *Germinal* [*April 20*].—I'm fed up with doing nothing. I'm reading Mme. de Genlis's *Souvenirs*. There are fifty amusing pages mixed up with two hundred pages of sermons, and the sermons spoil the laughter. This book has strengthened my determination to be simple, natural and sincere when out in company.

I was to have been introduced to Mlle. Duchesnois, but I won't be until one of these days. All the better, she'll have read Junius—that is, unless Crozet has thrown it into the fire.

1 *Floréal* [*April 21*].—I'm still playing the lottery. I could have a room for 18 francs at my 51-franc boardinghouse, which makes 69 francs, with 11 francs for spending money, 80 francs. 12 x 80 = 960 + 240 francs for clothes. Consequently, it's possible to live in Paris, going to the theater once a month, for 1,200 francs [a year]. I know that there are rooms for 8 francs in the Rue Jacques. You can have dinner at Mme. Desbenet's for 28 sous, which makes, by the month, 50 fr. + 10 fr. expenses = 60 francs. 12 x 60 = 720 + 200 francs for clothes = 920 francs. You can live on 900 francs. If I had only 1,200 francs, I'd prefer not to be obliged to spend more than 60 francs a month so I

could have 25 francs for entertainment each month. Thank heaven, I haven't been pinched for money yet this year.

3 Floréal [*April 23*].—I'm still waiting for my trunk. Perhaps I shouldn't have constructed THE TWO MEN as well six months ago as now; the division of man into soul and mind enlightens me more and more.

4 Floréal [*April 24*].—I read Fénelon and glanced through Beccaria (*on style*) at the Bibliothèque Nationale; I was pleased to find that Fénelon is in perfect agreement with me. In the evening, *Agamemnon:* the scene of the murder proposal was divinely played by Talma and Mlle. Duchesnois. After the play, Crozet introduced me to her. Her face, I found, is "in masses," something very well adapted for the portrayal of passions. In the future, when I'm going to be introduced to someone, I should write out beforehand the compliment I wish to pay, for when the time comes I'm confused. Crozet went out, I embraced Lemazurier (I mustn't forget to give a dinner or lunch for him and to tell him that M. Dubois quoted him in his class, and to pay for the carriage when we go to Versailles). I'm delighted with my evening, although, like a fool, I went and lost six francs at No. 113.[1] I was trying to win enough to buy the stereotypes FOR FRANCIS, MY SISTER AND ALPHONSE.

The only thing I said in Mlle. Duchesnois's presence was that *La Mère Coupable* and *Agamemnon* were the two most moral modern plays.

5 Floréal [*April 25*].—I received my trunk. I went for a walk with Crozet, Mante and Barral from five till nine. I came home very tired. Mante and I said good-by to Crozet in the Tuileries at a quarter past seven. Crozet urged me to go to see Mlle. Duchesnois tomorrow at noon.

Mante finds me much better this year than last; he said I had a diabolical energy last year. We have the same ideas on many things; he's discovered everything that Hobbes has said about laughter.

6 Floréal [*April 26*].—I finally started in on *The Two Men*. I had composed 306 lines at Grenoble, and I began on the 307th:

> *Le ciel m'attacha seule au soin de ton bonheur.*

I read over what I had already written, and the last two hundred lines seemed to me good.

I have just seen *Oedipe,* followed by *L'Amant Bourru.* I liked *Oedipe:* it has some very fine lines, in which Racine's manner may be clearly recognized. The subject is magnificent, there are some general maxims which are the exact opposite to what is needed in order to have an effect. There's nothing in the world as ridiculous as the bluster of

[1] Notorious gambling hall of the Palais-Royal, described by Balzac in his *The Wild Ass' Skin.*

Philoctète; his love affair with Jocasta, who is a grandmother, is displeasing.

Mlle. Raucourt spoke three or four lines almost well, all the others badly. Talma acted excellently; his expression was sublime in the last acts; he shouted a bit in the fourth, he shouted, "You are trembling, madame . . . ," which, it seems to me, should have been spoken with the despondency of an unfortunate who sees his sentence confirmed.

I'm going to see Mlle. Duchesnois tomorrow. I must ask her when she's going to play the role of Jocasta so we can thoroughly enjoy the scene of the double confidence.

7 *Floréal* [*April 27*].—About two o'clock, I learned from the porter of the house in the Rue Saint-Denis that M. Rebuffel was dead. The excellent man fell ill Easter Monday and succumbed three days later. Before that, I went to Mlle. Duchesnois's. They told me she wasn't home, I left a note.

8 *Floréal* [*April 28*].—I'm hard at work on the prose OF THE FIFTH scene. After dinner I went to the Luxembourg, and from there, about six o'clock, to the home of M. Daru [the father]. I found him with one foot in the grave. I found Martial, who greeted me with friendliness; Mme. Daru didn't say anything. M. Daru was so upset by a consultation the doctors had just held on his condition that I don't know whether he purposely failed to invite me to dinner. From there, I went TO THE GATE,[1] where I found gaiety. I expected as much OF THE MOTHER, THIS OF THE GIRL revolted me; EVEN during THE ACCOUNT OF HER FATHER'S DEATH she laughed boisterously. SHE EVEN HAS SEEMED TO ME HAVING HATE FOR HIM upon my saying that he would have settled his affairs had he lived. "He might at least have given some explanation," she said. This lack of feeling is frightful. I found her prettier, with more color (possibly given by the contrast with her mourning clothes). She told me her age was fifteen years, six months and five days. Last winter, she frequented the dance hall in the Rue du Bouloi which is popularly known as the Bal des Vestales. It costs only thirty sous and is open every Saturday. Its name shows how severe the entrance examinations are.

I stayed about an hour at Mme. Rebuffel's. I was in mourning.

9 *Floréal* [*April 29*].—*Bajazet, Les Deux Frères.* Never has Mlle. Duchesnois appeared more lovely to me than she was today as Roxane, and possibly never has a tragedy so consistently interested me as *Bajazet* did today: everything contributed to my illusion. My work tends to increase my sensibility. Desprez was very good as Osmin; Saint-Prix was good throughout, sometimes excellent, as Acomat. Mme. Talma

[1] Beyle frequently uses the English words to refer to the Rebuffels, who had a house near the Saint-Denis city gates.

was the only one who was detestable, with her doleful singsong as Atalide. Mlle. Duchesnois was above all praise. I went to see her after the performance; she greeted me again with the same naturalness, without compliments. Chazet arrived; he's a fine-looking man, he appeared to be surprised, I believe, at my natural and composed manner. He talked comedy and tragedy, making us laugh and being witty: as for myself, I expressed several apt opinions. While waiting for Mlle. Duchesnois, I saw Talma in the passageway: he's my size and was wearing a blue coat, knee breeches and black stockings. He was talking to the porter of the theater; his voice was the same as on the stage. Seeing him made an impression on me, he had the tragic look. I felt that I was coming into contact with fame. After all the illusions of acquaintance and friendship with great men, I had at last come across a little reality. I hope that in a year or two I'll be friends with Mlle. Duchesnois and him through THE TWO MEN.

I thoroughly admired Racine tonight. He has an elegant sincerity that is charming. It's not the draftsmanship of Michelangelo, it's the freshness of Rubens. Tonight, I had a thousand ideas which, it seems to me, would have made a good commentary on *Bajazet*.

10 Floréal [*April 30*].—Ten verses and the prose of *Le Raccommodement*.[1] At dinner, I displayed my skill at discussion. I have a pain in the mesentery from drinking a cup of coffee. At the Consul's side at yesterday's performance of *Bajazet*, I saw a woman who looked exactly like a skeleton: she had the bleached appearance of a well-washed skull, she really made your blood run cold; I've never seen anything like it, I stared at her a lot so as to retain a clear idea of her. She was very well dressed. It was the horror produced by death—that alone, without any other horror.

11 Floréal [*May 1*].—I've just been to see *Iphigénie en Aulide*. Not a line of this tragedy touched my soul. It's true it was played in as spiritless a manner as possible. Saint-Prix pitiful, Talma and Mlle. Duchesnois mediocre, Mlle. Raucourt unbearable.

After the performance, I went to see Mlle. Duchesnois with Favier; we found her in great anger against Mlle. Raucourt, who threatened her because she herself was hissed; it seems that Mlle. Raucourt has the manners of a fishwife. Favier spoke like a man who is conscious of his dignity. If his heart corresponds to his manner, and if he really owes his position to Mlle. Duchesnois, he is an estimable man and one with whom I ought to make friends. Second session of the Tribunat to declare Bonaparte Emperor.

12 Floréal [*May 2*].—I went to the Tribunat at noon, the session started

---

[1]*Le Raccommodement,* or reconciliation, was the big scene of Beyle's play, *The Two Men.*

at two o'clock. Several tribunes spoke like villainous rogues. Savoye-Rollin spoke in the manner of an intelligent man with a corrupt heart who sneers at everything. Costaz was not as bad as the others. I saw Carnot in the twentieth seat. I sat near a woman who slightly resembled Victorine. This resemblance enchanted me: what would it be then were I to see her herself! In the evening, I took a two-hour walk with Mante, WE SPEAK OF THE PASSIONS AND PHILOSOPHY.

13 Floréal [*May 3*].—I went to the French Museum. I well realize that you should never force your sentiment, as I did last year; it seems to me that only the center of comprehension can be forced. I worked all morning on THE TWO MEN. I began taking the herb juice. I put in an appearance at Mme. de Baure's and M. Daru's. Pierre Daru had just arrived. I went to see M. Le Brun, who displayed some wit, and consequently ought to be satisfied with mine. I feel that the time has passed to be a republican: I mustn't let ambition crowd out my plans for fame, but I mustn't do anything opposed to it. Publish AFTER MY DEATH. MY FATHER sent me TEN louis.

14 Floréal [*May 4*].—I came home at one-thirty this morning (consequently, the 15th). I returned from the home of Mlle. Duchesnois, to whose porter I gave a three-page article and a note. An hour earlier, Mlle. Duchesnois had hinted in her dressing room that she wished someone would take her defense. She received me very well tonight, invited me again to go to her house. Generally speaking, this visit was a series of victories, and to think that I hesitated to make it! Therefore, general maxim: I should go to see her every time, but should cut the visit short as soon as I see that I'm bothering her.

17 Floréal [*May 7*].—Nothing new from the 14th to the 17th. I'm working on THE TWO MEN. I stumbled on this line:

L'amour est un combat d'orgueil et d'espérance.

19 Floréal [*May 9*].—I see by the newspapers that the price of a copyist is three livres a day, or twenty-one livres a week; that's an indication. I'm writing this in my new room, Rue de Lille, No. 500, where I slept for the first time (19 francs).

20 Floréal [*May 10*].—I haven't worked on THE TWO MEN yet today; I finished moving. I read the gentle Vauvenargues; he charms me. I dressed at half-past nine to go to see Mlle. Duchesnois. I found her horribly tired and without a shift, the same as the day Crozet introduced me. A quarter to ten was striking when I passed the Tuileries, ten o'clock was striking when I passed it again on the way back. She had little to say; she told me she gave her porter a good scolding, etc. She repeated that twice, and asked me if my name wasn't Lebel, saying (I believe) that she wasn't able to read *my signature* very well. That was the only thing she said in connection with my errand of the 14th. I behaved well: I was right to see her, right not to go to *Agamemnon,* which bores me.

21 *Floréal* [*May 11*].—I got up this morning, went to the Régence for a cup of coffee, and returned home at eight o'clock. I worked without a break till four o'clock, and I couldn't compose the 353rd line of THE TWO MEN in a passable manner.

In the Tuileries I gave fifteen sous to a poor old man who had everything needed to touch me deeply, a moment later I saw a father playing with his daughter of about three years. These two little encounters touched me deeply. Later, I came across Dalban, with whom I'm well pleased, outside of his slight conceitedness.

This evening, I said something to Dalban which I believe to be true and of which he approved. It was that Racine lacks the qualities necessary to produce the greatest possible effect on the stage. I believe that these qualities can be reduced to concision and to dialogue that is spirited and condensed when passion requires it.

Everything, even the harmony of the verse, must be sacrificed to passion, which is the only thing that makes a play live.

The metromaniac's compliments (of my uncle's florid kind, ornate) pleased the pit today, 21 Floréal, and it seems to me that this pit was composed of the happy few. I was pleased with them myself.

I'm still of the opinion that it's better to express the genuine badly than to express excellently something that's not genuine, no matter how near it may be to the genuine.

21 *Floréal to 1 Prairial* [*May 11–21*].—I have too much to write; that's why I don't write anything. I dined IN FATHER DARU'S HOUSE and in that of Carrara. I saw *Phèdre* twice: Mlle. Duchesnois showed much progress, firmness in the details, sublime; better the first time than the second; the first time I was with Mante.

The 30th, Sunday, I passed an hour FOR THE FIRST [time] at the home of Phaedra [Mlle. Duchesnois].

I'm at the 375th [line of *The Two Men*].

The 30th, Sunday, I spent an hour with Ariadne [Mlle. Duchesnois] on the balcony of her apartment, Rue Saint-Georges, No. 18, her diction instructor made the third. That hour was too long by half. As I was leaving, Ariadne paid Basset a compliment which I took as something nice for me.

Am writing this 26 Germinal XIII [April 16, 1805] after rereading the above; I remember perfectly all my mistakes, I still see very distinctly all I did a year ago: the outline of the Théâtre Français, the trip at one in the morning to Ariadne's, etc.

Edouard Mounier (aloof and conceited) has just left my room. What asininity to worry about the future! Victorine is here and I haven't seen her: how happy I would have been a year ago if I'd been told that she would be in Paris in Germinal XIII!

Third Voyage to Paris

Second Notebook

Notes on cover.—All men on earth are seeking the things that will benefit them, the poet alone is in quest of nothing but our happiness. *Divina poeta!*

I should regard everything I've read up to now on mankind as a prophecy, and should believe nothing but what I have seen myself. JOY, HAPPINESS, FAME, ALL IS UPON IT.

It seems to me that the two characters of this century are the egoist and the vainglorious man, the first being capable of more vigor, the second of more gaiety. We mustn't permit ourselves to be swerved from our course.

Delaharpize and *degagnonize*[1] my taste by frequently reading the greatest dramatists in existence: *Aeschylus, Euripides, Sophocles, Shakespeare,* Corneille, *Alfieri,* Racine, *Aristophanes,* Molière, Goldoni, Plautus.

4 Prairial [May 24].—After racking my brains from ten in the morning till four in the afternoon trying to write two and a half lines [of *The Two Men*], I went to the Montansier [the present Théâtre du Palais-Royal]. Everything there appeared detestable to me. From there to Frascati and the Mille Colonnes.

5 Prairial [May 25].—Eleven lines: I've reached the 401st. During the past month, I've spent two hours and fifty-six minutes on each line.

Andromaque (for the second time), followed by *Sganarelle*. Talma acted perfectly, especially in the second scene of the second act: *"Oui, oui, vous me suivrez."* What an actor if he'd played like this throughout! Mlle. Duchesnois put far too many chromatic scales into her lines. I saw her after the performance, she received me superlatively; she was

---

[1]Beyle means by this that he must get over the influence of La Harpe and his grandfather, Dr. Henri Gagnon.

angry at the audience, which didn't insist on a curtain call; besides, she realized that she had been eclipsed by Talma.

Favier told me that Talma arranged for Napoleon to be admitted free to the Français in his youth.

15 Prairial [June 4].—I'm thinking of *Le Faux Métromane*. The idea came to me while thinking of Geoffroy's extract from the M. The newspapers are therefore worth the trouble of reading.

From a letter to Louis Crozet, June 8.—I certainly hope the comic, in which it's almost necessary to have sang-froid, will pick up in speed. Otherwise it will take me three years to write *Les Deux Hommes*. One day I'd turn out eight lines, and the two following days I'd turn out one. In other words, I'd compose forty bad ones, and then the good one would come to me ready-made. It was in this way that I produced

me croyant meprisée encore je t'adorais

which I consider excellent (I'm talking to you as I would to myself) because it shows the triumph of love over vanity (pride of little things), which is saying not a little, as I believe that women are all vanity, at least $\frac{99,999}{100,000}$.

The last twenty lines took me nearly two days each.

18 Prairial [June 7].—I'm trying to cool off in order to be able to correct my plot of THE TWO MEN.

I went to the Bibliothèque Nationale. I read the third volume of Goldoni's French *Mémoires,* the least interesting of the three. I must examine the French style of this Italian, there is something pleasing about it. I believe it's the extreme clarity; his sentences are short, and he prefers to repeat the subject rather than to employ a pronoun. I must examine it at leisure for my major work on style.

I read one of his comedies entitled *Il Cavaliere di Buon Gusto,* thinking that I might discover therein something in common with *Le Faux Métromane.* The subject isn't at all the same. *Il Cavaliere di Buon Gusto* is the model man of the world. This play is charming, the nuance of the young man who has just left school is very well grasped.

I could do over in French a number of the subjects that Goldoni has dealt with in Italian. If I were to follow up this project, my plays would have absolutely nothing in common with his, outside the subject matter. His plots aren't substantial enough for me, and his humor isn't delicate enough for us. For instance, *Il Cavaliere di Buon Gusto* gives me the idea of a play entitled *L'Homme du Monde* which would offer a model of the conduct of a thoroughly agreeable man of the world. It would be necessary to place him in the principal circumstances of life, to show him in at least four acts of sang-froid. He'd emerge honorably and gracefully from all the circumstances in which he found himself, he'd be very witty. I'd show him in all life's relations, I'd be able to show my century through the characters on the stage with him—a merchant, a young man entering society, etc., etc. An idea to be followed up.

When you finish reading Goldoni, you're amazed at how little dramatic talent our authors have. All the characters of this amiable portraitist have relief, they live; they're not very animated, he hasn't attained the heights of his art, but he's always gay, completely natural, and, from what I know of him, I place him immediately after Regnard, so that the comic Parnassus is composed of Molière, Regnard and Goldoni.

19 Prairial [June 8].—Goldoni thinks as I do about the majority of those comedies in verse which were given in France around 1750: they were lacking in everything.

Here is what Goldoni says of Diderot's *Le Père de Famille* in the third volume of his *Mémoires:* '. . . He is one of those unfortunate beings who are to be found in real life, but I should never have dared to put him on the stage.' What's the use of showing life under an unfavorable aspect? It's a poor merit.

21 Prairial [June 10].—At ten o'clock, I went to the reading room, where I read Palissot and learned of Moreau's sentence. From there to the Luxembourg. Two pictures by David, lack of expression.

Le Cid and *La Maison de Molière.* The audience was avid of applications against Bonaparte and in favor of Moreau. In the *Maison,* at the words, *"Les originaux sont à la cour,"* only one person applauded, but everyone was pleased.

The *Maison* enjoyed a complete success. It's a sort of dialogue between actors and audience. The actors speak, the audience laughs or applauds. The naturalness of this play is charming. Goldoni is perhaps the most natural poet in existence, and naturalness is one of the principal parts of Art.

A poet is made up of a philosopher and a versifier: the versifier can be held up to ridicule, reason never.

It was almost without thinking and while writing offhand that I discovered this truth, which I believe to be a capital one: *Tragedy is the development of an action and comedy of a character.*

In order to be as you should be in life, you mustn't live for yourself; in order to write sublime works, you must live for your genius, form it, cultivate it, correct it.

I'm so worn out by my thoughts that I can't write them down, in spite of a bottle of beer I went out to buy at Blancheron's.

25 Prairial [June 14].—The anniversary of Marengo. In the evening, a walk in the Tuileries with Fortuné [Mante], who told me a lot of details about the judgment of Moreau.

27 Prairial [June 16].—I read Hobbes's excellent work entitled *De la Nature Humaine.*

5 Messidor [June 25].—The end of two wrangles: George [Cadoudal] was guillotined at 11:35, together with the rest who weren't pardoned. *Les Tracasseries [The Wrangles],* a comedy by Picard, was a failure. The accused who were let off were condemned to deportation; Moreau is leaving for the United States, which, in the same century, will have seen Washington, Kosciusko and Moreau.

11 Messidor [June 30].—At one in the morning, M. Daru the son arrived; at five, M. Daru the father expired.

The day before yesterday I went AT THE Saint-Denis GATE. I found Adèle alone, she received me better than ever, with all sorts of attentions, kindnesses, etc. I stayed for half an hour. Three weeks before, in front of her mother, she received me in exactly the opposite way.

Today, I went up because of THE DEATH OF Daru, and stayed three quarters of an hour. I found the mother with an agent; a minute later, the daughter arrived, a thimble on her finger. During the conversation, she took the defence of virtue; what's more, she and her mother discussed what would happen if she got married—that she would remain in the same house as her daughter and son-in-law, etc. Unhappily, I felt my face growing red. I went away, joking as I left. I concluded that she was casting eyes on me FOR A HUSBAND.

But, as everything is a matter of chance, I didn't find her as pretty as the other day; I found her homely today. I wish she might learn for certain from some other source than me that, when I wrote her love letters, I was head over heels in love with Victorine.

I ought to stay away for ten days. I'll bet it was Baure who made them cast eyes on me. But I hope to have her someday; she'll be a charming mistress, but for me she'd make a poor wife.

12 Messidor [July 1].—At seven this morning, I went to Saint-Thomas-d'Aquin to attend prayers for M. Noël Daru. I noticed the base and occasionally malevolent physiognomy of the priests; those with the best faces had a stupid appearance.

For several reasons, it's good manners to join in what everybody is doing. Tabarié singing. A simple and natural air in all that was done.

It's the custom to go to the house of death. You get in a black carriage, you go to the church; after prayers, you accompany the dead person to his last dwelling. Summer house, winter house.

13 Messidor [July 2].—Summer rain at four o'clock. I dined in the Rue de la Loi opposite a lath; the people who went upstairs amused me a lot with their character traits. The rain put me in that divinely tender mood I used to experience in Italy.

16 Messidor [*July 5*].—At the Bibliothéque Nationale, I read the *Menagiana ed il Cavaliere e la Dama, comedia di tre atti in prosa del* Goldoni.

The *Menagiana* depicts a pedant who is witty but extremely boresome. This man is a contemporary of Molière. This great man, Corneille and La Fontaine are free from the least suggestion of pedantry; Boileau and Racine have a shade. I must correct myself of pedantry, for it exists in this century, as it existed in the time of Molière. Our pedantry is, I believe, to philosophize interminably about the least bagatelle—I believe my conversations with Faure last year should be excellent models for that. I'm indebted to Tencin [Louis de Barral] for getting over this weakness. Few acquaintanceships have been as valuable for me as his. He has shown me the man of the world in his entirety, he had shown me this man's heart. He had furnished me with this fine rule: of all writers, I should be the one who offends the vanity of my readers the least, I should appear completely natural to them without their noticing it—for a deaf woman would be displeased at your shouting if she were conscious of it.

[*July 12*].—In the newspapers of 23 Messidor, XII (*Publiciste, Journal de Paris, Journal du Soir*).

Still another example of the Othello catastrophe in Italy, near Genoa. A jealous lover kills his mistress, fifteen years old and of a rare beauty; flees, writes two letters (invaluable testimonials), returns to the body of his mistress, which was in her father's oratory, about midnight, and there shoots himself dead with a pistol, the same way that he killed her.

Seek the truth in this fact.

That's the sort of thing that makes me realize more and more that mellow Italy is the land where people feel the most deeply, the land of poets.

According to the *Journal de Paris,* it's possible for a man to give birth to a child and for both of them to live afterward. The thing happened in Holland.

23 Messidor [*July 12*] (*while reading in my sensations*).—My need of self-assurance comes from my being habitually without money.

When I lack money, I'm bashful wherever I go; since I lack it frequently, the bad tendency to find reasons for my bashfulness in everything I see has become almost a habit with me.

I must absolutely get over it. The best way would be to carry a hundred gold louis in my pocket every day for at least a year. The constant weight of the gold would destroy the root of the evil.

Journal of My Third Voyage to Paris

From 26 Messidor to 24 Thermidor, XII, exclusively

Edouard Mounier tells me he'll be in Paris early in Thermidor. MY FATHER announces an allowance of 2,400 fr. for me EVERY YEAR.

July 14.—A superb day. Upon getting up at ten o'clock, we went to the Régence. The Abbé Hélie arrived, and we went together to the Tuileries, where we stayed till one o'clock, with him all the time. He amused us no end. What he told us confirmed my principles. We saw Bonaparte perfectly. He passed on horseback fifteen paces from us; he was on a beautiful white horse, in fine new attire, a plain hat, uniform of a colonel of his guards, aiglets. He saluted a great deal and smiled. A theatrical smile, in which the teeth are displayed but the eyes don't smile.

The Invalides was jammed for the ceremony. He left the Tuileries at noon and returned at half-past three. There was some space left at the Tuileries. At his passage the crowd shouted, "Long live the Emperor!" but very faintly; even more so, "Long live the Empress!"

The evening of the thirteenth, he was at the Français, where *Iphigénie* was given free. He wasn't applauded at all. The night before, he was at *Les Bardes*. The receipts at the Opéra when the house is full go as high as 12,000 francs. The house was more than full, and they didn't go past 6,000 francs. Consequently, he was applauded.

I went to Mme. Carrara's at eight o'clock tonight. There I saw M. Cass[ini?] with his uniform and decoration. It was the first time I ever had an opportunity to observe the asinine vanity and prattle of a savant, and the avidity which a man unaccustomed to commanding respect has for constantly reminding himself and others that he's commanding it at present. It must be admitted that if all men of letters are like this one they are a very boring and ridiculous lot indeed. Phrases of this kind popped up constantly: "It's up to the savants like us . . ." "It's up to us, the savants of the Academy . . ." "He (Borda) was greatly appreciated by all the most learned men of the Academy, we thought very highly of him." There ought to be a Molière for people like that.

30 Messidor [*July 10*].—This morning, I bought *Le Opere Varie del divino* Alfieri as an antidote against the mephitis of baseness that surrounds me. In the evening, I went to *Iphigénie*. I was bothered a little by fever. Duchesnois performed well. George isn't very pretty, she has one of those insensitive faces, utterly lacking in character expression, nothing agreeable, nothing indicating a soul. She has a cabal, that's quite obvious; and she interpreted the role of Eriphile very badly.

Saint-Prix was flabby and bombastic, Talma firm and bombastic. Bombast is the general defect of our actors; I believe that this may be due in part to the everlasting verbosity of Racine's and Voltaire's plays. They write ten lines where two words would be enough; the debit has to be attributed to something. As soon as Talma slips back into naturalness (once yesterday), I am really stirred. Near me there was a pretty and nice-looking girl who wept. That's rare.

The pit has, to some extent, got over making allusions, but it's still aware of the places where they might be marked.

I persist in my opinion that *Iphigénie* is a bad play. It's possibly the one the vulgar appreciate the most genuinely. All the characters are mediocre, and consequently seem natural to the vulgar. If it hadn't been for my fever, I'd have gone to see Ariadne.

Two things that I must get rid of: the bombast of Racine in *Iphigénie,* and the execrable conceited and pedantic manner of M. C[assini?]. I have a tendency to be pedantic. I frequently say things that should only be done. In that respect, I must base myself on Martial's manners and the *Mémoires* of M. de Choiseul.

Remarks on July 14.—The Abbé Hélie, who has been a confessor and has studied mankind in man, told us that out of a hundred marriages there are twenty-five successful ones, where there's love, and fifty where husband and wife tolerate each other, where they even love each other, although the husband is frequently a cuckold. I spoke to him about the absolution that was asked of him in Grenoble for a poisoning.

He pointed out to us that the chiefs of all the parties in the present administration are Jacobins. They said to Sieyès, who is invariably against the government, in speaking of the Duc d'Enghien's death, "It's a very great crime, it's a horrible crime." "So be it," he said. "A great crime as much as you wish, but the important thing is that it's a great error."

I must correct myself of a shortcoming. It comes from lack of practice in talking to people whom I wish to please. A subject is spoken of, my slow mind doesn't find the striking thing (within reason) to say on this subject until the conversation has turned to something else. Then I sometimes yield to the temptation of saying what I had to say, which makes me seem ponderous and dull. The Abbé Hélie has swift and complete transitions. That's very good and should be imitated.

While the Abbé Hélie was with us in the Tuileries, a woman passed; there was nothing in the least remarkable about her except that in her eyes and look she resembled Victorine ever so slightly. That overwhelmed me, and I was beside myself for a couple of seconds.

1 Thermidor [*July 20*].—The queue in front of the Opéra for *Les Bardes* was drenched by a terrific downpour. We couldn't get in.

2 Thermidor [*July 21*].—I've just been to *L'Eté des Coquettes* and *Les Bourgeois à la Mode*. These two plays by Dancourt are as boring as they can be, everything languishes in them and nothing is interesting. *Les Précieuses Ridicules* still makes the audience laugh. Everything in it is vigorous: what power this play must have had in its day, when everything struck home! There's the *vis comica* that must be acquired, and without which there can't be any comedy. I didn't have any notion of that last year. I thought I was being comic when I painted passions vigorously. I must study the manners and morals of my contemporaries —what appears to them to be just, unjust, honorable, dishonorable, good breeding, ill breeding, ridiculous, agreeable, etc. That's the sort of thing that changes every half century.

4 Thermidor [*July 23*].—At the library, I read *L'Esprit de Mirabeau,* a work to be meditated and discussed thoroughly. I read the part: Philosophy. I'm in one of the most delightful states of mind I have experienced in my life. In *di quel grande* writings, I've come across several ideas I've already had. On Montesquieu, for instance, that his *L'Esprit des Lois* won't be read long; my ideas on incontinence, a vice which is harmful only to the person who has it, more or less.

5 Thermidor [*July 24*].—I had a long conversation with Mante, who believes my latest discoveries are true; he found Sieyès's phrase excellent.

7 Thermidor [*July 26*].—Tencin [Louis de Barral] and I have just been to *Rodogune,* followed by *Le Florentin.* We left after *Rodogune* in order not to let our impression weaken. Tencin almost fainted when Mlle. Fleury said:

> "*Voyez ses yeux*
> *Déjà tout égarés, troubles et furieux."*

Talma was superb. I haven't seen him act so well since *Andromaque,* 5 Prairial, XII. He interpreted all the sweetness of friendship excellently. He began with perfect naturalness, and didn't emerge from it during the first four acts; a bit of screaming in the fifth, but quite pardonable, about the frightful situation of Antiochus. Superb, however; in all his postures, he looked exactly like Raphael's fine faces. He was dressed in white during the first four acts, in red and a diadem in the last. He interpreted the prostration of grief excellently. This great actor is sometimes lacking in ideas, and sometimes in naturalness. Geoffroy & Co. almost blame him for having too much; according to them, he has an untamed naturalness.

Rodogune never impressed me so deeply. There are beauties of the highest order in the delineation of character (are they equal to Shakespeare's fine scenes?), but there are great defects in *scenegiatura*. These might easily have been avoided. I believe the study of Alfieri will make me strong in that respect.

I noticed two defects in the character delineation: the first is that Cleopatra, in speaking to Laonice, looks as though she was giving a lesson in politics. The politics are very fine, but they're out of place and chill the play. What should have been done is to apply the maxims to the facts without mentioning them.

The second defect, I believe, comes from the Spaniards. It is a false sense of delicacy which prevents the characters from going into the details, with the result that they are never terror-stricken, as in the plays of Shakespeare. They don't dare mention their room by name, they don't speak enough of what surrounds them.

Generally speaking, all the characters are loquacious; moreover, there are some great defects of *scenegiatura,* but what wouldn't the fifth act redeem! There's nothing finer in Shakespeare.

Tencin was delighted with this play, especially when, after one of the characters said something and it seemed as though there were nothing that could be replied, his interlocutor said something even more forceful. The beauties of *Rodogune* affected him much more than those of *Andromaque* and *Phèdre,* which he says are good for ardent people, for women.

"Those are beauties for people of sentiment," he said, "while in *Rodogune,* by God, you feel it!"

"That's because it deals with life," I answered, "and everyone loves life."

Besides, I have there the confirmation, by a perfect experiment carried out under my eyes and by myself, of this truth, which I wrote long ago:

Shakespeare, so natural, so ardent and so vigorous, seems as though he needed only Alfieri's art of *scenegiatura* and Corneille's manner of composing verse to attain the height of perfection.

Moreover, all that I've just written wouldn't have been understood by Tencin or another person if I'd told it to them. They don't see the things on which these truths are founded. Consequently, I must never talk about literature.

15 *Thermidor* [*August 3*].—Curiosity plays an important role in love. I, to whom drawing has given the habit of seeking the nude beneath the

clothes and of picturing it to myself distinctly, am consequently less susceptible to love than another person might be.

23 *Thermidor* [*August 11*].—I've seen Tencin, Martial and Mante. I've been to the theater frequently, thought little about my former castles in Spain of happiness through love.

This month has been passed in the study of noble philosophy in order to find the bases of the best possible comedies and, generally speaking, the best poems, as well as the best road for me to follow in order to find in society all the happiness it is capable of giving me.

I've had a slight fever every evening, and yet I've been happy; I only wish that the rest of my life might give me proportionately as much pleasure as this month. I have succeeded in knowing myself, and have seen that I must knock at the Temple of Memory if I am to find happiness, and that, for me, love is the sole passion that won't be crowded out BY THE LOVE OF GLORY, but that it will be subordinated to the latter, or at best will only be capable of usurping a few moments now and then.

Note added a year and a half later.—I reread this notebook January 10, 1806 at Marseille; it seems to have filled its purpose well enough. At times, there are some moments of profundity in the portrayal of my character. These moments of profundity have come to me by fits and starts since that time: I hope that Tracy's *Logique* will enable me to stabilize them.

(January 10, 1806, AFTER seventeen months.)

Journal of My Third Voyage to Paris

Notebook containing from 24 Thermidor XII to . . .

This notebook starts auspiciously today, Sunday, 24 Thermidor [August 12]. Having taken for the first time some extract of gentian and a tisane of lesser centaury and orange leaves, I'm as happy as a lark at three o'clock in the afternoon, bright sunshine after the rain, discovering the excellent ideas which open the notebook on *firm volition*. It's a milder variety of happiness, but it's every bit as intense as that of the Sunday at Claix when, after composing the first good verses I ever discovered in my life, I dined alone and informally on some excellent spinach and gravy and good bread. Man being what he is, such ecstasies can't last.

As accurately as I can judge, still being so close to the events, the three most delightful moments of my life have been: Adèle leaning against me during the fireworks at Frascati in Year X, I believe, the Sunday at Claix in Year . . . , and today.[1]

I remark that, since MY LOVE FOR Adèle IS cooled off, the memory of Frascati is gradually losing its charm and becoming effaced. Apply this generally: nevertheless, at the moment itself it was extreme; the only thing is that the sum of what happiness will procure for me in my whole life will be less because the pleasure of recalling it has lasted only two years, whereas the recollection of the pleasures procured by the love of glory will last longer. Glory, at least, is one mistress I'm not likely to desert.

It seems to me that, with my *head* of today, seeing as I see, I can find these lively and, so to speak, divine pleasures nowhere but in Paris.

I spent Friday with Martial. We went to see Mme. Rebuffel and La Rive. A course of twelve lessons at twelve louis, that's a bit steep.

After dinner, in the mahogany desk on the third floor, I saw the folders containing the letters and replies of more than twenty-five mistresses. We skimmed through all of those of Adèle . . . , whose virginity he had. More wit than passion, but at any rate it's a chance to study love in real life. That's well worth six louis.

30 *Thermidor* [*August 18*].—We embraced upon returning from the luncheon given by Diday and Moulezin. From there to the museum, where the picture of the judge made almost no impression on them. The reason for this, I believe, is the agitation of the soul, which is too much taken up with living (in newly arrived provincials) to be capable of sympathizing. A thing to be remarked: the soul has only *states* in stock, never *qualities*. Where's the joy of the man who weeps? Nowhere. That's a state. The deadly boredom inspired in Tencin by Diday and Moulezin. It seems to me that Moulezin is in about the same class as Rouget. What a difference! The one is ridiculous, the other isn't even worthy of being so. My bases of comparison make me more severe than most people in my opinion of mankind, and make me try to have all the sentiments OF MY SOUL sublime and worthy of the stage. I must stop having this kind of enjoyment, as it's too severe. Will this passion be a compensation for me in other pleasures?

I've been a score of times to see Mante, who's laid up with gout.

2 *Fructidor* [*August 20*].—We've just been to *Il Matrimonio Segreto*, which appeals to me more and more. I've thought often of Victorine. It seems to me that when I see THE FATHER AND THE BROTHER IN Paris, I WILL CAN try OF WRITING TO HER.

[1]Beyle several times refers to the evening with Adèle Rebuffel at Frascati, an open-air café and dance hall formerly at the corner of the Boulevards and the Rue de Richelieu, but under the dates indicated there is no mention in his diary of this evening or of the Sunday at Claix.

5 Fructidor [August 23].—Tencin won 129 livres at 113 and I lost 16.

I've just been to *Andromaque,* in which Mlle. Duchesnois played the part of Andromaque; Lafond is hopelessly mediocre. There are several things in the style of *Andromaque* which ought to be banished from mine. All that business of chains, fire, the power of your eyes, etc. smacks of La Calprenède's novels and is taken from them. When tragedies reach their second act, I'm invariably full of ideas which I don't remember when the play is over. When I see a play acted, it seems to me that the auditorium is illuminated and peopled in proportion to the warmth of the play. I can't imagine *Andromaque* performed in the desert.

6 Fructidor [August 24].—One of the most agreeable days I've spent in Paris.

At nine o'clock I called for Martial to go to La Rive's. We had breakfast and went there at ten o'clock. We spoke the first scene from *Athalie* and the first from *Venceslas.*

Leaving there, we went to take a lemonade at the Café de Foy, he invited me to dinner, I went to see Mme. de Baure a minute, I returned home at two o'clock. I set to work and decided to do *Le Bon Parti.*[1]

I worked till five o'clock. I went to Pacé's, we talked over Mme. Cardon's plan to marry him to Mlle. Pauline Auguié, the one who's the present wife of Marshal Ney. I saw that he'd prefer to take some nice little girl who'd bring him the pleasures of the heart, rather than obtaining some high rank that might be offered. Coming after other things, this decided me: he's a man worthy of being loved, and I want to merit being his friend.

He declaimed a bit from *Ladislas.* M. Le Brun arrived, we went out to go to the Tuileries. Near the statue of Diana, in the path parallel to the palace, we found the ladies with Adèle; we joked, and I was as pleasing to them as Pacé. I was delighted with this brief moment. We left them; Pacé introduced me in a comical way to Mme. Hanet, who happened along and whom he's had.

From there he suggested taking me to the Opéra. I put up some objections and asked him how much it would cost. "Nothing." I went along, and we went to the grilled loge on the stage at the left of the actors. They were giving *Les Bardes,* the eleventh performance, I believe. Bonnet, the manager, said the receipts were between 75,000 and 76,000 francs.

I understood that the loge and, I believe, the one above it are rented in common by Pacé and M. Lajard. The latter arrived, their manners

[1]This was a one-act play that Beyle was thinking of writing. The idea was later expanded into *Letellier,* the full-length comedy upon which he worked spasmodically for thirty years without ever finishing.

were those of perfect equality, but that's the only equality that exists between them. Lajard is far from being what Pacé is, a veneer of vulgarity is constantly spread over him; in my opinion, he has the appearance of having been for long a banker at Lyon, and that's possibly the job best suited to spoil a man. I examined these gentlemen's manners. I saw that the correct manner was the most simple. Pacé, whom I'd do very well to study and frequently to imitate, invariably says what comes into his head. This manner is a good one in that it can be adopted only by people whose heart is the kind that may be put on display. It seems to me that I'd acquire it very quickly if I had an occupation which obliged me to see these gentlemen daily for a couple of months.

I well digested this evening as far as observation is concerned, and it was delightful for the happiness it gave me; I was really beside myself. I didn't in the least lose ground to the extent of being afraid of being swamped, I felt myself being gently carried away.

Therefore, I should merely say what comes into my head, and say it simply and without affectation. I should always avoid any attempt to produce an effect in conversation; equality is the great law to follow if you wish to please.

8 Fructidor [*August 26*].—A year ago I was at Claix, all alone during the intense heat . . .

I thought about comedy and discovered some good principles on the ODIOUS. The comic poet who makes things odious goes out of the character of comedy. The study of comedy is more or less the study of society, and it's the study that's best suited to form me.

When I get a start in the poetic career, I must take Martial and the girls of the Opéra as my models in order to ward off that veneer of inferiority which, ever since Racine and Boileau, this art has given in respect to people of high society.

I should adopt the manner of Chapelle,[1] an epicure whose verses are the accessories of life, not the principal thing.

Today has been such as I imagined life when I began to think seriously of becoming a great poet. The morning devoted to fruitful work, the evening passed in the highest society. After dinner, at seven o'clock, I went to the Tuileries with Tencin. There I found Pacé giving his arm to Adèle AND TO HER MOTHER.

I'm not going to continue this description, for it would require too much working over if it were to show that magnificent happiness which I tasted for the first time, and after so intensely desiring it.

The better you know mankind, the more you are able to overlook the little shortcomings of your friends. The exalted way protagonists

[1] A character in his play *Letellier*.

have when they are at the maximum of passion (tragically) or of affinity (comically) would send me off to a desert if I took into society that inflexible severity I have for the figures I portray.

I must be very careful of that; it's my great failing and might make me as ridiculous in the opinion of society as La Harpe would be in mine if he were imprudent enough to criticize *Cinna.*

10 Fructidor [August 28].—This morning, I went to La Rive's, who told us he wouldn't be able to find two pupils with our ability in all Paris.

13 Fructidor [August 31].—This morning, I was with Pacé five hours on end; we went twice to La Rive's, the art of making an audience laugh at subjects I consider odious still plagues me a lot. I dined at five o'clock at Pacé's with Prévost and Dufresne, under-inspectors of reviews and division chiefs at the War Ministry, and Maisonneuve, a poet employed at the War Ministry under Prévost. He wasn't amiable at all, Pacé says, because he talks of nothing but verse. He has written eight plays, comedies and tragedies, of which only three have been performed and none published. We talked about verse from seven to ten; he recited two satires that he's written and a poem on the re-establishment of worship; they all seemed to me extremely good, especially the satires.

He told me his *Roxelane et Mustapha,* which was given 80 times, yielded him 15,000 francs up to the twenty-eighth performance, which he gave to the Comédie; otherwise, he would have made 25,000 francs with it.

Pacé is launching me in every way; never were six louis put to better use than those I've paid La Rive.

14 Fructidor [September 1].—Voyage to . . .[1]

In addition to my allowance, my father owes me 327 trancs from 1 Vendémiaire, Year XII [September 24, 1803].

If I leave 1 Vendémiaire, I'll have 200 fr. of my allowance. I'll need 100 fr. for expenses, consequently I'd have to ask Pacé for 200 fr. By economizing like the devil during the month of Vendémiaire, I'll be able at the very best not to make any new debts. Therefore, on 1 Brumaire, Year XIII [October 23, 1804], I'll have 100 fr. of debts. At that time, if my father doesn't give me anything, Martial will have to give me 200 fr., in which case, by not paying my 100 fr. of debts, I'll be the possessor by 1 Brumaire, Year XIII, of 300 fr. and the wearing apparel necessary for my departure.

Regarding Les Sonnettes [Rennes], it's consequently not impossible to go there. Clothes to take: my dress coat is all right; 6 shirts; 6 cravats; 6 handkerchiefs; 2 pairs of nankeen breeches; 4 pairs of silk stockings; 1 pair of new shoes.—To buy: green trousers; boots at 48 livres; 1 waistcoat.

[1]Rennes, the capital of Brittany, where Victorine Mounier was living.

Moral possibility, to be thought over. But next winter, no more out-ings, no more good times. Consequently, I have a month and a half till 1 Brumaire, and that's a long time.

16 Fructidor [September 3].—Pacé sent for me at four o'clock, I've just been to his house, he told me the dinner was for today. I barely had time to rush to the Palais-Royal to get a haircut, to return home and to rush back to Robert's, restaurateur, in the Rue des Bons-Enfants, where I arrived at six o'clock. There were twelve of us: Pacé, the sincere and consequently very agreeable Valmabelle, Possel, Aug. Janart and de Possai; the divinities were: Millière, Louise, the elder Mlle. Janart, the younger Mlle. Janart, Emilie, who's an extremely ugly dancer, and two old ladies. We sat down to table about half-past six, we got up at about half-past nine, and left Robert's at a quarter past eleven. I took leave of the other gentlemen, walked around the Palais-Royal and went to bed.

Undated—probably 19 Fructidor (September 6)

The 17th, for the first time, I experienced the lassitude of high society. I went to Pacé's at ten o'clock, and we went together to La Rive's. We went to lunch at the Café de Foy, then paid the rest of the bill at Robert's (the dinner cost 163 francs, there were twelve of us, plus 12 francs for the waiters). I saw Martial in that state of semi-boredom they often experience; as for myself, I was really bored with this life passed in the midst of amusements which, although you tell yourself that they're the *ne plus ultra* of good breeding, don't amuse you in the least. It was the first time I experienced boredom in the highest society. I examined myself, and I realized how much a good work of literature would appeal to them when they are in this state.

Yesterday I saw the right kind of pleasantry, not refined but clearly illustrated by M. de Possai. He said and did nothing but absolutely ridiculous things which didn't fatigue the mind in the least, but which made you laugh. Nothing is as appealing as that kind of foolery which doesn't seem to imply any wit in the person who indulges in it, which makes you laugh without being obliged to admire and doesn't weary you the least bit mentally.

At first blush, it seems as though genuine amiability would always be to say things that are charming and full of wit—but nothing would be more tiresome for your listeners. Laughter must be produced with the least wit possible.

Once it has reached a certain pitch, is laughter always of the same intensity? I wasn't able to solve this problem upon leaving the table. All I know is that women must be made to laugh by giving their minds the least effort possible. I must try to attain this frivolous manner as much as possible, and to get away from that heavy wit of mine which is tiresome and gives the impression of being ponderous and pedantic.

Nothing is as effective as sentiment employed in the right measure; I realized this when I said an agreeable and appropriate word to Louis, the waiter in Le Caveau; he let me see by his actions that I'd given him a very agreeable moment, he even showed a bit of affection for me.

One of the surest ways of consoling an afflicted person is to turn his attention to the analysis of his grief: at once it will diminish; pride invariably carries the day, wherever it may be placed. That shows the full extent of the nonsense in Voltaire, whose characters say, "I feel such-and-such a thing." There couldn't be any worse nonsense.

2nd Complementary Day [*September 19*].—Martial and I went to La Rive's home at Montlignon, in the Forest of Montmorency. Pleasant day, charming visit. We came back at nine o'clock. Martial went to Millière's. I stopped in at Lenoir's, borrowed *Timon of Athens,* an excellent comedy by Shakespeare, and came home to go to bed.

In its natural sense, taste (rules for producing such-and-such an effect) is half of genius, and it's the half that Pacé lacks. Returning by moonlight in the cabriolet, he recited some verses he'd written about the mistress of a Knight of Malta, in which there were some good things. There was some sparkle to it, because he'd sought the witty-emotional manner, but emotional people aren't like that, and he doesn't realize this, not having sufficiently studied the human heart.

5th Complementary Day [*September 22*], *last day of the Year XII.*—Got up. While conversing with me, Tencin admitted he was depressed because he'd lost 700 francs at 113. We were able to borrow 400 francs.

Went to the Museum, where I again saw the pretty girl who looks like Antinous and whom I saw at the distribution of the Legislation prizes. We looked at each other in a way that was full of meaning.

I returned at two o'clock, found Mante and we went to Mme. de Rezicourt's. We stayed there three quarters of an hour, and I talked incessantly; she didn't ask me to return. I think she was very glad to see me because she'd dined at my father's house in Grenoble, but my uncle was probably the cause of my undoing with her.

Mante told me he didn't have a chance to get in a word, and that's the great mistake I made: during first calls of this sort, the conversation shouldn't be allowed to fall off, but, while bearing this in mind, the introduced should let the introducer do the bulk of the talking in order that the tone of the conversation may become intimate as soon as possible.

It so happened that I didn't follow this rule, and that the conversation was quite different from what it usually is, according to what Mante told me.

During the course of the conversation, Mme. de Rezicourt told me that she finds informal gatherings as charming as visits made three times a year are detestable, that she has greatly curtailed her acquaintances, etc., etc. All of which seemed to tell me, and as a matter of fact did tell me, "Don't come back."

If my lotteries of Octavien-Arrigo-Fair-Montfort and of *Le Pervertisseur*[1] succeed, I may have between 2,000 and 6,000 francs to squander this winter. I may HAVE A FAIR WOMEN OF THE SOCIETY, THIS IS NECESSARY FOR LOVING ABSOLUTELY Vict., even IN THE CASE *nel quale trovarei in lei quel alma, grande e veramente amante, che forso ho sognata. E cosi finisce l'anno duodecimo della Republica.* [I may be able to possess a beautiful society woman. That's necessary in order genuinely to love Victorine, even in the case that I find in her that lofty and really loving soul of which I have possibly dreamed. And thus ends the Year XII of the Republic.]

Here is my scheme for making a fortune:

Go in July 1805 to Marseille, stay there six months working with Mante, from there six months spent in the same way at Bordeaux, from there four months at Nantes, from there eight months at Antwerp, from there finally to Paris. My father lends me thirty or forty thousand francs, and we establish the firm of Mante, Beyle & Co. in 1807 (Year XV). I'll be twenty-four years old at that time.

If by 1 Brumaire, Year XIII [October 23, 1804], I succeed in obtaining 200 francs in addition to my allowance, I can leave for L. [Rennes].

FOR THE morale, she must know that I've gone there.

Don't forget that 18 Brumaire, for the coronation, I'll find her alone. In that case, there's no further obstacle, as she'll be the only one who knew I was in L. I can see her while she is out walking without compromising her in the least. The only thing is that the mayor's records might inform TO THE RETURN [upon the return of Victorine Mounier's father and brother from the coronation ceremonies in Paris] that I had been in those parts.

She would realize that waiting for them to be away was what had held me back so long, and she'd be appreciative of my voyage. Maybe she'll be greatly changed AFTER TWO [years].

I reach L. . . . 20 Vendémiaire, Year XIII [October 12, 1804].

Voyage.

Sojourn.

I can leave a letter for Messrs. Périer with Mante, asking for 200 francs around the 20th, he could then send me the money at L. . . .

[1]Beyle himself and his many-titled play *Letellier*.

If I intend to go to L. . . . , what am I doing here? Remit to Sua., and leave.

But ought I to go?

Third Voyage to Paris

Journal of 1 Brumaire, Year XIII, to . . .

LET US SEE THE WORLD IN WRITING OF THE COMEDY, I SEE THAT IN MY SENSA-TIONS.

I must force myself to work.

You can't compose THE COMEDY properly IN THE TOO continual solitude, the ridiculous details become dim, and you no longer see anything but general precepts.

During the last days of Vendémiaire and the first of Brumaire, I was pestered by gastritis, which prevented me from *lavorare al Buono Partito* [from working on *Le Bon Parti*] as much as I should have liked.

3 Brumaire [October 25].—I went to the theater six days in a row, which kept me from working and made the after-dinner period painful.

I ran into Penet with three Grenoblois standing in the queue at the Français, and all five of us went to the pit. *Cinna* played by Talma, who's back from Bordeaux. This play aroused my admiration but didn't interest me. I'm again finding traces in myself of that old feeling I had five years ago which led me to find many tedious passages in all tragedies, except, I believe, *Le Cid*.

I was too peremptory tonight with Penet's three companions, and not comic enough. This manner frightens them off, and it's invariably my failing at the first meeting. The same thing happened at the dinner a fortnight ago with Rey, Mante, Durif and me.

4 Brumaire [October 26].—*La Jeune Femme Colère,* third performance, by M. Etienne. A poor play, no comic verve. It looks as if the author didn't know the play on the same subject OF THE GREAT ORIGINAL SHAKESPEARE.

Behind me was a man to whom I said, "It's amazing, monsieur, how much you look like the Emperor at the time he used to fight in a gray coat." "I'm not the Emperor, etc." The serious tone of this answer made it ludicrously asinine. The fellow took off his hat, and I saw the brow of a nincompoop.

6 *Brumaire* [*October 28*].—I've just been to a dinner where I met a man who was really friendly to me.

Mante came to get me at three o'clock, we went to the Rotonde, in the Palais-Royal; we first found Allegret there with two provincials, then the amiable Penet with M. Dupuy, a commercial traveler for a firm in Laval, who came from Spain a fortnight ago after living there for four years.

We went to Grignon's for dinner, it cost us five livres eight sous. There were seven of us, two idiots from the provinces who didn't open their mouths. M. Dupuy told us about the honors given Moreau in Spain, the Governor of Cádiz put him up at his home; when he went out on the street in the morning in a blue coat and round hat, with a pipe in his mouth, the little children followed him around, shouting, "Long live Moreau!" Dupuy and eighteen other Frenchmen, discovering that they were staying at the same tavern as he in Barcelona, gave a dinner for him. His wife was invited, but was unable to attend; he came and told them quite simply of his battles.

The Prince of Peace, who had been a mere bodyguard, was more powerful than the King in Spain because he was sleeping with the Queen. The Prince is thirty years old and is a fine-looking man.—The meeting in the street at the head of his guard.—The anecdote about the Archbishop.—The story of the rosary. He's universally hated, although he's not unkind, but he wounds the pride of others. Because of him, the Queen slaps her son, the Prince of Asturias, a youth of eighteen who hates the Prince of Peace and whom Spain worships, perhaps for that very reason.

Don Quixote is still rated highly; Dupuy prefers the edition in modern language. Dupuy appears to me to be wholly on the level of his class; therefore what he told me forms the *front* of a commercial traveler in Spain. This man has a strangely intelligent face, similar to the one I attribute to Miguel de Cervantes, Raphael's kind of eyes (the portrait with his master of arms). His account gave me a mental enjoyment that literally drove me out of my wits, my entire attention was devoted to the consideration of the things he told me.

The theater in Madrid is superb, they give practically nothing but French plays in translation and for the most part mutilated. Recently, they played Chenier's *Fénelon,* which had a run of fifty-seven performances. The staging of this play, which had been clamorously demanded for a month, was a thumping victory for Spanish youth over the Inquisition.

Incidentally, the Inquisition is powerless, the worst it can do is to prevent the free circulation of books. Our newspapers, however, get into Spain. When a man speaks unfavorably of religion or writes something against it, the Inquisition calls him up and asks him if he intends to keep on; he says he doesn't, and the whole business is over. If he errs a second time, he's clamped in prison.

12 Brumaire [*November 3*].—I forced myself to work TO THE GOOD PARTY, having not the slightest desire to do so, my lunch even being heavy on my stomach; I ended by DO THE BEST COMIC SCENE THAT I HAVE EVER MADE, THE THIRD OF THE FIRST ACT.

Consequently, you must force yourself to work every day.

13 Brumaire [*November 4*].—I read with much pleasure a selection from Montaigne that I hadn't seen for a couple of years. His style portrays his character excellently. It's the style with the most brilliancy in France.

I read a selection from *Le Génie du Christianisme* and was fascinated by the fine writing as long as the absurdities weren't too obvious.

17 Brumaire [*November 8*].—I'm reading Shakespeare's *La Méchante Femme* (THE TAME [sic] OF THE SHREW). At each scene I admired the genius of this great man, and the anti-dramatic minds of our playwrights.

I've only reached the seventh scene of the first act, and Shakespeare has already given me an idea that might make a charming comedy. Ever since I've felt myself capable of character portrayal, it's true that I seem to realize that any subject would be a good one in my hands. I'm no longer afraid of running out of subjects. Say to a dauber, "Paint Phaedra." Even go so far as outlining the action for him, he'll do no more than turn out a smear; Guérin, who possesses artistic genius, would paint a masterpiece.

In Shakespeare's place, I'd have made a very amiable Petruchio of thirty-five, fed up with love, no longer believing in it and desirous of a wealthy wife. Katharina would have had the same character, but with a wit so delightful in its originality and sallies that Petruchio would have ended by falling in love with her, after having started out by merely seeking to know and correct her in order to have a wealthy wife.

I believe that would be a fine comedy, but rare in nature, amusing and useless, made worth while solely by the artist's talent, and scarcely a masterpiece; provided the painter has genius, it's better for him to seek the finest subjects; in that way, he may hope to compose works that will last forever.

The pretext for Petruchio's anger is invariably the great respect which he desires to be shown Katharina, and he desires this respect to be shown her because, he says, she is subject to fits of anger, which is a horrible shortcoming.

23 *Brumaire* [*November 14*].—Lunched at the home of Adèle OF THE GATE, where I found M. Durand, painter. I ran into General Michaud, who said, "Bring me a model certificate and I'll sign it."

In order to steer clear of the slow-moving sort of thing I observed so clearly last night in Bièvre's *Le Séducteur,* I must decide on the *compass* of a character before portraying it; i.e., a list of all the actions it is capable of doing.

I worked till five o'clock, I went to the Palais-Royal, I found Dupuy, Penet, Allegret and three or four other Grenoblois at the door of the Café de Foy. As we were going in, poor Allegret took my arm, he's still very ill with the pox; Dupuy's face and manner never fail to delight me.

Penet, Mante and I each gave him six livres for fun, as a joke; we went up to 113; Penet lost seven livres, Dupuy twenty-four, I thirty. This loss, the heaviest I've had in Paris, comes at a bad time. Because of it, I was filled with wild gaiety all evening. I understand now (eleven o'clock) the cause of this gaiety, it still continues: it comes from my chimeras of *society* and my character of a poet.

25 *Brumaire* [*November 16*].—I read Voltaire's letters to Maupertius with much pleasure at the Bibliothèque Nationale. His handwriting is very similar to M. Daru's and my own. Afterward, I read some autograph letters from Henri IV to the Marquise de Vaudreuil, one of his mistresses. They fascinated me, there's no other word for it; they're as good as La Fontaine for the study of naïveté. Study naïveté?—Yes; when, as yesterday, I don't feel very well, when I have subtle ideas and at the same time perceive mentally, my soul studies naïveté and learns to perceive it.

The letters of Henri IV seem to me to be worth infinitely more than those of Mme. de Sévigné; this great man could have made his reputation by being nothing more than an author. I must read all his letters, but not when I'm in a highly enthusiastic state, they'd bore me; I must read them only when my soul is receptive to them. This is one of the most useful studies I could undertake as a poet; what a treasure-trove of naïveté they are, and not in the least marred by any thought that they would one day appear in print! These letters are full of mistakes in spelling.

26 *Brumaire* [*November 17*].—I've just been to the Montansier; there were four plays, one of which I didn't stay to see. The play that made me laugh so heartily at Grenoble seven or eight years ago appeared to me very asinine and lacking in the comic; yet it's spoken of as a master-

piece of comedy. I hope to show a more compact comic art, even in this kind of play.

Mante found *La Pupille* bad and *Les Etourdis* full of real comic art. My judgments on these plays are far different. In addition to his slowness of thought, Mante is perhaps slightly lacking in sensibility of the Jean-Jacques kind; a person only possesses this in proportion to his way of looking at women a little wildly, and Mante is too rational.

A Grenoble girl said to Penet, "Once you've had it, you can't get along without it," which confirms the maxim of Jean-Jacques: "Refuse everything to the senses unless you wish to be led to the ultimate weakness."

27 Brumaire [*November 18*].—I went with Mante at ten o'clock to see Rey, who told us about the way Destutt [de Tracy] introduced him to Cabanis: "Your master and mine."

To *Le Philosophe Marié,* a bad play, but liked by the vulgar because it's easy to understand. Tonight, I saw a thousand characters to portray in society because my imagination showed me literally every detail and its comic affinities with the audience.

28 Brumaire [*November 19*].—I must fathom the principle of the minor talent of the epigram and acquire it, read Catullus and make a collection of fifty or sixty, or thirty or forty, of the good epigrams of Jean-Baptiste Rousseau, Racine, Boileau, Le Brun. I must read Catullus.

29 Brumaire [*November 20*].—I must heed the natural in my conduct and style, and follow it more closely.

La Rive told me (and he says what he thinks) that there's something about me that is naturally attractive when I enter a place.

30 Brumaire [*November 21*].—I realize that the works I've written stink.

The ridiculousness of La Rive and many another consists of expressing the sentiments of a lofty soul in regard to the commonplaces of life, and belying them in the same breath through their actions. La Rive saying he scorns all the honors in the world, and in the same breath taking pride in the reply, totally without importance for pride, he wrung from Prince Louis Bonaparte by going to present him, for no reason at all, with some apple trees to sell. It's in the motives leading up to the present action, it's in these previous actions, that the vigorous sort of comedy is to be found and that the thoroughgoing connoisseur of mankind reveals himself.

1 Frimaire [*November 22*].—I'm getting along satisfactorily in my work. Rey spoke to me again about my lack of naturalness; I went to get Cler, the deaf mute, who wouldn't go with Mante and me to the tavern dance; as a result, we were driven back to the Français. *Le Préjugé à la Mode,* followed by *Les Deux Pages.*

I still had some recollection of the *Préjugé* from my childhood reading at Claix, that which turned me toward the dramatic art. All that was a long time ago, it was possibly before the day the two priests were killed[1] and I was expounding Virgil's *Bucolics* with M. Durand when, about eleven o'clock in the morning, shouts arose at their death. When I go to Grenoble, I must look up the dates of those early studies. Destouches, whom I now find so bad, and for whom I even have a pronounced antipathy, enchanted me with his love roles, which were embellished by my imagination and which turned me toward the theater. At this period, I had little appreciation of Molière: Racine bored me to death. I had more appreciation of Corneille. I had an antipathy for tragedies and the tragic manner. In all tragedies, except *Le Cid,* I found long passages that bored me, and, when I arrived at Paris in the Year VII, these passages still depressed me.

3 Frimaire [*November 24*].—I happened on Fatty Durif, and we took a walk together for nearly an hour in the Palais-Royal. He told me his story. Mme. Jubié's trait: "Have you got an income of thirty thousand francs for me to spend?" "No, but I've got twelve thousand." "That being the case, I prefer to remain where I am."

A measured reply is one which offends the persons to whom it is made only the degree necessary to produce the desired effect; it is consequently one that spares their vanity as much as possible. Had my father proposed last year that I go to Mass, I'd have replied in the manner of the younger Horace, in such a way that a man who still had some sense would be overwhelmed. This year, I'd say to him, "According to my principles, that would serve no useful purpose; according to yours, it would be a sacrilege. Therefore, it seems to me fruitless to go."

4 Frimaire [*November 25*].—I'm lacking in sensibility when it comes to comic traits; it's only after reflection that I find good ones. That comes from two causes: lack of social experience and the habit of regarding society like a passionate man, in the manner of Rousseau. Familiarity with men has led me to have contempt for the judgment of the great majority. This is composed of fools, but Rousseau himself said that, in indifferent things and within the range of his intelligence, even the fool is usually a good judge.

In order to get over this shortcoming, I must read Molière and Goldoni constantly.

The heartless abandonment in which my father is leaving me, as well as various traits of his life that I recall, leads me to think that he may indeed be nothing more than a Tartufe whose sole objective is money;

[1]This event, which took place in the Place Grenette, Grenoble, in June 1794, when Beyle was eleven years old, is recounted in his *Vie de Henry Brulard.*

when you come to think of it, where could he have acquired any generosity? At the law courts? Through religion?

This being the case, how long it has taken me to suspect the truth! What a difference if I had Mante for a father!

18 Frimaire [*December 9*].—I have many things to write since 11 Frimaire, last Sunday.

There have been few weeks in my life during which I've been the witness of events so interesting for me; there were several days when I returned home with enough material to fill several pages, as, for instance, a whole day I spent at Martial's and M. de Baure's.

Sunday, 11 Frimaire, the day of the coronation, neither Mante nor I had a sou; he came for me at half-past seven, we simply went to the Rue Saint-Honoré, near the Café Français; we happened on the delegation from the Isère National Guard, Penet, Durif, Chavand, Reverdy, Thénard, etc., etc., and, staying with them, we were able to see perfectly the little prig carrying the Pope's cross about a quarter past ten, then the Pope, and, an hour and a half later, the Emperor's carriages and the Emperor himself.

At half-past four in the afternoon, as I was going to Mme. Rebuffel's to see the procession go by, I encountered it en route and saw it clearly.

I reflected a great deal all day long on this quite obvious alliance of all the charlatans. Religion coming to crown tyranny, and all that in the name of the happiness of mankind. I rinsed out my mouth by reading a little of Alfieri's prose.

Martial and I took Mme. Rebuffel and Adèle to see the illuminations at the Tuileries, which were really very fine, but it was very cold. Pacé AND GATE [Adèle], who were walking in front of us, looked like two lovers who were quarreling.

I went to bed at two o'clock in the morning; I was awakened by my Uncle Gagnon, who had come from Les Echelles and who is now (half-past eleven at night), while I'm writing this, in my bed, where he got in first. Since then we've dined at Mme. Sauzay's; the conceited Samuel Bernard, a living character observed. On the morrow, the day that Bonaparte went to the Champ de Mars to distribute the Eagles, my uncle, Mme. Rebuffel, her daughter and I saw him pass from the Legislative Corps. That day, we stayed with the ladies fourteen hours. A spark OF LOVE emerged from the embers. We made another call, during which GATE, being more natural, began to please me again; I believe I also pleased her,

Au moins comme un ami, si ce n'est pas comme amant.

She had two or three moments of *naturalness* with me which enchanted me, especially the one in which I advised her to read the fifth book of *Emile, De l'Esprit* and Duclos's *Considérations sur les Moeurs.*

Divine naturalness, whither does your dominion not extend! The men of the most limited capacity don't always notice that what they are shown isn't natural, but it seems to me they permit themselves to be delighted only by what is.

I'm rushing through this because I haven't enough time to dwell on things; otherwise, I'd speak at length of a three-hour visit to Pierre Daru, of another with Pacé and of the completely sustained character of a conceited ass (of the civil servant variety) shown by the little S. Bernard, Sub-Prefect at Rochefort.

It seems as though the last will-o'-the-wisp of love for GATE has re-appeared in my heart merely to place it precisely in the position it occupied in Floréal, Year X.

I've seen Héloïse [Victorine Mounier] again. I wasn't in one of my tender moods: that diminished my pleasure, but at the same time kept me from behaving like an ass.

I've seen her again, I said but a word to her: "How do you do, mademoiselle?" Thereupon, she bowed briefly and fled to her room; I added, "Is Edouard in?" She replied, I believe, "He's in, monsieur." I don't recall her reply, I was too much taken up with scrutinizing her. I found her face very elongated, very much thinner. Is that real, or is it the result of the pleading of the Lawyer *Against,* who continually told me, "She isn't pretty," based on what Alexandre Mallein told me about her? He said she was stout, and I consequently imagined her as too stout. Anyway, I thought I saw that her face was greatly troubled, but I'm not sure of that because of her thinness. What leads me to believe it, however, is the fact that a servant coming into the antechamber where I saw her announced in a loud voice, "M. Beyle."

In accordance with my dramatic system of *maxima,* I ought to have taken advantage of this moment to let her see my love; I didn't do so, and yet I believe that she is the woman I will always love the most. That's something to make me think twice about my love of glory.

From there I went into her father's study, where Edouard greeted me, *but coldly.* "You've blossomed out like a Parisian!" As a matter of fact, my clothes, although common, thanks to my bastard [his father], had that agreeable disorder which betokens a young man accustomed to living well and to frequenting the elegant social circles of the capital.

After a quarter of an hour of *coolness,* I left with two men who were there on a visit. We promised to see each other again, but coldly on his part. I found his face very handsome, far handsomer than I had imagined. The Lawyer *Against,* basing himself on Mallein's opinions, had made my memories of beauty too exaggerated on the bad side.

In connection with my lodgings, he repeated his old phrase about my *natural fickleness,* which seems to be a set opinion with him.

Generally speaking, his conduct was quite proper, if he wants to break with me politely; everything tended in that direction, all the warmth and vivacity were on his side.

During my brief audience, at which a young man from Rennes who had been brought up in Paris was present, Philippine came in to say that her sister wanted to see him; he said, "I'm coming," and stayed where he was. She came back, he went out and returned a minute later by another door, with the look of a person who intends, as I've just said, to break off politely. Maybe Victorine didn't recognize me and asked him if I was that Beyle fellow; that would be a bit thick, but it's possible.

My appearance was good, as much as was permitted by my face, which has nothing but character in its favor; frill, cravat, waistcoat were all that could be desired; my hair wasn't piled up in the "genius style" because I had it cut at noon. Generally speaking, I probably gave her the impression of that *Parisian elegance* of which Edouard spoke. But I realize myself how misleading all the signs given by ardent people may be; this account, although written rationally, may be a thousand leagues from the truth.

She was wearing a straw hat of the German kind, tied under her chin with ribbons—blue ones, I think. I ought now to seek some means of seeing her again. How I would like to scrutinize her at leisure at the theater!

Here's a map of the battlefield,[1] all of it on the third floor of No. 558 [Rue du Bac], for which I hunted a long time before finding it. Incidentally, I'm far from blaming her behavior with me, I find it rational, and that's due to my experience; in my moments of sensibility a year ago, I'd have judged it far differently. Midnight is striking. I'm tired, tomorrow I'll add a few details if they come back to me. Thus, this week I've seen the Pope, Bonaparte on his way to be crowned, my uncle in Paris, Adèle fourteen hours on end, a visit of three hours with Pierre Daru, and, above everything else, my Héloïse.

21 *Frimaire* [*December 12*].—Martial took me to Dugazon's; we each recited the speech in *Cinna. I can conceive nothing better,* nothing more candid (less affected) than what that consummate actor told us; it's not often that I've conceived anything better. Guérin's *Phèdre* is possibly the only thing that has produced this effect on me.

I'm delighted with Dugazon; he's going to comment, truthfully and

[1]Follows a sketch of the apartment in Beyle's manuscript. It will be recalled that he always wrote of love as a "battle."

spontaneously, on all the roles he gives us, and he'll teach me to conceive them properly. He's so far superior to La Rive that there's no comparison between them.

He's in love with glory. He didn't voice this feeling in pompous phrases; I discovered it by a casual word he let drop.

Being acquainted with Dugazon is one of the best things that could happen for my talent.

I tired myself out, with the result that I felt fine all the rest of the day.

I've just been to Ducis's *Macbeth,* played by Talma; I was so worn out by this morning's lesson that it made no impression on me; it was extremely monotonous.

Ducis's play, which bored me throughout, is detestable; it's a caricature of the terrible. That's one of the most detestable ways possible of spoiling the superb play of Shakespeare.

Ducis seems to have overlooked the fact that there can be no sensibility without details. This oversight is one of the capital shortcomings of the French theater. Recently, I read Alfieri's *Orestes,* fully appreciating it; I found the same shortcoming there. I haven't the slightest intention of comparing Ducis with Alfieri; the Frenchman has as little good sense as the Italian has much. I found that the first act of *Orestes* is nothing but exposition, and the second is practically the same thing; the action doesn't move from the first line. Shakespeare comes much closer to the kind of tragedy that I'll perhaps never execute but that I conceive.

I must have the courage to put an abundance of details on the stage, and to make a character say, for instance, "The King sleeps in this room."[1] Too, I'll compose an absolutely new kind of tragedy by putting character portrayal into it.

The *Macbeth* of Ducis is literally not worth a pipeful of tobacco. Mlle. Raucourt's physical appearance, clad in white and with a large torch lighting up her villainous face, would have filled me with terror had it been well carried off.

Il zio [the uncle] saw Beauharnais; when I returned, he told me about the friendly greeting he had been given, and this made me have illusions of ambition for two hours.

28 *Frimaire* [*December 19*].—I've let events slip by since the day of *Macbeth*. I saw the play *Ariane* on the 26th. Mlle. Duchesnois was lovely and excellent; but too many of her lines were spoken in a singsong voice, like chromatic music. Mlle. Mars ever more perfect.

[1]No mention was ever made in the French classical theater of any specific details.

The Emperor came at the second act of the tragedy and left during the last. My uncle and I saw him clearly; his forehead and nose are more this way   ⟨   than I thought they were; these two effects of the forehead and nose being parallel are very common in France, and form a menial aspect.

I let many agreeable moments go by without describing them. Dugazon's second lesson was charming. Pacé didn't come.

But the greatest happiness that society at large has given me was produced the third time I went to Dugazon's. N . . . , Mlle. Rolandeau and Pacé came; I arrived at half-past eleven and left after two o'clock; left Pacé at three in the Rue Saint-Honoré, at Mme. Hanet's door, I believe, after having shopped around for a *pâté de foie gras* (four louis).

I'm a long way from having Pacé's social experience and particularly his facility, but it seems to me I'll have the exquisite taste an extremely sensitive soul gives. It seems to me that Pacé doesn't feel all these little things, for he would speak of them occasionally, and I'm sure that Locke [Mante] doesn't feel them. This exquisite sentiment is the cause of my bashfulness, and the lack of this sentiment possibly accounts for Mante's assurance.

This interval from noon to five o'clock was delightful for me. It was, it seems to me, the greatest happiness that society at large has ever given me. I was at the height of contentedness.

A long conversation I had with Pacé on leaving Dugazon's contributed not a little to this feeling.

In the evening I went to the Français, and for the first time sat elsewhere than in the pit. I found a seat as near as possible to the actors, later I made the rounds of the loges, looking vainly for Victorine. I was astonished at the beauty of Mlle. Contat, the astonishing delicacy of her nose and the Grecian beauty of her eyes.

Mlle. Contat was detestable in *Le Préjugé à la Mode,* a play written by La Chaussée, I recall that from my childhood reading at Claix, in my father's study, *che mi hanno decidato per l'arte dramatica* [which led me to decide for the dramatic art].

I hummed, "Ah, we'll find our judges," to the tune of *Ha, Pietade Troveremo!,* applying it to myself, Voltaire and other dramatists. I was thinking of two thousand years hence, of 3805.

Notes at end of notebook.—Voyage from Grenoble to Paris, Year XII.

I left Grenoble with 562 livres and 12 sous on 28 Ventôse, Year XII. I arrived in Paris on 18 Germinal in a Gouge cab at half-past six in the evening.

My trip from Geneva to Paris in five and a half days cost me

84 livres   84 l.
Tip at Lyon to the driver (a former artillery quartermaster) 1 l. 10 s.
Tips en route, about 4 livres   4 l.

I spent the sum of approximately 346 livres en route and at Geneva
from 28 Ventôse to the evening of 18 Germinal. In nineteen days of
traveling to Geneva, Lyon and Paris, 346, which makes 18 livres

$\frac{4}{19}$ a day.

"A Future Young Dramatic-Bard with a Future Young Actress"

PROBABLY no single day in Beyle's life was more momentous than the one which brought the year 1804 to a close. It started with his meeting Mélanie Guilbert, his first mistress and the only woman with whom he ever actually lived, and it ended with him trudging through the snow to buy the *Idéologie* of Destutt de Tracy, his philosophy master and the man whose influence on his thought was the greatest. At the moment, however, he had little time to give to new acquaintances, for he was far too occupied with rage at the "miserliness" of his "bastard of a father" and with rekindled love for the lovely phantom bearing the name of Victorine Mounier.

Although his financial situation had become desperate by the end of the year, his tirades against his father in the diary and elsewhere need not be taken too seriously. Most of the elder Beyle's money was tied up in property, and he had lost large sums in what his son contemptuously calls his "agriculturomania," yet Beyle's accounts of the period show that his allowance, with one or two exceptions, was paid regularly, that he received several extra sums from home and that, in all, his father gave him 3,184 francs during 1804. If he not infrequently lacked the bare necessities of life, it should be borne in mind that he had borrowed recklessly, lost 157 francs toward the end of the year in the gambling dens of the Palais-Royal, gone almost nightly to the theater, bought books constantly and started declamation lessons at twenty francs each—all of which was difficult to do, even in those days, on 200 francs a month.

In any case, during the month of January, when his finances were at their lowest, his love for Victorine soared to its highest. He moved as though in a dream, his imagination transformed the muddy streets of Paris into a glittering fairyland, the pages of his diary took on an unaccustomed lyricism—in a word, he had, as he would later have said, "crystallized."

The exaltation of the entries in his diary became more and more accentuated until his lyricism abruptly broke off on January 15 with the explanation: "I stop because I feel a dizzy spell coming on: my attention and emotion are too intense." He marked the day and the hour, and then wrote rather incoherently of other things. But as soon as he felt sure of himself again, he analyzed his threatened attack under the characteristic heading: "Ideological Physiology." This significant entry strikingly illustrates the strange duality of his character—mad emotions coupled with a cold, analytical intellect. It is typical that, driven to dangerous frontiers by his exaltation and concentration, he should turn around and conduct an ideological examination of himself with the objective interest of a scientist noting the results of an experiment.

Late the same night he went by moonlight through the silent streets of the Left Bank to stroll romantically beneath Victorine's window—as Lucien Leuwen was to pass his evenings outside Mme. de Chasteller's window and Fabrice del Dongo that of La Fausta. As the days passed and he received no answer to the letters he had sent to Victorine, he gradually gave up hope. Nevertheless, his ecstatic mood gave way to a blissful calm. He seemed to be floating through an exquisite dream that was prolonged from day to day. He had no money, but what of it? Everything enchanted him. In the middle of February he wrote his sister that those first weeks of the new year had been the happiest of his life. But by then the magic period when Victorine alone had been responsible for his felicity was a thing of the past, and, in the susceptible heart of her lover, a rival had moved into the place that had been hers for three years.

Having decided that if one was going to be a "dramatic-bard" one should know the art of acting, Beyle, together with Martial Daru, had started taking declamation lessons from La Rive in 1804, but at the end of the year they changed to Jean Dugazon of the Théâtre Français, who had the double advantage of being considerably cheaper and infinitely more talented. This declamation master was the animator of a bohemian group of aspiring Talmas and Marses: there was Félipe, a little hussy who had been brought up backstage; there was Wagner, a ponderous German youth; there was Mme. Mortier, "a vulgar wench who'd like to be refined," and, above all, there was a slender, sad-eyed young lady whom the village priest had christened Jeanne-Françoise-Mélanie Guilbert, but who, in somewhat premature anticipation of making her debut at the Théâtre Français, had rechristened herself Mlle. Louason.

The initial appearance of Mélanie in Dugazon's class the last day of 1804 caused no undue commotion in her future lover's heart, which was still devoted to Victorine and Glory: indeed, if he noticed her at all, it was merely to sneer at her "petty manners." Before long, however, he seemed to detect a certain friendliness on her part, even an appreciation of his "understanding soul." Finally, after a month of indifference, he walked home with her, an action that gave rise to the reflection that a passing love affair with this "little Louason" might cure him of his love for Victorine and would at least occupy the time pleasantly until he departed for his summer visit to Grenoble. "But," he added severely, "in that case, it's necessary that she have a soul."

As it happened, Mélanie really did have a soul, and a "melancholy" one at that. She was, moreover, pleasing to look at. The wistfulness of her "immense blue eyes," the suggestion of mystery about her "severe Greek face," the frailty of her graceful—albeit "somewhat skinny"—body made her, in Beyle's eyes, "a very beautiful woman."

Exactly three years his elder, she had been born in Normandy, the third and last child of an obscure and apparently not very harmonious family. An early love affair terminated in the traditional manner: the lover faded out of the picture, and Mélanie turned up in Paris with a baby daughter, the remains of a meager fortune and the ambition to become a famous actress.

In the capital further misfortunes awaited her, not the least of which was meeting Henri Beyle. Simplicity itself, Mélanie was cut out to lead a banal bourgeois life with a not too imaginative husband or lover. But what with an ordinary man might have been a happy little love affair became with Beyle a highly complicated relationship, constantly disturbed by his chimeras, shifting between tenderness and suspicion, and inevitably crashing in mutual disillusionment.

Up until this time the loves of the skittish Beyle had always been phantoms, merely so many euphonious names symbolizing his ideal Julie, and no unkind reality had ever intervened to expose their flaws. In Mélanie Guilbert he fell in love for the first time with a real woman, a woman he could see day after day, whose voice he could hear, whose actions he could witness, whose changing moods he could study. It was a cruel test that no human female could survive.

No sooner had Beyle confessed to himself that he was in love with Mélanie than his imagination galloped ahead to sketch a brilliant picture of what he described in his own brand of English as "a future young dramatic-bard with a future young actress." He multiplied his visits to Mélanie's apartment, discoursed lengthily on the soul, love and glory— and, once in the street outside, invariably reproached himself for not having seduced her. Soon he was in a state of violent jealousy and was tormented by all manner of speculations, most of them highly insulting to the woman he loved. But with his provincial gravity and his Dauphinois terror of being duped, he solemnly weighed the pros and cons, and, in the end, Mélanie's soul triumphed over his doubts.

The delightful ups and distressing downs of Beyle's interminable courtship, as told with an abundance of details in the following pages, never dulled this sentimentalist's appetite for the cold precision of rules and logic. He would return from Mélanie's apartment to analyze the day's emotions and, shutting his mind to love's uncertainties, immerse himself in the clean-cut verities of Destutt de Tracy's *Idéologie,* the only work, he afterward said, that brought about a revolution in him.

This philosopher's *Eléments d'Idéologie* (all but forgotten today) consisted of a trilogy on "the science of thinking"; the first volume treated of "ideology proper," or the *formation* of ideas; the second of "grammar," or the *expression* of ideas; the third of "logic," or the *combination* of ideas. This methodical and materialistic philosophy, which was considered by its inventor as a branch of zoology rather than of metaphysics, completed and codified the sensualist doctrines advanced by Bacon, Hobbes, Locke, Helvétius and Condillac.

Tracy's lucid, straightforward doctrine, expressed in a clear, simple style and reducing the hypothetical to a negligible minimum, at last revealed the secret springs of thought and provided a foundation for Beyle's future philosophical or, as we would probably say today, psychological researches. On first acquaintance he was less impressed by the *Rapports du Physique et du Moral de l'Homme* by Tracy's colleague, Dr. Georges Cabanis. Its vague style and the confused manner in which the material was presented irritated him, and only several years later, "conjecturing the ideas which lay behind the phrases," did he realize that "the father of materialism" offered a passkey to the human body as precious as that of Tracy to the mind. For Cabanis, man was a product of his "climate," which not only produced his "temperament" but, taken in its widest sense, included the vital influences of diet, education, government, mores, etc. Theories regarding the influence on the human character of climate and temperament were anything but new; in the early nineteenth century, however, they had lapsed into oblivion, and it was to Beyle's credit that he recognized their value and incorporated them into that peculiar system to which he himself gave the name of "Beylism."

Thus it was that he was able to devote his intellectual energy to the study of dry philosophical and psychological works at the same time that his emotional ardor was being consumed in the courtship of Mélanie. But Beyle would have had no difficulty in reconciling his two apparently incongruous occupations: was not a combination of the practical and the theoretical essential to the mastery of any subject; did not both Mélanie and the scientific philosophers reveal the workings of the human heart?

Another interest soon competed with love and philosophy. Exasperated by his poverty, and despairing of making an immediate fortune by means of his comedies, he had been casting about for some scheme which would assure him of an independent income, and out of his endless conversations with Mante a great idea was born. The latter, nearing the end of his bank-ing studies, was planning to serve an apprenticeship in the principal maritime cities of France, and then, with money supplied by his father, to establish himself as a banker in Paris. And why shouldn't Henri join him? Beyle, of course, was totally ignorant of banking, and nothing was more remote than the possibility that "the bastard" would advance the required capital. Still, where there's a will there's a way, and, with his customary optimism, he went over his prospects:

The property he would inherit at his father's death would provide him an annual income of 12,000 francs a year. On the property producing this revenue he would borrow 100,000 francs at 6 per cent to use as capital in his business with Mante. The bank would yield an average profit of 20 per cent; therefore, deducting the interest, he would earn 14,000 francs in addition to the 12,000 francs from his property. "Thus, as a bachelor, I'll have an annual income of 26,000 francs, and in society, I'll be de Beyle, epicure, wealthy banker, and writing verse for my own amusement." He would go even farther: he would marry a woman with an income of 19,000 francs, and become a tribunate at 15,000 francs, bringing his yearly income up to 60,000 francs. Gratifying prospects indeed for a youth who, in the meantime, was obliged to get along on 200 francs a month!

His hopes had become more modest by the time he got around to sound-ing out his family on the prospects of floating a domestic loan. "Pencil in hand," Mante and he had calculated that "very probably ten years from now" their bank would give each of them 15,000 francs in annual profits. However, and here was the rub, the bank's existence depended on "the bastard's" problematical generosity—30,000 francs' worth of it. Beyle did not have many illusions about the matter, but, resourceful as a good banker should be, he proposed a way out. Since his allowance was 2,400 francs a year, all his father would have to do would be to turn over the capital producing this amount of interest, which would be, "supposing we found it at 10 per cent," 24,000 francs.

No encouragement was forthcoming from Grenoble, but Beyle, un-daunted, went right ahead with his plans: as far as he was concerned, the affair was settled. Consequently, when Mante left on March 10 for Grenoble and Marseille, it was understood that Beyle would join him four months later at the Mediterranean port.

In all these arrangements, it will be noticed, no provision had been made for Mélanie, who, to all appearances, was to be abandoned by her capri-cious lover in favor of a career. But Mante had hardly left Paris when—incredible coincidence—Mélanie, who also had been thinking about the future, announced that if she were not accepted by the Théâtre Français she intended to accept an engagement to appear four months later at the Grand-Théâtre of Marseille! Beyle, who undoubtedly had been at a loss as to how to break the news to her of the banking project and his own departure, turned this announcement to his advantage with Machiavellian cunning. "There's an amazing stroke of luck for me," he rejoiced. "I didn't tell her I was planning to go there, but simply that, if she went, I'd follow her and sacrifice Paris for her."

During the ensuing weeks, commissions and percentages replaced states of passion and habits of the soul in his studies. But this sudden interest in commercial affairs should mislead no one. Never for a minute did he lose sight of his ultimate goal: "five or six years of boredom and unprofitableness for his studies" was the rather exorbitant price he would have to pay for the leisure to do what he wanted. Beyle, the wealthy banker, was merely to be the respectable mask for Beyle, the seducer of women and the successor to Molière.

Matters were abruptly precipitated at the end of April, when Mélanie signed a contract to appear in Marseille at the then amazingly large sum of 6,500 francs a year.

Beyle, who had been letting things slide, was forced to act, and act quickly. He decided to accompany her as far as Lyon, whence he would hasten to Grenoble, attempt to argue his father into lending him 30,000 francs, and then triumphantly rejoin his sweetheart and his best friend in Marseille.

There remained the question of taking the step that would make Mélanie his mistress. Time had passed; he had evasively promised himself that he would possess her tomorrow, next week, next month, and, when the day arrived, his courage had always deserted him. How many times had he seen Mélanie in negligee! How many hours had he passed alone with her in the intimacy of her apartment! And now it had come to a showdown. "It's absolutely necessary for me to possess her during the voyage," he told himself. "If I only dared to dare! The more I love her, the more bashful I am."

And to prepare himself for the bridal night, he deliberately set about "drying up" his emotions. He sneered at his sentimental self, determined to "attack" every woman who crossed his path, to be "as scoundrelly as possible" and to allow his natural tenderness to reappear only when he had finally become Mélanie's lover. A strange preparation for the pleasures of a honeymoon! Yet Beyle knew himself: he knew only too well that, when he was "all soul," he was bashful, awkward, silly. If he could succeed in reducing himself to cold-bloodedness, he might perhaps become the Valmont he had so long pictured himself as being. Only after having proved to his own satisfaction that he was capable of being a Valmont could he return with safety to his natural role of a Saint-Preux.

The never-to-be-forgotten period of the garret room across from the Louvre, the pit of the Théâtre Français and the declamation lessons at

Dugazon's was at an end. The time had come for new scenes, new occupations, new acquaintances. Early on the morning of May 8 the future young dramatic-bard and his future young actress went to the old Cour des Messageries, where, in the midst of chickens, barking dogs and piles of luggage, the horses were being harnessed to the stocky stagecoach that was to bear them toward the smiling future. Beyle, his heart thumping joyfully, inwardly rejoiced that this voyage gave every promise of being a "charming one."

1804-5 Paris

Journal of My Third Voyage to Paris

Notebook containing all that happened from 1 Nivôse, Year XIII to . . .
SOCIAL HAPPINESS

1 Nivôse, Year XIII [December 22, 1804].—Very cold; everything is fuzzy with snow.

Voltaire's note on Pascal.

Is the soul *substance* or *quality,* is it placed in the body with the *eye,* or is it the result of the *eye's* existence? Locke's theory that we receive all our ideas through our senses, together with the anatomy of passions such as is found in Helvétius, shows that in man we see no effect produced by the soul, that there are only effects produced by the senses, and that man therefore doesn't possess a soul.

Before everything else, it's necessary for a poet to have experienced an immense number of emotions, from the strongest—the terror of seeing a ghost—to the mildest—the murmur of a faint breeze among the leaves. For example, most men are indifferent to this latter phenomenon, which has often given me exquisite pleasure.

Without that *treasury of experienced emotions* which study not only does not create but actually prevents from being created, one makes blunders like d'Alembert, who, in the loge of his friend, Mme. Geoffrin, whom he'd just lost, spoke of people who are led to torture, a blunder perceived at once by the sensitive Jean-Jacques, who, moreover, was far less capable of reasoning than d'Alembert.

In this case, d'Alembert was like a man trying to write in English without a dictionary and only understanding a sixth of the words. He'd do like Adjutant General Petiet, who, wishing to pay a compliment to the daughter of his hostess at Constance, I believe, told her that she was a wench.

The fourth lesson on Bernadille [Dugazon] on 28 Frimaire, XIII, gave me the greatest happiness that society *at large* ever made me feel. It wasn't Bernadille, or Mlle. Rolandeau, or Pacé, or the other Mme. . . . alone who put me in this state of contentment, it was the union of them all. This state lasted from noon till five o'clock, at which hour my uncle repeated to me what Mme. Daru told him this morning, what Pierre had told her before the fireplace in two hours and a half of time.[1]

10 *Nivôse, the last day of the year 1804.*—I can rightly call this day a happy one; it would have been completely so if my father had the character of, say, Mante, and did not leave me languishing in destitution.

At noon, I went to Bernadille's, where I found Mlle. Louason and Mlle. Nourrit, of the Opéra, who looks stupid. Ariadne arrived and gave me her hand as she came in. Bernadille had her rehearse the fifth act of *Monime,* he weeps at will. Pacé arrived; a thousand slight nuances in his behavior with Ariadne showed me that he's had her; he admitted it to me and denied it a second later.

I went to *Le Philinte de Molière,* and never did a play make such an impression on me. Tonight I was more of a man of the world than an artist. The play filled me with enthusiasm for virtue, and I saw it only as a whole, energetically beautiful.

The audience, which was a rare one, appreciated it thoroughly and applauded ten or twelve times, as heartily as possible. At the climax in the third act, it applauded every word; the smiles, the talk I heard on all sides showed me that the audience thoroughly appreciated it. There, witnessed by me, is the small and select audience one should aim to please; the circle starts at this point, gradually grows smaller, and ends with me. I might compose a work which would please no one but myself, and which would be recognized as beautiful in the year 2000.

My enthusiasm for virtue was so strong, and I felt so thoroughly that one can possess virtue only in proportion to one's power of mind, and that, in works of literature, the virtue of the characters is an important part that, in spite of the snow, I went to Courcier's, on the Quai de la Volaille, to buy the first part of Tracy, and that, with no fire

[1] What Pierre Daru said is suggested more fully in *Pensées,* where Beyle writes, "He took me from my arrival from Grenoble when I had, he said, the air of a little nun and didn't dare blow my nose in a salon, up to the present, when, remaining in Paris without a job, I'm making a bad reputation for myself. This opinion of me certainly isn't a favorable one, since it interprets my whole conduct as continual hypocrisy. And yet, so deep-seated is man's conceit that it gave me pleasure."

in my room, I've just read the first sixty pages of it. There, it seems to me, is the strongest impression a play ever made on me. The noble pride it inspired in me affected even my bearing. I was superb as I passed down the corridor and stairs on my way out.

This strong impression perhaps came from the fact that my soul had no *sinews,* in Bernadille's sense, and, on the contrary, let itself go. In that respect, he's taught me a very valuable truth.

This play really filled my soul with happiness, a happiness more in keeping with my bearing, nobler, more deeply founded than that which the performance of *L'Optimiste* gave me last summer.

This day is not the happiest one I might conceive: for that, I'd have had to see the play beside Victorine, loving me as I love her, and being assured of a fortune—for instance, an income of 6,000 francs. In that case, there would have been nothing to bother me except the slight consciousness of fever, but probably it wouldn't have existed then, happiness would have driven it away, as unhappiness, I believe, gives birth to it.

This day's happiness has consequently been of a superb mediocrity, and this performance the one that has made the deepest impression on me of any I've ever seen. For me, the theatrical illusion was perfect because I didn't think of noticing the non-illusion in it. I gently let myself go, and, I repeat, I believe that I experienced so much emotionally because my soul was not *sinewy,* did not *stiffen.* I am indebted for that to Bernadille.

Here is a fact: the worst tragedies draw large audiences; everything is full up; the best comedies don't draw anybody; the actors are unimportant as a reason for people to come to see a play. This perfectly certain fact is a truth for the history of the Revolution.

January 1, 1805.—I read the first hundred and twelve pages of Tracy with the greatest satisfaction and as easily as a novel. Tonight I had a little fever; it wasn't painful, during that time I read a volume of Voltaire's correspondence at the Saint-Jorre reading room. I lack money —let's go to Grenoble. But yesterday I saw *Philinte,* I bought Tracy yesterday, I'll spend three hours tomorrow with Dugazon, Duchesnois and Pacé—let's stay in Paris. My position is consequently the best possible with a barbarous father who allows my machine to be undermined by a daily fever which a little cash would cure.

And this father may love me! If, contrary to all appearances, he is only a Tartufe who at bottom is only a miser, he's a fine example to show me, at my expense, the errors into which lead the passions I love so much; what material for the character of agriculturomania!

Crozet and Barral arrived on . . . Crozet has changed marvelously to his advantage. EVER TOO VANITY, too much of that false dignity which believes it lowers itself by approaching the simple things of ordinary life, a bourgeois mind, the opposite of Barral's. He's in love with Mlle. S. R. [Blanche de La Bergerie] and, what is astonishing and nevertheless appears *riamato,* having Penet for a rival, he's thinking of leaving the Ponts et Chaussées to become a lawyer. He's only twenty years old.

12 Nivôse [January 2].—If my grandfather speaks to me about reasoning with my father, I'll be like Count Almaviva: battle is my forte.

In strict justice, a father owes board, clothing and the natural necessities to his children. But every man should keep his promises, and my father promised me a thousand écus.

If my father, like Jean-Jacques, had put me in an orphanage, supposing all chances of hazard to be against me, *it would be impossible for me to be more unfortunate than I am at present.* Indeed, I'd be more unfortunate had I never read Jean-Jacques, whom I read in spite of him and who gave me THE CARACTER LOVING AND THE GREAT LOVES.

13 Nivôse [January 3].—*Quest' oggi il giorno dei due soldi; faro une descrizione dello stato nel quale mi lascia mio padre. Ecco un terribile effetto d'avarizia.* Tencin GIVE ME SIX LIVERS *ch'egli mi doveva.*

[Today is the day of the two sous. I'll write a description of the state in which my father has left me. This is the terrible effect of avarice. Barral gave me six livres which he owed me.]

16 Nivôse [January 6].—Last night Crozet, I and Barral went to the latter's house after Andrieux's lesson, and stayed there until midnight chatting and drinking tea.

Milan [Napoleon] almost perished at the large crucifix on Mont-Cenis, and jumped down a staircase of fifteen steps; all Turin knows about this.

A fine trait of pity in Barral, who, at eleven o'clock at night, set out from the Rue de Lille to take forty-eight livres to Charvet, in the Rue de l'Arbre Sec; all the circumstances augmented the beauty of the trait. Fabre's Alceste wouldn't have acted any better than this, I believe, in Year XI.

17 Nivôse [January 7].—It's strange that, in spite of the terrible abandonment in which I'm left by my bastard of a father, I'm still happy. For several days I've been putting off drawing a picture of my misery. Yet such a picture, together with one of the happiness I'm enjoying, would be curious.

M. Thorenc-Tardivy came to see me at seven o'clock to ask for the twenty-five livres I owe him and can't pay him, having but three livres lent me by Crozet. I'm hardly humiliated any more by little borrowings like that, which a year ago would have been the death of me.

I went to Dugazon's without declaiming, and from there to Pierre

Daru's in negligent attire to ask him for 200 francs (given me by my grandfather). In the library, I found Mme. Daru, Pacé, Mme. Rebuffel and Adèle; I, as well as the ladies, was asked to stay to dinner; I left them there, departing at seven o'clock, although I'd have liked to stay, but I had only twenty-six sous in my pocket and I might have been obliged to pay for a fiacre to take them home. That's a sample of the fine considerations to which a father's avarice has reduced one of the noblest characters I know.

In spite of that, I'm happy tonight; this is due in large part to the prospect of 200 francs tomorrow. I was quite badly dressed today.

Mme. Daru (Pierre) has no wit, and everything about her indicates a petty character. All day I recognized the conversation and character of Louis XIV's courtiers, such as I picture them. Full details about the Marshals' Ball yesterday; it cost, I believe, 180,000 francs, the finest that has been given in a long time; 4,000 candles, renewed every two hours, 1,200 women, 3,000 people in all; two quadrilles of honor; the Emperor arrived at half-past nine and left at midnight; the women had been there since six; the boredom of the long wait, a little pug dog who came in was taken for the Emperor, afterward a diversion was provided by a woman fainting.

The silliness of the things all my companions think about. What is a noble character? The notion of asking this question is the first fruit of reading Tracy's *Idéologie*. Only women of a noble character are capable of providing me happiness; I recognize the happy fruits of *Idéologie* by a thousand sprouts of new ideas.

A comedy representing a *noble character* among people like those with whom I dined, a comedy aimed at defending noble characters, like *La Métromanie* aims at defending poets in society. A scheme to be examined later.

One of Arsinoé's lines in *Nicomède* was a revelation to me on the subject of women, and made me see that the majority of them have petty characters which would be incapable of doing anything for my happiness.

The characters that I attribute to Portia, Pauline [Beyle's sister] and Victorine [Mounier] are rare. The discovery of this truth will remove my bashfulness in the presence of women.

Prince Louis dances very badly. It seems to me that all the petty ways I observed this morning in Mesdemoiselles Louason and Rolandeau, and even more so tonight in Adèle and Mme. Pierre [Daru] would very soon bore me.

If I were to be put in the exact place of the elder Daru today, I'd die of boredom in less than six months, and in Martial's place in less than a year. In either case, I'd hand in my resignation. I must seem queer in society, not entirely stupid and ponderous, but still not a man of wit.

Mme. Daru, the mother, overwhelmed me with kindness; I dined in a thoroughly agreeable manner between Martial and Adèle. I was aware of it as I took my place at table, and scarcely had the time to refrain from saying, "You are putting me between the ones I like best."

21 *Nivôse* [*January 11*].—I've just come from *Les Horaces;* Duchesnois took the role of Sabina, for the first time, I believe.

La Mère Jalouse by Barthe, very well acted and amusing; I was unable to judge it well, I was looking at the Emperor.

Throughout the first play I strained my eyes, from the second tier where I was, looking for Victorine. I thought I recognized her a few loges away, but it wasn't she, especially the gestures. I ogled so much that I'm cross-eyed.

24 *Nivôse* [*January 14*].—If the state we are in while our fate is being decided is a good omen, Victorine ought to love me. I spent a delightful afternoon at Bernadille's, from noon till half-past two; Nourrit, Mlles. Rolandeau, Louason and the German were there. There's no getting around it, Mlle. Rolandeau is out to tease me, once today I saw what was coming a long time ahead. I had the courage to come out of my reserve; a little joking is all that's necessary. The little wife of General Lestrange came, and I believe that with her and Mlle. Rolandeau, if we found ourselves alone, all would be finished. Bernadille said before everyone, like a man who sees something, and in three or four different ways, that it's not blood that flows in my veins, it's quicksilver.

Being heartened by the little successes resulting from my boldness, I became expansive, he saw that I had some mettle; he was very well satisfied with the way in which I recited the first scene of *Le Misanthrope;* he said with enthusiasm and truth that I would be an excellent actor; he told me he wanted to put the play on in society and have me act in it. Mlle. Rolandeau applauded; when I was going out, he said to General Lestrange's wife that I'd get over my accent, like Lafond, and that I would act like him, meaning that I would succeed in acting well. He said what I myself have said about my manner of acting, that I have great ability and warmth of soul, and that I lack the rest. Today was the first time that what I might become in declamation was discovered. Bernadille said what he thought, perhaps it wasn't the same with Mlle. Rolandeau, who predicted that someday I would act in comedy: I think there were two things in that, she said what she thought and was teasing me. It's absolutely the case you find in novels: she wants to take my education in hand and she likes me. *That youthful fervor,* as Corneille says, appeals to her. If, when I have a frock coat and some money, I want her, I'll have her: it's not that any of these things are necessary, but I myself need them in order not to be bashful, and bashfulness paralyzes all my means. I only begin to be myself when I am accustomed, blasé as she says. "He needs to become blasé," she said one day in front of me. She guessed rightly; if I took the trouble, I could also have Mlle. Louason and General Lestrange's wife.

So much for worldly things, for the pleasures of vanity; I went into detail because they are very rare for me, who have a sensitive soul and an avaricious father, and because I have need of being disgusted with them in order to give myself up entirely to my love for Victorine and THE FAME; but that will come, I'm sure. A year of luxury and the pleasure of vanity, and I'll have satisfied the needs given me by the influence of my century, I'll return to the pleasures which are really pleasures for my soul, and with which I'll never be disgusted.

But during this period of folly, I'll get over my bashfulness, something that's absolutely necessary in order for me to appear as I am; until then what will be seen will be a formal and artificial person who is almost the complete opposite of the one he conceals. I thoroughly experienced this in the letters I wrote to Victorine yesterday and the day before; they were detestable, they didn't at all show my heart as it is, and I couldn't correct them, and my facial expression wasn't there to furnish a commentary on them; they showed me as quite a different person than I am. If I frequented the same social circles as she, I'm sure she'd love me, for she'd see that I worship her and that I have a soul as lofty as the one I attribute to her, which her education (by her father in adversity and in a foreign country) must have given her, and which she undoubtedly has; it seems to me that, once we knew each other and realized how little the rest of humankind is suited to merit our love and make us happy, we'd love each other forever.

My letters came far indeed from showing my thoughts naïvely, and I feel that what I am writing here is still just so much phraseology, that it's not yet my thought, bare and stripped of all literary effect; for this, I need social experience, and for social experience I need money; I feel that I'm made for the best society and for the best of women; I desire these two things too poignantly not to make myself deserving of them.

Finally, from two to four yesterday, I wrote Victorine a letter entirely different from the preceding ones, much more natural, but still a little *inflated,* and that in spite of myself because, flustered as I was, I lost all naturalness in trying to make corrections. From four to seven I copied it *in these characters*[1]: there were three large sheets of vellum paper. I made a packet of it, with a little return letter addressed to

[1]The italicized words are printed in the manuscript.

M. Victor Alfine in care of Crozet. Crozet added the address, and I put the packet in the post in the Rue des Vieux-Augustins at the café on the corner of the Rue des Colonnes.

The weather was as balmy as an evening in spring: that and the step I had just taken, the pleasure of being rid of a necessary action and one which upset me, that and my hope, all made me happy. I dined contentedly with Crozet at Mme. Debernet's; from there we went to Barral's in a spring drizzle that took me back to Italy; we spent the evening there; I had a slight headache about eleven o'clock. I tumbled into a puddle in the Rue de Poitiers, slipping as I put my foot on a stone in the middle. Being all wet, I went to spend the night with Crozet. We got up at nine o'clock this morning and walked for an hour and a half together in the Tuileries. In this weather, which makes me happy through sentiment, the air is *charged with love* for me. Crozet only left me at half-past twelve at Dugazon's door. I left at half-past two, a bit recovered from my love because of the *pleasures of vanity,* but at present I'm only the more given over to my love. If Victorine repulses me, she'll be refusing another person. My letters don't show me as I am, and, the opposite from usual, show me up terribly badly. I don't believe they'll ever express the goodness and candor of my heart, and those ecstasies of love—the ones I experienced a few days ago while crossing the Louvre (west and east), going to dinner at three o'clock, and also when leaving Bernadille's. Only all my actions taken together, after three days of uninterrupted familiarity, continually in her company, could make her see me as I am.

What I ask is too much; if my bastard would send me some money and if I'd had Mlle. Rolandeau, my bashfulness would be over, I'd be myself.

The noble and republican principles that I have, my hatred of tyranny, the natural impulse that leads me to see through false respectable people, my imprudence in saying what I see in their soul and the energy that is to be seen in mine, the natural and occasionally ill-concealed impatience aroused in me by mediocrity—all these things result in my being considered a Machiavelli by feeble souls like my uncle. What they call a Machiavelli is, in their opinion, the animal that is the most terrible for them. Superiority breeds their most implacable hatred.

Indeed, the animal the most dangerous for them would be an agreeable chatterbox of their species whose purpose is to plague them and whose soul is a trifle superior to theirs.

These qualities, together with my defects, possibly at first dim my glaze of simplicity and candor in my friends' eyes; Faure is a case in point; Mante, whom I believe to be a quite different sort of man, has completely changed his mind. In the opinion of Tencin, I'm perhaps the man most worthy of being loved.

These are all the disagreeable circumstances that a *lofty* and *virtuous* soul, formed in solitude and without communication, has to contend with when it enters society. This is my confession, it is the way I see myself, and it is the gist of what I'd say to Victorine if, being at her feet, I should be asked by her, "What manner of man are you?" In this soul, perhaps still sullied by a few imperfections, she would see the noble passions at their maximum, and my love for her sharing the commands with the love of glory and frequently proving to be the stronger. And I venture to believe that, being at her feet, I'd show her my love in a manner worthy of her and it, through traits of immortal beauty.

All in all, if this soul isn't purified of every vice and filled with every virtue—and it's undoubtedly far from it—it's at least fired with all the noble passions that lead to this end.

The passion for being as enlightened and virtuous as possible forms the basis of all this; the love of Victorine and the love of glory alternately prevail. There, save for humanity's weakness, and with all possible sincerity, is what I am at twenty-two minus nine days, 24 Nivôse, Year XIII.

Generally speaking, I lack only good looks and—especially if Victorine loves me—money to be perfectly happy.

A quarter past four: Victorine has decided my fate, or my letter has fallen into the hands of her brother or father.

There's a good entry in my journal finished, written offhand, and consequently being all the more sincere and less inflated.

As we were going out of Dugazon's salon, the German took for himself what Dugazon said about me, that I would get over my accent like Lafond and, I believe, that I would act like him. Dugazon said, pointing to me, "I'm referring to him," and the German, although I consoled him as much as I could, was *white*.

25 *Nivôse* [*January 15*].—*Love*.—This preparatory passion puts you in a melancholy state, you see an *angelic happiness,* you feel yourself worthy of it (the desire to be worthy leads you to many an action), you say to yourself, "I deserved a better destiny than the one I have, fate has been unjust to me." I've said that to myself a thousand times, especially when the places where I was, or the suave air of spring in midwinter, or the sound of a street organ, made me better see this divine happiness I had imagined.

This melancholy state, it seems to me, can be caused only by an ardent imagination. What caused it in me, I believe, was that I thought

I'd find in real life the *happiness* I pictured to myself when, as a child, I read Destouches's *L'Homme Singulier* (that's the work which made me conscious of the charm of a portrait), the pastorals of *Don Quixote* and the restrained loves depicted in the *Novelle,* and a little those of Tasso (my grandfather's praise, mingling them with real life, spoiled them).

I stop because I feel a dizzy spell coming on: my attention and emotion are too intense (26 Nivôse, a quarter to four).

This explanation, which is difficult for *petty souls,* is dull for them. The loftier one's soul is, the better one will understand it, the less unfeeling it will appear.

For I understand the extreme of variation in myself, I see it clearly in the memory of my feelings, and it affects me.

[*After a few rather incoherent paragraphs, Beyle wrote the following marginal note in his diary:*]

Ideological physiology.—I feel that this change in the subject of my thoughts has prevented me from having the dizzy spell. It was the recollection of the sentiment that was fatigued. I feel it about to return after perhaps a quarter of a second of directed effort. If, during that time, I desire to recall my mellow impressions of Italy, instantly my head throbs and I am threatened with a dizzy spell. I see that as distinctly as I distinguish white from black.

With senses and inner faculties so variable and sensitive, it is quite possible that I shall become insane.

In such a case, I hereby beg to be taken to *Claix,* it is only there that I shall perhaps be able to recover. May I be spared all impressions that would require me to formulate an intricate judgment. It's the judging faculty that will be ill, I feel it.

In composing, I want every word to be perfect; I consider the conditions of the word's perfection and their bases; in connection with this, I discuss them for fear of being mistaken, and for fear that an error, becoming habitual, be noticed. Two years ago, possibly, I stopped rejudging everything on every occasion that arose; I do it, that leads me astray and makes me spend the time reflecting when I could be acting.

Men who have always had the right philosophy and have enjoyed themselves as much as possible every day—Mante, for example—and have given themselves over little or not at all to melancholy sentiments are not susceptible to the kind of love I feel for Victorine, the kind of love Héloïse and Abélard probably felt for each other.

In order that this love be extinguished, one of two things is necessary:

1. either that the first judgments—that happiness is to be found beside a woman who, with that shade of sublime melancholy which may be felt, or placed on the faces painted by Raphael, at nightfall in summer, on the shores of the Bay of Naples (the little picture in the Museum of a woman and child, shown to Basset and Crozet), looks at you in such-and-such a way in such-and-such a circumstance—appear false;

or 2. that he who says a certain woman—Marini, Pietragrua, Victorine—will give us this happiness, appears false;

or 3. that one places his happiness in other things, as, in my own case, the love of glory (that of Homer).

This analysis, read in my feelings, indicates where one must strike in order to recover from love.

I have paid not the slightest attention to my words; in such a subject, it was necessary to give them the *physiognomy* which I said might be attributed to the figures of Raphael, for instance that of St. Cecilia, by clothing it in another fashion, giving it another action and another background, but my whole attention was absorbed by the things themselves.

(Half-past four, a slight headache.)

25-27 *Nivôse* [*January 15-17*].—I'm reading Diderot's *La Vie de Sénèque,* a good work, and the letters of Héloïse and Abélard, a good work in that it shows a naturally sublimated example of love in two lofty souls.

But something better than all the love letters I've seen up to now are the twelve letters of a Portuguese nun to Chavigny, who was later a Marshal of France.

Hers is a case of really loving to distraction, she sacrificed everything, and without the least struggle, for her lover. In that respect, these letters depict a love stronger than that of Julie for Saint-Preux.

Rousseau depicted the strongest love possible in very *virtuous* souls; there still remains to be depicted a love between two souls as *enlightened* as possible, Héloïse and Abélard, for instance; and the advantage of this second subject is that it can be depicted as hopeless, like that of the Portuguese nun. Chavigny's letters are a curious example of *simulated love* beside one of the strongest passions that ever existed.

Today, the 26th, a lesson at Bernadille's from half-past twelve to half-past three; Rolandeau, Louason and Lestrange perceived MY UNDERSTANDING SOUL.

When Milan [Napoleon] was thinking of re-establishing religion in France, he employed some caution in dealing with the enlightened people with whom he had attempted to fortify his government; he consequently summoned Volney to his study, and told him that the

French people had asked for a religion and that he felt he owed it to their happiness to give them one.

"But, Citizen Consul, if you listen to the people, they will also ask you for a Bourbon." Thereupon Milan flew into a terrible rage, called his servants, had him thrown out, even—so they say—kicked him and forbade him to return. There's a good example of the ridiculousness of the advice-seeker.

Poor Volney, who's in bad health, was ill as a result, but that didn't stop him, as soon as he had recovered, from drawing up a long report on the matter, thinking that the affair would be brought up in the Senate. It became known, and he was told to desist if he didn't want to be assassinated; since then, he has scarcely left his home. IF TRUE, FOR A FUTURE Tacitus.

27 *Nivôse* [*January 17*].—Crozet and I have just come from *Mithridate,* followed by *Minuit*. Mlle. Mars in this little play gave us more pleasure than all the rest of the performance. Mlle. Duchesnois, who was playing Monime for the first time, played it in a very dull and unoriginal manner; she made not the least effort to bring out the *modesty* which, it seems to me, is the general color of the role. Mme. Talma gave us more pleasure. I saw her a moment in her dressing room.

Mlle. Mars was divine in the role of Séraphine in *Minuit:* she communicated the idea of the most exalted love: her facial expression during the time her cousin sings his romance to her was enough to make you fall in love with love. That's the facial expression I must attribute to Julie and Victorine. That dear girl hasn't answered my letter. I SHALL WRITE AFTER DAY.

The day before yesterday, I went with Tencin after midnight to walk in front of her No. 558[1]; the moon was shining, and the solitude of the quarter seemed odd.

28 *Nivôse* [*January 18*].—I've just been reflecting for two hours on my father's conduct toward me, being deplorably worn down by a strong attack of the slow fever I've had for more than seven months. I haven't been able to recover from it: first, because I didn't have the money to pay the doctor; in the second place, because, having my feet constantly in the water in this muddy city owing to lack of boots, and suffering in every way from the cold owing to lack of clothing and wood for the fire, it was useless and even harmful to wear down my body with remedies to get rid of an illness which poverty would have given me even if I hadn't had it already.

If you add to this all the *moral humiliations* and the worries of a life passed continually with twenty sous, twelve, two, and sometimes noth-

[1]Victorine Mounier and her family were staying at 558 Rue du Bac.

ing in my pocket, you'll have a slight idea of the state in which that *virtuous* man has left me.

For two months I've been planning to put a description of my condition here; but, in order to describe it, you must regard it, and my only resource is to distract my attention from it.

Just calculate the effect of eight months of slow fever, fed by every possible misfortune, on a temperament which is already attacked by obstructions and weakness in the abdomen, and then come and tell me that my father isn't shortening my life!

Were it not for my studies, or rather the love of glory that has taken root in my breast in spite of him, I should have blown out my brains five or six times.

For more than three months, he hasn't deigned to answer the letters in which, describing my poverty, I asked him for a slight advance, *to buy some clothes,* on my allowance of 3,000 francs, reduced by him to 2,400 francs, an advance that he would get back himself in the spring months when I'll be in Grenoble.

I asked him for this advance, which a stranger wouldn't have refused to a stranger who was sick and suffering from the cold a hundred and fifty leagues from home, in the month of Vendémiaire, Year XIII, at a time when he still had 2,200 francs of my allowance in hand.

From all this and from twenty pages of details, all of them horribly aggravating, it results that my father is a *wretched scoundrel* in his treatment of me, having neither virtue nor pity. *Senza virtù ne carita,* as Carolina says in *Il Matrimonio Segreto.*

Should someone be surprised at this judgment, he has but to tell me so, and, starting from any definition of virtue *he chooses to give me,* I'll prove to him *in writing,* as clearly as it can be proved, that all our *ideas* come to us through our senses—in other words, as plainly as a moral truth can be proved—that, in regard to me, my father has behaved like a dishonorable man and an execrable father—in short, like a *wretched scoundrel.*

He promised me 3,000 francs in order to induce me to abandon the military life; I was a sub-lieutenant in the 6th Dragoons in Vendémiaire, Year XI, at the age of seventeen years and seven months. To appreciate what this means, the internal political state of France must be considered.

Other considerations, which he doesn't know about, resulted in my finding happiness in this arrangement; but observe that the man who fires at me with a shotgun, aiming as well as he can, and who nevertheless fails to wound me because I am protected by armor, is a murderer. This great truth wins my case at the outset.

I finish this entry, still having enough material for fifty pages, by re-

peating my offer to prove *quantum dixit* in writing before a jury composed of the six greatest living men. Were Franklin alive, I'd name him.
I designate for my three men Louis-Gabriel Gros, Tracy and Chateaubriand to set a value on the moral suffering in the soul of a poet.

If, after that, you accuse me of being *an unnatural son,* you are incapable of reasoning, your opinion is but a vain sound and will perish
with you.

Remember that, before all, it is essential to be *sincere* and *just,* even
when the exercise of these virtues decides in favor of a man of twenty-
two against one of fifty-eight, although you may be nearer fifty-eight
than twenty-two, and of a son against his father.

Either you *deny virtue* or my father is a wretched scoundrel in the
way he treats me. Whatever weakness I may have for this man, that's
the truth, and I stand ready to prove it to you in writing at the first
request.

Written offhand 28 Nivôse, Year XIII, at half-past eleven in the evening, having twenty-five sous and a fever as my sole possessions.

H. Beyle
(22 years old minus 5 days)

P.S.—I write this solely for the happiness of my children and as a
guarantee against being a miser myself thirty years from now. Tell me,
at the bottom of your heart, aren't you blushing as you read this in
1835? Would you need me to write out the demonstration in minute
detail?[1]

Withdraw into thyself.

1 Pluviôse [January 21].—Combat on the frontier.—Sensibility.—All your
thoughts serve to work you up to the erethism of passion, your whole
body is taut. When that happens, if the subject be love, your thoughts,
engaged in making you taut, are unable to leave room for the promises
of happiness given you by the face, the manner and the words of your
mistress.

The habit of seeing whores leads to that. A man's imagination gets
excited each time he holds one of them in his arms while picturing a
woman who has more appeal for him. I discuss her beauty, I say, "Her
eyes are dark for such-and-such a reason, because they're the most
beautiful, etc. She resembles Angelina Pietragrua." While I'm trying
to recall where the resemblance lies, and, *so to speak, to build the up-
rights of the arch, I'm far from being conscious of the impression she'd
give me if seen from the exterior.*

And yet this impression is the whole pleasure of passion.

I must get to the bottom of this great idea. That's what sometimes

[1] The Beyle of twenty-two is talking to the Beyle of fifty-two.

makes me disgusted with passions: they haven't any rewards or pleasures for me.

(It was snowing, I took the little wife of General Lestrange home in
a cabriolet. She invited me to go up to her apartment with her; I refused. She hinted that I might go to see her on the days she doesn't go
to Dugazon's; I have no desire to do so. Wagner accompanied Louason,
who's as nice as can be with me. Generally speaking, a happy day.)

On 27 or 28 Nivôse, Pacé showed me the outline of the first scene of
his comedy entitled *La Vengeance*. This comedy has the same merit
among plays that its author has among men. It's absolutely him himself, it's naïvely his nature.

Journal of My Third Voyage to Paris

From 1 Pluviôse, Year XIII, to the 23rd of the same month, inclusive

1 Pluviôse [*January 21*].—HAPPYNESS GIVED BY THE WEATHER, AND MERRY
RESIGNATION UPON MY FATHER'S AVARICE.

3 Pluviôse [*January 23*].—I WRITE TO VICTORINE WITH MY OWN HAND, AFTER
I GO AT DUGAZON'S HOUSE. What I saw there made me resolve to come
out of my indolence. I've let Wagner take the places I was offered, and
at present he's filling them. After my refusal, he's perhaps having
Louason. Things are only to be had by those who take them. I must be
enterprising in declamation like he is, he gets twice as much out of his
lessons as I do out of mine. I must assume a little of the mummer's
manners, which are the best in this case, and above everything else I
must talk frequently. Being with Crozet makes me realize that it's
absolutely necessary to become amusing: nothing is easier, practically
all that's necessary is to talk.

4 Pluviôse [*January 24*].—I went to the Medical School at ten o'clock to
read Pinel's *L'Aliénation Mentale:* the library was closed. I went to the
Panthéon, I read the first discourse of Cabanis on the relationship between the physical and the moral. His manner of stating facts seems to
me so general that it's vague. This author doesn't please me at all, I
should read Bacon and Hobbes.

I went with Barral to *Il Matrimonio Segreto* tonight, we found
Crozet and Basset, who had come in the hope of finding us there. I
can no longer picture Victorine in any position, my imagination is ex-

hausted, but not my love. I feel these two things perfectly. I no longer am conscious of the positions in which I want to picture her, because I've seen her in them too often; but the idea of her loving me still enchants me.

I see in Cabanis that we frequently act to satisfy needs which come as the result of the ideas which come from the interior of the body to the brain. The union of desires thus brought about is called *instinct*. Condillac completely overlooked instinct: two birds taken from their paternal nest immediately after hatching and reared by hand certainly have no notion of *nest, eggs* and *birth;* yet at the mating season, at least a fortnight before the female lays her eggs, they build their nest.

Women have admitted experiencing keen pleasure in their breast and womb while suckling their child.

The feathers are plucked from a capon's stomach, which is rubbed with nettles, and afterward the bird is placed on some eggs: the eggs soothe it, it remains on them and becomes attached to the chickens when they are hatched.

Therefore, in the case of *instinct,* as in all others, the individual is again following what seems to lead him to the greatest happiness.

How is it that we didn't see instinct in Condillac's school? Because we didn't clearly make out all the subjects of science. I remember asking everybody why little pigs sought their mother's teats. I got no answer. We are all amazed when, from some little thing we'd scarcely noticed and from which we'd drawn no conclusions, we see a rule or result derived which changes the state of science.

14 Pluviôse [February 3].—Since the 4th, I've had some delightful days at Dugazon's, some of the happiest days of happiness, possibly, that mankind at large is capable of giving me. That's perhaps the nuance that may lead me from the pleasures of a lofty melancholic soul to those of a brilliant fop. Whatever the reason, these days have been divine and they're the happiest I've yet found on this earth. The love of glory contributes a great deal to this mellifluence. Yet, seen from without, it's possibly one of the unhappiest periods of my life, in the opinion of my uncle, for instance—and he's the man whose word is the most likely to be accepted on my present state, and the one who has seen me in the direst poverty. That's something that should teach me to pay no heed to public rumor. And my reputation of a rake and a man already blasé, with this soul so tender, so bashful and so melancholy! Mante the philosopher at last knows me, but I was obliged to help him to see me as I really am. After that, have faith in the reputations of the great!

I took Louason home; I've got half a mind to become attached to her, that would make me get over my love for Victorine. With my little Louason I'll taste all the sweetness of a happy love and gaiety until my departure for Grenoble; but, for that, it's necessary that she have a soul.

Victorine scorns me or else hasn't received my letters. I learned last night with the greatest of pleasure that her father had been appointed Councilor of State or Senator. The first thing I did this morning was to read *Le Moniteur* of yesterday; I saw that he was a Councilor of State. I strolled through the Faubourg Saint-Germain and the Tuileries, guided by a secret desire to see them. On the Pont Royal, I ran into the son, who greeted me admirably.

He was so delighted with his father's appointment that he possibly didn't recall my relations with his family. We'll see how he is at the first meeting.[1] He said as affectionately as possible that he'd come to see me one of these days.

Duchesne considers him to be full of presumptuousness, having a little knowledge and a bad heart. That's more or less my own opinion, but the more he might be my enemy, the more good things the Lawyer *For* has to say about him. Generally speaking, I realize that I am very impetuous and consequently a bad judge, with the result that, without my being conscious of it, the lawyer opposed to ardor goes too far. I saw this in the plainness I attributed to Victorine and HER BROTHER EDWARD, as well as in the judgment I didn't dare pass on the latter, although probably more firmly based than those of Duchesne. I was wrong in all three cases. For the same reason, I constantly erred in the Adèle affair; I must look for examples of this, I'll get over my bashfulness in that way.

Speaking of the sisters, Duchesne said *they didn't amount to much.* That's something to be examined. Does Victorine share her brother's character or suffer from it? That's perhaps what might settle the question. I should never overlook the fact that moral truths aren't demonstrable like those concerned with properties appreciable in exact quantities.

At present, my reason is still based on passion; that's of small value, and yet I feel myself very reasonable. I've just read the first volume of Mme. de Staël's *Delphine,* and I put myself almost entirely into the character of Delphine. The experience I've acquired at Dugazon's has been very helpful in getting to know myself. Pacé said to me one day, "You're all passion." Mante is of the same opinion. I feel it myself. As far as he knows me, Dugazon is of the same opinion. Whatever may be the objections of the Lawyer *Against,* that's a truth which appears to me proved. I may not have THE MOST UNDERSTANDING SOUL, but I at least have a soul that is all passion. If a man is to talk well, he must

[1] Just as friendly, see the 23rd. [Note by Beyle.]

be in possession of himself; if he is to write well, he must perhaps be *in possession of his soul* and have one that is UNDERSTANDING for a desired passion.

I'm so reasonable that, although I feel I have possibly twenty pages of important and true ideas on my art and the means of procuring more continual happiness, I'm going to bed because it's one o'clock in the morning and I feel that I'm injuring my health.

As a consequence of my rules concerning my art, my first work would have contained parts closely resembling *Delphine* if I hadn't read this novel at the present time, and perhaps parts will still resemble it, even though I've read it. But that will be because I want it so.

15 *Pluviôse* [*February 4*].—It seems to me I've only known habitual happiness since reading Biran. This evening, the 15th, I spent a delightful evening with what would have put me in the dumps a fortnight ago. Read Cabanis (death of Mirabeau) and Hobbes in the reading room at the end of the Rue de Thionville. On the way home, ate a *brioche* with exquisite pleasure, more than I've ever experienced at the best meals. I thought of Mélanie, and this memory charmed me as much as the pleasure itself (AS THE PLEASURE ITSELF).

16 *Pluviôse* [*February 9*].—The most divine grace I recall is that of Imogen (*Cymbeline*) and, for men, that of Arviragus and his brother.

What a *felice* brush Shakespeare has for the figures of women! Ophelia, Desdemona, Imogen (in her category), Pauline, Constance (another) and finally the hostess Quickly (in the last).

O divine Shakespeare, yes, THOU ARE THE GREATEST BARD IN THE WORLD!

Yes, thou art the greatest poet that ever existed! And yet his work is almost prose for me. Consequently, it's possible to be a poet in prose; but verse gives an added charm.

It eliminates the notion of the *commonplace* by giving a slight veneer of strangeness.

20 *Pluviôse* [*February 9*].—*Mlle. Mars.*—I've just experienced the liveliest enjoyment the comedy has ever given me as far as laughter is concerned. Mlle. Mars, whom I'm used to seeing so modest, nearly put me beside myself in the role of Agatha in *Les Folies Amoureuses;* at her first two entrances, I was obliged to look away in order not to fall in love with her. I'm surprised even now to have escaped safe and sound. I was frequently compelled to repeat to myself that there wasn't any hope. For me, it was a Bacchanalia of beauty, such as I pictured the Bacchanalia of Rome in my youth at Milan.

It was one of the liveliest enjoyments the arts are capable of giving; it exhausted me, and I'll describe it all the more poorly because it made such an impression on me. That's something entirely lacking in the Gagnons Juniors, the Mazeaus and the blasé and obtuse souls: they'd give all their treasures for it if they suspected its existence. *I never saw anything so divine* as Mlle. Mars's first two scenes in this role.

That is one of those divine pleasures which are to be found only in Paris and which nothing can replace or even make you forget.

I was in the orchestra, since it must be confessed, and I went there in the hope of finding Louason, who wasn't there any more than she was yesterday, after telling me the day before that she went there every day. On the other hand, both yesterday and today, I saw Wagner, who's thick-witted but who's perhaps having her. At least, he was there with her seven or eight times and took her home afterward. Dugazon thinks he's having her. I'm dying with jealousy.

I change my mind about her two or three times a day. At the reading room this afternoon, I thought of making her another Clairon, of telling her all I know of the dramatic art, of being her Valbelle.[1] I've even started taking down the dates of the birth and death of the most famous dramatic authors. Or I'd lead her from the expression of the passions described by them to the general principles of philosophy, and thus to become the greatest actress possible.

I saw everything in this scheme as quite easy. Really, we're a treasure one for the other, and a relationship so perfect has never been seen. Will she love me? With my brilliance in conversation, will I be pleasing to her? A FUTURE YOUNG DRAMATIC-BARD WITH A FUTURE YOUNG ACTRESS, I ought to be worth a thousand Wagners. I base my hopes on his asininity.

I'm mad at her tonight and want to forget her.

Existence is a burden for me as a result of the conflict of passion that makes me love Louason and almost hate her. I'm weary from thinking and feeling, I have a continual headache. I need distraction, this is the first time I've felt that way. My love doesn't have the violence of fondness that I had for Victorine. I haven't enough hope for that.

22 *Pluviôse [February 11].—Breakfasting at the Café de la Régence, a quarter to nine.—Declamation and composition.*—In order to enlist the spectator's sympathy, you must be in possession of yourself and get warmed up little by little; otherwise, seeing you in a passion right off the reel, the spectator reckons with you instead of sharing your sentiments and seeing himself in you.

Once the spectator's heart is won over and allied with the actor, the latter's moments of vehemence produce sublime sentiments in the spectator's soul. Otherwise, these moments of naked vehemence can do no more than inspire interest in an unusual spectacle, or, in the case of

[1] Beylistic hero of *The Two Men*.

provincials, by persuading them through quackery that it's the height of art.

The same thing applies to composition. The moment when I'm the most worked up myself is not the one when I'm able to write the things that will have the most effect on the spectator. The proof of this is obvious: were I to come across Victorine somewhere, as in a salon, and during a game or joke she were to squeeze my hand, I'd certainly be in no state to write anything for the next two hours.

It's a good thing to have these states of the *maximum* of passion, for without that it would be impossible to portray them; but these moments of *maximum* aren't the best moments for writing. The best ones are those in which you're capable of writing the most stirring things: *physical tranquillity* and *serenity of soul* are necessary.

Up to now, I have especially lacked the latter in writing. I always bear in mind that, while writing *Letellier* three months ago, I was so worked up FOR THE FAME and so deeply worried about whether or not I'd attain it someday that I was no longer sensitive to the *comic,* the *terrible* or the *pitiful*.

Certainly the moment was not propitious for writing. Frequently, I can't write because of my ardor; for the past quarter of an hour, I've been making an effort to write, my feelings are so strong that writing (the physical action) is hard work for me. The result is that my thought is slowed up.

If I don't change my ways, I shall have been THE GREATEST BARD for myself alone, and, never having shown myself to others, I shall pass on WITHOUT FAME.

I must follow Shakespeare's example; how he flows on like a river that floods over its banks and sweeps all before it, what a river is his verve, how broad is his manner of painting, it is all nature! I continually pass from the fondest love to the keenest admiration for this great man—as late as last night, when I happened to reread the first scenes of *Othello*. For my heart, he's the greatest poet that has ever lived; when speaking of the others, there's always a mixture of esteem based on their reputation; with him, I always feel a thousand times more than I say.

His characters are nature itself, they are sculptured, you see them act. Those of the others are painted, and often without relief, like those of Voltaire. La Fontaine is the only one who touches my heart the same way as Shakespeare. Pascal's prose is what comes the nearest to him, as far as I am concerned. I should reread Homer to see whether or not he appeals to me like this.

I was carried away by my feeling when I was interrupted by Mante coming in. A little more and I'd have been in no state to write.

Mlle. Louason (*22 Pluviôse, XIII*).—I went out at a quarter to twelve wearing a new suit (cinnamon bronze) of light cloth. I was fraught with that *filtered* sensibility which makes you enjoy yourself with other people and is the basis of the amiable man's talent.

As I neared Dugazon's, I felt myself forgetting everything that, yesterday and this morning, I felt I had to say to Louason; so strong is the force of habit in good things and bad that I was also a bit flustered. At Dugazon's, I'm nothing but an artist; I must grow accustomed to laughing and talking while I'm there; by the time three lessons have passed, the habit will be formed, I'll cultivate it for a fortnight and then I'll be in shape.

I found no one there but Wagner and Mlle. Félipe. Wagner is on better terms with her than I am for two reasons:

1. Because his soul is more on the level with hers.
2. Because he talks more than I do.

Mlle. Louason came in as I was reciting Philinte; after a moment she went to sit beside Dugazon, in front of me. I put much gusto, I believe, into the big couplet:

Il faut parmi le monde une vertu traitable, etc.

and I believe she saw it clearly.

After that, Dugazon had me recite the big scene from *Le Métromane.* I began to get hold of myself, in accordance with this morning's reflections: the habit wasn't yet formed; I acted with gusto, verve, and a charming vocal beauty. I'd have filled a theater. I'd have acted much better if I had been in fuller possession of myself. Dugazon said, smiling, "Good, good!" and said a few words about me to Louason, ending with, "What warmth!" The other replied, as though she were persuaded, "Yes, he has a great deal"; she even said that with verve. I had a superb bearing of loftiness, enthusiasm and confidence while speaking my lines.

She didn't look at me with interest today, she was cool toward me, that probably resulted from two things: she has, I believe, *il marchese,* she hasn't been feeling well for two days; and afterward Pacé arrived and started to treat her like an actress who's been had, being restrained only by the decency required in Dugazon's salon; she submitted to all that with embarrassment, without daring to defend herself; he tapped her lightly with his riding crop while she was taking the part of Monime; he kissed her, he was charming; Dugazon believed it, or wanted to make him believe that he believed it, and told him so by the tone of his voice in asking him this question, "Why don't you come any more on Saturdays, etc.?" (to Joinville's, I believe).

Louason defended herself against all that like an agreeable woman who's been *had*. Pacé appeared to be, and really was, worn out and bored, but he was no less brilliant because of that. I was, a little.

I told him he'd had her, he said no. He said:

"Don't sleep with her, she has the clap."

"I know it."

"How so?"

"I gathered as much by the pimples on her face."

Ponderously, through a remnant of my old habits, I asked her whether she had it. This question, which was meaningless, annoyed her. I wasn't any wiser than before, I took no heed of the warning. I'm merely putting the facts of the conversation here, the skeleton, without either charm or gaiety.

Louason said that, if she didn't succeed in getting into the Français, her mind was made up, she knew where she'd go. Words from her to me are rare; in spite of myself, I was haughty and distant, through bad habit. She was completely upset by her indisposition. I took her home.

Passing before a dress shop at the end of the Rue des Fossés-Montmartre, near the Place des Victoires, she noticed an embroidered gown on display, and said, "It's extraordinary how artful they are in Paris in displaying goods . . ." That was entirely outside the ordinary tone of our conversation. Was it embarrassment, distraction or the desire to have a present? Farther on, in the Rue des Petits-Champs, she looked at some hats on display at a milliner's with an air that meant the same thing.

She told me in front of the Ministry of Finance that two days ago she went to see her little daughter, who, as she ran to meet her, fell down two or three steps, and that this, *coming at this time,* had upset her and made her ill.

She emphasized this. It amounted to telling me quite plainly that, at the time of my visit, she had *il marchese*. It was only then that I thought about the clap. We reached her door, and I left her at the foot of the stairs, she must have been surprised.

The asininity of my behavior on the previous days, as well as my bashfulness, made it easy for me to leave her, but I was no sooner outside the door than I no longer knew where I was going. I was like a man who, with a great effort, has just made a great sacrifice and who surrenders everything to his weakness. I really didn't know where I was; I reproached myself for having left her. Finally, since the rain kept me from going to see Cheminade, I came home and started writing.

Here are three possible defects:

1. it seems to me that Pacé was on the verge of having her, and that

she told him she had the clap, or that someone else told him about it; anyway, it seems to me that she knows that he knows she has it;

2. she probably has the clap;

3. perhaps she wants to be paid. I'm not rich enough for that, and even if I were, once paid, she'd have no further attraction for me.

During my two-hour visit Friday, she had a voluptuous, tender moment, tears in her eyes, blushes, etc., which I didn't have enough sense, spiritually, to take advantage of: it seems obvious that she wanted to say to me today, "I had *il marchese* then." If that was on purpose, it could only mean, "If it hadn't been for that, you would have had me." If that's the case, I did well not to go up to her apartment.

But it will be necessary Wednesday to show much love for her, and I'll need only to dare to say what I feel. I was about to fall in love with her tenderly, and I haven't recovered yet.

I want absolutely to make her my friend. If I discover that she's a whore, I'll blush a year hence when I read this, but why blush? I've known for long that I'm overly sensitive, that the life I lead has a thousand asperities which torture me; these asperities will be removed by an income of 10,000 francs, a fortune isn't necessary to me as it is (in the same way) to another, and it's more necessary because of my excessive delicacy—a delicacy that is lifted to the height of happiness or dropped to the depth of despair by the inflection of a word or a scarcely noticed gesture. I hide that under my hussar's cloak.

The bank and an income of 6,000 francs earned with a friend as reliable as Mante will eliminate all difficulties and permit me to enjoy all the pleasures of this sensibility, which no one will ever know. What I need is a poetic soul, a soul like my own, a Sappho, and I have given up trying to find it; but if I should happen to find it we'd experience a happiness that is superhuman.

My sensibility, not being employed in this world, will be poured entirely over the characters of Shakespeare and will augment my genius. It seems to me that the sensibility of Jean-Jacques at my age was not as filtered, as refined; in a word, to go back to my expression of last summer, it doesn't seem to me that he had as good a head, or mind, as I.

Therefore, I must take Louason home next Wednesday, go up with her and overwhelm her with tenderness in order to show her that I'm not just an ordinary man of the world.

Mlle. Clairon is her idol; she repeated to me yesterday for the second time, *"She's a great woman."* She told me she'd read her memoirs ten times, that she had them; she told me she didn't believe the story about the ghost . . . We were interrupted. What a soul to appreciate what

I wanted to do for her Sunday night, and what I started! What a soul I'd be for her!

Wagner brought her Geoffroy's first article on Mlle. Amalric [Contat], saying, "Here's what you asked me for." When could she have asked him for it? What is the date of the article? And yet it seemed to me that they hadn't seen each other since Friday's lesson.

The tenderness I'll show her on Wednesday ought to make her explain. It seems to me certain that she desired me, at least the day she was standing against the pier glass and took my arm after acting the role of Monime.

I absolutely want to be her friend and, with the exception of financial assistance, which I'm unable to give her, to show myself as such on all occasions.

Whatever risk I may take of finding her no more than a common whore instead of a sensitive woman, I ought to tell myself that perfection, in good or in evil, has never existed; I must take a chance and say to myself that, if her sensibility isn't developed, perhaps so fine a soul will give birth to it!

The worst of all the duperies that may result from the knowledge of women is never to fall in love for fear of being betrayed.

Louason feels about Clairon exactly what I feel about Shakespeare.

Little Félipe told me that George [the actress] lives with Martin; it seems it's a case of passionate love; she went to see him in Flanders, at Lille, while he was playing there.

This pretty little Félipe, brought up in the backstage company of the Favart and the Conservatory, hasn't, I believe, the first idea of what modesty is.

I've been to Louason's FOUR times; THE FIRST, tête-à-tête, spoke of art half an hour, THE SECOND WITH MISTRESS MORTIER, A OLD MAN COMES IN, AND IS greeted with all the respect that might be shown a protector or a PHYSICIAN.

The 3rd and 4th: Wednesday and Friday last, 17 and 19 Pluviôse, I SPOKE OF MY LOVE; a moment of strong emotion the 19th which might have been the end of everything—but perhaps on the other hand I SHOULD HAVE THE *caldapissa* in the bargain.

All my words of love-making were artificial, not a single one was natural. All I said to her was Fleury pure and simple; I'd almost have been able to point out the play from which I took each gesture—and yet I loved her. After that, how can you have any confidence in appearances! But the reason was that I felt confusedly that my love was of too lofty and beautiful a nature not to be ridiculous in society, where abbreviated sentiments are all that's needed. My love is like that of Othello before his jealousy. When I have enjoyed an income of 6,000 francs for six months, I will have enough self-confidence to be myself, even in love.

In the past month, Percevant and I have composed the character of Ouéhihé (Camille Basset the younger), four folio pages, and begun that of Perrino (Dausse). This is the most useful work that I could do.[1]

M. Maisonneuve told me the other day that Marmontel went up to ten without tiring himself; that this was responsible for his success in society and the greater part of his literary reputation. With him, a woman could be sure of having pleasure, he said. He was five feet seven or eight inches tall, with black eyebrows and wide shoulders; in short, he was a genuine Auvergnat.

He also told me that he'd seen Chateaubriand a few days earlier at his bookseller's, that he's a thin little man half a head shorter than I am, that his vivacity is unequaled, he can't keep still.

23 *Pluviôse* [*February 12*].—Esprit[2] came to see me about two o'clock today, and we only parted company at half-past four.

He was as friendly and candid with me as his distant and would-be witty character permitted. In the past, he has always treated me with a coolness that was pronounced and even haughty, bordering on impertinence. The change was striking and complete. I find that very inane. Gripoli shares my opinion.

I made no attempt to disguise my character, he took notice of that; I showed myself as I really am, with the exception, however, of the traits of LOVE FOR GLORY and of GREAT SENSIBILITY THAT ARE NOT BUT FOR THE intimate FRIENDS. He saw the disorder of my books and notes, and said I was crazy.

He's the least sensitive man I know, although he tries hard to be so. He told me calmly that I was as impulsive as the Germans. It's just like *il zio,* who'd like to be sensitive, and whom I endow with reason rather than sentiment. Tonight, Gripoli roared with laughter at this phrase, which my family has been repeating to me for the past ten years.

Moreover, in regard to Esprit, you can see he's making an effort to produce witticisms, and that removes the last shreds of urbanity from his character, making him stilted and dull. He's a long way from possessing Pacé's amiability, and if Pacé had his brains Pacé would be a rare man. I shouldn't be surprised if Esprit were obsequious and well equipped to make his way in the Court. If he doesn't get ahead

[1]These "characters," or character studies, which Beyle wrote in collaboration with Louis Crozet, are among the most interesting writings of his youth.

[2]Crozet SHALL BE CALLED Percevant; Ed. Mounier = Esprit; Mante = Gripoli. [Note by Beyle.]

this way, it will be because he will sacrifice his fortune to his wit.

The important thing is to know whether Charlotte [Victorine] shares this character or suffers from it.

This character is common and disagreeable. Some knowledge, not much intelligence, haughty, a disagreeable man.

After he left me, I was returning (very well dressed, in boots) toward the Pont Royal by the Rue du Bac, reading a letter that Crozet had given me, when I encountered a tall young lady with a graceful form, wearing a gray-blue satin gown, who was walking very quickly and had a handkerchief before her face. I believe it was Charlotte. I found her charming, and I saw I hadn't forgotten her, as I thought I had, and that a couple of words from her would have made me fall more deeply in love than I am already.

If it was she, I believe she saw me.

24 Pluviôse [February 13], 11 o'clock at night.—I could have had Louason tonight if I'd wanted, and I'll have her when I want her, that's the story of my day. I must go to see Martial tomorrow to find out the truth about the cl. I'm *sul orto della felicita* [on the border of happiness].

I went to Dugazon's this morning. She was there with Mme. Mortier, little Félipe and Wagner. She was very gay, her complexion had cleared up and she recited the role of Monime like an angel, really very well. She treated me well; I kissed her.

We left at a quarter to two. Wagner was with Félipe; all three of us went to Mortier's, who displayed all the details of a base soul that would like to be good-mannered. We stayed there three quarters of an hour. Louason had the enthusiasm that success gives to a soul in love with glory. All the noble sentiments surged into her heart. I took her home and stayed until four o'clock, only speaking of my love incidentally. She told me she was going to the theater.

Mante lent me six livres and I went in the orchestra. Louason arrived, I gave her a seat beside me. I offered to take her home, she accepted. When we reached her door, she asked if I weren't coming up. I went up, we lit the fire, spoke of her, then of my love. During the first half hour, she listened to me with tender emotion and dreaminess, later her interest flagged and I believe I bored her for a moment. I should take advantage of the first moment of tender emotion to have her. She's in love with me, or at least wants me to think she is, for she said she quite understood my behavior Monday when I left her at the door; she dwelt on this; then I spoke of the state I was in when I left her. This moment was the maximum of tender emotion. As I was going out, I asked her for a kiss, and, after putting up some weak resistance, she let me take one, obviously on purpose and with complaisance.

Everything proceeded well up to this point; she displayed a lofty character; but, as she was telling her maid to see me to the door, I saw her eyes, which were very bright and seemed to say to the maid, "He hasn't had me yet!"

This look had the effect of strangely dampening my enthusiasm. Perhaps, though, it was merely the eyes of an alert temperament that hasn't been satisfied. I am to take her Shakespeare tomorrow.

I'll have her Friday if I want to.

As I was writing this, a family of provincials, very good folk and very gay, got lost on the landing; a girl, very gay, with black eyebrows, young, pretty, a bit plump, knocked at my door and asked for an artist named Mademoiselle N. We went together, laughing like mad, to arouse the lady artist. This little episode of unconstrained gaiety gave me pleasure. The father, who was in a uniform embroidered with silver, showed great politeness toward me, and the daughter treated me with the familiarity of gaiety and youth which comes naturally to provincials.

I spent eight hours with Louason today.

25 *Pluviôse* [*February 14*].—At half-past ten, I went to see Pacé, who told me that he only told me Louason *aveve il mal francese* because he saw me laying siege to her. He said he didn't know anything about it.

Mante and I went for a walk on the Terrasse des Feuillants from two until a quarter past four. Louason was there. Mante considers, as I do myself, that she has a heavenly face; she was with two men. We thought we noticed an air of understanding in her smile when she looked at me. She has a manner of walking that's full of sentiment and grace.

Tonight I went to see Adèle OF THE GATE. What a difference! I found a spiritless character, wholly lacking in sensibility, occupied solely with petty impressions of vanity. She spoke to me of a young man who'll have an income of 250,000 francs, with a cupidity that showed through her protests of disinterestedness. She's forever occupied with play-acting; I observed her face from behind her mirror while she was combing her hair, brightly lighted by a lamp, having my own face entirely in the shadow; I saw nothing on it but *lack of sensibility, absence of gentle passions* and *even cruelty.* How sensibility (the real thing) makes beauty more moving! What a difference had Louason been in her place! Even without loving her, how much interest her toilette would have had! Instead of that, I saw only stupidity in the mother and badheartedness in the daughter.

For a man whose eyes had been opened by Lavater to physiognomies and who has himself tested out the significance of the facial traits, it's a curious experience to be present casually at the toilette of a pretty woman. For her, it's a matter of the greatest importance; she's herself, and you are in a position to judge her. All that I saw was: an insensitive soul, absence of gentle passions, cruelty. What made me love her the most three years back was that, in line with my ideas on love, I thought I ought to be loved. What remained of this love was killed tonight. She wouldn't even make Pacé happy, and he's goodhearted. I was with her from half-past five to eight.

26 *Pluviôse [February 15]*.—The contrast to the two women of yesterday, in whom I didn't notice an ounce of sensibility, made her dearer than ever to me; I had some charming things to say to her. When she arrived at Dugazon's, I forgot them all. I was alone with Mme. Mortier; she inspired me with such disgust that I found nothing to say to her. I tried to cover this up by means of all sorts of gallantries which were a continual mystification. This flood of words and gestures fell on little Félipe, who's pretty, who lends herself to it quite readily and who's perhaps even making some advances to me. After acting the role of Monime forcibly, she sank into a deeply serious mood which became melancholy while we were roaring with laughter at Dugazon, who was going over the role of *Iodelet* the way Wagner reads it, which made us hold our sides with mirth. Perhaps my attentions and gaiety were what made her sad. I only thought of that tonight. Even were she to deceive me, what could deprive me of the pleasure of feeling what I've felt during the past few days? But I don't believe she's deceiving me. Gripoli believes, like myself, that she may have a lofty soul. I came away from her home at four o'clock after having stayed there an hour and a quarter. I wasn't witty at all, I was too flustered; on the other hand, after leaving her I thought of a host of tender and witty things. When I'm more given over to *perception* and less to *sensation,* I'll be able to say them to her.

When we reached her apartment, she started out by giving me an account of the people she was with yesterday in the Tuileries. The young man who was holding her hand is M. Lalanne, poet; the other is a certain M. Le Blanc, a relative of Prince Joseph's wife, who, so it seems, has some elevation of soul.

A letter was delivered which we read together, after that she told me that Mme. Mortier had come over to her this morning and, speaking of me, had said, "That young man comes from a good family, he looks as though he had a fortune, undoubtedly he has." Thereupon, I said, "By way of conclusion, I'll say the first chance I get that I have a job in the War Office which pays me 1,500 francs." "And that they give you a hundred écus as a favor (from your family)," she added with vivacity.

This is only a summary. That makes me believe she loves me.

Gripoli even believes it's possible that what she told me about Mme. Mortier was invented in the hope of making her lose out with me. We talked with the intimacy of two lofty souls who understand one another; from time to time she looked at me with haggard eyes (slightly charged with love) without saying anything. She told me with natural and entirely unstudied decency that she didn't want to have a lover before her debut for fear of becoming pregnant. She said that without employing these terms, and in a way that was as delicate as this is vulgar. I lingered over the same notion, which I repeated in a thousand ways; I had too much emotional pleasure to take the trouble of inventing another one. She then told me in a charming way that she didn't love me.

The conclusion was that I kissed her and she gave me permission to go to see her tomorrow between two and three, the hour when little Félipe will be there. Since I can't muster up enough composure to display some wittiness, I must at least be simply myself in order to have the grace of naturalness; otherwise, I'll be between the devil and the deep blue sea. Not enough composure to follow out my plans for being a roué, and no grace or emotional appeal, not simply saying the first thing that comes into my head. If I'm wise, however, I'll try paying some attention to pretty little Félipe in order to make her a bit jealous. It's strange that I only have pleasant, even tender things to say to her when I'm far away from her. I must explain this thing when I can.

The role of Ariadne seemed charming to me. I must read *Manon Lescaut* with her before she takes this role. I was gracefully dressed today, at least the bust, and *at her home* I had all the appearance of the liveliest emotion.

27 *Pluviôse* [*February 16*].—Today should have been one of the most agreeable of my life, and in fact it almost was. I worked with Gripoli on Biran three hours and a quarter. The weather was superb. I spent four hours at Louason's. I saw her for only a second tête-à-tête; she rehearsed the second and third acts of *Ariane*. I found M. Lalanne there, saw M. Paillette arrive and depart; saw arrive and leave M. Le Blanc, the relative of Joseph's wife.

I was downcast when I came away from Louason's at five o'clock. I thought I saw that she was a whore. I'd be delighted to learn that she's being kept by Le Blanc. The only thing needed for my happiness was lacking because of my father's avarice. It was the ball in the Rue du Bouloy, where Adèle is dancing at this very minute. Strictly speaking, I could go anyway, but my soul, exhausted by violent emotions, needs some rest.

Louason, after rehearsing the charming passage of Ariadne and Theseus, which ends with:

C'en est fait, tu le vois, je n'ai plus de colère,

which she addressed to me throughout, leaned against me and I kissed her.

It was one of those days the like of which it's forever impossible to have in the provinces. Gripoli well sustained me when I was dejected this afternoon, he's a rare friend and all the more precious to me because he has the rationality I lack.

28 Pluviôse [February 17].—Walked in the Tuileries with Gripoli and Durif. Read Mme. Roland and Tacitus this morning. Found that the monarchy, by introducing deference between nations, mixes passions with government.

At Pacé's, I see every day the increase of respect for the law and the decline of its authority.

I didn't see Louason in the Tuileries. Worked all evening with Percevant on our *characters*.

30 Pluviôse [February 19].—After rehearsing Gripoli in the role of Desronais in *Caroline,* I went to Dugazon's at noon; I was informed that there would be no lesson. I went to Mélanie's, a bit tremulous. She greeted me with visible pleasure and gaiety; her chambermaid was curling her hair. I didn't have enough wit to be witty—that's a fact. I fanned the fire myself while she was doing something else. This little task, which bespoke intimacy, delighted me. Her chambermaid went out at last. We remained together two hours. I was very happy. I'd have liked a lot for her to be as much so as I. I have reason to believe that she was part of the time. What should have been accomplished by skill was brought about by chance; she told me her life story, it showed that she has a soul as sensitive as mine, because she told me things that could have been discerned only by a sensitive soul.

My mind is tired as I write this, I've just carefully gone over four hundred pages in three hours of time; but I don't want to go to bed without writing.

Her name is Mélanie Guilbert; she was born at Caen. She has a brother, a sister and a mother. Her father is dead. It looks as though her father made a misalliance in marrying her mother, who, an only daughter and very beautiful, brought into the household all her defects of character—to such a point that, on his deathbed, her father answered her sister, who told him she was going to write to her absent mother, "No, no, my daughter, let me die in peace." Another time, she slapped his face in front of the children; he pretended to laugh at the affront.

It appears that Mélanie's brother is quite a bad lot, even a low fellow, but conscientious when it comes to money, going as far as to return to the family of one of his friends 6,000 francs in bank notes which the friend had left him when he died. Her mother sank into avarice.

She was divine while telling me this story. I was sitting beside her, looking into her face, not missing a single one of her traits, holding her hands in mine. She was quite conscious that her tender soul was producing its effect. She was really moved; while speaking of her father, she twice dabbed at her eyes, in which there were no tears. I stole twenty kisses and she didn't go out of her way to stop me; I believe she loves me. The proof of it lies in the smiling joy and delight of a sensitive soul which she manifested upon seeing me. Yet I bored her a bit the last time, for when I said, "Choose a signal to give me when I'm boring you," she said, "Ah, yes!" with an accent of satisfaction. I joked a bit about it. This signal is the question, "Is there a ball at the Opéra?" I urged her to tell me whether she was in love with someone, she said no, at length yes, looking at me; in spite of my efforts, she saw that I was crestfallen (it was largely put on), she quickly said no; the suave grace she put in this whole conversation proved that she's in love with me. Anyway, I succeeded twice in making her laugh boisterously; I began to recover my composure. Still, I continued to have those moments when my lips alone speak, my heart being busy feeling while my lips forever repeat the same thing.

At two o'clock, I accompanied her to the office of Talma the dentist, where I'm to go tomorrow. On our return, she wanted to work, I saw that by the expression on her face. I went up a minute; it's agreed that I'll call her Mélanie and she'll call me Henri. I gave her a good kiss and left her at three o'clock.

She told me again today that she didn't want to have a lover, that all she thought about was making her debut; that's another reason for working with her. She read Shakespeare's *Othello* and then the *Othello* of Ducis; she preferred the second; the great beauties of the first failed to achieve their effect because of the Barbary horses and the beast with two backs; I must teach her to appreciate the sublime Shakespeare. She was delighted with Desdemona's premonition of her death; she made two or three sentimental criticisms of Shakespeare's *Othello* which (whatever their merit) could have come only from the soul of an artist. I'll see her tomorrow at Dugazon's, Thursday at *Le Bourgeois Gentilhomme,* or rather at her home and at the theater, Friday at Dugazon's. Now, on account of our signal, "Is there

a ball at the Opéra?" I'll go to see her oftener. I must acquire the
habit of making compliments; she joked about a little tap she gave
me in the eye, and said, jesting fondly, "Those big eyes!" I ought to
have answered, "Oh, you're used to your own, you don't find any big
ones, but, etc., etc." This day, which has been a delightful one and
filled with a happiness I would never be able to enjoy in the provinces
(the arts and the delicate love of an intelligent woman), didn't make
the same impression on me that it would have a few days ago; I'm
beginning to get used to happiness.

Journal of My Third Voyage to Paris

From 1 Ventôse, Year XIII, to . . .

Ventôse, XIII.
HAPPINESS OF Mélanie.
6 Ventôse, XIII.—SEE.—TO SAY TO HER IN EVERY INSTANT WHAT I THINK
and feel at the time; HERE IS THE UNIC WAY TO HAPPINESS, READ IN THE
NATURE THE 20 Ventôse AT THE THUILERIES GARDENS. TO HAVE EVER CARRIKS.

My whole behavior in this affair has been, and probably will be, that
of a child. 27 Ventôse, XIII [March 18, 1805].

*Le vicende di amore: spiritoso il 6 Ventoso, provo tutte le furie di
gelosia e d'incerta corrisponza il 13, teneva le mani nelle mie il 30.*
[Vicissitudes of love: witty 6 Ventôse; I experienced all the fury of
jealousy and uncertainty regarding my own love the 13th; I held her
hand the 30th.]
Ventôse, XIII.—The time this journal opens is perhaps the happiest of
my life. Dugazon's lessons, my love for Mélanie and perhaps hers for
me compose my happiness; and yet possibly never ought a time to
have been more unhappy: my father hasn't given me the advance to
buy clothes for which I've been asking him since Vendémiaire. In a
few days, I hope to have 1,000 francs, of which 300 francs will be an
advance from my father and the balance a loan.

I have quite nice lodgings in the Rue de Ménars, No. 9. That's my
physical situation. I'm very well dressed.
1 Ventôse [February 20].—This day has been one of the happiest in my
life. I spent three or four hours of the sweetest intimacy with Mélanie.
Everything showed me that she loved me. Her gentle and entire con-

fidence, her astonishment upon learning, when a man she'd invited for dinner arrived, that it was five o'clock.

WITHOUT LOVE OF GLORY, *diceva io ieri* TO Gripoli, *credo che io mi* DID DO AC. AND *sequerei l'impiego del* Molé. [Were it not for my love of glory, I said yesterday to Mante, I believe I should become an actor and follow the career of Molé.] THIS IS TRUE. THIS LIFE IS CHARMING.

2 *Ventôse* [*February 21*].—Ever since last night, I've had an epistle to Mélanie in my head, or rather my heart. I still have the feeling of it; it would undoubtedly give her pleasure, but I still recall the difficulty I had last summer in composing four lines of verse in eight hours of abominable labor. A hundred lines of verse would be necessary. It's impracticable.

I've perhaps never loved her as much as yesterday, and she never appeared as pretty to me as today, at half-past two, when she was atremble as she was about to recite the first scene of *Phèdre*.

11 o'clock.—I've just left her after spending the evening with her (eleven o'clock is striking); and I wish I might cease to exist until noon tomorrow, when I'm seeing her again.

My soul is too exhausted for me to be able to write down everything I've felt today. Yesterday was the happiest day in my life, everything convinces me that she's in love with me. At two o'clock today, I went to her home, she received me very well, she was all dressed up, charming and quite flustered. As for myself, on the way there I was unable to hold in my happiness, in the Rue Neuve-des-Petits-Champs I had to make an effort to get out of the way of the passing carriages. At her apartment, I found a M. Martin de . . . , an openhanded man with a mediocre mind, I believe. She was expecting a M. de Châteauneuf, to whom she was to recite her lines. He arrived a minute later, introduced by M. Le Blanc, the same one I made so impatient one day that I stayed until five o'clock—who looks to me as though he dined there frequently, who looks to me as though he were an *entreteneur* because with everything I see I associate his words, "Mademoiselle is afraid," whose ambiguous status is beginning to displease me singularly, undoubtedly as much as I displease him, and whom I'd take the greatest pleasure in throwing out the window. That man is no fool, he has piercing black eyes and a bad breath, according to what Mélanie gave me to understand tonight, and a mind that repeats; he's already said before me twice, "Yes, it's permissible to copy—but when you kill your man." I've read that somewhere.

M. Châteauneuf, a man of thirty-six, heavy-witted and handsome of face, with no expression other than nullity of character, is a bad and very dull copy of La Rive; moreover, the same character in what he says, with more baseness. Fatuous in an asinine way.

To tell what Mélanie made me feel, I'd need fifty pages and a fresh mind, no desire to sleep and no fatigue. All these reasons likewise prevent me from going into the lofty views on the human mind that the sight of these characters gave me this morning. I experienced so much emotionally tonight that I have a severe stomach-ache.

Mélanie recited the first scene from *Phèdre* with a rare soul; you can see that she feels more than she expresses.

She also recited one of Aménaïde's passages. But what is beyond description is the divine soul she unconsciously revealed. She has Desdemona's character in everything. At first excessively shy, then becoming assured, but paying no compliments to Châteauneuf, lacking the falsity that society gives, in a word, divine. I came away at half-past four, leaving M. Le Blanc and Mme. Mortier there.

I reached the orchestra through an uproar in the queue; they were giving *Le Bourgeois Gentilhomme*. (Same judgment as when I read it: the traits are true but of the vulgarest, the characters undeveloped, the outline of a great master. Dugazon good.) Wagner had kept a seat in the orchestra for me. She arrived with that little Mortier, who throughout displayed the character of a low wench; she [Mélanie], from the beginning to the end, the modesty of Desdemona.

GOOD, AS SHE THE WORLD HAD NEVER SEEN,

really without social experience, as modest as Mlle. Mars; I at her side, enchanted, immobile, brilliant, but not telling her all I wanted to tell her.

With this character, it's possible that she is compromised a great deal by her behavior and that she's had very few lovers; she admitted to me that she's had one; I believe Lafond has had her. We left, wearied by the ballets, at a quarter past eleven. I accompanied her as far as her door, but didn't go up out of discretion. I could have kissed her; tomorrow I must make her appreciate my effort to hold myself in. Tonight, she was wearing a black hat and a rose and she was rouged, like a piquant beauty playing a concerto of beauty, and her face was that of Desdemona—sweet melancholy and innocence. This discord was ill-becoming.

This was a day when I saw her only in public. I feel that I love her more every day. Today, I was with her from two till a quarter to five, and from seven till eleven, six hours and three quarters; yesterday, from three till five. Who wouldn't believe that I have her? And yet, that's not the case. I read in her candid soul; she's so candid, in fact, that I shall always believe her in preference to anything that may be said about her. Sometimes I'm furious at the thought that she may have given herself without love.

Were I to see Victorine, the other love might possibly come back; as I don't see her, Mélanie fills my life and I don't think of her. Adèle is driven from my heart forever.

I'm going to bed with the desire to sleep, to obliterate myself until I see her again. I took her *Cymbeline* and *Manon Lescaut*.

3 Ventôse [*February 22*].—As I write this at midnight, it seems to me as though the events of this morning took place several days ago. When I woke up at seven o'clock this morning, I had enough surplus energy to provide stimulus for several bodies. I went to Dugazon's at noon. I found Wagner and Félipe there. Mélanie came in a moment later. Dugazon had me recite Çinna's narrative twice; I spoke it in four voices: the artificial voice of Talma, my own voice distended, a silly voice and still another, but none of them was the real one. I'm not blasé enough. What makes me speak badly is my excessive sensibility.

Mélanie finished with Monime and began Ariadne. We left together at two o'clock; she was crestfallen because she thought she had given a bad interpretation of Ariadne, whom, on the contrary, she established with deep feeling. We went along the Boulevards, then the Rue Montmartre to the Tuileries, in the loveliest weather in the world. From there, as we were both dying of hunger and she wouldn't go in Legacque's, we went to her apartment, where a fire was burning. Her chambermaid heated up a little dish of potatoes for us, we put a chair between us and ate them with delight, because, in the first place, we were hungry, and because, I believe, at the moment she was as deeply in love with me as I was with her. We were about to go back to the Tuileries when the inevitable Le Blanc came in at a quarter to four. Maybe he eats there. I stayed until five, she smiling divinely at my restrained wrath and the smile (somewhat put on) with which I masked it.

If I only could have felt that I had some claims on her, I'd have had one of the most violent fits of anger possible. My anger without claims and my jealousy without any reason to show that I was jealous put me in a cold rage that lasted until seven o'clock. A word, a fissure through which to escape, and I don't know what could have held me back—nothing but death (mine). This state was not disagreeable, I thought that at bottom she was in love with me, and she said this morning that she would be going to the Français.

I went there, she didn't come. I saw Félipe and Wagner in the balcony, I joined them in the second act. That little Félipe is charming, but it's extraordinary how lacking she is in acquired ideas.

They were giving *Iphigénie*, which is positively the play that bores me more than all the others in the world, with the exception of cheap dramas. The characters have nothing but vanity, a sentiment with which one reckons but doesn't sympathize.

I lead a very brilliant existence, to Félipe's way of thinking. Wagner is certainly a goodhearted plodding animal, thoroughly German in the full meaning of the word, a thousand leagues from refinement.

We've just taken Félipe home. Tomorrow, I'm going to Mélanie's at noon to take her to the Luxembourg. The time of the day when I'm able to express my love least well (in my opinion) is always the one that I'm with her; I spent five hours in her company today. Her character seems to me to have a general tinge of melancholy. Perhaps her soul is too delicate for her situation.

She told me this morning of a thousand vulgarities she has observed in Mme. Mortier, whom she must stop seeing.

If Louason had come tonight, I'd have got ahead with my affairs, I had all the necessary audacity that comes with composure. I experienced feelings that were very keen and different today. Never was I in a better mood to appreciate *Iphigénie,* I only asked to be moved, and yet it displeased me mightily.

Perhaps it isn't impossible to have Félipe. That would be amusing.

The general opinion at Dugazon's, the opinion that everyone holds and expresses in front of me, is "that I have too much of what the others haven't enough of." "You have too much soul," as Félipe and Wagner told me tonight and this morning while I was acting.

Can it be that this charming girl has some terrible secret sorrow which gives her that melancholy? I'm inclined to believe so for several reasons—several of her words which said as much, and the firmness of resolution with which she devotes herself to the theater.

Or is this melancholy a game to mask the silence into which she is forced by the fear of unmasking herself? But why go to so much trouble in order to be loved by me? To have some money? But the tone she has adopted is the farthest removed from that; it even makes such a thing impossible.

Just let the Lawyer *Against* try to stop me from worshiping a lofty and sublime soul whom I've come across by the greatest of hazards, whom I worship and who's in love with me, according to what Gripoli believes! I must be all eyes tomorrow; I've been courting her since 15 Pluviôse [February 4] at the most. On that day, I spoke to her of my love for the first time jokingly, I speak to her far too often in this manner; her soul is too tender, hasn't enough social experience to be so pleased by the comic.

How natural the role of Ariadne is!

4 *Ventôse* [*February 23*].—Some time ago, Milan went hunting daily. Four days ago, he was at Malmaison, in a gloomy mood; they say it's

because he's just had Lucien assassinated. Louis is sick in bed, and Joseph has accepted the kingdom of Lombardy.

I went to Louason's at noon. Her chambermaid told me she'd gone out. I returned at half-past one, same reply; maybe she shut herself in again. That would indicate that Le Blanc is keeping her. If such were the case, would she have the courage to tell me? Wouldn't the shame of admitting it overcome her love? All that worries me. Gripoli thinks I oughtn't to see her before Monday.

I went for a walk with him two hours in the Tuileries; he told me what a terrible effect my kind of wit produces in society. We're going to develop what he said and write it in this journal. That brings me even closer to my Louason. She possesses the soul of an artist; it will be a long time before I'm able to explain my opinions well enough to be considered by her as even an equal in declamation. When that time comes, she will love me and I will find happiness with a soul as tender as my own, while the idiots, mistaking my jokes for considered statements, will conclude that I am a dangerous man, and hence a *bad-natured* one. If I live, my conduct will show that there never has been a man whose pity is as easily aroused as my own: the tiniest thing moves me, brings tears to my eyes. My sensation invariably triumphs over my perception, thus preventing me from carrying out the slightest plan. In a word, they'll realize that there never has been a man with a better disposition than mine.

Mante, who has known my character, will bear witness to this; and anyway, don't trust reputations. He told me that Rey and I had minds as far apart as possible.

All that redoubles my love for my divine Mélanie.

6 Ventôse [*February 25*].—MAXIMUM OF WIT IN MY LIFE.—I left Louason's at half-past three; for the first time in my life, I was brilliant with prudence and not in the least with passion. I was aware of what I was doing all the time, but without being bothered because of that, without being embarrassed. I don't believe I've ever been so brilliant, nor filled my role so capably. I was wearing a waistcoat, silk breeches and black stockings, with a cinnamon-bronze coat, a very well arranged cravat, a superb frill. Never, I believe, was my homeliness more effaced by my character.[1] I arrived at Dugazon's, I found no one there but Félipe, who opened the door for me. She was enchanted with me and gave me a good opportunity to make a declaration to her; I brought her a copy of Racine.

After four minutes alone together, the doorbell rang, no one opened the door, I went myself to open it. It was Louason with Mme. Mortier.

[1] My whole soul appeared; it caused my body to be overlooked; I had the appearance of a very handsome man, of Talma's kind. [Note by Beyle.]

Reaching the fireplace, Mme. Mortier said, "It's impossible to be better-looking," etc., a compliment on my dark clothes. Louason regarded me and felt the compliment. I replied with a noble gaiety and the most offhand and extreme politeness. The whole lesson period was in that strain, especially toward Louason, but this politeness was a long way from the tender and abandoned love of the other days. I looked at her very little while putting her through her rehearsal. This was the only thing that might have appeared affected (to her alone; the others only noticed a slight letup in my usual ardent manner), and it fitted into my role perfectly.

I told her that yesterday I was at the Français, where she was; this appeared to surprise her. From that moment, passion was awakened in her, she started to pay attention to what she was doing.

While speaking her role, she frequently took my hand with all the tenderness of the role; it seems to me she even squeezed it three or four times. I was extremely polite, but I didn't squeeze hers.

While playing the role, I manifested a charming gallantry for little Félipe. I mustered up all the beauty and grace I was capable of. I danced with her a second. She had to leave the room, she said she'd come back, and she actually did come back, something I believe she's never done before.

Louason, it seems to me, was surprised, attentive and immobile: that's the spirit of her behavior.

She complimented little Félipe on her sea-green hat, on the fact that she was able to wear such a color, and said at the same time that it was badly made. I went over and said some agreeable things to Félipe; she took off her bonnet, there was some question of putting it on Louason; she wouldn't let us, finally she started to put it on me; I agreed on condition that she would take it afterward. I believe she found pleasure in the act of putting it on me.

I took it off, and, as I urged her to take it, she whispered to me, "Do you want to become disgusted with me?" This word seems to me decisive. I think I answered, "I have need to."

I next recited the second act of *Le Misanthrope,* and I said to Félipe with all the grace and half passion (in the world) possible, "Divine Félipe, come and rehearse with me."

The charming grace of my declamation dumfounded Louason; she stood there astonished, immobile, breathless. After twenty lines, Dugazon told Mme. Mortier to take the part of Clémentine. Félipe went to Louason's side, with Wagner, who was the maximum of the German sort today, between the two of them. Louason, I believe, spoke to them about me.

Dugazon complimented me on a four-line rejoinder; he told me it was perfectly in character, etc. In the middle of my role, I saw Louason ask for some paper to write a note. She wrote it, I went over to her without affectation and asked her if she were leaving; she said she was dying of hunger, and sat down.

During his role, Dugazon sang us—particularly her—a charming couplet from Moncrif with all the gaiety and grace possible:

"Pretty shepherdess! You have all the shepherds, one after the other. But I have no complaint, you make me pass such a lovely day!"

That meant, "After Wagner, you have Beyle." I was interrupted a few minutes later, she rose to leave. Dugazon told Mme. Mortier to begin. I left a couple of seconds after her, employing this time to give Dugazon my note.

When the two of us were alone on the stairway, she was silent, abashed, without resoluteness in her actions, telling me she wasn't giving me her arm so as to be able to raise her skirt, but giving it to me at the same time.

She had her book and handkerchief in her hand, she didn't dare give them to me. I asked her if they bothered her, she said *yes* and gave them to me.

We continued like that from Dugazon's to her apartment, she speaking of her roles, without love. We arrived at her door, I asked her if I might come up, she seemed surprised at this question, and answered it with a look that said, "Why, yes, of course." I happened to be holding her book the same way as on the day I gave it back to her in the same place and went away without going up. She was upset by that, I believe. She said a few words I didn't understand, she was embarrassed; she said, "It's because you were holding my book the way you were the day you gave it back to me and went away." These were more or less her words. When we reached her apartment, the same tone continued, agitation on her part and also a bit on mine—everything needed for me to act my role properly.

On the way back, she had told me that she'd go to the Français tomorrow (because of *Phèdre*).

When we reached her apartment, she started singing the praises of little Félipe. That seems to be her way of treating all the people she fears; she's clever. I was very moderate and polite in regard to this praise. She started out by telling me that I took her home the day before yesterday and that the little girl told her I cracked all sorts of jokes as we were passing through the Palais-Royal, that she roared with laughter all along the way. The little girl must have let her see by these words that I had been as amiable as possible with her.[1] I

[1]The truth is that I made her laugh two or three times, the rest of the time I was much occupied with her. I kidded her mildly and subtly about Lafond,

replied that I didn't believe it was difficult to make her laugh a lot. She told me, after a few embarrassed words as she walked about the room while I was fanning the fire, that my grimaces when M. Le Blanc came in the other day made her laugh heartily. I put up a graceful defense, broaching the subject of love in connection with the word "grimace"; she replied, pausing in front of her mirror, that when I was her lover—which I'm still a long way from being—I mustn't stop her from seeing other people. The explanation we'd both been waiting for was about to start.

Instead of getting up and going to the center of the stage, as I have the bad habit of doing sometimes, I kept on fanning the fire; I told her some jokes she didn't understand. Without stopping to putter with the fire, I had my ear out for what the chambermaid might say to her; she told her in a whisper, "M. Le Blanc came at a quarter past two, thinking that it was three o'clock." I took it all in. We were at this point when Châteauneuf came in for the second time. We were about to have the explanation, the reconciliation was bound to fail, as M. Le Blanc was due to arrive at three o'clock. I saw M. Châteauneuf come in with a pleasure that astonished me; I thought I would be depressed because of his coming, and instead I was pleased.

I greeted M. Châteauneuf with extreme politeness, he recounted his life to us; his conversation was ponderous and arid with the best possible material. The man is thick-witted.

I soon took the conversation in hand, and made it wander around and change subject with an ease that amazed me. He asked for *Le Cid,* Mlle. Louason went to look for the book, finally handed it to him; he'd scarcely started to talk about this role and Lafond when I made him talk of something else, book in hand.

After making my man gallop through everything under the sun, I led him up to Alfieri; it turned out that he knew him well and once stayed a month with him in Florence. On hearing this, my enthusiasm for this great man was revived; he had been saying that he knew Italian, that Alfieri used to like him to read his plays, etc., etc., etc., etc. I drank in these details, I bided my time. Finally, he asked me casually, as though out of duty and as though sure of a *no:*

"Do you know Italian?"

(With the best pronunciation:) *"Si, io capisco molto, sono stato tre anni in Italia,"* etc. [Yes, I understand it well, I spent three years in Italy.]

His face expressed utter astonishment and pleasure. I was majestic

---

who's had her, or is still having her, and with whom she's a bit in love. Therefore, people must be occupied with themselves. [Note by Beyle.]

to the point of being *sublime* for him, and, indeed, I began to be *sublime*. (Terms from the art of moving people, or poetry.)

Louason was attentive.

After this sentiment had been exhausted, he recited for me the sonnet of the great Alfieri, the sixth, seventh, etc. lines of which are magnificent: great and profound and lofty truths expressed as well as they possibly could be in a language that is pompous and crammed with sentiment. I let my own sentiment burst out, it was the expression of the keenest admiration. Louason said, "If you keep on, monsieur, he'll go out of his head." After that, I restrained my admiration a little.

The bell rang, I changed places three or four times with embarrassment, as at the approach of a person one hates and before whom one wants to put on a good appearance, all this was taking place while Le Blanc was opening the three doors through which you have to pass to enter the room. I forgot to say that, before the arrival of M. de Châteauneuf, I spoke to her of Le Blanc with hatred, and, as she was preparing to ask me what right I had to hate him, I saw the question in her eyes and replied, "There are eyes I don't like; he's a man I don't like. You aren't going to prevent it, I hope." That's the gist of it. Her nervousness increased, she said while arranging herself before her looking glass, "I think you're crazy." Châteauneuf came in. By the time Le Blanc came in, I had made up my mind. Châteauneuf liked me because of the deep feelings he'd just aroused in me. I said, "Let's put on a front of enthusiasm and pretend to be completely absorbed by what Châteauneuf is saying, I'll make him talk to me while my ear and attention are trained on Louason and Le Blanc." I carried this out so effectively that there were several times when I had no idea what Châteauneuf was saying with the liveliest interest for my exclusive benefit. I smiled and frowned from time to time, the least ineptly possible.

Here is what was done by the two persons I was observing: Louason put on the look of a woman who's receiving the man who keeps her, a look of feigned tenderness and friendliness; she took an armchair, giving her place to Le Blanc; the latter, seeing that Châteauneuf and I were deep in conversation, began talking in a low voice (the *low voice* of Parisian society, which isn't a *whisper* like the *low voice* of the provinces). He squeezed her knees, he started out saying things like a man who's keeping a woman, among them, "After the days of plenty!"

"After the days of plenty, what?"

"You'll see."

Some pleasant surprise he's preparing for her after the days of plenty. She thanked him with a smile, but not with her eyes, feigned.

During this, the form of her upper lip changed completely, she lost her angelic tenderness and assumed the wantonness of a wench. Her lip is usually almost as straight as mine, it became almost as arched as Mante's.

(Night and hunger are driving me out, I'll continue after dinner. Two hours and a half to write the foregoing.)

The whole object of my conversation with Châteauneuf was to induce him to form a troupe in which Louason could play. At this point the conversation became general. Le Blanc said he had a theater in view but that the scheme was still in the air. Some minutes later, Châteauneuf said, "I too have a theater in view,

> *"mais nos mystères sombres*
> *Doivent s'ensevelir dans la mort et dans l'ombre."*

I told him he was terrible with death, that one should flee it. Thereupon, not seeing the joke, he told me that the two lines were from [Voltaire's] *Mahomet;* I continued to joke, I took my hat and went out. I bumped my head as I passed through the first door. Louason said, not very tenderly but with much warmth and curiosity, "You'll kill yourself," and then, to the others when I had closed the door, "He's such a hothead!" This word with great expression. I couldn't have ended the day with a better exit.

This was undoubtedly the finest day in my life.[1] I may enjoy greater successes but I'll never display more talent. My perception was just strong enough to guide my sensation; a little more, and I'd have let myself be carried away by the latter.

And I had an audience worthy of me! Loüason, with her soul, her kind of studies and her experience, is possibly the most difficult woman to deceive when it comes to the expression of love.

I displayed great talent; it's the first time I've seen it in myself to such a point; assuredly, this is the time to enjoy the pleasures of vanity. Well, I felt it yesterday, and I still feel it today (7 Ventôse), I'm absolutely incapable of anything. Love alone makes me find mellowness in the memory of my day. I desire nothing but the happiness I can enjoy through loving Mélanie, *the rest is of little importance*.

In the evening, I was absolutely exhausted, I was incapable of doing anything; I'd have needed a society in which I could relax, a concert in a home where I'd be entirely without constraint; not having this, I went to bed at eight o'clock.

To express the perfection of the sort of thing in which I excel, I

[1] As far as talent is concerned. The day I possess her will be far finer. [Note by Beyle.]

might say that I filled a role such as Molière might have written, being the actor as well as the author.

7 *Ventôse* (*Mardi Gras*) [*February 26*].—I saw the fatted ox, it was pitiful. Generally speaking, I can hold all this sort of spectacle in contempt.

A year ago, quarrel at Grenoble with Colomb and d'Avignonet. Two years ago, quarrel at the Bal de la Cité between four loafers and F. Faure, Boissat and me. I was certainly a child in those days, I was all soul, I had no conception of vanity, I was taking Legouvé's course. I was in love with Adèle OF THE GATE and I thought I was making her fall in love with me. I flooded myself with coffee, the only moments I counted as happy were those passed in mental erethism. That had a tendency, it seems to me, to drive me insane. By his contagious gloominess, Faure darkened that whole period of my life, otherwise so fine because of the sentiment, the days when I thought of *Hamlet* and was taking lessons from Deschamps.

I didn't go to the Français because I wasn't sure of finding her there, since George was playing; because I'm not very rich; and especially because it was good policy not to go, although she told me in advance that she'd be there. She even told me in advance in this fashion, "For instance, I'll be there tomorrow," etc.

Which seemed to me a bit emphatic.

8 *Ventôse* [*February 27*].—I went to Mélanie's at two o'clock, she was wearing an attractive negligee. I never in my life saw her so gay. All my resolutions gave way, I kissed her a thousand times, she put up no resistance. I took her in a fiacre to see an agent in the Rue des Mathurins; she stayed there a quarter of an hour. We returned and I left her at five o'clock, four minutes after the arrival of M. Le Blanc. She gave me all sorts of explanations about him: he has composed three tragedies and two comedies, he doesn't take his meals with her, but he comes there every day from four to five. What for? I'll go tomorrow. She saw me leave with regret and nodded to me charmingly, saying, "You'll come tomorrow to rehearse me in Ariadne." She said that to me from behind the door; I being already on the stairs.

She told me with feeling that M. Le Blanc and M. Châteauneuf found me amiable the other day; she said, "And I didn't say a word."

9 *and* 10 *Ventôse* [*February 28 and March 1*].—Yesterday and today, I saw the lovable Mélanie. My love increased amazingly. Tonight it was my whole life. I believe that M. Blanc, far from keeping her, is merely a man of letters who talks over her roles with her, but has exacted secrecy. In that case, what an angelic soul! She was far from even imagining my suspicions, and how far my coarse words are from interpreting her delicacy! She's in love with me and won't tell me so; tomorrow, I should let her see that I'm sad.

I'm going to bed at half-past nine tonight because I feel *che mi distruggo pensando a ella* [that I am wearing myself out thinking about her].

Ventôse [*March 3*].—Since that day, much misfortune has befallen my love. I wasn't able to go to the Français in the evening, and it was a great misfortune. I'd have been sad, I'd have asked her to pardon me for my indiscretion, for it was one, and even a very stupid one; that would perhaps have ended everything and at this moment I'd possess her.

But there, as elsewhere, we have a bastard. It seems to me that, at the moments when I need to go forward, I hear a voice above me crying, "You would like to fly and you haven't got wings, crawl!" I frequently desire the passions in order to be happy; that's not asking for pure happiness, it's asking for anxiety. But that kind of *anxiety* trains me in gallantry, makes me know man's heart (FOR THE GLORY), and, all in all, is worth more than the profound boredom in which Tencin wallows because of the absence of all passion. His hope is of the destructive kind, of that kind which waits for an event which cannot be hastened by any act of ours.

I consequently didn't see Mélanie at the Français. It was Friday the 10th. In the evening, I was in a mood of that tender sadness that comes entirely from love, and that affects you so deeply.

Yesterday, I went to Mélanie's at half-past twelve. I was told that she wasn't home. I went to Mme. Daru's; Adèle came in. From there to M. de Baure's, who greeted me as though he had seen me the day before, although two months had passed since I last saw him. I never so much appreciated the pleasure of conversing with a man of parts. That is still another enjoyment that is impossible in the provinces.

I tore myself away with difficulty at half-past two. I hurried to Mélanie's. She opened the door herself. Before I had taken two steps, I noticed a hat on the sofa. I found the poet Lalanne. I looked crestfallen, I've just left him. I was more witty than amiable. I felt that I was unable to say anything to Mélanie, so I was in a bad temper and scarcely paid any attention to her. I talked well, but I was *in such a temper* that two or three times I prevented Lalanne from leaving.

At this point in my visit, I noticed that she looked very sad. She said she expected an agent at half-past two. She rang; she said to me (speaking to me):

"As it's an agent, I'll ask you to leave us alone a moment." That more or less. A *moment* meant, "You'll go into the next room," but the *inflection* said, "You'll leave me alone, I hope."

"That was certainly my intention," I said.

Today I went there, my heart beating, at one o'clock: "Madame isn't in." I went to the Tuileries, where I found that booby of a Wagner. I left him to return to Mélanie's at two o'clock. Passing by the porter's lodge, the idea came to me to ask if Mme. Louason was in:

"Yes, monsieur," looking very assured. I went up; the chambermaid, with the look of a deceitful soubrette in a comedy:

"Madame isn't in."

Yesterday she replied to me with a truthful look:

"Madame has just gone out."

Consequently, it's obvious that Mélanie shut her door to me today and perhaps yesterday. Undoubtedly, M. Le Blanc, whom I saw arriving and with whom I went out two days in succession, told her, "You're making me ridiculous, either he doesn't keep me from giving you a lesson again, or I stop coming."

Thereupon she presumably decided to shut her door to me, renouncing me, at least until I become more reasonable.

I shouldn't be in the least mad at her tomorrow; that's a lesson she has given me, and I deserve it.

I should be tenderly melancholy, completely tender and languid, even in my role in *Le Misanthrope,* which I'll have to denature if I'm to achieve this. Dugazon will correct me, I'll maintain my sentiment, which will result in my being asked, "What's the matter with you today? You're not at all like you usually are."

I mustn't let on that I noticed that she shut her door to me today. I must be the first to speak to her of my stupid obstinacy on the 10th, and I must tell her I did everything I could to drop in at the Français a moment in the evening to ask her forgiveness.

Thereupon, I must redouble my tender melancholy, *without the least shade of somber despair.* I must tell her that my departure has become necessary; in speaking to her about my stupidity of the 10th, I'll look as though I were humiliated by it and I'll give her my word of honor: "I give you, etc., to leave as soon as M. Le Blanc comes in."

Friday, during my obstinacy, Le Blanc being present, I struck up a conversation of the eyes with her; she said to me, "It isn't what you think," with the most sincere and sustained tone possible.

In speaking to her of my departure, if we have reached her apartment, I should break into restrained tears; I must be at Dugazon's at half-past eleven so we can leave at two.

That's the right road. But, above all, *not the least shade of despair.*

She's really taking an astonishing ascendancy over me. I missed a victory this afternoon on the Terrasse des Feuillants, and perhaps let myself be beaten by that booby of a German.

He said to me, "Mlle. Louason is very intelligent." I approved heartily and stopped short; whereupon, a moment later, he said in a pronounced way that he enjoyed nothing more than making people jealous. I didn't taunt him as he deserved after that quip; on one of my days of verve, if there had been a gallery, I'd have sent him packing to all the devils in hell.

But my chief stupidity is not to have exaggerated the praise of Mélanie beyond all measure. I don't give a damn about his quips, and he would have repeated my words of praise everywhere, if it had been ingenious, and it would have gotten back to Mélanie. That's what comes from lack of attention and not having my wits about me.

I saw the Pope quite clearly this morning at Saint-Germain-des-Prés; in particular, I saw him giving the communion and benediction. I heard him pronounce: *et spiritous sanctous.*

13 *Ventôse* [*March 4*].—I've never recited these lines [from Molière's *Le Misanthrope*] as well as today, and I never felt them so deeply. Dugazon was as pleased as possible with the way I acted this scene, and if I had been sensitive to the pleasures of vanity I should have passed the day in a state of delight. Instead of that, I passed it in fits of fury and in the most frightful jealousy and the cruelest uncertainty.

I'm about ready to believe that Louason has never loved me or else wants to break off with me. A kiss stolen by Wagner this morning set me beside myself, and yet it was possibly only a bit of stage play. She came to Dugazon's at half-past twelve. I accompanied her as far as the Rue Coquillière. I scarcely said a word to her. Later I met her in the Rue des Petits-Champs; she said she was going to the Français. I've just been there and she wasn't there.

What drives me to desperation is that she treats me politely; no more familiarity.

I felt, as I was passing the Château des Tuileries at three o'clock this afternoon on my way to see Mounier, how sublime is that passage from *Othello,* "They say there is a noble race of horses, etc."[1]

I longed to do something desperate, I'd have taken keen pleasure in stabbing myself. As I recovered from this mood, I experienced the pleasure of melancholy. I repeated with enthusiasm and enchantment that other passage from *Othello,* "It is the destiny of generous men and lofty characters that, etc."[2]

I experienced indescribable pleasure in pronouncing the word *generous.* I possibly experienced more emotionally today than Pacé, Tencin

[1] This phrase, frequently quoted by Beyle, is not to be found in *Othello* or, apparently, anywhere else in Shakespeare.

[2] Possibly Beyle, whose quotations are notoriously inexact, was thinking of these lines spoken by Othello in Act III, Scene 3: "Yet, 'tis the plague of great ones; . . . 'Tis destiny unshunnable, like death . . ."

and Ouéhihé in their whole lives. What commotions! Mante was of the opinion that I shouldn't go to the theater; as it turned out, I'd have done well to follow his advice. I told Mélanie I was leaving, I was exactly as I had planned to be. Maybe she came to the Français and was prevented by the crowd from going in. She wasn't there the 10th for *Zaïre*.

To make matters worse, the bastard hasn't sent me the money he promised for the end of Pluviôse.

I've lived more on this Monday than in two months at Grenoble.

Can it be that I displeased her BY THE *due cappelli?*[1] If it's that, O too fatal bastard, O experience which is costing me dearly, the heart of my Mélanie! Tomorrow will decide.

14 Ventôse [*March 5*].—I was so unhappy that I didn't have the courage or time to write this entry on the day itself. I went through all the torments of unrequited love. The frightful humiliation experienced produces moments of fury (of cruelty), then sadness and tears; when later you are able to attain melancholy, the state becomes less cruel. If I had written the same day, I'd have written twenty pages. I find the character of Hermione very natural; she's not a cruel woman at all, she's an amorous woman who does cruel things.

Once a trait of passion has been written down, there's nothing to correct. For instance, the other day after having written, "I long to do something desperate," or, noblifying the thing like Shakespeare, "They say there is a noble race of horses, etc.," there remained nothing to add or to take away. It seems to me that such things are spoiled by retouching them.

I got dressed at noon; I went to Mélanie's nearly beside myself with emotion. I rang; there was no answer. I went to the Palais-Royal to while away a half hour which was possibly one of the most painful of my life; my sole distraction, and it was an enormous one, was to observe my state. I should employ this means of consolation if ever I have to console an intelligent person.

I went back to Mélanie's at a quarter past one, still nobody. Despite the violent objections of the Lawyer *Against,* I went back at half-past two. I was admitted and found her with Châteauneuf.

Then began a scene which seemed extraordinary and terrible for me; a single observation consoled me. It happened that, because of

[1]"By the two hats." Reference to the scene on February 11, when Mélanie remarked on the hats in a shopwindow. A similar scene takes place on March 29. Because of his father's failure to send his allowance regularly, it was as impossible for Beyle to buy presents for Mélanie as it was for him to take her to the Théâtre Français.

lack of experience and composure, I judged all that badly, or at least it's quite possible that I judged it badly.

Mélanie, after one of those smiles with which she greets everyone, constantly looked away from me. Whenever her eyes fell on me, they were cold and polite. I realized that she intended to make me understand that she wanted to break off with me. What reassured me a little was that she appeared to be very upset. Sometimes her eyes were moist with emotion, at other times her features seemed to be obliterated and to have a deathlike pallor. She was very distracted.

I delighted Châteauneuf during this visit, and my conduct was full of love for Mélanie. I left discreetly at four o'clock, a minute after M. Le Blanc came in.

In the evening, I went with Crozet to the pit of the Français. I saw Mélanie in the orchestra. I saw her leave with Dusausoir; she bowed to me very politely and coolly, as though it were unavoidable. I was disconsolate. I sought a distraction by going with Crozet to see Ariadne in her dressing room.

15 *Ventôse* [*March 6*].—I thought I wasn't loved any more. I went to Dugazon's, intending to be gay in order to have a chance to say in her ear, "What have you got against me?"

I went there, I played the fool with Félipe, who let me go ahead. Mélanie finally arrived after nearly an hour. I played the fool with her, I kissed her; she replied to me coolly and politely. I thought everything was finished. I was no less gay with Félipe.

I went to look for a book in the library, I called her to help me, she came, I kissed her, she let me go ahead. We had already had a little explanation in Dugazon's salon. She had answered my question by saying, "Why, nothing," etc., etc., naturally enough.

She recited the role of Aménaïde enthusiastically; this worked her up to *metromania,* which took her heart a bit away from love. At the end of the lesson, she said to me, "Let's go to the Luxembourg." I told her the Luxembourg wasn't open. Finally, we agreed to go to the Jardin des Plantes.

I didn't feel this happiness as keenly as I would have on the preceding days of unhappiness. I was worn out by physical and mental fatigue. I had rushed around all morning to get away from despair; I was worn out.

(I'm breaking off here, 16 Ventôse, eleven o'clock in the evening, to get the first real rest I've had since the 13th. I slept two nights in succession with Crozet in order to avoid being alone, I'm literally capable of nothing more, and this entry shows it. Since my disgrace on Friday, I haven't stopped rushing around in order to numb myself.)

We took a fiacre in the Rue des Petits-Champs; we went to the Jardin des Plantes, we lunched in the simple, cool thatch-roofed cottage on the sign of which are some verses from Virgil; afterward, we strolled through the whole garden; we saw the animals and the greenhouse in detail. In the great owl, we remarked a superb way of holding and turning the head; Mélanie, who made this remark, observed that some excellent poses are to be learned from animals. We left at half-past four.

We were happy that day, but not with all the verve of love I some-times feel. I've already said why, I was tired out; she was in one of her moments of metromania for glory.

When I told her I was all the happier because I'd thought for four days that she wanted to break off with me, she didn't understand how I could have imagined such a thing; she told me that the day before Châteauneuf had bored her to death, and that this was what had given her that look; that, at the theater in the evening, she saw me and bowed to me three times; that I didn't appear to see her. " 'He's in one of his moments of . . .' I told myself." (I don't recall the word she added, I believe she only indicated it by her expression.) She displayed charm-ing grace in saying it.

"But that bow, so distant and polite?"

"But *in front of everybody,* how would you have wanted me to bow to you?"

She twice repeated *in front of everybody.*

All considered, this way of explaining boredom is peculiar; I must observe her the first time she's bored. I have always *felt* more than I have *perceived,* which makes me as fresh as a child; and, as I moreover know the possibilities, I'm inclined to be suspicious and susceptible—very serious defects.

I asked her permission to go to see her the next day, she said, "Yes, but not for long, because I want to learn *Hypermnestre."* I kissed her without difficulty. My acquaintanceship with Ariadne raises me in her opinion, that's the advantage in going out in society. She told me that Richerand (the physiologist), who's had Duchesnois, told her that she needed three men at a time; I'm inclined to believe this of the sensi-tive Duchesnois. (*Sensitive* isn't used ironically, she does that the same as children and savages steal. She's experienced too much to have learned that there's anything wrong in it.)

Mélanie told me that Alibert told her that Pacé was a man who de-ceived women, and that's all there was to it. Mélanie thus told me, with much wit and delicacy, that Pacé was a mediocre man. I rather think so too, but he's goodhearted and has excellent manners. He's not the best I might conceive, but my present fortune doesn't permit me to go to the homes where I might see the best.

It appears that Mme. Legouvé is a *virago*. She has had all the society men but one, who's fortunate,[1] as Louason said (that's nicely put, she said it much better than I'm writing it). She advised Duchesnois before George's debut to have someone get her with child. That's terrible. Legouvé is a benign husband.

16 Ventôse [March 7].—I didn't go to Mélanie's. I slept at Crozet's. We went together to see Duchesnois. I was struck by the divine beauty of her eyes and voice. Mélanie is far beneath her in those two respects. Perhaps she's less carried away by her roles than Duchesnois. On the other hand, Louason has far more wit and intelligence. When I got home I found an insolent letter from Douenne. I shook off my spell of dumps, counting on my star, which invariably brings me some money when I need it. I'm beginning to be pleased with myself on that score; my association with Mante and Crozet is beginning to cure me of the infinite harm done me by that with Félix Faure. I believe Faure has absolutely the character of M. de Valorbe in *Delphine;* he's a man who is essentially unhappy. There's nothing easier than to shake off unhappiness (of this kind), all you need is sufficient will power.

Wit.—Yesterday, I thoroughly enjoyed the pleasures of society. After the interesting visit with Duchesnois, I dragged Crozet to Cheminade's. There I learned that the Mounier family frequently sees his own. He told me that Edouard was very fatuous. I'm beginning to realize the advantage of *natural* and entirely *unstudied* wit over the rehearsed wit of Crozet, Edouard and even Pacé; after a couple of months, you can see right through theirs. Even the charming (as far as wit is concerned) M. de Baure is in this category in the long run; at bottom, nothing is as agreeable in my opinion as *natural* wit, the kind that's invented constantly by an amiable character under all the circumstances of the conversation. The reason for this is simple: it presents a comedy of character in which the protagonist is amiable. Therefore, if you want to be witty (inform yourself of all the studied wits, frequent them in order to be entitled to hold them in contempt), work on your character and say what you think on every occasion.

This kind of charming wit is invisible to the asses; it's necessary to have a very sensitive soul or infinite wit yourself if you are going to appreciate it. Among my acquaintances, Mlle. Duchesnois for the first reason, and M. de Baure for the second are possibly the only ones to whom it's visible.

For this wit to win the respect of asses (such as, for instance, my uncle and Ed. Mounier) and dull souls (such as Adèle OF THE GATE, Mme. le Brun, etc.), it has to have a label; then they *respect it because others do,* and, when they glimpse a bit of it, they call it *originality.*

[1]Fortunate = fortuné—apparently a pun referring to Fortuné Mante.

Destutt-Tracy's son and Wauthier (a student at the Ponts et Chaussées) were charmed at the first sight of my candid and *natural* wit.

The first made Félix Faure indignant. I was really terrible in his opinion; it was like yesterday in that of Cheminade. I'll never be enough of an ass to appear goodhearted to him. I've sometimes been the dupe of my *vanity* with people of that kind; I see them in admiration and awe; without realizing it, I allow myself to be carried away, I lay it on, awe them even more, with the result that they more and more come to the conclusion that I'm ill-natured.

I'm a scoundrel for my uncle because, in his opinion, I'm energetic.

Gripoli is afraid my wit will make me considered ill-natured, and I have occasionally appeared so to him because I tire his mind. A multitude of sallies annoys a man who's accustomed to conceiving things slowly because he conceives perfectly.

For the same reason, I'm probably ill-natured in J. Rey's opinion.

Mante got over this when he saw my soul, the most sensitive he ever encountered, and he's had experience. Faure can never be cured; my strength offends his weakness, as it does that of Rey, but, in addition to that, my wit irritates his vanity. That's what can never be cured.

Judith, Angelina, Adèle, Victorine and Mélanie know that I have a sensitive soul. I must develop myself a bit in the opinion of Duchesnois and M. de Baure, they'll understand me.

As for Pacé and Edouard Mounier, I must resign myself to being considered by them a blockhead (like La Fontaine) all my life.

Mante lent me four louis until my money arrives.

18 Ventôse [March 9].—I left her apartment at five o'clock. How easy it is to be witty in a circle of people! I went there at two o'clock, spent three hours with her, including a tête-à-tête of a quarter hour, she was sick. Later, Châteauneuf, Le Blanc and two other gents, one of whom, a Royalist and stupid, wore his character in his expression. Châteauneuf bored her. Tomorrow, we'll go to the Luxembourg. Félipe came and sang, *"De tous les pays pour vous plaire,* etc."

A delightful day. I'd spoil the pleasure by describing it.

19 Ventôse [March 10].—I loved you before; I worship you now. I got home at half-past one.

I got up at six o'clock, I went to Mante's. We got in a fiacre at seven o'clock; we called for Dard and Rey, and went to La Vache Noire, where I embraced him [Mante] and left him at a quarter past eight, he departed.

At eleven, I went to Louason's; she was getting dressed. It was raining a little, a spring rain. We went to lunch at the café on the corner of the Rue de la Michodière and the boulevard, from there to the Luxembourg. We looked at all the pictures and the rooms in the

Senate. We went back to her apartment at a quarter past three. I stayed until a quarter past four; M. Le Blanc arrived at four.

I returned at a quarter past six; she was dining with her chamber-maid. Mme. Mortier arrived and left when she saw that Mélanie was getting dressed. We got into a fiacre, like this morning. We arrived at the Théâtre du Marais, Rue Culture-Saint-Catherine, about half-past seven; we found the tragedy of *Othello,* which we had come to see, in the second act. We stayed until the middle of *Les Visitandines;* eleven o'clock was striking as we came out.

She began talking to me of Mme. de Caux, that infernal shrew; the conversation in the fiacre continued at her apartment until a quarter past one, when her porter came to tell her what time it was; I stayed a moment longer.

Two o'clock is about to strike (of 20 Ventôse). Today I have lived twenty hours. This day has been one of the most interesting of my life. Does a woman confide such things with the wit that she has to a man she doesn't love? We spent twelve hours together. The details to-morrow; I'm going to bed, thanking heaven for having so sensitive a soul. I've probably done more living in this one day than Percevant or Pacé in a week.

20 *Ventôse* [*March 11*].—I absolutely must change my system of love with Louason. I'm learning through my successes. I was genuinely amiable with her in the main path of the Tuileries at a quarter past three when I said to her, "You ought to show your wit more, etc."

The thing to do is to appear amiable to Mélanie and not to tell her I love her. As I see her frequently tête-à-tête, nothing would be easier than to bore her by everlastingly repeating the same words, "I love you, I worship you," in connection with everything.

I must never plan in advance to tell her such-and-such a thing, under penalty of talking *spropositi* [nonsense]. I must simply say constantly to her what I think, and, in the moments of silence, speak about her.

I'm afraid I'm too unattractive to be loved by her. I'm afraid this fear gives me an awkward appearance, it must be conquered.

There's nothing so disgusting as a man who, at the very minute he's boring you, starts talking about his love.

Therefore, I make the resolution to speak to her of my love only when the time is appropriate, and yet to make it apparent enough for her not to think that it's extinguished, I see her daily, it's up to me to try not to be boring.

I was at Dugazon's from noon on, she arrived at one o'clock. I was distant at the outset; that, I believe, is one of the results of my unfortunate habit of thinking about what I'm going to say to her. She was the first to say a few words about last night, and these finally made a strong impression to set my soul in action instead of my mind.

Louason started reciting the fourth act of *Ariane,* she wasn't in form, but she gradually got into her stride. She recited the fifth, and was superb in these two verses:

> *"Prenez soin d'Ariane! Il viole sa foi,*
> *Me désespère, et veut qu'on prenne soin de moi."*

Since she recites two lines like that, she is capable of reciting them all by only heeding her soul. I believe therefore that she may become an actress who is superb in the expression of love and the moods of *metromania.*

She stirred our souls so deeply that I was as silly as a goose. I was all *athrob,* as certain asses say. We left Dugazon's at three o'clock after having snuggled together a minute.

The weather was agreeable. We went for a walk in the Tuileries. I believe I was agreeable to her for an hour, because I told her exactly what I was thinking at the moment.

I tasted pure contentment, our souls communed. She was charming as she talked to me. During this time, I said to her what I was thinking, "Even if a person were not in love with you, he would become so while listening to you."

These words aimed at reaching her soul, and I'm convinced they did so. The only thing that might have spoiled the effect was the memory of the same sort of words I said to her at a time when her soul wasn't stirred.

21 *Ventôse* [*March 12*] (*before seeing her*).—I reflected that I'm a damned fool. She spoke to me about THE THREE CARRICKS Sunday like a woman who's surrendering herself, I'm a damned fool not to have some with me always so I could take advantage of an opportunity like this; she had *il marchese.* I must buy some tonight and always have them with me.

At Dugazon's today (20 Ventôse) she looked at Wagner smilingly. I turned toward her by chance; at once, her look became serious. I shouldn't be at all surprised if Wagner had had her. But I'm afraid my character is suspicious because of my sensibility. If she'd had him, that loutish German would have gone through with it with his fresh face and his ponderous good sense; but in that case, she's embarrassed on my account, therefore she would like to have me.

23 *Ventôse* [*March 14*].—I feel that she fills my whole soul. I haven't enough sensibility left to be conscious of anything else. Everything I do is done mechanically; my thoughts are constantly centered on her,

she is constantly before my eyes, and, since my experience keeps me from confiding in anybody, my sole relief is in writing. For everything else, I'm listless.

In this state, everything becomes a matter of indifference to me. I could make the greatest sacrifices without being aware of them. Generally, you don't have a precise idea of the sacrifices caused by a great love. If there are other sacrifices like those of love, those who make them aren't aware of them.

Today, for the first time in my life, I desired a fortune. To be sure, I've often desired it vaguely, but today my desire was strong enough to make me submit willingly to several years of office work.

If I'd had some money, I'd have possessed her today, that's certain, and my day would have been charming instead of utterly dismal.

Perhaps that's the reason I'm not making any progress with her; I love her so much that when she tells me something she gives me so much pleasure that, besides no longer having any perception, and being all sensation, even if I had the strength to perceive, *I probably wouldn't have the strength to interrupt her in order to speak myself.* What she does is too precious to me. Perhaps that's why true lovers frequently don't possess their belles.

Here's the history of yesterday and today. In the first place, I don't know whether it's the absence of Mante, but whenever I'm not with her, I'm conscious of an intolerable void which soon turns into a slight sadness. The superb weather of yesterday and today is repugnant to me. Lack of money contributes to this; yet it seems to me that, even if I had some, the void would still be there. It's Mante, I believe.

Yesterday, 22 Ventôse, Tuesday, I went to Dugazon's at half-past one, wearing a black cravat. I found Félipe and Wagner there. I recited the role of Sosie for the first time; had a very bad lesson. She didn't come. Dugazon arranged not to give a lesson until Sunday.

I went to her apartment at a quarter past two, leaving Dugazon's with Wagner, who is most assuredly ponderous and stupid, exactly what is meant by the word German. The maid told me she wasn't there; at a quarter to three, the same reply; I went back at three, she opened the door, the sight of her delighted me:

"How unhappy I am!"

"Am I in the way? I'll leave."

"Not at all, not at all, come in; I've just sent for M. Le Blanc to take me for a walk. If I'd known you were coming, I wouldn't have done so. How unhappy I am!"

That *how unhappy I am* was as tender as could be, it increased my delight even more.

I don't remember what I said; all I know is that I said to her what I was thinking, and that I loved her more than myself. She must have seen my love.

That *how unhappy I am,* several times repeated, was said with the sincerest and broadest *inflection.* I told her, "I'm too happy now that I see you." The conversation led us to explain that *how unhappy,* etc.

"How do you interpret it?" she asked me. I recalled the scene from *Deschamps* and pretended not to hear her.

"That I'm unhappy to see you?" she said. "Oh no!"

Everything considered, it seems to me that that *how unhappy,* etc. was love. I paused too long over the enjoyment of what I was feeling, I didn't venture to kiss her, maybe I was wrong. I'm so familiar with the game of love that I have to hold myself in like the devil in order not to be suspicious, and I'm never sure of anything for the reason that I see all the possibilities.

Nothing will hold me back tomorrow; the first time I see her tête-à-tête at her apartment, I must firmly propose the *carricks;* I must insist on them, make that the subject of the conversation, recall it. All considered, I'm a fool, she didn't turn it down Sunday. I was a fool Monday, since the opportunity was lacking yesterday and today.

27 *Ventôse* [*March 18*].—I haven't written since the 22nd through foolishness; it would have been too much work to describe what I felt, but the facts at least ought to have been written.

It was on the 22nd that I discovered there are 820 paces in the Tuileries from the palace to the statue at the end of the main path. This action, which is ridiculous if the details aren't considered, was only, it seems to me, so much kindness for her; she ought to have said to me:

"Beyle, I've got something to say to M. Le Blanc, leave us while we make a couple of turns, and then come back and join us."

The 24th and 25th were perhaps the unhappiest days in my life. She gave orders for me to be told she wasn't home, although she was. I had no more than a glimpse of her in the Tuileries the 24th. The 25th, Tencin came to see me a minute as I was coming back from her apartment the first time; we walked in the Tuileries through a charming spring mist that reminded me absolutely of Milan.

I ought to have written these past days, I'd have depicted the unhappiness of love perfectly; but I saw her yesterday and that obliterated everything.

It's very difficult to describe from memory what has been *natural* for you; the *factitious,* the *shammed,* is described more easily because the effort that's been made to *sham* it has engraved it on the memory. I should practice recalling my natural sentiments, that's the study that may give me the talent of Shakespeare. While *shamming,* you see your-self going forward, you have *perception.* This sensation is easily re-produced by the organ of *memory;* but, in order to recall, *natural senti-ments,* it's necessary to start with *perception.*

That's where the study of *Idéologie* (Tracy and Biran) is useful for me.

I was quite natural yesterday, Sunday, during the four hours I spent with her; I didn't manage to achieve *perception,* so I don't yet know how I appeared to her. In order to be entirely natural, which is genuine wit, it's necessary to be accustomed to it. In order to arrive there, I'd have to be with Mélanie constantly, then I wouldn't be in the least hurry to speak, and, after a couple of days, I'd have the charm of naturalness.

26 *Ventôse* [*March 17*].—I got up at six o'clock. Rey came in to bore me for an hour, I read forty pages of Tracy, then *l'Inconstant* by Collin, an inane work if ever there was one, which dried me up. I got dressed at noon, I was inclined to be bored because it was Sunday. I'll go crazy if this keeps up. Today was terribly *odious* for me.

I went to Dugazon's, and I was superb: large black curls, lofty char-acter, good appearance, cravat, frill, two superb waistcoats, perfect frock coat, cashmere breeches, fine-knit stockings and shoes. In my whole life, it was one of the days when I was at my best physically. I had the noble and self-assured bearing of the highest society.

The weather was superb. As I was saying, I went to Dugazon's at half-past twelve. "Monsieur, there will be no lesson; he waited for you until one o'clock and, seeing that you didn't come, he went to Ver-sailles." I was a little disappointed. I kept from being unhappy by my firmness in saying to myself, "Let's hurry to Louason's." On the way, I said to myself, "She didn't come to Dugazon's, all that would be lack-ing now is for me to be told, 'She's just left for the country.'" I didn't think that in this case I'd be able to find Crozet at home.

I went up to her apartment: "She's just left for Dugazon's."

"You think so? There isn't any lesson."

"She's just this minute gone out."

My *you think so* said, "I don't believe you." I decided to go slowly and be on the lookout as far as Dugazon's; I found her returning in the Rue des Fossés.

We went back to her apartment. I don't know why, but I was a bit cool (I think it was because I lacked money). I jokingly reproached her for having shut her door to me; she didn't agree that she had. I must have appeared a bit put out.

I returned at half-past four, overwhelmed with sadness. The weather, which is suffocating, puts tenderness in my soul. I'd have keen pleasure in going to the Français tonight, but I haven't got any money; even the anxiety caused me by this month-end and the beginning of Germinal is one reason for my sadness. But the main, or rather the sole one is this:

I arrived at Louason's at half-past three. M. Le Blanc was there. She was seated in front of the looking glass with her head wrapped up in an embroidered handkerchief, a thing which removed almost all that was touching from her expression. She was holding *Phèdre* in her hand, with an appearance of deep thought. During this time, M. Le Blanc passed into the antechamber. I was behind Mélanie's armchair, I was terribly tired. M. Le Blanc came back in, took his hat after a moment and went out. I stayed where I was. Louason went on reading Clairon's *Mémoires,* the part about *Phèdre* and several others in succession.

I had entirely the disadvantage of natural wit; I was alone with her and I didn't occupy her with my love; I only kissed her twice. The time slipped by; I was happy. I would have been perfectly so if I'd had four louis in my pocket; I would have had that boldness without which there's no beauty. She was in her armchair, her appearance exceedingly serious, and no gentleness in her expression, because of that wretched handkerchief. There was a brief moment during which she turned back to Clairon. Assuming that her gestures reflected her sentiments in the same way that mine do, she must have been very intent on her art. Yet, I believe it was the moment to speak of love; but *a skillful turn* was needed, feigned wit, and I was all soul. I was trembling a little and I sighed (it was partly put on; I added to nature).

When I thumb through a book after having read parts of it, my head seethes, I'm entirely taken up with my art. At the moment when she was making the same gestures that I make myself on these occasions, I told her with all possible precautions for Ariadne, and after exacting her word of honor not to say anything about it or where she heard it, that the latter was at Legouvé's when a deputation came in to ask that she make her debut [at the Français]; that Ariadne said it was impossible for her to be received, but that she was nevertheless of the opinion that she would be allowed to make her debut so she could get a good engagement in the provinces. That renewed her interest in her debut. We talked about it for some time. Then I told her I would go again to Ariadne's on Monday for her birthday and then wouldn't go any more because I foresaw that it would soon be necessary to be on two sides at the same time. She told me to keep on going.

I believe I oughtn't to say anything more about Ariadne. I behaved like a gallant man today; but if Ariadne were to cabal against Mélanie, I'd be obliged to be a traitor to one or the other. At the slightest sign of a cabal on Ariadne's part, I won't go to see her again, and I'll be on Mélanie's side.

Afterward, I paid her some compliments in action which made her laugh and pleased her.

I was in a happy mood when I was brought down to earth by the return of M. Le Blanc. That was too much for me. I thought I saw my foolishness, she laughed for four minutes while reading Clairon. I left, she said quite casually, "Good day, monsieur."

I came home, crushed by the thought of my bashfulness. I hadn't the heart to write this; finally, I thought of the advantages of a witty character (natural). I eventually thought that, since she was entirely taken up with her art, my love had appeared inopportune to her, that perhaps, having appeared to her amorous and bashful, I was at my best. The thought that maybe I wasn't as stupid as I at first believed acted as a slight tonic on my soul and gave me the strength to write.

If I could go to the Français tonight I'd be happy.

I must go to see her early tomorrow and propose firmly to get it over with. I must write out everything beforehand, because as soon as I'm happy I don't write a word.

I must say to her tomorrow, "You were so taken up with your roles that my poor little love didn't dare show itself."

It occurred to me only while writing this that M. Le Blanc behaved like a gallant man today.

By this, I saw as clearly as possible the influence of the *head* on the *heart*. My heart has far more experience than my head; I have loved much and judged very little.

Continuation of Sunday, 26 Ventôse.—When I arrived at her apartment, she was getting dressed. I'm too chaste on these occasions. We went to the Tuileries. I have few memories because I didn't see myself talking; I was natural and too taken up with the effect of what I said for that. We laughed at the faces we encountered; that's the sort of thing in which I might be like fireworks, brilliant and comic—but I'm only that way when it comes naturally, I can't feign it.

We went to the Champs-Elysées. At the moment, there was a slight chilliness in our conversation; that's the shortcoming of people who are natural, but it's at this price that sublime moments are purchased. We took a turn in the Champs-Elysées; on the way back, our souls were in communion. We looked for a name for me to take if I go to Marseille as her cousin. If she doesn't make her debut here within four months, she's going to Marseille. That's a rare stroke of luck for me. I didn't tell her I had the intention of going there; instead, I said that, if she went, I'd follow her and give up Paris in order to be with her.

I haven't any right to complain of my fortune in small things when it favors me to this extent in such an important one.

"Yet," I told her, "I'm sacrificing my interest to yours, and I wish you would stay here." That's true; our souls were in communion, I was happy.

(*There indeed is the man of nature and not the man of a novel. I feel that I ought never to stop loving Adèle or to forget Mme. Nardon* [Mme. Rebuffel], *and yet if my Mélanie is at Marseille with me, I'll be the happiest of men.*)

The name I am to take there is Le Boullier, the name of one of her cousins in Versailles. It was three o'clock. We went back to her apartment, as she was expecting M. Lalanne. I was happy, I was holding her under the arm when we came out of the passage leading from the Tuileries to the Rue Saint-Honoré; a smile of happiness was on my lips when suddenly my eyes fell on Victorine. She was in a carriage, and she saw us perfectly. She must have seen a little emotion on my face at seeing her. I didn't bow to her. I couldn't make a sign to Mélanie because Victorine saw me too clearly.

The excellent thing about it was the fact that I had warned Louason we might run into a little society girl whom I was courting. As soon as the carriage had gone by, I told her that the girl was in it.

That was one of the most exquisite pleasures of vanity I could have. I said to myself, "There is a great pleasure of vanity." My knowledge of the passions made me regard it as a curiosity, but I was scarcely conscious of it. If Victorine has a soul like mine, this meeting must have driven her to despair, and, at the same time, inclined her to look on me favorably the first time we see each other.

We returned to Louason's. She wrote a note to Lalanne. We went back to the Tuileries. I was again too chaste during the moment we were alone. In such moments, I'm not a lover, I'm an amiable society man and nothing more. I have no idea myself of what a child I am.

There was a moment during our walk when she thought I was offering to take her to dinner somewhere; she declined. It was doing me a great honor.

I spoke to her of my bashfulness; she said I had an audacious air. She believes it and I do too.

We spoke of my love, she told me that I didn't talk like a man who was imbued with it. I parried the blow by touching her heart, but it's none the less true that I speak of love in too light a tone. An excellent shortcoming, but one that I acquired through my fear of being too sentimental and consequently sad.

She finds me a libertine. She launched out against Martial and the irreverent tone of the fashionable young men.

Le Blanc didn't see us at first in the Tuileries, where he came; then he came over to us. At once there was a silence, in spite of all the efforts I made to get the conversation started; he stuck to us like glue and played a sorry role, thanks to me. I made him thoroughly ridiculous by talking in a low tone to Mélanie. Finally, at a quarter to five, we took her home. We went up, and I left him there.

I forgot a little battle of sentiment, which is very essential; I'll write it when I think of it.[1]

In the last analysis, I see clearly that I'll have to be getting somewhere with Louason, but I love her too much to do so voluntarily; what I need is her aid, or the right occasion. I'll give the right occasion a chance to arise as soon as I have some money. At the moment, I have very little feeling, I'm in no mood to go through with it; but when I'm near my divine Mélanie I'm too much in love to do anything.

My journal is now up to date, except for the history of last Sunday, which I won't write because at the moment I feel nothing.

The 28th, I took it upon myself not to go to Mélanie's. I read sixty-six quarto pages of Helvétius, a hundred of [Adam] Smith and the tragedy of *Andromaque*. I'm reading Smith with great pleasure.

The 29th, I went to Pacé's at ten o'clock; I found Ariadne's chambermaid there, and him deeply engaged in replying to her. She went out, he unburdened himself to me; that interested me a great deal. Came an under-inspector and M. Pelet (des Verreries); I let myself go, the solid character of this man pleased me and mine him. I enjoyed myself hugely until one o'clock.

I arrived at a quarter past one at Dugazon's, badly enough dressed; I was very gay and hardly looked at Mélanie. Dugazon rehearsed me in the whole first scene of Sosie; he's charmingly natural.

I took Mélanie home about half-past two; at half-past three, Félipe arrived. She shut the door to everyone. She asked me to go there to rehearse Theseus tomorrow at one o'clock; I interested her. She was the first to ask for news of the little girl we encountered coming out of the Tuileries. That battery is a good one.

I believe it would be easy to make her afraid of Félipe.

I'm going to finish Helvétius, the first volume of Tracy and then

[1] "I'd have to see you for a week to become blasé." The second time passing through the passage from the Tuileries to the Rue Saint-Honoré. [Note by Beyle.]

Letellier before leaving. I must work on these all the time I'm alone, and spend the rest of the time with Louason.

I have, I believe, at last found the road to follow. This has been a happy day.

30 Ventôse [March 21].—At eight o'clock I went to breakfast with Cheminade; important and very agreeable conversation because I had the presence of mind to lead it up to a subject which was of equal interest to both of us: trade in Pondichéry.

Here is what this trade is: you arrive at Pondichéry, in peacetime you make 50 per cent a year. An agent *contracts* cloth for you twice yearly. You pay two thirds of the price before delivery, and the merchants who came to Pondichéry twice a year give you 25 per cent profit on the authentic bill of the contract price.

If you want to go into the interior yourself to make your contracts, you'll make 80 per cent. These profits (the first) will only be 30 or 40 per cent as long as the French have only two leagues around Pondichéry.

A young man twenty years old arrives at Pondichéry with 24,000 livres, the second year he has 36,000, the third 54,000, the fourth 81,000, the fifth 121,500, the sixth 180,000, the seventh 270,000, etc.

Consequently, in eight years, a fortune is assured. For that reason, young men should be made accustomed to the sea early in life.

In Pondichéry, with 120 louis a year, you can have horses, carriages and eight servants, a life similar to that procured in Paris with an income of 20,000 livres. The servants do only one thing, are olive-colored and cost seven livres ten sous a month.

A thing to be followed up if ever I am ruined, or, being poor, have many children.

The climate isn't unhealthy.

I see that a good mind is the best capital for the bank, as for everything else.

Cheminade gave me a thousand details that were very interesting and sincere.

Wouldn't it be better to lead this kind of a life for eight years than to languish in an office for a whole lifetime?

30 Ventôse [March 21].—I was a tender and submissive lover the day before yesterday, I had a glimpse of the good effect that can be produced by fatuity; today I was fatuous the way I should be, I mingled very tender things with my fatuity, but things that were said with a little less breadth than they should be in pure sentiment, and never did I appear so amiable to Mélanie.

I find that I weaken my sentiments and give them a solemn, austere appearance in writing them out. The reason is, first, that, in a word, I'm not able to write them the same way that I experience them; the second, which comes from my trade as a poet, is that I explain them as I describe them.

I had a charming fatuity which didn't offend her, which showed her I wasn't a man for her to disdain, and at the same time offered her the hope of correcting me.

This fatuity throws still another excellent light on my behavior of the past fortnight. The sentiment was pure and simple during that time, today I appeared charming and witty to her, and she believes I'm a little less smitten with her; therefore, she should conclude from this that I loved her very much on the other days.

I'm delighted with her. I'm very pleased with myself, I'm very happy.

Six years from now, I won't take a month and a half to reach this point with a woman who pleases me; I'll probably possess her at the end of a month. Will I be as happy at the end of six weeks? Happiness is everything. "The heart is everything," says the tender Ariadne. Will I have the heart that I have now?

This has been a very happy day, and who would have predicted that it would be so? On the contrary, it ought to have been very unhappy. Two years ago, it would have been nearly desperate.

I arrived at Mélanie's at one o'clock. I thought it was later. I was well dressed, and the breakfast with Cheminade had left me with a character full of gaiety and tenderness. I could not have been in a better mood. I found Mélanie with a little boy (a relative of her maid). I was very amiable, frivolous but rather distant. She told me she was going to the Rue des Blancs-Manteaux.

I started off by telling her, with all the grace possible, that I had spent the morning in a room I had there:

"You're a libertine!"

"You do me a great honor!"

This beginning produced an excellent *mass* (design) of conversation, all the details of which were of the amiable fatuity I explained above.

I told her I was there with another Mélanie, a woman who was getting a divorce, who was from Normandy; that what made me laugh the most was that I knew we were together for the last time, and that she talked of our future happiness there together.

That's the framework. This fatuity interested her immensely. She asked me if I'd seen the little girl; I told her that everything was going fine, that she was still weeping; thereupon, she became softhearted a moment.

I told her (during the second visit) that yesterday I hadn't said two words the whole evening, that I played bouillotte opposite *Eudoxie,* to whom I spoke with my eyes.

Eudoxie is the name I give to the young lady we encountered Sunday as we were coming out of the Tuileries.

She was getting dressed to go to the Rue des Blancs-Manteaux at two o'clock. I told her I'd employ this time to go to the home of the old ladies where I'd find *Eudoxie*.

We left her place at a quarter past two; I went to see Barral. As his gloomy mood would have bored me and spoiled my manner, I made him very gay by telling him of how to get rich in India and promising to make him refuse to go there if I ever decided to go myself. I had some *coquetry* at the end of this conversation. In order to be very gay again tomorrow, I must go to Pacé's for breakfast; we can go together from there to Dugazon's.

I returned with a triumphant expression to my *Princess's* at three o'clock sharp. I had what makes up the beauty of expression: I was gay, I was happy, I saw myself as enjoying one success after the other for the past two hours, I was perfectly dressed.

I went in, her first look (the result of her resolutions) was casual and indifferent; but her indifference was exaggerated, and only the first look was like that.

It was during the second visit, which lasted from three to a quarter past four, that I appeared really amiable to her.

She asked me if I had seen that young lady; I told her, "At the end of my visit, but things are going badly with her, she spoke to me with a wholly casual air, etc., etc."

"You're going to fall in love with her."

That's the general tone of her conversation: tender, her eyes moist with tears. We were seated, I was holding her hands, she sighed frequently; there was a moment when her eyes were moister, her hands were very warm, they had the sweat that is given by the anxiety of love (in a certain degree). I squeezed her hands slightly at this moment, she also squeezed them slightly. She loved me at this moment. Her face showed the tenderest emotion.

That was possibly the strongest impulse of tender and deep emotion that I have ever caused.

She didn't dare look at me, I'd have read her soul in her eyes.

This state lasted more or less throughout the three quarters of an hour of my visit. We talked slowly; we savored our happiness, the kisses she let me take registered. She was far from having the will power she had yesterday, when she told me, as I asked for a kiss in leaving:

"Not the tiniest."

I confess that it was delightful for me. We said a thousand things during this time. She frequently brought up the subject of the other Mélanie and Eudoxie.

I told her I was tempted to tell the other Mélanie that the chocolate we were drinking gave me more pleasure than her, saying that in an obscure and consequently a subtle manner.

She told me that what I was saying was vulgar, that I said things like that to women, that I said one of them to her the other day that was terrible.

She recounted the strange anecdote about Mlle. Sainval putting her lover out of the house in a nightshirt at their first meeting, closing the door, then reopening it and letting him in, her finger on her lips: "Be careful of my father, my friend, we mustn't wake him up." She amused me a lot, she had just complained of a cold.

"Is that the way you caught cold?" I asked her, laughing. This joke was led up to perfectly by the conversation. It may have been insolent, but it wasn't asinine.

She reproached me for my jokes today, etc., etc., saying that one of them had appeared indecent to a gentleman who was there. It seems to me that only Châteauneuf and Le Blanc were there, therefore Le Blanc was the man who was shocked. I begged her pardon for it, kissing her hands; I believe my kisses registered, and I excused myself, saying I didn't consider my joke insolent, that the very excess of its absurdity made it amusing.

The bell rang: "It's he, devil take him!" I kissed her three or four times in succession. My kisses registered.

M. Le Blanc came in, she had the tact to start a charming general conversation. No one could have more wit. She said everything about God and the soul that Mante and I think, and, in this discussion of deep philosophy, she had the complete advantage over M. Le Blanc, who defended God—and she's never read Helvétius, Tracy or Bayle.

That's the best possible proof of a rare natural good sense. She came on everything she said all by herself. Find me another woman who could do as much. If there had been six people present, I'd have been sparkling with lightness and eloquence. I restrained myself while joking. I was wrong; I ought to have been *myself*, natural.

Finally I left: "Good-by, I'll see you *tomorrow*," in the tenderest voice. She held out her hand, I didn't kiss it. Le Blanc didn't see us, it would have been amusing to make him hear the sound.

That's the lifeless skeleton of a charming hour, the outline of the Borromean Isles and the shores of Lake Maggiore, exactly that.

Mélanie is truly destined to be a Ninon—with this difference, that she'll have three or four lovers in her life. This is all the truer since she hasn't a character which is *attaccato,* feigned; she hasn't read the character of Ninon, she doesn't seek to have it on principle as the happiest or most amiable; she has it quite naturally.

Well sir, that's a merit that will be forever invisible to Pacé.

M. Le Blanc told us that the Comte de Lauraguais, speaking to the Queen, was not a little licentious, and that the Queen was frequently the same (they were a frivolous couple).

The Queen: "I can't imagine how a woman can sell herself!"

"But, madame, she was given a million."

"Bah, what difference does that make?"

"Ten, a hundred."

"Ah, you don't say so!"

"There's the woman that's ready, the only thing lacking is a buyer." (A word less vulgar than "buyer.")

Motet-Daleville, general stagecoach proprietor, twenty years ago gave a *million* to Dutor, I believe, the mistress of the Prince de Condé, and carried her off. There's a good fact.

Farewell notebook, I'm tired of writing.

She asked me for a history of Charles V. We had spoken of the one by Robertson, she's burning to read it. She's *burning,* show me a Councilor of State's daughter, a society girl of Paris, who has such a desire.

Being no longer able to see, I'm humming to myself and making music with my fingers on the table, I feel it to the depths of my heart, it makes me quiver, I feel my eyes filling with tears, so true it is that a sensitive soul makes one a musician. I must take the score of *Il Matrimonio Segreto* to my divine Pauline [his sister]. It will make her as happy as an angel. I'm writing this without being able to make out a single letter.

There is one of those pleasures that are thirty million leagues over the heads of all the unfeeling people. There's the poet.

If I had this feeling to interpret in a tragedy, obviously two days after having written it and cooled off a bit myself it wouldn't be as pleasing to me. Nevertheless, I'd have left it in.

There are details which can't be put in the French tragedy as it now is, but it will change—have no doubts about that.

                                                                    H. B.

Third Voyage to Paris

Germinal, XIII

Qui vedrai le vicende d'amore [Here you will see the vicissitudes of love].
1 Germinal [*March 22*].—I'm going to bed so as to be sure the day is really ended. And yet, all considered, it's been a happy one for me—but what kind of happiness is it to be near a woman you love and don't possess?

Thriftiness spoiled my day. Yesterday I didn't sleep at home. I returned there at eleven o'clock. At half-past twelve, I went to Dugazon's. He was expecting a Russian; at a quarter past one, he sent me to get Louason and to tell her to put on some rouge. I found her in the Place des Victoires, running, charming. We went back to her apartment, she arranged herself, laughing. We left Dugazon's at half-past two without him giving a lesson.

We went for a walk and returned at a quarter past five. I received 200 francs this morning, out of which only 27 were left for me; that made me as miserly as those who furnish the money. She told me she was going to *Nicomède*. I saw her there all the time from the second gallery. I went down to the pit at the fifth act. The curtain was scarcely lowered when I saw her go out, running with her usual gracefulness. I went to her house three times and went up twice; she wasn't there.

I hung around a minute in front of her door. I thought I saw M. Le Blanc go in; in that case, it's clear, she hurried away from the theater, where it was agreed I'd come to get her, in order to receive him at her apartment. Perhaps she had business with him. Perhaps she's deceiving me. Nothing would be easier for her.

But it was a saving of four livres eight sous that made me lose her tonight. If I'd gone to the orchestra, I'd have been beside her all the time. I'd have had a brilliant evening. I needed that today, I didn't display any wit when I was with her—not a particle of yesterday's verve. I don't know why, but the first minutes I'm with her are always chilly.

The best thing of the day was that, sitting in the Champs-Elysées, she confided to me that she was reciting verses before Fontanes; she told me to come along, that we would recite them together, that she liked better to recite them with me than with M. Le Blanc, and thereupon she fell on M. Le Blanc with might and main.

Later, when we returned to her apartment at five o'clock, she looked at me and sighed.

If, for a silly reason of health, I hadn't gone without wine at lunch; if, for a silly economy, I hadn't gone to the pit, I'd have had a charming day. I especially regret my evening. Having seen her this morning, I was sure of being charming tonight. I must go to see her at noon tomorrow.

My body and soul are terribly tired. Today has been full of events, various passions and running around town.

It's agreed that tomorrow I'll say to her at the fifth act, "Unlucky at cards, Eudoxie didn't come." I should joke about the fact that I seemed jealous in the Rue Neuve-des-Petits-Champs. Then watch her way of laughing. I'll see whether M. Le Blanc joined her, and, if it was he, whether he recognized me.

I'm really a child; if she's playing with me, she has no merit. Still, if she's playing with me, what does she want of me? She can take charge of my education. She told me this morning that I ought to put more subtlety into my manner of scoffing. There's a real friend for you.

Mightn't she be just a *whore* like so many others? This morning, she pointed out a pretty bonnet to me.

But I get desperate when I think that she's deceiving me. I must go to Pacé's tomorrow in order to laugh, and leave there at noon.

Tomorrow, I must be sure to follow up the indication of fatuity given above. She didn't see me at the Français, while I saw her all the time. The sight of that straw hat gave me pleasure. I must be sure to follow up that fatuity tomorrow.

I've lived more fully today than in two months during my trip to Grenoble in the Year XI.

2 Germinal [*March 23*].—The finest day possible.

After passing the morning in court intrigues and in Martial's cabriolet, I went at noon to Mélanie's. We fooled around until half-past one. She really has designs on me. But I feel forever incapable of possessing that woman by an assault.

There are a thousand charming details that I haven't the time to speak of. An hour and a half of happiness, a talent that was neither too great nor too small, an excellent mediocrity.

I returned at half-past two. I found Le Blanc and Châteauneuf there. The latter bored her to death until five o'clock. During the conversation, I said something to her that was downright insolence. My talent was the cause of that.

I advised her to study the roles that are the farthest from her character, Cleopatra for instance. I said to M. de Châteauneuf:

"Mademoiselle won't bite you."

The meaning given in high society to *won't bite* carried it off. The habit of giving each word its exact inflection was put in play; my inflection said broadly and naturally:

"It's well known that everybody possesses Mademoiselle."

That was as stinging as possible. I believe tears came to her eyes.

Messrs. Le Blanc and Châteauneuf, who see me there constantly, must have believed that I had had her and was fed up with her.

That was a piece of foolishness; I repaired it by my sudden sadness, if reparable it was.

I must make endless apologies the first time I see her; I must start with that.

She told me a yarn about last night. The fact was that she spent the evening either with M. Le Blanc or the devil knows where.

Châteauneuf is a bore, there are no two ways about it.

I must play around with her again the first time I see her at her apartment.

4 Germinal [*March 25*].—I need to reflect a little about my behavior. I'm doing it with pen in hand; that diminishes the influence of passions on the opinions that are formed about me.

Yesterday, I was at Dugazon's at noon. At half-past one, Louason arrived with Mme. Mortier, well enough dressed. Louason said that she was ill, that she would recite nothing, and she was charming. There was love in her eyes; my dumb play was good, and it increased her love.

Mme. Mortier recited the first lines from *Zaïre;* my dumb play rendered all Zaïre's sentiments so well that Louason remarked it and called Dugazon's attention to it in a whisper. I overheard it, things only went along the better. After the line, Dugazon expatiated on it and forced me to recite the line. That shouldn't do me any harm with Mélanie.

She recited *Phèdre.* A Portuguese named *Castro* arrived; Dugazon acted the mountebank a bit, and Mortier the wench a lot. We left at a quarter past three, Louason indignant (according to what she said) at the behavior of Mortier. She told me some other anecdotes of the same kind. Her jealousy was aroused a bit, I believe, by Mortier.

She was cold, we returned to her apartment. I suggested that we go and eat some cutlets at the café in the Chinese Baths, she eagerly accepted, and it seemed to me that her soul was entirely unveiled at this unexpected happiness.

She was exceedingly gay, and no longer seemed to have any reserve with me, this was on the way to the café and back home. My soul is too delicate, she no longer dared speak, seeing that she was being invited to lunch.

If I had had the talent that I'm seeking to acquire, I'd have engaged her in conversation at this moment and I'd have been brilliant and

charming for her. Instead of that, I was amiable in the manner of
Montesquieu.

Journal of My Third Voyage to Paris

From 6 Germinal, Year XIII, to Sunday, the 17th of the same, breakfast at Martial's

5 *Germinal* [*March* 27].—I went to Dugazon's as usual; at the start I was
rather cool, as is my laudable custom; Louason arrived and didn't even
deign to look at me. She had some charming glances for that booby of a
Wagner. That brought me out of my coolness and made me amiable,
but not for her. I began paying compliments to little Mortier and titil-
lating her breasts, the whole quite decently. I didn't think I was being
very amiable; far from that, it seemed to me that the session was, like
the weather, freezing cold. I took Louason home with Mortier. Félipe
arrived, I was genuinely brilliant; but it wasn't real wit, it was merely
a young man's ardor. Mortier said she'd go to the Bourgoin ball in the
evening with Wagner.

I looked at Mélanie at the same time: she was so pale she was green.
Is she in love with Wagner and is she jealous?

I was enterprising with Félipe, who didn't object.

These ladies left: "How you've taken on the manner of those women!
How you talk! If you're deceiving me, if you're making fun of me!"

She twice repeated the words "making fun of me," and said these
and other words of the same kind with the most natural and broadest
intonations. That's the finest success of vanity I've had with her; it's
superb, it gave me pleasure only because it advanced my love, and today (8 Germinal, Year XIII), it's ancient history for me.

After pausing a long time between: "Perhaps you're deceiving
me . . . , you," etc., etc., looking at me fixedly, she concluded in the
negative. At the time, I didn't understand what she was telling me, I
behaved very well with her after these words.

It's plain that in her opinion I was very amiable with Mme. Mortier
and Félipe. If I've ever been an ass when I was with her, that will show
her it was because I was in love.

It was a superb success of vanity with the woman with whom I like
best to have one.

She was the first to speak of Eudoxie (Eudoxie has a mother).

7 *Germinal* [*March* 28].—I called at two o'clock; she sent me away so she

could work, was annoyed to see me there. She told me to come back at four o'clock; I went, brisk, spruce, amiable. I was refused admittance because she was dressing.

In the evening, I went with Crozet to the dressing room of Ariadne, who's just taken the role of Camille for the first time. Her face was more ardent than I've ever seen it, her eye superhuman. She thought her acting had been bad, she told us that she'd spoken the imprecation badly, that she didn't feel it at all because of Lafond.

And we, base flatterers that we were, pumped her full of praise; we perhaps prevented her from becoming sublime. Lemazurier was so abject he was disgusting; Pacé praised her through conviction and little knowledge of the art; Crozet and I praised, but I more than Crozet; I'm ashamed of myself.

My eye held that of Duchesnois; our eyes are friendly much more than the rest of us.

Leaving her, we went for a walk in the Palais-Royal. Crozet was superb, I never saw so much genius in him; he felt a noble and vehement indignation at Ariadne's flatterers. He was exactly like d'Eglantine's Alceste, perfectly so; there wasn't a trace of that slight apathy he usually has; he was sublime in the manner of Alceste; that's how I must picture this character, the finest that exists on the comic stage.

In my opinion, it was Crozet's finest day.

8 *Germinal* [*March 29*].—I've been in a witty and gay mood today which makes my whole behavior of the past few days appear stupid. That too is philosophic genius. I had a fiendish desire to show everybody what man is when flayed. I was like a painter who, wishing to distinguish himself in the manner of Albani, might have started judiciously by the study of anatomy, and for whom, as a useful object, it might have become so agreeable that, instead of painting a pretty breast with the desire of delighting men, he would paint, bare and bleeding, all the muscles forming the breast of a pretty woman—all the more horrible because something more agreeable was expected. They furnish a new disgust by the accuracy of the objects which they represent; you would merely have contempt for them if they were false, but, being true, they haunt the imagination.

Women are undoubtedly guided by interest, luckless wretch! But let me forget that while I kiss my Mélanie, leave me a moment of illusion; will the knowledge of the truth ever be worth as much as that?

After this fine start in rigmarole, immediately turning into the emotional, I must repair Mélanie's honor, which seems to be compromised; she's still charming, in my opinion; her character hasn't belied itself. The only thing is that unhappiness gives the character a veneer of grandeur.

My genius for the loftily emotional, based on the lofty philosophy of Pascal and Rousseau's Héloïse and the passionate and sublime passages of Racine, Corneille and Shakespeare, has possessed me utterly up till now. It has never been poured out in naïve and gay speech, in follies that are agreeable through their lack of consistency.

Therefore, let's get away from the seriousness that is necessarily given by thought continually concentrated on all that's lofty. This is the currency with which immortality is purchased, but it doesn't purchase friendly smiles and tender hand squeezes.

I'm indebted to Mélanie for all that; she's serious, tender, frequently melancholy, interested in the same subjects as I. I can't yet explain my leading thoughts to her: the loftier they are, the more I see that I can make myself understood only by what I write.

Therefore, I should apply this wit to the production of agreeable things. All that has saved me up till now is my youthful ardor.

I have fire in my veins, I need to adopt a cooling diet. I must skip a few lessons at Dugazon's, that will result in my having better ones.

I arrived at Dugazon's at half-past twelve, Mélanie and Wagner were there. I have violent suspicions of Wagner, it's quite possible that he's had Mélanie; I'm too much of a child to dare decide; she smiles at him, that's the fact, I see it; but what does it mean?

Mme. Mortier arrived late, then M. Castro, Portuguese; Dugazon is a consummate mountebank. I took a place beside Castro and I mystified Mme. Mortier with my eyes; I made Mélanie laugh outright, and, without saying a single word, kept Mme. Mortier busy.

The latter made ridiculous advances to M. Castro.

Mélanie doesn't agree that the last four feet of this verse should be recited joyfully:

> Où me cacher? *Fuyons dans la nuit infernale,*
> Mais que dis-je? etc. . . .

She's wrong, she doesn't reason as well as I do on the passions. I ought to write her three or four pages about that one of these days.

Mme. Mortier's absurdity reanimated Louason, she was grateful to me for making fun of her; we left together. Passing by a milliner's shop at the corner of the Place des Victoires, she went into a store to try on a bonnet; they asked twenty-four francs for it, she offered eighteen.

Does she expect me to buy it for her?

We stayed together until a quarter past four in the closest intimacy, as though I'd just had her and we were both languid.

I went to *Britannicus*. I came home at half-past eleven. I must say to Louason tomorrow, "I didn't recognize Le Blanc from behind."

At her apartment this afternoon, my hands were in hers and she squeezed them as she spoke. She recounted with much vivacity several things that happened to her; she treated me like a successful lover. I made her laugh by repeating for her benefit my pantomime with Mme. Mortier, she told me laughingly that Dugazon said she had a tragic —— , that she required one as long as that.

These scurrilous things—in skeleton form here—were entirely comical between us. As for myself, I said Dugazon told me she had the clap; I hope that one was even stronger.

It seems to me that dear Dugazon is somewhat of a ruffian by trade; she said, "In the beginning when I went to Dugazon's, he made me some shameful propositions, he told me, 'You see that man at the Français who's looking at you; well, do you realize that he's in love with you? He's Bacciochi; if you like, I'll take you to his country house, he'll give you twenty-five louis a month.'"

She didn't know where to look, according to what she told me, and turned down the offer. Another time, Dugazon said to her, "Don't go and give yourself away for a *bonnet;* you ought to know how to make your way better than that, etc."

I was struck by the word *bonnet,* she treated me excellently today, and did so because she wanted to. If, in a few days, she neglects me or treats me badly, it will be clear that she's not following Dugazon's advice; she'd have given herself to me for a bonnet.

I believe she wanted to show me that she had some money today; she had her menu for dinner read before me.

She told me that Wagner's downfall was nothing more than a pretext. I told her that I had guessed as much and had given her credit for it; she denied being involved, saying, "When could I have seen him? You left here at half-past four."

If she's having him, what's the good of being circumspect with me?

To finish with Dugazon, I asked him this morning for a ticket to the pit; he owed me forty-four sous, naturally he didn't recall it; in our opinion, that shows him up as a pimp and a man who's unscrupulous in money matters.

I asked Louason if I could take her home tonight, she accepted with joy; afterward, as it was necessary to go to get her, it was only conditional. I must say to her tomorrow that I saw the tragedy from a loge, and that I entered the little room in the orchestra by tipping the attendants.

The fact is that my evening at the theater cost me three livres eight sous. After having swum and flown like Satan trying to reach heaven, I finally found myself behind her in the orchestra; I spoke to her, she asked flusteredly how I was, and went out with Le Blanc, avoiding looking at me.

Maybe she looks up to that rogue because he's written some tragedies and knows the theater; one of these days, I must compose a seven- or eight-page letter for her on my knowledge of the passions, in which I can show the head and the heart, the passions and the states of passion. This clearly worded letter, in which I'll speak directly to her, will place me on a level well above the others.

16 Germinal [*April 4*].—"You're my god, you're the directress of my fate; be my guide and I'll follow you to the end of the world."

She has seen into my soul; only an hour after coming away from her apartment did I understand what she said to me and it fills me with delightful enthusiasm. What would the effect have been in her presence!

I should say to her tomorrow:

"Mon génie étonné tremble devant le sien."

She refused weakly to give me a lock of her hair; I'll insist tomorrow, and I'll have it.

The course of our conversation led to what follows: I'm skipping the details, they take away from the *marked appearance* that things have here. In general, this warning holds good for the whole journal.

We were talking about me, saying that I would be witty at the age of twenty-eight.

"In that case, you'd lose your greatest merit, the real passion that can be seen in you."

Those aren't the terms she used. What she meant was:

"You haven't got the brilliant kind of wit that is amusing; you have passion, you'll lose the second without perhaps acquiring the first." Her meaning was perhaps not as severe as that.

She started telling me what I was. Fool that I was, my bad habit was my undoing! I'd have been sublime at her knees, like Rousseau at Mme. d'Houdetot's, if I'd taken the time to reflect. Instead, I replied with four or five grimaces in the manner of Fleury.

This face-making gave me a very expressive dumb play, and destroyed everything else.

General rule: I should always take the time to reflect when I'm spoken to, instead of playing the part of a braggart and comedy marquis.

She said while I had my hands in hers, "You're witty. . . . You're capable of doing anything. You have great ardor and a lofty soul."

"I'll attain glory."

"It isn't enough to want a thing, you must have the proper circumstances."

She saw into my soul; the conversation flagged because of my *Fleuryism*.

I must give her a guaranty in my handwriting against a lock of her hair.

Since she has seen into my soul, I should by all means fortify the idea she may have of my nascent talents; I should avoid the slightest falsehood, which forever destroys grace. I write better than I talk; I must take her my verse, our article on Phaedra, etc., etc.

I must adopt her as my guide—really, I couldn't do better. I'll take my verse to her tomorrow.

I'm not going to write my charming memories any longer, I've noticed that doing this spoils them.

I must learn to hold myself in while writing, and trim down my style; otherwise, the accessories make me forget the principal thing.

Palm Sunday, 17 Germinal [April 7].—Lunched at Martial's with Dugazon, Wagner, Fougeard, Prévost and Dufresne, a war commissioner with a face of wax and a well-powdered wig and a wit in keeping, Digeon the major, and Maisonneuve. M. Combe was present and Pierre [Daru] came in for a minute.

Maisonneuve spoke of d'Eglantine's *L'Orange de Malte,* of which the two plays yesterday were imitations. D'Eglantine's play was of the most elevated sort. I felt, as I listened to him outline it, that the comedy was among my first loves. Maisonneuve told us that he had talked with d'Eglantine six or seven times about the play, once from ten in the morning until eleven at night while thumbing through Molière and placing the scenes. I experienced indescribable pleasure in hearing this. If it weren't for my damned laziness, I'd render him the service of translating [Alfieri's] *Agamemnon,* I'd take it to him and we'd become friends, I'd have as many of these anecdotes about genius as I liked. It seems to me that d'Eglantine was the greatest genius the eighteenth century produced in literature.

Maisonneuve believes that the play was never written, Dugazon that the first three acts exist.[1] Maisonneuve is rereading his *Le Méfiant* at the Comédie tomorrow; by becoming attached to him, I could follow through all the things that happen to a man who's trying to get a play produced. I could take lessons from him.

Per le mio avro una eccellente via nel Dugazon [For my plays, I'll have an excellent interpreter in Dugazon]. It seems to me he'd be de-

[1]More than a quarter of a century later Stendhal gave the provisional title of *L'Orange de Malte* to the unfinished novel that was published posthumously as *Lucien Leuwen*.

lighted to create a new role. That's excellent for my *Letellier*. He regards the creation of a new role as the touchstone of an actor.

Dugazon is too much of the clown, remaining apart from the rest of society; besides, today he was in a company where there was no verve or gaiety; I believe he'd produce a far greater effect if he isolated his stories by six minutes passed on an equal footing with us. Dugazon doesn't have the good breeding of society, he hasn't any poise.

Dugazon is dauntless when he's telling stories; his listeners don't laugh; he keeps on; the laughter gathers force, it bursts out on all sides. I ought to acquire this self-assurance gradually.

Generally speaking, the guests had no verve. I pictured myself in 1815, having composed four five-act plays and enjoying an income of 20,000 livres, having Dugazon, the Talmas and the Lemerciers to lunch from time to time in the country with our mistresses. How charming this sort of wit is as an adornment of true happiness! But here it was placed on the empty and anxious look of a courtier.

Journal of My Third Voyage to Paris

Written in an Old Notebook on *La Pharsale,*
Epic Poem Begun about the Month of Brumaire, Year X,
OF 18 Germinal, XIII, TILL . . .

Last notebook. Year XIII. Third Voyage. THE STORY OF MY THIRD TRAVEL AT PARIS, YEAR XIII. LOVE INTRODUCING ME IN THE SOCIETY. FROM THE 18 Germinal, TILL THE DEPARTURE, THE . . . Floréal WITH Mélanie.

20 *Germinal* [*April 10*].—Mélanie's character must have become reasonable and solicitous of the future, since she has a daughter whom she loves and who would be without resources if she lost her. Perhaps this is one of the reasons for her melancholy; this reason ought to make her sensitive to kindness.

By the word "become" I don't mean any reflection on this heavenly girl who perhaps has a lofty soul. She'll change my character and make me more sociable. I'll learn to furnish my quota of agreeableness in society, and through that to be agreeable there for myself and for others.

I'm beginning to see that you must bother very little about the future if you want to be happy or merely reasonable. Yet I've been foolish enough to worry about it so often when it looked dark that I should be permitted to derive some joy from its contemplation when it seems to promise me happiness. It appears that I'll always have Mélanie for a friend, if not for a mistress, and I really love her with all my heart. If she can't make her debut upon the return of M. de Rémusat, it's probable that she'll come—while waiting for the favorable moment when they'll open their eyes to the state of the Théâtre Français—to Marseille, where she appears to have friends. Adèle will be there with her mother about the same time. There's a rare stroke of luck! I'll be there too, working in the bank with Mante.

I'm obliged to go to Grenoble for a few months, and even this obligation is a pleasure, since I'll see my dear Pauline there again. I think there aren't many brothers like me, who have the good fortune to be *amico riamato* of a girl with genius and the loftiest kind of a soul.

If I'm finally able to take life reasonably, I'll be capable of deriving pleasure from the company of even the most hopeless asses who people the dear home town. I'm obliged to go there, and as it happens Barral will be there too. He's an agreeable companion as far as the heart is concerned, although his wrongheadedness is depressing. Far better than that, perhaps Crozet will come. He's a friend of infinite wit, perhaps the wittiest of all my friends, and certainly the one who can help me to get the most gaiety out of the ninnies of Grenoble.

What more can I ask in my present situation? Misfortune, or what I've called misfortune up to now, can befall me only through money. Well and good, I have a miserly father, but am I alone in this? When my silly vanity has completely disappeared and has permitted me to own up to this shortcoming, I'll only have the more charm. It's a good bet that in the next two months I'll receive 1,000 francs. I'll pay off my debts and live gaily. I'll leave 1 Messidor if I can, after finishing *Letellier*.

I've done nothing in this direction, is it to be regretted? I'm beginning to amend my character; a charming woman and one I love is amending it. Heigh-ho, leap, marquis!

As soon as I've amended my character, which is melancholy through bad habit and infatuation with Rousseau, I'll have, I hope, a very agreeable one; gaiety in the best taste on a basis of extreme tenderness.

Will you love me then, Mélanie?

18 Germinal [April 8].—I went to her apartment at about three this afternoon. I found her still in curl papers, arranging her linen, which the chambermaid was ironing. She greeted me with a smile of happiness. Would she have had the same smile for any other man who might have surprised her at this moment, or was there something special in it for me? I don't have enough experience to decide.

I was in a witty mood when I entered; had there been a couple of men present with a conversation sparkling with wit and gaiety, I would perhaps have been as brilliant as they, and, if I had been so during the first half hour, I'd have been more brilliant than they during the second. Alone, I didn't have the verve necessary to *launch* myself, I was too worthy of being loved to be amiable. I suggested that we go out, she didn't want to. I gave her the scene of *Le Raccommodement,* copied in haste and not reread, she was about to read it in my presence, that would have been delightful. Without thinking, I said, "No, I prefer that you read it when I'm not here." That was exactly the opposite of what I meant. My words were silly in that they showed an author's pride, and never in my life did I have less. Accustomed to the delicate vanity of literary men, she immediately said in the low voice that one uses with a sick person in order not to hurt his feelings, "All right then, I'll read it when I'm alone."

What I meant to say was, *"It will bore you."* If she had read it, how well I'd have been able to declaim it!

Instead of that, many other things happened. We began walking back and forth in her little room, arm in arm and her hand in mine. We spoke of her debut and her plans in case she couldn't make it. She told me that she'd gone through half her fortune and planned to retire to the country with her daughter; there were tears in her eyes.

Finally, I offered to live with her in any corner of France she might choose. When she had fully grasped this idea and the fact that I was willing to give up everything for her and act as her daughter's schoolmaster, she turned her face to the window for some time so I wouldn't see her crying, later she asked me for her handkerchief. It wasn't in the bedroom, I went to look for it in the salon, where the maid was ironing. I didn't dare brush away those charming tears myself. At first sight, I was wrong, but perhaps, for anyone who recognizes grace, I was right.

She was weeping profusely. Obviously the tears came with the smile that results from the view of happiness[1]; she found me so goodhearted that she wept. After she turned her head, I spoke to her a bit longer before she asked me for her handkerchief.

Her soul experienced something comparable to liquefaction, to the division of the being experienced by the Chevalier des Grieux when Manon spoke to him in the cabin at New Orleans.

With a little more assurance or a little less love, I would perhaps have been sublime and would have had her.

The mood I produced is rarer than gaiety, and, above all, would require more talent to be introduced; but I didn't have this glory, I was

[1]"Tears are the ultimate smile," Stendhal wrote in *De l'Amour* two decades later.

entirely natural. We again spoke a bit of our plan, we thought of settling down on the shores of Lake Geneva.

Followed this conversation: ". . . They've missed me everywhere
I've been."—"I believe it, you have a kind soul." And she did believe
it. Unfolding my soul to her, and speaking of what we'd do in our
retreat, I told her I'd try to achieve fame through mathematics; she
said with astonishment and even a bit of admiration for a soul so extraordinary, "But have you told Martial about that? Does he know
you?"—"Oh, good heavens, no, he wouldn't understand me!" That's
merely the substance. By changing the name of the subject through
which I wanted to achieve fame, everything I said would have been
true.

I believe all that produced a great effect on her.

I left at six o'clock, at the end I bored her a little perhaps. That was
due to two causes: I have so much pleasure in being with her that I
can't tear myself away; the second, I give myself up to the pleasure of
seeing her, of worshiping her, and I no longer think of saying amusing
things. These are two results of love which aren't likely to give birth
to it in the object that inspires it. If I don't succeed, these will be the
two principal reasons.

She's going to spend six days at Saint-Germain-Laxis, the former
country home of M. de Juigné, near Melun, belonging to M. Biers, one
of her friends.

The next day, 19 Germinal, I didn't see her; this was almost a pleasure for me; I foresaw too much difficulty in maintaining the charming
emotion of the previous day.

I'm stopping, because this detail, instead of making me recover, has
only increased my love: and, as she left today (Saturday, called Good
by the simpletons) for a week, that would only increase my loneliness.

Since her departure, I've worked a little on *Letellier*.

5 *Floréal* [*April 25*].—Yesterday, the 4th, to *Le Philosophe Marié,* followed by *La Gageure:* Fleury and Contat. From there to pleasure with
Barral, Vincelles, Crozet and Basset.

I went to the theater with the latter three. All the men were shameful urchins, old libertines, gamblers, military men who don't know
where to go, young men of good breeding who are lost in that milieu
or who want to rinse out their mouths after a tedious evening. I grew
very fond of Percevant. The departure of Tencin caused me a slight
pang in the heart.

I took a stroll with Crozet until two o'clock.[1] The sight of the nascent

---

[1] That was one of those bad days of melancholy and tenderness that make me
sink back into my old malady. If that becomes a habit, and if I don't find a
Julie in the woman with whom I happen to fall in love, I'll blow out my brains.

verdure in the Tuileries and the gardens giving on the Champs-Elysées cast me back in the midst of my ideas—romantic, alas!—of happiness through love. This gentle melancholy prevented me from working on *Letellier*. In the evening, I sought refuge in the wit of Chamfort and the Opéra-Comique, where they were giving *Le Chapitre Second, Les Confidences* and *Le Calife de Bagdad,* of which the music consoled me somewhat after the racket of the other two. It was full of youthful gaiety. The audience there has quite a different character from that of the Français, but it's more childish, especially the pit. I was struck by Pingenet's resemblance to Mélanie. Were I to see Pingenet after leaving Paris, she'd make me forget what Mélanie looks like, as the laundress at Bergamo did in the case of Signora Marini *della contrada della Bagutta.*

Mélanie was at Dugazon's without my knowing it.

6 *Floréal* [*April 26*].—Lunched at Blancheron's with Vincelles, Basset, Crozet, and Barral. The first two, who gave the lunch, left at eleven o'clock, the first for Mont-de-Marsan, the second for Tours.

From there I went to Dugazon's. I recited Oreste before Mme. Clairval quite well, according to what Dugazon told me, playfully slapping my face. Mme. Clairval said, "Good, good."

If I'd gone there yesterday, I'd have found Louason, Mme. Mortier and the leading actress of Rouen. Louason said yesterday that she wouldn't come today.

9 *Floréal* [*April 29*].—Crozet, who's just left at ten o'clock, slept with me. This morning I read Chamfort's *Pensées*. At noon I went to Dugazon's, where I recited *Oedipe*. Mme. Mortier was there, I said all sorts of smutty things to her without her getting mad. By the greatest hazard in the world, she said she was going from there to Mlle. Louason's; I went with her. We took a cabriolet at the Place des Victoires because it was raining a little. We went in to Mélanie's: I never saw her so pretty. She was wearing a white frock and a straw hat trimmed in pink. M. Le Blanc was there. As I was going out, she followed me to say, "I'm leaving. I've got something to tell you, come back at five."

I took Mortier home. I could have had her a thousand times if I'd wanted to, but, my faith, that's not to be, as Matta said.

I had a snack with Crozet, and hurried back to Mélanie's. She told me she was leaving in a week for Marseille, where she had an engagement at 6,500 francs a year. I said, "Very well, I'll go with you as far as Lyon."

Haven't I already thought of doing so for Mélanie? [Note added by Beyle three days later.]

That surprised her. I was all soul; if I'd had the comic composure I had a week ago when I was reading *Figaro,* I'd have been much more amiable.

I took her to dinner at Robert's. From there to the Français. I was four seats away from her in the orchestra. *Esther,* same judgment as the first time. Talma, perfectly in the spirit of a despot.

From there to her apartment, she was charming. I told her what Mme. Mortier had done to have me. If I'd dared to dare, I'd have had her. I left her to rejoin Crozet.

I told her this morning that I'd had Eudoxie [Victorine Mounier]. Therefore it's clear that I'll leave in a week, 17 Floréal probably. And *Letellier?* I'll have it presented by Rey. I absolutely must have her during the voyage. If I dared to dare! The more I love her the more bashful I am.

For the voyage, I must take along *Fél.,*[1] *Figaro* and some selections of jokes and puns. This trip may turn out to be charming. She desires very much that I accompany her as far as Marseille. She's afraid of robbers. The Bronzes [?] will decide this affair. I've never seen her as pretty as she was tonight when she returned home, after she took off her hat (21 livres). I'm to see her again tomorrow at one o'clock.

Crozet owes me 38 livres; I owe Barral 96. I'll have to settle up with Dugazon, the landlady, Douenne, Mercier, Silan, Pidançat. Pack my trunk. Take out a passport. Say good-by to my relatives and Father Jeky. Buy Say and *Félicia.*

FINANCES:

I have	250 livres		To be paid:	Douenne	170 livres
	150 "			Silan	48 "
	200 "			Mercier	72 "
	—			Bal.	12 "
	600 "			Leg.	60 "
				Astley	30 "
				M.	60 "
					—
					452 "

Balance: 148 livres.

I'll have to give Douenne only 70 livres and Mercier nothing; thus I'll have 148 + 100 + 72 = 320 livres. It's not too much.

Find out tomorrow the price Gouge charges for seats in his coach. Write to La Roche. I'll send the latter a letter of exchange for 172

[1] *Félicia, ou Mes Fredaines,* well-known pornographic novel attributed to Andrea de Nerciat.

livres. In Marseille, the first of the month, I'll draw 100 francs on one bank, and the 15th, 100 francs on another.

10 Floréal [*April 30*].—Lunched with Martial. At two o'clock, to Mélanie's. From there to Adèle's, an hour of tête-à-tête; *gli piglio le cioccio*. From there to Mme. Martin's. From there to Mélanie's, with whom I intended to dine; I didn't find her. I went out to dinner after writing four letters. From there to the Français.

I was up to my neck in sentiment, and consequently in a melancholy mood of tender regret at leaving Paris; that was certainly a bias: (outside N.) what am I leaving behind me? What can I do here without money? What would I do here without Percevant, Tencin and my friends? I need to go some place where I'll be forced to see society and mankind. I must sacrifice everything to that in Marseille.

Duclos helped me regain my common sense. I was gay all the rest of the evening. At present, I fully feel the possibility of taking the thing I so desire. In order to remain in this mood when it comes over me, I must act a great deal and not give myself time for reflection; I'm lost if I take it. Tonight I saw ALL THE THEORY OF THE BEST CONDUCT IN WORLD; TO WRITE THAT. It must be granted that I'm emerging from a strange state of madness; Rousseau's moments of exaltation had become my customary manner of being. I took that for genius, I cultivated it complacently and looked with pity on those who didn't have it. I must keep that for myself alone, otherwise I'll be everlastingly unhappy in society.

TO WRITE THE PLAN OF CONDUCT, AND TO SAY THAT TO NOBODY BUT PAULINE. I must follow it point by point in Marseille, and definitely set the ideal goal I wish to attain.

IF I HAVE NOT MELANIE IN THE WAY, I SHALL BE EVER UNHAPPY WITH HER. In the opposite case, I SHALL BE THE HAPPIEST OF MEN TO MARSEILLE. I'll put my new plan into execution daily with her, and she'll end up by becoming attached to her pupil.

Le Barbier de Seville was played without verve because of Saint-Phal, who paralyzed everything. I saw clearly what he lacked in this role to be as good as Fleury. His pauses were too long, his face too expressionless and immobile.

That's probably how I am with Mélanie because of my excessive bashfulness. Do you want to know the reason, you simpleton? It's because you've only had the strength of passions in your favor up until now. You believed yourself good and strong because you were impassioned; you haven't any character; sublime in your castles in Spain, extraordinary, but no good at all in society. You've got to grind yourself down constantly in Marseille, and have but one goal—to produce laughter: and, once you are *natural,* you'll see where you'll go.

As Félicia says, add the happiness of numerous passing tastes to the happiness of passion in love. I've got to attack every woman I meet (until my return to Paris, then I'll heed my heart); only then will I deserve to have a real love.

In a word, I must form my character. My character consists of doing what I've set out to do, upheld or not by passion, with verve and gaiety. I should pretend that I'm always in the presence of Pacé or M. de Baure, I should try to be pleasing to them and not to think about the people in whose presence I actually am. I must possess all the Mme. Mortiers I meet.

Instead of kindling my passion when I'm bashful by means of reading novels or other things appealing to my heart, I must read only books that will dry me up, like Duclos.

If Mélanie were to tell me tomorrow that she had a chance to take the post chaise and couldn't leave with me, I envisage the possibility of supporting this reverse. There will be time enough to give way to my too tender character after the victory; until then, I should consider her as just an ordinary woman, analyze my heart and play on the passions; otherwise, I'll be forever bashful and silly. You'll be amiable and yourself only after the victory. I'm convinced that she herself will be amazed at the result. One thing alone can restore me in her opinion—my ardor at Dugazon's.

I must devote myself exclusively at Grenoble to the outline of the *beau idéal* FOR MY CONDUCT, which is merely a sequel to the principles of the comic art. I must arrive at Dugazon's tomorrow the most *dried up* and scoundrelly possible. I already feel that I am no longer that; I'm carried away by rhetoric; I could be eloquent all night.

Remember that this natural talent can be brilliant in society only after I've supplied myself with an adequate fund of comic conversation; and for this kind of comic, I must always recall Pacé at Ariadne's: "My breast hurts." "Which one?" "I have a cold." "And I'm in heat."

I realize that I am a thousand times above this sort of nonsense, and this nonsense came from a man who triumphs. I must take a lot of chances.

The state of reflection which is usual with me is contrary to that of experience, without which I'll never be A TRUE BARD. It isn't a question of knowing what those who have had this experience are (Durif, for instance), but of knowing what a soul like mine would be after having it. In my future conduct, I should seek all occasions to go ahead, I should get into action continually, even though it be through nonsense. I should make a habit of that (examples: Cardon, Tencin, Favier himself). The example of my conduct with Châteauneuf shows me the way to please men; I must employ this way with *everybody* without exception, save Pauline. She has a soul sufficiently lofty to understand mine.

12 Floréal [May 2].—I reserved TWO PLACES AT THE DILIGENCE.

In the evening, *Le Tyran Domestique.* A few little traits that would be effective in La Bruyère, but that are of too little interest for the stage. A dull play. Mlle. Mars was perfect.

It was Crozet's enthusiasm that made me regard her with all the attention she deserves. I found her charming, but I didn't enter into the detail of her perfections.

I must reckon well with my passions.

The first, the strongest, the sole, THIS OF FAME; I must speak of it to no one, and satisfy it in silence.

That passed, being completely indifferent in society, I ought to be charming. To preserve me from stagnation I have my bank and the love for women.

What has spoiled me up to now is the false opinion I've had of them. I believed them to be Julies, and they're merely the *Parisiennes* of Dancourt. (See the nice comedy of this name by Dancourt.) Gaiety, brilliance, audacity—especially the latter—and you'll succeed a thousand times better than you will by displaying the most sublime character by your deeds.

Keep the conception of the *beau idéal* FOR THY WORDS [works?]; but in society, Pacé is almost the *beau idéal.*

Sadness, when one knows life, shows that one possesses passions which the impossibility of satisfying them hasn't yet been able to cure.

The sadness of him who doesn't know life reveals the kind of cowardice that despairs of succeeding.

13 AND 14 Floréal XIII, ALL THE DAY WITH MELANIE. THE 15 WE GO TO NEUILLY FOR SEEING THE YOUNG M. [Mélanie's daughter.]

I must leave good conduct and the love of study. My example shows where these qualities lead. You must give yourself up to intrigue alone.

30 Prairial [June 19].—Your true passion is that of knowing and experiencing. It has never been satisfied.

When you impose silence on yourself you discover ideas; when you make it a rule to talk, you find nothing to say (SEEN IN THE NATURE).

Love and Groceries

THE six days spent sitting beside Mélanie in a crowded stagecoach and the five nights the two slept in the same country taverns hardly constituted the "charming voyage" that Henri Beyle had anticipated. When they parted at Lyon, she to continue on to Marseille, he to return to Grenoble, the future young dramatic-bard, to his disgruntlement and humiliation, was still the platonic lover of his future young actress.

In his native "mudhole," too, things went badly. The somber Chérubin Beyle and the doddering Dr. Gagnon, canny and old-fashioned, failed to be impressed by Henri's incontrovertible mathematical proofs that, entrusted with 30,000 francs, he could not help making a fortune.

In the end, however, the elder Beyle went so far as to promise vaguely that, provided he was able to sell some property at Cheylas, he would advance the required sum in eighteen months or two years. Uncertain as it was, this was acceptable to Henri, for he had not given up his two-year program to gain business experience in Marseille, Bordeaux, Nantes and Antwerp before establishing his bank.

Unfortunately, there were no banking positions open at the moment in Marseille, but if he would care to take a temporary job with Mante in the firm of Charles Meunier & Co., Wholesale Groceries, matters might be arranged. Thus it was that, in order to start his career with the woman he loved, the Molière of the new century sacrificed glory to groceries.

His decision taken, Beyle lost no time in getting out of Grenoble. By a resourceful combination of mail coach, river boat and diligence, he managed to arrive three days later in Marseille, where Mante had tactfully reserved a room for him in M. Rambert's rooming house, where Mélanie was staying.

Here it was that, after the months of hesitation, the two finally became lovers. Beyond a cryptic allusion in English in the entry of July 29, his diary passes over the event in silence, which is typical. "Happiness," he believed all his life, "is like a delicate fruit, it spoils if touched."

For other reasons, probably, he was similarly reticent about Mélanie's histrionic talent—although his diary shows that he was appropriately indignant to note how little impression her restrained brand of acting made on the lusty Marseillais.

Indeed, he soon developed a cordial contempt for these earthy, vulgar southerners whose lives were divided between sordid business deals and boisterous pleasure-seeking. On Sundays, husbands, wives, mistresses, lovers, sweethearts and children swarmed over the surrounding countryside to devote the day to eating, drinking and love-making. During the week, the wives, left to their own resources, looked after the household and sought lovers whose generosity could be relied on to round out the budget, while the husbands loafed contentedly in their clubs and gaming rooms or in the hospitable salons of their mistresses.

"What a sojourn after you've lived in Paris," Beyle wrote. "Nothing is as materialistic as the people of Marseille . . . They haven't enough intelligence to be bored by their churlish pleasures; they gather to play whist or boston—and this at ten o'clock in the morning . . . The women are hyperpromiscuous and expect to be paid. The men are boorish and only know how to play the market: when it's bad, they go bankrupt; when it's good, they keep wenches."

The city displeased him almost as much as its too primitive inhabitants. He had not been a Parisian long enough to regard with indulgence the colorful life in Marseille, its pagan morality, its naïve religious processions, its conglomeration of races from all parts of the world. He saw only its provincialism, its vulgarity, its base materialism—all of which, inevitably recalling Grenoble, filled him with loathing.

For the first few weeks, however, Beyle was divinely happy, so happy, in fact, that he zealously set out to make his intimates as happy as himself. After prescribing daily doses of Tracy's *Idéologie* for Mélanie, he decided that the souls of his mistress and his sister Pauline were so much alike that they were "bound to love each other," and accordingly engineered a correspondence between the two. Nor did he neglect Mélanie's daughter, whom he would henceforth consider as his own. He wrote Pauline, asking her, if anything happened, to adopt the little girl, and telling her that he was leaving his entire fortune (?) to his mistress. The understanding Pauline wrote back that she herself had decided to bequeath two thirds of her possessions to Mélanie and her daughter.

These matters settled, Beyle turned his attention to arranging a match between his sister and Mante. As soon as Mante and he had made their fortune, the marriage could take place, and Pauline and Mante and Mélanie and himself (nothing was said about the latter two getting married) would live together in a house on the Boulevards of Paris, where they would entertain Tracy, Cabanis, Talma—all the leading figures of the literary and theatrical world.

And then there was poor little Louis Crozet. His engineering studies had taken him to Auxerre, where he had promptly fallen in love with Blanche de La Bergerie, the sixteen-year-old daughter of the Prefect of the Yonne. His timidity, homeliness and lack of money proving insurmountable obstacles, he had grown despondent and finally desperate. He bought some opium and romantically resolved to take his life. "Happily," said Beyle, "he wrote to me and waited for my answer. Time and I have induced him to form new habits: he's working like a madman."

While getting the others started on the road to felicity, Beyle himself was enjoying that "rustic and poetic happiness" of which he had so often dreamed while wandering through the Grésivaudan Valley or the green plains of Lombardy. Like the Marseillais, he and Mélanie packed a picnic lunch each Sunday and spent the day in the country. He was delighted with the picturesque roads, the streams, the cool glades, all of which, poverty-stricken as they were after the majestic scenery of Dauphiné, formed a welcome contrast to the dreary town. As the autumn advanced, however, the hours of pastoral solitude became fewer and fewer. The well-meaning Mante frequently tagged along, and, in the presence of his friend's misplaced enthusiasm, it was impossible for Beyle to recapture his Rousseauesque moods. Even worse were the days when he and Mélanie went picnicking with a band of eight or ten Marseillais, whose vulgar chatter kept him from feeling anything but ill humor.

It must be admitted that the people with whom Beyle and Mélanie associated—mostly odds and ends of the local mercantile and "artistic" crowd—were a sorry lot. The most picturesque was one Jean-Pierre-Aaron Seimandy de Saint-Gervais, a retired brigadier general and a would-be gentleman of the old school. Turning his distinguished appearance and his fifty-seven years to good advantage, Saint-Gervais paternally fondled feminine newcomers and, at the appropriate moment, hinted that they would do well to take him as a lover. At the other end of the social ladder was Mme. Cossonier, an ambiguous female who roomed at M. Rambert's and who, despite her bad reputation, seems invariably to have been present when anything was happening. A Parisian divorcée, proud to have had "a multitude of lovers," she was a washed-out blonde of thirty-five, shapely, crafty and gossipy.

In between the general and the divorcée were a score of pretentious nonentities. Besides these there were a few slightly more distinguished people whom Beyle visited without Mélanie (their liaison was not supposed to be known)—as Mme. Pallard, the hostess of one of the most select salons in Marseille, and Louis Tivollier, an old acquaintance from Grenoble, an easy-going bourgeois, given to boasting of his successes with other men's wives, and himself the possessor of a comely young spouse whom Beyle in turn hoped for a time to conquer.

As for the "bank"—that is, the office of Meunier's commission house —Beyle was obliged to "work like the devil" in the mornings copying letters which, after Shakespeare and Tracy, he found "horribly botched as to style and thought." In the afternoons he frequently had to go to the crowded, dusty docks to get merchandise out of the customs, help load casks of brandy for transportation to the warehouse and trudge through the hot streets dunning Meunier's debtors.

Casting about for a less drastic way to become familiar with the commercial life, he decided that it would be a good idea to go into partnership with his employer! He had little respect for Meunier's ability or his "wheedling ways," yet the firm was sound and, with a little new blood (Beyle and Mante, for instance), was capable of great things. A request was dispatched to Grenoble for 3,000 francs, which, placed with Meunier, might easily become 10,000 in a year or two. But "the bastard" refused to be convinced that Charles Meunier & Co. was as solid as the Rock of Gibraltar: there was always danger of bankruptcy was his argument, and he stuck to it.

As events turned out, he was right. Business in France had been bad since the rupture of the Treaty of Amiens in 1803, and just three weeks after Beyle indignantly scoffed at the possibility of bankruptcy the Battle of Trafalgar took place. The French fleet destroyed, the British soon organized a blockade that paralyzed the life of Marseille. Ships no longer entered or left the port, the quays were deserted, trade languished, employees were thrown out of work, and the firm of Charles Meunier & Co., fulfilling the predictions of Chérubin Beyle, was left hovering on the brink of ruin.

Then began a period of obligatory leisure which Beyle at first thoroughly enjoyed. But not for long. With the advent of 1806 and the return to the Gregorian calendar, it became increasingly evident that his honeymoon with Mélanie was drawing to a close. Five months of daily life with her had left him with few illusions that she was the ideal Julie he had been seeking. Instead of possessing the anticipated stormy passions, she had turned out to be cold and passive. He saw that the melancholy he had admired was nothing more than a chronic gloominess. Already jealous of his liberty, he rebelled against the "bondage" in which his mistress held him. But, worst of all, he had made the fatal discovery that Mélanie was stupid. His disenchantment having reached this stage just when his revived interest in study demanded solitude,

Beyle could not help realizing glumly that he had burdened himself with a clinging vine that must somehow be shaken off.

For Mélanie, the situation was even worse: having all but lost her lover, it now looked as though she was going to lose her livelihood. Owing to the blockade, which had impoverished the Marseillais, the actors of the Grand-Théâtre were playing to empty houses and the management was no longer paying them. On January 15 the company refused to continue. Mélanie, her savings almost gone, was faced with the prospect of returning to Paris, and Beyle with that of following her and living on what she could earn—or of abandoning her to her fate. He became very evasive about the future.

To make matters worse, his best friend, like his mistress, had failed to stand the test of daily association. Mante had turned out to be a thick-witted, insensitive boor, with no knowledge of social customs, no delicacy—all he knew was his *Idéologie* and his groceries. There it was: Mante had about decided to go into business with Meunier, Mélanie was returning to Paris, and Beyle frankly did not know what he was going to do. "I've embarked on a plank," he said wryly, "and a great many portions of this sorry plank are rotten." Henceforth, Mélanie's soul, the bank, Pauline's marriage with Mante and the house on the Boulevards were conspicuously absent from his letters to his sister.

But, far from being exhausted, his enthusiasm, after having successively embraced glory, love, happiness and fortune, soon found a new outlet in *ambition*. This unfamiliar seduction was the result of well-timed letters from Félix Faure, his grandfather and his uncle Romain Gagnon, all of whom drew attention to the fact that Pierre Daru, the benefactor whom he had neglected during the past four years, was now a Councilor of State, Napoleon's confidant and one of the most influential men in France. For Beyle to continue in a provincial commission house when he might be launching himself on a career in Paris was, his correspondents hinted, sheer insanity. Dr. Gagnon volunteered to patch matters up with Daru, while Romain suggested that he might drop a helpful word to Martial.

Overjoyed, Beyle immediately wrote his uncle and grandfather, urging them to spare no effort to get him a government job in Paris. Followed many letters but few results. Overburdened with work in Vienna on the morrow of the Battle of Austerlitz, Pierre Daru, now Intendant General of the Grande Armée, had other things to think about than hunting a job for his harum-scarum little cousin. When his reply finally came, it contained nothing more than a vague promise that he would "avail himself of the first opportunity" to place Henri in a suitable position.

Meanwhile, Mélanie had started back to Paris, and Beyle, at first delighted at his new-found freedom, soon became familiar for the first time in his life with the devastating effects of boredom. Was it a longing for Mélanie, whose shortcomings seemed less glaring with the passage of time, or was it some weakness in his own character? He analyzed the situation and decided that the key to happiness was held by Pierre Daru, not Mélanie Guilbert.

The weeks dragged by with Beyle sinking farther and farther into the morass of blockaded Marseille's banal, vulgar life. Eventually the letters he received from his grandfather began to be "terrible" ones urging him to come back to Grenoble. Indeed, what was keeping him in Marseille? He was no longer working for Meunier, he was bored to death, the hot dusty summer was approaching. But Beyle had his pride: there was glory in being summoned to the capital to enter the service of Napoleon, while to return empty-handed to his family was a shameful admission of failure.

But he did not have much choice in the matter, and after a solemn conference with Mante he resigned himself to the inevitable. The two erstwhile banking partners took a few last strolls around this crass southern town where Beyle for the first time had had his nose rubbed in reality and which now seemed shrouded in a poetic mist. Mante, who had finally gone into partnership with Meunier, accompanied him to the stagecoach. As the horses started out, he waved farewell to his old friend: he never saw him again. The port, Marseille, the blue slice of the Mediterranean disappeared from his thoughts almost as soon as from his sight, and he slowly made his way through the Alps, now by coach, now on horseback, dreaming of the honors and women he hoped would be his.

1805-6 Grenoble—Marseille—Grenoble

TRAVEL IN GRENOBLE IN THE SPRING OF 1805[1]

[*Grenoble*] 2 *Messidor* [*June 21*].—I feel that I'm spoiling the anticipated pleasure of my trip to Marseille through stupid, depressing and degrading discussions about it with my father and grandfather. They oppose me with stupid reasons (these are the reasons for those three adjectives), they predict a gloomy future for me in general, and in particular they show me in detail the humiliating steps that will have to be taken. They have both become misers. My grandfather sees

[1]Title in English in the manuscript.

obstacles everywhere, and wants to put off everything until some other time. My father starts all over again discussing the obstacles and wailing about them after it's been pointed out to him a thousand times how they can be surmounted. Is this on purpose, or is it from weakness of head and heart?

That such people, and, generally speaking, stupid heads and unfeeling hearts, or both together, should be able to influence my happiness is a great piece of nonsense on my part. In the first place, even giving them credit for good heads, all they can do is to show me the sensations they've experienced in such-and-such a situation in which they've found themselves and through which I have yet to pass; and, as our hearts are quite different, it's more than likely that I'll have quite different sensations in the same situations. The proof is clear: if I had their position in society, wouldn't I make my life entirely different from theirs?

Their sensations have value for me only because, being separated by the connection between me and them, they forecast those I'll have myself. This is all the benefit I could derive from them if they had an excellent head, but it's a very bad one. Therefore, everything they tell me ought to be considered just so much *sound, empty words,* and nothing more. It's the height of nonsense to let myself be affected by it.

Fortunately, it seems to me that I let myself be less affected by it each day. Today, they were little more than a subject of reflection for me; two years ago, their contemptible ideas would have completely sullied my future for a day or two, and would have brought about my unhappiness.

I ought to tell myself that I'm living in a madhouse. My reason is aware of this, but my soul is too sensitive. If I were unfeeling like all the stupid animals I see here, there would be no need of my being upset.

It's impossible for them to give me any pleasure when I converse with them; practically nothing of what they say to me is not disagreeable. The words they use to remind me of all the things they've done for me are almost always false, their manner of doing these things is humiliating. Remain the facts that they might teach me, but they are few in number, usually badly observed and even worse told.

Only the absurdity of their actions saves them from being odious. For example, my father gave me twelve livres eight or ten days ago, the eve of my departure for the Grande-Chartreuse; I spent them an hour later for my share of the expenses of the trip; ever since then, I have literally been without a sou. I've just asked him for some money, experiencing, I don't know why, a feeling of contempt and repugnance because I foresaw the ridiculousness, and I foresaw too that I'd have to struggle a minute in order to see only the ridiculousness of the action, instead of the odium that it would represent for me the first minute. He gravely handed me two little écus. What is there to reply to such a procedure?

Since then I've ordered a pair of shoes that will cost me six or seven francs. I've had my boots cleaned, and taken ices or beer regularly at the expense of my comrades, without ever buying a round in my turn. By spending the least possible and contracting some debts, I have consequently spent, previous to 2 Messidor, today, more money than he gravely gave me to spend in the future. In addition to this, I had the pleasure of never having *a single sou* in my pocket for unforeseen expenses, and yet I am a rich young man, and the young men are considered rich in this town, and they really are rich.

My father is short of cash, but he experiences a secret pleasure in being so, because at bottom he feels he isn't spending money he doesn't possess. He's full of fine words, he argues because he feels that the only thing he has to show us is his straitened circumstances; if he sells his house tomorrow and has some funds: 1st, the sight of so much money is going to put him in a holy state of anxiety; 2nd, he'll be in a temper, and fly into a rage in order not to have to argue with us.

When he talks to us, I'm obliged constantly to restrain the indignation given me by meanness, or at least the impulse to restrain a man who is visibly in error. I see them driven by contemptible reasons to argue, and, through arguing, to reach false conclusions. FOR MY HAPPINESS BY THE FAME OF GREAT BARD, I must accustom myself to return easily to a maxim . . .

6 Messidor [June 25].—I'm rereading most of my notebooks. I find them filled with commonplaces, but perhaps they wouldn't appear so simple if I had not discovered them laboriously.

I believe that in the future I'll write nothing but THE WORLD [society] itself in the form of anecdotes.

They bore me and make me depressed.

3 Thermidor [July 22].—I AM PARTED FROM Grenoble THE 3 Thermidor XIII AT 12 IN THE BARIOT'S DILIGENCE FOR Valence WITH A CONDUCTOR NAMED France, MISS Revol AND MISTER Le Roux, I BESIDE.

Mlle. Revol was haughty with me. I replied to her very civilly, I did this quite naturally because of Mlle. Talencieu. The conversation got going little by little, with the result that, when we reached the beautiful countryside around Tullins, she made my ears ring with the names of the property owners along the road. She next took me into her confidence regarding her affairs, and explained that she and her brothers had a trusted servant at Alba. The garden of M. de Lupé, seen through the grille, appeared to me really fine in the manner of Le Nôtre.

Journal of His Life

From 9 Thermidor, Year XIII, to April 15, 1806

The beginning of this notebook still smacks too much of the pedant of the Rue d'Angiviller. (January 30, 1809.)
I'll love you till death and I'll never survive you.

READ

I have no need of warning that this notebook, because of its childishness, is written for absolutely no one but myself.

Consequently, I beg anyone who may find it not to read it: 1st, in the name of honor; 2nd, in that of the inevitable boredom it would give him.

Forgive me the pedantry and the ridiculous self-importance of which I haven't yet been able to purge myself entirely.

9 Thermidor [July 28].—I MOVED FROM Paris THE . . . Floréal YEAR XIII, WITH HER, WE WERE AT Lyon THE . . . OF THE SAME MONTH. SHE MOVED FOR Marseille THE 24 Floréal, I BELIEVE. I ARRIVED IN Grenoble THE . . . AFTER TWO MONTHS AND . . . DAYS OF inaction, somber boredom AND SOMEWHAT DESPAIR, I finally left for Marseilles 3 Thermidor XIII.

I left in the mail coach at noon, arrived the 4th at six o'clock in the morning at Valence, the sun shining full on the cliff opposite, on the other side of the Rhône. Had I believed what I was told, I'd only have reached Marseille a week later, BUT LOVE HAD GIVEN WINGS TO ME. However, it wasn't by flying that I arrived at Avignon, but in a boat which was transporting two millstones, one weighing fifty quintals and the other forty, and each worth 1,000 francs.

I left Valence at eight o'clock under a bright sun, having as companions one of the most prodigious asses I ever met, M. Boissieu of Saint-Marcellin, such an ass in general and at times so inane that I was ashamed to appear to know him, and some workmen, among whom were several characters worth observing; found the characters about the same as their facial expressions showed them to be. A gay, straightforward, candid and strong character in the master of the millstones, a character similar to that of Rebuffel. The chief: same character, but not as good a head; his gravity, standing on his plank, his oar in his arms, gravity of the circumstances.

Shadowless and burning heat in the boat at noon. On the banks, ugly little rocks, peeled and burned by the sun, surmounted by some old fortifications of the light and elegant variety, of the svelte variety, but with the unsubstantial appearance of the Arabs. Morals of the boatmen, seeking the happiness of the present, and thus being comparable with military morals.

The banks became less arid a few leagues above Bourg-Saint-Andéol, the noonday wind rose and cooled us off, we were obliged to call it a day at Saint-Andéol. Pretty hostesses; southern morals, far different from the highway morals of Paris and Dauphiné.

We stayed in Saint-Andéol from five in the evening until three in the morning. The boatmaster sang, vulgarity of Boissieu; striking superiority of the boatmaster's character over his. Boissieu, claiming that he had seen me at M. Belair's six years ago, tried by every means to get to know me, and even took it upon himself to address me in the second person singular.

We passed the Pont-Saint-Esprit without the least danger and at quite an ordinary speed; absurdity of the reputed peril. I've already noticed the same thing at the Saint-Bernard and Mont-Cenis. The bridge is elegant, still in the same style of architecture, Saracen or Arab, I believe. Elegance, lightness, cleanliness of the brick constructions. This bridge has perhaps forty arches, of which twenty-six, I believe, are large ones; the others are cut through the arches, and the Rhône doesn't flow through them except during the heavy floods. I thoroughly examined all that and the number of arches; but, as those physical details, which have no effect on the emotions, don't interest me, I've forgotten them. The same thing has happened to me on all my voyages.

The boat stopped on the shore of Avignon at noon. We went to Saint-Omer, quite a clean inn, a very honest landlord.

I didn't have time to observe anything. Only the mayor of Avignon, a man of great energy. They told me later that Bonaparte had made him independent of the Prefect.

The white houses, full of dust, blinding as in Italy, some resemblance to the grandiose style of Italy. In the towns of the North (Nevers, Chalon, Lyon, Grenoble), the dirt on the house walls is damp and blackish, greenish. Nemours, Fontainebleau and Paris have a whiter and cleaner appearance. Avignon, Aix and Marseille, on the contrary, are white, dry, full of dust.

A young porter, handsome, vigorous, with a cheerful face (the valet who served us at table told me he could carry 900 pounds), came to offer us his services; he arranged all our affairs for us, struck a bargain with a boatman who promised to take us to Beaucaire. The porter carried our luggage to the boat at two o'clock.

Fine bridge falling in ruins, from which, nevertheless, there is only one arch missing. Its appearance is quite grandiose. We passed through an arch, fine color (worn olive = mat gray) of antiquity.

Our boatman, a face out of Raphael; there must have been refinement on this face at one time, it now bears the marks of hard labor; fine features, a mind stultified by the desire to make a few sous. A man avid of his subsistence, seeing nothing else—for me that was touching. A twelve-year-old son whom he mistreats in order to lose less time in ordering him around, clad in a horribly coarse shirt, unconcerned. An elder son (I believe), a young man of twenty resembling Raphael painted by himself at the age of fifteen. (His head resting on his hand, tricornered hat, Napoleon Museum). Only he was darker, more energetic; in a word, he was dark and twenty years old. Raphael was only fifteen. His eyes absolutely like those of Raphael's subjects, shadow on the upper eyelid, much more pronounced than in the sculptured Greek heads.

These people touched me, I saw excessive labor—the result of bad government—become a punishment. At the same time, I told myself that one must not hate work because of its bad reputation, that my work at the bank would be far less painful.

The boat was horribly crowded with common people. Continually increasing asininity of Boissieu.

We arrived at Beaucaire, I didn't get off, I finally left on some log rafts, and had myself landed on the Tarascon side with a porter whom I took with me. But right now I feel too deeply to keep on with details which have so little effect on the emotions; I feel that my soul is worthy of contemplating *Apollo* and of working on another one if I had some modeling material at hand. I've passed the time since two o'clock far from Mélanie and Mante, who are in the country, I've passed the time alone. That's what forms, intensifies, the soul. I've had time to enjoy my feeling.

I am stopping to describe because I've already observed that I thus spoiled my memories, that mellow part of life. I'd need fifty hours of work with a burning sensibility, flowing like an all-inundating river, to describe what I felt between three o'clock and nine (now). That isn't possible; I'd consequently describe badly, and a fortnight from now I'd no longer recall what I'd written down. Therefore, I'll only write ridiculous and satiric anecdotes; I'd be crazy indeed to spoil my tender memories. Therefore, I'll speak only of what influences me, of the sentiment that fills my every moment; I feel almost nothing that's foreign to it.

6 Thermidor [*July 25*].—I arrived at Marseille at six in the evening. First view of the sea in my life, from the *Vista*. The diligence stopped in the

Rue Beauvau. I went to Mante's, he arrived. H, H, H, H[1] at eight o'clock in the evening. I went to bed at half-past eleven. I SEE HER AT THE GREAT THEATER; Gavaudan WAS ACTING *Aline* THE QUEEN OF *Golconda.*

7 *Thermidor* [*July 26*].—I SEE HER IN HER CHAMBER AT ELEVEN O'CLOCK OF THE MORNING. I had dinner with the Tivolliers.

8 *Thermidor* [*July 27*].—I began at the bank.[2]

9 *Thermidor* [*July 28*].—I mystify Miaille. I write this.

SAID TO THE FATHER, THAT MY TRAVEL FROM Grenoble TO Marseille HAD COUTED [COST] TO ME six louis AND HALF.

10 *Thermidor* [*July 29*].—Mante and I crossed the bridge and went to look at the open sea. THE EVENING TILL THE MID-NIGHT, FOR EVER.

12 *Thermidor* [*July 31*].—Saw *Les Templiers* AND SHE FOR THE FIRST TIME. *Les Templiers,* BAD play WITHOUT characters OR INTEREST. SHE HAS A CHARMING WHITE CROWN.

14 *Thermidor* [*August 2*].—WE GO TO THE APPLE,[3] Mélanie, Mante AND I, FROM THE 6 O'CLOCK ½ TILL THE 10½, BEAUTIFUL LITTLE WAYS [paths].

16 *Thermidor* [*August 4*].—THE EVENING SHE, MANTE AND I, WE COME TO THE CASTEL BORELY. WE WALK FOR IT AT THE HALF AFTER SIX, AND WE ARE AT THE CITY AT THE A QUARTER PAST ELEVEN. The seashore.—The sound of the waves.—The two fishermen who passed along the strip of land between the Huveaune and the sea.—The star above the Château d'If and disappearing behind it.—The darkness behind us, the daylight toward the Château d'If.—We sat near the sea.—This is the first time I've seen it, roaring thus and so vast in extent.

Returning at half-past nine, we found that our coachman (WHAT HAD GONE FOR 10 livres) had left. He hadn't been paid, a trait typical of the provinces. We returned afoot, and arrived at a quarter past eleven.[4]

20 *Thermidor* [*August 8*].—M. de Saint-Gervais blaming the bad manners of the Sub-Prefect of Aix, and repeating *with child* instead of *pregnant,* playing the grammatical pedant and dwelling lengthily thereon, finding Mme. de Genlis's *Les Veillées du Château* a model of *all those little things you have forgotten.* Apparently he considers these to be of great importance.

How true it is that an artist should believe only in himself! Once he's sure of having translated his soul for the public, he should no longer see in his verse, for instance, the emotion he experienced in composing it and which it makes him remember, but only that emotion which he has expressed, and the manner in which he has expressed it;

[1] Probably happy, happy, etc.

[2] More exactly, Meunier's wholesale grocery house.

[3] La Pomme, then a rustic spot, outside Marseille.

[4] That's one of my finest memories. (January 31, 1809.) [Note by Beyle.]

he should no longer believe anyone, but he should listen to everyone. Other people make him rejudge his work; hence, you shouldn't listen to absurd opinions unless you feel like rejudging.

On the 18th, I believe, we went to Les Aygalades, a spot similar to the cascades of Font-Belle, a little shadier perhaps, but not worth the woods at the Château de Tencin. Leaving at half-past five with Mélanie, M. de Saint-Gervais and M. Baux, we arrived at the château, saw a view which was vast but arid and not in the least appealing; we took the wrong road to Les Aygalades, and didn't reach there until nightfall. Returned at half-past ten, somewhat bored. To go to see a fine site isn't sufficient to amuse and affect you, your impressions depend on the persons you're with. SHE, M. AND I alone would have amused ourselves as much as the dull, vain, narrow-minded Saint-Gervais and the stupid Baux, annoying SHE AND ME, bored both themselves and us.

I've been to La Pomme three or four times, as many to the Château Borély, twice to Arrailh. I'm describing nothing in order to spoil nothing.

25 *Fructidor* [*September 12*].—Eccentrics to characterize: Saint-Gervais, Meunier, Baux, Tivollier, Faure, Miaille the elder, Miaille the younger, Petit, Girard, Victor Tivollier, Mme. Tivollier, Mme. Chauvet.

Among all these, there are but two, M. de Saint-Gervais and M. Girard, who are eligible to appear in high society. Girard ought to be more successful there than M. de Saint-Gervais. Meunier and Saint-Gervais are the two men we know best.

Since I've been here, the only thing I've read is Mme. de Staël's *L'Influence des Passions*. The truths this book presents would have given me much more pleasure if it hadn't been for the detestable bombast which, I believe, Mme. de Staël mistakes for eloquence. I read, thoroughly enjoying it, half of the first volume of Cardinal de Retz and Ducis's *Abufar, ou la Famille Arabe*.

On the other hand, I've thought a great deal. It seems to me that I'm recovering a bit from the literary nonsense I got from the host of minor artists I used to read indiscriminately. My way of thinking is acquiring more truth, forcefulness and profundity. The mercantile spirit, which calculates everything and is enthusiastic about nothing, is useful to me. I haven't any desire to read the philosophers I already know, they'd put me back in the rut where I was six months ago. Yet, I'm tempted to reread Hobbes, as well as the thoughts I wrote out in Paris, in order to get whatever is good out of them. I might get one notebook of truths out of the ten or twelve of junk that I brought along with me; and that notebook would perhaps be again reduced next year when I see things with more profundity.

Since my arrival, I haven't read twenty lines of Racine, Corneille or Molière.

Barral has written me four or five letters from aboard the *Neptune,* on which he has embarked. Crozet hasn't written me since Grenoble. It seems to me that trade has given me a little curiosity about political events, while the habit of reasoning has given me a little contempt for the delicate articles of *Le Publiciste,* which I liked fairly well in Paris.

9 Vendémiaire, XIV [October 1].—Mélanie told me that I saw that M. Wildermeth had some subtlety because he talked to Mme. Cossonier and Mme. Blanc. "Well, you see, he doesn't talk to me the way he does to them, he doesn't say the same things to me."

From which I conclude that one of the most flattering things for women is to address them from the outset in a different sort of speech from that which they think you have with other women.

Today I reread part of the notebook *della Filosofia Nuova,* written in Messidor, Year XII. I found its contents very youthful, not very profound, even not profound at all, they aren't thought out: I BELIEVE THAT MY TALENT IS PERHAPS FOR BE THE BARD, but I feel that I lack philosophic genius (turn of mind). I believe I'll have to apply myself seriously to *idéologie* and to rereading the philosophers.

Besides that, there's the arrogance of ignorance in this notebook. I'm more satisfied with my notebook OF POETRY.

17 Vendémiaire [October 9].—Simple [Mante] said some things that were very jejune tonight. It appears that, pretending (or believing) "it doesn't mean anything," that "they're only bits of nonsense" (these are his terms), he'd permit himself to do many things that are opposed to delicacy, and even to honor, if he felt like it. In this respect, Mélanie regards him as completely dishonored.

The subject came up in connection with the matter of opening Mme. Quesnel's letters. Mélanie's look when I went in at half-past ten, a moment after the exit of M. de Saint-Gervais, she having already knocked three times.

She was looking forward to telling me right away all she'd just heard; Mante, who followed me in, put a damper on everything. After his departure, as while he was present, she was distracted, she no longer talked to me with impetuosity.

If I could get down to writing four pages a day on M. de Saint-Gervais, I'd have a superb character in a short time. I must tell his story (but it's for myself; if anyone ever finds this notebook, I beg him to stop here).

Mélanie didn't believe me when I told her he was in love with her; his line is always the same, a few jokes—only a bit more off-color.

"If a person could ask for something, I'm sure I know what you'd ask for."

"And what?"

"Some bosom. Anyway, be consoled; that's the shortcoming of women of quality."[1] Etc., etc.

That appeared impertinent and was displeasing.

"Love isn't a natural thing, it's the product of society."

Every day he would give her a delicate little present: a coral necklace for the Saint-Nicolas Fair, some quail at dinnertime, a frock of embroidered percale, purchased before her for five louis from Mme. Cossonier, a flask of tea, a bottle of old Malaga.

Always arriving with a ready-made compliment, this compliment frequently a bad one, invariably inept; I've seen him say twice on the same occasion, at a week's interval: *"Medicus sum, non sum coquinus. Do you know Latin? Etc."* That means absolutely nothing. From time to time, a timid face displaying emotion permitted me to see his love.

At length, about a week ago, I found Mélanie very upset at six in the evening; she swore me to secrecy about what she was going to tell me.

"M. de Saint-Gervais is in love with me."

"Aha, at last!"

"The poor man touched me." (And she was very much so: he'd produced the impression of magnanimity in her heart.)

M. de Saint-Gervais: "A very great misfortune has befallen me."

"Really? Is it something irreparable?"

"Yes, I shall never see you again."

"What, you'll never see me again!" (Turning around on the sofa, clasping her hands tightly and ending by taking one of his, which she squeezed.)

"No, I'm leaving Tuesday for the Army of Germany. You know my position, when I left the service I was the senior brigadier of the Army. (Etc., etc., etc., etc.) Kellermann is my friend, he's in command of an army corps in Strasbourg, and I'm leaving Tuesday. Anyway, I'd have been obliged not to see you any more. Since I'm leaving, I can confess to you: I'm in love with you. At my age, I well realize that I cannot entertain any hopes." (Etc., etc., etc.)

In a word, he played the modest, and so successfully that I found Mélanie as affected as possible by his loftiness of soul.

I shared this impression, but it lasted a shorter time with me than with her, because the self-interest of my love made me reckon too much with M. de Saint-Gervais to sympathize with him for long. I wasn't at all jealous of Mélanie's exaltation; I saw that this impression was a cold one, and, as it can't be renewed daily in an intelligent woman

[1] Mélanie was a little too thin even for Beyle's taste.

unless there are very real sacrifices, as it almost entirely excludes grace, I saw that this impression of admiration couldn't last long.

He came back the next day, spoke of his love and made a nuisance of himself at the end of a quarter of an hour; he let a day go by without speaking of it, and then he spoke of it again; he finally asked Mélanie's advice, and told her that perhaps it might be better to wait for Marshal Kellermann's answer before taking such an important step as to go away. Mélanie began to have some doubts as to his sincerity.

Since then, he's pursued her to the point of becoming importunate. He used to see her a half or three quarters of an hour, from three to four or a quarter past four [sic]; for the past few days, he's been coming at two o'clock and even earlier, he returns in the evening and stays on interminably. He seeks to have the appearance of being a lover, continually whispering to Mélanie, and that right in front of me and M. *Leases* [Baux]. He scores up tallies over the latter in an outrageous way, endlessly talking of good manners and devoting the time to giving lessons in them that he ought to use in practicing them.[1] He's taken the liberty of making the strangest declarations to Mélanie.

Having, moreover, previously advised Mélanie to live with a man who would be good to her.

"Love is an artificial sentiment that isn't natural, it's only love of self. —I am generous with women, and known to be so; the benefits of my favors would follow you wherever you went."

In a word, all the remarks showing the most consummate vanity, the purest and most thorough; not the slightest sensibility tempers it.

His literary judgments are in harmony with his actions in showing this character. "Crébillon is the most charming novelist in existence. *Tanzaï* (ah, what a tale!) and *Le Sofa* are delightful. Rousseau is lacking in taste." Etc., etc.

I've been a fool not to write every evening. At length, yesterday, Tuesday, 16 Vendémiaire XIV, I came to see Mélanie at four o'clock. Madelon [Mélanie's maid] said she went out at seven, she was at Mme. Cossonier's. I heard her come in. I was jealous of M. Wildermeth and very angry.

I saw her, I could not help loving her, literally. She told me she was having one of her gloomy days, I urged her to come to the theater. The weather was so mild that we went to the Cours and as far as the end of the Allées de Meilhan, having gone to learn what had become of M. Truci, Junior, her doctor. She confessed to me during this charming walk that she had passed the whole day crying, at first sobbing so much that she was prevented from crying, that she shut herself up from

[1]Not bad. [Note by Beyle eight years later.]

everybody. M. de Saint-Gervais had come at one o'clock and made the strangest scene possible. He started by asking her for a moment's audience.

"I'm ready to listen to you."

"But tell your maid to say that you're not in. M. Baux or M. Beyle may come and interrupt me."

". . . I can't give an appearance of mystery when there is none. You may talk as much as you wish, but I don't intend to close the door."

"Not a woman in town would refuse me that."

I'll continue tonight, I'm obliged to go out. At eleven o'clock, having reached a decision, Mélanie calmed down completely. In my presence, she wrote M. *White* [Le Blanc] everything that had happened to her, that she was frightened; and it was true. M. de Saint-Gervais is the sort of man who would take her to an isolated house in the country, have her held down by four men, and violate her. He might do this with Cervoni, and, with the aforementioned general, by whom he constantly swears, buy off Madelon and the whole household in order to have the appearance of success, and certainly to try to dishonor her when he sees that he isn't able to have her. She's going to tell the good Leases about M. de Saint-Gervais's love at nine o'clock this morning.

I was frightened myself in the Allées de Meilhan when she repeated two anecdotes that M. de Saint-Gervais had told her, undoubtedly with a purpose, but that look as though they were true. He confesses that he is vain, makes no bones about it, shows it by the strangest kind of conversation. "Be it said without vanity, I have wit and social experience, I'm pleasing to women—I least I have the reputation of being so." I'll take down his words textually.

In fine, this unprincipled man, possessed of a vanity that turns everything to misfortune, a mind best suited for vengeance, not a shadow of sympathy, of social experience, of consideration, might well be a deepdyed scoundrel.

4 Brumaire [*October 26*].—I've just been to see the role of Phaedra played BY Mélanie. I'm learning to imagine a whole audience being mistaken, and consequently the opinion of a single man being worth more than that of two thousand, but, SEEING Mélanie abandoned by Leases, Little, AND ALL HER FRIENDS BUT Seym,[1] I've thought that, even AT Paris, SHE DID CAN WELL PERFORM AND NOT BE APPLAUSED.

8 Brumaire [*October 30*].—I've just been to Michel's [reading room]. Excitement of all the readers over the victories at Ulm.

17 Brumaire [*November 8*].—Last night before going to bed we said we'd

[1]The reference is to Beyle himself. Seym = *Seymours*, the name of his first dramatic attempt.

get up at seven o'clock this morning and go on an excursion and return at ten o'clock.

This morning we got up at half-past eight and filled a black half bottle with wine. I took it, I went to the pastry cook's next door to Casati's, where I bought two cold thrushes, a lark and two little pies, one with jam and the other with cream. We reached the Montfuront fields by going across some private properties. We had a delicious lunch under a tree, enjoying that rustic and poetic happiness I've so often imagined, particularly at Saint-Vincent and in Italy. Under the tree, we left some bread and almost a whole pie, which we scattered about for the happiness of some birds. Here is how the Montfuront fields are laid out, four regiments of dragoons could easily make a charge in them.[1]

After taking our time over the lunch, being fully conscious of our happiness, she delighted with the fine weather and only complaining from time to time of the pain between her shoulders which she noticed yesterday as she was leaving the theater, we started making a tour of the fields.

Two men, O and O', who were talking, of whom O' had a rifle, prevented us from going to the end of the fields on the north. We rested at R in a charming spot and at R', our feet in the sun and our heads in the shade of the trunk of a large poplar. She told me that I looked as though I was dying to do that; it was true, but that wasn't all I desired. I'd have liked a few more transports on her part—or, more exactly, a few transports. As far as beauty was concerned, no one could be more fortunate; I had, in a measure that surpassed my hopes, a sublime beauty, the grace of the most beautiful Grecian heads; but what I would have liked was a few of the transports that I imagined Angelina [Pietragrua] had. I was ready to soar, but, in order to do so, I had need of that (a remarkable thing in MY LOVE FOR HER).

While we were resting, at R I believe, I told her that her character was better adapted to love a man who inspired confidence and a certain admiration. At the word "admiration," she burst out:

"I've admired too much, my admiration is exhausted."

"You're a clinging vine, you've attached yourself to a little tree, and the result is that you're worried; what you need instead is a big tree in which you could have full confidence."

More or less that. She said I was perfectly right.

Talking about my love and M. Leases, we went as far as L, to the gate. We returned by the line WW. I said that I would bet he addressed

---

[1]Follows a rough sketch in the manuscript, to which the letters in the text refer. To the end of his life, Stendhal retained the habit of covering his manuscripts with sketches of the scenes he was describing.

her in the second person singular; she denied it, then admitted it, losing patience a little. "Well, yes, then, I address him in the second person singular."

She said it was a fine question to ask her IF Leases had been HER LOVING; I repeated that I'd be delighted to learn that he was the one; she told me I could wait five months and a half if I wanted to, she asked me if I feared him at a distance of two hundred and fifty leagues. I told her that he had addressed her in the second person singular at least when he said, "I love you [*Je t'aime*]."

"Oh yes," she said, "we're always quarreling."

"But the reconciliations . . ."

"Do we become reconciled, then?" (For so little, she meant . . .)

"But when you were mad at him?"

She repeated a bit of conversation in order to cover up the gesture.

"He took my hand, he kissed it, he bent over it, and I believe that he . . . that he . . . was crying, from the way he choked."

"I see."

That's the general sense of the conversation. We went to the gate M, I went out, she didn't. I said, in an attempt to make her tell me whether Leases was in the habit of addressing her in the second person singular, that several things would take place within me; I explained the mechanical effect that would produce, and that existed—and I didn't at all feel the things that I told her would happen or were happening.

At length, at E, she said:

"There's the tree under which we ate our lunch," pointing to P. I, who, as I passed, had remarked our pieces of gray wrapping paper under the tree H, and who moreover, recalling perfectly the scene of the lunch, saw clearly that it wasn't P, said no.

Everything that follows, with the greatest vivacity.

Henri: "Let's make a wager: if it isn't that tree, you'll tell me whether Leases addresses you in the second person singular; if it is that tree, I'll do anything you wish."

"But what could I ask of you? You have nothing to tell me."

"Anything you want, I promise to tell you everything you ask me in the future."

"Well then, if it is that tree, you won't sleep with me for five months and a half . . ." (stressing her words and observing me), "until our return to Paris.—Even if I beg you to, you'll resist, you'll be firm."

I pretended to hesitate a little; actually, I didn't hesitate. In a strained manner, and a bit tragically: "Well, all right then; I promise."

At once I leaped over the ditch, I ran from φ to P. I made sure it wasn't our tree; on the way back, I saw the paper from our cream pie, I said to her, "It's not that one, come and see the other."

She returned slowly—pensive, inwardly upset. I leaped across the ditch at B, she passed it, she came within range of H. Then at +, turning back two paces after, she said: *"Well then, yes, he addresses me in the second person singular."* (Declamation of avowal, deeply felt and a bit restrained.) Wager at E.

Immediately we became silent. She lowered her eyes, had a disturbed look, and tears even flowed from her eyes.

I'm tired, I'll close as I have very little feeling anyway.

She remained serious until the moment when, tying her shoe, I smiled at her; she smiled back at me.

We separated in the Rue Saint-Ferréol. I returned at noon to the store, and, as there was nothing to do, I wrote this right away.

Around 20 Brumaire [*November 11*].—Fetes two Sundays in a row.

The first, at Arrailh, Mme. Cossonier, Mélanie, Messrs. Saint-Gervais, Baux, Garnier and I.

An impromptu party, gay because everyone satisfied his dominant passion.—Mélanie became animated, was even prettier than usual, had that kind of grace which Mlle. Mars, ordinarily so reserved, had for me in *Les Folies Amoureuses.*

M. de Saint-Gervais, as pedantic and affected as ever. Mme. Cossonier didn't become animated at all. Her behavior at the end of the meal appeared tame and like that of an old woman.

I don't know what was the matter with her, but she's usually licentious in such circumstances.—She took me into her confidence.

A week later, Sunday, a party arranged in advance, the contrary of the first, depressing. Everyone was irritable. We went to La Renarde.

Six hours in the carriage; the ladies, going, and I, returning, were sick to the stomach. A good dinner next to the column in the Rue Paradis. They talked of nothing but me, a brilliant role in a sense, and one which offended Saint-Gervais (the perfect example of the vain man, worthy of the stage; his character is really sufficiently unadulterated for that, the only thing lacking is a plot that would completely develop it).

A brilliant but very awkward role in my position. I assailed false love, analyzed the true, and saw nothing but temperament and vanity in that, which made me seem insensitive to our four guests, who suspected me of being the *amante riamato di* Mélanie.

Carried away by vanity without realizing it, I was foolish enough to let them talk about me.

Baux was simple and asinine, pretty much of a fool.

Mme. Cossonier stood up for me, pretending to be my dupe. Mélanie was grateful to her for that.

Garnier, silly as a goose, led me on and repeated thirty times that I wasn't showing my hand.

Saint-Gervais played host at the dinner, and a fortnight later, having lost hope of succeeding with Mélanie, called on his guests to pay for it.

Since then, I've drunk punch and flaming rum and brandy two or three times with Mme. Cossonier and Rosa; I could have the latter without the least trouble, but *non voglio esser infedele alle dive, e mi disgusta* [I don't want to be unfaithful to the goddess, and she disgusts me].

22 *Brumaire [November 13].—The Geffrier Ball.*—At half-past nine, Mante and I went to M. Baux's in the pouring rain, just about the first since my arrival in Marseilles. Our stockings were so wet that Mante went to get some others. At about a quarter past ten, we reached the home of Mme. Geffrier, who was giving a ball for the whole town.

Asininity of most of the men's faces.—Idiotically vain appearance of the young men.—Crozet the younger, alone, the gracious manners of a Parisian.—His elder brother, the best manners of the ball. Wildermeth would have them too, were it not for his consummately cruel face.—Belville danced very well, the steps of the gavotte well, but a bit awkward and bashful in the body.

Birdlike high spirits of Mme. Blanc, who looked as though she wanted to be in everything for fear of not being in anything.

Mme. Thibaudeau's appearance of a gawky wench, especially striking while she was dancing. Idiotic dignity, self-satisfaction.

General Cervoni, like all athletic figures, improves when seen at close range; his face has character, of the kind of the salesman Rossi's, but looks cleaner.

We left at two o'clock. It seems to me that balls bore me. I'd soon be boring at them. I danced only one quadrille.

[*Frimaire*].—Mme. Cossonier is lewd in the full meaning of the word after three glasses of flaming rum; after one, she's only gossipy. During the first session, she told us the whole story of her divorce, in the second that of her second child's death.

She's been making advances to me since around 1 Frimaire, and wants to have me.—JEALOUSY OF Mélanie THAT LOVE ME MORE FOR THAT.

21 *Frimaire [December 12]*.—We've been reading a lot of Tracy's *Logique* since 14 Brumaire, XIV. I started it again today, 21 Frimaire.

I've closely observed Saint-Gervais, Baux, Mme. Cossonier, Meunier; these are four good characters. I've put several of my observations in my letters to the discerning and sensitive Crozet.

I agree with Tracy: *nosce te ipsum,* know thyself, is a source of happiness.

I've often thought I had passions that I really didn't have in my life from Year X to the middle of Year XIII, the time IN WHAT I BEGAN TO LOVE Mélanie.

This erroneous belief has caused me to lose much time and has given me many moments of despair.

But *love* (as it is understood by Cabanis) formed the prime mover of my character, the other passions could do no more than distract me from it.

The love of glory has again taken the upper hand; it has made me read Tracy.

I must now fathom an old judgment which, I believe, is but one of Condillac's ideas: it was that it's useless to read books of logic; it's essential to try to reason correctly, and that's all.

The rules that Tracy prescribes at the end of his *Science de Nos Moyens de Connaître* are so simple that I can quite well try to put them into practice. They consist in retracing the memory of the thing on which one wishes to reason, and then in being careful to see that the subject always contains the attribute given it.

All our errors come from our memories. Therefore, it's an immense advantage to have a good memory. I have, I believe, a very good one: Crozet calls Beyle "the man with the terrible memory." I must cultivate mine, not by learning things by heart, but by practicing recalling facts with all their circumstances.

24 *Frimaire* [*December 15*].—At Mme. Cossonier's, I suggested giving a comedy. They spoke of *La Petite Ville;* Mme. Cossonier put some rouge on me. I got away at eight to go to get Lambert at the theater. He . . . (Madelon interrupted me here, and I went to spend the evening with Mélanie. I rehearsed her in *Andromaque,* which she's playing tomorrow; afterward, while she was removing the peplum from her dress, I read the first volume of Marmontel's *Mémoires,* which I read last year in a very different situation. I made some tea, which I took with some fresh butter patties. I returned at midnight, and am writing this on Monday, 25 Frimaire, Year XIV.)

He introduced us at the home of M. Truchet, a retired trader living on his income, as they say, and giving five times a week—especially on Thursdays and Sundays—an evening's entertainment that costs him about four livres, an entertainment for twelve or fifteen rather bourgeois and ridiculous girls and as many young men, among whom the outstanding guests are Lambert and Laforêt, aide-de-camp of General Calvin, killed at Mincio.[1]

When they don't give parties costing two thousand écus or when

[1]Bourgeois society, the most inanely bourgeois I've ever seen. [Note by Beyle.]

witty people aren't present, I prefer the good-naturedness of this party of young girls to that of mature women.

That's probably because of my bashfulness. Second cause: the desire to observe natural characters, not at all polite through social experience, and beginning to be developed.

I danced a quadrille. I played bouillotte.

All that is gay, animated, but asinine. However, I'll return there with more pleasure than to any other place where I've been introduced.

December 24, 1805.—Or rather, the 25th, since it's half-past two. Mante, Mademoiselle Rosa and I spent the evening at Mme. Durant's, drinking punch, tea and flaming rum. We were going to midnight Mass, but everybody told us there wasn't any.

That's precisely the happiness I wanted last year at the same period in my loneliness in my room, Rue de Ménars, No. 9. It gives you an occupation, but doesn't satisfy. What I might still desire is that, instead of Mante, who was half asleep, and Mademoiselle Rosa, who is stupid, there had been seven or eight amiable men.

THE NEXT NIGHT WAS PERFECTLY HAPPY; THE MORNING, TWO IN THE ARMS OF Mélanie: voluptuousness and happiness.

It seems to me that THE PASSION FOR THE FAME quiets down only to burst forth anew.

I'm rereading Tracy's *Logique,* I began this author December 31, 1804. He'll have been of the greatest usefulness to me; I owe the fact of having read him to the hazard of having become friends with Mante.

At half-past two, after everybody (Rosa and Mante only) had left, I went up again to Mme. Cossonier's to ask her for a candle; a formal nuance in her manner, quite natural therefore when one is tactful. She's been making advances to me for two months in a marked way. This evening, Rosa desired me.

December 25.—A superb Christmas Day, the sky a beautiful clear blue, a little cloudier, however, than two months ago, but this almost imperceptible cloudiness isn't to be compared with the cloudiness of Paris. Two days of rain and five or six of clear cold—that's the weather we've had up to now. It has frozen twice, I believe.

Christmas Day WE GO, Mélanie AND I TO Arrailh. A day of surprises. In the morning, Mante entering the salon by the corner facing the sea; slightly JEALOUS SHE WAS MORE amiable FOR [in order to] counterbalance HER rival.

In the evening, one leg on my lap: "May I come in?"—It was Mme. Cossonier, who'd taken advantage of the fact that the door was ajar. Dryness of Mélanie's "yes."—"I'll leave . . ." Mme. Cossonier let her anger be seen a moment, then recovered her natural manner.

It appears that she has the greatest control over herself, she says nothing would stop her from getting revenge.

FOR PLEASING TO Mélanie, I HAVE MISSED THREE OR FOUR DAYS OF GOING AT HER CHAMBER [Mme. Cossonier's] FOR HER LESSON. She can't hide her spite, she continually complains, and said to me before Mélanie, "I'm choking with anger." There's nothing official, however, everything's in hints; even less than that, in allowing things to be understood.

8 Nivôse [December 29].—This evening in Mélanie's dressing room, she and Rosa appeared as though they wanted to talk to me in quite a clear manner about Mélanie. It appears that she's talked about me a lot with Rosa. "He's capricious, eccentric . . ." She tapped me lightly on the head.

As Rosa was on me, she pinched me. We had spoken jokingly of jealousy. I said, *"It's out of jealousy!"* She hid her feelings, but the word appeared to sting her. She told me several times that she'd get her revenge for it. We'll see. She repeated for the tenth time that every night, as she goes to bed, she looks at my door.

December 30.—I must be sober if I want to retain the use of my mind: the least disturbance in my stomach has an influence on my head, makes it ache, or prevents me from seeing my ideas clearly through a disorder of another kind. Bitter chicory restores the use of my mind, and, as the free use of my mind is one of the things I desire the most, it makes me gay.

Saw *Tancrède* played, went to Mme. Pallard's at half-past nine, found Mme. Cossonier there, who came in with Mante and Garnier, played bouillotte. Observed Wildermeth, he was courting Mme. du Bâton, not frivolously but with the tenderly attentive appearance of a man who's smitten; but his manner was elegant as usual.

I left at midnight, having discussed Shakespeare a moment with M. Samadet.

Wildermeth carries on his courtship according to my rules of last year, as it should be done with lofty souls. By letting it be seen that he's deeply smitten, he offers himself with the merit he has, he isn't agreeable directly, and it's to be feared that the woman won't believe you to be more amiable after you've won her.

The rule of continuous amiability has the opposite advantages, but it hasn't the look of being smitten, amiability in this case appears an inanity to lofty souls.

Perhaps it's necessary to mix the two appearances, forming the base of the one that is analogous to the person's dominant characteristic.

Last day of the year 1805 and of the republican calendar: 10 Nivôse, Year XIV.—I've received 100 écus THAT MY GREAT FATHER GIVE TO ME FOR MY DAUGHTER. I DID DEBT [I owe] 120 TO THE HOUSE [Meunier's firm], AND I

SPEND THIS EVENING THIRTY IN GOODGOODS [bonbons] FOR Mélanie AND MISTRESS Cossonier.

WHAT A DIFFERENCE between THIS DAY AND THE SAME, THE NEXT [last] YEAR! THE HALF A livre TO GIRL OF THE GATE.

(Wrote what follows January 1, 1806, at noon):

I'm far happier than last year. I went to see Mélanie AND Mme. Durant at the theater, where they were giving *Les Deux Petits Savoyards;* we sat through it rather gloomily. From there, we returned, Mme. Durant and Garnier went to Mélanie's. Ponderousness and inane stupidity of Garnier.

I kissed Mélanie at midnight, BEING IN HER BED WITH HER.

Reading the third volume of *Jacques le Fataliste,* a work which produces the effect of the most agreeable wit on me, I thought two days ago about what wit is. Here's what it seems to be:

Wit consists of speech composed of more or less subtle and more or less lengthy enigmas.

That's wit proper, the ultimate nuance of laughter. Taken alone, it would soon be boring, it's usually to be found mixed with grace.

What a difference between my fate today and on December 31, 1804! I saw Mlle. Louason for the first time at Desnerf's [Dugazon's], I went to *Philinte,* which filled me with enthusiasm. With my love of virtue, I went in thin-soled shoes to Courcier's at eleven o'clock at night, I returned to read sixty pages of *Idéologie* in my room, Rue de Ménars.

I was too sensitive to the things of society (the little events at Desnerf's) to be able to observe them. It seems to me that I observe better now: the *Logique* [of Destutt de Tracy] has done me a great service.

1806

January 1.—I got up at eleven. WE TAKE THE RESOLUTION to draw up constitutions for our instruction.

January 6.—I'm writing this on my window by moonlight without being cold; I can see fairly well, I left my lamp with Mélanie.

After the theater, I went to the home of Mme. Pallard, who had company. At the same time, I took her some bonbons. I had a moment of embarrassment before going in, fearing it was improper to give them to her before other people.

Nonsense: I went in with my bonbons, and chance produced the right thing to say.

January 7.—I wrote to M. Daru today, and to Mme. Daru yesterday.

Saturday night, January 4, I had possibly the most violent burst of passion I've ever experienced. It was so violent and left me so little liberty to be attentive that, although only three days have passed, I've almost forgotten it.

The passion that was brought into play was ambition. A letter received from my grandfather a day or two before aroused it. The word is apt here: I was reading *L'Avare,* I had thoroughly appreciated the first acts; the letter arrived, I read it out of a sense of duty, I then went back to my book, but I was no longer attentive, I began imagining the happiness I would experience were I an Auditor in the Council of State or anything else.

I turned over these feelings in my soul. Finally, Saturday evening, dining with Mélanie contrary to my habit, I should have been the happiest of men through love; it seemed to be entirely extinguished, and gradually I became full of a mad and almost furious ambition. I'm ashamed to think of it, I found myself considering the most ambitious actions I know.

In order to portray an ambitious man, you must assume that he would sacrifice everything to his passion; well, I'm ashamed to say it but I was like that Saturday evening. I DID THINK TO *sposar* MY OLD *vicina* FOR HAVING *per me il credito dei suoi* BROTHERS [I thought of marrying my old neighbor in order to win the credit of her brothers]. I felt myself capable of the greatest crimes and infamies. Nothing mattered any longer. My passion goaded me on. I was perishing from rage at the thought of doing nothing at the very hour for my advancement, I'd have taken pleasure in beating Mélanie, with whom I was. The next day my passion diminished, the second day it became reasonable. I'm still thinking of it today, January 9; it's in vain that I read Saint-Simon in order to see what I'd have to submit to in becoming an Auditor of the Council of State, nonetheless, at the bottom of my heart, that's what I want.

January 9.—At half-past four, beginning of the most profound grief without despair, a dismal disgust, dejection with nothing vigorous, after HAVING SEEN Mélanie, WHAT HAD SPOKED TO ME OF HER WANT OF MONEY FOR LIVING AT PARIS, AFTER HER DEPARTURE FROM THIS COUNTRY. SHE WAS sad. I GO AT MISTRESS Durant's CHAMBER, HER SHE DOG distracted her a moment; MISTER LEASES COME IN. There was a bit of intentional detachment with very little feeling of anger. SHE again became sad.

For the past three days, I've had a very violent cold that partially paralyzes my brain, prevents me from sleeping, etc.

During the past fortnight, I've unconsciously fallen into the habit of not talking to Mélanie any more, being disgusted with her slowness and those remarks which, after keeping you waiting for a couple of minutes, have no particular meaning. I'll have to tell her that this sadness comes OF MYSELF.

Reading Saint-Simon (I, page 378), I think:
History, Christian Religion.—It makes true virtue inaccessible through reasoning.

Since the priests have warped their dogmas, and even formed some of them, for the purpose of flattering the kings, this religion, one of whose principal advantages is supposed to be to bring the truth to the attention of the kings, can tell them nothing but what is harmful, as happened to the Duc de Bourgogne.

Consultation of the Sorbonne, which allayed the fears of Louis XIV when he was alarmed at a new tax, by demonstrating to him that all the property and subjects belonged to him.

This morning, January 9, while I was reading the newspapers at Michel's, the latter, with his bombastic and serious eloquence, brought in a poor little girl with disheveled hair and an expression of astonishment who had just seen her foster mother murdered by her brother. The brother, pursued, killed himself.

Tonight at Mme. Cossonier's, tales of robbers and murders which distracted Mélanie, who could not be touched (at that moment, I am sure) by anything moving outside of similar tales.

January 20.—Blanchet (of Voiron), contractor for the hospitals of Toulouse (a coarse man, but with wit in his coarseness, who stole, in this and the fodder business, 200,000 francs in Italy, of which he squandered 100,000) was Meunier's guest. I had already eaten, I didn't sit down at the table, all through the meal I read *Cinq Années Littéraires,* a sort of journal without any profundity, without even any flashes, the pleasantry of last century; at the end of the lunch, bored by my inane book, I joined the conversation a moment.

I soon saw that in Blanchet's opinion I had an immense value because of the look of restraint and of difficulty in concentrating that my reading had given me all through the lunch.

He spoke to me lengthily of the education he was giving his two children. I saw that he saw the truth, but had never sought it in books. Soon he was no longer talking to the others, and was only talking to me. Meunier took on his cold and serious appearance, beneath which I detect passion. He flushed from time to time, he was humiliated by the subject of the conversation and the redoubled interest Blanchet showed a short time after starting to talk to me; like Blanchet, he's coarse, all his moods are quite visible.

His little eyes flashed and gave a bit of expression to his face, which is really that of a hospital treasurer, of a low rogue gnawing the meat of the poor patients and possessing the cruelty needed for that. He [Blanchet] told me that his children were very good musicians, that they were in the fourth grade, writing Latin verses and learning English. The poor man spares nothing to give them a good education and make well-bred men out of them; he told me that one of them had the character of Pasquin, seeking only to make others laugh, while the eldest had nothing of all this; that the eldest would be excellent in the manufacturing business; that he sometimes listened to them when they were in bed.

The eldest: "When you're married, your wife will lead you by her apron strings. If I had a wife, I'd take good care of her, I'd be very careful of her, I'd take her her coffee in bed, but she wouldn't lead me around. You only try to make other people laugh, etc."

Blanchet told me that the upper schools were places of corruption, that his children remained eight months in the one here, and that, when he came to see them, they said to him, "Papa, take us away from here, they do horrible things that we can't tell you, etc.," and he took them away.

He said he saw the eldest losing his health. He took him aside and said, "You touch yourself, etc.," the whole thing laughingly. "I'm my children's confidant, I've made myself their best friend." The youngster said it was true, but it was too strong for him: "Well, sir, have your brother tie your hands behind your back every night." The youngster did so, and since then he has completely regained his health.

Blanchet stressed the fact, and repeated it several times, that when they asked him for money he gave them some at once—one sou, two sous. "I ask them what they want it for, etc."

The rigid economy of a man who has made his fortune.

Well, there's a man who has excellent intentions for his children's education, he puts their instruction ahead of everything, then their present conduct, and he pays scarcely any attention to the *formation of their characters;* in 2006, he would be primarily concerned with this important objective, and he would have detailed historical treatises read to them, from each anecdote of which a Helvétius-like character would be taken, he would teach them to reason by showing them what they do by reasoning; the usual reading of these children would be Tracys and Helvétiuses stripped of everything these philosophers have put down to combat the errors of their predecessors.

For all his care, poor Blanchet will perhaps have nothing but asses for children, and will consequently conclude that education is useless: "I've given them an excellent one, and yet they haven't any intelligence!" He and those others who have followed this education will be thoroughly convinced of the truth of this falsehood.

My happiness has increased through the loss of my virtuous indignation; I scarcely have any more regrets for the republican calendar. Is this because I have grown reasonable, or merely because my love of the country has decreased?

Three quarters the latter cause, I believe, and the other quarter the first.

January 23.—My twenty-third birthday. Agreeable. I went (at one o'clock) with Meunier to the warehouse he wants to rent for his brandies, opposite the château that can be seen from the start of the road to La Pomme. An elevated situation, view of all the country homes arranged like an amphitheater, lit up by the setting sun.

I thought of *Letellier*. Engaged in manual labor for two hours; pleasures of the mind keenly enjoyed after this distraction. Means of happiness. It's necessary, I believe, that the physical labor be shared with another and have a useful purpose.

In the evening, I spoke of debauchery before Mélanie, that increased her love and, as a result, my own. A truth to be developed, and one that I've remarked for the past month.

January 24.—I must write out a description of the manners and morals of Marseille; undoubtedly, it will be far from perfect, and even from the sort of thing I'll be able to do ten years from now when I have acquired the habit of seeing the boundaries of truths, or of not letting myself be carried away by my imagination, and of attaching a constant and determinate sense to each word expressing a character nuance.

My principal study should be to know and determine the sense of these words. That's one of the most useful works FOR THE FAME AND, IN THE SAME TIME, FOR THE CONDUCT.

I must compose this Marseillais *character* from what Samadet and Mme. Cossonier tell me, obtain some enlightenment from Baux, Samadet, Tivollier and Meunier, and study it in Garnier, the only Marseillais I see regularly. When I travel, once I am wealthy, I should see scarcely anyone but the people of the region, at least during the first month, in order not to let myself be influenced in my views by outsiders living in the region.

I must write out a description of my days last summer and of my days at the present time in order to draw a good picture of myself.

January 26.—January 23, beginning of energy; I recaptured my ardent and somber soul, loving comic profundity, choloric, going to the bottom of ideas with vigor, will, impetuosity. A result produced by an excellent cup of coffee at Mme. Cossonier's.

But today, the 26th, the same state continuing, a pain in the mesentery. While in this state, I should accustom myself to the happiness OF LOVE, which I have so much desired and which has given me so much melancholy.

January 23 and 24, superb sunshine, not a cloud in the sky, it was too hot in the sun; today, the evening of the 26th, it has rained all day and I wouldn't be able to stand a fire. Magnificent weather, a winter passed incognito, I suffered from cold only in Brumaire, before Meunier resigned himself to lighting the fire. Back in Paris, I'll often regret this weather.

There has just been a scene in the house. A man asked for M. N., on the fifth floor; he went and listened at the door; fearing that he was a thief, someone lit up the hallway; forced by that, he went in and began boxing a woman who was there and who said, "Stop it!" He sent her packing down the stairs by means of kicks in the backside; on the floor below, he gave her such a violent one that he made her miss an entire flight; she tumbled with her head against the door of the main salon. The four servant girls of the house (Victoire, Rosette, Madelon and Rosette's sister, who's pregnant) witnessed the whole business; they thought the poor wretch was going to break her neck, so great were her falls.

This spectacle delighted Mme. Cossonier, it amused her, gave her a thrill. Victoire was amazed by it, as I am by a good tragedy. Madelon, who was superior to the sensation, not being concerned with it like little Victoire, was furious not to have been able to collar the man.

The poor little woman's host was too much of a coward to defend her.

She was a dressmaker, possibly twenty years old, very pretty, Victoire said, already with plenty of experience. If we'd arrived a minute sooner, Mante and I would have run into the people on the stairs.

I don't know who it was that said Victoire was the daughter of Mme. Cossonier, who had her before her marriage, being still a spinster. I'm rather inclined to believe in an accident of this kind, but there's no proof.

Under my window yesterday I saw a dead man whose bier was open; you could see his face, his crossed hands, covered with a drape, a small cross at his breast. That made my blood run cold. At the dinner table (a quarter of an hour later), I told a story, and, as I was telling it, identified myself with the situation of the hero; that, or rather the pleasure of seeing the story succeed, or rather that *and* the pleasure, distracted me.

The spectacle of a harmonious household makes respectable women gain in value. Tivollier beside his wife, who was stretched out on a cushioned armchair because of her grippe. His pleasure. That's as much of an argument in her favor as her zeal in playing cards every day makes her appear disagreeable to me. But such occasions are rare, and the card-playing is an everyday affair.

January 28.—Here is my life during the past two months; I get out OF MY BED at nine, ten or eleven o'clock, I go to the office, I have lunch, I read in front of the fire, I copy some entries, a page every other day, out of the scrapbook into my diary; when there are two or three pages, I enter them in the large book. I've gone out to collect money two or three times, I've got a score of kegs out of the customs, I went once to the warehouse past the Cours Gouffé.

For the past month, I've been going fairly often to take a demitasse of coffee at Casati's. For the past month, I've been going to Michel's to read the papers. This poor man is becoming insane through his foolishness, which is driving him to melancholia. I've been twice to read at the club, for which M. de Saint-Gervais gave me a card. I'm afraid of being importunate.

At four o'clock, I go back to Mélanie's, sometimes to my own room; I go to dinner at half-past five, and usually find dinner already started. After dinner, at half-past six or seven, I used to go to Mme. Cossonier's, then to the theater. The past week, following the suspension of the performances, I haven't been going so often to see Mme. Cossonier, who always overwhelms me with compliments on my hands. I pass the evening with Mélanie until half-past twelve or one o'clock. When M. Baux comes, I read in my room from seven until eleven or half-past.

I bought six livres' worth of firewood, which I won't be able to use up. It was due to my delay in making this purchase that I caught the grippe January 6 while writing in this notebook by moonlight. It lasted ten days.

28. In the *Moniteur,* I read an important declaration on the freedom of the press.

Anything may be printed, but the author takes the responsibility for his book. He is accountable for it to the courts, in accordance with the law, or with a decree of His Majesty. The offenses are to outrage morals or to attack the sovereign authority. The government, like virtue, should hold itself between extremes (*Moniteur,* January 22).

Last night, observed at Tivollier's the asininity and prattle of Mme. Hornbostel. She lives in the most extreme frugality, she's a widow and has six children, only one of whom is in a position to earn any money.

He's at Tivollier's. This Tivollier is the *kindest* man I've ever seen. Taking Mme. Hornbostel home, he talked a bit smuttily to her; he justifies himself by claiming that what he says is true, that at bottom she thinks the same as he. The poor woman was embarrassed.

That's exactly the way I talked two years ago when I didn't know what vanity was.

Mme. Hornbostel talked for twenty minutes to Tivollier and me, and told me forty pieces of nonsense, that Voltaire started *Zaïre* at the age of eighteen in the monastery where he was brought up.

Tivollier had a woman of Grenoble for four years without anyone suspecting it. But, to do so, he could never be at ease: nearly always dog-fashion, behind the door, with his coat on. "A thousand times, I've buttoned up my breeches as I walked about the room in front of the husband, when he returned unexpectedly."

Once you have a woman, she's more imprudent than you.

January 30.—I was able to work only a minute on *Letellier*. Mélanie wanted to go for a walk at three o'clock.

Tivollier promised to have me to dinner with a M. de Saint-Amin, a quack who is, I believe, a M. Renard of Grenoble, and who is an eccentric in the bargain, so it seems. He wasn't able to have him yesterday. Consequently, there were at table Samadet, Jacques Pey, Tivollier, Victor, Mme. Séraphin, Séraphin and I. The dinner was a good one, it amused me greatly and was very good for me.

February 2.—I HAVE DONE THAT TWO TIMES, AFTER THAT AT MID-DAY WE ARE GONE TO THE *passagio,* we went as far as the mill in the Montfuront fields, passing over the plain in one of the most violent *mistrals* I've seen since I've been here, BUT SHE DID WILL [she wanted to go].

I was dying from cold, she wasn't any too gay, somewhat nettled over the affair of Mante, which I told her about, not lending herself to any conversation that might have satisfied us a bit. After being chilled to the bone by the wind, being cold, having a headache, an arid heart and desiring nothing, I went to take a demitasse of coffee.

We saw some almond trees in bloom. We talked of the man who died of love for her, his name was Dacier, Daussy, or something like that. We're going to the masked ball tonight.

February 2.—Mme. Cossonier ejected from the ball.—Yesterday, the 1st, there was a subscription ball at the Français. Mante went to it with Mme. Cossonier; a minute after their arrival, the committee members summoned Mante, and, with all possible decency, even with some embarrassment, asked him by what right he was at the ball. This point cleared up, Mante having told them the truth, they said that Mme. Cossonier would not be permitted to stay at the ball. Mante went to tell her that, as his ticket wasn't good, he couldn't stay, and asked her if she wanted to stay; she said no, pretending to take what he said at its face value.

News of this affair spread like the devil. Today, it's the main thing they're talking about in connection with the ball. After telling Mélanie about it this morning, Mme. Cossonier asked her not to speak of it to Mante because he would feel badly about it.

Mme. Pallard and M. Baux were told that I was the one who took Mme. Cossonier. M. Baux said that that was impossible because he saw me in my street shoes at half-past ten last night, the time the scene took place.

Lambert and he are of the opinion that Mante oughtn't to have stood for Mme. Cossonier being put out, and that, rather than standing for it, he ought to have put up a fight. That's my opinion too.

I believe it wasn't through outright cowardice that he acted as he did, but through childishness, lack of character, stupidity.

They say that Mme. Cossonier lives publicly with M. Garnier. At the ball there were a score of women who are wenches just as openly as she, but they have husbands, they pay their respects to society by concealing themselves.

A fortnight ago, M. Baux of Toulon, going home at one o'clock with Mme. Cossonier and M. Garnier, was shocked to see M. Garnier go in with her. "That's a bit too much," he said. And yesterday Mme. Cossonier was put out of the ball. Society, which is merely vanity, offended by several acts such as the first, gets its revenge through the second.

What's more, all the women here have lovers in the sight and knowledge of everybody. Several of them allow themselves to be taken out of town, live three or four months with their lovers in Paris or elsewhere, and are considered no less respectable for that. Very few of them haven't been shown up at least once in their lives by some adventure that set tongues to wagging.

Mme. Pallard, who teases M. Samadet publicly at her home before her two marriageable daughters and any other people who happen to be there, is admitted everywhere. She had Lambert ask me amicably for the details of what happened so that, if things had gone too far, she wouldn't risk taking Mme. Cossonier to Mme. Filip's tonight.[1] That's how Mme. Pallard treats Mme. Cossonier, who goes to her house every evening, and Mme. Cossonier always speaks badly of her, makes fun of her really hideous face, especially when she's dressed up, and of her childish ways with M. Samadet, and of her dog Lutin, which she treats almost the same way.

[1] I was mistaken. Mme. Pallard, on the contrary, proved herself to be on Mme. Cossonier's side, and wanted Garnier to avenge her; she said heatedly that, if it weren't for her daughters, she'd take her everywhere. [Note by Beyle.]

Her elder daughter Henriette laughs at everything, and without ever saying anything herself. The other one is a fat stupid creature who never produces anything more than a silly smile.

Mante is becoming duller and more thickheaded every day, say Mme. Cossonier and Mélanie; unfortunately, that's the truth, it seems to me he was better two years ago. His confidence in himself because of his philosophy and *idéologie* keeps him from forming himself through social experience, results in his frequently being wrong, even with Meunier on business matters, keeps him from acquiring any delicacy, even causes him, I believe, to resist it.

(February 1.) Had coffee at Tivollier's with M. Eynard, alias Saint-Amin, quack physicist, who gave a performance Friday at the Français, where I was. Ignorant of physics, uninventive in his tricks, performing them with gaiety; you can see that he's having a good time, you can see that society has polished him as far as his speech is concerned, but no natural talent, no brilliant facility, no grace; good nature, an anxious look on his common face; you can recognize the Dauphinois stamp. This man needs two years of social experience in Paris.

This Eynard used to be a criminal court judge in Nîmes, he was a war commissary for fourteen years, so he says, in Italy, a lawyer, a captain, and finally succumbing to his taste for the rank of a conjuror. Nothing brilliant that might make him succeed in this sort of thing, excessively common appearance.

Funny little enthusiasm of Meunier, his little oldish face alight and quivering while talking to him about physics, a subject which, I believe, the one understands about as much as the other.

Tivollier thinks that Meunier is very well informed; in the land of the blind . . . , etc. Tivollier, perhaps without being conscious of it, at bottom aims at having the reputation of being quite a ladies' man, he's always talking to me about them, gives me methods. I ought to draw him out on this subject.

(February 2.) I took Mme. Cossonier and Mlle. S. to Mme. Desplaces's masked ball, and from there to the ball at the Français. Coming home at ten o'clock, I read Euripides' *Alcestus* to prepare myself for that of Alfieri. I find the dying words of Alcestus almost perfect.

I had to leave my tragedy to get dressed. I entered Mme. Desplaces's with boredom at a quarter past twelve with the ladies, they intrigued Lemey, who soon recognized them. Mme. Cossonier told me some anecdotes about Mme. Langlade: the lover's room, 15,000 francs' worth of furniture; the scissors pricks that she gives him on the thigh; when her husband goes to sleep, she leaves the house. I told that to Mme. Langlade, she was intrigued.

I intrigued Lemey a bit about Mme. Grimblot, we changed masks, we returned to Mme. Desplaces's, there was no one left but the rabble. We went to the Français, ditto. We went home at half-past four, I experiencing only a very slight pleasure of vanity.

A superb night, the moon lighting up the Allées de Meilhan, sharpness of the light, which made the shadows deep and hard. Thirty francs.

The ease with which you recognize a person beneath his mask once you're used to doing it.

I notice that I no longer have any enthusiasm for balls, masked or otherwise.

February 3.—Reading *Le Publiciste,* I saw the death of M. Mounier [Victorine's father], who died January 26. It affected me deeply.

A story that would be curious to write, the one of this man who, from being the son of an obscure drapery merchant, suddenly became an outstanding member of the Constituent Assembly, waged civil war in the provinces, as he said to my uncle in front of me, went to establish a school at Weimar, was a Prefect and a Councilor of State. I should point out how each of these events was a product of his character, his mind and the circumstances. I should evaluate these things. His character was more remarkable than his mind.

There's an interesting spectacle, a story I'd read with extreme pleasure. Poor Victorine is going back to Grenoble. What a comedown! What a misfortune! I must make her a friend of my sister.

Mante is certainly an ass, he didn't understand a single one of the reflections this event inspired in me, and they were just his kind of reflections. His dullness comes from an extremely unfeeling heart and a slow mind; if there was a mechanism in him, it might accurately be said that it turns slowly and painfully.

Mounier's entire estate amounted to only 30,000 francs, according to what he told my uncle.

(February 3.) My uncle sent me a copy of a tactful letter that he wrote in my behalf to Martial January 26.

He told me, truthfully I believe, in speaking of my father: ". . . In spite of the mask (and perhaps *genuine* sensibility), he is governed without realizing it by a genuine passion for speculation and a future which diminishes the value of the present, etc."

That seems to me quite exact; in my opinion, much light is thrown on my father's character by that of Meunier, a man who is sensitive, hypocritical, religious, egoistic, etc. I received a fine letter of affection from my father, I happened to glance at the closing lines, and I saw that Douenne had written and hadn't yet been paid. That so disgusted me with the lofty phrases of sentiment that it still keeps me from reading the letter.

February 6.—In order to know yourself, it's necessary to have gone through frequent alternations of happiness and unhappiness, and that's something you can't give yourself.

(February 6.) I returned at a quarter past one from Mme. Roland Filip's ball, where I went at a quarter to twelve.

During seven or eight days, I drank too much coffee, with the result that for the past two days I've had a slight headache in the evening; this state was coming to an end when I entered Mme. Filip's. I don't even know whether I ought to attribute to this the boredom that remained with me throughout. The ball was a fine one, a few fresh faces, but not a single head that was beautiful in the manner of Raphael. Mlle. Antoine, I believe, appears to be excessively coquettish, with large mobile features that give her a kindly appearance. Mlle. Baux, a pretty round apple; her immobile features portray nullity. Some women of thirty-five, ridiculous as soon as they start dancing. I played a hand of bouillotte, taking M. Samadet's place next to Mme. Pallard. All that didn't liven me up in the least, I'd have needed some very amiable people to liven me up tonight. For some time, I observed General Cervoni playing bouillotte; he yawned continually and looked like a consummate bore. Generally speaking, a word foreign to bouillotte was heard only at quarter-hour intervals. After an hour of this, the general went home. A fine sort of an evening for a man holding a position that has become important, who is envied and who undoubtedly considers himself happy!

I'll have to choose a role for the days when I go out into society feeling bored like this; I mustn't take a role that's too difficult, I wouldn't carry it off. The role of a man of the most noble politeness would suit me fairly well.

A button dropped off my coat, I thought of it several times during the evening, I'm only a fop when my dress is irreproachable.

[*End of February or March 1*].— . . . at half-past one at Saint-Louis, I believe, a league from Marseille and half a league from the *Vista*.

One of these days, the details of a leave-taking,[1] its effect on those who leave. How to be at your best at a leave-taking, whether you are leaving or remaining—something to study. Similarly, compose for myself in advance the principal scenes of life. This is sad, but experience shows me the need of it.

March 2.—I wrote to Mélanie. She left from Touchet's, at Saint-Père on Le Jarret. A dinner for sixty-five people at three tables.

I spoke a minute to Mme. . . . , the mother of Pauline and Félicité, feeling Pauline's backside and Félicité's thighs; it would have been

[1]Mélanie left for Paris March 1.

perfect if I'd had my thigh against that of Colette, the third daughter, as I had during dinner.

Mme. Tivollier continues to greet me in a very friendly fashion. I used to think that a year and a great talent would be necessary in order to have her. Perhaps I could have her without either in two months.

March 4.—I received a letter from Mélanie dated from Aix which gave me the greatest of pleasure. Garnier came in to bore me half an hour at Meunier's on the excuse of giving me fifteen livres ten sous from M. Samadet. I went to read the newspapers: a French prince at Naples[1]; the death of Collin d'Harleville. I bought the *Théorie des Sentiments Moraux* for ten francs. By midnight, I had already read forty pages of Sophie Grouchy's *Lettres*. In the evening, I played six games of checkers with little Joseph Blanchet of Toulon. I played with pleasure, therefore gamblers aren't ridiculous.

March 9.—I bought Collé for six livres WITH THE GAINED MONEY, he still puts me in high spirits.

What Samadet told me is quite true. I don't yet possess stability, the kind of stability that makes you want the same thing today that you wanted yesterday.

I'm still in a state of ebullition, that's the reason I'm trying to find myself. I mustn't stop at what I believe myself to be. I must get over my arrogant pedantry before everything else. Where in the devil did I pick it up?

March 11.—I finished Miss Bellamy's *Memoirs* in bed at seven o'clock this morning; I read these memoirs several years ago, and retained the idea that they contained nothing for me. The same passion (LOVE OF BARDISH FAME) that made me judge them thus at the time now causes me to find a multitude of details in them that depict English manners and morals.

Very useful reading as a comedy of character; I was carried along by a mild interest. A work written without vivacity, unfeelingly. And yet it seems to me that Miss Bellamy was a very lively person, she says so. She was a little brunette. It appears that English vivacity scarcely comes up to the common wit of a Frenchwoman.

Englishmen have no prejudices against actresses.

This reading is also very useful to me, as it gives me prudence.

Debts were the cause of Mirabeau's and Miss Bellamy's unhappiness. I must be careful to make none. Up to now I've detested the very word prudence, I liked only enthusiasm.

I'm starting [Adam] Smith, he's an author who will be very useful to me. A year ago, my liking for enthusiasm of the Rousseau variety—minus the misanthropy—would have kept me away from him.

[1]Joseph Bonaparte had just been made King of Naples.

For *Letellier*.

I've thought up some scenes, I believe they're good ones. I'll remain where I am until I can make the outline. I don't feel any inclination to do so now.

Yesterday, I went back to Mme. Pallard's. I'm bored there, but it's a house of very good breeding, and I'm warmly welcomed there.

I want a lot to have a job in Paris, but I'm not counting on it. Loneliness frequently saddens me, Mélanie's shortcomings are beginning to be effaced.

It's hard not to exaggerate the happiness you haven't got. I'm going to read Smith.

March 14.—I went to Mme. Pallard's after being half an hour at Mme. Tivollier's. Very well received by her. Guilhermoz pretended to be agreeable; being jealous of the way Mme. Tivollier received me, he exaggerated while pretending to be agreeable, in general his features resembled gaiety, but, recalling my having been in the same position with Adèle, I very quickly recognized his position for what it was.

From there to Mme. Pallard's. Samadet's incredible frivolity. He wants at all costs to make an effect, allows himself to be carried away by this sentiment, hasn't enough social experience to conceal his self-esteem. "I'm convinced that if we, the people of talent . . . (*correcting himself*), that, if a company of talented people, etc." All that for the purpose of leading up to a subject of conversation in which he hopes to shine. He discourses, but doesn't reply to what others say.

Garnier was there. We talked of brave actions. I left him with that feeling of grandeur, of enthusiasm, of fear (I haven't the time to look for its real name) which is produced by extreme pleasure, and which I frequently experienced in childhood. After leaving him, everything appeared to me sublime—the rain, the house on the corner of the Rue Paradis and the Rue Sainte, which was dimly lit up.

I went back home, I finished Mirabeau's *Lettres sur Berlin,* I found them far below the opinion I had of them a year ago. They bored me, there's no pleasure in their information. Generally speaking, Mirabeau has fallen from the esteem my hatred of the numskulls gave me for him.

I believe I haven't found myself yet, I don't yet know what my character will be; with my ambition, I'll perhaps always believe that happiness lies somewhere else, therefore I'll never rest easy until I've enjoyed everything. I'll have to moderate this gloomy disposition.

(Thursday.) I wrote a letter without any gusto to the good Mélanie. Smith (from page 125 to 160, I) bored me so much by his dearth of clear-cut ideas, or the triviality for me of the ideas, that I was really wretched. I fell asleep, and, when I woke up, I was still wretched. What susceptibility!

Daru doesn't answer my letters; that is, he doesn't answer them satisfactorily; the same with Martial. He doesn't want me, or, if he does, I'll be tried out for a year or two in an office, otherwise I'll be in Paris working in business with a salary of 100 louis a year. Show me the way to happiness with that amount of money! Therein lies the great problem of my life. As far as money is concerned, I'd be happy if I could live in Paris as I am doing in Marseille.[1]

March 16.—Remark.—The end of this diary is cut up into various fragments, but the dates easily show what composes the picture of my life.

(Saturday the 15th.) I went to Mme. Tivollier's very well dressed, she didn't appear to notice it, but she really treated me wonderfully today; she hasn't done anything yet of her own accord, but she accepts my little attentions; I'm on quite another footing with her than Meunier, Guilhermoz and Mante, who are nothing but spectators. Meunier and Guilhermoz sometimes intimidate me.

(Sunday, the 16th.) I was rather bored this morning. I went for a three-hour walk with Lambert. Garnier stopped us for half an hour, he was dying of boredom. That stupid man isn't insupportable, because he knows how to express himself; but no ideas, he's dying of boredom. Lambert told me about the siege of Lyon (from inside the city), we dined together at Mme. Pallard's. She thinks she can reason and mistakes her personal feelings for the truth, she defends these with ill-humor, flies into a rage, her little eyes flash with dark fire. I observed this in the discussion about Carnot, who is a knave because he didn't have her released under the Reign of Terror. I held myself in so as to spare her vanity, but not enough. Samadet was completely against her, he knew Hérault de Séchelles well; he was just the kind to fall into the latter's snare, and consequently did.

M. Triol told us that Mme. de Staël is at present in Geneva, where she's acting up in society.

Music before Mathias Stabinger, composer. That rather bored me, but not excessively like the concert tonight (Monday), from which I've just come. I was observing mankind.

Generally speaking, I was bored at Mme. Pallard's. I go there only because of the good manners, but these fine manners inspire a sort of embarrassment that can be paid for only by gaiety. This gaiety, how-

---

[1] I DID NOT HAVE slept THREE MOUNTS [months] WITH LOVED WOMAN, I was in love with love. It was, I believe, an intellectual love.

May 22, 1819. I reread all this for the first time fourteen years later.

These memoirs are tiresome because I didn't describe my happiness between August 1805 and February 1806 for fear of spoiling it. [Note by Beyle.]

ever, isn't what pleases Mme. Pallard and M. Samadet the most; what they need is arguments in which they can get the upper hand and confound their adversary. Their vanity isn't refined enough to be satisfied with gaiety, their minds haven't got the necessary frivolity.

I left at half-past eleven, rather tired but taking along Ancillon,[1] which M. Triol lent me. This work appears to me excellent in general and excellent for me in particular. It will instruct me quite a bit in history after the fall of the Eastern Empire.

It will be enough for me to read a history from Caesar to Augustus and the last Emperor of the East. Then I'll be familiar with the past eighteen centuries. The portions on Mohammed and the conquest of the Roman Empire by the barbarians are charming.

March 17.—I'm reading this history, which makes me happy. I went to see Rosa and Mme. Lavabre. What a horrible day!

I spent an hour with Mme. Tivollier, with whom I'm making great progress. I put my hand on her thigh without any objections on her part. I'd sleep with her with pleasure for a month.

I had several moments of satisfaction with her; yet nothing is less sure than success. I accompanied her to Mme. Arnaud's at seven o'clock. From there to the concert, as full as an egg; this gathering of women at first dazzled me, but before long I got bored with the stupid appearance of them all and the bad taste they showed in their way of dressing. I saw the little Claustrier girls, all three with Agamemnon, we smiled at each other fully a score of times. I left at nine, went to Mme. Pallard's, where there was nobody in spite of the fact that it was her at-home day, and here I am.

March 18.—Tonight ought to make me recover completely from the fear I often experience that my conversation lacks interest. I realize that the world is full of people who can't bear being alone and to whom a remark, however uninteresting it may be, is better than nothing at all.

I accompanied Mme. Tivollier to Mme. Etienne's. From there I went to see an act of *La Mère Coupable*. How the dialogue and sentiments of this play have fallen in my estimation! What trash! What bombast! What prattle! What concern with one's vanity in moments of haste! What bombast! Mme. Turbot, who shrieks but who possesses boldness and a voice that carries, ought to be appreciated far more than Mlle. Louason. I left at the fourth act, indignant as the Vicomte. I went to Mme. Pallard's, whom I found alone with her two daughters. The conversation lingered on uninteresting things. Samadet arrived and tried to start an argument; he hastened to say a few words, and

---

[1]Jean-Pierre-Frédéric Ancillon's *Tableau des Révolutions du Système Politique de l'Europe depuis la Fin du XVe Siècle,* a work that had considerable influence on Beyle in his youth.

then, in connection with nothing, launched out on a story of a couple of speeches he'd made.

We went to Mme. Filip's. It was decided that Mlle. . . . had been hissed at the concert. I heard it. Mme. Filip wouldn't believe it, and said afterward that it wouldn't have made any difference to her. There were seven or eight old women on hand, Mme. . . . , a *bonne vivante,* gay, continually saying vulgar things, sanguine temperament, eating like the devil, a good character. She contrasted perfectly with the six old women (between forty-five and sixty), consumed by vanity, talking of nothing but themselves, endlessly going into details about their lunch, wrangling bitterly, saying rude things to each other. Anyone who goes in such society must be thoroughly miserable at home!

Could there possibly be any conversation that wouldn't be delightful amid such nonsense!

THOUGHTS

Clarity, accuracy of terms, absence of
all eloquence, avoid it purposely.

Fondamenti dell' arte nella conocenza dell' uomo, e pensieri ri-formatrici di me stesso per rendermi più atto a pensare profondamente e veder chiaro nel proffondo del cuore umano. [Foundations of the art of the knowledge of mankind and thoughts of reforming myself to make me more capable of thinking profoundly and seeing clearly to the bottom of the human heart.]

I wrote this 30 Thermidor XIII [August 18, 1805], after my second trip to La Pomme WITH Mélanie AND Mante, I BELIEVE.

I would have been perfectly happy had it not been for the nuisance of playing the successful lover, and had I not been the host: these responsibilities bothered me, and, after eight or ten trips, perhaps, made these excursions boring for me. (March, 1806.)

March 25. Holiday.—I've just spent two hours with M. and Mme. Tivollier. I believe Tivollier is a little jealous of me, his wife didn't greet me as warmly as usual.

What a profound boredom is preying on these good people! They owe their belief that they're not the unhappiest of mortals only to the fact that they haven't enough imagination to conceive a happiness superior to this state. Even if they were rich, they'd wallow in the same way. People say, "Tivollier is happy in his family life." I mustn't let myself be misled by tales of such a kind of happiness.

Boredom is beginning to make me feel the void of Mélanie's absence. Sunday, I was absolutely invulnerable to any agreeable sensation. Lambert, Mante and I killed the time lengthily by going for a walk. I went to Trouchet's, where P—— kissed me. From there to Mme. Filip's. My deadly boredom pursued me.

Yesterday, Monday, I was as open to pleasure as I was shut on the previous day. The Fridzeri concert amused me, Lambert's conversation interested me. One of these days, we're going on a picnic with Mmes. Filip, Pallard, etc. Lambert told me that Samadet and Mme. Pallard believe me to be a Werther in everything that's lofty in character.

The bondage in which Mélanie kept me was frequently oppressive, the abandonment in which I'm left by her departure bores me. I must consequently correct myself if I expect to be happy. I have need of giving new habits to my desire for happiness.

26, *Wednesday.*—Mélanie doesn't write, I don't know what that means; but her last letter, which was the first of any length, was cold in tone. Is she only mad at me, or doesn't she love me any more?

I have violent suspicions of Leases AND Girard; that angers me, diminishes the happiness I've enjoyed, but I must know the truth.

I left Mme. Pallard's at half-past twelve, I lost nine livres there and enjoyed myself very little; but that initiates me into society, I'm still far indeed from having the desired composure.

There was a lot of talk about the picnic Saturday; it's getting under way without any enthusiasm.

We agreed with Samadet that the American individual is the most disagreeable possible, a fine fruit of the most tolerable government in existence! Especially are they of an incalculable avarice and servility. Is this the result of the government or something entirely different?

They say that the May fetes are going to be postponed, as the Emperor is going to Italy via Marseille to have himself crowned King of Naples, apparently.

Today I finished the second volume of Ancillon, a work that is exceedingly useful for me. I believe it will make me abandon my love for the pure republic in favor of a modern state.

March 27.—I'm writing this in my new room, which reminds me of the one I had at Reggio, where I wrote with so much enthusiasm. I'm staying at Mme. Tournier's, I pay her twenty-seven livres a month, and three livres to the valet.

I went to the Montfuront fields with Samadet, we left at a quarter past two and returned at five. I talked almost without stopping. I'm still worn out as a result.

I've just been to Mme. Tivollier's, where I found the Messrs. de Montvallon, the son still full of spirit; he's just been telling me anecdotes for two hours.

The Montvallons, father and son, never refer to a gentleman of Provence without adding, "He was a near relative of mine, he belonged to our family," and, a moment later, "One of the greatest lords of the region." That and the appearance of telling stories because it pleased him to do so and not in order to give you pleasure were the only two things that were ridiculous in the son.

Meunier didn't fail to notice that I'd taken lodgings across the street from Mme. Tivollier's. "That's exactly what led me to do so," I emphasized.

Today I received a five-page letter from Mélanie, but still chilly in tone; one of six pages from Crozet, whose sustained and abundant naturalness filled me with a feeling of friendship. Barral is in Trieste. *March 30.*—I was gay in bed when I awoke this morning. Then I had to go and remember that it was Sunday. I had made up my mind to read Vertot (*Portugal*), at once I began to doubt that I ought to read it. It's five o'clock, and I haven't read it; as soon as I had this thought this morning, I felt myself being overcome with boredom.

I consequently still need an occupation. I haven't enough wisdom to know what to do with myself and to fill up my spare time, that's obvious. Paris and a job with my cousin would therefore suit me wonderfully; but it looks as though that's not to be.

I ought to examine myself thoroughly so as to find out what I ought to desire; I believe that, at bottom, I haven't the slightest idea.

I desired passionately to be loved by a melancholy and slender woman who was an actress. I was, and I didn't find sustained happiness.

The reason, I believe, is that sustained happiness is a chimera, that I haven't the rationality necessary to derive all possible happiness from my situation. Generally speaking, I am immensely lacking in wisdom; the fact is that I don't know what I want. In general: Paris, Auditor, eight thousand livres a year, life in the best society and having women from it.

I don't dare to say to myself, "I'm unhappy," but frequently I'm cruelly bored, like last Sunday, and like this one a little; the energy which makes me think what I write and then write it has to some extent rescued me from boredom.

The basis of this boredom is that I'm disgusted with the pleasures of others.

The party of yesterday, Saturday, for instance, didn't bore me; the picnic was in the Montfuront fields.

I went there conversing with Samadet. How unnecessary it is to fear the true talent of the men I may meet! What a man Samadet is! Led on by his passions, which are of Meunier's kind, but on a much higher plane; believing himself an enthusiastic admirer of true beauty in music and character; at bottom having nearly all his sensations falsified, and yet possessing a bit of sensibility, but very conceited, like everybody. Constantly making himself utterly ridiculous.

I was on the way to judging him very badly on January 30 when Lambert stopped me: I was about to consider him a consummate hypocrite because he had defended religion eloquently and praised everything, even Mme. Tivollier's servant. Not at all: he hasn't enough mental vigor for that, not enough *constancy, will power* (that's the word); he merely wanted to shine by his conversation, to be eloquent, to work himself up.

I have been very near this absurdity several times in my life; at the age of seven or eight, on the way to Claix, I gave my father the description of a superb land, telling him that I'd read it in La Harpe's *Histoire des Voyages;* I made believe that this land was Ceylon. I was lying, I worked myself up by my tale, I experienced pleasure in swaying my father, I believed myself very eloquent; all these things made me enthusiastic, and I kept on until I was tired out. This, I think, is what takes place in Samadet. All this sort of thing makes him a child, always carried along by his taste of the moment.

We found that the ladies had arrived. No pleasure, general chilliness; they went to sit down at B, and from there soon came to seek some sensations in a game of faro which they started . . .

All that amused me very little. We returned, dinner was served; nothing was said during this dinner.

Mme. Filip, on my right, got drunk on white wine; prattle without imagination or gaiety. Mme. Decrai continued to appear to me superior to these women: she told them the unpleasant truth with the rest of good nature. They sang, the whole business dismally, Wildermeth in a ridiculous manner. I'll have to learn one or two table songs. Little Teissier kept on with his little mouselike amiability. He's at home in that role. He talked throughout to Mme. Collavier, Mlle. Filip and two or three old women, whom God confound. This disgusting old age would make me sick to my stomach. Mme. Pallard, wearing a felt hat, was of an ugliness and bad taste that were absolutely matchless, the whole assemblage very ridiculous. But this was nothing: on

leaving the table, she took me by the arm to go to gather some haw-
thorn blossoms for her *pawr lil girruls*—the language in which she
talks to her dog, and in which she and M. Samadet sometimes talk
together in front of everyone. I nearly burst out laughing, and was
unable to muster up the courage to say anything to her.[1]

Louis Tivollier, sitting beside Mme. Tournefort, looked like the
most bored man in the world; that sort of thing was a thousand leagues
from his cigar and habits. Perhaps for him that represented high
society.[2]

We left, Mme. Filip taking my arm. All along the way, she witlessly
bothered the buxom Mme. Decrai, whom I gave a slap on the backside
which she repulsed with genuine dignity. I had held Mme. Filip's
thighs all through dinner; her drunkenness and her horrible ugliness,
which literally made her a market woman, so disgusted me that yesterday, Sunday, I had no desire to go to see her.[3]

I no longer recapture, except in moments as fleeting and rare as
lightning flashes, the delightful sentiments I used to be given by a
rainstorm, a fog, etc. when I was in the land of chimeras about women.
The weather we had while returning to Marseille reminded me of
Milan. What emotion I used to experience in similar circumstances
while returning from a walk with Angela Pietragrua! I can conceive
old age after that.

We arrived pretty much soaked at Mme. Filip's. She fainted and
had an attack of nerves.

The stupidity of all these women, her friends, who were not in the
least moved; it was really hideous. She was aided by me, Mme. Decrai
(who, in this hole, is perhaps considered her enemy), Mante and
Tivollier, at my request. It was the first attack of nerves I've ever
seen.—The indifference and stupidity of her daughter; it seems that
her soul is as vapid as her face.

Mme. Filip was stretched out on a day bed in her yellow salon, to
which her indolent daughter finally found the key. She *belched,* which
completed my disgust with her. A voluptuous face and sighs, the latter
running up and down the chromatic scale; these sighs were particularly voluptuous when she was inhaling punk smoke.

That's the way you die! In the interest of friendship, those present
trying to cover up this natural tufa[4] with a show of forced tenderness.

She recovered and went into her salon. One lamp was put out, the

[1] I OUGHT BE BE ANIMATED. (1809.) [Note by Beyle.]

[2] Yes. [Note added later by Beyle.]

[3] I ought to have had her. [Note by Beyle.]

[4] Beyle uses this word figuratively to designate the basic material under the
surface,

other lowered. *Les Revenants,* a song by Wildermeth. Arrived several women, among them Mme. Grimblot, invariably the same naturalness full of sensibility in her manners and the same enchanting breath.[1]

Earlier, Samadet made himself thoroughly ridiculous—but only to a score of people, like Pacé and myself. English duets, a falsetto voice. What a need of sensations this poverty-stricken society has! How little you should be afraid of boring it by the futility of the subjects, provided you're not obscure—and you become so as soon as you're witty. Wildermeth's tufa was clearly visible that day.

This man has a dignity that is studied; his neat appearance, his physique, something cruel about him, something slender and distinguished in his figure. Everything contributes to making this style the most appropriate for him. Were this character to be of his own choosing, it would imply more intelligence than he shows. Moreover, stiff, having no taste or grace; nevertheless, he's the Lovelace of Marseilles, a seductor through sentiment.

His manner of telling stories while hunting for ideas, having few of them, incessantly groping, embarrassment in all the habits of the body and, in the end, choosing his ideas badly.

It seems to me that he's nothing but a pompous and distinguished ass, well suited for women, a veritable hero, undoubtedly giving all the attention necessary to details. Therefore, he's possibly the most distinguished conquest in Marseille.

I left Mme. Filip's at ten o'clock, went to see Mme. Tivollier. She cooled off my blood: she is young and simple in comparison with the others, and I'm courting her. I returned to Mme. Filip's, and stayed there until midnight.

April 1.—I'm still so much of a child that, being obliged to write my grandfather a letter in which I spoke of my ills, going into detail about them and even exaggerating them a bit, I ended by convincing myself that what I said was true and being affected by it and very sad. These letters make me almost unhappy. I began reading Machiavelli's *Il Principe,* a genuine remedy for this mobile sensibility which makes me effeminate and is disguised beneath my reasoning faculty; but this faculty doesn't give me the habits I need. Machiavelli doesn't entertain me, but I understand him, and that's a lot. Perhaps I'm only now ripe for history and will acquire a great taste for it.

I saw Rey yesterday at Fort Saint-Jean. Guilhermoz and Dufay considered me brilliant because, like Samadet, I worked myself up. I got dressed and went to Mme. Tivollier's, where there were some English people and Samadet. He sang, as usual; as for myself, I was considered brilliant by Mme. Tivollier.

[1] A stolid hussy. The drowned child. [Note by Beyle.]

April 2.—Arrival of Périer. I dined at the Tivolliers', Madame was charming to me, I played boston FOR THE FIRST TIME.

April 3.—The Paradises.[1] All the girls of Marseille were in the streets to visit them. A real holiday, a good day to see young and pretty faces. I went for a walk with Samadet and Tivollier; Samadet was very expansive, republican out of vanity.

I spent three hours with Périer, a man governed by his own ideas, who comprehends those of others only with difficulty, yet not stupid.

I learn that Daru is in the Academy,[2] a good occasion to write him, but the letter embarrasses me.

April 4 and following days.—Lunch with Voisin, the stupid speech of General M. The influence of an education that is entirely military. The contrast to the delicacy of his associate. P. told me there were some bad stories going around about Lambert. From there to the Armory. Tivollier had a woman; the eternal remorse of this woman, who fears that her son is Tivollier's.

Second lunch (Sunday) at the Tivolliers', more agreeable than the first, but nevertheless degenerating into boredom when only two or three people were left. Boredom, idleness of Périer; he owes the fact that he doesn't believe himself unhappy to the dullness of imagination which keeps him from conceiving another happiness, and to the conceitedness which impels him to believe himself happy.

Finally, on April 9, a six-page letter was sent to Daru.

Four days previously, I was in bed thinking of the letter I wanted to write him about the Academy, when Mante brought me a letter from my grandfather, in which was enclosed the one from Daru. I wrote my letter, a long session with Lambert to correct it. Lambert made me think, and settled my uncertainties. At last, it left the 9th; with a little activity it would have left the 6th. If something happens between the 6th and the 9th (eight days later, the 14th or 15th), it will be my own fault.

It's possible that I will receive the answer the 24th. This is one of the most important events of my life.

[*Among notes at end of notebook*].—
Notice to my sister Pauline Beyle

If I die, employ every means possible to take possession of everything I may have, I give it to you. I confide *my daughter Mélanie* to your keeping. M. Paillet, father-in-law of M. Sauzai, Prefect, Rue Vivienne,

[1]Wayside altars put up on Holy Thursday.
[2]Pierre Daru had just been elected to the Académie Française to replace Collin d'Harleville, whose death Beyle mentions in his entry of March 4.

M. Blanc de Voix, son-in-law of M. Geffrier, of Marseille, living in
the Rue Sainte, will tell you where she is. I know you, and she is my
daughter in spite of the false appearances it has been necessary to
give her. Adieu.

Henri Beyle
March 10, 1806

Such is and has been my wish.

Henri Beyle.[1]

Journal of His Life
From April 15, 1806, to May 3, 1810

Voyages.—Left Paris for Grenoble WITH Mélanie 18 Floréal XIII [May 8,
1805]. Arrived in Grenoble . . . Left Grenoble for Marseille . . .
Arrived in Marseille 7 Thermidor [July 26] Year XIII. Left for
Toulon May 20, 1806. Arrived in Marseille the 22nd, and left Marseille for Grenoble . . . Arrived in Grenoble May 31, 1806, having
seen Aix, Orgon, Lambesc, L'Isle, Cavaillon, Vaucluse, Apt, Forcalquier, Sisteron, Gap, Corps (the most dangerous precipices I've
passed), the Lakes of Laffrey, Vizille and Brié. Left Grenoble for
Paris July 1, 1806. Arrived in Paris July 10, slept for two nights at
Plancy with Crozet, saw Bray, Nogent, Méry-sur-Seine, the barren
plain of Champagne. Two trips to Clamart, one to the Bois de Romain-
ville, one to Montmorency, two days (August 30 and 31) near Saint-
Gervais.

Marseille.—I've just read, in the March number of the *Bibliothèque
Britannique,* some reflections by Ferguson on the principle of per-
fectibility in man which developed the reflections I've had continually
during the past few days.

In what way is it important for me to perfect myself, and have I
sufficient passion to make me attain this perfection? Lambert isn't
lacking in wit, yet he bored me cruelly during a five-hour visit yesterday. Whence comes this boredom? From a habit given me by the
desire to perfect myself in the art of knowing and stirring my fellow
men. I consider each day lost during which I don't instruct myself.
It seems to me that the only exception I made to this rule a year ago
was for the art of having women. I passed whole days pleasantly, and
even rapturously, in Pacé's company because what I got from him

[1]This is the first of more than two dozen wills or fragments of wills that are
scattered through the papers and manuscripts of Stendhal.

that didn't instruct me in the art of having women gave me the social habit. His grace also played a large part; in his company, I found a happiness from which I am very far indeed when sitting at my desk.

I believe Samadet was right when he said to me, in speaking about me, "You're still in a state of ebullition." I don't know what I'll be in the end; I experience extreme boredom during the time passed in society, with people sitting looking at each other, and this boredom is only expelled by the still greater boredom to be found in solitude. This state bores me so much that it puts me in bad humor.

The work in Meunier's office, which certainly wasn't attractive, made me unhappy for two months when it came to an end.

During the next year or two, my dominant passion is probably going to be that of occupying a favorable situation in society.

In order to do that, I must acquire:

1. The amiability necessary if I am to be welcomed with pleasure.
2. The talents of my position.

I must acquire these talents without adding to them the things that are usually detrimental to those possessing them, as pedantry, pride, etc., etc.

My letter to Z [Pierre Daru] left April 9, perhaps I'll copy it here, I've been awaiting his reply since the 21st. A letter from my uncle gives me some hope: "I shall avail myself of the first opportunity to place him *in a suitable manner.*"

I must acquire some talent in this line. I tremble in advance, and yet those men will be like the ones I've met here—Meuniers, Tivolliers, Samadets, Guilhermozes, Saint-Gervaises, and the women will be Cossoniers, Pallards, Rosas and Filips.

I'm getting cautious; in Persia [Paris?] I may stop writing this diary. The preceding notebook was forgotten for four hours in Meunier's office.

April 19.—At two o'clock, Meunier, Lempereur, Guilhermoz, Dufay, Mante and I left by the Porte de Rome to go to Sainte-Baume.

A ridiculous and boring assemblage: Meunier, a sorry ass with sensibility and timidity; Lempereur, a disgusting swine, mentally and physically; Dufay, a stolid ass; Guilhermoz was the only one who interested me a little, like a fledgling in spite of his breeding, etc., etc.

We covered about eighteen leagues in forty-eight hours; much more tired the second day than the first. We slept at Gémenos after drinking a good bottle of wine at Saint-Marcel and a bad one at Aubagne, on the Toulon road. We left Gémenos at five. Shady and rather pleasant road at the bottom of the little valley; a stream bordered with Italian poplars in all their freshness; copper and paper factories. Saint-Pons, a hole where there are some pretty trees that I didn't see very well.

A mounting zigzag road, three hours; from the top you can see Marseille, the islands and the sea as well as on a good map; we came down, a damp plain, cold and treeless, in an hour, an unkempt wood before Saint-Pilon. We climbed up, rather tired; Sainte-Baume fell away. A hole in the rock like a man's mouth; a little Gothic temple inside, a wooden staircase, broken statues, dankness. Those people were incapable of feeling or making felt anything agreeable in such a spot, a dozen peasant men and women were going in or coming out.

We dislodged a couple of stones, crossed the plain, trudged alone for three hours, and reached Saint-Zacherie. A little girl lying dead, her hands crossed, the intense coloring of death, her eyes half closed, her mouth as though uttering her last prayer, the great expressiveness of her whole body, of her eyes; nothing of the horrible. She touched me deeply.

As I'm not sensitive in the manner of the composers of country songs, I won't stress the fact that there was a *train*[1] in progress forty paces away: that, as well as the appearance of unconcern and going about the daily business as usual, touched me nevertheless. I imparted a bit of my sensations to my dull companions, who attempted to ruin them. "They've crossed her hands like that," said Dufay, etc. They aren't people of this sphere. With my eyes, I followed a priest who was there in a stole; he mumbled a bit, then went to the cemetery, the woman was still carrying the little body in her arms, without a coffin.

The little girl did not possess the Grecian type of beauty, but she had everything necessary to be touching, nothing of the repulsive, the appearance that Tasso gave to the knight killed by the infidels. I'm going to look it up.

We had supper at Saint-Zacherie, the *train* continued under our windows until eleven o'clock at night; pretty promenade and cascade belonging to M. de Tournefort. The next day I started out with Guilhermoz, execrable road along the bank of the Huveaune; Auriol, Roquevaire, the fertile basin of Roquevaire, fine olive trees, but all this was far inferior to what is to be found in the Dauphiné. The hillsides were superb because there were some pine trees. Aubagne. We arrived in Marseille worn out after again seeing La Pomme, a cherished and pretty spot.

I believe the situation that will take me out of this society will bring me nearer to happiness. We each spent 13 livres 5 sous x 6 = ... I wasn't as tired as I was the second day, and I livened up.

May 1.—Since Sunday, worry, not the low-spirited kind, but just plain worry. That day there was a great spree with Guilhermoz, Trichand

[1] A country dance to the accompaniment of a tambourine.

and Blanquet. I did that with the fat girl of the sr . . . and with Théreson. She's charming, but Trichand was told that she has the pox.

I'm waiting every morning with extreme impatience for Z's reply.

At midnight April 29, Guilhermoz, Mante and I left for La Pomme. Superb moonlight. I felt like having romantic adventures. We were at Saint-Marcel at a quarter past one, after having missed La Pomme. Good-naturedness of the stableboy, who let us sleep in the hay. We set out again at five o'clock. Shadiness of La Pomme, which we crossed. Nightingales.

My grandfather writes me disheartening letters. I'm burning with impatience to get some sign of life from Daru. I'm tempted to write to the *good* Martial.

May 3.—Twenty days ago, I was in a state of ebullition. I was full of ideas, I had new ones every day. Since the 23rd, the possible day for an answer from M. Daru, I've no longer been the same. I live only for the arrival of the mail: the rest of the time I'm bored. It's a devastating hope. If only I had two hours of necessary work, I wouldn't be so bored. But, since I'm able to put off what little work I have, I let it pile up, and I'm behind in many things.

I'm gaining experience: it's necessary to have suffered if you're going to be capable of reflections on the means of avoiding boredom, and to keep on suffering if you're going to get the strength to contract the habits indicated by the reflections.

My grandpa is growing angry and is writing me disheartening letters; I'd die if I have no one to love me. Mélanie is also growing angry; Crozet has stopped writing me.

I haven't got the pox yet today, Saturday I went to see the slaughter-house.

May 4.—A nice day for Marseille. Future centuries, look on my wretchedness! Yesterday gloomy, apparently from too much virility. I did that once last night, I was gay. From three till a quarter past six with Lambert and little Mimi Olivier, the father, mother and her. She's of the wench variety, and has a face that will bring her customers.

We dined together gaily and philosophically. From there to Mme. Tivollier's; I was affectionate and quite at home with her, if it's possible to be so with such a wet blanket. From there to Mme. Filip's, whence I've come at one o'clock in the morning after losing twelve livres.

I was really happy the first two hours we were with Mimi. The pox hasn't appeared so far. I'm writing to Martial tomorrow.

May 6.—I received Cheminade's terrible letter containing the conversation between Mme. Jaubert and Mme. Daru. It didn't lay me low, it gave me energy. Could that be pride? In any case, I wrote nine pages to Cheminade and seven to my uncle about this important affair. In view of Daru's letter dated March 23 and that of my uncle containing an extract from the one written by Mme. R., Lambert believes there's still some hope, that Mme. Daru has a grudge against me as a result of my desertion.

For my own part, I believe I shouldn't have any more hope of being an auditor. Cheminade is improving infinitely, this is the second charming letter he's written me.

Wrote to Martial yesterday, the 5th; both my letters will leave to-morrow, the 7th.

Wednesday, 7th.—A picnic lunch at Mme. Pallard's; boredom from noon till half-past three. Visit to little Mimi Olivier; deep pity: the three living with forty-nine livres; her coquetry. I arrived at Mme. Tivollier's heartbroken. Played boston, went at ten o'clock to Mme. Pallard's bouillotte. Her uneasiness, her bad temper; as she was leaving, the vindictive, susceptible Mme. Decrai saw that they were eating in the dining room. Mme. Pallard, while telling me how she put off Mme. Decrai yesterday, employed the same smile she uses for everybody, me the first of all. Change of men; I had a confidential talk with Samadet: I had courage in my soul, and my mind excited by business and society when I left a house that I had entered heartbroken and with the deepest pity.

May 11.—I'm reading Hume's *History of England;* after forcing myself to read the first volume, I began to get used to it a bit, and this took me a little out of my boredom. I'm waiting for every mail delivery as for the Messiah.

I'm learning English.

Sunday. A walk with Mme. Hornbostel, Mme. Tivollier and five or six children on the banks of the Huveaune from five till nine. Country house belonging to M. de Saint-Jacques, charming with its shade, at a short half league.

May 15.—Last Tuesday I saw the Meindret and Reynaud sugar refinery.

In the evening, Avrain's dinner; vulgarity and stupid gloominess of all the guests. Craftsmen, not being held back by decency, would possibly be gayer. Not the tiniest spark, the whole business nothing but the most stupid asininity and the most repulsive baseness of sentiments. Bouillabaisse, truffles and *brandade:* five livres ten sous.

I'm still waiting for the mail every day as for the Messiah. I'm beginning, nevertheless, to become reasonable; however unfavorable Z's reply may be, I'm prepared for it. I'm also beginning to put up less impatiently with the lack of letters from Crozet, who hasn't written for fifty days.

Yesterday I read the second volume of Hume's *History* in bed until one o'clock with more interest than any novel has inspired in me for the past two years. The stay in Marseille has ripened me for history.

Whatever hole I'm relegated to by the will of Z, I must have myself introduced upon my arrival at the Prefect's home and to everyone belonging to the best society. I'd be less bored at M. Thibaudeau's than at Mme. Pallard's. The society of Mme. Pallards has only served me to make the conquest of Samadet and, to a small extent, her; but they don't do anything but argue, and, to complete the sad picture, M. Samadet and she have minds as far as possible from being filled with good sense. She praises Fouquier and tears Carnot to pieces: the former received her well, the latter badly. Samadet's invective against any man who doesn't believe in God. A genuine subject of Chateaubriand. Chateaubriand could lead him to the devil. No knowledge of true virtue. Vulgarity of Mme. Pallard and M. Samadet in regard to Ardisson, who's abandoned them. The collection of disgusting old women, seven or eight of them. Mme. Decrai is the only one who's passable; this rabble is in league against her.

My extreme disgust and boredom with all that.

I haven't opened Racine or Corneille for three months, a week ago, I read a thousand or fifteen hundred lines of Tasso, who enchanted me in spite of his conceits at each octave. I feel that I love Shakespeare more and more; for me, he is the greatest of poets. Molière is the only one who can be compared with him.

I'm beginning to find Mélanie stupid. I recall a thousand and one traits showing little intelligence; immediately after her departure, joy at my freedom; forty or fifty days later, stirrings of regret. At present, a balanced appreciation, I believe: a great deal of friendship, even love if she wouldn't try to tyrannize me and always be complaining. *Ecce homo.*

May 17.—I've been drinking a demitasse of coffee every day for the past month, I didn't drink any today and I'm infinitely gayer, more on a level with other men. It would seem that coffee produces genius and gloominess; I've already experienced this result, which is striking in my case, several times.

Lambert left last night without our being able to see each other yesterday.

Yesterday, a ballet which bored me but entertained the Marseillais. These people have a mortal loathing for tragedy, they don't understand it. Since they laugh at comedy—occasionally in the wrong places

—they dislike it less, but it yields to the opera, which in turn yields to the ballet, which they like better than anything else.

May 18.—After reading a letter from my uncle, I decided to go to Grenoble. After that, I went for a walk on the Cours and the Allées with Mante, who had helped me reach this decision. From there to the club for an hour. From there to the house, where, after setting the dogs to fighting, we dined—Guilhermoz, Trichand, Mante and I. From there with Guilhermoz to the Montagne Bonaparte to look for Mme. Tivollier; she wasn't there. We took a turn around the mountain, and, by a fine sunset, I saw perfectly this city and this sea I'm going to leave. We went to the knoll on the right of the Chartreux road, the usual goal of Mme. Tivollier's promenades; she'd been there for two hours with her husband and M. Pey senior. We returned after an hour; there were some loiterers on the boulevard in front of Th. Gilli's baths. We took some ices. We returned to her house, remained there half an hour with nothing to do because there weren't enough people for a hand of boston. Finally, Victor arrived from a Sunday party (with the old men; they entertain themselves in fine fashion for their five livres, said Guilhermoz). We played a few hands, with him being bored stiff. I won four francs through the mingled smells of the dog and the feet of the gentlemen and Madame. She started a hand of piquet with Guilhermoz; I watched them play a moment. I've just left them; since then, I've written my English theme, and here I am.

That's the life I'm leaving, it must be admitted that it wasn't taking me very far.

I'll go to Toulon tomorrow during the night, but alone. I've about decided to go to Grenoble via the secondary road: Aix, Manosque, Sisteron, Gap, La Mure, etc., etc.

May 20.—*Trip to Toulon.*—I left for Toulon May 20 at three o'clock in the morning. The night before, I left the Tivolliers' as midnight was striking. I went to take a glass of brandy at the Café Chinois. Profound solitude and silence of the streets. Street lamps burning in silence. I encountered only two people, one of whom was the elder Crozet, who went on his way singing.

This silence and solitude as midnight was striking.

I left as three o'clock was striking. It cost us eight livres apiece. Three companions. Esprit Alléon, possessing the least possible *esprit,* gross ignorance, forty years old, one of those faces that women consider handsome, evincing nothing but much petty vanity, getting mad at the least contradiction and refuting you with assertions that are the height of absurdity. He amused me the first day, I tried emerging from my character of steel, appearing to approve opinions which I detest the most. Wasted effort. The second day he bored me to the point of nausea. I scarcely spoke to him after that.

M. d'Heureux, son of a captain of a ship of the line, twenty years old, going to Dalmatia; a good fellow but what ignorance! It's really rare. He looks like a dressed-up peasant. It seems that the hunt is the only thing about which he has meditated a bit—and a bit about women.

The third was a good bourgeois, I believe he's employed in the artillery, he's been at Toulon for three years, has a tender face. He was wearing a little hat *à la Pamela* belonging to his little girl, aged seven; a great enemy of higher education. He told us that he had had the misfortune to lose his wife, etc., etc., and things of that stamp. Great enemy of the Navy: he reproached the cowardice of the officers in this branch. He has a sense of honor, he replied with heat to young d'Heureux, who, speaking of the military career, weighed it with the danger involved; inflexible on the subject of duty.

We had a bad lunch at Cuges. From there to Beausset; Gorges d'Ollioules, of the same kind as the grotto at Les Echelles, excellent military positions.

We came out. Orange trees on the open ground. First view of the roadstead, superb view; six ships in line. On the way, we passed a garden belonging to Admiral Ganteaume which seemed to me ridiculous, and which is considered superb. For this sort of thing, generally speaking, there is a total absence of taste in Marseilles.

We entered Toulon; ramparts, drawbridge and city gates in very good condition. My bourgeois told me that there were thirty-six forts in the mountains around Toulon.

Toulon is built on a strip of land half a league wide, coming down as mountain slopes to the sea. The mountainside is carpeted with an infinite number of olive trees; they are less agreeable to see than oaks.

Toulon has twelve thousand inhabitants, all those who aren't connected with the Navy live on what they sell to the sailors.

Wretched streets, like those of Grenoble but even uglier, paved with sharp little stones. We entered by a long curve, a wretched street paved in a way calculated to break your neck, named the Rue Impériale.

May 27.—Left Humières at four, arrived at Apt at nine, left again at ten. We stopped a moment at La Garde de Dieu, hurried on and arrived at Forcalquier at seven.

Hills, mountains, great quantities of oaks. No longer the dull nature you find around Marseilles; but, as nothing was grandiose, I didn't have any deep impression.

The villages on the mountaintops; some of them, like Mont-Saint-Justin, put up in a manner as inconvenient as possible.

We passed Céreste. Fine roadway of walnut trees. Demolished château, like that of Villemus, like all of them.

Forcalquier, with its high steeples and towers, has a far more dignified look than Apt.

I've just written Mélanie; it's half-past eight, I'm dead tired. I'm going to Sisteron tomorrow for six livres.

May 28.—I'm writing these lines at Sisteron in a room looking out, it's true, on some latrines and a beastly drain, but affording a glimpse in the distance of the suburb of La Durance and a few trees.

A horrible, stinking town, but a pretty view at the confluence of the two rivers. Yet the arid nature of mountains.

The smell of the provinces is redoubling, I'm in them for good this time. The bored look of the customers camped in front of the cafés, the asinine look of everybody. Self-important bad humor of the servant woman. Sour look of the mistress.

The stinking street. Four pretty girls at work, unfortunately eight or ten paces from the door of Le Bras d'Or.

The stay in Marseilles has helped me tremendously in getting over my bashfulness, has formed my character (made me acquire habits conforming to my reflections). I'm inclined to take everything gaily, and I'm getting over my melancholy—a proof that it was wounded pride. Let this be a warning to worshipers of melancholy.

Yet it's still hard for me to bear the sight of a small town. *Transeat a me calix iste.*

I'm bored with traveling. The boredom of not seeing any society is largely responsible for this. I'm getting over my melancholy, but I'm contracting new needs.

From Pertuis to Sisteron, wretched appearance of the mountains, but nothing reminded me of the drabness of the country around Marseilles.

Invariably villages perched on the mountain peaks. I've got to find someone to sleep with in Grenoble to keep from being bored, otherwise I'll die there.

May 30. Gap, Marchand's Tavern, 10 o'clock in the morning.—I wasn't active enough the night before last at Sisteron; I was punished for this by a twenty-four-hour stopover at Gap. I'm only leaving today by the mail coach, at one o'clock (twenty-four livres). Stifling heat, the skin over my cheekbones hurts me. The annoyance of trying to arrive at two o'clock, and of being mounted on a worthless nag.

Gap is only a small town, and Sisteron nothing but a filthy burg. Gap is a Prefecture. They say Ladoucette [the Prefect] has an income of sixty thousand livres at the age of twenty-six. What a bore it must be to spend five or six years of your life in a hole like this! It seems to me that a Prefect should be delighted to be in Grenoble.

Gap, in a basin surrounded by fairly high mountains, thinly wooded, and after that by mountains entirely covered with snow (all that you can see).

Inside the town, what idleness! What boredom! At the café yesterday, a victim of boredom complained of it out loud, and showed that his complaint was well founded by the uninteresting things he said.

Mine host has several daughters, the three eldest of whom were all the time in a room joining mine by a double door, of which one side was ajar when it wasn't entirely open.

I realize too thoroughly what good manners are to say and do the bad-mannered things necessary to take advantage of the open door. That will come.

Yesterday, they sang and talked loudly as soon as they knew I was in the room, they got dressed at nine o'clock to go to a dance in the neighborhood. An old woman who was out of time and out of tune had them dance; they started singing; I heard sounds that were extraordinary for their discord. About ten o'clock, loud cries: "Fire," I got up. It was a few pieces of amadou burning in a shop opposite my room.

I read a canto of Tasso, it touched me; last night, walking around the crumbling walls of Gap, my soul was inclined to be melancholy. This morning, I meditated an epic poem; how far I feel my mind beneath such an enterprise! An epic poem might be composed that would be entirely new through the sensations it would give the readers.

Owing to lack of experience, I can't describe what I feel, but I feel a very marked shade of difference between Marseille and Gap, as I do between Marseille and Paris. A look of boredom and acrimony that is utterly unknown in Marseille.

What I write in the provinces (with the exception of Marseille) is usually intolerable to me because of its bombast and ridiculous gravity.

Everything seems flat and tasteless when you come from a place where the seasoning is high—that's one of the causes of the boredom experienced in the provinces by a man of the world. What piquancy was there in last night's dance after those of the salons or even at Mme. Filip's? What piquancy was there in the latter after those of the Duchesse de Clèves?

What piquancy do the women of the provinces possess when a person is accustomed to those of the Court? Novelty, innocence, naïveté, a lofty soul, WHAT CHARACTER SHALL I HAVE AT THE Court?

One exaggerates the shortcomings of the place one is in.

Maybe that is the reason Helvétius says nothing of the provinces. Rousseau was led by his error to love them as getting closer to the savage state. The things that are simple frighten the provincials and appear naked to them, all the more so when they accompany something lofty. That's what keeps them from ever being in style. The magnificence of my mop of hair appalled the barber at Sisteron.

Grenoble, June 27.—It's a long way from Toulon to Grenoble; I haven't written a word since then, out of disgust with writing. Neither Daru nor Martial has answered a word.

I've done everything I wanted here, but my contempt for mankind has greatly increased. I've seen a few virtuous actions, but nearly all of them with vicious motives. I believe I've got over my arrogance a bit.

The thing that has best shown me to myself is the ease with which I am affected to the point of tears.

When that happens, all my bases of judgment change at once.

I've lost nearly all my enthusiasm for the great writers. Their servile and petty vanity has ruined my admiration. I see them as I see MY *zio* [uncle], charming (outside blind spots in taste) in his letters; petty, ridiculous and odious when his behavior is seen.

My father has drawn closer to me, and this has given me pleasure; with more candor on his part, we'd get along well, we'd make each other happy.

The art of living well, which a year ago seemed to me nothing but words, now seems to me very difficult: it requires much wisdom. To live constantly on good terms with someone is the point to be reached. Faure is right, it's very difficult.

Nothing gives me much pleasure. Rapture is dead in me, except a half hour of rapture for women. Last night, for instance, an hour of keen pleasure with Mme. Galice while returning from the Porte de France, but very soon spoiled by the desire to be amiable. Nevertheless, a pleasant evening.

Still, I don't believe I'll have her.

The German Adventure

BACK in Grenoble, Beyle had the novel experience of finding himself in complete agreement with his family regarding the future. He had had enough of commerce; literature would have to wait: his ambition had been aroused, and, for once docile, he asked nothing better than to have his grandfather and father start him off on the right road. With open arms, Dr. Gagnon and Chérubin welcomed the black sheep back to the bourgeois fold. There were to be no more unconventional notions about leading an artist's life in Paris, no more wild talk about investing the paternal capital in banking schemes: henceforth he would lead the life they had always planned for him, that of all respectable folk. Taking advantage of his cousin's influence, he would advance in a functionary's career, he would win official honors, occupy an estimable place in society. Henri agreed to everything; his respect for his grandfather was revived, he was even momentarily reconciled with "the bastard."

Returning to Paris early in July, Beyle took a room he had formerly occupied in the Rue de Lille—conveniently near the Daru home—looked up his old acquaintances and appeared regularly at the places in vogue.

Running about town was pleasant, but the important thing was his campaign against the Darus, which was methodically conducted. The schedule was to win over Martial, get into the good graces of his mother and relatives, and then, supported by loyal partisans, open the decisive attack on the terrible Pierre.

All went well in the preliminary skirmishes, but when he was invited to a dinner at the Darus' country home in Clamart, a drive of half an hour from the Emperor's palace at Saint-Cloud, he was so frightened that he almost convinced himself he was ill and would be unable to keep his engagement. At the last minute, however, he gathered up his courage and presented himself to Pierre's young wife.

Mme. Daru caused him as much uneasiness as her mighty husband, for he scarcely knew the one, was awed by the other, and suspected, not without cause, that they both regarded him with disapproval.

In the summer of 1802, Pierre, then aged thirty-five, had married Alexandrine-Thérèse Nardot, sixteen years younger than he, and a few months younger than Beyle. On this occasion the latter had turned up to kiss the bride. Following that, he had let four years slip by with but a visit or two to the home of his cousins. It later pleased him to imagine that his single appearance had aroused Mme. Daru's curiosity:

"She asked who that young man was. THE HUSBAND probably answered in an angry tone that he was a ne'er-do-well who had just handed in his resignation," to which Martial had hypothetically added some information about his escapades in Milan and particularly "the famous affair over Signora Martini." Thus, undoubtedly dismissing him as a youth of evil ways, Mme. Daru had thought no more about him until the beginning of 1806, when he, his family and his friends began importuning Pierre to find him a job. At this time she was informed that he was working in a wholesale house at Marseille and living with an actress, whereupon she told a friend that her husband had no intention of doing anything for such a wrongheaded lad. However, she had chanced to see a letter "full of sentiment and wit" which he had written to Cheminade, and she possibly had come to the conclusion that this strange little cousin who fought duels over women, shared in Martial's adventures, preferred working in a grocer's office to being a sub-lieutenant and, withal, was capable of composing charming letters might, in spite of appearances, be an interesting person.

In consideration of all this, Beyle felt some uncertainty as to what kind of reception awaited him at Clamart, and he was no little relieved to find Pierre amiable and his wife gay and friendly. The latter was a vivacious young woman, short, a bit plump, elegantly dressed, with chestnut hair, heavy eyebrows, ardent dark eyes and a merry face. Beyle, whom she had previously left indifferent, now began to find her to his liking, although for a long time he was intimidated by the superiority of her social position. Reassured by the cordiality of his host and hostess, he forgot his self-consciousness and spent what he considered a triumphant evening.

This visit restored his confidence in himself but did nothing to change his situation. Soon there was again talk of war. Relations with Prussia had been growing strained just as those with England appeared to be getting better. Friedrich Wilhelm, learning that Napoleon was flirting with the idea of restoring Hanover to England, mobilized the Prussian Army and ordered France to evacuate Germany within two weeks. At the same time, Fox died, and, seeing all hope of peace collapse, Napoleon hastily departed for Germany.

Public sentiment in the two countries was at fever heat, and, with war in the offing, Beyle decided that what he wanted to be was not an Auditor but a war commissary. Finally, on October 16, after nine months of job-seeking by letter and in person, he drove out of Paris with Martial Daru, not as an Auditor, not as a commissary, but, reminiscent of his departure for Italy six years earlier, as a simple supernumerary.

Nor did he, as he afterward affirmed, witness the battle of Jena—which was fought two days before he left the French capital. However, he did reach Berlin in time to behold Napoleon's triumphant entry along Unter den Linden on October 27. Two days later, Pierre Daru, under the pre-text that he could not wait for additional commissaries to be sent from Paris, had his protégé appointed provisional deputy commissary and ordered him to proceed "without delay" to Brunswick. But Beyle, as usual not taking his orders too seriously, lingered on in Berlin for another pleasant fortnight. On Christmas Day he set out from his new post for Paris to confer with Minister Dejean on the finances of the conquered duchy, and by February 5, 1807, he was back in Brunswick, which was to be his headquarters for the next two years.

What a contrast this old German town presented to everything he had previously seen! The picturesque houses, with their steep and varicolored tile roofs, their overhanging upper stories, their leaded windows, their carved and brightly painted walls; the ornate public buildings of a naïve and toylike architecture; the neat, cheerful streets with their quaint statues and fountains—all this was curiously new for eyes used to the severe architecture of Paris and Milan and the dreary lanes of Grenoble and Marseille.

Beyle, however, had already demonstrated his indifference to the physi-cal aspect of cities: scarcely a line of his diary or letters is devoted to description of the towns he had visited. His attitude was defined once and for all when at the age of eighteen he disdainfully dismissed Brescia as "a collection of more or less handsome houses, like all cities," and declared that the only thing of interest to him in a city was the life of the in-habitants. He might also have mentioned the surrounding countryside and the sundry urban annoyances, for these things were constantly the subjects of his comment in Marseille, as they were to be in Brunswick.

The annoyances of the latter city were several. For one thing, the climate was the worst possible for a man who was easily brought down with a cold or fever. Now it would be freezing, with a cold wind and an abundance of snow; half an hour later the sun would come out and a thaw set in, and between times it rained; all of which not only made the country roads dangerous, but filled the city streets with mud—and no one in the world loathed mud more than Beyle. Summer came abruptly with no springtime transition and was apt to be as intolerably hot as the winter had been cold and disagreeable.

Obliged to go on frequent errands in the vicinity, he was exasperated by the postilions, who recklessly cut across fields to avoid the boggy roads and drew up before every inn to drink a glass of schnapps at their passenger's expense. Indoors it was as unpleasant as without: the taverns were filled with gloomy beer drinkers who lived "a purely animal life"; the assembly rooms of the houses, overheated by porcelain stoves, were kept hermetically sealed, and, when the floor had been wetted down and sprinkled with sand, the stifling heat, together with the mingled odors of stale tobacco smoke, sand and wet wood, gave him a splitting headache.

The food, too, was a cruel ordeal for a French country boy with a healthy appetite. Did he drive all morning? At noon he would find a lunch consisting of four or five bread-and-butter sandwiches, some punch, cake and a bit of chocolate. Did he sit down to a meal in a tavern? He would be served a ghastly repast of soup made from wine or beer, an immense platter of sauerkraut ("a stultifying dish"), a roast accompanied by foul-smelling coleslaw and some tasteless boiled vegetables.

But worst of all were the German beds! One was engulfed by a feather mattress, while a mountain of pillows held one in a sitting posture despite the bravest efforts to stretch out normally. There were no sheets: instead, an enormous sack filled with feathers pinned down the prospective sleeper, "so that, since everybody sweats under this cover, to which the heat gives a thickness of two feet, you have the pleasure of being in communication with all the voyagers who have sweated under the same bag before you."

There were, however, many compensations for these discomforts, especially during the hot summer months. Only a short distance from Brunswick lay forests and hills and green fields and limpid streams. The hunting in the hills and woods was excellent, the rural roads were ideal for horseback riding, and pleasant excursions could be taken to the Harz Mountains. When his duties detained him in town, he found fruitful material for his observation of the human heart as it manifested itself in the curious German people—preferably, of course, in the female of the species.

Appropriately, he began his sojourn in Brunswick by falling in love. But this time he was more reasonable than in the past: with the memory of Mélanie still fresh, he did not seek an ideal Julie with a melancholy soul. He was content to take his sweetheart for what she was, to play at being in love and philosophically to accept defeat.

Wilhelmina von Griesheim was a beautiful, slender and graceful girl of twenty-one—"that blonde and charming Minette, that soul of the North," he called her. She was the daughter of one of the oldest families of the Thuringian nobility: her grandfather had been a Chamberlain in Saxony, her father was a brigadier general of the Brunswick army and a favorite of Duke Karl Wilhelm Ferdinand.

During the winter and spring he flirted timidly and with his usual lack of success. "I nearly had Minette's heart in my hand," he told his sister. "I said to myself, 'It can't fail!' Yet it did fail, and cruelly."

The fact was, as he soon found out, that a Dutch youth named von Heerdt had been courting Minette for four years and was only waiting for her father's consent or death to marry her. After that, he became more circumspect, looking for a means of winning Wilhelmina's heart without jeopardizing her marriage prospects. He fell back on his first rule of seduction, attempting to arouse her jealousy by flirting with her friend, Fräulein von Treuenfels—with results no more satisfactory than with Adèle and Mme. Rebuffel.

Besides these two, their entire circle and many of the townspeople welcomed him to their parties and outings. Among the men, the most curious was the Grand Chamberlain von Münchhausen, middle-aged, untidy, avaricious, "a pitiless chatterbox," with a weakness for bragging and a great respect for official decorations. Among the women were Charlotte von Oeynhausen, who permitted a moderate amount of love-making, and the "fat" but "heavenly" Philippinschen von Bülow, for whom Beyle retained a permanent admiration.

Philippinschen, who was destined to enter a convent and die an abbess, was the sister of Amelia von Strombeck—"a perfect nonentity"—and was loved in a silent, hopeless manner by her brother-in-law, Baron Friedrich von Strombeck. Beyle soon became the intimate companion of the baron: many years later he wrote him, "You are the only friend I have in the language of *ja*."

Strombeck was a kindly, sentimental German, a bit of a dilettante and a skillful lawyer who was to preside at the court of Celle, Hanover. In his *Scenes From My Life and Times,* he says of Beyle, "At that time, he was a young man of scientific culture, aged about twenty-six, who was distinguished by a thoroughly French vivacity heightened by an unparalleled good nature." Beyle returned the compliment in his *Histoire de la Peinture en Italie* and *Promenades dans Rome,* but in 1807 he considered Strombeck "ponderous," and accorded him only the bourgeois and domestic virtues.

The two friends explored the neighboring country together and even took two or three longer excursions to the Harz Mountains, including the Brocken of folklore fame. More frequently, however, they strolled out for target practice or to take refreshment with the Brunswick girls at Der Grüne Jäger, a rustic open-air café with a Bohemian orchestra, set in the woods a short distance from town.

It was during the twilight hours of one of these soft summer evenings, sitting with Minette and Strombeck at a little painted table beneath the lofty elms of Der Grüne Jäger, that he heard for the first time the light, spontaneous airs of Mozart, the sole composer he was to admit to his heart by the side of Cimarosa. The musician of the South and the one of the North satisfied his two dominant moods—gaiety and melancholy. "On the days of happiness, you unhesitatingly give your preference to Cimarosa," he wrote a few years later. "In the moments of dreamy and enchanting melancholy that you find at the end of autumn in the vicinity of an ancient castle under the long pathways of sycamores where the all-embracing silence is disturbed from time to time only by the rustle of the falling leaves, it is the genius of Mozart you love to come across. You wish to hear one of his airs played in the forest by a distant horn."

Together with the awakening of his love of music came an increased interest in painting, an art which he was before long to consider as the sister art of music. But, as ever, his chief interest lay in literature, philosophy and the facts they contained about the human heart. Eagerly he devoured all the printed matter available in Brunswick. He took up the study of German and announced confidently, "In six months, I'll know two thirds of German and be acquainted with German literature," but, after a brief exposure to its multi-syllabled complexities, he dismissed the language as the "cawing of crows."

It was during the pleasant stay at Brunswick that, discarding what little remained of his "pure republicanism," he decided to elevate himself in rank by the simple device of adding the noble particle *de* to his name: henceforth he was known officially and socially as "Monsieur *de* Beyle"— a name he retained all through the Empire. He wrote home for his father's coat of arms ("these bits of foolishness have great value in Germany") and, dressed in that "Parisian elegance" of which he was so proud, succeeded in commanding the respect not only of the local aristocracy but also of the French generals who visited him.

In the summer of 1807 he occasionally went with Pierre or Martial Daru, the latter of whom was acting as the Intendant of Brunswick, to the mountains to hunt deer, but because of the long waits and the sight of the stags' suffering he had little taste for this sport. He preferred to shoot hares and partridges with comrades of his own rank. He made a reputation for himself one day when, driving with some soldiers, he suddenly drew out his pistol, took quick aim and sent a bullet through a crow forty paces away.

A new direction was given to his thoughts in September, when the pretty young wife of Pierre Daru passed through on her way to Berlin and, during her stay in Brunswick, manifested "a great deal of friendliness" for her cousin, even, as he wrote four years later, "a tender kindness that made him tumble down from the clouds." She went so far as to propose that he accompany her to Berlin and there act as her escort—a project that was nipped in the bud by Pierre, who remarked dryly that, at the moment, such an arrangement was out of the question. Mme. Daru continued her journey, and Beyle found himself persistently musing about a pair of mischievous black eyes and a merry smile that had seemed (or was it his imagination again?) to hold out a promise of something more than friendship.

The year 1808 passed by agreeably enough with no serious love affair or momentous event. Minette had gone out of his life, he continued to see Strombeck, he made new friends, attended official dinners, played cards and billiards, rode horseback, hunted, read, went to the theater, dreamed and flirted with sundry servant girls. He experienced a touch of regret upon learning that Adèle Rebuffel had become the wife of Alexandre Petiet, and was immensely interested in the marriage of his sister Pauline to a neighbor, François Périer-Lagrange, "a genuine bourgeois" of thirty-two, "goodhearted and thick-witted." Happy memories came flooding back when he heard that Victorine Mounier had returned to Grenoble, but no such effect was produced a few months earlier when the forsaken Mélanie, under the name of Mme. Saint-Albe, finally made her debut at the Théâtre Français in *Andromaque* with Mlle. George and the famous Talma. In February, Pierre Daru had given him the duties of Intendant of the Emperor's Domains. How wonderful his present position would have seemed in the spring of 1806, when he was marooned in Marseille. Life was pleasant and easy, there was no denying that, but . . .

The truth was that he was bored. For the second time military life had proved to be an illusion: even his ambition often seemed empty, and his only moments of deep happiness were those when he was able to dream in solitude. He lingered on, amusing himself as best he could. There were no regrets when, on November 11, 1808, two years almost to a day after his arrival in Brunswick, he was handed the order that permitted him to speed back to Paris.

1806-1808 Paris—Germany—Brunswick

Voyage to Paris to Obtain a Position

August 10.—I'm writing this August 10, I arrived in Paris July 10 after going to see Crozet at Plancy-sur-Aube, in Champagne.

The Champagne plain: chalk, large trees, an absolutely round horizon in an absolutely flat plain. I passed through Méry, and arrived at Plancy, a burg that has become wealthy through business.

The dignity of Crozet, well-developed words, gestures aimed at being noble, but what sterility of ideas! Only for brief moments did I find the Crozet who used to read *Polyeucte* with me. I was prepared for disappointments, otherwise I'd have been unhappy. I didn't at all find the Crozet I was looking for.

M. de Plancy's grounds, the charming woods along the Aube; really striking. I left after a stay of two days.

We talked of LOVE (he was going to jump out the window); BOOKS; my affairs with Daru; Mme. de Staël.[1]

I explained the English Constitution to him. He accompanied me as far as . . . , on the Troyes highway. There I took the diligence to Paris at eleven o'clock. Vanity pesters him like the devil and takes away all his naturalness and earnestness.

August 16.—I tasted the solid pleasure of having done my duty today, a duty of ambition. I read attentively the first seventy-eight pages of *L'Esprit des Lois*. After that, to Martial's (at three o'clock), he took me as far as the Boulevard Coblentz. Excellent visit. From there to Mlle. Duchesnois's; a couple of turns in the garden, her superb eyes. I went back to Mme. Badon's; genuine pleasure.

From there to dinner with Faure and Michaud; I was unusually animated today. After that I saw Mars in *L'Intrigue Epistolaire*. She's a true beauty. What pantomime!

Mme. Rebuffel is coming at seven o'clock tomorrow to take me to Clamart.[2]

August 20.—*Theater.*—Since July 20, the day of my arrival, I've done so many remarkable things for my objective (in the two houses of the Rue de Lille and the Rue du Sentier) that my laziness has kept me not only from describing them, together with their motives, but even from noting them down.

I've seen *Henri IV* twice, the first time with tickets given by Duchesnois and coming from Legouvé; I didn't applaud any oftener because of that. The first time I went to the Français, I was very displeased.[3]

I went to the Feydeau, the plays made me sick to my stomach. I didn't go to see Duchesnois; I made a big mistake: Pacé, Legouvé, Maisonneuve and Chazet were there.

[1]Crozet had recently met Mme. de Staël at the Yonne Prefecture.
[2]Suburb where Pierre Daru had a country home.
[3]Went once to Dugazon's, saw the Prince of Bavaria, an ass playing at being a prince. Dugazon stupid. Wagner more so than last year. [Note by Beyle.]

Tartufe, Mlle. Mars, the ideal of beauty; at moments she seemed to be a living face out of Raphael.

Gaston et Bayard. Everlasting bombast, monarchical heroes who make me writhe. This play delighted Mélanie's soul; after that, trust a woman's judgment, put your happiness in their hands, artists; that's the kind of judgments they make.

At the Buffa the opening day: *Il Matrimonio Segreto.* A worthless troupe.

To the *Matrimonio* a second time. I was completely conscious of my soul, which had been awakened by the first performance. Since then, twice to the second act; I was too busy to get there earlier.

Once to the *Cantatrici Villane,* which Faure had the nerve to prefer to the *Matrimonio.*

Today (exhausted after having done that twice with Mélanie and having sweated horribly all night) I find the overture nice.

I'm reading *L'Esprit des Lois* with great pleasure. I was received as a Freemason about August 3 (123 livres).

August 21.—I've just been at Martial's (a quarter past ten). Saint-Vincent, his assistant, lacks good sense, yet has character. Later, I found M. de Pacé reading the [marriage] contract[1]; dissatisfied with it, he went to Z's to have him send it back. Pacé busy, peevish, angry. Myself, very well received, friend.

August 23.—Got up at six o'clock, went with Faure to the Tuileries. Read Tracy. From there to the Régence. Returned to my room, wrote three letters. Went to Pacé's, found him at table with Messrs. Châtenay and Saint-Floriant; they were amiable, Châtenay serious; I was quite at ease, I left after half an hour so that Martial could be alone with M. du Châtenay.

I believe I'll go to the *Matrimonio* tonight.

Hobbes, *Nature Humaine,* page 217:

". . . Likewise, men of prompt imagination have, all things being equal, more prudence than those whose imagination is slow, because they observe more in less time."

That's what makes me hope that I'll have some talent. I observe better, I see more details, I see more accurately, even without centering my attention on a thing, than Mante and Faure.

Shortcomings: 1. I reflect on everything I see, I sometimes devote too little time to observation. When reading the newspapers, I frequently skip words or parts of words.

2. Excessive enthusiasm: I realize all the happiness that could be given by something assembled in a single moment, and I wax highly

[1]Martial Daru married Charlotte-Xavier de Froidefond du Châtenet (Châtenay) a month later.

enthusiastic; if I happen to speak of it, I convince myself by my own eloquence; two days later I grow disgusted.

I got excessively enthusiastic about a job as Auditor; I went to Court, I was disgusted by the sight of so many stuffed shirts who didn't seem to be very happy. I noticed this vice several months ago, it seems to me that I've got over it a little.

I slept this morning and read eighty-four pages of *L'Esprit des Lois* and twenty-two pages of *Nature Humaine*.

August 26.—I've just read Hobbes's *Nature Humaine*. With the exception of Chapter IX, this book is on the level of the notebooks I composed two years ago in the same place I'm writing this one (Rue de Lille, No. 55). He bored me because what I read was nothing but the words of a man of good sense who hadn't gone to the bottom of his material, or else truths that were pointless. Chapter IX[1] is the only one that's useful, it starts out in the right direction, everything should be analyzed like this. This book, which had left me with so much admiration, bored me.

Yesterday, the 25th, I went to take Mme. Rebuffel and Adèle to the Jardin des Plantes at half-past eleven; I left them at eight. Eight hours spent together; I gradually became less stiff with her, but I never experience a very intimate pleasure with them because of the dearth of ideas.

We set out in a fiacre, arrived, I didn't give anything to the custodian of the stuffed animals, forty-five sous to the first doorman, twelve to the animal keeper. I must keep some thirty-sou pieces in my pocket to give to these people.

We remarked the bats, the monkeys, the septicolor (bird), the female elephant, but especially the monkey . . . , which has red stripes on its face, and backsides of the brightest colors, violet and red, and a fiery-red penis. His intelligence, the human expression of his eyes. I gave him some pineapple lozenges, he trembled, his nervous spells.

After dinner, Adèle and I talked about things that interested us; her mother's lack of ideas excludes her from any conversation that is at all sensible, from which I conclude that Mme. Petiet's friendship with her is aimed at marrying off Alexandre.

Anecdotes about the people in the street; the lady getting into the cabriolet; the former dancer; the streetwalker; the love of the muslin merchant whom I saw smoking at his door; the performing dogs; a little chorus girl whom I know.

Adèle told me: "You must get over that; I'm telling you this a bit for myself; if you don't get over that, you'll fall into bad ways, and we

---

[1]The reference is to the section in Hobbes's *Discourse on Human Nature* dealing with the subject of laughter. Stendhal tried all his life to develop a theory of laughter, but he never got far beyond that of Hobbes.

won't be able to see you any more. It's all right to see George, Duchesnois, the principals, but you must stop seeing the others. Martial had detestable manners when he was frequenting them."[1] She told me a great many things that ought to make me lose my stiffness, make me natural with her, and, to my shame, these things, without exactly carrying me away, gave me a great deal of pleasure.

Buffon is her only profane reading. History of man. In what we read on monkeys—she reading with her eyes and I reading half aloud—I skipped phrases like this: "The females, like women, are subject to a mensual flow."

I thought I noticed that she was blushing a little, but she kept on talking. She hasn't got the kind of a character to let herself be disconcerted by such things.

Leaving me: "You won't be long before seeing me again."

I believe it's to shield Alexandre [Petiet].

I've received 300 livres from my father, it's the first money he's sent me.

In the evening, went to Mme. Daru's, saw M. Daru, left after a minute and a half, read Virgil.

Every morning, Faure and I read Blair (six pages) and Virgil (one). The first twenty pages of Blair appear to me common, very flabby and inane.

September 1.—I've skipped several very interesting days, pleasure is often spoiled by describing it. I'm writing now because in this way I increase the pleasure I experienced the day before yesterday and yesterday.

Didn't I have the weakness to go and fall a bit in love with Mlle. de Cossé [Adèle Rebuffel]?

M. Laguette-Mornay, artillery lieutenant of the Guard, came to my room at seven o'clock Saturday. Faure and I got dressed, we had breakfast and went to the Porte Saint-Denis.

We left for Montmorency (six livres). An uninteresting plain. Laguette talked about the little German girls he's had. We arrived at the church: spire, view. We passed through Montmorency (2,000 inhabitants), we arrived at Leduc's: a room with three windows. We went to the hermitage of *Janques* Rousseau, as we were told by a woman of the region.

A wood of large chestnut trees, charming; the hermitage, a very ordinary house and garden. Grétry, who owns it, was there. The part of the house in which Rousseau lived; garden; lawn seat near a plum tree in the eastern corner against the wall on the east where he used to

---

[1] Adèle's sermon about actresses was, of course, aimed at Mélanie, with whom, on the same date a year earlier, the fickle Beyle had gone on an excursion to La Pomme which he said he "would remember all his life."

go to read; it's kept in repair; bust of Rousseau with some verses by Mme. d'Epinay, false sensibility and what one owes oneself in society.

The terrace where he composed *Emile,* said Grétry's good servant woman, who was our guide. We gave her thirty sous, and went to spend an hour in a little wood a hundred paces from the hermitage; Grétry was there with his nieces, one of them played a few simple notes on the piano.

Laguette read us a few pages of Mme. de Staël's letters on Rousseau, which we had unluckily brought with us, as well as an insipid travel book by M. Damin. Mme. de Staël's bombast and preoccupation with herself spoiling a few concise ideas.

Fine view from this little wood, recently built ancient tower.

We returned via some secluded roads. The War of the Vendée; Laguette's brother-in-law; the cavern where they suffocated some children, pointed out by an old woman whom the inhabitants were incautious enough to leave behind.

The father accompanying his son, who was coming to hand over his rifle; the son was shot. Soldiers slitting open the pregnant women, tearing away their child and bearing it on their bayonet. Soldiers complaining at being used in this war, desiring the fate of those who were waging it on the Rhine, at the sight of the children suffocated by the smoke in the cavern.

We dined. Grounds (thirty-six arpents) of Mme. Daumont-Mazarin, a middle-aged woman; charming, the prettiest I've ever seen; view from the pavilion on the summit, immense view, reminded me of that from Bergamo; less life in this one, however; long horizontal lines; eleven villages; spire of Saint-Denis; dome of the Invalides; the heights of Montmartre (300 feet) hide the rest of Paris; nothing worth mentioning in the view to the east.

The Parisian amiability of our little driver (sixteen years old) because of a little girl of ten (ugly, bad teeth) who had the door keys and who followed us; pleasantness, playfulness of the young man; the little girl's looks, similar to those of a woman of twenty-three.

My companions took no interest in these kinds of observations, or didn't understand them: they were entirely taken up with more serious things. I began to regret not being there with two or three women like Mlle. de Cossé and two or three Bellisles and Pacés. I was gently moved, I had tender and delicate thoughts, the enjoyment of which would have been tenfold if I had seen them augmented by those of others, if I had seen other hearts touched like mine.

I had serious and reasonable companions, not too sensitive and a thousand leagues from all that.

We left; the little boy resumed the indifferent and unoccupied look of a young man of good breeding. The grayish evening. The rising of the moon, a strange effect: it was red and broken up by slate-colored clouds.

September 2.—I'm all in, I'm worn out, exhausted to the last drop, mentally and physically; but I want to employ that last drop to say what put me in this state.

Dinner with C. Story of Mélanie.

Ten o'clock is striking; I slept with Mélanie last night.

September 4.—I've decided not to leave any more blank spaces, I'll go back to the accounts of the previous day when I have time.

Since I've been in Paris, I haven't yet hustled around in a carriage as much as today (seventeen livres three sous).

At Faure's, I translated fifty lines of Virgil.—I went to M. Pacé's, who wasn't home. I got in a cabriolet at twenty minutes past ten, I went to Mme. Mélanie Durfey's, from there to Mlle. de Cossé's, where I found Pacé, from there to Joseph Périer's (young tough), from there to the Rue du Bac, passed by the Rue de Babylone, to Quesnay's carriage stand (noon till evening, fifteen livres), from there to my room, from my room to Legacque's at half-past one.

Alphonse and Joseph [Périer] arrived, Dominique too, with a berlin. We rode from three till half-past four to the camp; we drove around the camp, to the Château de Meudon; very extensive view (Paris, Saint-Cloud). We were back in Paris at a quarter past nine. We went to their house, from there to Mélanie's, from there to Frascati (a hundred and fifty persons, pretty), from there to my room, where I'm suffering from a headache and the fatigue of riding in the carriage.

I must go to see Mme. Z [Daru] tomorrow at Clamart. Mme. Durfey is there. Yesterday, the 3rd, dined at the home of Mme. Z, the mother, with M. de Z, Pacé, Le Brun. The frankness and gaiety of Z, I'm satisfied with this dinner. Thirty others like it would fix me up in great shape.

I went to Pacé's at ten o'clock, I left there at half-past twelve. The most intimate confidences.

Inspection of the Guard. Role of M. de Z; pride, nobleness, virtue. THE husband. ALL IS DONE, AT THE END OF THAT MONTH THE END.

I wrote a ten-page letter to my grandpapa.

Excellent morning. That, with some dinners like the 2nd over a period of six months, and I'd be anchored. Fifty lines of Virgil.

September 6.—This morning I thought I had quinsy, and was an imaginary sick man. In the evening, all worked up about my visit to Clamart. I left at a quarter past six. Joseph. Details concerning the purchase of cabriolets and horses (nine livres, fifteen sous); fifty minutes from Châtillon to Paris. I found M. Z, his wife, Pacé, Mme. du Châtenay, the bride-to-be, an indifferent woman, the children. Martial went to the billiard room on some pretext or other. I said to him in English that that was his intended; she seems to have some soul, she was all aquiver. They left. I was leaving, Mme. Alex [Pierre Daru's wife] told me to stay, that we would play billiards. We played, she against Mme. Estève and me! I played badly, but now and then I made some good shots.

M. Z came in, I played with M. de Z, against him and Mme. Estève; I wasn't too much of a fool, as M. Jourdain said. Daru invited me to dinner tomorrow. Mme. Alexandrine invited me to stay. Daru said, "We have a bed to offer you." We played six games, I left. I'm satisfied because I became a little familiar with them and showed a little wit. I'll never again tremble to make any visit after having made that one. I became a little acquainted with Mme. Estève, who looks like, and is, a very goodhearted woman.

Visits like this one do much for my hopes: I'm indebted to Mlle. de Cossé for having encouraged me along this line. I believe I'll be entirely attractive to Mme. Martial. I believe he'll be much happier with her than with Mlle. de Cossé.

Sunday, 7.—I dined at M. Z's, I wasn't overly amiable; I forgot to bow to Mme. Estève as I entered; I said two or three witty things before Digeon and Pacé.

Monday, I saw the Mmes. de Cossé. I dined at their home Tuesday (September 9) with M. Delmotte, Mlle. de Cossé's confessor. We went to a garden, from there for a walk on the Boulevards; I'm invited for dinner Thursday, the 11th; we're going to Mousseau [the present Parc Monceau].

September 10.—Today, the 10th, I feel unhappy because of my lack of a job. I went to take a bath, met M. de Baure, played billiards with Faure. I don't feel any genuine genius FOR MY COMEDY; that's what makes me the unhappiest.

September 18.—Paris, a war town. Napoleon said to M. Mollien: "I'm leaving soon, I'm going to preside at the Frankfurt Diet, I don't know whether I'll have war, but I want to throw some fear into them."

Everybody is excited. I've just said good-by to Laguette. All the carriages of the Faubourg Saint-Germain are piled up in the streets.

The gunner of Vincennes who died because he couldn't leave; the sick soldiers at the Ecole Militaire who jumped out the windows. The tried and proven ardor of the Guards.

Yesterday I saw four or five of my relatives here. Increasingly close friendship with Martial; he came to see me this morning. I've just been to Mme. Al. Z's, who wasn't home.

If everyone leaves, what will become of me? Am I to remain a bourgeois of Paris this winter? Am I to go to win honors in the North? I'd prefer the latter, especially with Martial. Nothing would be easier for Z than to find me a place there. If I made good, it would mean a commission: if I bungled, it would be overlooked in the disorder of war.

But will Z think of me, 1st? 2nd, will he tell me, "Come"?

They say His Majesty is leaving Wednesday. Within a fortnight, I'll know my fate. MY LOVE FOR Mélanie has revived a little. I've been happy the past few days.

September 23.—I was consumed with ambition all morning long, so much so that I could scarcely read. At two o'clock I went to see Martial, whom I found in anger at his assistants, who really are lifeless and conceited machines; I dictated a legal document to them until four o'clock; I went downstairs, numb with work, to see Mme. Daru the mother. I felt what I already knew—that I can be a hard worker.

Listless conversation, friendship and trust on her part; she invited me to dinner without insisting, as she had enough only for herself.

At seven, M. and Mme. Z arrived. Monsieur greeted me in a very friendly way, he was very tired, he had to go to Saint-Cloud at eight.

I went to Mme. de Baure's: Mme. de Laussat, a Senator. The Emperor is sending them a message tomorrow. Mme. de Baure and I went to Mme. du Châtenay's to sign Martial's contract. A quarter of an hour later, Mme. Rebuffel and her daughter arrived. Adèle looked like a woman of the Court, tall but completely lacking in feeling, even perhaps cruel, occasionally without ideas, narrow-minded.

M. and Mme. Z were there. A reply I made to Z about Pacé was apt, he admitted it.

He left at eight, Martial not having arrived yet.

The signature took place at half-past eight. I wasn't in the least bashful, but I wasn't what you might call amiable. Sulky look of Mlle. Chanceny [nickname of Martial Daru's fiancee]. I played bouillotte.

Martial at first wanted us to joke, and he joked himself, he asked me my opinion of his intended, soon a happy look came over him; right now, at half-past eleven, he has it completely.

At a quarter to eleven, Z arrived from Saint-Cloud. "I'll look after any errands you may have on the Rhine: I'm due to be at Mainz, that is at Frankfurt, on the 6th. The Emperor is leaving the day after tomorrow with the Empress." He appeared to think he had been told that as a favor.

I was a little irritated by the departure of my cousins. I talked for an hour and a half with Faure, who's naturally slightly pessimistic in general and a great deal for me in so far as I am living on hopes and plans for the future; he himself has none at all, and feels excessively the rubs that I scarcely notice.

This conversation made me gloomy the rest of the day.

I found some relief, however, by doing that with Mélanie. My relief would have been complete if I had been in love with a woman who slept with her husband.

The tragic character into which I've lapsed is more to Mélanie's liking than my usual character.

September 27.—I've just been to *Il Matrimonio Segreto;* the overture and first scene (that of love) gave me exquisite pleasure. The lightest touch of the bow on the instrument is perceptible to me, I begin to enter into it through the melody.

Mlle. du Châtenay played me a charming one yesterday. I went because Mme. Rebuffel had told me in the morning that the family would be there. Mlle. Chanceny complimented me on my patience in listening to Martial, who was playing the piano, I realized that I was trying hers by staying. I left. At Martial's for two hours this morning; at the end, I talked to him about himself in a way that was led up to by the conversation; he told me that I could leave with him if I wished, that he'd speak about it to M. Daru *this morning* so that my fate may be decided at once; I'll be:

2. Either a subordinate going with Martial;
1. Or a war commissary ditto;
4. Or a war commissary going elsewhere;
5. Or a subordinate going elsewhere;
3. Or nothing, staying in Paris.

It seems to me that, in order to justify the latter contingency, Daru will be obliged to promise that I'll be an Auditor. That upsets me a little today, we'll see tomorrow which supposition will be confirmed.

I'd like to be a war commissary, employed with Martial; if the war lasts a long time, as the chances are that it will, a year or eighteen months, Daru being the only talented man in the war administration and I being with him, I'd have a better chance of promotion that if I were an Auditor.

In any case, it seems to me that my situation is going to be decided, and that gives me pleasure.

If I leave, I'll take more than 3,000 livres with me; I've bought a map of Germany from Lesage which clears up that chaos for me entirely.

September 28.—I went out at half-past eight, I ran into Martial in the Rue de l'Université, we made the rounds of the saddlemakers, jewelers and others till five o'clock. I went to see the Mmes. de Cossé at half-past six. Alexandre drove me out at eight. From there, happiness until midnight; happiness of reason which I thoroughly enjoyed, the first in my life, I believe. Superb moonlight. Coblentz. *Mémoires sur la Russie.* An ice at the Café de Foy; the woman on the corner. Walk. The whore. Happiness.

Tuesday, the 30th.—Martial's marriage. I was returning to my room at a quarter past eight from Mélanie's, where I had spent the night, when I ran into Martial in his new carriage, who said, "Aren't you coming to the church? etc." I went there at half-past eight, Mme. Daru spoke to me in the sacristy, there were tears in her eyes. She spoke to me confusedly about a scene Alexandrine made with her husband Tuesday night at Mme. du Châtenay's. Daru said to his wife, "It would be unseemly for you not to come, etc.," a little reprimand. But his face was scarlet, he was sweating profusely and, as a result, was ill during the night.

That seems to me to show weakness of character.

The wedding; Mlle. de Chanceny's agitation. We went into the sacristy, I displayed some wit with Messrs. de Baure, Le Brun and Nougarède. It was the first time in my life that I wasn't the last word in awkwardness in front of the latter.

I'm a great ninny, I must confess; I take all my pleasure in being sad. I detect sorrow in my heart because Martial hasn't yet told me definitely whether I'm to go along on the voyage to Mainz, and that is not because it's of major importance for my situation, but because, were I sure of leaving Paris, I would have the pleasure of getting an impression of sadness from everything I see here.

I'd be plunged into a fatuous melancholy at the sight of the trees in the Tuileries, of those beneath my windows, of the highway between here and Clamart.

This feeling may have its good side, but it serves as a counter-incentive to action, it casts you into boredom and into the English manner, it makes you boring for others, it brings you vexations in society and greatly increases your susceptibility to vexations.

October 6.—My mania for making back entries keeps me from describing what happens to me; too, I frequently prefer to act rather than to describe my actions, frequently I would lessen my happiness if I attempted to describe it.

At nine o'clock, breakfast with Faure; four games of billiards. I went to Martial's. I'd consider it a very great misfortune to fall in love again with Mlle. de Cossé, although I now have means of succeeding whose existence I didn't even suspect three years ago.

October 9.—I don't know why I'm not very happy. Certainly, if my luck was the contrary, I'd be very sad.

This morning at a quarter to twelve, Martial, in his cabriolet, agreed that I should go along with him; he isn't going to take anyone from his office; we're leaving Saturday or Sunday.

Since then I've been hurrying around (seven livres four sous), I saw

Mlle. de Cossé; I dined with her yesterday at Pacé's. Is hope about to reawaken my love for her? When I told her of my departure, she had a few moments of reverie, her eyes are hurting her.

Alexandre [Petiet] came to get his orders for Burgundy; thus, she will be simultaneously without the man she loves and the man who loves her. (In loving her, I felt all my old absurdities returning; I'm not wealthy enough to be her husband, therefore to the devil with the whole business! It's better to leave.)

I'm leaving, but without any rank. That's the reverse of the medal.

Thursday, October 17, I believe.[1]—I believe we're going to leave with Martial in three hours.

I went to Mélanie's, who, at five minutes past eleven, wasn't there. I wrote to her.

Mme. de Pacé wept; I'm on splendid terms with M. de Pacé. I'm leaving alone with Martial; I'm taking about 2,000 livres with me; 1,500 on my father and 1,000 on Périer, I paid out about 400 livres.

Leaving today, I'll have been in Paris three months and seven days, or ninety-seven days, having arrived here July 10. I haven't any very intense pleasures, but I've frequently been contented.

The most intense pleasures I've had were given me by the consciousness of my progress in the knowledge of life.

Adèle gave me a moment of sentiment at the performance at Olivier's when she drew back against me, pretending to be afraid. She talks of nothing but the Petiets. I think she'll marry Alexandre.

We were to have left Saturday, then Sunday, then Wednesday; we're finally leaving Thursday.

I think that's true.

From letter to Pauline Beyle, Metz, October 18.—We left Paris the 16th at 6:03 in the evening. Leaving Paris, we were rather sad. We concluded from that that we should laugh more than ever. I'm perfectly satisfied with the way Martial treats me.

We're going to Coburg, but the Emperor is undoubtedly far ahead. We're going from here to Mainz, from Mainz to Würzburg, from Würzburg to Bamberg, from there to Coburg and from there to glory.

From letter to Pauline, Münnerstadt, October.—We slept, for the 1st time since leaving Paris, at Münnerstadt. We haven't a second to ourselves. We are the first French to come into this region, which calls for precautions. If you wish to follow the march of a heart you never leave, look on the map for Metz, Homburg, Mainz, Frankfurt am Main. We only left this beautiful river yesterday, from Frankfurt to Hanau. From Hanau to Aschaffenburg, from there to Würzburg; from Würzburg

[1]It was October 16.

to Werweck and finally to Münnerstadt, after fifteen leagues partly covered on foot in the midst of a violent windstorm, our terrified horses threatening to upset us every minute. At the height of the storm, the rain pouring from my hat over my shirt and into my boots, I thought of you. This storm, at six-thirty on a boundless plain in the middle of a forest in Saxony, without encountering a single companion for five hours, gave me unknown sensations.

From a letter written thirty-four years later, on August 10, 1840, to the fourteen-year-old Eugénie de Montijo, the future Empress Eugénie.— I thank God for having entered Berlin October 2[7], 1806, with my pistols carefully charged and primed. For his entry, Napoleon put on his dress uniform of a division general. It was possibly the only time I saw him in it. He rode twenty paces ahead of his soldiers; the *silent* crowd was but two paces from his horse; he could have been shot down by a rifle from any window.

From letter to Pauline, Berlin, November 3, 1806.— I believe we're going to Brunswick; it's said to be a fine city with a French theater.

The weather was cold and damp the day before yesterday; we went to a review at Charlottenburg at nine o'clock; I had been hurrying around since seven; I had a little chill; last night I noticed that I was cold, that I had a peculiar feeling; this morning I had the symptoms.

I'm afraid it's my slight fever of two years ago. I want to cut it short; it used to plunge me into a horrible gloom every night; it's true that I had only my intellectual faculties to make me happy in those days; I was in Paris without a fire, without light, without a coat, with holes in my boots; it's quite different here. I must have three or four hundred louis; I'm quite well dressed, though not entirely so; I'm badly lodged and well fed.

On the other hand, my mind is unable to make me either happy or sad, the poor devil is obliged to remain dormant.

I'm opposite the arsenal, a superb building next to the King's palace. We're separated from it by a branch of the Spree, whose waters are the color of green oil. Berlin is situated on a strip of sand which starts a little this side of Leipzig. In all the places that aren't paved, you sink in up to your ankles; the sand makes a desert of the city's environs; they produce nothing but trees and some turf.

I don't know what gave them the idea of planting a city in the middle of this sand; this city is said to have 159,000 inhabitants.

Here, a thousand rumors of all kinds cancel out each other in a trice; you can hardly depend on anything you haven't seen yourself. I've only seen the battlefield of Naumburg. I'm only a provisional war commissary.

From letter to Pauline, November 9.— I'm writing you from a wretched village called Schönebeck, near Magdeburg on the road from Berlin to Brunswick. We dined on an omelet of six eggs, which Martial and I made, and some soup of bread crumbs, beer and eggs. Yesterday, we visited Potsdam, the apartment of Frederick the Great, his tomb. At Sans Souci, we saw some specimens of his handwriting and a volume of his poetry with manuscript corrections by Voltaire. The man who showed us all these things was one of the hussars of his chamber who was relieved two hours before his death. He showed us a clock given to Frederick by his cherished sister and which he used to wind himself. It stopped at 2:21, the moment of his death.

From letter to Pauline, Brunswick, December 25.—I'm leaving today, Christmas Day, at five o'clock in the morning, for Paris. I was to have left a week ago, but the government and the Intendant wanted me to await more complete materials for my mission.

All the preparations for the voyage are finished at last. The weather is terrible, a mixture of rain, hail and snow; it's as dark as an oven; the wind blows out all the candles in the wagon's lanterns.

From letter to Pauline, Strasbourg, December 30.—As nine o'clock struck, I was climbing up the filigreed steeple of the Strasbourg Cathedral, higher than the bells and in a raging wind. I thought the tower was going to collapse. I'm on my way to Paris; I expect to be there in sixty hours, and to stay for twelve or fifteen days.

From letter to Pauline, Brunswick, March 16, 1807.—I got out of bed to-day for the first time in a week; I had a rheumatic fever accompanied by a swelling in the extremities and a skin eruption; it went down a bit this morning; I haven't any fever at the moment, but I expect some in a couple of hours. I was afraid, and the people called my friends were afraid, that it was scarlet fever, a dangerous and contagious malady which isolates the patient from society for two months. I'd already planned to make considerable progress in German during this period of solitude.

I've been prevented from sleeping almost every night by fever; a subject of reflection I could not escape was the need of uprooting vanity from my heart. That's the front door to unhappiness.

It's necessary after that, I told myself, to have independent pleasures. Would you believe that one of the fruits of my nocturnal reflections is going to make me learn to play the piano? Si, signora, in order that I may better appreciate good music! I'm becoming more sensitive to this fine art every day, and every day I'm growing more disgusted with the common run of men, who are much too base and vulgar: they end by making me sick to my stomach.

There's a rather strange society here, which I'll describe when I have more strength. I was trying my best to become a little smitten with a damsel in this society; my sickness came along and interrupted me in this noble enterprise. All the women here are pretty, but hardly inspire anything more than boredom and scorn.

From letter to Pauline [Brunswick], April 30.—I was to leave for Thorn. I conquered love with great difficulty and, since it must be said, with weeping; I was so excited at seven o'clock in the evening—the time when I was going to decide on my departure—that I ran through the streets of Brunswick like a madman; I passed before the windows of a little girl I like; I felt myself torn between honor and love. But love was the stronger; I went to tell Martial that I wanted to leave; he didn't want me to, he was relying on love to retain me, he said everything needed to make me stay.

I'm staying, I consider myself happy; I don't know why Minette [Wilhelmina von Griesheim] has taken it into her head to keep me waiting; prudence, vanity and pity order me not to worry about her any longer. At a famous ball, I courted another; surprise, unhappiness, disappointment on the part of Minette. This other one offered an easy victory to cover my retreat.

Yesterday, I finally became reconciled with Minette; I could tell you two or three volumes of little foolishnesses, but I don't want to take advantage of your friendship to bore you. Yesterday, Minette *squeezed my hand,* nothing more; you'll laugh at me, but, after the life I've been leading for the past six years, that's the reason I've been so upset during the present month.[1]

I no longer have more than a liking for Minette, that blonde and charming Minette, that soul of the North, the like of which I've never seen in France or Italy; the proof of it is that I'm going to try to go to Falkenstein, the headquarters of the Army. After what Grandfather tells me of M. Daru's letters, *if he has the occasion to write him*—I say *if,* for he mustn't be provoked—ask him to say that I desire *to serve in the active army,* don't forget my errand.

This evening, great battle at the ball, where I'm going to be between the two rivals; perhaps tomorrow I'll be as upset as the day before yesterday; but my plan remains the same, I'll join the Army if I can. What attracts me to it is the desire to get a close view of those barnyard dogs called men.

From an undated letter.—I wrote three days ago, and I meant it, that my liking for Minette had entirely passed; I gave her up for Fräulein von Treuenfels, whom I love not at all; I was amused by the agitations of the two rivals; I finally turned to philosophy for the emotions which love was no longer giving me.

[1]Years later, Stendhal wrote in his *De l'Amour,* "The greatest pleasure that love can give is the first hand squeeze of a woman one loves."

Fräulein von Treuenfels as much as told me that she was in love with me. It happened last Thursday; this love confession consisting in confessing to me the love she had had, and no longer had, for Herr L. . . . For the first time, I saw Minette with a lover who's been courting her for four years and is only awaiting her father's consent or death to marry her; even if she doesn't love him, she ought to prefer him to me, who have no desire to marry her. That evening she held the scales even between the two of us, but yesterday, Monday, she seemed to love him. Would you believe it, for four mortal days I've been thinking of nothing but that! When my soul doesn't upset my mind, it's completely devoted to finding means of making myself loved by her without harming her in the least with her future husband, and there's no doubt that, the day after I became sure of her love, she'd be almost unbearable to me. Finally yesterday, with rage in my heart, I recalled the influence of the physical on the mental: I drank a lot of tea, and I partly recaptured my reason, enough at least to be amiable; but she has too much intelligence and passion to be sensitive to this kind of merit. In my unhappiness, I turned to all my tastes in search of a distraction: I took some little trips. I was bored by books. This morning I reviewed them; my eye fell on a volume of selected thoughts from Helvétius; I took a horse; I galloped to Richmond (a very pretty English garden as far from Brunswick as the Piquepierre bridge is from Grenoble, in a flat countryside with light-colored vegetation). Arriving in the cool shade, I flung myself down on the lawn: Helvétius consoled me for two hours.

From letter to Pauline, Brunswick, May 28.—I haven't received my orders from headquarters yet. If I don't get any in the next fifteen or twenty days, it will mean that M. Daru prefers to leave me here, and I'll stay.

That will suit me for my instruction. In six months, I'll know ⅔ of German, and I'll be familiar with German literature. I'll have made some progress in the great art of traveling, which is far more difficult than is generally believed.

I'm still working on my sentiments, that's the only road to happiness.

Journal from June 17, 1807 to . . .

I am starting this notebook with all the humility a good Christian could ask of himself. The Minette adventure is a lost battle: that will teach me the value of time. If she hasn't given me a sublime moment, like that with Adèle at Frascati, I have had some with her that were very delightful.

Je ne veux en aimant que la douceur d'aimer.

This line is almost true of my soul and not of my pride, it's the latter that has put me in a bad humor since Thursday. I've just taken my second music lesson from M. Denys (forty-four francs for twelve lessons), I take two a week, and two others from Herr Maucke, three from Herr Koechi.

I expect to learn to ride a horse any time now. It appears that M. Daru found me forward to ask to be changed. Martial is beginning to treat me well again, because I'm getting to be a flatterer. I'm on good terms with all the French.

I'm reading Tracy (*Logique*), Biran and Helvétius's *L'Homme*.

I have my pistols, on which Rasch has just changed the trigger guard, I've gone shooting a dozen times, seven or eight hundred shots at the most. My entire possessions consist of 71 fr. and 50 louis.

If, as Biran says, we possess musical memory only through the sounds we can reproduce, it's necessary to learn to sing in order to remember beautiful melodies.

Minette: "I'd be ungrateful indeed if I didn't love him, he's loved me so long."

June 17.—I was exposed to a great danger this morning: Brichard read the beginning of this diary, fortunately not to the bottom of the first page.

Yesterday I was almost beside myself with the pleasure I used to picture to myself in childhood when I looked at M. Le Roy's *Baigneuses*.[1]

Music at Der Grüne Jäger,[2] after walking home with Fräulein von Treuenfels, who told me her story with Liby.

[1]"In M. Le Roy's studio, there was a large and beautiful landscape: a steep mountain close to the eye, adorned with large trees: at the foot of the mountain, a shallow but wide and limpid stream flowed from left to right at the foot of the last trees. There, three women who were almost nude—or without the 'almost'—were gaily bathing . . . It was a blend of tender sentiments and gentle voluptuousness. To bathe thus with such amiable women!" Stendhal: *Vie de Henry Brulard.*

[2]The Green Huntsman in English, or Le Chasseur Vert in French. This rustic open-air café made an indelible impression on Beyle. In *Le Rose et le Vert* he transplanted "Le Chasseur Vert, an English garden, celebrated for its old elms," to the vicinity of Königsberg. "It is there," he said, "that two or three times a week, at five o'clock of a summer's afternoon, all the girls and young women of the town meet to take their coffee in the open air. There is invariably some troupe or other of Gypsy musicians who play wind instruments in the distance, concealed by great elms which are the contemporaries of the

Minette's expression made her pretty.

Strombeck and I fired thirty pistol shots, I very badly.

You may make believe for a month, two months, but you return to your true character. I don't invest my capital in the possession of women. Between the ages of sixteen and thirty-one, Martial has had about twenty-two women, of whom a dozen came after a genuine love affair. I'm twenty-five years old; in the next six years I'll probably have six. I'll have twenty horses between now and the time when age prevents me from riding.

June 18.—Minette at the Intendant's. "You put some questions to me the other day, I'm entitled to put one to you in my turn: is what you're doing to Fräulein von Treuenfels serious or are you making a fool of her?"

"In order to answer you, it would have been necessary that you answer me otherwise the other day. I loved you to distraction, and I still love you; there's no sacrifice, no folly, etc., etc. . . ." (A vehement declaration which was probably listened to with the pleasure of coquetry.) "Will you receive me when you are Frau von Heerdt?"

"Certainly, but I won't be that for a long time yet."

The arrival of her intended cut short our conversation, showing me that I'm not yet relegated to a place among the indifferent ones, and that her feeling for Heerdt is not passionate love.

Minette and Philippinchen asked Herr von Strombeck a number of questions about me.

Minette told him, "I'm sure Mina [von Treuenfels] doesn't love him, she has someone else in her heart."

Philippinchen: "Tell me, was it by chance that you came to Der Grüne Jäger the other day?"

Strombeck started telling her that he didn't know anything about it, that I'd come on horseback to get him, etc.

Strombeck to Mina, who was reading a letter in German:

"Ah! You receive billets-doux!"

"Can it be that Beyle has told you something?"

I interest their coquetry, I talked a lot to Herr Emperius, who is intelligent but in whom you feel the lack of soul (in conversation, he hasn't a spark of Corinne's warmth); he entirely eclipsed Strombeck.

last masters of the Teutonic Order . . . Hearts that are ripe for music and love delight in these melodies of the wind instruments played at a rather slow tempo. The most barren hearts . . . are not shocked by it." And, in *Lucien Leuwen* (which he thought of calling *Le Chasseur Vert*), he again speaks of these musicians "who execute in an enchanting manner a variety of music that is sweet, simple and rather slow. Nothing could be more absorbing, more in harmony with the sun setting behind the great trees of the forest."

June 19.—At five o'clock, I went to take my first riding lesson from Quartermaster Lefaivre, a narrow mind.

I went shooting with Münchhausen and Herr von Heerdt. I shot quite badly. This company makes me sick.

Herr von Heerdt is a handsome likeness of M. David [of Grenoble], mathematics professor, physically and mentally. Small stature without either grace or strength, some good sense, speaking several languages well, but he isn't, it seems to me, what could be called an intelligent man.

Heerdt said to Herr von Strombeck:

"I'm delighted to have M. de Beyle go with me, he pleases me greatly, etc." (This is a translation.) He finds everything good in me, he doesn't treat me at all like a rival.

I'm in wrong with Frau von Strombeck for having been a bit of a Valmont one evening. It's not the first time I've gone too far.

Herr von Lauingen invited me to dinner at Lauingen, afterward Frau and the two Fräulein von Griesheim, Herr von Heerdt, Herr von Strombeck and I are going to Grossen Twilpstedt [Gross Twülpstedt, Strombeck's home].

This morning at one o'clock, returning from La Mache, where I had spent two hours with Herren von Heerdt and Münchhausen, I experienced a couple of hours of disgust with everything in the world, even with Helvétius's *L'Homme,* which I was then reading and which seems to me good sense itself. I find more in one of its chapters than in whole volumes by others, both more clearly stated and better demonstrated.

Strombeck agreed with me tonight that the Germans' weak point is to be too meticulous. Their legislation undoubtedly leads them to this. How many receipts, how many cashiers' offices, how many employments there are in the Brunswick financial administration! What complexities in the distribution of justice!

June 23.—Voyage to Twilpstedt.—I returned last night from Twilpstedt. Strombeck and I left Saturday at half-past eight. Frauen von Strombeck, von Griesheim, Philippinchen and Minette had left half an hour before the carriage; Herr von Heerdt escorted them on horseback.

We arrived at Lauingen at half-past eleven, lunched well, as a German would say, on rum, *bischof,* cakes, butter and chocolate; nothing hot.

I was satisfied with myself all day, I was occupied with my situation with Minette and Herr von Heerdt. Minette constantly sought me out, I was a bit bashful till dinner, it brought about a revolution.

After dinner, I saw clearly that Minette was in an amorous ecstasy that wasn't a matter of sentiment but the opposite of it; this points out a great means of seduction. I ended by speaking to her very well of my love in veiled but unmistakable words. From that moment until we left, Herr von Heerdt was sad: he really loves her.

I didn't know anything about Holland, he gave me the first elements of a description of its position.

Shamefully pillaged. Capital diminished by two thirds. The King wanted to seize the money in the bank, he was warned that there would be a revolt, ruining their credit: he ruined them. A strong and genuine spirit of liberty. Hatred of the Spaniards is still national. Generally speaking, all Holland is under water; some places sixty feet. Dutch character, as unpleasant as it is grave. Peasants near Amsterdam who have possessions worth eight hundred thousand or a million francs.[1]

Herr von Heerdt himself, a Frenchified Dutchman, but only slightly so. You always feel his fund of good sense. He told Strombeck not to aid in marrying Philippinchen to Herr von Lauingen, it wouldn't be a success; i.e., he'd be a cuckold. Yet he himself is deeply in love with Minette, he's with her all the time, he talks to her incessantly; that's in absolute opposition to French mores: such an unconcealed preference shocks society, disrupts it. The Germans, being less civilized, are concerned much less than we with what disrupts society.

The husbands are forever fondling their wives, but in a phlegmatic and listless manner.

All the Germans of Strombeck's acquaintance married for love, namely: himself, Strombeck; Herr von Münchhausen; his brother Georg; Herr von Bülow; Herr von Lauingen.

I must ask Faure for a list of twenty or thirty French husbands with the reasons for their marriage; in general, convenience, which is related to vanity, the usual passion of the French.

June 30.—Quite a happy day, this morning on account of the money from my father. I went to Der Grüne Jäger at one o'clock, I fired thirty shots at twenty-five paces: two bull's eyes. On the way back, the first good trotting weather I've had this year. I returned tonight with Strombeck. Fräulein von Griesheim and Fräulein von Oeynhausen were there. I made the latter a bit amorous during supper, from what I was able to guess. Strombeck came back with me, we looked at the stars.

This morning, July 1, 1807, I sang with M. Denys for the first time the duet, *"Se fiato in corpo avete."*

July 3.—A happy day. The Griesheim girls, their mother, Frau von Strombeck, Fräulein von Oeynhausen, Herr von Heerdt, Strombeck and I went to the Hasse Mountain.

[1] I am extracting this piece from the present diary FOR LOVE June 23, 1820. [Note by Beyle.] (The lines immediately following, as well as the entry of July 6, are the nucleus of Chapter LVIII of *De l'Amour.*)

Through experience, I am realizing a truth from which my laziness was taking me away: namely, how useful it is to choose the proper moment. I'd have done well to put this into practice with Pacé and some women.

I've seen Philippinchen, the fat and sensitive Philippinchen; she could have been made to understand things that day which were impossible on the other days, yesterday, for instance, at Frau von Lefzau's.

She, Minette, Herr von Heerdt and I got lost.[1] Frau von Griesheim's anger, the embarrassed look of the susceptible Lauingen, the host; his detestable dinner.

I was (as much as my stature permits) a handsome man that day. First day of my gray coat. I seemed to notice a little agitation on the face of Φιλιππιδιον[2] at half-past eight in the morning when I went into Strombeck's. She's here for four days. Very happy day.

July 4.—At Frau von Lefzau's. Boredom. What kind of a face should you put on in society when you're bored or sick?

A person is quite right to say, *Audaces fortuna juvat;* with all due respect, what subterfuges are necessary in order to pinch Fräulein von Oeynhausen's thighs! From sheer boredom, I did so yesterday with success. I even touched the spot where the ebony must start to shade the lily. But I'm afraid that Frau von Strombeck, who was filling the functions of a mother, noticed it and was angry.

All in all, as Mirabeau said, I've had enough of Brunswick.

Sunday, 5.—A hot day. I wrote to the little Italian girl I never saw. I fired seventy pistol shots at La Mache.

I received a letter from Faure well describing those moments of happiness which the Théâtre Français has sometimes given me. The day before yesterday, I received about 580 francs from the government. I've been getting 4 écus (3.877 x 4) a day since May 24. That's one of my faults: my laziness and bashfulness are costing me 30 fredericks and an écu a day as long as I'm here.

July 6.—Very nice party at Wolfenbüttel, given by Strombeck. Frau and the two Fräulein von Griesheim, Fräulein von Oeynhausen, Frau von Strombeck, Strombeck, Herr von Heerdt and I left at two o'clock. I was well mounted and dressed with elegance. (Here is what I understand and wish to make understood: you may wear a suit costing five hundred louis and not be elegant; elegance comes from clothes being adapted to the character of the day, different from those worn the day before, etc., etc., an important thing for a man who is ugly.)

---

[1] I was devilishly and ridiculously romantic eighteen months ago. [Note added later by Beyle.]

[2] Philippinchen von Bülow, Strombeck's sister-in-law, whose name Beyle frequently writes in Greek.

Heerdt's good nature. His anecdotes, which he tells well for this country, win over Strombeck completely. He's frankly and openly in love with Minette, he follows her everywhere and all the time, talks to her incessantly and very often at ten paces from the others, most often in French, in a serious, ponderous way and without grace. He has an ignoble figure, a dull face, much smaller than I. No wit or intelligence (new ideas, sallies, vivacity), but good sense. He tells stories with clarity and sufficient warmth, constantly mixes Dutch with German, which has its charm.

As ass, said Lichtemberg, is a horse translated into Dutch. Dutch is the height of the ridiculous for a German ear.

Yesterday and today, I made the mistake of wearing Strombeck out with talk about myself. I lose all my grace by having an accentuated manner with him that perhaps frequently bores him.

Now that he's going to have supper alone with his wife, I should regain my grace by going more rarely to see them in the evening.

The open manner in which Herr von Heerdt courts Minette would be the height of indecency, ridicule and rudeness in France.

But then, Strombeck told me as we were returning that, of all the women in his family (very large), he didn't believe there was one who had made her husband a cuckold.

His strange proposal to his sister-in-law, Frau von Knisted, whose family is going to die out through lack of male heirs and all the property to revert to the sovereigns, received with haughtiness, but, "Don't ever speak to me of it again."

He hinted something about it to Φ [Philippinchen] in very veiled terms; unfeigned indignation, diminished by the terms instead of being accentuated: "Have you no longer any respect at all for our sex? For the sake of your honor, I choose to believe that you're joking."

During one of his voyages, Φ leaned on his shoulder while sleeping or pretending to sleep; a jolt threw her a little on him, he squeezed her, she moved over to the other side of the carriage. He doesn't believe her to be unseduceable, but he believes that she would kill herself on the morrow of her crime.[1] It's perhaps his pride that makes him believe in this sequel, he loved her passionately, *ne fu riamento, e non l'ebbe* [was loved in return, and didn't have her].

On the other hand, a married man convicted of adultery can be sentenced by the courts to ten years in prison. The law has fallen into desuetude, but it still keeps this matter from being treated lightly. It's a long way from being, like in France, a quality that one can scarcely deny in front of a husband without insulting him.

[1] If I die, I beg, in the name of honor, that this diary be burned without being read. In the name of honor, Frenchmen. [Note by Beyle.]

A few years ago, a woman told her husband, a man of the Court here, that she'd made him a cuckold; like a fool, he went and told the duke about it, the man who made him a cuckold was obliged to tender his resignation from all his employments and to leave the country within twenty-four hours as the result of the duke's threat to apply the laws.

I've said elsewhere that the majority of the men marry for love. They aren't cuckolds, but what wives they have! Chunks of wood, clods destitute of vitality. Not that I don't prefer this sort of thing to Mme. Pacé badly playing the role of a Frenchwoman, playing it like an incompetent debutante, with no flexibility, no progress.

To finish with the subject of women, their dowry. It's just about nothing because of the fiefs: Fräulein von Oeynhausen, daughter of a father who has an income of 30,000 francs and who makes a profit from his landholdings, will possibly have a dowry of 7,500 francs (2,000 écus): Frau von Strombeck had 4,000 écus (4 x 3.877), she'll have 1,500 or 2,000 more at the death of her mother. The supplement of the dowry is payable to the court in vanity. "Among the bourgeoisie," Strombeck told me, "parties of a hundred or a hundred and fifty thousand écus are to be found, but you no longer have any chance of being presented at Court, you're isolated from all society where there is a prince or princess; *it's frightful.*"

A German woman with the soul of Φιλιππίδιον, a great deal of intelligence and the noble and sensitive face she must have had at the age of seventeen (she's twenty-nine or thirty), being respectable and natural, judged by the country's standards, for the same reason having only the small dose of religion necessary, would undoubtedly make her husband very happy.

"But he was married!" she answered this morning when I blamed the four-year silence of Corinne's lover, Lord [Oswold].

She stayed up until three o'clock to read *Corinne,* it had a deep effect on her, and she answered me, *"But he was married!"* There's a woman who'd be bound by marriage.

But, without being pretty, even found to be prudish and insensitive by the petty minds set on petty souls like Christian von Münchhausen,[1] for instance, she made me walk four long leagues this morning. I accompanied them (at eleven o'clock) as far as Ordorf, a long mile away, I came back to Der Grüne Jäger, fired twenty shots at twenty-eight paces; went to bed with the host's daughter for the first time, and began writing this at four o'clock.

She's the first German woman I've seen who was totally exhausted after sex. I made her passionate by caresses; she was very afraid.

[1] I was wrong; he's a good fellow, one of the best-bred men in the region, but witless and with an ordinary sensibility. October 1808. [Note by Beyle.]

I'm gradually learning my trade.

Yesterday, I saw a fine black dog nine months old for which the Wolfenbüttel dogcatcher asked 2 fredericks (2 x 20 f. 80 c.).

July 10.—Bought the black dog, which I named Brocken, 11 écus: the écu is worth 3 f. 887 thousandths.[1]

Voyage to the Brocken.—Monday, July . . . , Herr von Strombeck and I left for the Brocken in superb weather. We went in his barouche, drawn by two military horses; he had his servant with him. Our trip lasted sixty-four hours and cost each of us . . .

We reached Videlah about nine o'clock. The countryside takes on some character as you approach the Harz. At one o'clock, we dined at the inn La Truie Rouge[2] at Ilsenburg.

We started out for the Brocken at four, and reached it about eight, tired out, although Herr von Strombeck was less so than I. There's nothing unusual about the little valley leading up to it; the people of the region admire it because it's the first mountain they have seen. The Ilsenstein, or Ilse cliff, in my opinion merits no attention, and yet it's famous. On the Little Brocken, a half hour before the real one, there's an abandoned house. On the summit of the Brocken, Graf von Wernigerode, sovereign of this region, has built a house with walls five feet thick. It's made of granite, like the mountain itself. The house is exactly on the summit. This summit is covered with big blocks of granite, everything indicates a mountain falling to pieces. This house, I believe, is noteworthy in that it's possibly the only one in the world at this altitude from which the view extends to every side. The plains leading to the forest of Thuringia, toward Gotha and Weimar, can be seen as clearly as those of Brunswick and Hameln. The Brocken is the highest inhabited point in Germany. We found it cold there, with a wind, the like of whose violence I have never encountered.

I was all in. After drinking some rum, beer and tea, we took a turn about the house and went up in the tower. The wind was so violent that it seemed warm to me, it seemed as though we were hearing forty or fifty drums being beaten continuously. Our view extended over about a quarter of a league, all the abysses surrounding us were filled with clouds.

We ate quite a passable supper, considering where we were. The rooms were clean; if it weren't for the rabble from Göttingen and Helmstedt, who come there in swarms and smash up everything (they're students for the most part), the count would have the rooms

[1] Stolen a few months later. [Note by Beyle.]

[2] Beyle's French translation of the inn's name means "The Red Sow." The actual name was apparently Zu den Roten Forellen, which means "The Red Trout" and in French should have been "Les Truites Rouges."

kept much neater. The host he engages has been there for five or six years; three of his children were born in this end of the world, he's separated from the rest of the earth for three months; he told us that his children were baptized at the return of the fine season.

He showed us some small quarto volumes in which it's the custom for each foreigner to put his name and a platitude on the Brocken in the form of a motto. They usually admire, in bad spelling, the might of God, who plucked the Brocken from the void. The volume before the one in which we put our names started with: *Friedrich Wilhelm I, Luisa, Königen von Preussen,* written in German script. I was surprised at the small number of foreign names; I came across two French inscriptions and one Italian as I thumbed through it. I was also surprised at the dullness of such a collection, but that didn't prevent a bookseller from having the first four or five volumes printed. That's the limit, but it seems to me that more is printed in Germany than in France.

From letter to Pauline, August 10.—You've undoubtedly met Victorine [Mounier] by now. Tell me exactly and entirely your impression of her and the character you believe her to have. I'm asking you for a snap judgment, for you've seen her very little; at the same time, I'm eager to have this judgment.

From letter to Pauline, September 2.—But write me at length about that charming Victorine. I believe you're right; she's a very rare soul. I loved her dearly, and I saw her seven times in my life. All my other loves have been but reflections of that one. I loved Mélanie because she reminded me of her character. You must realize how precious the tiniest details on Victorine are to me. Does she love her brother as much as they say? He's one of the most insensitive persons I know, really made for the society of this century.

Try to find out whether she's in love in Paris or Rennes.

From letter to Pauline, October 6.—Here are the principal works of Mozart, a musician born for his art, but a soul of the North, better fitted to depict unhappiness or the tranquillity produced by its absence than the ecstasies and gracefulness that the mild climate of the South bestows upon its inhabitants. As a man of ideas and sensibility, he's infinitely to be preferred, the artists say, to all the mediocre Italian composers; but, as a rule, he's far beneath Cimarosa.

Music consoles me for many things: a little aria that I hum in a falsetto voice refreshes me after two hours of red tape.

November 9.—It takes too many words to describe well. That's what has made me interrupt this diary since the beginning of July. It would be useful to write the annals of your *desires,* your *soul:* that would show you how it could be corrected, but it would perhaps have the drawback of making you meticulous.

My bay horse got the staggers; I bought a gray one in October for 35 fredericks, light but not sturdy, handsome however.

I've killed three partridges on the wing, to my great surprise.

I've gone to Elme several times with M. Daru. He again spoke of our former differences with extreme benevolence.

Grand Marshal von Münchhausen has entirely satisfied me by his sort of excuses. This affair is closed and good to be forgotten about.[1]

I've got over my love for Minette. I sleep every three or four days, for physical needs, with Charlotte Knabelhuber, a girl who's kept by Herr von Kutendville, a wealthy Dutchman. I'm pleased with myself on that score.

Mme. Alexandrine Daru passed through here and greeted me in a way that seemed friendly.

I took a pleasant trip to Hanover.[2] I've had Jeannette. I won 34 or 35 napoleons from the amiable Digeon.

I was absent from Brunswick with Réol eight days minus a few hours (October 26 to November 2). An agreeable trip about which I plan to write a separate journal.

Yesterday, a lively ball at Frau von Marenholtz's, with whom Brichard spends all his time very conspicuously. Strombeck was miserable while we were having a good time. He wrote me these very words: "Last night was one of the most terrible of my life: my wife disconsolate, and myself in no condition to console her. All night long, the image of my Karl was before my eyes.—That will finish as everything finishes."

He lost his son Karl from the croup. I was at his house several times the day of his death.

1808

January 14.—Of all our acquaintances in Brunswick, the only really intelligent one is Jacobsohn. Together with intelligence, he has all the finesse of the Jew he is, and two million.

A great deal of imagination of the oriental kind; but he doesn't

---

[1]For an unknown reason, Beyle almost had a duel with Münchhausen. In his *Vie de Henry Brulard,* he says, "At Brunswick, my clumsiness might have sent me *ad patres* with the Grand Chamberlain Münchhausen, fortunately he was not brave that day, or rather, he did not care to compromise himself."

[2]Apparently meaning Hamburg. A long letter to his sister, dated November 25, describes a trip to Hamburg with Réol.

speak French well, and his vanity is too unguarded. By flattering his vanity at the baths of Helmstedt, they made him spend two thousand écus. By handling him properly, you could make him spend ten, but in his household he's miserly like a Jew.

Herr von Siestorpf, master of the hounds, intelligence No. 2.

A man of sixty, 80,000 francs income. A physiognomy expressing finesse and malice. Badhearted; he's never given financial aid to anyone. He ordered a telescope from a poor young artist of Brunswick (Herr von Siestorpf is a very great enthusiast for this sort of endeavor); he was to have given the poor young man 200 écus; when it was finished, he would no longer give him more than sixty.

They say he was little affected by the death of his only son, who died at the age of twenty-four, and disapproved of the latter's love for a natural daughter of the Duke of Brunswick, I believe, but having the title of countess, lady of honor, received at Court, etc. A hard man with no consideration for misfortune. Somewhat resembles a boar.

No. 3. Herren von Münchhausen, Ambassador; von Strombeck, Councilor.

These two men combined would make two charming men. They have a merit that is quite different the one from the other. Herr von Münchhausen, a man of high society, a pitiless chatterbox, is forever recounting fairly diverting anecdotes. Puts himself forward a bit too much, is always reminding you indirectly that he was present when Prince Heinrich, M. de Boufflers, M. de Nivernais, etc. said such-and-such an amusing thing. An income of 36,000 francs, life annuities for the most part. Miserly and unkempt to the last degree. Placing his whole happiness, his whole existence in decorations, ribbons, badges, etc. At bottom, a man of the Court.

A good musician, playing the harmonica, piano, etc. well, having published music. All told, a specimen of the upper society man. Fifty-five years old.

All of which is the contrary of Herr von Strombeck, who looks like an apothecary. Heavy, ponderous and slow-witted; and yet ideas, which are neither sound nor accurate, on the subject of virtue and governments. A good friend, a very fond father, a good son, a good brother. Loving the arts, having a little knowledge of astronomy, well educated but lacking the philosophic spark, unable to unify his ideas. HIS LOVE FOR Φ. Thirty-five years old, and an income of 12,000 francs.

His wife is a mother, nothing more. A perfect nullity, mildness, virtue, but ghastly sluggishness; a German woman as much as it's possible to be one.

4. Herr von Bothmer, Grand Chamberlain. Is sixty-six years old. If he were only forty, we should undoubtedly have placed him as No. 1. Ravenous appetite, eating as much meat as three ordinary men. Knows six languages, has composed some nice German dramatic compositions. Has the literary taste that prevailed in Germany under Frederick the Great. The great Germans—Goethe, Wieland, Klopstock, Bürger, Herder, Schiller—have changed that.

Herr von Bothmer is no longer anything more than a shade of what I believe he used to be. He has nothing to live on but his salary, 6,000 or 7,000 francs; he's commander of the Protestant branch of the Teutonic Order. He's kindly through philosophy and also, I believe, through tenderheartedness; and, he deliberately sings everybody's praises with an appearance of candor, which makes everybody delighted. Has a great love for Frau von Marenholtz, his daughter, an accomplished coquette who completely captivates Brichard.

Father of a witless savage, a genuine military man, excessively strong, well fitted to disgust any man thinking of following the profession of arms. This son, named Ferdinand, didn't want Brichard and me to call him that.

Herr von Bothmer doesn't have liberal and settled ideas about anything. He's a mediocre and amiable little philosopher. Jacobsohn, on the contrary, is really the most intelligent man here. No one would have any doubt about it if only he knew French passably.

January 17.—Dined with General Rivaud, division commander.

A bit upset by dizziness for the past three days. Herr Haeur, a reasonable doctor.

Martial is still in Cassel with his brother; I'm here, occasionally building castles in Spain and seeing myself a war commissary in three months, and, what's more, going with M. Z to Portugal or Greece. I'd be delighted with such a voyage. All in all, I'm contented with my position and rank; the climate is the only thing that puts me in a bad humor from time to time.

February 1.—I received M. Daru's letter assigning me to the Domains.[1] I'm not enthusiastic about this favor; I don't know yet what I ought to do about it.

February 18.—I dined for the second time at the Prefect's. Brichard rather bores me. The inhabitants and I don't have much affection for each other. I've bought *The Last Supper,* the portraits of Frederick and Raphael, a beautiful landscape by Lorrain and a view of the midnight sun at Torneå.

[1]Daru had entrusted Beyle with the duties of Intendant of the Emperor's Domains.

I'm going to put under these portaits and landscapes: "The North and the South, both of them great; which was the happier?"

February 19.—I'm going hare-hunting tomorrow. We're leaving at half-past six; it's at Wolfenbüttel.

I'm still sleeping with Fräulein Charlotte from time to time.

I have strong but fleeting desires for several women. Moreover, the ethic I described last year in the notebook before this one has almost turned into habit. In this respect, I've gained. My bashfulness is disappearing too.

Were I serving under an Intendant General other than M. Daru, my relative, this sentiment would be almost unknown to me by now.

A month ago I wrote Tracy a letter that Faure didn't like very much.

Adèle is marrying M. Petiet.[1]

I must get rid of a bit of pedantry in my manners, possibly the result of bashfulness.

February 25.—Since the last entry I've killed three hares, the first quadrupeds in my life.

Wine and music give me pleasure.

Magnificent weather, frost and sun for the past week.

I gave a dinner, for the first time, for seven people (ninety-two francs). A semi-official dinner that was a success.

The next day, duck-hunting. The only things we killed were two crows.

Yesterday, the 24th, I was bored with Brunswick, I was in good shape, no longer suffering from fever in the past few days, but always unhappy out of boredom.

March 2.—I left Herr von Siestorpf's at eleven after having written, with this pen, until eight a long letter to the Intendant General.

I also wrote Lambert one, in which I told him what I think of this country—namely, worse than hanging. That made me inclined to be gay tonight, and I was so, not bashful in the least.

I lost three écus, a week ago ten; I won twelve or fifteen a fortnight ago.

Lambert's letter contained some things on Calabria and the music of Naples that confirmed my ideas instead of modifying them. I'd find mankind almost natural in Calabria.

My eyes took keen pleasure tonight in Fräulein von Klösterlein's beauty.

March 3.—Dull company and faro game at General Rivaud's. Madame had a fever. Saucerotte taught me how to win by observing the sequence of the cards, because they don't shuffle them.

[1]The marriage took place three days earlier.

March 4.—I received a very friendly letter from Martial, who speaks of the Guard, but I don't believe it would be to my interest to go into it. Z would be jealous of the way in which it was done. I'm taking an examination in which I hope to come off well. Once in the Guard, I'd no longer be available. I'm probably going to be a commissary. This intendancy may lead to a real one.

March 6.—The population of Brunswick took the oath. Gothic ugliness of the building where the authorities were gathered.

The ignominy of the bourgeois during official ceremonies always makes me sick.

The Burgemeister of Brunswick, a ridiculous figure, read a speech which nobody heard. He didn't have the presence of mind to inform the public when it should raise its hand; this movement was made partially, and everybody laughed. The Germans swore allegiance by raising two fingers.

Ceremonies of this kind always make me sick because they recall the ignominy of Grenoble. They'd have a much worse effect on me were I to see them in Grenoble itself.

March 11.—I write all my official letters beneath Raphael's portrait, whose expression changes with the hours of the day. This handsome face, which extracted happiness from its heart, keeps my soul from shriveling up completely. I also have Morghen's *The Last Supper,* copied by Rainaldi.[1] I'm very pleased with it, especially with the figures on the right of Jesus. I also have a beautiful landscape by Lorrain, the midnight sun at Torneå and the portrait of Frederick II.

I want to put Frederick beside Raphael, and under Frederick: *North;* under Raphael: *South;* under Lorrain: *South;* under Torneå: *North.*

This gives a little of my impressions.

At eleven last night, there was a knock on my door. It was the excellent General Michaud and Durzy, who were staying at the Hôtel d'Angleterre. General Michaud's excellent greeting, his extreme kindness. How pleased he looked, how he embraced me on entering and leaving, how he lit my way right to the last landing!

I was contented as I returned at one, with that rare joy given by men's contentedness.

He joked with me about Adèle's marriage. A queer panegyric of Petiet; he believes he's going to become tubercular.

I received a letter from my sister; there's a year of experience between this letter and the last one. Agitation forms a person. She has become very friendly with Victorine.

[1] An engraving of Leonardo da Vinci's *The Last Supper* was made in 1800 by Raffaello Morghen and copied by his pupil, Francesco Rainaldi.

Voyages.—Since November 13, 1806, the day of my arrival in Brunswick: December 25, left for Paris, arrived back in Brunswick February 5.

Went to Wolfenbüttel	9 times
To Hamburg	once
To Cassel	ditto
To Blankenburg	ditto
To the Brocken	ditto
To Helmstedt	ditto
To Twilpstedt	ditto
To Halberstedt	ditto
Hunting at the Elme	seven times
To the Hasse	twice[1]

It will be sixteen months the day after tomorrow, March 13, 1808, since I arrived in Brunswick.

March 17.—I'm very glad that I happened to be taken a long way from the Court, where I desired a position two years ago. That was one of my great mistakes, and it ought to make me circumspect in two things: marriage and resigning from my post.

It's possible that I may have these two desires, but I must reflect on them a long time.

The experience I've had in being attached to a single person for a year confirms my idea that I'm absolutely unsuited for the Court. An independent and solitary job like the one I have now suits me much better. It's true that I'm no end bored.

I didn't go horseback riding for a whole month. For the past six days, I've been riding every morning. Strombeck is at Einbeck. Brichard and I don't get along together, it's about the same with Lejeune, so I'm living absolutely alone, liking no one and liked by no one, I believe.

I have 400 francs a month from my father, and I owe 3,000 francs.

March 18.—I took an excellent English lesson from Herr Emperius. I expounded *Richard III,* I was extremely affected by it. Instead of keeping my imagination to myself, I was stupid enough to dissipate it by telling him two good stories.

March 25—For me.

An efficacious remedy for love: eat peas. Tested today, March 25, after going for a very pleasant horseback ride and feeling a strong desire for the little girl who lives near the Bevern Palace.

---

[1]Although he apparently did not visit it, there can be no doubt that Beyle often heard talk about the nearby town of Stendal, the birthplace of Winckelmann. He later referred to this town as his "bailiwick."

What's the best way for me to put my periods of listlessness and illness to use?[1]

March 29.—For two days, I've been reading with the learned Herr Emperius the work on the London police by Colquhoun, whom I find damnably verbose. I'm reading the works of Gozzi, who appears to me to have more intelligence and a better manner than Goldoni.

I regret and desire Charlotte now that I don't have her any more.

I was delighted with the taking of Constantinople by the Crusaders, as recounted by Simonde de Sismondi at the end of the second volume.

April 8.—A huge flood reached my door at half-past one on the morning of April 8.

I'm reading Johnson's preface to Shakespeare. Judicious and worth discussing.

Shakespeare wrote thirty-five plays.

April 11.—I received a letter from Réol, who tells me that M. Z has been called and that Martial is leaving for Spain.

I wrote to Mme. de Baure, to Mme. Daru the mother, to ask to go to Spain when my work is finished here. I wrote to my grandfather to write to M. Daru, Martial and Mme. Daru for the same purpose. That will make all the strings vibrate and make them say, "Spain."

On April 23, Herr Bothmer repeated to me that there isn't a single good tragedy or comedy in the German language. What slightly invalidates this verdict for me is the fact that I find some merit in the four plays of Schiller that have been translated into French. At the same time, Herr von Bothmer told me that there was an excellent comedy in Dutch entitled *Gisbert van Aemstel,* by van Vondel. "But a bit too much like the Shakespearean sort of thing," he added.

On May 1 I chanced on a society, at the home of the presiding judge, where everybody had been invited except the French. I made some good observations while playing faro. Frau von Marschall, although she has a marriageable daughter, would suit me; she appears intelligent and not prudish. But I feel bashful with her, and anyway there wasn't any opportunity for us . . .

May 3.—I'm writing this at exactly eight o'clock. Until this minute, I've been reading the *Vie de Johnson*[2] without any difficulty. I don't believe it would be possible to read at present in Marseille or Madrid.

Here's my life today, which will serve me as a sample in order to recall how I lived in the spring of 1808: at eight o'clock, the barber woke me up in the grand salon, where I slept for the first time—a

[1] See Beyle's remarkable autobiographical letter to his sister of March 26. It may be found in *To the Happy Few.*
[2] *An Essay on the Life and Genius of Samuel Johnson,* by Arthur Murphy.

circumstance which made me go for a military promenade at four in the morning, sword in hand. I heard a noise in the adjacent rooms, I was up to my neck in dreams, and, as soon as my imagination is awakened I'm timorous. I'm only brave when I'm stupid, the reason being that then I have my feet on the ground. I'm speaking of genuine bravery, my imagination fortifies the bravery coming from the passions. My anger is so intense that it makes my stomach ache for twenty-four hours.

After the barber, I read a few pages of the *Vie de Johnson,* which Herr Eschenburg lent me. Herr Köchi arrived: German lesson, I expounded three pages of the history of des grosses Friederich [*sic*]. These three words, in which there are undoubtedly at least three mistakes, show my progress in this language spoken by bores, and which has few words that are expressive. After Herr Köchi, I put in order the reports on the payment and distribution of a sum of 16,000 talers in gold. I drank a bowl of soup made out of bread, water and butter.

I went to Herr Emperius's to take my English lesson. As my watch (the old one) was fast, I got there a quarter of an hour too early. In a room next to the one where he was, I read a prologue by [Samuel] Foote. I must read this modern Aristophanes.

Herr Emperius had me write in English from an English book which he read in French. I then expounded the fourth and fifth scenes of the first act of *Macbeth.* I made a great mistake in not taking Herr Emperius upon my arrival in Brunswick, I'd know English and Latin by now. He's unintelligent, but an excellent man for teaching languages.

After an hour and a half at his house, I returned home and read the *Vie de Johnson* until three o'clock. All in all, I read a hundred octavo pages during the day with pleasure and without a dictionary, for I haven't got one.

At three o'clock, I worked three quarters of an hour at the office, where Rhule told me in his jargon of a wheedling German that he was going to leave me to work for Herr Voigt, war commissary, Westphalian. The rascal wrote me a letter tonight which corresponds with my opinion of his behavior. I answered it with a contempt that's invisible to a German, and with dignity.

At a quarter to four, I dined on grilled lamb, fried potatoes and salad. The first two dishes came from Janaux's and cost six bongros apiece (eighteen sous).

After dinner, *Johnson.* I went horseback riding at six, and returned at a quarter past seven. I passed by the cobbler's daughter, who smiled and went into the house. My whole day yesterday was animated and happy as the result of the rendezvous I had with her and which was very original. Afterward, at nine o'clock, I met Charlotte, and we took a walk together by moonlight. But the little girl I had just left made me insensitive to this beauty of twenty-five who looks as though she were thirty-two.

Coming home today at a quarter past seven, I drank some tea, three cups, in order to divert myself with my mind in the evening. I read until eight, and I'm finishing this at thirty-five minutes after eight.

I saw the first buds April 15, and nature in full bloom April 26. A warm rain is lacking for the good of the plants and of my nerves.

May 4, after reading *Tom Jones.*—The notions of propriety and danger recur much oftener in a *given* English volume than in a French volume on the same subject.

I must see if this *given,* which generalizes the observation that comes to my mind, is well founded. Then, if this observation is correct and general, I must hunt for the notions that recur the oftenest in Italian and French books.

I have a bad habit of immediately generalizing my observations; this comes from pride in making an important observation, as well as from laziness, since it's much easier, by means of a *given* or a *generally speaking,* to generalize an observation than it is to consider carefully whether or not you really often have the occasion to make it.

On April 15, nature awakened a little; the 26th, generally; on May 5, summer arrived. I'm writing this in shirt sleeves on May 8, 1808.

From letter to Pauline, May 26.—A few days ago, I was thirteen hundred feet underground: it was in the depths of a mine in the Harz Mountains called the Dorothea. It's queer, but the sight which afforded me the most amusement was the one I provided myself. I have such an aversion to bad smells that they immediately change me; I was afraid of the smell of coal sulphur you find in foundries. That was the first thing that made me hesitate; the second was the fear of falling. You go down by means of vertical ladders; if you miss your hold, you become a mess of slag; the greasy rungs are so covered with slippery mud that your hand continually slips. That gave me the same feeling —on a reduced scale—as fighting in a swamp on horseback.

Four years ago, I was in Paris with a single pair of boots full of holes, with no fire in midwinter and frequently without a candle. Here, I'm a personage: I receive numerous letters in which the Germans address me as *Monseigneur;* the leading French personages call me *Monsieur l'Intendant;* the generals who arrive in town come to call on me; I receive requests; I write letters, I get mad at my secretaries, go to formal dinners, ride horseback, and read Shakespeare; yet I was happier in Paris. Could I set my life at the point I please, like a pawn on a chessboard, I'd go back to take declamation lessons from Dugazon and to call on Mélanie, with whom I was in love, wearing a ragged coat that humiliated me. When she wouldn't let me in, I'd go to a library, and finally in the evening I'd take a walk in the Tuileries, where I'd envy those who were happy. But how many delightful moments there were in that unhappy life! I was in a desert where, from time to time, I came across an oasis; now I'm at a table laden down with good things, but I haven't got the least appetite.

This monotony is perhaps going to change: they think we're going to punish Austria for all her insolence; as for me, I'm not one of those *they*. I don't at all desire war, and I'd prevent it a thousand times over if it were in my power; but, once this business is decided, I'd be delighted if it were waged and I were there. This is a case where it may nearly always be said, "You never see again what you've already seen," and I'm beginning to notice that this is the only thing that makes three quarters of men and things bearable.

September 20.—I'm writing this on the day that I've had my books brought back from Richmond,[1] September 20, 1808. It isn't cold, however, but I lost too much time in coming and going.

I've just been to *Cabale und Liebe,* or *Love and Intrigue,* drama by Schiller.

The principal defect of the Germans, in my opinion, is lack of character. Outside nature, which I observe every day, it seems to me that this is to be clearly seen in the difference between the German and Spanish styles, even in translation.

Next, their government has given them the spirit of formality, the talent of the jurisconsult.

Next, reading the Bible, too, has made them silly and bombastic. This factor likewise affects the English character.[2]

The stolidness of the Germans is explained by their food: black bread, milk and beer—still, they drink coffee, but what they need is wine, and the headiest, in order to put some life in their sluggish muscles.

They can't live without women, many children. Few cuckolds.

Remarkable honesty in the nation. Shown by the numerous shipments of money by post.

Since about a month ago the prejudices that concealed the German character from me have been falling off, and I'm beginning to see it clearly, I believe. The greatest sovereigns of the eighteenth century, Frederick II and Catherine II, were from this nation. But I haven't

[1] Attractive summer residence ten minutes from Brunswick. [Note by Beyle.] He had moved there early in June.
[2] True. [Note by Beyle.]

yet found that, since it has degenerated from the character given it by Tacitus, it has produced any ardent geniuses, like the Prince de Condé, for example.

September 26.—I've been in Brunswick nearly four years, which gives rise to the following reflection: I've regarded the people of this land like a real young man, like a real Frenchman, finding fault to their face—as though they were philosophers who were above prejudices— with what seemed to me faulty, and even allowing my contempt for their ponderous thick-wittedness to be seen.

In the first garrison I'm sent to on the banks of the Ebro or the Elbe, I must declare as soon as I arrive that I'm enthusiastic about the country.

October 3.—I built a fire for the first time on September 22, 1808. It was indispensable on October 1.

National vanity makes the French unconquerable, they'd regard it as a humiliation to be subject to a foreign sovereign. If they submitted, the foreigners would soon drive them to revolt through the severity with which they would try to avenge themselves for the contempt the Frenchman produces by poking fun at them.[1]

October 13.—Style of History.—Solemnity, solemnity . . . My style will have a character all its own by scoffing a bit at everyone; it will be apt and concise, and it won't put the reader to sleep.

October 14.—In point of taste, sovereigns have a great advantage; it's to be surrounded, in the role of artists, by the cream of those who live in their time. The Emperor has just accorded an audience to Goethe at Erfurt, and discussed German literature with him. The poet probably explained his guiding thoughts. Consequently, the Emperor is in a position to have much sounder ideas on this literature than the common run of men. And the same applies to everything.

Louis XIV used to converse with Boileau, Molière and Racine about poetry.

October 28.—The finest autumn day I've seen here.—Charlotte jealous and full of love. The *Bibliothèque Britannique* has finally arrived.—I composed my first German theme.

November, 1808.—Charming voyage to Cassel. Left the 13th with an order to go to Paris, returned the 20th. Very agreeable voyage. There was no one, not even the little Westphalian girl, who wasn't good-natured on this voyage.

It cost about 120 francs.

[1]Precisely the most interesting truth in 1815. [Note added by Beyle.]

The Austrian Campaign

IN Paris, "Monsieur de Beyle" plunged into the life of pleasure that befitted a young man intent on becoming a cog in the wheels of Empire, taking dancing lessons, studying Spanish—for he still had hopes of being called beyond the Pyrenees—indulging in a flirtation or two, frequenting the fashionable cafés, dropping in at the theater or opera every evening and following the ambitious Félix Faure when the latter went to pay his social calls.

Especially was his attendance regular at the salon of Alexandrine Daru, his tantalizing young cousin, who, after her friendly treatment in Brunswick, now "overwhelmed" him with kindness. Thus encouraged, he promptly "crystallized": in other words, he was in love, or thought he was, with the wife of Pierre Daru!

The situation, with its danger and piquancy, was a flattering one for a youth who had always dreamed of becoming a "seducer of women." The "immense distance of rank" that separated them, the "insurmountable obstacles and the great danger for both" made his position that of "a courtier in love with a queen." An open courtship being out of the question, he regarded her "as a woman whom one loves timidly and without thinking too much of possessing," relying on the eloquence of his flashing eyes to communicate his sentiments. With Angela Pietragrua and Victorine Mounier, this method had failed miserably, but with Mme. Daru, it seemed to him, there was a response—and it was favorable. "She looked at me as though I were a powder barrel," he later assured Félix Faure.

At the end of four months of this agreeable routine in Paris, he was obliged to resume his duties as deputy commissary. Reports at the beginning of 1809 that the Austrians were rearming warmed up the military situation, and on March 28 Beyle received orders to go to Strasbourg and there await further instructions from Pierre Daru.

After marking time for a week in Strasbourg, he made an auspicious re-entry into Germany one sunny April morning, admiring the Rhineland countryside and skimming through a book while his carriage companions sang.

During the next six weeks he laboriously advanced in the wake of a murderous campaign that cost upward of a hundred thousand lives, but the fatigues, annoyances and horrors of the voyage only momentarily dampened his spirits. "This life fascinates me," he exulted. "I'm in my element." There was much work, but he tackled it with his usual passionate intensity; there was also much leisure, and he devoted it to reading, appraising the girls in the villages he passed through, observing the topography and engineering works of the various regions, and, above all, enjoying the springtime beauties of the German mountains, plains and forests. At length, he arrived on May 12, the eve of the capitulation of Vienna, at Schönbrunn, where Napoleon was already established in the palace.

Vienna delighted him: during his first days there, he experienced "that inner contentment and perfect well-being" which had been inspired previously only by Geneva and Italy. At that period, the city proper was still surrounded by massive fortifications (whose line is followed by the present "Ring"), while outside the walls was a wide band of verdure cut by innumerable paths leading in every direction beneath the dense shade trees. The nucleus of the capital, with its magnificent cathedral, its palaces and its fine houses, presented an appearance of cleanliness and opulence. The Viennese women, Beyle found, were exceedingly attractive, with perfect complexions, a refreshing naturalness of manner and a suggestion of languidness, mingled, however, with considerable sophistication and a taste for coquetry.

To complete his joy, he soon discovered the famous Prater, at that time still possessing all its virgin beauty, and equaling anything he had seen in Lombardy. "The Prater, fertile like all the islands of great rivers, is filled with superb trees which seem to be nobler there than elsewhere," he wrote five years later in his *Vie de Haydn*. "This island, which on every side presents nature in all its majesty, unites pathways of magnificently laid-out chestnut trees with the wild aspect of the most solitary forests. A hundred winding roads cross it, and when you arrive at the banks of the superb Danube, you continue to be charmed by the view . . . of the picturesque slopes on the other side."

In spite of working day and night on the complex preparations for the battle of Wagram, he found time during those weeks of early summer to become acquainted with several Viennese girls, to take solitary horseback rides through the Prater and the Wiener Wald and to pass numerous evenings at the opera.

Such things occupied his thoughts far more than the momentous military events that were taking place about him. It was his fate to just-miss most of the important battles of the Napoleonic era, and, if he experienced some regret at his absence, it was merely the regret of an artist not to have witnessed a thrilling spectacle. Thus he was safely seated at his desk in Vienna May 22 while the Army was engaged in the almost fatal encounter of Essling, across the Danube; and the day of the battle of Wagram, he was stretched out on a chaise longue with a splitting headache.

As a matter of fact, Beyle's health at this time was far from satisfactory. After his long illness in Italy and his intermittent fever, headaches and dizziness in Paris, he had enjoyed a year of comparatively good health at Brunswick, suffering only occasional fever and rheumatic pains from the humidity of the climate. Early in 1808, however, he had had some dizzy spells, and, by the time he had returned to Paris, symptoms of the disease he had contracted in Italy had again appeared. Dr. Richerand, of the Hôpital Saint-Louis, prescribed mercurial massages, but these didn't prevent the symptoms from reappearing in Vienna and causing him considerable suffering through the summer of 1809.

His morale, however, seems to have been very little affected, and his amorous propensities not at all. After two years of sentimental in-activity, he decided that it was time to be falling in love again. During the summer he wrote Mme. Daru four or five letters which he considered to be adequately tinged with affection, but something nearer and more certain than Pierre's wife was required. "I still have to encounter that perfect happiness I have been pursuing," he wrote, "I need a woman with a noble soul."

Women with noble souls were unfortunately no more common in Vienna than elsewhere, but he apparently found several acceptable sub-stitutes among the blonde and buxom lasses of the capital. The principal of these was a girl he called Babet, with beautiful eyes and "an angelic face." He was more or less in love with Babet for several months, but, although they spent many happy hours together, their affair was not of the tranquil sort that he would have preferred, for, as in the case of Mélanie, he was jealous of all rivals, real and imaginary, past and present. He even had an "arranged duel" in the Prater over her with the future General Raindre, according to a couple of vague references in *Henry Brulard*.

The involved negotiations that eventually resulted in the Treaty of Vienna retained Napoleon at Schönbrunn until the middle of October. In addition to the purely political phases of the situation, the Emperor, by now having determined to divorce Joséphine, was taking the first steps toward arranging a marriage with the Archduchess Marie-Louise. If

Romain Colomb is to be believed, Beyle "participated in the work and negotiations that preceded this great event." A note at the beginning of this section of the diary likewise implies that he had extensive personal relations with Napoleon at this period. There may be a bit of truth in the statements, but they should not be taken too seriously.

What is certain is that, at the time, Napoleon was of less personal importance to Beyle than Mme. Daru, who turned up in Vienna that autumn. Their curious and slightly ambiguous relationship is suggested with sufficient eloquence in the following pages. Beyle wrote in 1811 (giving her the pseudonym of the duchess and himself that of Banti): "It seems to me that, during her stay in Vienna, the duchess made as many advances to Banti as was consistent with the character we assume her to possess. At least, she seemed to cast aside all prudence, she frequently gave him proofs in front of everyone of a very marked preference, by her conduct she led several society people to believe that Banti possessed her, she gave him a thousand chances to declare his love, was continually alone with him, had a tender manner, etc." Yet, in spite of all the opportunities, real or imagined, "Banti," true to character, did nothing.

The truth of the matter was that he was not the least bit in love with Pierre's wife. For all his cynical rules of "attack," what he really craved was the "melancholy" of a Mélanie Guilbert, the "understanding soul" of a Victorine Mounier: alas, the plump and matronly Alexandrine Daru—already the mother of four children—was as full of gaiety as she was devoid of sensibility. At the very period when, had he felt any love for her, he should have been the blindest to her defects, he was engaged in cold-bloodedly analyzing her every action—a practice that speedily convinced him of her "total lack of character." Yet the absurd idea of being "a seducer of women" was firmly rooted within him: all his reading and observations had convinced him that the proper thing for a self-respecting young man was to have a married woman, preferably of a superior social rank, as his mistress. His determination to possess Mme. Daru was as passionless as that of Julien Sorel to possess Mme. de Rênal: the only difference was that he gave his hero the aggressiveness that he himself had lacked.

Time passed, and Vienna lost the charm of the first full months. The trees that had been turning green when he arrived were now losing their leaves; the chilly winds of early winter were sweeping the town. Napoleon had left, the Darus had left, the French troops were preparing to leave—the time had come to seek new adventures. He had already acquired a taste for traveling, and, expecting the victory of Wagram to be followed by an immediate peace settlement, he had built many castles in the air. At first it had been Spain again, then it had been a jaunt with a comrade to Warsaw and Naples [?], then the brief hope of visiting Italy with his sister, then various other projects for touring Italy alone. Suddenly, in October, he dropped all these plans and again began to concentrate his efforts on advancing in an official career.

The negotiations at Schönbrunn appearing to have ended warfare for the time being, he no longer desired to be a commissary, but, instead, returned to the ambition he had held—a little prematurely—in Marseille three years earlier, that of being an Auditor of the Council of State. As in Marseille—and again in Brunswick—he organized his family to launch an intensive epistolary assault on Pierre Daru.

The new siege producing no more results than the old ones, Beyle, probably as a subterfuge to regain Paris and continue his suit in person, wrote General Dejean, the War Minister, applying for a post in Spain. His request was seconded by General Villemanzy, the Intendant General, who at the same time authorized Beyle to return and hold himself at Dejean's disposal. Accordingly, early in January 1810, he set out across Bavaria for Paris, where the most brilliant period of his life awaited him.

1809 Paris—Germany—Vienna

My Sojourn in Paris in 1809

AT Brunswick on November 11, 1808, I received the order to come to Paris. I arrived here December 1.

I'm writing this February 3, 1809. I've just been to the Vaudeville, where I sat beside a woman whom I took for a mistress of one of General Hulin's aides-de-camp. Her name is Elisa, living in the Rue Neuve-des-Bons-Enfants, and she's prepared to receive me tomorrow at eleven. Her face, which is rather pretty, has an expression of gentleness. I took pleasure in courting her.

A day of gaiety, produced, I believe, by the spring weather we've been having for the past week. Got up at nine o'clock this morning; translated three pages of *Don Quixote*. Took a dancing lesson with La Bergerie, WITH WHOM I HAVE WIT. From there, went for a walk in the Tuileries. There were a great many men there of the same class as Faure and I.

At half-past four, we didn't go to dinner at Legascque's; for a change, Faure took me to a little restaurateur's in the Rue d'Argenteuil. From there to the Café de la Rotonde; I went to take an ice at the Café de Foy. From there to the Vaudeville. I took a very weak coffee with milk this morning, a thing I've abstained from for six weeks.

Everybody in this country acts dignified, from M. de Baure's porter to the Prince de Bénévent. That bores me—especially in the young people. Someday, the squirrels will abandon their graceful frolics in the branches, and come down to the ground to assume the solemn gait of the sheep they see grazing. In England, they write that good breeding is to be found in Paris, and here in order to be *well bred* you must have the apathetic and impressive look of an Englishman.

February 4 and 5.—The whole day of the 4th was livened up by the thought of going in the evening to see the girl of the Vaudeville, whom I endowed with a thousand charms. I went to her house at five o'clock, she'd just gone out; at six, I preferred to go to the second performance of Mozart's *Così Fan Tutte.* Suave music, but it's a comedy, and Mozart is pleasing to me only when he expresses a mellow and dreamy melancholy.

At noon today, the 5th, I found Elisa in bed, I got in: fine thighs, but a face that looks stupid and lives up to its promise; twenty-four livres.

I put in an appearance at Mme. Z's, whom I hadn't seen since Tuesday; she wasn't there. The only one I saw was Mme. Daru the mother. There was much talk of changes in the Ministry. I spent the evening at home, I've just skimmed through Besenval.

February 6.—We arrived at eight o'clock at the home of Mme. Dubarret, a thin and lively little woman, the wife of a respectable inspector of rivers and forests. Those folks decided to give a ball, and Mme. de Bézieux was kind enough to present us at it. She overwhelmed me with attentions.

A musician who accompanied his violin-playing with facial expressions inspired me with a desire to laugh that was difficult to conceal and which, added to some absurdities that I pointed out to Mlles. Mimi and Amélie, gave me the reputation of being a *bad man.* The mistress of the house frowned on me. We returned at four o'clock, very gay.

February 7.—Dinner at Mme. Bézieux's. I was seated opposite her at the table. Bad breeding was revealed through the compliments, which fell thick and fast.

I danced a quadrille, and arrived at the party of Mme. Nardot, which abounded with distinguished persons: Messrs. Barthélemy, Estève, Clément de Ris, etc.

Mme. Z overwhelmed me with kindness, told me that she'd write M. Marescalchi that evening to ask for a ticket for me, invited me to dinner on Thursday at eleven o'clock, etc. I owe her much gratitude.

February 8.—Spanish lesson, dancing lesson, bath, dinner, read Crébillon junior with pleasure. Portrait of Mlle. Jules sent to her brother, the impression it made on me . . . I WILL OF HER NOTHING BUT FRIENDSHIP I SAY TO Félix.

Vienna Campaign in 1809

OUT OF PRUDENCE, I wrote nothing: 1. about military events;—2. about the political relations with Germany and especially with Prussia, stupid enough not to attack; 3. the relations between Dominique and the greatest of men [Beyle himself and Napoleon].

This is nothing but a diary composed for self-observation, nothing in the least interesting to others.

Parenthesis.—Out of prudence, not knowing where to put my papers, nothing political, all names changed.

Campaign of 1809. From Strasbourg to Vienna. Out of prudence, nothing political, I noted nothing but observations UPON MYSELF.

I LEFT Strasbourg April 12, 1809 at half-past two with M. Cuny in his carriage. The wooden bridge over the Rhine, with the footwalks separated from the roadway in the middle, appeared to me to be a useful construction, but didn't inspire the least admiration in me. That was possibly on account of the waters of the river being very low. There was a bright sun, a little later there was a fine storm of the North (neither thunder, nor heat, nor heavy rain, but just plain hail). We followed the Rhine, leaving to our right the mountainous region which forms its basin on the east and which is called, I believe, . . . [the Black Forest]. That inspired me with a feeling favorable to Germany. It was fortified by a very pretty girl whom I saw at the window of the Kehl posthouse.

After the storm the evening was very fine and the sky, after the sunset, was magnificent in its purity and the gradual fading of the red aurora-like color it had taken on. We sang in the carriage, or rather M. Cuny—who sings very well—sang some Italian arias, among them the beautiful ballad from Mozart's *Figaro: "Voi che d'amore,* etc."

This aria seemed perfectly in harmony with the character of everything that has appealed to me in Germany. This is mildness and frailty, united with something heavenly, but it's the touching frailty produced by passion and not the inane frailty that inspires contempt. My ideas will perhaps change with the passage of time, but everything that appeals to me now in Germany invariably bears the image of Minette.

I endeavored to see a great deal of the peasants and to make them like me. Thus it was that at . . . I went into the posthouse, joked with some working girls who were eating supper, and ate boiled potatoes the same as they.

We had a glimpse of Karlsruhe at four o'clock in the morning, we left the north road to turn abruptly to the southeast toward Stuttgart. But why didn't we go there directly from Strasbourg?

The Grand Duke of Baden had the bright idea of raising the price of his post horses and deciding that people should pass by Karlsruhe to go to Stuttgart, which lengthens the road by three leagues. The countryside we crossed between Karlsruhe and Stuttgart is covered with mountains which aren't high, but which, most of the time, present agreeable points of view. They looked like some engraved scenes I saw in Switzerland.

In spite of the small amount of space in the road and the small amount of talent of the peasants who were driving us for lack of postilions, all went well until we neared Pforzheim, as the road had been trodden down in the past few days. But when we reached this fatal spot, a postilion—idiocy personified—was unable to hold in his horses, and set us down in a ditch. A brigade of twenty-four subordinates on their way to rejoin the Army got us out (22 fr.) and we finally arrived in Pforzheim, being afraid all the time of landing in a ditch.

Upon arriving in Pforzheim, we went to see the war commissary (M. Duché), there weren't any post horses. M. Duché promised us some, but shortly afterward ten carriages arrived one after the other. The master of the post tried to make trouble for us because we hadn't taken any horses from him. After five hours of waiting, I got hold of some horses which had already gone twenty-four leagues. Everyone passed us on the road, and we were the last to reach . . . Upon arriving at the inn, I found two girls with fresh complexions and with eyes . . .

These girls had pretty faces. I took the less pretty one by the a., I could have had her, but I found that unwise at the beginning of a campaign. That rid me completely of the bad humor that had been gnawing at me since Pforzheim, and I was happy all the way to Stuttgart, where we arrived about ten o'clock. On the way, I read the *Vie d'Alfieri* (Volume II).

Beneath us, before reaching Stuttgart, we saw Ludwigshafen, the Versailles of the King of Württemberg. This pretty little town lies against an oblong hill isolated in the middle of the plain.

The part of Stuttgart that we saw was very well built. At the post-house, I was told that there weren't any horses, because "tomorrow the Prince Royal and several Ministers are going to pay their court to the Emperor Napoleon at Ludwigshafen."

We found five or six comrades at our inn; our supper, unanimously judged to be a bad one, was good for me because there were some fried potatoes that just hit the spot.

There weren't any horses, or any indication of any arriving, we decided to go to bed. I hastily threw myself under one of those depressing feather cushions that serve as quilts in Germany. I suffered tortures under it till five o'clock, when I was roused by M. Cuny. Discouragement and general despair; we had visions of being detained indefinitely in Stuttgart, there weren't any horses.[1]

As soon as I was able to get my boots, which had gone astray in the immense building, I went out; upon reaching the square in front of the posthouse, I saw the arrival of some horses that were going toward the posthouse, I decided that it was useless to stop them. It was obvious that German peasants, coming from such a distance to go to the posthouse, would repulse me with losses. Fortunately, there passed enough of them to give me the time to reflect that the worst that could happen to me was a quarrel with seven or eight furious people who, they said, were smashing everything in the posthouse. These quarrels annoy me greatly, not to go through with them is a shame, to terminate them by taking drastic measures would make a bad impression on M. Daru. I consequently seized some horses by the bridle; resistance; but finally my uniform and a two-florin piece persuaded them to come to the hotel. I only stopped shouting and arguing quite a way along the road, where a woman came to make us pay the post.

At the edge of town, we noticed a very fine English garden that was being planted; a few paces farther along we had to make our peasants take the road to Donauwörth; we asked our way repeatedly, and went along a very pleasant road bordered by hillsides covered with vineyards where the earth was held in by stone walls. Several times, I counted as many as sixteen, one above the other. The plots of ground behind the walls were sloping, they were separated by narrow paths provided with steps, leading directly to the summit of the mountain. I imagine that when it rains they serve as a drain.

We crossed a rather high bridge over the Neckar. After this bridge came an agreeable town which also had a filigree steeple, like that of Strasbourg. A league farther along, we learned that we weren't on the Donauwörth road but on that to Ulm.

A lucky mistake! We had no more worry about the horses until

[1] Juvenile memories of my voyage in Germany. [Note added later by Beyle.]

Dillingen, where we rejoined the right road the next day. We were on the one to Ulm—Florian, Jacqueminot, Richard, Mme. Jacqueminot and two or three comrades. From the enemies we had been, because to the scarcity of horses, we became friends, lunched together in a nice inn (nice for Germany: a well-lit room without wallpaper or furniture) at thirty paces from the still-tiny Neckar. We had found some warmth in its valley. The sky was superb; I saw a storm gradually forming in the north, to our left. Afterward rain and cold as far as Ulm, where we arrived at nine o'clock, I very bored, having read until a quarter past seven, finished the *Vie d'Alfieri* and read a hundred pages of Moore on the Court of Vienna.

I had covered a league on foot with Florian, M. Jacqueminot and his wife. We went up a passage like that at Les Echelles: an ascending roadway beside a mountain torrent, an austere countryside without anything magnificent, rain that was cold, the same as the countryside. Going up, I was very occupied with moral considerations and vainglorious sentiments.

I arrived at Ulm with a cold.

Letter to Félix Faure, Donauwörth, April 16.—I haven't time to do anything; there are always fifteen or twenty close friends who read what I am writing over my shoulder. I sleep in an office with M. Cuny; we're traveling together. As a result, I don't know where to write or where to keep what I have written.

This morning at four, awakened; at twenty minutes past five, departure for Augsburg; a charming day. I saw the Alps all of a sudden: a moment of happiness.—People like Wilhelm III, for example, never have moments like that. For me, these Alps represented Italy.

Three leagues from Augsburg, which is twelve from here, countermand, and we returned to our lodgings.

I want to keep up my diary as much as possible and to send you the pages as I write them; two advantages: shortening of my letters and security. Only don't lose the pages.

Travel appeals to me more and more. I feel that my love for Paris has greatly diminished, but not my sentiment for the charming C . . . , whom I loved before my departure; this sentiment has, on the contrary, increased.

April 19.—Today has been fertile in sensations for me.[1] We got up at six o'clock, not having any horses to rejoin M. Daru at Ingolstadt. German honesty obtained some for us. M. Cuny had reserved some the night before at the posthouse, which has sixteen, I believe, and in spite of the departure of H. M. and that of eighty or a hundred

[1] Beyle here goes back to his trip before his arrival at Ulm and to his departure from Donauwörth.

carriages which followed him to Ingolstadt, the master of the post faithfully kept his promise. We finally started out about ten o'clock, after stuffing ourselves as a precaution. We arrived without accident at Burgheim, after crossing the Lech, quite a swift river, on a bridge before which a bridgehead had been erected in the past few days. We passed through Rain, a miserable town.

At Burgheim, we saw the German regiments of the Rhineland Confederation (Reille Division) fall on some geese and kill them with their sabers, this sight amused me hugely. The master of the post wasn't willing that the horses go any farther. All my German eloquence barely prevented him from coming to ... but finally, taking advantage of the deep-seated conviction held by every German that he counts for less than the man whose coat has more braid than his own, we ended by agreeing that the horses should feed for an hour and afterward take us to Neuburg. During this time, Cuny, Paris, Bénard and I drank some coffee; it was made in a kitchen above which there was a hole in every floor, the smoke thus rising to the roof sixty feet high.

We left at half-past one, and, in order to reach Neuburg, passed through a majestic countryside similar to those of Claude Lorrain. We proceeded behind the slopes which border the course of the Danube, the summits of these slopes were crowned with clumps of trees on our left; to the right, we had an almost unbroken forest with some clearings; from time to time, between two slopes, we could see the Danube at a distance of three quarters of a league; the whole formed a superb landscape and one of the most beautiful that could be seen which lacked nothing but a lake and some high mountains. A league from Neuburg, I thought I heard the sound of cannon fire, and, in the midst of this thrilling countryside, it gave me intense pleasure. But, alas, it was only thunder! Gradually, a superb storm approached us, pelted us with hail for half an hour and whitened the ground like snow.[1]

It was in this beautiful weather (beautiful for me, but quite uninteresting for all the others) that we crept into Neuburg at the rear of a convoy. We found three rows of wagons in the street, and, on the square, two regiments with their baggage. We walked twenty paces every five minutes, and the hail changed to heavy rain.

I heard my name called, I raised my eyes, someone said, "Lower them," and the amiable Montbadon held out his hand to me through the bars over a ground-floor window of a fine inn. "Come on in and eat some excellent fricassee I'm making."

I went in: three pretty girls. Bénard and Paris obtained some horses, M. Cuny dejected because he didn't have any, I indifferent, afraid

[1]Written at Ingolstadt (upon returning from the Emperor's) April 20, at nine o'clock. [Note by Beyle.]

to let it be seen by my busy comrades, going from the kitchen to the common room. At last, the fricassee appeared. I fell to. Cuny didn't show up. But the three pretty girls, one of whom wasn't overly so, the second not at all, because of pockmarks, but built like an angel, if angels have fat behinds, Montbadon said; the third had an inflammation, but an expression full of gentleness and pleasantness. We laughed and joked with them for an hour. This variety of pleasure produces in me a complete diversion from all other varieties of thought, and proceeds FROM BASHFULNESS and my unreliable imagination, but I yield to the latter's error—being conscious of it at the same time—which represented to me the character seemingly promised by these amiable faces and kept me from seeing their ugliness. The illusion I experienced was similar to that given by the theater. I was finally obliged to leave them. Our carriage sped along the steep road by which you leave Neuburg. Going out, we crossed the beautiful Danube, which slightly resembles the Rhine at Geneva. The Danube is cut in half by a dike whose purpose I didn't have time to see.

Leaving Neuburg, the countryside was superb. Everything at Neuburg was charming for me: fine region, fine storm, well-built town; pretty girls—who gave a charming veneer to all the rest. We'd have had them if we had passed the night at Neuburg, and I'd have been rather glad if the lack of horses had forced us to do so.

Dull weather and at length darkness as far as Ingolstadt. Half a league from the town, we saw some fires and passed by a bivouac. We entered the town and went to the commandant's, at M. Daru's, to get billets, to M. Desermet's, war commissary. We went around for an hour in the black darkness looking for our lodgings with the aid of a little lantern belonging to an officious old woman. We finally reached the home of a priest, the face of an old codger (Beneficiis Haus, No. 20), where we were lodged; this man, a dastard by nature, plied us with insults and went to the Municipality. We waited an hour at his house for him to come back, I won the favor of an old serving woman, we went through the place and saw for ourselves that there weren't any lodgings. We went with her to the Municipality. It was ten o'clock and pitch-dark. Here began a scene worthy of a comedy. We arrived in front of a scrawny little man, with a large head and a rather intelligent face, who was in charge of lodgings. But, as he had been working for three days, he was dead-tired, he smiled at us, leaned against the table as if to look for some papers, fell asleep and awoke only as he was about to topple over forward or backward. We remained with this worthy man from ten o'clock until a quarter past eleven without getting mad and without being able to obtain billets. Montbadon served as our interpreter, I had an impulse to laugh at seeing this tottering figure. We finally got billets and went to knock at an inn (No. 17) after wandering around for a long time trying to find this fatal number. Everything was full up and everybody was in bed, the door was opened only after a full quarter of an hour. We went through all the rooms, notably one where the master of the house kept his child and where the heat was intense. Finally, a friend of M. Cuny's allowed us to sleep on the straw in his room, whence I emerged in the morning covered with dust and dirt.

April 23.—Landshut, April 23, in the home of Count von Portia, beside the bell tower.[1]

M. Daru will never like me: there is something in our characters that is mutually repellent. He has spoken to me only seven or eight times since the beginning of the campaign, and invariably in vehement exclamations: *"The numskull! A numskull like you!* Stay away from there, a numskull like you would get into a quarrel immediately with those people."

He said last year, in connection with I don't know what, "Young men must be led with iron rods, that's the only way to get results from them." I don't know whether M. Daru applies this maxim to me, and, believing me to have a thoroughly heedless and bumptious character, is trying to master it through continual disgrace, or whether . . . One thing sure is that his eye falls with benevolence on M., a young man to whom I assuredly wish no harm but to whom I'm superior by experience, and I have never received a look like this.

Consequently, I'm neglected (*negletto*) among the sixteen or seventeen war commissaries attached to M. Daru, and my comrades have no liking for me at all. The asses started out by finding that I have an ironic look. The one who is ambitious saw a rival in me and flattered me, but his hatred was obvious to me. The semi-ambitious ones possibly like me even less. The young men find me severe, and Florian, walking with me the other day, endeavored to find all the most serious subjects he could think of to talk to me about.

Anyway, since this page already contains things that might be compromising, I might as well sink the personnel of our headquarters completely.

Fromentin, who calls himself de Saint-Charles. The pure man of ambition; that is, I've never seen him do anything that doesn't lead to his objective, which is to win over M. Daru. There's no standard for such characters other than the wit that goes with them. This man has enough of that; he talks incessantly and jokes about everything, but

[1] I was working with the Emperor continually. All my relations with the great man are passed over in silence in order not to compromise myself. 1813. [Note by Beyle.]

with such a forced gaiety that from the very first day it inspired me with an aloofness I haven't concealed. He looks on all the others in the *shop* as children; I am, I believe, the only one he considers worthy of some notice. This may well end in a duel, not because of his principal goal, not because M. Daru believes him the most outstanding young man among his subordinates, not because he's having him decorated, that doesn't prevent me from being so, but I'll perhaps be forced to resist some of his private usurpations. Place, table, chairs, carriage, horses, he grabs everything. This morning, in connection with the horses, he had a run-in with Lacombe, who said, "You damned troublemaker, I've seen through you a long time."

"Shut up, I'll slap your face twenty times, etc., etc."

It's not hard to see that, even were I fired for it twenty times by M. Daru, the only way I could answer a threat of twenty slaps would be by giving one to be deducted from the total.

Fromentin is thirty-two or thirty-three years old and doesn't look it. An ashy complexion, made up of freckles, a false and scheming look. He's tall and well built, except his legs. He has served previously, and has carried out, they say, a good act, being only sixteen years old at the time, and for that reason he's applying for a decoration, for which he wrote directly to the Emperor last year. Only he stamped his epistle with the seal of M. Daru, who unfortunately was with H. M. when the letter arrived. He opened it, and later returned it to Fromentin with his apologies, "I opened it by mistake."

If I'm not mistaken, Fromentin would appear rather coarse in Parisian society, since his manners have something of the guardhouse in them.

Lajard is a young old man of twenty-five. His weakness is all charm, ignorance of everything, rather than the science and practice of petty means. He has the manners of present-day good society: weakness, freshness and charm. He sings very well. He has the eyes of a jaded man, half closed, he's very thin, medium height, a very long nose. He's a nephew of Chaptal and the brother-in-law of . . . Fromentin, who sensed this, got himself introduced by him to his family, quite sure that the family would take into account what he did for him; and this family, which probably hesitated to let their young man go out into the midst of the Army's hubbub, would reward Fromentin's protection. He's bound to succeed everywhere that he doesn't come across somebody who's able to see through him first.

I haven't anything else to say about Lajard, a bleached-out plant, amiable, good-natured, but quite insignificant.

I'm terminating this at Landshut, at five o'clock April 23 in the office, a fine room on a fine street, in the midst of all those whom I'm describing, and shivering. This town pleased me greatly this morning; compared with Ingolstadt, it's the Italy of Germany. I was kept busy all morning by the necessity of talking. We saw thirteen enemy corpses and some doors riddled with balls and bullets.

Landshut, April 24.—We *got ours* this morning in fine style at Neustadt; we set out on the wrong road, encountered M. Daru, who told us we were numskulls, and unfortunately he was right. To go from Neustadt to Landshut, we'd passed by Geisenfeld, and there was a direct road.

We crossed a mountain range, but I don't know its name. We passed by a burned bridge where there had been fighting the day before and where I saw three dead *kaiserlicks* [*sic*]; they were the first. The road was surrounded by bivouacs, parts of it were as picturesque as possible.

We finally arrived at Pfeffenhausen. I had a scare on arriving there. I'd been on foot for an hour, all of a sudden I saw a calash behind our carriage, I thought it was M. Daru reaching his lodgings ahead of us; it was the excellent Joinville. M. Daru arrived only two hours later and was pleased with his lodgings. He asked what we had for supper, I answered, "Some potatoes and half a calf." He had a good laugh at the half a calf. I believe it was at me for using an incorrect expression, but I also believe he began to realize that it was on purpose. Nothing seems to me so inane as bookish language in conversation. Richard, one of our comrades, is that kind, and he grates on my nerves all day long.

In the evening, we had some excellent fried potatoes, some veal which was almost cooked and in large quantities, some excellent beer, and M. Daru extremely gay, but with the kind of gaiety that seems to be only semi-gaiety.

After this good supper, I spent a good night in a good straw bed. I stayed there from ten to three o'clock in the morning, when we left. The road from Pfeffenhausen to Landshut was very fine and quite picturesque. Only near Landshut did we see some corpses, but we noticed many helmets in the fields, notably in a little square field.

The Landshut city gate was riddled with balls, the brick part was shot out a foot and even in some places two feet. We crossed the Isar, which looks quite a bit like the Isère, but which is larger; this river forms an island above Landshut.

This town impressed me like Italy. In half an hour, I saw five or six feminine faces of an oval that was far more perfect than is usually found in Germany. I waited a couple of hours for M. Daru and his suite so as to give them their billets. They finally arrived, and since then we've been staying in Landshut. After dinner yesterday, M. Daru put Florian in charge of a hospital. Bénard and I went there as amateurs, and did a little of everything until midnight; we helped the patients out of the wagon, and I, who am not indulgent for myself, found no reason for self-approach.

We came twice to see M. Daru, who bawled us out good and proper the first time, not very much the second, and he was right the first. He asked us the number of patients; Bénard, who did the talking, said a hundred and sixty. "Ah bah! There were four hundred and fifty this morning!" Fortunately, he was sleepy and the matter ended there.

Nothing new; the details of a hospital in disorder. A knavish treasurer and ill will. A single Austrian surgeon for everybody, full of good will. We talked in Italian and arranged everything for the best.

This morning (24), I came to M. Daru's, and from there went with Senneville up to his hospital, situated on an oblong hill in the town. From the top of the castle that crowns it, there's one of the most magnificent views possible. The whole course of the Isar. It's really beautiful and rare. We had lunch and here I am, with a strong desire to sleep.

Landshut, April 24.—I didn't take off my clothes all the time we were at Ingolstadt. We lodged at No. 17, an inn where the mistress wasn't all she should have been. I'd nevertheless planned to have her, but the time lacked. At the office, we received the news of a big victory. I saw the effect of it on everyone, it was hardly good for anything but that, for it faded away a bit. Yet we've seen three or four thousand wounded.

On the 22nd, we left to arrange for lodgings on the road to Landshut and at Landshut itself. It was one o'clock, I'd been in bed only a little while, it broke my heart to get up. We were driven by two peasants and their horses, which they didn't know how to drive. We started out by going over the bridge to the imperial castle, we turned in the courtyard with great effort and continued on our way along a very fine and narrow road. About three o'clock, we noticed some fires on both sides of the road, and the Danube. It was a fine bivouac, very picturesque, but it was devilishly cold. We crossed the Danube on a bridge that looked as though it had been built in a hurry, and then went through the little town of Vohburg, set in an agreeable manner in relation to the Ingolstadt road. From there to Neustadt, the road was agreeable: a plain between two hills.

Upon approaching Neustadt, we came upon the bivouacs. We finally entered, bringing up the rear of a convoy, this pitiful little town which had the aspect of devastation: no inhabitants, everything open, everything smashed, everything filled with straw and uniforms of all kinds. In the midst of that, the good German peasants, each casually driving a wagon to which were hitched their horses, having no sorrow other than that given them by the annoyance which the wagon of their *master* might give them. A NATION BORN TO SERVE . . .

Arrived at Neustadt, Cuny didn't show all the activity necessary, we whiled away the time, saw the chief of ordnance, Chambon, were held up two hours in the town by the Oudinot Division, which, entering by one gate and leaving by the other, barred us from the one through which we had to pass in order to go to Pfeffenhausen. We made a big mistake, and, relying partly on the false information we were given on all sides and partly on the map, we thought that, in order to get to Pfeffenhausen, it was necessary to return to Geisenfeld.

Enns, May 5.—I'm dead with sleep as I write this, and M. Cuny is asleep on my left; to the right, Mure and Richard look like ghosts.

I'll start in again at Lambach. Leaving the home of the sick woman (the first idea she recalled to me was the manner of German actresses in acting tragedy. It exactly resembles this woman's way of talking. These actresses give all their roles the slow, frail and dreamy hue of that of Ophelia). Leaving the home of this woman, I was saying, we went to look for some meat and wine at the convent. I almost received a saber wound in the belly from an officer who was pommeling a soldier with the hilt.

Going and coming, I continually admired the situation of Lambach. I said to myself, "There's the most interesting spectacle I've ever seen in my life." Seeing some cannon set up beside the convent door, I said to Lacombe, "All that's lacking here is the enemy and a fire."

We returned, we slept on chairs at the commandant's, we supped and went back to sleep. At two o'clock, there was talk of leaving. I went down to the square. While walking there, I noticed a large amount of light behind a house; I said to myself, "That's a very brilliant bivouac!" The light and smoke increased, a fire broke out. The disturbance at the outbreak of the fire was observed by me in all its gradations, from the calm of sleep up to the galloping of the horses hitched to the ammunition wagons coming from all sides.

The flames couldn't be seen; with the exception of that, the fire was superb: a column of smoke filled with light crossed the town transversally, it lit us up on the road for a distance of two leagues.

The hill north of the town was lit up so brightly that, from below where I was waiting with my carriage for the arrival of Cuny, I could count the trunks of the pine trees on the summit. The kiosk and all the little houses situated on the slope stood out perfectly.

The brilliant light that the fire cast on the tops of several edifices.

The callousness of the grenadier of the bivouac:

"The fire will come this far," pointing to a house separated from the burning one by fifty or sixty other houses. We learned that forty had burned. They said at first that three cavalry officers, drunk from the buckets of wine distributed at the abbey, had been roasted alive; that was reduced, I believe, to one quartermaster horribly burned but still alive.

There's a sample of horror, but agreeable horror, if it may be so described. That of yesterday was horrible horror, affecting me so strongly that I was sick.

We reached Wels at about five o'clock, and were comfortably quartered in the home of a worthy man. We had come in a light wagon. The peasants who were hitched to the heavy one cut the traces and left it standing in the middle of the road.

Charles came up laughing to tell us about this. He laughs at all the accidents; that's his way of making excuses for taking the trouble to remedy them. That rascal of MYSELF, about whom I think and say so many bad things, and of whom I am nevertheless very fond, is sometimes ambitious like that. I was getting rather fed up with pacing back and forth in my host's big gloomy room when the carriage arrived with the horses of a surgeon who knew Cuny slightly.

At three o'clock, we left Wels for Ebersberg, on the Traun. A superb road in a plain bordered by pretty hillsides, but otherwise very flat, as far as a signpost; beside the signpost, a dead man. We took the road to the right, the going became difficult, the wagons were squeezed together, and finally a single file was established. We finally reached an extremely long wooden bridge over the Traun, which was studded with sand bars.

Marshal Masséna's corps had a hard fight to cross the bridge, and it turned out to be a futile one, as the Emperor had outflanked this bridge.

As we started over the bridge, we found bodies of men and horses, there were still about thirty on the bridge; we were obliged to shove a lot of them into the river, which was excessively wide; in the middle, four hundred paces downstream from the bridge, a horse was standing erect and motionless; odd effect. The whole town of Ebersberg was still burning, the street through which we passed was strewn with corpses, most of them French and nearly all of them charred. Some were so badly burned that the human form of the skeleton could hardly be recognized. In several places, the corpses were heaped up; I examined their faces. On the bridge, there was a worthy German lying dead, his eyes open; German courage, faithfulness and kindliness were portrayed on his face, which had a slight expression of melancholy.

Gradually the road grew narrower, and finally, beneath the city gate and ahead of it, our carriage was obliged to run over these corpses disfigured by the flames. A few houses were still burning. The soldier who came out of a house with a look of irritation. I confess that the whole thing made me sick.[1]

I didn't see this impressive spectacle very well. Montbadon, whom I found again at Enns, still being admired wherever he went, had gone up to the castle, something that was far worse than the street, as a hundred and fifty corpses were burning there at the time, the majority French light infantrymen.

A very handsome dead officer; wishing to see where he had been wounded, he took hold of his hand; the officer's skin remained in his palm. This handsome young man was killed in a manner that didn't do him great honor—by a ball which struck him in the back and lodged in his heart.

The cold rain, the lack of food, the insurmountable obstacles between my thoughts and my comrade's brain—all this resulted in my nearly being sick at the spectacle.

I've learned since that it really was a horror.

The bridge was attacked by the infantry skirmishers of the Po, who numbered 800 (not more than 200 are left) and by the Claparède Division, which was 8,000 strong and which is said to have been reduced to 4,000.

It appears probable that there were 1,500 dead. This devil of a bridge is enormously long, the first platoons to reach it were mowed down. The second shoved them into the river, and succeeded in crossing. They took the town, and put *great numbers of the wounded in the houses.* The Austrians returned and recaptured the town, driving back, I believe, the 26th Light Infantry Regiment. Fighting took place in the town, shells were showered down on it and ended by setting it on fire. Obviously, no one made an effort to put it out, the whole town burned up, as well as the unfortunate wounded in the houses.

That's how they explain the horror to be seen while going through the streets. This explanation seems to me a probable one. For where else would so many burned and dead soldiers have come from? But no one was killed inside the houses, the dead were not carried into them; therefore, these poor devils were burned alive.

Those in a position to know say that the spectacle of Ebersberg is a thousand times more horrible than that of all the battlefields in the world; there, you see only cut-up men and not horrible corpses with the nose burned away and the rest of the face recognizable.

[1] In a letter dated Wels, May 3, Beyle wrote to Félix Faure: "I really wanted to vomit while going through Ebersberg and seeing the wheels of my carriage make the entrails gush out of the bodies of the poor little infantry soldiers. I began talking in order to take my mind off this frightful sight, with the result that I am considered ironhearted."

We arrived at Enns, where we are now. Nothing remarkable. The amiable Martial promised to fix up my affair here. I slept last night (the 5th) in Richard's lodgings. You get nowhere in the Army without a usurping, intriguing, brazen character.

Enns, May 7.—We're still in this huge gloomy room of the Municipality. About thirty of us sleep, work and eat in it; it's not hard to guess what kind of humor, smell, etc. there is.

Not having anything to do and being obliged to sit at a table with pen in hand, I gossip while the others smoke.

We left Burghausen about eleven o'clock on the morning of the . . . Our carriage was on the verge of backing us into the Salzach after we'd crossed the bridge. M. Cuny went to great pains without his energy being well applied; he got covered with mud, fell down twice and ended by thinking he was dead, which resulted in us going from Burghausen to Braunau with the windows closed. At first you're on a plateau two or three hundred feet above the Salzach; you have some charming vistas, a hollow in the hillside permits the Salzach to be seen, as well as the plain beyond, which is very picturesque; you finally go down the hillside and follow the river about a league, after which you come to the hole of Braunau. There's a single street, I think, but quite wide and well aligned. I've found the same thing in nearly all the towns of southern Germany; in this, they differ greatly from those of the North.

May 11.—On May 11, we went through the outskirts of Sankt Pölten. I'm enjoying the summer and a very cool habitation. It used to be a cotton mill, a hundred paces outside the town, with a fine body of water. I went in bathing. We were surrounded by fire. Last night, thirteen were counted all around the horizon. This morning, I saw only two columns of smoke, but they were on the horizon at the height of the sun; two hours before it set, there was a huge horizontal cloud, reddish-gray in color, which we all thought was a cloud of smoke.

In the evening, I began writing about eleven o'clock, in the midst of four snoring comrades, and about two o'clock I finished A LETTER OF TWO PAGES TO MILADY [Mme. Daru].

May 12.—On the 12th, I was sound asleep when I was awakened by Ameil, who said, "M. Daru wants to know which of you gentlemen are the ones who slept here." A minute afterward, "M. Beyle, he wants to see you."

It was to order us to prepare the orders for the departure of headquarters. He bawled out everybody. I couldn't discover what the moral reason was for this matinal bad humor. He was very anxious to rejoin the Emperor. I concluded from this that he had a lot of bile and was in that state where it's natural to be in bad humor. Yet, in my opinion, he's far from being a bilious character.

Unfortunately for us, there was no one at the ordnance house. He consequently distributed among us some letters to be delivered. I left about six o'clock and walked for two hours and a half in Sankt Pölten. I was in a bad humor, a very bad one, my weariness was the only thing that kept it from bursting out. Finally, I couldn't find the addresses of three of the letters. I returned to the house, they had finished their coffee and were leaving. Ten minutes later, Martial's carriage, in which I was traveling because I'd let Lacombe take my seat in Cuny's, I found that everybody had left.

Consequently, I scrambled into the carriage, still with an empty stomach. We arrived about one o'clock in . . . , quite a small town. All the houses open and pillaged, but nothing burned. The posthouse and the house of the parish priest were the only ones inhabited. The priest behaved very well. They say he did the same three years ago, and that this time H. M. had a hundred napoleons given him, telling him he would remember him.

We had a dinner that wasn't too bad at the priest's house; it cost us four paper florins each. I paid for M. M., who was with us. I gave ten florins; when I asked for the two florins change, nobody knew what had become of them. This is less than nothing, but it illustrates the selfishness and ill will with which we're filled in our relations with each other.

Later, I loafed with Lhoste, today's resource. A genuine Frenchman; he doesn't know anything, but his first impulse is always generous and candid, and then he hasn't any education, low morals, because his mother has a trade, I don't know which one.

I suggested to him at three o'clock that we go up the hill back of the village, from the top of which you're supposed to be able to see the Danube. We climbed it and didn't see the Danube, which can hardly be seen a full league from there, but we saw a pine woods that was quite strange. It was made up of trunks thirty or forty feet high, with a very small clump of verdure at the top. These straight trunks were very crowded. We came down, enjoying the beginning of spring, which started for us the day of our arrival at Melk (the 8th or 9th). The chestnut trees at Melk were only in bud, those of Vienna are in full leaf and ready to bloom.

After examining the valley behind the village of . . . , we turned to the left and went into a pretty little hamlet. At the entry, we found an army valet plucking a hen, with two wooden buckets filled with flour and eggs beside him.

Lhoste and I started going to the houses and looking for eggs. We didn't find any. We plainly saw the character of the French. Everything that couldn't be taken away had been smashed. In the village, we found a little dog that was still yelping and a cat that looked very weary. Finally, we returned to the village. All the carriages had just left, notably our own.

(*I'm all in, the rest tomorrow.*)

From letter to Félix Faure, Vienna, May 18.—During my first days in Vienna, I've experienced that inner contentment and perfect well-being that, since Italy, only Geneva has given me.

The adorable Martial Daru was appointed Intendant the day before yesterday; this morning, he asked his brother to have me with him because I was familiar with his way of working. M. Daru answered, "Prepare the letter, I'll sign it." Thus, to all appearances, here I am a Viennese for a year or two.

At the theater at the Carinthia gate, they play excellent music, and there's a ballet like the Italian, with grotesques.

The stay in Vienna is delighting me and producing a strange sadness; too much inclination toward love, a pretty woman at every step. How I regret not to have consecrated my life to the talents which Montbadon possesses in such abundance, to the talent of pleasing them!

From letter to Pauline, Vienna, July 14.—All considered, from the time I arrived in Paris up to the beginning of last December, I've been happy with my happiness, which would be intolerable anxiety for anyone else.

In Paris, I was in love with Elvire, the immense distance of rank separating us resulted in a passion of this sort having no other interpreter than our eyes, as they say in novels; this diverted me, especially during the last days of my stay. Elvire hasn't much sensibility, or at any rate this sensibility hasn't been much exercised. I believe that, while she was with me, she was astonished to have emotional experiences. Three or four times, we had some of those impulsive moments in which everything fades except what is desired. Insurmountable obstacles, as well as the greatest danger for one and the other, kept us from speaking otherwise than through expressive glances. But who is this Elvire?[1] I'll tell you the first time I see you. As for all the details of our behavior, imagine a courtier in love with a queen: you'll realize the nature of their dangers and pleasures.

Since my departure from Paris, I've seen many new things. I've suffered much, but physically. At last, I suffered from an attack of fever which prevented me from going to the battle on the 6th of this month,

[1]There can be little doubt that Elvire is Mme. Pierre Daru, with whom Beyle was beginning to fall in love.

a spectacle forever to be regretted: 500,000 men fought for fifty hours.[1] Martial was there: I ought to have gone with him, but I was stretched out in a chaise longue, with a splitting headache and the fidgets; each cannon shot could be distinguished; an armistice has just been arranged, and it's believed that peace will result. If so, I'll probably go to Spain.

If I have time, I'll leave here and go with one of my friends to Warsaw, where he has some business; from there we'll go to Naples, Rome, Genoa and Grenoble. I'm saving up my money in order to be able to carry out this plan; I have some good servants and excellent horses; I've proved to myself that I can stand the greatest fatigue. But I haven't yet found the perfect happiness I've been looking for. I need a woman with a lofty soul, and all of them are like novels—interesting as far as the denouement, and, two days later, you're surprised at having been able to be interested in things so common.

I'm still sick with a fever; I've been given the hope that six days of calmative will fix me up again; but the morale is feverish, the doctor knows nothing about such things and is astonished at the little effect his drugs have on me.

It's possible that, sooner or later, the boredom of vegetating in a post beneath what I've now shown I'm capable of filling will make me shed my uniform and retire to Claix; but I can see nothing certain in this distant possibility of my present destiny.

If you come across any poor German prisoners to whom I can be of service, write me at once. During this campaign, I've saved the lives of two German prisoners and two hundred merino sheep. That, I believe, is a good action.

From letter to Pauline, Vienna, July 26.—I'm still suffering from the fever of which I've already spoken to you, but that doesn't have much influence on the situation of my soul. I'm happy, although upset by the passion of which I've already spoken to you.

Recently, I was given a mission to Hungary; I promised myself upon leaving Vienna not to think of what it contained for twenty-four hours. It was possibly the only chance in my life to see that celebrated Hungary. I found a superb country, magnificent vineyards, a narrow and superb road with a row of young chestnut trees on either side, the road set off in white amidst the verdure of the prairies and crops, the view changing every half hour; to the left, at first the imposing Scheeberg (or snow mountain), and afterward the road going off in the distance to this white summit, the countryside simultaneously became peaceful and majestic: instead of mountain peaks, there were extensive

[1] The battle of Wagram. At this period Beyle was suffering from "a horrible case of pox."

prolonged hills and, at the horizon, a large lake. Upon leaving Vienna, I went to Laxenburg, where there are beautiful gardens and an astonishing fifteenth-century castle.

From Laxenburg I went to Eisenstadt, and from there to the shores of the lake which you'll find on the map. There I found the Croat costume in all its purity: it's absolutely the same as that of our hussars, the plume, the small boots trimmed in silver, etc., etc.

I've told you, I believe, that, before returning to France, I was going to Warsaw and Naples. I'll have need of doing so. To leave Vienna will break my heart; but a fortnight later I'll no longer think of it, except agreeably, especially while traveling.

Haydn passed away here about a month ago; he was the son of a simple peasant and elevated himself to immortal creation through a sensitive soul and studies which gave him the means of transmitting to others the sensations he experienced. A week after his death, all the musicians of the city gathered at the Scottish church to execute *Mozart's Requiem* in his honor. I was there, and in uniform, in the second row[1]; the first was taken up by the great man's family—three or four poor little women in black with mean faces. The *Requiem* appeared to me to be too noisy and didn't interest me; but I'm beginning to understand *Don Juan,* which they give in German nearly every week at the Widen theater.

Diary of Kahlenberg and Leopoldsberg (or liaisons of Colonel L. with Princess P.)

BASHFULNESS AND wounded indifference in the manner of Rousseau
1809, Vienna, COMING-ON OF LADY Palfy.[2]

October 21.—On October 21, I went with M. Feck to buy a pipe in the outlying district of Widen. On my return, I learned that Mme. Z had arrived from Pressburg with her two brothers. I was told that she couldn't be seen until three o'clock. I wrote some letters. But I was so flustered that I felt myself changing color each minute. At half-past four, I made up my mind to go in. I was with J. Her first gesture was exactly what it would have been for another. She stood up for me to kiss her; I didn't dare to (from lack of social experience) and merely took her hand flabbily.

[1]Stendhal recalls this event in Letter XXII of his *Vie de Haydn.*

[2]Princess P. and Lady Palfy are two more names for Mme. Z—that is, Mme. Pierre Daru.

We spoke of Berlin. "Have you been there?"

"Yes, for a month."

"When was that?"

"At the beginning."

"I didn't think you would want to come for fourteen months."

"You know quite well why I didn't go."

"I thought that the pretty Brunswick girls were holding you back."

No answer on my part, my wits failed me, granting that I have any wits—something that remains to be proved.

A minute later:

"It's a very long time since we've seen each other. Have you been very bored?"

"I was very sorry that you didn't come sooner, when Vienna was at its best and everyone was expecting you. But I haven't been bored in the least."

I believed myself obliged to make this answer because of J., whose unintelligence sees the bad side of everything.

"I was told that you had been ill. Is it all over now?"[1]

"Yes, entirely."

Ca. came in, I effaced myself until dinnertime, went to open a package of books, cut the pages of Roussel's *Le Système Moral de la Femme* and skimmed through it.

In this first interview, it seems to me that I was offered a much more elevated place than the one I've held up until now; with a bolder manner, I'd take it and acquire an immense superiority, but also I'd be showing off.

THE LIFE AND SENTIMENTS OF SILENCIOUS HARRY
THE LIFE AND OPINIONS.—Relations with Princess Palfy in Vienna
THE MAN PERHAPS, THE MEMORY LITTLE[2]

November 1809.—He got up at nine o'clock because he had read the *Mémoires de la Régence* until half-past one. He had a fever. He signed some furloughs and had five or six business visits. M. Pacotte arrived. Little Joséphine (de Lhoste) came; he had her, after which he got dressed quickly and breakfasted ditto. He jumped in a carriage and arrived at Princess Palfy's. There he found Mme. Guérin, with whom

[1] Still marveling at this indiscretion, Beyle wrote two years later: "An odd trait of naturalness and kindness, for the point in question was the pox—nothing less than that."

[2] Like all the words in capital letters, this title is in English in Beyle's manuscript.

he was gallant and gay. Mme. de Palfy was in a brown study for a moment, after which she was amiable with Henri, but with the same sort of amiability she has for everybody, which lets the absence of any other feeling be seen. She hadn't slept. We went shopping. She said something to Mme. Barthomeuf and Mme. Guérin in an agitated voice and almost with tears in her eyes, which showed her deep attachment to Mme. Barthomeuf at the same time as her displeasure, equally rational and deep-seated, with the Duke of . . . [her husband, Pierre Daru].

We returned at one o'clock; still coolness, not what's called coolness in society, but cool manners as compared with those she had on the previous days.

Yet she had an amiable smile as she came in and said, "Go quickly and look for your horses," but far indeed from what it was yesterday and from the little finger-tap which accompanied it. Jacqueminot, she and I got on our horses at half-past one; we went to the Lusthaus. This role put me at ease, Jacqueminot talked just enough to permit me to be sensitive and to give me a chance to talk. We happened to go into the story of Jacqueminot's marriage. He offered his father to remain ten years without seeing his mistress, without writing her, and to take a job wherever his father might wish—which the latter was blundering enough to refuse. But in all that there were two or three traits that showed more and more the total absence of character in Z [Pierre Daru].

That led the princess to tell us the story of her marriage. "I had an aversion to young men, so when they told me, 'He's a middle-aged man,' I wasn't afraid . . . It was in accordance with this principle (that love matches don't work out well) that I didn't want to marry someone I loved."

There, it seems to me, is something that cuts the taproot of all love for the Duke of . . .

During the entire ride, scarcely two or three glances. We galloped through all the bridle paths of the Augarten, and returned via the rampart. It was half-past three, I went with her, but she left me at the B. In the evening, the beginning of *Don Juan*. I returned home at half-past ten without going to the Burg.

November.—All day yesterday was spent at the property of the younger Comtesse Triangi [Mme. Pierre Daru]. It seems to me obvious that this day was the zenith of my credit with Mme. de Triangi. She was going to Mts. Kahlenberg and Leopoldsberg, she seemed to be attempting purposely to get rid of her traveling companions, she was gay with the natural and enterprising gaiety that is given by the approach of an event that gives pleasure.

As we were leaving, we almost ran over a wounded soldier on the corner of the Herrengasse. The people in the street were indignant, I got out and arranged the matter. We went in the berlin as far as the little road halfway to Leopoldsberg. We got on horseback and went, nearly all the time at a gallop, to Leopoldsberg. The weather was clear enough to distinguish the view; it couldn't be seen as well as in summer, but still it could be seen well enough. We got off the horses to enter the courtyard of Leopoldsberg; she got down in my arms. That gave me quite a bit of pleasure. My big error was not to have assumed at the outset that air of gallantry which permits you to risk anything, since nothing has the appearance of being said seriously. I didn't do so at all. A gallant remark isn't far from the tone of sentiment. She was cold and her cheeks were rosy. That called for a quite natural compliment; I saw the place for it and didn't pay it. After passing a moment at Leopoldsberg, we galloped to the Kahlenberg. Arrived there, we looked for the view, we arrived at two pavilions which appeared to terminate in terraces. Her spirit of enterprise made her want to go up on these terraces. It happened that the only access was by means of the worst of ladders, going up to the narrowest of holes. We climbed up: "You go first." From there, by means of a kind of catwalk, crawling on our hands and knees, we reached the place where the terrace should have been, but in reality there were only two shingle roofs; these roofs were very slippery; by means of a little ladder, we reached the balustrade, she walked around it on the inside with charming courage. I went through the hole in the roof first.—"I want to go through it like this," she slipped through head first; I wanted to go down the ladder first: "No, no; I want to go first; your coachman is quite enough." I was too concerned with her safety and not enough with being gallant. It's true that in Paris her companion is usually the faithful M. D. . . . , whose seriousness and lack of wit on the road are conspicuous. These subjects of comparison must have made me appear less ridiculous.

We came down from the Kahlenberg by an agreeable road, I believe she was pleased with her excursion but less so with her companion. We returned to the city gate on horseback. I'd planned to speak to her about: 1. what's going to become of Prince Sulkowski; and 2. what's going to become of me. She was the first to say, "You ought to speak to my husband if you want to find out what they're going to do with you."

"I'm afraid of getting bawled out like the devil."

That was a crazy thing to say.

This trait shows at the same time what's lacking in my character and the frame of mind I attribute to her. I had some fine things to say, and I didn't say anything. I'm affected by too many things. If I'm to believe what she told me, M. Z SHALL NOT COME TO SPAIN AND HAD FOR THE SECOND TIME REFUSED THE PREFERMENT OF THE GENERAL D. HE WILL LIVE AS A SIMPLE COUNSILOR OF STATE AND GO NEXT SPRING TO ITALY AND SWIZERLAND [sic].

We were reserved coming back, I silent. In the evening, to *The Crusaders;* a devilish reserve, both physically and mentally. THE FOOT, THE HAND. I see nothing special, as far as I am concerned.

November.—I have a bad cold. This morning, I saw Mme. de Triangi, who told me with all possible graciousness, that I was invited to the general's ball. My name was even first on the list, a thing that will shock M. M., whom I suspect of a bit of envy. But enough of all this.

November 20, at a quarter to 2 in the morning.—Mme. Daru left at half-past one.

This morning, after three or four scenes which showed the bad side of mankind, I went to the Burg at eleven o'clock, full of the reserve that in my case is the result of wounded sensibility. I was received at lunch by M. and Mme. Z, the Mmes. Jacqueminot arrived. We went to Mass. But F., having seen her on the way, gave her his arm. We were only able to get in downstairs. The Mass was finer than usual, but I had little taste for it. I was busy chatting to Mlle. Lucrèce in order to let . . . see that, if I don't talk to her enough, it's because of bashfulness rather than stupidity. The Governor took her home from Mass, F. and B. having deserted. The Jacqueminot ladies went on. The embarrassment of a tête-à-tête increased the reserve, and I went on to await orders at the office.

We went out. I took her, as well as M. Daru, in my carriage to the home of Mme. Bertrand, a woman who appeared to me to be very amiable because she found me somewhat so. We found a dozen generals there. Mme. Bertrand was especially attentive to me, and invited me in such a way to come to see her in Paris that I intend to accept. She's thoroughly English, worships her husband, speaks English, etc., and, in her opinion, I have the great merit of appearing to please another woman who's more attractive than she. We went to the home of the Prince of Eggmühl, but I stayed in the carriage reading. We left Mme. Daru behind, and went to pay a call on Mme. Guérin, a fat good-hearted Polish woman with a German character.

We went to the home of Mme. Ott . . . This little hunchback appeared to me to have some sense. She and her husband at first mistook me for M. Daru, and at length contented themselves with calling me M. le Baron. A gay visit which rid me to some extent of my bashful reserve. We came back for a minute. Then to the steeple of Stefansdom. The tête-à-tête in such a safe spot made me curse MY BASHFULNESS, and consequently intensified my reserve. From there to the benediction at the Franciscan church; nothing remarkable. From there back home. Some people were there, my reserve was somewhat dispelled. I was hoping that Mme. Barthomeuf would arrive; she came, we had supper. I talked and was amiable, possibly even very amiable as long as she was there.

My amiability seemed to please Mme. Z, and I saw its effect because she immediately became more amiable with me. She said once to Mme. Barthomeuf, "I leave you my cousin."

While waiting for the horses, which didn't come, we asked riddles. During this time, Mme. Z reclined on a sofa that M. D. and I had brought in from an adjoining room. When the time came to leave, she appeared to soften toward me. She even had tears in her eyes, but I'm far from believing, first, that they were sincere, and next, that they were for me.

As the departure drew nearer and nearer, I took a seat on the foot of the sofa. I toyed with her gloves, I gave them back to her, she in turn gave them back to me. Once she held out her hand to me for me to return them, but she did so very gracefully and possibly even with some tenderness. I lowered my head on the sofa and kissed her outstretched hand. I must have had some grace and feeling, for I was animated, not too animated, and I did nothing to restrain myself. All that, the same as the rest of my behavior, was rather imprudent. The spectators perhaps believed she was in love with me, the asses perhaps went as far as to believe I was having her.

Finally, it was announced that the horses would return only the next day; Mme. Z became angry, they arrived. A moment of agitation, we took leave, we embraced each other, I made no move. Senneville offered her his arm to go down, she took mine. I squeezed the arm she gave me, she undoubtedly noticed this action.

Below, at half-past one, near the carriage, she turned to the left and, advancing her head, said to me, "Farewell, my dear cousin." I embraced her, her veil cut our kiss in two, but in any case it was soulfully given and received without reserve, as I saw it.

By chance, I've written the diary of her arrival (October 21) and of the day of her departure, adding that of our ride to the Kahlenberg, in a few years I'll be able to form an idea of my behavior. With more boldness, had I assumed a gallant manner at the outset and had she been continually with Mme. Barthomeuf, I believe I'd have been close to happiness. I mustn't fail, if I see her again, to assume a manner of gay gallantry right from the start. A little more boldness, and our numerous tête-à-tête, which must have appeared reserved to her, would have been charming, for, once the ice is broken, I'm sure of myself in that respect, I'd have appeared more to my advantage.

What must she think of me?[1]

[1]I've lost the diaries containing the sequel and the end. All that came to an end in six minutes two months later, and I had her during a whole year, six times a week. Parenthesis. [Note by Beyle.]

The diary and other private papers eloquently prove that this curious note could not possibly apply to Mme. Daru—or to any other woman. Henri Martineau furthermore points out that Beyle put parentheses around false statements in his diary, and in this case he writes the word out. The note was apparently written in to mystify a possible reader, but its exact object remains obscure.

The Harvest of Ambition

ALTHOUGH the four years that had elapsed since Marseille had yielded nothing more than the post of deputy commissary, Beyle returned to Paris undaunted and with the firm resolution this time to let nothing stop him from advancing. Like Julien Sorel, he adapted his ambition to current conditions. In 1806, upon the outbreak of war with Prussia, he had abruptly abandoned his attempts to become an Auditor, and had followed the Army to Brunswick; but, once peace seemed in prospect, his interest in the Army evaporated and he again turned to the Administration as offering the best promise of a career.

The center of this structure under the Empire was the Council of State, in which "Napoleon had gathered together the fifty least stupid Frenchmen" to elaborate bills before they were submitted to the debates of the legislative bodies.

In the service of each Councilor were several young men known as *Auditors,* for whom this apprenticeship might easily lead to important administrative posts. Beyle's plan was to be appointed Auditor through the powerful influence of Pierre Daru; this achieved, he would seek a place in society, try to obtain a title, possibly make a wealthy marriage—and, in three or four years, become a Prefect! Then, possessing a sinecure, honors, wealth and leisure, he would at last be able to devote himself tranquilly to the composition of his comedies. Worldly success was but a means to a never-varying end; in 1805 he had considered it necessary to become a banker, in 1810 a Prefect, in order to attain this end.

Now fairly launched on his lifelong "pursuit of happiness," he resumed his life in Paris with the same contentedness he had experienced in Germany and Austria. He was free to devote himself entirely to his ambition, to change his attire three or four times a day, to call on the people who were in a position to help him, to appear at the theater and fashionable restaurants, to attend the social functions that were so numerous at the period of Napoleon's marriage with Marie-Louise. Most important of all, he overlooked no opportunity to be at the home of his protectors—now the Comte and Comtesse Daru. The latter's smile seemed more encouraging than ever, and even Pierre, no longer harassed by overwhelming duties, displayed a patronizing affability.

During the six months he waited before being appointed Auditor, he found several old friends and made some new ones. Chief of his new friends were Louis Pépin de Bellisle, an Auditor, handsome and amiable, although a bit avaricious and inclined toward haughtiness, and Bellisle's mistress, the Comtesse Beugnot, wife of a well-known politician.

Mme. Beugnot, a homely woman possessed of much intelligence, character and charm, was perhaps the first person in Paris society to understand and appreciate the complex character of Beyle. He responded gratefully to her sympathy, and their mutual affection only strengthened as the years passed. It was to "Mme. Doligny"—as she was christened in the lingo of Beylism—that he dedicated his first book. Some dozen years later, her daughter was to become his mistress.

By summer, the most accessible portion of Empire society had become aware of the thickset, immaculately dressed and studiously amiable young courtier who called himself "Monsieur de Beyle." He was making gratifying progress along the road which led to the kind of success he was seeking. But for success to be complete, it was essential for a bachelor to have a reputation as a ladies' man. This was an item on the program that Beyle had by no means overlooked, and during the years 1810 and 1811 he spent as much time as possible in feminine society—although his successes were scarcely more noteworthy than in the past. "Possibly," he says with humility in *Henry Brulard,* "no man of the Emperor's Court had less women than I, who was believed to be the lover of the Prime Minister's wife." This lady—variously referred to in the diary as the Comtesse de Palfy, Mme. Z, Elvire, Mme. de Trautmand, Marie and Mme. Petit—was not exactly the wife of the Prime Minister: she was merely Alexandrine Daru, the wife of Beyle's protector.

At the same time he was bashfully and awkwardly "courting" her, he overcame his timidity sufficiently to carry on eight or ten other love affairs, flirtations and sentimental intrigues. Unhappily for posterity's curiosity, he had grown cautious since the days of Mélanie Guilbert, and in his diary will be found nothing more than laconic and often deliberately confusing references to the women of uncertain identity who played ephemeral roles in his life at this period.

Money, the remaining essential ingredient of success, was not as easy to find as women. It may be wondered where Beyle obtained enough to cover his numerous expenses, for he was still only a deputy commissary drawing a monthly salary of 300 francs—and he was spending four or five times that amount. In fact, not merely had he provided himself with a costly wardrobe, acquired a fondness for the spitted kidneys of the fashionable Café Hardy and otherwise established a luxurious way of living, but in April he purchased a team of horses, a cabriolet costing 2,100 francs and hired a coachman!

But all this was part of the program: the only way to get ahead was to mix with the right people, and the only way to mix with the right people was to give the impression of being wealthy. He was gambling everything on the one hope of eventually becoming a Prefect with an annual salary of 26,000 francs. In the meantime, he counted on an auditorship to give him 2,000 francs; if he were attached to the Court he would have another 6,000 francs. He estimated that 14,000 francs would be required to live properly; therefore, he would borrow the missing 6,000 francs annually for, say, the next four years, and as soon as he was appointed to a prefecture he would start paying off his debts.

But where was the loan to come from? He beseeched his father to obtain the all-important 6,000 francs—8,000 would really be better. He went further; he suggested that Chérubin turn over an estate to him as a *majorat* and advance him the money to purchase a barony. These proposals failed to open the purse of "the bastard," who—as his son did not know—was himself so far in debt that he could have done little even had he so wished. So nothing was settled, and "Monsieur de Beyle" went on as before, borrowing where he could. By the middle of July, he owed 12,500 francs.

Then there was the matter of getting married. For him, saturated as he was with the morals of the *ancien régime,* marriage did not necessarily have anything to do with love; it was chiefly a means of procuring wealth and social position. He had about resigned himself to asking for the hand of a certain "lovely and gentle cipher" to whom he gives the name of Jenny Leschenault when he received disturbing news from Grenoble. Victorine Mounier, it appeared, was being courted by a local swain, and Pauline proposed attempting to arrange a match before it was too late. Giddy at the thought, he read his sister's letter "twenty times," but in the end his good sense for once asserted itself. He had worshiped the image of Victorine for eight years. There could be no doubt that, with her "exquisite sensibility" and her "nobility of soul," she was infinitely superior to the "insignificant dolls" of the Parisian salons, yet at heart he could not deceive himself; he knew that he was in love with a chimera and not with the real Victorine, whom he had seen but "seven times" in his life.

Moreover, returning to practical considerations, he reflected that to wed Victorine would be to defeat his plans, for she would bring him very little in the way of a dowry, and he could hope for no more than a subordinate place in a family headed by the aloof Edouard—now Baron Mounier and secretary of the Emperor's office.

While occupied with his social duties and his plans for success, he managed to continue his "pursuit of happiness" through aesthetic sensations and intellectual interests. He spent much of his time reading, as always. And, wistfully recalling the days of the Rue d'Angivilliers when he was fired by the love of glory instead of worldly ambition, he turned back to his rules for laughter and the comic, and his classifications of "the passions, states and habits of the soul, and means of passion."

Finally, on August 3, when he was least expecting it, he received a letter from the Duc de Bassano, Minister Secretary of State, notifying him that he had been named two days before as Auditor of the Council of State. Beyle regarded his watch, as he always did at important moments in his life, and then solemnly recorded the historic event in his diary. Not long after, Pierre Daru, as Intendant General of the Emperor's Household, obtained for him one of the two posts of *Inspecteur de la Comptabilité du Mobilier et des Bâtiments de la Couronne;* moreover, he was placed on the civil list in charge of the Holland office. He successfully applied for the privilege of retaining his position as deputy commissary. In addition to various gratuities, he was now to receive, as he had anticipated, 2,000 francs a year as Auditor, 6,000 as inspector of the Emperor's household furnishings, and 900 as a retired deputy commissary. The first step of his projects was accomplished.

1810 Paris

Diary from February 15 to . . .

February 15.—I was at Martial's at five o'clock this afternoon; he read me a note his wife had just received from M. du Châtenay, which started out like this: "I'm giving you as information, and sure information, that M. Beyle has been appointed Auditor, but under the name of Reile, etc."

That gave me some well-founded hope. My desire to be an Auditor wasn't as great as my horror at resuming my sorry trade of being a war commissary.

February 16.—I wrote to the Minister of Justice from Crozet's. Lunch at Hardy's. Cardon is of the opinion that our hope is well founded. From there, Crozet and I went to see the Pont d'Iéna, and, as we were coming back, we saw the Emperor. In the evening, to the Opéra, *Saul* and *Paul et Virginie,* a ballet that wasn't very pretty. I SPEAK WITH Pacé a large part of the time. I saw Clotilde and, what's much more, Mars; Martial believes I've been appointed; from there to Mme. Viel's. I spent the night with Emilie. Sunday, I'm to see the little girl of the Rue Traversière who's scarcely been touched.

Saturday, 17.—I went about town this morning, and tried out my horse's speed. I went to the Legislative Corps a minute, went to the Bois de Boulogne with Crozet, and from there to Mme. Z's. I was a little freer because her mother was there. I dined at Grignon's with Crozet and Ouéhihé. Then *Le Mariage de Figaro.* I WAS WITH Pacé.

19, Monday.—It's confirmed that I'm an Auditor. M. Mounier said so, according to what Faure was told. This morning, I went with Crozet to the Collège de France, where an ass was expounding Virgil; I almost burst out laughing before the scandalized audience.

The evening at Mme. Z's. I went there at ten o'clock with boredom and making an effort on myself. I was natural and right in my element. I was as satisfied as possible with Marie [Mme. Daru]. M. Daru spoke to me with all possible good grace of my little letter. When I told him, "This will be the last," he said, "Why no, keep on; we'll try to arrange your affair." I'm going to be introduced to Mme. Estève, an excellent woman, judging by her expression. I'm happy.

February 20.—This was the day, I believe, that I threw my thumb out of joint at the Palais-Royal. This accident put me on sick leave; I'm trying to get a clear notion of the history of the Revolution.

I dined at Mme. Z's the day after the accident.

I was greeted by Marie with tender friendliness.

February 24.—I was introduced to the La Bergerie ladies, whom I found less Raphaelesque than I had expected. Blanche and Emilie resemble Ursula too much through their intellectual character to please me greatly. I like Mlle. Jules better, but her merit is still a "maybe" in my opinion. It was today, the 26th, that I saw beauty itself. I experienced the strongest sensation of beauty that I can recall: Mlle. Mars as Suzanne in *Figaro.* I was enchanted to the point of feeling myself about to fall in love. Had I known less about the difference between conduct and expression, I'd have perished.

I saw Marie this morning in the Tuileries; HER ASTONISHMENT AT MY sudden APPEARANCE; PERHAPS SHE HAS SOME LOVE FOR ME.

I was with Bellisle at this delightful sight.

February 28.—I've just been to *Figaro,* Mars's delightful face. A spring day, long bath, *Tom Jones,* happiness. Mlle. Mars made me recapture my heart, which I thought was dead.

March 1.—Happy tranquillity, won during the past two years. In the evening, visit to Mme. de B. . . , a moment of gaiety. *La Forteresse du Danube,* vacuous. Many people, charming reverie during my long excursion on the Boulevards.

March 2.—Took a bath at Tivoli, read with Crozet. Crozet was as dull as dull can be. At midnight, I went to take an ice at the Café de Foy, and returned CONSCIOUS OF HAPPINESS in weather that was almost like spring.

March 12.—These divine beauties, as we call them, are assuredly devilishly boring. Amélie [de Bézieux] is a thousand times more amiable, but her lover [Faure] is jealous, even pettily so. I went to see the ladies with the best dispositions toward them, but I had to submit to the weight of the evidence.

Moreover, a day filled with happiness through . . .

My thumb, which is slowly getting well, still keeps me from going around in a carriage.

March 13.—I HAVE BREAKFASTED [lunched] WITH HER; I HAVE SEEN HER AT HER MOTHER'S. This affection has nothing gloomy about it, almost no constraint, almost no boredom.

March 14.—I've just seen David painting. He's a collection of pettinesses, both in his manner of tracing his name and in the difference between a historical painter and a miniaturist in connection with a page's costume which he *sent* to the Emperor. People of that sort wear out their souls over trifles, it's not surprising that they haven't anything left for lofty things. Moreover, David isn't intelligent enough to hide this petty vanity and not to show constantly the vast importance it has in his own opinion.

I was perfectly at home there. I went at one o'clock, she wasn't there yet; returned at a quarter past two, she was waiting for David. He signed the picture as four o'clock was striking.[1] OUR EYES told each other THAT THEY LOVE THEMSELVES [*sic*]. I HAVE SEEN HER AN INSTANT, embarrassed and not daring to raise her eyes to meet mine, which were worshiping her. All comparisons and grace apart, THERE IS MUCH OF Chérubin's PART IN MY AFFAIR. It's our position. I'm invited tomorrow, and for the purpose of showing me something that she knows that I already know well and that she's already shown me; but I don't know what it is that I'm invited to, to lunch, I think.

March 17 and 18.[2]—Intimacy between Marie and me is beginning to appear. I'm natural and reap moments of happiness.

19.—On the morning of the nineteenth, I took her some flowers, but because of my bashfulness, I wasn't happy; I didn't see her. In the eve-

[1]The picture is David's portrait of Mme. Daru, included in this volume.
[2]This and the following two entries were written by Beyle in his own peculiar brand of Italian.

ning, I went to the ball at nine o'clock, I started out with a bit of nonsense, I took her hand in front of everybody in the dining room. She somewhat resented this nonsense; otherwise, she was very kind to me and invited me for lunch today. I've just been to it.

March 19.—I was also amiable for the first time with the terrible Daru. I had come from Mme. Beugnot's, I had gone there to get into the right tone and I succeeded very well, for I was also at home in Mme. Daru's presence. Her words were of affectionate friendship, and her husband joked with me. The Hôtel du Châtelet [where the Darus lived] won't have seen me bashful, and the period of my acquaintance with Mme. Beugnot will be that of my wit's happy maturity. I'm reading Malthus's book on *The Principle of Population* with the greatest of pleasure.

March 20.—I'm beginning to feel with genuine satisfaction that I've contracted the reasonable habits that ensure happiness. I felt this clearly, down to the details, an hour ago.

This morning, all alone, I was busy and happy until half-past one, when I began writing this. My situation, free from all passion, was such that the company of another person would scarcely have added to MY HAPPINESS. I enjoyed my sentiments and thoughts in the English manner.

Through the same effect of reasonable habits, I'm able to affirm that yesterday I experienced the greatest quantity of *pure boredom* (free from any depressing feeling) that I've ever felt in my life. It was at the home of the La Bergerie ladies. Crozet, Ouéhihé and Bellisle were there. Not the tiniest little idea, not the tiniest little sentiment; we kept on talking like people doomed to maintain a conversation, we listlessly amplified the most trivial topics. When I left, I almost had an attack of indigestion as the result of yawning. It was the second time in my life this has happened to me, and both times were in the Rue Thérèse [where the La Bergeries lived].

I have but one observation to make—I talk to Mlle. Emilie, I look at Mlle. Blanche practically all the time, and I do neither with Mlle. Jules. All that is in inverse ratio to the interest these persons arouse in me; it's undoubtedly ONE EFFECT OF BASHFULNESS, the effect of a formerly acquired habit, for I experience none with them.

In my opinion, the mother and the two younger sisters are as crammed with social experience as they are void of ideas. They probably have much tact, but not a tact of the *soul,* but a tact of education, of experience, well versed in the things their soul has led them to remark, and this soul is wholly French; from which it results that baseness, for instance, is invisible to them, the same, I believe, as all refinement of soul.

Mlle. Jules is undoubtedly extremely spoiled, tainted (may I be allowed the use of this term, I see no other for it) by a constant intellectual company that is vicious. Her mother hasn't left her for half an hour since her birth. Since Crozet, Bellisle and Faure say she's mentally alert, I'm willing to suspend judgment until it's demonstrated to me; up to now, it seems that I've intimidated her. It really seems that we have produced this effect on each other, an effect which is, however, weak on my part.

Ottilie (THE BOOK OF) [Goethe's *Elective Affinities*] seems ridiculous to her. We'll pass over that: with a French head, a soul like that of Mozart (the tenderest and most profound sensibility) would be required to appreciate this novel.

Mlle. Jules, be pleasing through your charms, but stop pretending to be possessed of sensibility, or stop mistaking your lassitude for sensibility.

Mme. Beugnot is extremely amiable and, at her house, I was too. It would be very odd if she were to have a remarkable sensibility, I want very much to see her often. As for HIS LOVE[1] I BELIEVE, the indifference of profundity without profundity shouldn't be preferred to the charms and brilliant vivacity of youth. *Allegro vivace* is preferable. His manners, sad, serious, solemn, are probably a result of his bad health; he'd be reasonable if he were governed by ambition, but I believe him incapable of taking and sticking to a difficult decision unless it were propped up by the whole scaffolding of society's petty ideas. Besides, he's beginning to have a great love of money; he has succeeded, he says, in saving up twelve thousand francs. He's another of those asses who are excellent for their heirs.

Ouéhihé still has jerky little movements, and openly appears to be what we know from another source that he is—a very mediocre man.

Crozet, who really has extreme sagacity and some sensibility, and who incontestably is an intelligent man, is at a disadvantage when with those *divine beauties*—that's the word for them—through his pedantic appearance. I'd like to see him at ease, unrestrained, cheerful, with the noble facility of *Wakefield,* from which, moreover, everyone was far removed. As for myself, I was bored and must have seemed unamiable.

With a dash of political genius (the art of attaining an objective with the elements one possesses), the evening, instead of being so *dull,* would have been very agreeable. There were all the elements of happiness: 1. youth; 2. wit; 3. beauty; 4. health; 5. pecuniary ease; 6. social experience.

The inane habit of being dignified spoiled everything. In a village, we'd have had wild gaiety, in Germany we'd have had fun, in Italy

[1] Beyle apparently means "her lover," a reference to Bellisle, Mme. Beugnot's lover.

voluptuousness would have arisen in our midst and we'd have obeyed its gentle laws. *French corruption* was so great that the most amiable of men would have appeared unhappy at this gathering, would have given rise to envy rather than joy.

These six pages, I'll wager, would be found spiteful; in that case, I'm spiteful, this is the way my soul rings. Princess de Palfy has much less beauty, youth and wit, but I believe that she creates in me, and feels herself, more happiness than these damsels.

Mars was perfect in *Les Fausses Confidences*. At the end I had a heavy heart, a little more and I'd have burst into tears. This has been a day during which I've felt a great deal. I'm thinking of returning TO MY TRUE TALENT, IF I HAVE A TALENT, THAT OF COMIC BARD.

March 31.—Friend Ouéhihé, talking to Crozet about the ladies, started out with an exclamation:

"Ah, but I found that Beyle didn't stand on ceremony at all with the ladies! He was stretched out in a chair, his hand over his eyes, looking at them from time to time as though he was examining what was going on, and scarcely condescending to speak. La Bergerie couldn't have done more. How do they find him, the ladies?"

"They find him extremely nice."

Ouéhihé: "Oh! In the first place, he's got plenty of wit . . . and then . . . even if he didn't have, they wouldn't dare to find him disagreeable . . . Yes, yes, yes, oh! he's got plenty of wit; yet I found that he said things that weren't spontaneous, things that didn't entirely produce a good effect. For instance, he repeated a comparison of lumps of sugar and said it twice over, that's the worst. All in all, I said to myself, 'Beyle, friend Beyle, isn't all he ought to be with the ladies, and in general (*puckering up his lips*), I see that the young men who go there—and no doubt it's the fault of the ladies—go there the same as they'd go to a bawdyhouse.'"

The talk turned to other things; an hour afterward, Ouéhihé said:

"How much has he got, Beyle?"

"Oh, he'll be very rich."

Ouéhihé: "Very rich, very rich or not, the question is how much? Ten or twelve thousand francs?"

"Oh, more than that!"

"But at present, at present, how much has he got at present?"

"At present, his father will give him eight thousand francs for his auditorship."

"Ah, ah, that will do, that will do! That will make at least ten thousand francs in Paris. He'll have to be careful though. How many horses has he got? Two?"

"Four. He's trying to sell them."

Ouéhihé: "He'll do well to cut himself down to one."

History in dramatic form.—June 8, 1789, Arthur Young, who was in Paris and recorded his conversations, gives me the quite simple idea of a history of the French Revolution in dramatic form: Mirabeau, Cazalis, Lally-Tollendal, Sieyès and the fatuous d'Epréménil talking together.

The biographical details would make the lovers of the afore-mentioned finesse swallow the historical part. This racy and instructive work would make a man's reputation.

A. Young arouses the desire to go traveling in France with his book in hand, but it would also be necessary to have passion in the heart to find as much pleasure as he in doing so. I myself, mixed with Crozet's sagacity, would make a blend that would be good for a book, although not gay enough to get along together agreeably: we'd need a third person, a gay, reckless chap full of enthusiasm. We would write a description of French character in the country's various provinces.

13th April.—A very pronounced look of love. The rest of her behavior showed friendship at least, outside of a moment of boredom; but there were fifteen persons present. Marie must have been in a very affectionate mood for my presence alone to keep her from musing after six hours of performance. A man of experience would possibly say to me, "Young man, you're only able to read things written in large letters."

A full day: sentiments and thoughts. Yesterday, still fuller, and I was ill; I had the pleasure of getting the upper hand over my discomfort, of ridding myself of it and of working on [Malthus's] *Population* from eleven to six without interruption.

Since last writing, it seems to me I've seen twenty proofs of love, but our rather cool tête-à-tête kill everything. If she had a few more relations with me, we'd already have confessed our love for each other.[1] I've been nettled without any cause for three days. Since her soul hasn't enough affinity with mine for a big battle to decide everything, I must become familiar, joke, make myself intimate with her. I am (during the absence of her uncle) the only lover she could conveniently have without it being apparent.

April 14th.—Today I've lived on my thoughts and sentiments. I haven't talked to a living soul except café waiters and my servant. On the other hand, I've read seventy pages of the first volume of Malthus. I came across some good ideas FOR MY BASHFULNESS in the third volume of Arthur Young. Dined hurriedly at Lambert's in order to go to *An-*

[1] Our eyes are in agreement, but they haven't spoken. [Note by Beyle.]

dromaque. I'm busy nearly all the time with two women: a foreigner, brunette with a character of the same kind as Mme. Le Brun, a woman who isn't pretty, but voluptuous: I suspect her of being a bit of a wench because she ended by ogling me in a very human manner.

April 16.—Today and the 15th I lunched at Mme. de Trautmand's [Mme. Daru's]. The 16th, tête-à-tête, embarrassment on my part. She really must have some love for me, or a diminutive of this sentiment, to make such a fuss about me.

April 17.—I'm working a great deal. Through reflection, my afternoons and evenings are occupied, and with pleasure. Today, for instance, I dined at Beauvilliers' at six. Charming little German girl. I took a demitasse at the Café de Foy, from there I went to Brigitte's reading room, where I read the *Bibliothèque Britannique* with pleasure until half-past eight. I came home in the fine moonlight, but Kamenski [his servant] wasn't there. That almost didn't put me in a bad humor, I went out to look for him, and afterward took a cab that must have been the world's worst. All this gave me a slightly astonished manner at Mme. Nardot's, but I think my slightly too virile expression concealed it. Mme. Daru bantered me on my solitude of yesterday, she asked me to go with her to Longchamp. I didn't say much in reply to all that. Pacé seemed a little *sostenuto* [distant] with me. I came back and am writing this at a quarter past twelve, consequently the first day of Longchamp. All considered, I believe I love the Comtesse Palfy a little.

It appears that Mme. Doligny [Beugnot] is very well disposed toward me. On the other hand, the divine beauties still bore me to death. Félix has a gloomy character which always makes him see the disagreeable side of things—the ridicule he may incur, and which he fears like all the devils in hell. Besides, he's always on the side opposed to all action. It's a great pity.

April 18.—First day of Longchamp. I got up and saw that the weather was magnificent, the finest day of the year. It was less clear in my soul. I was downcast because of my alleged asininity of the day before, I was displeased with myself. I recalled Marie's jokes about my solitude, I thought of gracious ways in which I might have replied to her. I was in a bad humor when I left the Café de Foy. I dressed and went to see Mme. Doligny. I was at ease, she was very nice to me. I went alone to Longchamp. I found Faure at the wicket, my bad humor ended. At four o'clock, I went to Mme. Estève's. Mme. Palfy arrived, we got into a carriage; as we left it at the entrance of the Champs-Elysées, I offered her my arm. This gave me more pleasure than it was worth. I began to feel at ease; this feeling intensified and ended by being almost amiable—altogether amiable, I believe—, dining alone with her and M. Z, I paid no attention to Ma. She was very nice to me (IN THE MIDDLE OF THE WALK A GLANCE OF LOVE) and, as I left her at eight o'clock, she called me back to ask me to go to Longchamp with her Friday, "but if it's convenient for you," and this in a manner she's never had with me before: no more superiority, the tone of equality of two persons who are beginning to be in love (the sequel of the respect I commanded during dinner). She said whatever she was thinking; as she returned fatigued from the walk, I saw that she was saying to us whatever she was thinking. It was seven o'clock, we were in the office of M. (Roger) [Daru?], M. . . . was reading, she was holding a bouquet negligently in her right hand, this bouquet was right beside me. I began to stroke it, and, true to my romantic character, I experienced a lively pleasure; finally, after being conscious for some time of my action, she gave me a tap on the fingers.

All this is badly described, but it was a happy day, even a very happy one, the first time in my life that I was witty two hours on end in the presence of the terrible Z.

Thursday 19.—Rain. I went to Hardy's for breakfast at half-past eight, from there to see Louis [de Bellisle], who brought me Mme. Beugnot's invitations. I went to see M. Renauldon; this man, although an ass, is probably a good mayor, his genius and self-esteem are on a level with this distinguished position. He recited I don't know what inane proverb for me: "Work, wretch; wretched work," which, however, showed that he felt where the shoe pinched. From there, home, where I read Malthus from noon until a quarter to six. From there to Longchamp, almost nobody. I dined quickly and well at Legascque's, I went to Mme. Bézieux's, where I drank some good tea until half-past ten. From there to Mme. Shepherderie's [La Bergerie]. I saw as soon as I entered that I'd been seen on good terms with Mme. Roger. There was a shade of difference in the greeting a woman gives a man who she knows has chosen her rival. Respect and the *sostenuto* sort of thing, the Italians would say. I tried not to be listless, and left at half-past eleven, after a visit of twenty minutes. With me was Louis, who told me that Mme. Doligny was surprised not to see me at lunch.

I'm not in the mood for writing. All I've just written is badly written; but I wanted to note down yesterday's happiness. This feeling has so often made me unhappy that it's only proper it should give me some happiness. The first day that the verdure of the Tuileries is abundant enough to form a mass.

April 20.—I'm not in a writing mood, but I will have to provide some laughter for next year. Here goes then, the third day of Longchamp, I arrived at four o'clock sharp; she was dressing and I was denied admission to her room; when she was ready, I found her very gay, with the high color sometimes given by the presence of the loved object. She was wearing a little white frock, short and narrow, which showed her feet. She spoke to me with the sprightliness, the gaiety that one has for what one loves, and which is lacking in the succeeding period.[1] I don't say it can't be explained otherwise, but I'm writing in the way that seems the most natural to me. I was too pleased with what I saw to have the time to be witty. I ought to have limited myself to some spontaneous exclamations, instead of that I said some rather insignificant things. Perhaps I appeared distant to her. There's so little of the romantic in her head that I'd almost think this was the case if it weren't that women didn't have an innate tact in everything that's connected, near or far, with the great affair of their lives, and in this sort of thing they have more intelligence than in all other (indifferent) things. Her white thin gown outlined her whole form perfectly, I noticed several defects of design. If it weren't for that damned respect which separates us, we'd settle our business in fine shape. She hasn't got the age, or the beauty, or the morals necessary to have a brilliant young man of the Court, one of the ordnance officers, for example, whose uniform, I know, pleases her immensely. My heart happens to be so disposed that I desire her, and certainly the first months, even the first year, of our liaison would be delightful for both of us. In order to bring things about nicely, gay and slightly unrestrained gallantry on my part is required.

Her father came, her husband, and a bit later the Comtesse E. It was decided that the ladies would go in the berlin with the father and daughter, and that M. Paul and I would go in my cabriolet; as we were going down the stairs, I said graciously, "A fine arrangement, to exile us like that in the cabriolet!"

"Why, what a child you are; we can't all go in the berlin, we'd look like a wedding party! Besides, you're going to dine here."

While she was thus consoling me and going down the stairs, she squeezed my hand very markedly. I only left her at half-past ten; our hands met, but she withdrew hers. In the evening, she didn't look at me; I don't believe it was indifference.

Easter, 1810 [April 22].—A superb day. I bustled around like a Basque. A delightful cold lunch at the Café de Chartres. From there to Saint-Eustache, an abominable din; from there, back home, forty pages of Smith; from there to the Conservatoire: agreeable music, I'll return; from there to the Tuileries, a good dinner at the Frères Provençaux; from there to *Manlius*. After that, I waited for my cabriolet half an hour without getting too impatient, walking in the Palais-Royal and reflecting on what sort of conduct I ought to assume with Mme.

[1]The most intense moment OF THE PERIOD CALLED PASSION. [Note by Beyle.]

Robert [probably still another name for Mme. Daru]. From there to the home of Mmes. Shepherd [La Bergerie], less gloomy than usual and even gay and, what's more, natural. I was amiable and withdrew at half-past eleven. I read a scene from *Othello* before going to sleep.

I forgot to say that the day before Easter, the 21st, I ate some excellent ham at Mme. Doligny's and that I was very amiable—to the point of not returning because I'll never be so to such an extent again. It's not in my nature to be amiable with women.

April 26.—I got up at seven and am writing this after midnight. I spent an hour and a half at the Albert baths, which put me in a perfectly reasonable mood. I read until two, when, after leaving in a calash to go to the Comtesse Beugnot's, I lunched abundantly at Hardy's; from there to Mme. Beugnot's and Mme. Shepherderie's; her two eldest daughters came with us to Saint-Denis. I wasn't very malleable, the party was lifeless. From there to the Bois de Boulogne, etc.

But to come to the essential: returning at nine from Mme. Beugnot's, I found a letter saying that Babet is coming to Paris soon. The hope of seeing those beautiful eyes *e angelico sembiante* [and angelic face] filled me with an intensely voluptuous feeling.

I don't want to speak badly of Bellisle, yet it must be said that his soul is moved by the tiniest little events which affect his vanity. There's where you can see that he's still young. Ten years from now, his soul will be the same, but his experience will shelter him from emotion. Thus it was that three days ago he was immensely put out by the ladies' quips about his alleged drunkenness; on the way back in the carriage with Mme. Beugnot, he reproached her sharply. What shocked him a lot was the unanimous *laughter* of the ladies over nothing at all.

Moreover, his avarice is continuously apparent, and in a way that, for THE COMIC BARD, is very conspicuous. Thus, yesterday I came across him in the act of shaving, he told me he was going to do it every day, I opposed this plan: "You haven't got a heavy enough beard, that'll make it grow." "Oh no! It's neater, and besides when I don't shave, it's like a rasp the second day, and *right away it cuts my cravat.*"

A good way to portray a character. It's his sole outstanding trait. Susceptibility comes afterward perhaps.

April 27.—First day at Mme. Estève's. I was immediately at ease. We played games. I'm satisfied with my deportment there; anyone who had paid attention to me would have found me one of the four or five gayest men, and there were twelve or fifteen present.

Previously, I'd gone to Mme. Romain's, where I found Comtesse Palfy, who regarded me constantly with interest: "You've come very late!"

She still sought to take my hand. I squeezed hers slightly, but I made a mistake in not kissing her in the little room; there was only one other man present, and I was entitled to do so by the penitence she underwent. I'm gathering up all my courage, and I've decided to kiss her cheek or hand at the first opportunity. One ends by scorning a numskull who never takes advantage of anything. He'll kiss the hand that happens to recline on the mantel. She'll say to him, "What a child you are!" He'll reply with a tender expression, "Yes, I am a child. You have nothing but friendship for me, and what I feel for you is a quite different thing." He'll add, "When I'm with you, I do nothing but make blunders."

If Mme. Romain is receiving Friday (and if Comtesse Palfy doesn't go to M. de Schwarzenberg's), I must be very amiable and brilliant with a couple of chubby-cheeked damsels in order to show her that, if I'm awkward and bashful with her, it's because I give her the preference.

A happy day, full of ideas and sentiments up to seven o'clock, when I dined, a day full of amusement, of agreeable sentiments and of the sight of what I truly love, from eight until midnight.

If I had had a carriage instead of a cabriolet, I would have taken her home; at least she asked me that question, and if it hadn't been for Pacé, who had his carriage, I would have had a tête-à-tête.

April 28.—Got up at a quarter to seven; Tivoli, coffee at Hardy's; bought Gray, whom I read until two o'clock. I then went to Mme. Palfy's. I was wearing a military costume, a bit ponderous. My conversation was the same. I was full of ideas of quite another kind. After the brilliant evening the day before, I ought to have done better, yet I'm wrong to find a reason for dissatisfaction in my behavior with Mme. Palfy. She welcomed me with pleasure, had much confidence in me.

April 30.—CHARMING EVENING.—I'm afraid I paid her a visit that was a little long. Pure, fresh, charming pleasure during the evening passed at Monceau. I dined very well at the Provençaux's, where I saw a very lovely feminine face. From there to Mme. Doligny's, and we left for Mousseau, where we found a lady whom I had seen in the morning at Mme. Doligny's and who, having arrived at the position where one may or may not have lovers, looked upon me with pleasure and respect, the same as we men look upon a young widow of twenty-five who shows signs of having some amorous disposition. We had some ices and punch in a charming pavilion surrounded by columns. An evening of the Italian kind, dark, cool, a beautiful landscape (for Paris) and excellent iced punch.

I know quite well the secret of the pleasure I experienced, but I won't tell it in order not to dim it.

The nicest evening I've spent in Paris.

May 1.—Yesterday I bought a very fashionable cabriolet for 2,100 francs, and some seals for 163 francs. This morning, I went to take *Ottilie* to Mme. Z. I found her making out her accounts. From there to Mme. Robert's; she was busy AND THE LOVE APPEARED NOT. I was very well dressed. I went to see Mme. Bertrand, who was in Brussels. To the Tuileries, where everyone looked at my getup. From there to Pacé's, who looked at it too, but who didn't say anything about it, so as not to stress my triumph.

May 2.—Got up at half-past seven. Bibliothèque Imperiale, which hasn't got the prose works of Gray or those of the immortal Millin, member of thirty-seven academies. I didn't employ my morning as though I weren't going to see Mme. de Palfy. (I went to her house, she wasn't there, I went for a walk at Monceau, from there from one to four o'clock with Mmes. D. and E.; from there to Mme. Marie's.)

I was quite at ease with Marie, especially at the beginning, when, having completely shed my inane cheerful look, I took on genuine dignity. I was at ease during the entire walk, it was like yesterday: friendly attentions, but THE TENDER INTEREST, *dov'è* [where was it]? Perhaps concealed in order not to be imprudent. It's certain that the passion of last week doesn't appear any longer. Yet, as we were on the way, our legs were pressed together all the time, and in a pronounced manner, she didn't try to change anything. As we were leaving, we stopped before a man who had some molten tin, I traced an A [for Alexandrine Daru] with my cane on the surface of the metal in fusion; she followed my movements, smiled when she saw the result and leaned heavily against me. All in all, except for the passion of the other day, there's nothing better than her behavior; coming home, she avoided looking at me, she's on a footing of the closest friendship with me, and I believe that, if the ladies were to talk about me, they would say, "He's very nice."

General character.—From April 15 to 28, tender interest, marked *con brio,* and braving the fear of compromising herself; from the 28th TILL NOW, close friendship, but no more *brio* (May 2, 1810, RETURNING FROM Monceau).

In the evening, I talked a great deal and very well to Mme. de Bézieux from half-past seven until half-past nine; from ten to eleven, I was ridiculously silent at Mme. Shepherderie's, it's probable that I was SEVERELY lapidated after I left.

May 3.—I GO AT BREAKFAST TIME AT PALFY'S HOUSE. I was natural enough and had sufficient dignity. I'm satisfied with this meeting. Her eyes seemed to be animated by my presence. I BELIEVE THAT SHE THINKS ME restrained BY SOMEWHAT, BUT VIRTUE IS RIDICUL [*sic*], I must arrange to make her understand that it wasn't this respectable motive, but solely the fear *di non esser corrisposto* [of not being loved in return]. She seemed to me to lack equally the coolness of the past week and the *brio* of the preceding period; it was rather (if it was) deeply felt affection, CONSCIOUS LOVE, tender, slightly melancholy, being conscious of every mood. Her face seemed to me to be covered with the colors of love when, as she was reading a newspaper aloud, I watched her instead of reading over her shoulder—and she saw this from the corner of her eye. All in all, I was satisfied with her and with myself. I was very well dressed in a way that went perfectly with my facial expression, which was handsome.

On my return, first and very good lesson by M. Goodson, from half-past twelve until two o'clock. This man shows that he has very clear ideas and a good deal of sensibility, without any bombast. He appears to be very learned in general grammar, and he declaimed *The Country Churchyard* like an angel, really in a superior manner.

Prudence makes me terminate this notebook here. Tomorrow will be the anniversary of a period in 1806 when, without hating (in the least), I cursed that which today I see through a very different eye.

DJORN'L, OR ANATOMY, OF THE THOUGHTS, FEELINGS AND EVENTS OF HARRY FROM THE 9th May 1810 TILL THE 12 August 1810

> The most beautiful woman is spoiled by dissecting her; it is her portrait that should be composed, but in portraying her you only learn the colors, and it is in the pattern that you seek instruction.

MYSELF

IF I HAD HAD MELANIE THESE 3 MOUNTS [MONTHS] AND THREE DAYS I SHOULD HAVE BEEN PERFECTLY HAPPY.

Notice

If some indiscreet person reads this diary, I wish to deprive him of the pleasure of making fun of me by pointing out to him that this aims at being a mathematical and rigid report on my manner of being, neither too favorable nor too unfavorable, but stating purely and severely what I believe to have taken place. It is destined to cure me of my absurdities when I reread it in 1820.[1] It is a written part of my intimate consciousness, and what is most worth while, what I have felt at the sound of music by Mozart, while reading Tasso, upon being awakened by a barrel organ, while giving my arm to my mistress of the moment, is not to be found here. Hence, I beseech you on bended knee not to make fun of me.

June 1, 1810, COMING BACK from Mousseau.

A TOUR TO *Versailles.*—A DAY HAPPY *con brio.* Ofchêne [Deschênes] and I arrived at Mme. de Palfy's at half-past eight; she was getting up, we took a turn in the garden. M. de Baure absurdly kept us waiting and tried to persuade us that he had only a minute to spare.

We left at half-past nine after a cold breakfast. We saw La Savonnerie; bold and brilliant colors, beautiful and rich rugs.

We reached the Manufactory of Sèvres, which at this season is surrounded with fresh foliage, at eleven o'clock.

At Sèvres, I found the handsomest living creature I ever saw: Adolphe Brongniart, son of the savant who is the manager of the manufactory. We likewise saw the loveliest manufactured articles I've ever seen: the round table, three feet less an inch, with the portraits of most of the marshals and that of the Emperor in the center. Isabey (who displayed nothing but a servile character being polite out of self-interest to the powerful man he fears but doesn't like, without the least vestige of CELESTIAL FIRE) showed us the table, which really gives a notion of perfection, especially in the portraits of Marshals Soult and Pontecorvo; the Princes of Eggmühl and Neuchâtel are the least well done. This charming work, which has already cost fifty-eight thousand francs, I believe, is soon to be baked, which may shatter it. The rest of the manufactory is interesting enough. A stained-glass window that admits the light through the pretty figure of a seated woman. I suggested to M. Brongniart that he try some night subjects, Gérard's *Ossian,* for instance, for boudoir windows. He was in favor of the idea, but replied that experiments along this line hadn't been successful up to now. The statuary was mediocre, they ought to ask Canova and Thorwaldsen for models; in general, they miss the majestic in the Emperor's face, which they reproduce continually. We saw an Emperor they were putting on horseback, a mean face, simpering and pretty, the accessories perfectly rendered.

A pretty road, very fresh verdure. We soon reached M. de Clédat's, in the Cour du Dragon. The streets of Versailles are those of a capital, the shops and inhabitants those of a provincial town.

We left for Trianon after a glass of excellent malaga. M. Clédat,

[1]Indeed, this gives me confidence in my determination FOR MY FUTURE HAPPINESS. [Note added by Beyle June 21, 1818.]

although somewhat of a Versaillophile, isn't lacking in intelligence, and he demonstrated it by having excellent wines, but not iced; it was too bad.

The Trianons are pretty; nothing gloomy, nothing majestic. The furnishings aren't fine enough for a sovereign who wishes to play the role, sometimes they're lacking in the comfort a voluptuous man would seek in shedding his sovereign's garb.

I remained all the time with Mme. Héliotte, an agreeable woman, though not pretty and thirty-one years old. I was surprised last week not to see any affectation or bashfulness in a provincial woman, but it turns out that she isn't one—she was brought up in Paris. I took pleasure in my visit to Sèvres, the pleasure stayed with me and became more intense up to ten in the evening, when I left Mme. Nardot's.

May 11.—I was in a bad humor yesterday not to have seen Marie, this morning I was excited and pleased at receiving an order from the Minister sending me to Lyon. I went to lunch at M. Daru's to talk to him about it, I didn't find a minute to do so.

I read, with the most sustained and lively pleasure, the XVIth Canto of *Gerusalemme,* the one in which Rinaldo abandons Armida. I constantly repeated to myself, "My God, how beautiful it is!" I was much more given to admiration six years ago than now. I'm obliged to force myself to read Corneille and Racine, I find fault with them at every step. I discovered that my admiration for Tasso was as keen as in those days of sensibility when I used to contemplate the stars with so much pleasure from the top floor of M. Paquin's in the Rue d'Angivilliers.

May 12.—I SPEAK TO M. DARU WITHOUT BASHFULNESS OF THE ORDER GIVEN TO ME BY THIS EXCELLENCE THE COUNT OF CESSAC; HIS INSIGNIFICANT ANSWER MEANS: "Get out of this little affair as best you can; I don't want it to make me contract an obligation toward A MAN THAT I DON'T ESTEEM."

In the evening, to Marie's, who IS NOT VERY TENDER FOR ME, however, at bottom she said two or three things to me that showed her interest. This morning, in order to assume a little of the indifference necessary with women, it being possible that I might spend a couple of hours with her, I preferred being bored by waiting.

May 19.—Two hours of such keen contentment that I was unable to concentrate my attention on anything. I went TO SEE PACE WHOM I BELIEVED A LITTLE COLD FOR OUR LITTLE DIFFERENCE. I FIND HIS SOUL SERENED BY THE FELICITY OF CUPIDITY. He offered to take me to see M. Nanteuil, who has promised to find out if I am on the list of forty.

This morning, amiable with Mme. Doligny, with whom I lunched. THIS EVENING AT BUFFA WITH MARIA, A SENSIBLE [sensitive] AND COLD

LOVER. THE LITTLE cousin. She leaned against me with pleasure. Maria was tired and rather distant. Yesterday, instead of love, it was perhaps boredom that she felt. There's devilishly little that's romantic and melancholy in that heart, she takes life gaily as it comes.

Mme. Doligny firmly believes that I am a lover and a successful lover. Count on appearances after that!

Mme. Le Brun told me that women start to have ideas of their own at the age of thirty. That seems to me exact.

Ermenonville and Mortefontaine.—I wrote Lambert June 1:

"I took a delightful trip to Ermenonville and Mortefontaine. There's an irregular body of water—four hundred arpents and a depth of twenty feet—where we were caught in a storm. We covered 3,100 toises, so we were told, in twenty minutes. We had two sails that swelled out a bit in spite of us, and three women who became rather pale at this sight. Our pilot chattered away agreeably and boasted to us, with the Parisian type of silliness, that he's never been out of Mortefontaine— a kind of life that's undoubtedly very suitable to form a sailor. (This touch of fear placed our womenfolk in the antipodes of boredom.[1]) This dash of pleasure—the enemy of enjoyment planned in advance—, this *brio*—so rare on the hither side of the Alps—livened up our trip."

June 7.—Laziness is the cause of my not writing since the delightful trip to Ermenonville. I'm letting myself be led along by the pleasures of the moment.

I wasn't very brilliant, I rarely am; what I need is people with an abundance of wit and naturalness (in the Italian manner), then BASHFULNESS entirely disappears, and I chatter away with gaiety and *brio*. Yet there were two women present, and everything was working out in such a way that, had the party lasted eight days instead of two, I'd have possessed them if I'd wanted to. This was noticed, I believe, *da Maria*.

Mme. Genet,[2] a juicy nun of twenty-eight (but witless and with the narrow-mindedness of the provinces), told Mme. . . . confidentially that I'd let it be understood in one of my letters to headquarters that I'd possessed her. I was told of this accusation under the pledge of secrecy, Marie said it was serious and that she knew several *frightful* things about me. She confided that to Mme. Héliotte. By the merest chance, I started jokingly to assume the appearance of a former lover with Mme. Genet. This bit of playfulness had its advantage, since it

[1] A recipe to be used in cases of boredom. [Note by Beyle.]

[2] One of those women who talk about indecency and bawdiness because they're interested in nothing else. She wanted to talk to me about it and to be taken to bed. 1815. [Note by Beyle.]

showed that I wasn't bashful with everyone. It succeeded and was kept up all the way to Paris.

The evening at the inn of Mortefontaine was extremely gay. There were just enough of us. M. Letx. [Lecoulteux de Couteleu], who, without having anything remarkable about his wit, and especially his appearance, nevertheless has ideas, and especially concerning women, and the philosophy given by travel, led them a merry chase. Marie was lying on a bed, I was seated on it against her knees with my hand on the bed at her side and encircling *il desiato corpo* [the desired body], my legs on a chair; Mme. Héliotte seated on the bed and unmistakably leaning against me, to the great scandal of the juicy nun, who was seated in front of us with Messrs. Dschns and Lex [Deschênes and Lecoulteux].

The tone of our little circle was perfect, very gay, aiming at voluptuousness and not the least sparkle of wit; we only talked so our words would serve to cloak our actions. That lasted from seven o'clock to ten, when the ladies went to bed, all alone to our great regret, which we didn't conceal, quite the contrary. I might had been a bit more enterprising; but the two acolytes were not of the same rank, consequently they were attentive and jealous; we were obliged to purchase respect with restraint. In spite of all, I managed to get away with A GOOD AND *sufficientemente saporito* [sufficiently appetizing] KISS.

I am fully aware that the loveliest party, like the loveliest woman, is spoiled by dissection. It's a portrait that ought to be composed, but this has all the austerity of a *study*.[1] In painting it, I'm learning the way to apply the colors (to write), and what I wish to acquire is the knowledge of what is concealed in the depths of the heart and mind.

My heart is too full of the Borromean Islands, of the forest that surrounds the lake, of the colossal statue of San Carlo Borromeo, the only saint I love. I think too often of Lake Geneva, of the approach to Lausanne, of the view from Bergamo and of the Grande-Chartreuse not to be a little unjust when it comes to English gardens.

It seems to me that in the environs of Paris all that can be done is to make something like the garden of Trianon; that is, forming an isle by cutting off the view completely and seeking isolation from a mean and shabby nature that shrivels up the soul on every side. Consequently, there is no room for a hill in such gardens.

Ermenonville is pretty, and even Jean-Jacques' crag becomes a very faithful imitation of nature, but of a petty nature; but when you're there, all you see is a bare plain or hills sparingly and monotonously strewn around. The isle where that sensitive man was buried for a few years is entirely lacking in the grandeur, the impressiveness and

[1]Painter's term. [Note by Beyle.]

the calm majesty it ought to have in order to harmonize with the man who, had he only been able to abstain from an unfortunate pedantry, would have been the Mozart of the French language, and would have produced a far greater effect on the heart of mankind. But he wanted to be men's legislator and not to charm them.

The soil has lent itself to the growth of trees worthy of this tomb; a man about forty-five years old showed us some trees that had been planted by M. de Girardin forty-four or forty-two years ago, when he came to Ermenonville after the death of the King of Poland, Stanislas. These trees, of the finest growth, frequently have two feet of coppice.

There's a spring that you can see coming from the earth at the bottom of a limpid basin, but here art has behaved pettily toward its associate, nature: M. de Girardin has built a trashy little grotto here, and, what's more, has had some verses engraved. *Qui, Maria fu veramente tenera con me, appoggiandosi a me* [Here Marie was really affectionate with me, leaning against me].

We went about Ermenonville with a man who said he had seen Rousseau during the six weeks he was here. He spoke to us of his [Rousseau's] wife. "We won't get married, my dear Josse, I don't want to give up the name of Rousseau, but it will make no difference, we'll live just the same as though we were." She was fifty years old. That's the opposite of the usual story.

We went around hurriedly, we didn't take the time to experience any feeling; Marie especially went very quickly, I gave her my arm most of the time, the others left me alone, and I'll bet they believe me far more advanced than I am (or wish to be, I may say truthfully so that, a few years from now, I won't believe myself worse than I am).

At length, tired of looking, as I am tired of writing, we left for Mortefontaine about three o'clock. We saw the château and the mean little park of fifty arpents that lies along the road. It's merely a prairie whose edges have been festooned. If the view of it were not flat, it would be quite nice. There are a few pictures in the château, and in the garden are some good verses by Delille that stand out because of those put up by M. de Girardin at Ermenonville.

We went to dinner, after which there was the charming evening of which I spoke at the start. The daisies: she loves me, she loves me not . . .

June 8.—I'm happy. I received my books from Brunswick. Faure came, and in talking to him I drove away the clouds that might have darkened my soul a bit. I went to Comtesse Palfy's at half-past eleven. I had all the appearance of happiness, *brio* and genius that could have been expressed by my irregular facial features.

Tonight, I went to the theater of the Court of Saint-Cloud. Being with Comtesse Palfy brings about a complete truce in my other thoughts. I'm completely taken up with her.

At midnight sharp, I reached Saint-Cloud, where we were subjected to one of the dullest and most sentimental rhapsodies that could be heard. The music was on a level with the words, and was sung off-key from start to finish. But I had a good view of the great man [Napoleon] and the Empress. Most of the women of the Court are ugly, they don't know how to wear their finery, they lose all grace when they're dressed up.

On the way back, I made love to Mme. de Gency the way I used to do to Rosa, and with almost the same success. I got as far as a busk, I found a skin that was very soft. She got mad, but only a little, and told me that in fifteen years she hadn't been able to grow accustomed to her husband's indifference, and she finally told me she didn't love me, and, in order that this declaration shouldn't hurt me too much, she gave me an extremely tender kiss on the lips at the same time. She slandered my charms, a minute later she told me she'd been in love with me from the first time she saw me at Monceau. She has a bit of amorous disposition; her disturbed and tender face at Tortoni's was very agreeable.

June 10.—To the journalists.

I notice daily in society that the young people who talk the most glibly about everything have no opinion to express concerning the artists who, by luck or merit, are frequently mentioned. I am consequently undertaking the composition of a thin octavo volume.[1] It will contain the lives of:

1. Raphael, Giulio Romano, Domenichino, Paul Potter, Rubens, Van der Werff, Poussin, Titian, Correggio.

2. Pergolese, Durante, Cimarosa, Mozart, Haydn; a notice on Canova, Fioravante, Paesiello, Monti.

3. Lope de Vega, Shakespeare, Cervantes, Tasso, Johnson, Schiller, Algernon Sidney, Alfieri.

Each of these three sections will be preceded by a notice which I promise will not be longer than ten pages. As a result of this work, and of the judicious and sound criticisms which the gentlemen of the press will devote to it, the number of absurdities heard daily about art subjects will, I believe, be slightly reduced. Etc.

I must write Crozet about this.

My interpretation of character from facial features.—1. Prince Schwarzen-

[1]This appears to be the first idea of the book that Beyle published six years later under the title of *Histoire de la Peinture en Italie.*

berg, Ambassador, a man four times as fat as Pacotte, sentiments and ideas of this size.

2. Finesse, haughtiness and princomania of M. de Kurakin.

3. His brother, Russian Minister of the Interior, a coachman full of sagacity.

4. Humoristic and gloomy haughtiness of a Metternich, grand cordon of St. Stephen.

5. Respectable seniority of Herr von Kalkreuth, a stagnating old grenadier, ridiculous coat allowing his breeches to be seen behind—and a big behind.

6. The asinine and vacuous look of my Minister.

7. On the contrary, the fine face and expression of a soul loving whatever is great, the simplicity of the new Minister of Police (Savary); I'm partial to that face.

8. Herr von Fürstenstein, the utter nonentity and good-naturedness of vulgar people who are beneath even the pretense of their position, an agreeable character.

9. The pedantic, bowing and protective ponderousness of Cambacérès, contrasting to the simple, active, military look of the prince major general [Berthier]; the slow, bowing entry of Cambacérès well observed.

10. The rationality of Marshal Davout, making him at ease with Mme. . . . , with whom he didn't dare to permit himself any impertinence. It's not impossible that he recognized me, I spoke to him.

11. The countenance of Iscariot (particularly in the small *Last Supper* at the Luxembourg) of the dull Dubois, whom they say the Emperor has invited to dinner in Paris.

12. M. Frochot, a large fat man bred on beer.

13. M. de Czernichev, squeezed into his clothes, which were about to split open all over, four decorations on his chest, the face of a fatuous young lord, talking a great deal with the politeness of the old Court which the émigrés, I believe, have grafted on that of St. Petersburg, a politeness like that of M. de Narbonne, the son of Louis XV, but a thousand points beneath it in grace and gaiety.

During my stay in Paris this time, I've seen good society, and seen it on a flattering level, such as was demanded by my pride.

June 18.—Yesterday I received this note:

"If my cousin Beyle has no engagement for tomorrow, it would be very nice of him to come to a family dinner tomorrow at the home of his cousin.

"A[lexandrine] D[aru]."

The welcome corresponded to the invitation. I arrived at a quarter to six, only a few people were there, including M. Camille Teisseire. Mme. Daru reproached me lengthily and complaisantly because it was a long time since she'd seen me. While I was caressing Napoleon [three-year-old son of the Darus], who really gives promise of having a likable character (worthy of being liked), M. Daru said to me, "I've written to M. Maret about your affair."

This morning, I looked through my trunk in vain for *Letellier* with Faure. I passed a cool morning in the Tuileries, thanks to a pair of dimity trousers, at the Café de Véry and in the shade. M. Camille Teisseire came to see me, afterward Alphonse Périer, whose wife came to get him, a really elegant figure. My self-esteem was gratified by her finding me well dressed. I read Faure's diary of his trip to Vienna, I was pleased with it; its defects are a colorless style, the defects it shows in the writer are a propensity not to act, but at the same time candor and sensibility.

A day of contentment. I repeat that Mme. Palfy was at her best with me, as in the good old days, as in the same place, about a month ago. Absence did its work perfectly. If Camille Teisseire speaks about me, he can only say that I'm at my best in this house. M. Z conversed with me, and about things of which he doesn't talk to everyone. I believe he finds some wit in me.

June 25.—At one o'clock this morning, I wrote in my small copy of Chamfort: "Anyone would certainly have to be possessed of the devil to be unhappy because he didn't go to a fete like the one tonight at the Ecole Militaire!"

I went to it at six o'clock with Mme. Daru, but I wasn't able to remain with her as I did at the fete in town, the whole business owing to lack of a plan of campaign; instead of going into the ballroom, we ought to have gone into the throne room, as we did in town. From there, we would have watched the races and fireworks, and, most important of all, we would have been cool, instead of being crowded in among a lot of cursed bourgeois and their tedious chatter, and from there come back with the Emperor to the ballroom. If this course can't be followed, what's best for people who see the Emperor frequently is to find the means of coming at midnight. Then you see a fine ball in an immense hall. Yesterday I was tired and bored. The degree of boredom, however, was tolerable.

Yet I'm a bit tired out this morning, it's because I drank too much currant water in this devilish heat.

Since writing last, I took a very agreeable trip to Montmorency. I perceived that I could walk four leagues in the morning without noticing it, just as I perceived a few days before that I could write four stanzas to my belle without noticing it.

The woods at Montmorency are nice, but what is less nice is the character OF MY BEST FRIEND [Faure]. He is steeped in chilliness and gloom, is provoked, vexed all the time, and never the least gaiety. If you monopolize the conversation in order to keep it from becoming frigidly sepulchral, he's annoyed because the PARTNER does all the talking. If you don't talk much, you sink into a horrible gloom. With the exception of this defect, he's a very virtuous and goodhearted man. But I must avoid traveling with him, especially in Italy; he'd kill my pleasure.

The next day, we went to Mme. de Charlot's [Bézieux]; I was gay there and nothing more, he was in a bad humor as a result, although I didn't kiss Amélie. He tried to make me see that I was quite wrong, it was like Louis, who scolds me because I have a merry look. In spite of these little clouds, I like them both very much, but they have taken a damnable road, for themselves in the first place, and after that a bit for the others.

Besides, if my friends are indifferent, it isn't the same with the mistress: her eyes and the ring of her voice are just as inflamed as ever. Four or five days without seeing her have done wonders.

Letter from Bereyter. Letter from Z⁻ to M. Maret. The hopes are being strengthened, but the dress is getting to be devilishly common. It was everywhere at the fete yesterday, and what mugs there were inside this garb![1]

M. Daru continues to be friendly with me, he talks and jokes with me, he realizes that I'm not an uncouth job-seeker.

I have more and more admiration for the picture by Raphael in the Luxembourg; the truly divine smile of Jesus.

July 7.—I haven't written anything from June 25 to July 7. Time was hanging rather heavily on my hands because I was doing nothing. I took up *Letellier* again on July 3, and since then the time has been passing more quickly and with happiness, which is the reason I have entitled the *Letellier* notebook *Felicita nel lavoro* [happiness in work].

I was at the Ecole Militaire fete and the burial ceremonies for the Marshal Duc de Montebello [Lannes]. Unfortunately, I wasn't present at Prince von Schwarzenberg's great contrast,[2] the most brilliant thing in the world for those common souls transformed into a thing that

[1]Beyle here refers to the uniform of the Auditors, whose ranks he was shortly to join.

[2]A temporary ballroom constructed by the Austrian Ambassador had burned down during a large ball. Beyle describes the event in a letter to Pauline dated July 2, 1810.

could inspire the most horror in them; and all that happened, M. Z said to me, *in a time of exercise*. Telling me about it the next day at dinner, he was still a changed man. His face was drawn and sallow. Mme. Palfy displayed courage, kindness and activity, qualities that can't be denied her. She gave all possible care to Mme. Tousard. Three days later, His Majesty invited her to dinner.

Yesterday at the Invalides. Odd applause given Canon Raillon, who —— on the memory of General Lannes. In the evening to Mme. de Bézieux's. An agreeable evening because I felt like letting myself go without any reserve. I wrote in my slippers, *"Un poco di freddo per producer il caldo* [A little coolness to produce warmth]." This maxim, put into practice with the appetizing Amélie, yielded me her continual attention and some soft glances. (But I protest that I don't want to follow in the footsteps of Félix.) Put into practice with Mme. Palfy, albeit a bit gropingly, same excellent result.

I experienced a mellow pleasure this morning before the panorama of Wagram, which recalled Vienna and THE PLEASANT ANXIOUS BEING [state of anxiety] which I experienced there, Babet, etc., etc.

Be sure to remember that veneer of *freddo,* without which one invariably plays the role of Orestes with women.

Nosography of passions and soul states.—I must read the first pages of Pinel's *Nosographie* and make out the one I need (July 9, 1810).

I'll keep a nosographic diary in which, under the title of *Vanity,* I'll put down the traits of vanity I've observed; under the title of *Avarice,* the traits of avarice; in the same way, under the title of each passion, soul state, etc., I'll make an entry of what I've observed. These symptoms will make an impression on my imagination, and double my mental strength. I'm liable not to be able to follow through an idea because of not being able to recall it without difficulty a minute after conceiving it. (July 11, 1810.)

July 27.—I'm resuming this diary after not having written anything for about a month. From the 3rd to the 26th, more or less, I found happiness in work—from nine till five, generally TO [on] *Letellier.*

Only one thing was lacking for my happiness, it was, after tiring my mind by working all morning, not to have had an amiable mistress with whom to spend the evening. But probably, if I had had one, a large part of my energy for work would have been lost in her arms.

With my manner of living, and my prestige being raised by my cabriolet and calash, I could easily have a little mistress, but I'm so lazy that I'm incapable of making the sustained effort necessary for that. In order that I may experience pleasure with a woman, nothing must intervene to disturb the illusion I've formed; at the first low thought my little grisette permitted me to have, my impulse would be to give her a frock and see her no more.

I've also been disturbed this month by fits of extreme impatience, notably toward Pacotte and Kamenski, a servant whom I discharged. I mastered these fits, which I hadn't experienced previously, they ended in some misanthropy, and there remains something of this misanthropy in my character.

It occurred to me that I was running up too many expenses. I'd have more pleasure by spending 200 francs less a month and taking a trip of a month to Switzerland.

As soon as I'm appointed an Auditor, I'll make out my budget with Félix. Here are the bases:

Two servants	2,000 francs
Two horses	2,000 "
Dinners	2,160 "
Lunches	400 "
Clothes	2,000 "
Upkeep of carriage and horses	500 "
Lodgings	1,500 "
	10,560 "
Plays, books, girls	3,440 "
Total	14,000 "

I'll see if that's reasonable, and swear not to go beyond it. It would suit me perfectly to be obliged, as Auditor, to travel four or five months out of the year.

1. That's my pleasure, and it's what I'd do if I happened to have, together with the same character (something that's not at all likely), an income of a hundred thousand livres.

During these four or five months of travel, I'd put aside some money which, divided up among the seven months of my stay in Paris, would permit me to live in a brilliant fashion for a young man.

I've devoted myself too much to the pleasure of working, I haven't gone out enough.

Remark.—With the present absurdities of this good city of Paris, which my ambition makes me neglect to enjoy,[1] my extra horse and servant might make me become a Prefect three years earlier.[2] I might take my

---

[1] RIDICULE TO BE PAINTED IN MY NOVEL: "THE TIMID." Refinement, and well written. [Note by Beyle.]

[2] To be a Prefect and married to a wealthy woman would no longer provide me with happiness in 1813, quite the contrary. [Note added by Beyle.]

meals at a boardinghouse, I could find a good one for 3 francs a day.
My lodgings might be reduced to a rent of 700 francs, like those of M.
Nanteuil, and the interest on 3,000 francs required for furniture, or 200
francs; total, 900 francs, instead of 1,500.

I'm going to see M. Duché and M. Lavollée today if I can, and to
write a little letter to M. Maret, backed up by one of those that
Councilor of State Jollivet wrote me at Brunswick with *Monsieur
l'Intendant* at the beginning, and in the end this title will differentiate
me from all the lucky little youths who expect to become Auditors as
soon as they get out of school.[1]

From which I conclude:

1. That I'm making a great mistake in not going out among people
more, since, had it not been for my laziness, I'd have been an Auditor
two months earlier, and perhaps better placed than I will be now.

2. That I need a mistress with good breeding, twenty-five years old
and an intrigante, to form me in this sort of thing.

3. That I must *make more acquaintances*. The three strongest interests of my soul urge me to take this decision, which is opposed only by
laziness and the bad habit of leading a cloistered life.

These interests are: A. THAT OF BARD;—B. THAT OF AMBITIOUS;— C. THAT
OF LOVE-PLEASURE;—D. FOR HAVING PLEASURE IN MY TRAVELS I MUST HAVE
THE PERSUASION OF HAVING WELL KNOWN PARIS.

The Marais. Went to Montmorency, a dance by lovely moonlight, a
walk in the woods with the two sisters, WITHOUT MOTHER.

July 28.—I was at the Café Véry in the Tuileries when eight o'clock struck.

[1] I'm going to buy the first volume of the *Confessions* and the volume of *Emilie*
containing Sophie, which I'll have neatly bound together, and on the back:
STYLE. I'll write on the first page seven or eight truths which I'll read as a
morning prayer every day.

July 27, 1810.

Thoughts to be read every morning upon awakening.

1. Think about making more acquaintances; you owe it to yourself AS BARD,
AS AMBITIOUS, AS LOVE-PLEASURE.

2. Think about acquiring the peace of mind that Beaumarchais maintained
in the midst of the most tumultuous position.

3. Try to observe absurdities without being affected by them, and without
seeking to be bitter toward these absurdities.

4. Don't go beyond your budget.

(This was wise, I see more clearly into my character today and find the noble
sentiments bought too much by boredom with the good turns of Fabio. March
13, 1813.)

(Precisely so. Instead of loving ambition, I've always been exasperated by
what had to be done for it. Industrious solitude in a big city, GOOD FOR MY
HAPPINESS. June 21, 1815.) [Notes by Beyle.]

I was thinking of how convenient the apartment in the Rue Mont-Thabor would be for me.

At half-past ten, I found Marie lunching, *un sorriso d'anima lampeggia in questo volto* [a smile from the soul lighting up her face]. All her actions called for familiarity, I was stiff and rather silly. I SEE, AND SHE GIVES ME TO UNDERSTAND THAT SHE IS PREGNANT, I BELIEVE, OF FOUR MONTHS. I was ridiculous enough to be a little jealous. I GO WITH HER AT Mme. Dubignon's, FROM THERE AT THE MOTHER, WITH WHOM I AM VERY WELL, BUT FLORIAN IS, I BELIEVE, BETTER.

I went to do my duty as a job-seeker with M. Lavollée, who, not having a post which gives him officially the position which he is filling because of his ability to intercede with the High Chancellor, received me not with impoliteness but with haughtiness, or rather self-importance.

I DINE WITH Mme. Z. I MUST SPEAK OF MY VISIT TO M. Lavollée. SHE SPEAKS AT SEVEN, THIS EVENING, WITH THE ALMIGHTY DUKE OF BASSANO.

Sunday, the 29th.—I missed Mme. Palfy at one o'clock. I worked from three to six on Bentham. I went for a walk on the boulevard. I regretted not having some circles of people to which I might go. A day full of bad humor.

Monday, the 30th.—I worked with Félix on the classification of the passions, states and habits of the soul, and means of passion from half-past seven to half-past three. I GO AT MARIA'S LODGING. Things that I regard as proofs of love, and that I cannot regard otherwise. I DINE WITH HER AT Mme. Dubignon's. From there to the *Due Rivali*. I was wrong not to follow M. . . when she went out.

I saw the ladies of Charlot STREET for a minute. I worked an hour with Félix. A happy day and one that was in harmony with my system, through work and the company of women.

It's through days as full as this one that I'll procure happy years. TOMORROW I HAVE THE PROJECT OF COMING FOR BREAKFAST AT MARIA'S.

I WAS WITH HER. SHE WAS PERFECTLY WELL FOR THE FIGURE, ANIMATED *e la fisionomia di* [and with the appearance of] counting on me.

SHE GOES OUT FOR A PETTY TOUR OF EIGHT DAYS, *non l'abbraccio e ho gran torto* [I didn't kiss her and I was wrong].

August 2.—I WRITE TO LADY MARIA. I DON'T KNOW WHETHER MY LETTER WILL BE WELL RECEIVED.

I read the letter about the dangers on the lake (*Nouvelle Héloïse*, Vol. III) under the huge trees of Saint-Cloud and those immense solitary paths. I was driven out by the cold at eight o'clock in the evening,

August 2. The weather of this country is the emblem of the souls to be found in it.[1]

I plied my trade of an office-seeker by writing a letter to *Probus* [Daru] AND THE OTHER TWO, THE FIRST TO THE DUKE OF BASSANO, THE SECOND TO LADY MARIA.

Mme. de Baure really is intelligent; I should get on more friendly terms with her. SHE CAN GIVE ME EXCELLENT COUNSELS.

August 3.—A remarkable day IN MY LIFE.

I took my coffee at eight o'clock, worked till noon, went driving in my cabriolet with Félix; I had the intention of going to see Comtesse Bertrand at Malmaison. She's in Paris, but not at her home. We deliberated and went for a drive to the Pré-Saint-Gervais. I dined at the Provençaux, from there to *Le Philosophe Marié,* followed by *Les Deux Pages.* I thought of a portrait to be done of that great Frederick whom Fleury shows us in this play, but whom the author has disfigured. I also thought a great deal on the way home of the auditorship; what I'd be obliged to do if, upon going in, I were to find word from M. Maret. I scolded myself not to regard this as sufficiently uncertain.

As I came in, I asked casually if there were any letters; I was told that there were some. I saw a packet addressed to M. Daru and countersigned: "The Minister Secretary of State." I opened it and saw the following letter:

"The Minister Secretary of State hastens to notify M. de Beyle that he was appointed Auditor of the Council of State by a decree issued the first of this month. He has the honor of returning to M. de Beyle the official letters which were enclosed in his letter of the first of this month.

"Saint-Cloud, August 3, 1810."

I opened this good letter at twenty-two minutes after eleven o'clock at night. I am aged twenty-seven years, six months and twenty days, having been born on January 23, 1783.

If, two years ago, someone had predicted that I was never to be a war commissary, I should perhaps have been grieved.

August 4.—I've had a strange series of fortunate happenings. I'm almost tempted to believe in the proverb which says that it never rains but it pours.

On August 4, I went at ten o'clock to show the good letter of last night to Martial. I said I received it this morning as I was going out. Martial showed me one from M. Daru in which he spoke of me with friendliness and advised me to go to Lyon.

I went to lunch at Mure's. Upon my return, I found a letter full of

[1]True. 1813. [Note by Beyle.]

kindness from Mme. Daru, who entrusted me with a letter from M. Daru, who advised me, with all possible grace and kindness, to depart for my destination.

Finally, at half-past six, at the home of M. de Baure, to whom I announced my appointment, I learned that I had a letter from M. Daru. Within myself, I feared that it was a severe reply to the letter in which I had asked him a little indiscreetly to write to M. Maret. My surprise and happiness can be imagined when, in the hired cabriolet which was taking me to the *Cantatrici Villane,* I read a first letter couched in these terms:

"Your letter, my dear Beyle, took a long time in reaching me: I paid my compliments to you two days ago through my wife. Here is a letter for the Duc de Bassano. Request Baure to send me a report in which I propose you, together with M. Le Coulteux, for the post of inspector of furnishings.

"With kindest regards,
"Daru.

"This August 1."

Enclosed with this letter was the following:
"Monsieur le Duc,

"I learn that, from afar as from anear, I have thanks to give Your Excellency. This time, it is for the interest he has been kind enough to accord M. Beyle, my relative. He has now been appointed Auditor. I desire, since one must always desire something, that he be employed in such a manner that he will work. He is twenty-seven years old, he has acquired experience in several campaigns and in the Intendancy of Brunswick, which he held. I believe him well fitted to draw up reports with clearness, intelligence and precision. My own wishes would be to see him attached to the Civil List and to my section; if one and the other, one or the other, of these things is possible, I beg Your Excellency to grant my request and accept my gratitude and respect.

"Daru

"Amsterdam, this August 1, 1810."

Both these excellent letters are dated August 1, and yet that of M. Maret would make it appear that the decree appointing the Auditors is only of the same day, August 1. And who could have informed M. Daru of my appointment? It seems to me that, if M. Maret had slipped that in at the end of some official dispatch, M. Daru would have thanked him for this attention.

However that may be, in my delight with these letters I made the mistake of not leaving the gay music of the *Cantatrici* at half-past eight in order to go to make the request of M. de Baure, as M. Daru told me to do.

August 5.—I only saw M. de Baure at ten o'clock this morning. He seemed to be very pleased with M. Daru's intention and very hopeful of success. He told me to give him a copy of M. Daru's letter, which he would enclose with his report to the Emperor, and that this report would be sent tomorrow, the 6th.

This morning, I saw a letter from LADY MARIA on my mantel; I hesitated to open it, I feared a refusal (it was in English) and it fully granted my request. That gave me keen pleasure. My appointment and all the agreeable circumstances that I've just described gave me a rational pleasure, but far less than the pleasure I'd have if I were the possessor of LADY Charlotte and loved by her.

Finally, to complete my happiness via letters, I've just received two, one from my commandant, the other OF MY BASTARD. M. Charmat was perfect with me, and told me to do as I saw fit; the other gave me 25 louis and hopes of 5,000 francs FROM MY EXCELLENT GRANDFATHER.

Thus, between eight o'clock on the evening of August 3 and today, the 5th, at four o'clock, I've received:

Letter from M. Maret	1
from Mme. D.	1
from LADY MARIA	1
from M. D.	2
read from M. D., favorable for me	2
a second from M. Maret	1
from M. Charmat, commandant	1
from MY BASTARD	1
	—
	10 letters

That makes ten letters, all favorable to me, and several of them excellent. It has certainly been the day of letters.

I wrote one dictated by my heart to M. Daru, one ditto to Mme. Daru.

August 6.—A day of errands, crowned by success. I got into uniform at half-past eleven, and went to get M. Depon-Delporte so we could go together to see the chief justice. He had just gone out, I went alone; the chief justice had just left for the Council of State.

I had my calash stop in the Champs-Elysées, changed clothes and went to Saint-Cloud, somewhat annoyed at being obliged to lie to a porter, but managing to get the upper hand of this slight annoyance, enjoying the fine day and the pretty verdure of the Bois de Boulogne, which was pretty today, and trying to stir up whatever ambition I may have by picturing imaginary successes to myself.

The porter didn't see me at Saint-Cloud. I went up, waited for a quarter of an hour in a lonely antechamber, finally went in. I was informed that M. Maret was at Sèvres. I went there, hunted his address for some time in Sèvres, where nobody but a gendarme was able to give it to me. I went up to his fine home. I was informed that he had left for Trianon. On the way out, I gave an écu to the woman at the gate, who said, "A woman's faith, you've been tipping me for the two years I've been here."

I drove back to Paris, reading Helvétius, it seemed as though I was reading notes written by myself in a loose style, so thoroughly do I agree with him.

When I got back, I found Faure, who gave me M. Michel's invitation to a dinner where Messrs. Versiat, Marchand and Alphonse were to be present. In accordance with my rule, *make acquaintances,* I went. We dined gaily enough at half-past six. I took Alphonse with me, and we drove to Sèvres in three quarters of an hour in fine weather.

August 11.—If, instead of the intriguing G., I had a pretty little mistress, a bit sensitive, with whom I could discuss my happiness of ambition and the new play, my happiness would be complete; but for lack of this little mistress, it is very incomplete. I took my volume entitled *Style* to the theater with me, but ought I to speak like Rousseau on everything that comes up? This is a question that worries me.

But I come back constantly to my lassitude with Mme. de G. and her cousin, and to my heart's need of a mistress I could love.

I'm daily awaiting the report in which the excellent Daru is requesting the post of inspector of furnishings for me.

August 12.—The happiest day was that OF THE TOUR TO Versailles, OR THE 3rd August 1810; I believe the happines of Versailles was stronger (August 12, 1810). Like Tancredi, I see a wall of flame, very rarely do I have the courage to spring forward, but, when I do, I realize that the flames are only an optical illusion. That's the result of my visit this morning to the beautiful E.

I went to Martial's, whom I found indifferent UPON MY HAPPINESS, and affecting to pay no attention to it, besides he's perhaps the unhappiest of men, with an income of eight thousand livres, thirty-three years old, an amiable appearance and what is called amiability here, but no soul, and the asininity to have placed his happiness IN THE AMBITION, ADVICE TO YOU, YOUNG Auditor.

I next enjoyed Goethe NEAR TO MY SOUL. I finished *Wilhelm Meister:* these ideas drove me wild, and it was in that mood that I began writing.

Ambition permitted me to leave Paris to itself for thirty-six or forty-eight hours. The law of *freddetto* [lukewarmness] made me go away from Maria, and I tasted happiness in the wood at Montmorency, thinking of *Letellier*.

Thus ends this notebook. At this point arrived my Auditor's dress uniform, which Léger sent me. I tried it on, I found this costume very good-looking, and decorated just enough to be becoming to a young man.

It is precisely in this way that should end this volume, which contains the history of my job-hunting from May 9 to August 12, 1810.

With a heart like that of Mélanie, I would have been perfectly happy. I have precisely what was lacking when love furnished me with happiness in Marseille, but, by a just compensation, I no longer have what I had.

The Man About Town

THE dawning season promised a brilliant new existence for "Monsieur de Beyle" in his double capacity of Auditor and household inspector.

As an Auditor, he was assigned to the War Section under the "admirable" Gouvion-Saint-Cyr, and was admitted to the debates between Napoleon and his jurists in the Council of State. His post and title of Inspecteur du Mobilier, besides acquainting him with the contents of the museums, gave him an entrée to the Court functions at the Tuileries and Saint-Cloud. He was presented by the Duchesse de Montebello to the Empress Marie-Louise; and, although he admitted that Napoleon "didn't speak to fools like me," he was proud to be treated in a friendly fashion by "the best of men," the Duc de Frioul (Michel Duroc), the Grand Marshal of the palace.

All the important figures of the Empire passed before his eyes—rulers, princes, generals and marshals, ambassadors and ministers. He saw the handsome but "vacuous" General Lagrange dance for the Court in a ballet with Queen Caroline Murat and the "divine" Princess Borghese. The charm of Mme. Récamier aroused his admiration. He was present at the session of the Académie Française when his idol Destutt de Tracy was welcomed into membership by the Comte de Ségur. Ministers and officers of the Crown received him in their homes. His life was "a mixture of serious and rapid work at the office, of visits and changes of costume"; people with whom he was unacquainted called to pay their court, wherever he went he was treated with consideration.

Beyle enjoyed these triumphs of vanity as much as another, but he had too much love for candor and simplicity, too much knowledge of the memoir-writing society of the *ancien régime,* to be taken in by the dazzling exterior of this fundamentally insipid society composed of the heterogeneous brand-new Napoleonic nobility. Above all, he detested the military "swashbucklers" who were to be found everywhere. "Posterity will never realize the vulgarity and stupidity of these people off their battlefield," he later said. "And even on this battlefield, what prudence! They were people like Admiral Nelson . . . , always thinking of what each wound would yield in the way of endowments and decorations."

He had little more respect for the other members of this society which passed its time with charades, rebuses and games of blind man's buff, and which was honeycombed with venereal disease. The princesses, duchesses and countesses usually had "fine dresses, but the faces of chambermaids." The men, often ignorant, were invariably puffed up with importance. Even his own cousin Pierre Daru could not begin a conversation except by, "The Emperor said to me . . . ," or answer a request without saying, "But have I time for it, busy as I am?"

This new life naturally demanded a great deal of money, and, as usual, the question of obtaining money was not an easy one. In August, 1810, his father had belatedly paid him the first installment of his maternal inheritance—a check for 2,373 francs, which, however, was dated a year ahead! During the following months, Beyle continued to bombard his sister with entreaties to plead the cause of the 6,000-franc loan with his father. The whole matter was so simple: all that need be done was to mortgage one of the Beyle houses or sell a portion of Claix! But "the bastard," weighed down by debts and undoubtedly regarding as insane a project to live extravagantly three or four years on the gambler's chance of becoming a Prefect, showed no inclination to sell or mortgage any more of his property.

So everything hung fire, the loan, the *majorat,* the barony; and, by June 1811, Beyle's position had become desperate—or so he painted it to his sister. "A man must live," he cried. In less than ten years he could, with his father's help, be wealthy, a baron, a Prefect: denied this assistance, he had but two alternatives—either he must marry Jenny Leschenault, whom he did not love but who had an income of 7,000 francs a year, or he must resign himself to settling down as a Sub-Prefect in some remote village. Even so, Jenny's parents would not consent to her marriage unless the husband had a title—while to leave Paris meant, after four years of efforts, to relinquish all hopes of promotion. The whole future was in the hands of "the bastard." "I'll sign anything in order to stay here," Henri wrote. "If he wishes, I'll renounce all claims to an inheritance . . . All I want is the means of living here until the Prefecture . . . If I remain here, within ten years I'll be sheltered from all need."

Wasted words. No money was forthcoming from Grenoble, nor did Beyle carry out his threats. He apparently arranged his own loans in Paris, for, in the autumn of 1810, he congratulated himself on the possession of 11,400 francs, and the following year he lived more luxuriously than ever.

Almost his first action upon becoming Auditor was to rent and furnish, together with Bellisle, "one of the gayest apartments in Paris," in the just-opened Rue Neuve-de-Luxembourg (today the Rue Cambon) at the corner of the Rue du Mont-Thabor, a stone's throw from the Tuileries gardens and five minutes from the Emperor's palace. "Drunk with contentment," he had taken up his duties in an office overlooking the Esplanade des Invalides. The new work was the kind he liked—it confined him to his office barely an hour a day. He looked on it as the "embroidery" of his life.

The "substance" was composed of things far more important. Immediately upon becoming Auditor, he drew up a will in which he explicitly instructed Faure and Crozet to employ any money he might leave at his death to found a literary prize in England. The conditions were curious but characteristic: Each year, one of the following subjects was to be proposed: What is ambition, love, hatred, laughter, tears, etc.? The answers might be in any of the chief modern languages, and were to be written in "a plain, straightforward and exact style, in the manner of an anatomical description and not of an oration," and were to be divided into three parts: "1. Examples from history; 2. Examples from art imitations (poems, novels, etc.); 3. Exact and dispassionate description." The prize was to be a handsome edition of Shakespeare's complete works in English and a gold medal bearing on one side the words, "Happiness in a temperate monarchy," and on the other, *Nosce te ipsum*"—the Delphic inscription which Beyle had found quoted by Tracy, and which he had adopted as his own formula for happiness.

He began frequenting the Louvre and the Luxembourg. He "more and more admired" the Madonna by Raphael in the latter gallery, and found the smile of the Christ child "truly divine"; Correggio gave him the greatest of pleasure, he had an engraving of the artist's *Leda* over his desk; the paintings of Titian, with their "vigorously laid-on colors," reminded him of Molière's *Les Précieuses Ridicules;* he approved of Domenichino, Giulio Romano, Poussin, Lorrain, but considered Rubens "ignoble" because of the plump breasts and knees he gave his women. He judged his contemporaries without enthusiasm: David was cold and pretentious; Gérard's coloring and lighting effects were praiseworthy, and the artist showed an understanding of aerial perspective; Girodet was "extremely energetic"; Gros cold. His artistic standards, then as later, were purely literary and psychological: the art of painting, he told Félix Faure, lay in the painter's ability "to portray passion by means of facial traits or body postures."

The source of the purest joy for Beyle at this period was the Opera Buffa, which was given three nights a week at the Odéon. He went again and again to hear Mozart's *Nozze di Figaro,* and declared that he went to his beloved *Matrimonio Segreto* "sixty or a hundred times" in 1810 and 1811.

But something more than the music of Cimarosa and Mozart caused him to gallop in from Saint-Cloud to the performance of the Italian troupe, for it was on the stage of the Odéon that he finally found that "little mistress" he had been seeking since he had an official position, money and a fine apartment. Her name was Angéline Bereyter, and she was a comely young Jewess who sang the roles of *seconda* and *terza donna*. Since June 1810, he had been writing her periodic "mash" letters which went unanswered until the following January. At this date, he was permitted to "pay his respects in person." His way with actresses had improved since Mélanie's time: during his first visit, he kissed Angéline, the second time he saw her he "attacked" and was victorious.

In the apartment of the Rue Neuve-de-Luxembourg, where she established herself, she would frequently sit down at the piano and sing those Italian songs that her lover adored. She was "cold for her art" and "her judgment had been warped by the vulgarity of the contemporary French school," but the important thing was that she knew all his favorite operas and taught him the arias of Cimarosa and Mozart. There can be little doubt, as M. Arbelet has written, that these afternoons played a large part in the musical education of the future biographer of Haydn, Mozart and Rossini.

They entered into their liaison with no illusions on either side. Beyle, for once reasonable, did not ask that his friend be a Julie. "Angéline, whom I never loved," was the way he afterward referred to her; but it flattered his vanity to be keeping an actress, and he had a great fondness for his "little angel" who was so loving and gentle.

The first week in February 1811, to Beyle's delight, Louis Crozet turned up for a visit to Paris. He was given a room in the famous apartment, and the two *idéologues* resumed their favorite pastime of studying and making notes together. Attacking Cabanis' *Rapport du Physique et du Moral de l'Homme,* which Beyle had been looking over again, they outlined "the most essential part—the temperaments"; but this theory of the temperaments, on which Beyle was to place such importance a few years later, was still regarded with some distrust by the pair: "It appears to us to be very little proved," they noted.

While thus engaged, they heard the momentous news that Martial Daru was about to be appointed Intendant of Rome, and that Beyle was to be sent along to aid him in taking over the museums and libraries. Deciding on the spur of the moment to accompany him, Crozet returned briefly to Plancy to request a leave of absence and a passport.

The days passed with no further news. While marking time, the two friends went back to their studies, drafting more ideological charts and analyzing the plays of Molière, Corneille and especially Shakespeare. Curiously enough, one of their notes on Shakespeare bobs up verbatim as a long footnote in *Histoire de la Peinture en Italie,* opening unexpectedly with the words, "Seyssins and I have just read *Cymbeline* . . ." (Seyssins, a village near Grenoble, was one of Beyle's nicknames for Crozet.)

On April 19, it was decided not to send Beyle to Italy after all, so he and Crozet, bitterly disappointed, took a consolation trip with Faure to Le Havre for their first view of the ocean. Back in Paris, Crozet changed coaches to continue on to Plancy, while Beyle turned back to his slow-moving "courtship" of the Countess Daru.

This strange campaign, which is related in eloquent detail on the following pages, continued through June, began to languish in July and finally flickered out in August. The last week in July, Baron von Strombeck put in an appearance. Beyle greeted his old friend from Brunswick with open arms, presented him to his acquaintances, took him about Paris and did his best to obtain him an audience with Napoleon, assuring Strombeck that it would be an experience he would remember all his life. But the latter did not possess a Court costume and was unwilling to spend six hundred francs to have one made. Disappointed, Beyle insisted on driving him to Saint-Cloud that he might at least catch a glimpse of the Emperor. With Strombeck's departure, he began to experience an abysmal disgust with the life he was living. In capital letters, he traced across a page of his diary the words:

I'M BORED.

His pursuit of Mme. Daru had lost its thrill, he was fed up with Paris and society, his time and money were wasted with no resultant pleasure, he was tired of playing the courtier, his official duties had all but ceased to exist, he was more than satiated with the even-tempered Angéline, he lacked the mental tranquillity to resume the everlasting *Letellier.* There was no one to whom he could open his heart: Mme. Daru, Angéline and the other women were out of the question; Pauline, now a busy housewife, was no longer the confidante of other days; Bellisle had left for Spain; Faure's morbid ideas were more depressing than ever. Like a persistent refrain, Italy returned again and again to his thoughts.

By the happiest of coincidences, the check for 2,373 francs which his father had sent him the year before was payable on August 24. Nothing retained him in Paris, nothing prevented him from returning to Milan. He cashed his check and reserved a seat in the coach. Early the morning of August 29, as Faure waved farewell and Angéline burst into tears, he started off on the same road he had followed as an adolescent eleven years earlier.

The active period of his ambition was over. For five years he had devoted his energy to advancing to a position which, while in itself hollow, would give him the leisure to travel and dream. Now that he had attained it, the sentimental philosopher of 1802–5 was to dominate the Imperial functionary of 1810–11. He was to recapture his soul in that fair Italy which from childhood he had considered as his real fatherland.

1810–11 Paris

DJORN'L FROM THE 16TH AUGUST 1810 TILL THE . . .

> Pleasure would portray them, knowledge
> dissects them.
> > Myself

MME. MARIE left for A[msterdam] August 16, 1810, I believe. I learned on August 3 that I had been appointed Auditor the 1st. I was fed up with Paris, I couldn't work freely on *Letellier*. Visits, the servants, the laundresses and other things of similar importance interrupted me five or six times a morning, stirred up my irascible character, and I got nothing done. Besides, I might have said to Faure what Mme. de Saint-Martin says to Chapelle [in *Letellier*]: "I feel that what I need the most is to be in love." And I'm not in love.

I sought happiness in a change of scene, and I found it at Plancy with Louis Crozet. The *country*, I mean the real country and not the village, is, like the people in it, as ugly as possible. But my heart thirsted for the country; M. de Plancy's park, the cofferdam, and especially the oaks across from the sand where we worked on *Letellier*, are worthy of a picture representing Italy. Even the dance, although vulgar, pleased me.

Louis was affected and distant on the days of my arrival and departure. Had it been only on the day of arrival, I'd have thought I was taking him away from some favorite occupation. I believe this coolness of his only comes from a vestige of the bad habit of sentimentality acquired at M. *Shepherderie's*. He has a perfect sagacity, he seems to me to be superior to me in that respect, and inferior in imagination and sensibility. At Plancy, I found him very much as he was this winter at Mme. *Shepherderie's*, the appearance of a savant and a timid man; neither EASE nor gaiety. Yet he isn't entirely wrapped up in himself, he observes extremely well. I don't believe he has that elevation of feeling which makes Italy necessary for happiness.

His first quality is, in my opinion, sagacity; the second, talent for managing things; perhaps it's from the necessity of managing that he retains that seriousness which is sometimes applied to petty things. He'd be an excellent director general of Public Instruction, he wouldn't hold his job in contempt as would Signora Pietragrua's lover [Beyle himself], a superior glory wouldn't be necessary for him.

I found his character to be extremely mild and malleable. Working up his soul a bit in order to appreciate the possession of a fat and slightly vulgar peasant girl, but, on the other hand, very stable and without either gaiety or naturalness. He isn't gloomy; rather, he's reasonable and distant, conversation would easily provide him with happiness.

I arrived by diligence on the . . . First thing of all, I quenched my thirst for hunting. I recaptured my talent for shooting birds on the wing which I discovered unexpectedly at Brunswick. The first three days, I killed thirteen swallows and a partridge; after dinner on the fourth, in an hour and a half, I killed twelve swallows. I haven't fired a shot since. The satisfaction of this desire left me entirely free for *Letellier*.

I took Louis into my confidence about it. His sagacity grasped and well understood the salient and comic situations. I feared this would make him a little envious. I saw only the sensation of a finger passing over a wound.

Once I experienced a touch of my *irascibility,* a quality that I hadn't been conscious of in myself and that frequently makes me unhappy. In the country around here, I've acquired the reputation of a *master bugger*. In the sense the people of Champagne take these words, that's the reputation I'd like to have everywhere.

The seventh or eighth day of my visit, upon returning to the charming cofferdam after working a long time and bathing, we found three letters from Faure informing me that, by a decree of August 22, I was Inspector General of Crown Furnishings, and that moreover I'd been summoned for the examination. I left the next day at three o'clock.

I arrived in Paris on the . . . I found it more disgusting than ever, and, once my examination was over, I decided one evening to leave at once. I did so without any hesitation.

I went to bed at half-past twelve at L'Espérance, a good inn of Brie. I didn't fondle the backsides of a very pretty girl enough; I had used up my sensibility before my departure from Paris.

This second trip, made with my horses and calash, was very agreeable. I read *Tom Jones*. I slept at Nogent. The weather was superb, that fine September weather which has such a potent effect on me and which bids me to fall in love. I regretted not having brought Babet[1] with me.

Not being happy through love, which, after all, I can't indulge in all alone, the only thing left was for me to do something great . . .

Advice on style to Felix.—Felix wanted to read Blair to mold his taste in literature. I wrote to dissuade him.

Passions can't emerge from the breast of those who are impassioned to be exposed to the eyes of everyone; to portray them, it's necessary to have felt them. Blair, an unfeeling man, is like a man who might wish to state an opinion on the nose of Punchinello, whom he has never seen. He might demonstrate very wittily that Punchinello has a small nose, because he has done no more than catch a glimpse of a ten-year-old Punchinello whose nose wasn't formed, and Blair comes along to say, like a good Englishman supported by aristocratic authority, to a poor Mlle. de Lespinasse who doesn't even know how to spell: "Love should go only to a certain point; beyond that, it is unnatural."

The trait, "I wish that hell were here, I'd cast myself into it for you," which a soldier said to a laundress, is outrageous and in bad taste; the same trait presented in fine language would be found a little more natural; in Greek in Homer, it would be divine. But, luckily for them, the poets of antiquity, born before the refinement and exaltation of the passions, possessed very few of these cursed follies to upset their system. There's probably not a single one in Homer.

But where is literature to be studied?—In Helvétius, Hobbes and a little in Burke, and many applications are to be seen in Shakespeare, Cervantes and Molière.

The whole of literature lies in five rules, i.e.:

1. That of this entry: you can't describe what you have never seen, nor can you judge portraits composed by others;

2. The sublime, sympathy with a power which we see as terrible;

3. Laughter (Hobbes);

4. The smile, view of happiness;

5. Study a passion in medical books (Pinel), in nature (the letters of Mlle. de Lespinasse), in the arts (Julie, Héloïse, etc.).

Being aware of these rules, one should look for their confirmation or refutation in Shakespeare, Cervantes, Tasso, Aristo, Molière.

But if one wishes to acquire the usual prattle and remain, or become, petty, one has but to study constantly the correct Laharpe, the judicious Blair and other worthies who have seen the passions face to face.

[1] Beyle's mistress of Vienna who was visiting Paris at the time, and to whom the end of the preceding paragraph refers.

October 2.—I haven't been able to work for myself since my return from Plancy. I've made two business trips to Versailles. I've set up an office and worked at the Hôtel du Châtelet. My work is worth far more than that of my partner; M. Z hasn't seen either yet.

Marie accuses me of indifference, she still shows affection for me. My carriage overturned and I broke a tooth. I often go walking with the Vicomte [Louis de Barral] on [the Boulevard de] Coblentz. I'm making an attempt on the little Jewish singer [Angéline Bereyter], her sister is too much of a tart. Superb situation of MYSELF: 11,400 francs, the barony.

How many others would have been perfectly happy in my place! The happiness of clothes and money is not enough for me, I need to love and to be loved. If I can't attain this chief of all happinesses, I must work on the things in which I place my self-esteem.

Mme. Palfy has given me some rather happy moments. After her, the two most fertile sources of happiness have been Sully's *Mémoires* and [Cimarosa's] *Impresario in Angustie.*

October 8.—*My work.*—A conspicuous trait of Probus's [Daru's] character is *to employ the first instrument that comes to hand.* And, as they say that asses are more common than intelligent people, he's surrounded by the dullest fools I know. Hence his work is doubled and his annoyances are centupled. This cause undoubtedly increases the number of outbursts coming from the rest of his make-up.

If I were making the choices for him, I'd take M. Catineau-La Roche as division chief or general secretary, a man like Blondin for the bookkeeping and some young men from Geneva as copying clerks. I'd clean out the stable of everything in it, and introduce the rule of silence in my offices. Add two large account books, and all would go smoothly, with a maximum of two hours' work for the supreme chief.

October 9.—*Ambition.*—What a dismal passion! I've just seen Jacqueminot in his dismal office, all alone, with his lifeless face which only livened up when he read us a trivial letter from himself to Minister Dejean, a letter written to contradict in some measure M. Daru, his benefactor. What a dismal existence! He's always unhappy, not the slightest magnanimous sentiment of the kind that does the soul good. If William Pitt and all the unfeeling men of ambition were like that, those gloomy figures are not to be envied. I believe, however, that the consciousness of great activity and power gives pleasures. But Jacqueminot hasn't got that power and isn't conscious of such things. He's one of the unhappiest men I know.

After him comes Pacé, who at least has some fire and is on a higher plane. After him, the amiable Joinville, so suited to be happy with

Angelina [Pietragrua] or any other woman if he'd settled down in Italy with the certainty of being a war commissary all his life.

Finally, there's Probus, who doesn't give signs of being any too happy. Compare all these folk with Gros! They consequently have a vague feeling of what it is, and, in order to avenge themselves, they take on a haughty look as soon as an artist is mentioned.

What illusions in these hollow dreams of ambition! Jacqueminot, who wants to be promoted from a war commissary to a Prefect!

I've had much happiness through having made out my budget, started my cashbook and not spending six francs without entering it in my cash book.

I reacted so deeply to the *Nozze di Figaro* yesterday that I have a pain in my chest from it today. Paul [Louis de Barral] and I were beside a rather pretty little Italian girl, with whom we chatted a bit. She's staying at the Hôtel des Arts, near the Abbaye Saint-Germain. Italy is my real country, everything that reminds me of it touches my heart. I had pleasure in hearing this girl speak Italian.

Earlier in the day, I was at Mme. Daru's, where I saw Charles Cheminade's elder sister, who was nice-looking. I discovered a bit of coquetry in her, however. I put on some *freddetto* and was quite at ease.

Florian, *che stava quà* [who was there], was more jovial than I and a thousand times more at ease; that's the good side, he was at the *Nozze* and almost fell asleep there, he just told me it was badly sung, that's the reverse of the medal.

Speaking of the reverse of the medal, I should be careful of what I say in my letters: Jacqueminot concluded that I'd possessed Mme. Genet, one of her lovers told him that she was charming in pleasure. And yet this woman is nothing but a goose at Mme. Marie's, apparently all her liveliness is reserved for sensuality; she ought to be all the better for that.

November 27.—It's been an age since I've written, the reason is that I've been very busy. I frequently write for five or six hours on end at Z's.

Yesterday at the Duc de Rovigo's, a very brilliant evening. Delightful sensation at the *Nozze di Figaro* during the voluptuous duet in which the count asks his wife for the key to the closet where Susanna has just shut herself. My heart, stirred by the contemplation of the beautiful bosom of Mme. Lacuée and the beautiful face of Mme. Pallavacini, drank in these sounds with avidity. My white breeches produced a great effect on Mme. Boucher, that pretty person makes too deep an impression on me.

27. Today I was so tired out at dinner that I sent Mr. Goodson away. I lunched as usual with Fairisland [Pépin de Bellisle]. These lunches are domestic happiness. I left at half-past ten and went to leave my name with those of Messrs. Cardon and Chevalier at the home of some fifteen Councilors of State. I went to my office at noon, I left it at half-past five, after working hard on a reply to M. Appelius on the Domains. I wrote a counternote that the asses would find bold to M. Z, but Clarissa's rule, PERHAPS MUCH LESS SHOULD HAVE TO BEAR. At six o'clock, dinner at Véry's.

From there home, Fairisland came to get me and we went to the High Chamberlain's. Upon arriving at his door, we learned that he wasn't receiving.

From there to M. Defermon's. Bourgeois and shabby gloom of the salon; my desire to laugh.

I shifted scenes for the third or fourth time, and Bellisle took me to M. Nardot's. I paid court to Mme. Genet, whose bare breast and shoulders gave me pleasure. Besides, Jacqueminot told me that he'd been told she does that very well and that she's almost witty in bed. I believe it, you can see in society that she must be entirely at home in bed. By chance, in conformity with the essential rules, I was gay and made my presence felt. That ripened Marie's heart.

Z seems to me a very disagreeable man, almost as devoid of generosity THAN [*sic*] HIS BROTHER; not a shadow of strength of character, and not much wit or executive ability. Having succeeded through an enormous quantity of ink spilled on blank paper.

November 28.—I haven't written because I was tired out, without any exaggeration. This mixture of hard and quick work at my office, of visits and changes of clothes nearly killed me during four days this week.

Tonight, visit to Comte Joubert and the *Shepherd* ladies, more insignificant every time; since they've ejected naturalness and it hasn't come back either at a gallop or at a walk, they're vacuous creatures.

Nevertheless, and in connection with vacuous creatures, they must be possessed, because a given woman who's very insignificant provides delightful pleasure in a good mahogany bed; 2. because the whole comedy is transformed the moment they are possessed. They're Tancredi's flames.

November 30.—Session at the Museum. I find that little M. Six assumes a bit too uppish a tone with me. The abominable thing about those animals is that they oblige you to play a role, prevent you from being natural. I stayed at the Museum a long time after the errand that brought good Mme. Palfy there. I'm incapable of feeling any admiration, although I try by every means to open my soul to it. All the princesses, duchesses and countesses in Paris were there: fine clothes, but the faces of chambermaids.

Genuine nobleness and naturalness seem to me to be very rare in France.

December 2.—Anniversary of the coronation. I remember my situation at that time.

The devilishly forced smile of Probus, in which *Fairisland* finds something extraordinary as far as I am concerned. A weak and indecisive character.

December 3.—Bellisle and I went shopping for prints and maps. Execrable foggy weather. We bought 200 francs' worth of prints. The maps were out of stock.

Tuesday [December 4].—This morning, worked at my office with great speed. Went to the High Chancellor's, the ridiculousness of the little club-footed man and of the High himself, whose silent and periodic movement amid twenty people standing up reminded me of a black bear.

My time is taken up with writing letters and going out in society. I hardly ever follow through an idea any more. When I happen to be placed at the beginning of an interesting series, I put it off until another day. Yesterday, I was struck by this habit of putting off and skipping over everything that requires too much attention.

When I happen to be home an hour, I don't know what to read.

What consoles me is that it seems to me that when you want to do something well, you must do only one thing at a time. I go out in society and write letters, that's my life this winter.

December 13.—Outside THE D. OF R. (whom I sleep with once a week), I'm as chaste as the devil. As the result, I'm getting fatter. It seems to me that since I've been an Auditor I've forgotten my amorous disposition. Possibly it feeds the fire of my head. I believe I could easily lose the habit of women. I lack almost entirely the talent of possessing common women, otherwise I'd have struck up a conversation a hundred times with Mme. Boucher (I believe), of the Buffa, and at the end of six days I'd have had her.

Yesterday, I wrote to the little Bereyter. I had some fun Tuesday with Amélie and Mimi. "YOU ARE VERY agreeable, I take great pleasure in seeing you." The next thing is to pinch their thighs and be capable of giving myself up to all possible gaiety. I sang aloud a superb song, for I composed the words and music as I went along.

The barony has given me some grief BUT *tandem* THE BASTARD is taking the leap, or at least is going to take it.

I wrote some letters to the terrible Probus, but I never speak to him and hardly ever see him. I haven't spoken to him about business in his office since the day he railed at me a bit after a three-hour conference with M. Six and M. Costaz. The latter is a model of self-importance. That's the only way to hold your own with a man of Probus's kind, and all the mighty ones are somewhat alike in that respect. It makes me indignant to be obliged to put on the soporific mask of the most kill-joy silliness in order to succeed with the bores in power.

(Thursday, December 13.) I've just spent a boring evening at Z's, from eight to half-past eleven. I took Bellisle to the Tuileries, and from there to Z's. Given his character, he stood on ceremony with me as much as possible. One thing that repaid me a little for my boredom was that I must at least have had a distant look, which is the only prudent one to have with a man of great merit who, in spite of that, needs to outrage people in order to breathe.

From there I went to M. Palfy's. He was highly pleased with him-self. He was to have dined at the home of the Comte de Cessac, Min-ister, at five o'clock. His Majesty sent for him and worked with him until half-past seven. Palfy consequently had the pleasure of breaking an engagement at the home of the Minister, who had certainly been officially informed that His Majesty had detained him. Perhaps the Comte de Cessac was good-natured enough to say to some guest or other, "We haven't got M. Palfy with us for such and such a reason." M. de Palfy had the pleasure of dining alone in his salon and of re-counting the affair to anyone who happened along, and of saying, "My faith, I'll not go to the Tuileries tonight because I've just come from there."[1] That's a reward for all his mornings of bad humor.

During the first of my visits, I put on a little too much *freddetto* toward the mistress of the house. I HAVE QUITED HER FOR SAY TO, FOR SPEAKING WITH [sic] Mme. Genet, whom I've desired ever since I was told that she was charming in bed.

All these poor rich people who were gathered together without lik-ing each other and without permitting themselves any banter, gaiety or other pleasures of the mind lack happiness and hence are ridiculous.

An absurdity to be throttled: dining in the Rue Charlot a fortnight ago, the great M. Achille proposed to me, with the servile and clumsy manners of a bourgeois trying to flatter, to introduce me to M. Con-stant, the Emperor's valet. I almost choked; however, I had enough strength left to say to myself, "He's going to tell me about some liberty he's taken with the Emperor." Sure enough; my idiot immedi-ately added, "He has said things to the Emperor that no one else would

[1] A good description because true. [Note by Beyle.]

ever have dared to say to him." Luckily, M. Achille left to go to a party where he was expected, otherwise I'd have burst.

December 18.—My faith, if it's coquetry, I'm caught, if you can call it being caught to experience keen pleasure.

There were fifteen or twenty people present, they were about to start some games; she was beside the fireplace, two women kept me from approaching her. She came over to me with that decision given by a keen desire to which one yields, in order to come over to me she took four or five steps, and stopped to speak to me in the middle of the salon. I'm not very sure what she said to me, I didn't pay much attention to it; in this salon I was like a prince who is vain and who finds himself among people to whom his ribbons, his orders and all his dignities are invisible. I happened to be near the sofa to the right of the door, I was playing with the children to give myself countenance. She suddenly came over, seated herself beside me and said:

"Mama told me to ask you if it's true that the louis is going to be demonetized the first of January, etc. . . ." (not altogether said in those terms).

I replied, and at once the conversation turned to what interested us. Her face, on which the expression of feeling is extremely rare, had such a look of loving me, and her eyes regarded me with so much happiness that I restrained myself just as I was about to take her hand.[1] We happened to change places a moment later, and, while seated, she spoke to three ladies who were standing up, I at her side. A man was mentioned, and she asked, "Is he young? Is he amiable? Does he look intelligent?" with the liveliest and warmest expression of happy love. She congratulated herself on her choice and took pleasure in praising, in his presence, the lover to whom she hasn't yet confessed her love, and, as she talked, in urging him to be aggressive. Her face was animated and full of passion. Her soul seemed to be stirred. If, during the past year, she'd had a quarter of this expression in one of our languishing tête-à-tête, it would at once have become delightful. I looked at her fondly, and her soul being stirred, she must have read in mine.

Surely it was the *freddetto* that was beginning to take effect. Every time she told me that she'd be home she added a phrase begging me to come to see her.

In all the time I've known her, this was the day when I saw the most ardent expression of love in her. Things had reached a point where all would have been over at once if we'd been alone. I had seen her before with penetrating and steady looks, occasionally with the gentle ways of love, but never with such a spirited, candid and poignant

[1]That was the best thing that happened. 1815. [Note added by Beyle.]

manner. I don't understand how she can help realizing how much she is exposing herself. There were four women present who, at the same time they were paying her their respects, were undoubtedly getting their revenge by observing her tiniest shortcomings through a microscope. These women were together, her conversation with me in a corner of the salon couldn't be overheard by them, they undoubtedly didn't assume it to be as innocent as it was. In addition, her ardent look and three questions, asked with less grace but more vigor than Mlle. Mars would have put into them, said quite plainly, "I've got all that in my lover."

Possibly she was livened up by a good dinner, the afternoon is the time when she rises a bit above her insipid life. Possibly, being livened up, she yielded to a very slight fondness she has for me, and, as the three questions in succession and strongly accentuated passed through her mind, she asked them out of the desire to be brilliant that is ever-present in women.

After duly looking on, I went out. The stupidity of the *Shepherd* ladies, the bad breeding, or rather the lack of ideas, at the dinner in the Rue Charlot quite reduced me to the keen sensations of an observer in both salons. *Freddetto! Freddetto, amico!*

December 19.—I talked to Félix about my *majorat* from half-past nine in the morning until half-past seven in the evening. HE WRITES TO MY BASTARD.

In the evening, *Fairisland* PRESENTS ME TO MISTRESS Gay [Sophie Gay]. This at last resembles the society described by Collé and Marmontel. We stayed an hour and saw Mme. Récamier, a charming face; it seems to be asking forgiveness for being pretty. It's still very much so. Mme. de Caraman (Mme. Tallien) came in, Mme. Récamier disappeared. Mme. Tallien still has a beautiful face which shows nothing but an imperious, dismal, common soul. I'd willingly walk ten leagues in order not to pass a fortnight with her, and I'd walk twenty in order to spend a little time with Mme. Récamier, who hasn't changed at all; she's a bit stout, that's all.

FROM M. Gay TO LADY Alexander.

I GO OUT FROM LADY Alexander at half-past eleven (I went to the Rue Saint-Honoré) THE EYES WERE NOT AS YESTERDAY. PERHAPS WHY *io non son venuto che alle dieci. La madre m'a fatto qualche rimproveri della mia tardanza* [perhaps because I came only at ten o'clock. The mother reproached me a bit for being late]. As for myself, I paid court to Mme. Genet, who's so witless in society that she must go to it wholeheartedly IN BED. I'm going to M. de Joly's at ten o'clock tomorrow to see about the *majorat*.

January 1, 1811.—My ambition and finances are to be thanked for the changes that have come about since this time last year, when, at Linz, I went in uniform to pay a corps visit to poor Villemanzy and the Messrs. Chambon and other people with ability and pleasant manners.

But the Ministry of Love has behaved badly; if it keeps on acting this way, it may well become useless.

But also there wasn't any pox this year, and in 1809 there was one dose of clap and two poxes. No illness of any kind.

Good work, THIS UPON *Letellier,* a hundred or so good English lessons from Mr. Goodson, BASHFULNESS defeated all along the line.

In twenty-three days I'll be twenty-eight years old.

My New Year's Day went off very well; there's a cold spell that's magnificent and dry, but rather rigorous, I stayed in bed till ten o'clock reading Chénier's criticism of La Harpe's *Lycée,* very good.

At noon, to the Tuileries in full-dress uniform with Delporte. A big crowd. At Mass, I was very pleased with the face of the Duchesse de Courlande's daughter; she had a pure expression. Were I not afraid of being misled by my present fondness for German women, I would attribute these qualities to the fact that she is German.

At the audience following Mass, Cardinal Maury presented the vicar-generals to the Emperor, who said to one of them (a lean, evil face):

"I don't trust you; the religion I profess and yours are as far apart as heaven and hell. I am a Christian of the same kind as Bossuet and Fénelon . . . I've got my eye on you . . . Don't forget that I carry a sword."

It appears that the Emperor was as handsome as Talma in his good moments. I have yet to see him speak severely.

We left the audience at two o'clock. Delporte and I agreed to pay our calls tomorrow at ten o'clock. The High Chancellor will be home at half-past ten.

Yesterday we went to pick out the toys at Labatte's, in the Rue Saint-Honoré near the Rue de la Ferronerie. I must buy them a week earlier for 1812. From there the fiacre took us to dinner at Legasque's. I left there to take my toys to the nice family in the Hôtel du Châtelet.

M. Daru was dining alone WITH HIS CHILDREN AND MISTRESS Nardot. I nearly didn't go in. Finally, I presented myself with the whirligig in my right hand and a big lamb in the other.

M. Daru didn't see me at first, he excused himself politely and got up to offer me a chair. THEY WANTED A LITTLE OF TOPICS: Amélie's lamb, which was big enough to hold her on its back, Napoléon's miniature billiard table, on which he played, Aline's whirligig, and especially Pauline's Pyrrhic fire, supplied some, with the result that everybody was brightened up by these toys. I made my escape as the others left

the table to go to show all these things "to mama." I THOUGHT THAT
THIS DISCRETION SHOULD PLEASE TO THE FATHER, AND I BELIEVE THAT I
HAVE NOT ERRED.

January 15, COMING FROM MUSEUM.—I perceive that it's utterly impossible
to acquire new physical habits, especially the kind that distract from
thought.

Consequently, although music gives me great pleasure, even though
it were to be taught by Cimarosa I don't feel the strength in myself to
learn *"Voi che sapete"* on the piano.

This mood comes from my love for my art, and consequently for
thought, through which I may perfect myself in it.

Dancing, which I learned three or four years ago, did no more than
run off me like water off a duck's back, in spite of my love for women.
Thus, that I might learn to dance, I'd have to get rid of my love for my
art.

Conclusion, which 994 men out of 1,000 would call absurd, but which
is true for all that: falsehood of the phrase, *Vox populi vox Dei.* A
proverb ought to be written saying that *Vox populi* never expresses
anything profound—whether it be in metaphysics or in sentiment—on
Newton, Tracy or Mozart and Raphael.

A TOUR THROUGH SOME PARTS OF ITALY IN THE YEAR 1811[1]

The gentleman who may find this notebook is requested in the name of
honor and of the boredom it would give him not to read it, but to return it by diligence to M. Fournex, Hôtel de Hambourg, Rue Jacob,
No. 18, in Paris.

Exact knowledge of mankind.

Notice: If this hodgepodge falls into the hands of an honest man, he is
requested not to read it. It is an *anatomical* work (undertaken on the
advice of the celebrated C.) solely for my enlightenment. I was born
violent; in order to mend my ways, I have been counseled to know
myself. This study had to begin with the knowledge of other men. It
will be realized that to dissect a paralytic is not to insult the paralytic
but to seek to understand paralysis.

If you go any farther, put your character down under the heading of
inanity.

[1]Beyle wrote this title in English in a separate notebook in anticipation of going
to Italy on an official mission.

March 9.—About the middle of February, 1811, I WAS WITH ANGELINE EVERY NIGHT, Crozet was staying in Bellisle's apartment; during the moments I was able to steal from my office, we read Burke ON SUBLIME together. We discussed his ideas, of which we approved very little. Their chief merit was to make us think. By attentively observing the circumstances of our sentiments and thoughts, we made some fairly accurate discoveries. Suddenly our thoughts were turned to another channel.

I went to see Mme. . . .; she said, "I've got something to tell you that will give you pleasure; you're going to Italy . . ." I was excited and delighted. I went back to tell the news to Crozet, who appeared indifferent, as he always does when he's really stirred. He said at once, "I'll go with you." I was agreeably surprised at this sign of character. He immediately returned to Plancy to ask for a leave and a passport. He got both. Since February 25, I've been afraid several times that I wouldn't see the Italy I love so much.

The excellent Mr. . . . planned to send M. L. . . . to Italy. That would have given me great pain, and him probably no pleasure. I refrained from speaking of M. L. . . . , but I took the liberty of allowing M. Daru to see my desire to go to Rome. I was left for three or four days in uncertainty; finally on March 6, at half-past one, M. de Baure informed me that M. Daru had told him to put my name on the report.

Usually, M. Daru works with [the Emperor] on Thursdays. It was otherwise this week. My report hasn't passed. That makes me sorry for Crozet, who has a two-month leave of absence, and who's obliged to be back at his sluice by May 1, I believe.

I'm in love with my voyage; by that I mean that I have almost no more sensibility for the opera buffa AND THE AMIABLE GIRL WITH WHOM I LAY EVERY NIGHT.

I've seen that the best way to spoil my pleasure is to read travel books. Crozet and I have agreed that the character of a nation must be studied in what has been said about it, but descriptions are to be guarded against. Unfortunately, what I know about the *Italian character* is very little indeed.

Mme. de Staël (*Corinne*) makes me sick. That stilted style, the least fault of which is to strive to command admiration continually, that wit which lays claim to the honors of genius and doesn't realize that the latter's most salient quality (naturalness) is entirely lacking in it, that farce which ridicules what I love most, makes me acutely ill. I attempted to ward it off by making an extract from the end of the first volume, where Corinne deals with the Italian character. By putting her phrases in a natural style, I saw that they enclosed practically nothing but commonplaces and feelings that are visibly exaggerated by the person who experiences them. I'm not going to put the extract here, as I had planned to do. I happened to come across Spon the same day that Mme. de Staël *dried me up*. I thoroughly realized the advantages of naturalness. I read with pleasure a hundred and fifty pages written by the Lyon doctor in 1675, I believe. I admired his genuine modesty, and the affected bombast of Corinne was all the more glaring as the result.

The dull, precise and complete Lelande is what we need. He mentions everything, and, since he feels nothing, he doesn't spoil the sentiments that might be given us by St. Peter's or the site of Florence.

We're going to Italy to study the Italian character, to get acquainted with the men of that nation in particular, and, as the opportunity arises, to complete, extend, verify, etc. what we believe we know about mankind in general. Fortunately for us (that's the advantage of our studies), our pleasure and work overlap.

Our judgments are exclusive and peremptory. I see nothing as asinine, for instance, as the travel book of M. Creuzé. But these words must be added to each sentence: "for our character and temperament." I believe that a tall, skinny young man, mild-mannered and well bred, with his linen carefully creased and his cravat well arranged, would find me very strange and disagreeable; but, after this warning, it's his own fault if he reads us. This diary is written only for ourselves and the three or four friends whose character resembles our own or whom we like in spite of the difference of our views. We are unable to realize the merit of others, and they are unable to appreciate our own. A horse doesn't become amorous of a cow; as far as sex is concerned, these two creatures don't exist for each other.

In the same way, as far as sentiments and ideas are concerned, the best thing that M. Creuzé, for example, and we can do is to be nonexistent for each other. His account is good for those who resemble him, ours for beings formed by the same climate, the same education, etc., etc. as we.

Any man who doesn't throw this book down at the fourth page should throw down our big notebook at the first line. Now our *profanum vulgus* is driven off. We're going to speak with an open heart, as we would to ourselves, sparing neither our expressions nor the proprieties. We're going to call senseless, idiotic, insipid, etc. what Mr. So-and-so calls pretty, majestic, beautiful, ingenious. He's right, but we're not wrong.

Don't go any farther, you bastards.

We'll only take Lalande, as a general directory, and Duclos, because his way of seeing things—outside a bit of pettiness—is our own.

Alfieri, in his autobiography, will give us some glimpses into the Italian character. He was a good judge of character. What he foresaw about the Spanish and Portuguese proves it.

I or *me* should be understood to refer to the one whose handwriting will be recognized, *we* or *us* to both.

March 15.—Our voyage is still being held up, which makes me feel very sorry for Crozet, whose leave is limited and whose return appears to be obligatory.

The amiable and good Martial was appointed Intendant of Rome by a decree of March 12.

I saw with my own eyes in M. Daru's portfolio today the report in which I'm mentioned. M. Daru hopes to work with His Majesty tomorrow.

I'm afraid His Majesty will find the voyage of an Auditor useless. Won't the Intendant be able to take over the museums and libraries alone? It might be useful to have an Auditor leave within twenty-four hours. It's probable that the Intendant won't leave before a fortnight from now. But this reason can't be given to His Majesty.

I consoled myself by thumbing through Lalande. I've just read in his book of description about the Quirinal Palace, which will be the Imperial Palace. It appears to be majestic, please God that it is. All our palaces are as shabby as can be.

I'm making a note to see Bernini's St. Theresa in the Vittoria Church. Lalande says that "the saint is swept by passion to the verge of frenzy." I'm not familiar with anything of this kind in the arts.

March 17.—I haven't written since January 15[1] owing to laziness and because I didn't have the time to make my descriptions with sufficient accuracy. Besides, this notebook was locked in a small table, the key to which I had mislaid.

The Minister of Love, who was about to be removed from office and who frequently diminished the happiness procured by the other Ministers, has finally redeemed himself. At intervals of several months, I had been writing to the amiable and gentle Bereyter. She finally permitted me to pay my respects in person. I'm indebted to Faure for this success; without his advice, I wouldn't have written the last letter. It was a long one and written in the most lofty and least impulsive tone of gallantry. Bereyter told me that, when I arrived at her home, I had tiny little eyes and a fatuous look. I must have seemed bashful. I kissed her tenderly the first day and possessed her at my apartment the second (January 29, 1811). I nearly missed her.

[1]This entry resumes the diary proper, which stopped January 15. The intervening entries are from the separate notebook in which Beyle expected to keep the diary of his trip to Italy.

We've been plagued by some anonymous letters, which frightened her and gave her what seemed to be an extreme fondness for me. A bilious pedant named Fournier, the private surgeon of the Princesse de Galitzine, is strongly suspected by me of being the author of the twelve or fifteen letters we have received. Their purpose was to make me believe that Angéline was a whore. It didn't succeed. In the six weeks that we have been together, I've given her an engraving (St. Cecilia) and a necklace. The letter writer later threatened Angéline with the violent wrath of a *grande dame* whom I had left for her. She believed it was one of my three mistresses: Aline, Pauline or Joséphine.[1]

This Fournier is bilious, tenacious, very adroit, well versed in the underhand tricks of princes' servantdom. His fortune is made up of three pensions. He scorns medicine and is writing a poem on love. This gallant personage, who is the color of a quadroon and about forty-five years old, is exactly like the villain of an English novel. In one of his moments of bile, he offered to marry Angéline, who refused. He brought on a quarrel between her mother and her, the next day he patched things up between them.

While all this was going on, I had the gentle and goodhearted little Angéline with me every night. She knows music very well, but her judgment has been warped by the vulgarity of the present-day French school. This good little thing had the nerve to tell me that *the erudite is worth more than the melodious.* She admires Berton, Méhul and Co.; but she's teaching me Mozart's and Cimarosa's arias exclusively. She tried to make me listen to *Montano et Stéphanie* [by Berton], which I couldn't stomach. We met Berton there.

In conclusion, as far as love is concerned, I'm happy. She writes like an angel. The worst day of the anonymous letters, she wrote me, "I'm desperate. Come, I beseech you, whatever hour of the night it may be, come."

Ambition.—I showed off my velvet suit. Pacé and Ouéhihé were offended by it. Their envy was expressed through their criticisms. Pacé's envy was particularly striking.

M. Z scolded me October 18; he hasn't scolded me since. I go to the office for two hours every day, and twice a week I work five or six.

The lovely Marie has the same tenderness for me, or the same sweet friendliness. She gives me proofs of it every day. Our tête-à-tête are still cool—through embarrassment, it seems to me.

[1]Beyle had apparently boasted to Angéline of a trio of imaginary mistresses, to whom he gave the names of Daru's three little daughters.

I'm still negotiating the barony with MY FATHER. Faure, the semi-official defender of bastards, has given up trying to justify mine. To all appearances, he's a man who is very cunning and yet narrow-minded like a genuine provincial who has very little sensibility, and who conceals what little he has under the role of a fond FATHER. All in all, a villainous man. The excellent Mme. de N. was going to lend him 15,000 francs to make me a baron; he didn't reply to that argument, which was too strong, but he wrote a letter of the falsest diplomacy adorned with cunning hypocrisy, rather well written.

My mind is engaged in double activity when I'm with Crozet. He stayed for a week or so in the apartment of Bellisle, who was at La Rochelle (from December 24 to March 15). We made some nice little discoveries on pleasure and pain in connection with the pompous prattle of Burke ON SUBLIME. In a word, we were working very well together in the direction I've chosen (as COMIC BARD) when, about the middle of February, M. Daru led me to entertain some hope of going to Rome.

Last night, Ferdinand misunderstood an appointment I gave him. He left at seven o'clock and waited for me until three at the door of Frau Mozart (Rue l'Echiquier, No. 36) [Angéline's home]. In the meantime, I went for a drive in a fiacre, and brought her back to the apartment, where we found ourselves with no supper.

At half-past eleven, I went out to stray through the Rue Saint-Honoré in front of the closed shops in an attempt to find something to eat. I returned with a loaf of bread given me by the porter. There were two or three glasses of Frontignon wine left and not a drop of ordinary wine, when the doorbell rang. I was all prepared to give a scolding, I opened the door, it was Bellisle.

He's going to be an Intendant in Spain, in the district of the Army of the North. I was afraid he wouldn't come to see Paris again before his exile.

The belles OF THE THERESE STREET squeeze my hand, especially WHITE [Blanche de La Bergerie], all of which doesn't keep me from finding them poor little creatures, very dull, bored and boring. To acquit himself, Crozet talks bombast to them. Crozet is still in love with A., piloting his boat like a nincompoop, and he's gloomy and spreads gloom as the result. That's what I keep on telling him in order to make him a bit of a Beylist; but he balks against it. Voluptuousness will never have a true worshiper in him, and he seems to me almost irrevocably devoted to gloominess and the respect it procures amid this people of monkeys.

In a word, since the middle of January, I've been in a happy frame of mind. But I haven't had moments of inspiration like last July, I believe. I've grown a little fatter, at least in the legs. The study of music has been good for my art. With the peace of mind that good music gives me, I reflect on this subject, and with fruit.

I'm tired of writing. This morning, I sent Mme. Daru a pretty bouquet of artificial flowers.

Classes for the Auditors have been spoken of in recent months. It happens that I'll probably be first, being in extraordinary service.

(End of the review of the first two months of 1811.)

March 17.—It seems to me that my physical happiness with Angéline has deprived me of much of my imagination. I MAKE THAT ONE OR TWO EVERY DAY, SHE FIVE, SIX AND SOMETIMES NINE TIMES.

I'm convinced that a COMIC BARD ought to arrange his life in a manner quite different from that of Alfieri. He'd have had more intelligence, talent and happiness if he hadn't attempted to struggle proudly against institutions that can't be changed; what he ought to have done was to look at life as a masked ball in which a prince isn't offended in the least when a wigmaker in domino crosses in front of him.

Taken on this side, Alfieri's character would have contained the material for a comedy destined to lead those virtue-stuffed bilious people back to Beylism.

Like all men who aren't out-and-out imbeciles, I need to be busy with work of some kind if I'm going to be happy. Holland kept me busy for two or three months; ambition, clothes, the Court for a month or two; not having much to do at present, I need a long voyage or *Letellier*.

I've just been to Pacé's, whence I was driven away by boredom. Yet that's what's called going out in society. The street jammed with carriages. Marie wasn't there. With her, since my happiness there depends on her, if she had paid some attention to me, I'd have been HAPPY, but without her the boredom was overwhelming. I didn't work with pleasure today. I need *Letellier*.

March 20.—I was sleeping with Angéline. The cannon woke her up at ten o'clock. It was the third shot; we counted the twenty-second with joy.[1]

At our nineteenth, which was the twenty-second for the public, we heard applause in the street. In the most retired places, as in the

[1] This was the announcement of the birth of Napoleon's son, the King of Rome. A hundred and twenty-one guns signified a boy, for a girl there would only have been twenty-one.

gardens of the Musée des Augustins, the twenty-second shot was applauded.

My barber told me that in the Rue Saint-Honoré the people applauded as at the appearance of a popular actor.

It's a great and happy event. At two o'clock, they already had the reply from Lyon.

The birth was at twenty minutes past nine, the *Moniteur* says; at ten past nine, the other papers say.

March 21.—A moment of sadness almost ending in tears, that in which I made out my accounts with Bellisle, who was leaving in the evening for Spain, maybe for three or four years. I didn't dare show it.

This morning we went pistol shooting, for the first time using pistols without flintlocks. They fire more quickly. An excellent invention. In the first three shots I hit two clay birds. Generally speaking, when I give my mind to it, I shoot well, very badly when I pull the trigger in bad humor.

Today's the day when the matter of the trip to Rome was to have been decided. The great event of yesterday prevented M. Daru from working today with His Majesty. That makes three weeks that he hasn't had any work, something extremely rare.

Yesterday, a pleasant dinner with F. B. and Angéline. She's gentle and loving, but has little feeling for her art.

This morning I ordered a brace of pistols without flintlocks for five hundred francs at the shooting range.

New demonstration of my shortcoming.—I'd have gone to M. Denon's only with the greatest reluctance. Yet it was an excellent show. Every month I miss twelve or fifteen very useful shows through my cursed horror of whatever is *low*.

In addition to this shortcoming, the *folly* of amusing myself by imagining that I have been insulted so I can compose some very haughty and insolent replies and picture myself handing out insults in return. This morning, as I was going to the shooting range at seven o'clock, I discovered myself indulging in this folly. That makes me extremely susceptible, like Alfieri killing Elie for having pulled a hair out of his head. My folly is almost of the same kind.

If I could uproot these two shortcomings from my character, I'd have much more talent and be far happier. These weeds possibly have a common root. I enjoy my thoughts, the company of other men brings me back to reality, and in a disagreeable manner. If I don't watch out, I'm punished by a humiliation.

March 22.—Bellisle left for Spain at half-past three. His taste for detail, his continual dignity, but also his gloominess. He's a prince, but princes aren't happy. That's what the Baron Séguier must be like, I saw him (the 23rd) at his solemn audience, where he was a clown. I expected to see a nincompoop, the same as almost all the bearers of great names. On the contrary, he is a man who is given to laughter.

On the evening of the 22nd, I went for a walk with Angéline in the Champs-Elysées from half-past eight until half-past ten. Her life story. She didn't find pleasure in the arms OF HER FIRST LOVER. A LITTLE MORE WITH THE SECOND AND EVER SO.

I conclude from this that she is only now reaching her real puberty. At the age of thirty, she'll perhaps have real talent, when the strength and luxury of health have arrived.

March 23.—I went with Faure to visit the law courts. M. Séguier's office gave me pleasure, all the rest is deadly bourgeois, petty and dull. Nothing new FOR MY TOUR. M. Daru takes his portfolio with him every day. His Majesty calls every evening for the list of people who have come to inquire about the health of Their Majesties the Empress and the King of Rome.

The head page (M. Sannois), I believe, fell off his horse as he was going to the Senate to announce the great news.

March 25.—I had him sing *Udite, sei Morella e La Vendetta. Andiamo al letto a mezza notte ed un quarto. L'amo sempre più teneramente, egli è il solo* . . . [We went to bed at a quarter past twelve. I love him more and more tenderly, and he's the only one . . .]. (WRITTEN BY Angéline.)

March 26.—We got up and went for lunch to a very cool mezzanine at Nicolle's, behind the Favart (seven francs fifteen sous). From there to Monceau. As I was coming back, I thought I recognized Victorine in two women walking one behind the other. That touched me, but I concluded from it that I'd forgotten her, even her face, but not the idea of her soul. For the past three weeks, Marie hasn't been looking at me with those eyes filled with love that I've observed so often. She has had enough of playing up to a ninny, or else THE HUSBAND has pointed out to her that friendship is all very well but evidences of friendship too frequently renewed might be unfavorably interpreted.

I frighten Probus. I believe he's what Helvétius said: a strong character, or having the reputation of being such, constantly stimulated by a little terror.

Nothing new on the trip to Rome. Never has M. Daru remained such a long time without working with the Emperor.

March 27.—Nothing new except those damnable rumors of war with Russia, which made me tremble for our voyage.

Crozet arrived. While waiting for him, I was unable to resume *Letellier,* and yet my mind has need of some intense occupation; I've digested those of my job. They can no longer do anything but occupy my time and not my mind. This act of digestion, mingled with enjoyments of vanity, lasted through September, October, November, December, January and February, 1811, which makes six months during which time I've composed enough to fill two notebooks as large as this one and of the same paper.

I've just skimmed through Brydone; although he doesn't describe precisely enough, he aroused some enthusiasm in me. I thanked nature to have a soul capable of finding happiness in majestic scenes of nature; they have the same effect on me as good music, things which make absolutely no impression on Pacé. Traveling will be a great source of happiness for me. I observe that you should go in a party of two or three.

Sicily, if ever I can go there, presents two advantages: human nature there is as distinctive and curious to study as the nature of plants and stones. I'd have rare sensations if I lived for a month in some wild cavern on Etna. I'm writing this in a perfectly suitable apartment (FOR ME AND MY POSITION OF AMBITION), and furthermore one of the gayest in Paris. But this capital of the greatest of modern empires is blunted for me, I'm blasé to its pleasures. I've leaped over most of them with my feet bound; that is, I didn't have them at the time they might have given me pleasure, and they seem to me insipid now that I'm able to attain them; as may be seen, I haven't the frivolous and vain character that is needed if Paris is to be enjoyed in its entirety. But, on the other hand, I could experience, in the caverns of Etna and before the immense crags of Norway, sensations that are invisible to the true Parisian, who would be aware of nothing in these places but the bad dinners and the beds stuffed with peach pits; instead of playing boston and having my charm admired, I'm going tonight to hear *I Nemici Generosi,* a product of that fine Neapolitan plant, Cimarosa. But, on the other hand, it would be folly to feel badly because I'll only be a Master of Requests five or six years after the people who pay twenty calls a day two hundred days out of the year, like THIS POOR FELLOW N . . . WHO WAS ONE OF THIS EVENINGS AT M. D[aru's] THE MOTHER, and who spent, WITH HIS PREGNANT WIFE, a long half hour listening to her spout twaddle.

You mustn't desire things that are incompatible.

It occurred to me that the Italian trip would separate me for a long time from Shakespeare, and I reread *Romeo and Juliet* with undiminished admiration; I observed how much this great poet had

Italianized his characters, I saw with pleasure his poetics in this passage
(ACT III, SCENE THE THIRD):

Romeo to Friar Lawrence

Thou canst not speak of what thou dost not feel:
Wert thou as young as I, Juliet thy love,
An hour but married, Tybalt murdered,
Doting like me, and like me banished,
Then mightst thou speak, then mightst thou tear thy hair,
And fall upon the ground, as I do now,
Taking the measure of an unmade grave.

Why put this passage here? To read the verse of the greatest OF
THE BARDS in Italy, before the most beautiful nature in the world.

March 27.—My mind has digested Holland, I need some substantial
occupation; if it weren't for the *speme del viaggio a Roma* [hope of
the Rome trip], I'd resume work on *Letellier,* but I may leave any day.
I certainly hope that tomorrow will see my report signed. THEY SPEAK
MUCH OF WAR WITH RUSSIA. It would be charming, upon returning from
Italy, to be transferred to an active army.[1] My two shortcomings resulting from *misanthropy* make it advantageous for me to be absolutely
forced to see and mingle with people.[2]

To while away the time, I tried to read *Cinna.* I admired the style,
but I didn't finish it. I thought of Shakespeare; I read Romeo, it
seemed as though I were rereading something I'd written the previous month, so naturally did the sentiments spring from my own outlook. I found Shakespeare's poetics in *Romeo,* page 110 (Act III,
Scene III); I was delighted to see that I think exactly like that
UNDERSTANDING SOUL.

March 28.—Crozet arrived at nine o'clock.[3]

I arrived March 28 at nine o'clock in the morning; Henri and I
went to M. Z's, who hasn't worked yet. I thought everything had been
arranged and that we were to leave tomorrow at the latest. It's impossible to write too clearly, even to people of intelligence.

April 1.—We went to M. Z's this morning at half-past nine. Henri
saw an order at M. Corbeau's to send M. Nanteuil to Rome and to write

---

[1] That happened. Charming isn't exactly the word that applies. February 25, 1813.
[Note added by Beyle.]

[2] That's impossible for me, it's too foreign to my character, it gives me too much
unhappiness through boredom and by depriving me of all happiness through the
arts. [Note by Beyle.]

[3] The following entry, as well as that of April 1, as far as the space, was written
by Crozet.

Pacé to do what Henri was to have done himself. We believed our-selves to be entirely out of the running.

At the same time, we thought that M. Nanteuil might be sent ahead to take care of the most urgent work: M. Z, not knowing when the report on this young man could be presented to H. M., might have taken this measure temporarily. This thought showed us that there might still be some hope.

On the other hand, the rumors of war with Alessandro [Alexander I], which are circulating with more and more persistence, are unfavor-able to our voyage. For, if M. Z wants to be Intendant and take Henri with him, he won't send him to Rome.

While we were making these conjectures, it was announced that M. Z was going to His Majesty's and working with him until five o'clock. We venture to hope that this work will hold up Corbeau's order. But we are afraid of Pacé's jealousy and intrigues, and we are all too aware that he can fill Henri's functions and spare H. M. 6,000 francs.

Henri tried to get in a word with Mme. Z before M. Z went to the palace, but he wasn't able to see her until after his departure. She seemed to have no doubts as to the success of the affair.

We retired rather worried, Henri very annoyed and even a bit angry, I rather out of sorts, and we began reading *Macbeth*. Félix came, and we made him acquainted with the circumstances. He bet 1 to 6 in our favor and that's all.

It's six o'clock and that's how things stand. M. Z is working right now with His Majesty. We're going to Henri's office to try to get some news. What would vex us more than anything else would be for the work to have been put off again.

A superb evening. I was acutely sensitive to it as I left the excellent M. Z's at eleven o'clock sharp. I had arrived there at half-past ten, endeavoring to be firm. Mme. Daru said, "Ah, here's Beyle, who's coming to learn whether he's going to leave! Well, there's nothing new, my husband didn't work with the Emperor . . . ," and the details.

I said, "Might I venture to ask you, monsieur, if you are still plan-ning to present the report in which I am mentioned?"

"Yes, but nothing has been done about it, it's there with the others."

A minute later, in connection with nothing, he said, "Get your Court cloaks ready; the Emperor won't delay in going to Rome . . . , he'll be going before long."

I embraced Martial with pleasure; his wife and he spoke to me of my voyage to Rome. Martial looked tired out. They only sat down to dinner at half-past nine. M. Daru had been waiting at the Tuileries since five o'clock.

This has been a day that forms the character; twenty a year like this one, and I'd almost become an Ambassador. I owe much gratitude to Mme. Daru.

April 1811.—Walk in the Parc Monceau the 3rd, Crozet's advice to be followed.

Intimacy is beginning with Probus; he himself had the impulse to invite me TO dinner THE 15th of April.

The hope OF THE TOUR THROUGH ITALY has kept Crozet and me in a state of agitation for a fortnight. I'm more and more disgusted with the human rabble, and am never so happy as when, shut up at home, I don't even hear the doorbell ring. This feeling attaches me to Angéline.

Faure, gloomier and gloomier, takes everything I say to him badly and appears to be getting more distant with me. Crozet is also sometimes irritated at jokes.

April 17.—Crozet and I worked reading *L'Avare* until four o'clock. At four o'clock, I went to the office. I was told that M. Daru had asked for me. Maréchal told me that M. Daru was Minister Secretary of State.

April 18.—Every day since April 1, we've been waiting for the work with His Majesty, the result of which would have sent us to breathe the air of fair Italy.

Faure and Crozet opened my *Moniteur,* I saw in it that M. Daru had taken his oath. Seeing decrees signed by him, I had a moment of keen pleasure on the Terrasse des Feuillants.

Finally at eleven o'clock I saw Mme. Daru. At five-thirty in the evening, I embraced M. Daru wholeheartedly, and he received me with kindness. The dog of ambition has bitten M. de Baure. "I find myself the brother-in-law of a Minister," he told me this morning. I believe he looks on me as something of a rival (he makes a great mistake).

April 20.—Faure, Crozet and I left for Rouen and the sea. The trip was a very good one. There's only one thing wrong with those fellows, and that's not to be jolly enough, but to get mad sometimes at jokes. That's what I call a bourgeois way of acting.

Everything's all right WITH MARIA. I continue TO LAY EVERY NIGHT WITH Angéline.

Diary of Our Voyage to the Sea
Left April 29, Returned May 3

We left punctually on scheduled time (4 o'clock, April 29), we traveled at a speed worthy of the most advanced civilization. It's sixty-three miles from Paris to Rouen, and we arrived there in four hours. The climate changed five or six times during our trip, it was cold and disagreeable in general, the opposite of what I'd imagined. At the 53rd mile, we descended a rather agreeable, and above all very fertile, valley; it's obvious that the soil is far superior to that surrounding Paris and presenting the accurate symbol of the warmth of the souls in that region. The souls of Rouen would be quite ridiculous if they were to be judged by the streets of that city. In general, its an execrable hole, even worse than Grenoble—everything that's the opposite of majestic. We saw the house where Corneille was born June 9, 1606, in the Rue de la Pie. There are some fine boulevards and a few passable streets.

April 30.—I've seen the sea again. The odor of tar reminded me vividly of Marseilles and Mélanie. Is it absolutely impossible for me ever to fall in love again? Still so young, shall I be obliged to renounce my heart? This is the sad result of being devoured by passion and having the misfortune to have been cast into the maelstrom too young.

The inhabitants of the coasts ought to be less narrow-minded than those of the interior. The sea, which encloses the idea of the infinite, is beneath their eyes, they talk incessantly of the dangers to which it gives birth, of the courage with which these dangers are surmounted, and the quick fortunes made in maritime trade. The conversation of the weary sailor returning to port is less stupid than that of the notary of Bourges. I thanked my good fortune to be no longer a soldier; when you see the life of those animals from anear, you're obliged to forgive them for their outspoken ways, it's the poor devils' sole pleasure.

The servant of the commissioner general of police pleased me through her honest and obliging manner. She was very useful to us, and her master was very polite. We saw the lighthouse, which was shown us by an intelligent young man. Here too was a new invention, which they are testing out tonight. The number of new inventions in details involving mechanics and chemistry is immense. The beacon can be seen nine leagues away. We could distinguish the coast going toward Cherbourg at a distance of twenty-five leagues. Le Havre is a pretty little town.

Forever skinned alive by the inns; the Council of State ought to do something about it.

May 1.[1]—Set sail at ten minutes after five May 1, 1811. The owner of the boat had an intelligent appearance, his name is Victor . . . and he's the father of thirteen children, of whom eight are girls. There was a second sailor who also displayed intelligence, and who had sailed around the world with Captain Baudin. On his face there was that contemptuous expression which indicates the true philosopher (Henri). The boat, which cost 6,000 francs fully rigged with nets, appeared to be an excellent one and sailed very rapidly. It pitched as it started out, a pleasurable emotion. For an hour, this pleasure was pure; lofty ideas of immensity, reflections on the ordinary influence of the sea on the sailors, who have more intelligence and character than people of a similar rank on land. Nausea. Low spirits. Vomiting. Crozet started by feeling dizzy, his eyes smarting; his head was affected, and finally going into the cabin, where he sat down, he vomited, with very painful convulsions of the stomach. The vomiting spell came after we had been out four hours, and it relieved him greatly for half an hour. Two hours later, a second vomiting spell, but not so painful as the first. At noon, when we tacked, a headache came on and remained with him as far as Le Havre, and even lasted a full half hour after we landed.[2]

May 2.—Left Le Havre at four o'clock in the morning. At the posthouse, Crozet had almost the same disappointment as I in leaving Strasbourg at the Kehl bridge two years ago. We were in the cabriolet with Henri. At lunch, Crozet joined us. Pretty countryside all the way to Rouen. Many trees. I especially liked the way the hedges were trimmed. The thatched roofs that can be seen through the great screens of beeches produce an excellent effect.

Arrived in Rouen at noon. Barber. Baths where the service was quite good, and from which there was a pretty view; as we were leaving, we had that of a little girl from Caux who was chatting with an old woman distributing tickets. This little girl had beautiful eyes and a pretty figure, we looked at her a long time, praising her (in English). I thought I noticed that during this time the old woman's eyes showed benevolence for us.

I climbed up the steeple of the Cathedral, which is very high. The

---

[1]The following three entries were written by Faure, but the manuscript has the annotation, "Written from Henri's dictation."

[2]Diaries kept of the trip to Le Havre by Crozet and Faure reveal that Faure and Beyle were also sick during the boat ride.

wind was very strong and the weather was good. This steeple is of wood covered with lead; the view from it is superb.

Rouen is situated in a sort of half nest formed by the hillsides that surround it and that are unfortunately not wooded. The diameter of the nest is formed by the Seine; opposite Rouen, the Seine's course describes a sort of crescent, it flows at the foot of the slopes which follow the same direction, and the terrain it encloses is a fine plain dotted with woods, prairies and arable ground. This plain rises imperceptibly in such a way that the line connecting the two extremities of the crescent are almost the same height as the slopes. The boulevards of Rouen are comparable to those of Paris, but are not, however, lined with such fine houses. We followed them on our return from the steeple, we passed before an orchard where some cows with enormous udders were grazing on very green and abundant grass, the whole belonging to a hospital.

After dinner, we went to the theater; they were giving *Crispin Médecin,* one of the farces in which I've noticed that the most is made of the jokes, good and bad; a very mediocre orchestra. Near me I noticed a woman sitting between her husband and her lover and looking sidewise at the latter, observing the former with an ardor and an expression that I wasn't near enough to make out.

May 3.—The same driver took us back to Paris. Unfortunately, we were inside the coach with two men who, I believe, were tradesmen, and a little woman with a gentle, almost distinguished face, and in whom Henri found a striking resemblance to his sister. I didn't share this impression. It appeared that, had the voyage been of some duration, and especially had we been traveling at night, we might have been able to tame her without much difficulty.

I slept quite a bit on the way. Read Franklin as much as the jogging of the coach permitted, and with much pleasure. There was nothing remarkable anyway. Montmorency. Arrived in Paris at four o'clock.[1]

May 18.—Matrimony.

Félix handed Mme. H. . . . a letter I had written her through him and in which I expressed the desire to obtain THE HAND OF HER DAUGHTER. Maybe she's thinking of remarrying. She has already been asked for HER DAUGHTER, she'll have quite a large fortune when she's between thirty and forty.

Félix gave me the very wise advice to speak of this to Mme. Z.

Mme. H. appears to me to have a mind that's not in the least bourgeois, she shows signs of having the diplomatic mind of a woman of the Court.

[1]Here ends the section in Faure's handwriting.

Mme. H. thought at first that it was a question of her herself.[1] She seems to be planning to settle her daughter's fortune, perhaps so she can remarry. Her son-in-law will have to affect the appearance of a very gentle character, to look as though he didn't have any character at all.

My father appears to be driven into his last intrenchment, his tender affection is probably going to be driven into doing me a service which is profitable to him.

I'll say to Marie, "It is fitting for my fortune that I marry, but my heart is not involved. I have never spoken to the young lady whose hand has been asked for me." She's the daughter of M. L[eschenault].

MEMOIRS OF MY LOVE, AMONG THE AMIABLE SEATS OF
MONTMORENCY Valley

June 3, 1811.—History of the battle of May 31, 1811.—On May . . . , 1811, I was returning from my office at three o'clock, bored with Paris, with the heat and with not being in the country with the woman I loved, when I was handed the following note . . .[2]

I left Saturday, May [25], at eight o'clock. I covered ten leagues in four hours. As I approached the château[3] my heart beat with timidity.

I was greeted with eagerness, gaiety and a shade of tenderness, which was especially manifest through the fact that ten minutes never went by without my arm being taken or something being said to me. As for myself, I had planned to say that I was in love, I reproached myself nightly for not having put my plan into execution. Driven by remorse, I believe I'd have spoken Tuesday, but UPON THE ARRIVAL OF MISTRESS Dubignon it was decided that I should stay until Sunday evening (June 2, 1811). That gave my timidity a little respite. I spent eight days at . . . ; this period was a happy isle for me. I was debonair, and Mme. Palfy was infinitely so with me.

On May 31, I wrote the following: The army I was commanding was full of terror and looked on the undertaking as beyond its capacity. That is what I told myself with rage on May 30 as I walked in

[1] A ludicrous mistake. [Note by Beyle.]

[2] Beyle neglected to include the text of the note in his diary, but it was obviously an invitation to visit the Darus at their country home in Bècheville.

[3] The Château de Bècheville, the Darus' country seat, which was not at Montmorency, but near Meulan, on the Seine.

the park alone at a quarter past eleven after everyone else had retired. Heavy clouds were passing before the moon, I contemplated their flight and I thought of the tender mythology of Ossian in order to take my mind off my dissatisfaction with myself. Five or six obvious reasons showed me the advantage and necessity of engaging in battle, but all my courage vanished at the sight of the enemy. Another step, and I'd have blown out my brains rather than tell a woman who possibly loves me that I love her. And I'm twenty-eight years old, and I've seen the world, and I've got some character! I understood perfectly why young German lovers frequently prefer to drink poison in a glass of lemonade to fleeing together.

My moments of remorse were terrible. The night of the 28th, to mention but one, was horrible. I realized that, wherever I went, the thought of having side-stepped such an excellent opportunity would make me unhappy. The next morning I was really ill. The following night, I didn't dare think of my cowardice, I drove out the thought and sought only to distract myself.

Wednesday, May 29, we went for a walk in the prettiest of English gardens (THE HERMITAGE). She left us and walked for some time with Mme. Dubignon. The ladies returned in my calash; seeing that my presence in their midst interrupted their conversation, I remained standing against the coachman's seat. On the return from the walk, as the night was falling, she took my arm:

"Come, my dear c[ousin], so I may tell you what I was saying to Mme. Dubignon." Inquiries UPON HIS SERVANTS.—ALL THE HISTORY OF THE MATRIMONY WITH . . . (ALREADY SAID TO ME AT PRATER, Jacqueminot WAS WITH US).[1] She spoke of her suitors. We weren't more than a hundred paces from the château; I made an effort and said to her:

"This role is ridiculous and I thoroughly realize it because before long I'm perhaps going to play it."

I told her that, yielding to the entreaties of my friends and of a quite near relative of mine, married in Paris (Mme. Joséphine Longueville), I had allowed them to ask the hand of Mlle. Jenny H. for me a few days before. She gave me a little sermon on marriage with a rather concerned look. When I went into the house, the children fell on me, and I told them a story; this story lasted at least half an hour. When I came back to the others, I found die Gräffin Palfy seated on the sofa between Mme. Dubignon AND HER MOTHER, her eyes red and looking straight ahead, the eyelids continually lowered, as when a person is holding back tears, and her face pale. That touched me. She began to sew, keeping her face turned away. I read a little dramatic

[1] See undated entry in November 1809.

piece; but I clearly saw that she didn't raise her eyes from her sewing, and that she held her head lower than usual.

I BELIEVED TO SEE IN THOSE TEARS AN EVIDENT PROOF OF HER LOVE FOR ME, and the following night, as I've said, was terrible for me. My bashfulness no longer had an excuse for deferring. I thought of two or three forms of declaration. This word was mentioned at dinner that day or the day before, and Mme. Dubignon, whom I believe to be in on the secret, an idea that was beginning to be given me by what she said at the time, said one should only make a declaration when one was sure of being loved, that at that time they weren't difficult, that one should speak out, etc., etc. She added some encouraging maxims.

Die Gräffin Palfy went out on some business WITH HER STEWARD. While joking with Mme. Dubignon during her absence, I happened to say, *"My spirit of enterprise."* Mme. Dubignon, a gloomy, bilious woman, desiring to be amused, who doesn't often laugh—and never except at something really ridiculous—, burst out laughing and then resumed her serious manner. From which I concluded that she was in on the secret. My melancholy was marked all that Thursday; I wanted to appear melancholy, and from my face it gained my heart. Mme. Palfy was possibly gayer than usual.

May 31.—Today, getting up, piqued at appearing as ridiculous as a bashful Orestes in Mme. Dubignon's eyes *e forse, forse dell' amato oggretto* [and perhaps, perhaps in those of the loved one], I resolved to be gay and to make a declaration *allegro risoluto.* I even wrote out two formulas in pencil, I carried this paper with me all day to aid me in case of need, and I'm burning it now.

When I went downstairs about nine o'clock this morning, we were alone in the salon. She was pale, depressed, her eyes tired; maybe she'd been crying. She told me that she's scarcely slept a wink. She has been complaining of that ever since she arrived here. She made an attempt to sing with her harp, and gave up, not being in voice. She played a game of billiards with me, and it was while we were playing that my gaiety began.

We went to accompany HER FATHER TO THE ferry OF Triel. FROM THERE, a visit to a country gentleman. Mme. Dubignon told me as we were going through a pretty wood in my calash that Mme. Palfy's religion was at stake, but that she was convinced it was genuine at present. It's quite in the above-mentioned lady's character to have sounded me out on this matter.

"Oh certainly!" I answered. "That's the result of education: her mother is so religious!"

A reply that I find a good one. IF EVER THE *gräffin* DID REPROACH

TO ME MY BASHFULNESS, TO ANSWER THAT UPON HER RELIGION, I SHOULD
FEAR being kept at a distance, which would be the worst of all evils. If
Mme. Dubignon wanted to sound me out, it's clear that I'm loved and
that religion isn't what it ought to be IN THE HEART OF Palfy.

My eyes ache from having a globe of fire [a lamp] between her and
me all evening, and I'm going to bed (May 31) at five minutes to
twelve.

The foregoing is copied from a sheet of paper brought from B., with
a few reflections added. I ought to have written the sequel the next day,
but, either from laziness or the fear of diminishing my pleasure, I
didn't write, and now everything is mixed up. Félix reproached me
for not having written TO HER.

About three o'clock, I was very debonair, she looked at me frequently and tenderly, there was possibly even some reproach in her
eyes because I was so gay. At a quarter past five, after the little girls
had become quiet, she left her loom and said, "I'll play the harp a
little." She sang, *Ruisseau* . . . , etc., and then, *Il est trop tard*.

She put an expression that seemed to me unmistakable into the
latter ballad; she had the passionate look that I've so rarely seen in
her and that so illy suits her character; her eyes staring straight ahead,
red and serious, her face pale, the movements of her head jerky. She
never took her eyes off me. There was one verse, the last I believe, that
almost made me lower my eyes, so unmistakable was the application:
it was absolutely my own position. A new stab of the dagger, because
I realized the necessity of going forward. We dined. A few minutes
after dinner, she said with visible agitation:

"My c[ousin], come and take a turn with me."

She usually says these things to me in a gay manner that covers
everything; there was less gaiety than usual, and especially a very pronounced movement of the head to urge me to come.

I went out by the window A, Mme. Dubignon took possession OF
HER MOTHER AND THE BOYS. They remained fifty paces behind us, which
didn't seem to me to be very natural. From A to B we were occupied
with nonsense which concealed a little mutual embarrassment: she
was surprised that I hadn't received any letters, asked me for news of
Fairisland, told me the name of a plant at *a*. From B to C, I attempted
to take heart a little; when we reached the poplar C, it seems to me
that I said to her:

"I'm certainly a silly fool, I'm not happy at Bècheville."

"Yes, it seems to me . . . , etc."

She talked to me, I believe, OF MY MATRIMONY WITH JENNY. I answered that it wasn't that that made me unhappy.

"You have only friendship for me, and I love you passionately."

I was upset as I pronounced these words; we held each other's arms all through the combat, at this moment I took her hand, which I squeezed; I even tried to kiss it. She replied that I ought not to think of such a thing, that I ought not to see anything more in her than a c[ousin] who was friendly toward me. I replied that I had loved her for eighteen months, that I had succeeded in concealing my love in Paris by not seeing her sometimes for eight or ten days when I felt I loved her too much . . . I told her, among other bright things:

"Yesterday, I was terribly unhappy."

"And why?"

"Because that affected me more than usual."

This is the only word in the entire conversation of which I am textually sure. It will be said that that's not worth the trouble, but I remember it precisely because it was remarkable for something else. It seems to me that Biran is right: he says we don't remember sensations that are nothing but acute and pure pleasure, or pain of the same kind.

She questioned me at length without looking at me (she was protected by her straw hat) on the marriage. I remember that, among other things, she said:

"A person gets married through ambition or love; do you believe you'll be happy with that young lady? Do you know her? etc."

I replied that I wasn't marrying through ambition, even less through love, since she herself was the only one I loved. She told me that she was an old woman who shouldn't be thinking about such things any longer . . . Her agitation increased because she was apparently speaking from her heart. She said:

"Young men say those things to women so they can boast of them and tell about them among themselves."

I even believe she added:

"She who believed (these things) would be unhappy indeed! . . . You'll go and repeat what you're saying to me."

I answered that with the indignation of an honorable man:

"What kind of an opinion do you have of me? etc., etc."

In her reply she said:

"Until now, I've kept myself intact." (That isn't the word she used but an equivalent.) This idea returned twice in a very conspicuous way.

If, in the vegetable garden, near G, I'd had the courage to follow up two or three slightly affectionate arguments, maybe I'd have heard her say that she loved me. She was terribly upset, and I was too. We arrived at the iron gate F, it was closed, we called a gardener, and went some twoscore paces to rejoin HER MOTHER AND Mme. Dubignon, who had been following us at a decent distance all the time. She let go of my arm, and took theirs; we went as far as the swans. The path wasn't wide enough for me to walk beside the three ladies, which prevented me from looking at her as much as I would have liked to, but I saw, while playing with the children, that she leaned against the other two ladies as though she were weak, that she was very pale, had red eyes, looked as though she had been crying, and amid all that there seemed to be something or other of the tender emotion of happiness. She didn't look at me and didn't say a word to me all the time the stroll lasted. Upon our return, she left us a moment, and came back looking as though she had shed some tears of happiness for a minute or two.

In the wood, I was happy with love, but the cessation of remorse didn't give me the immense pleasure I anticipated, in comparison with the mental suffering it caused me.

During the walk, Mme. Dubignon looked at me with a little smile of satisfaction, which led me to believe more and more that she was in on the secret. She let me take her out in a boat, I believe, in order to observe more closely my ridiculousness or my love. A man in this position is always a touching sight for a woman. Upon entering my little room in the evening, however, I experienced a feeling of joy to be free from remorse, but, as I said, the lamp had made my eyes and head ache.

The next day, Saturday, June 1, she neither looked at me nor spoke to me; she hesitated at the table as she said, "My cousin, will you have some of this?" As she had placed me at her side the first day, she was a little embarrassed to know where to turn her eyes. My momentary disgrace and her slightly passionate look seemed to me to be visible to the others; and if Mme. Dubignon isn't a voluntary confidante, she's undoubtedly an involuntary one. I think it's the same with Mlle. Camelin and Mme. Deschênes.

Saturday evening, we went to a charming wood. I was ten or twelve paces ahead with her, she kept me from speaking of my love by talking to me about herself with great volubility. However, I said to her:

"It seems as though you hated me since yesterday. You don't even look at me."

She replied:

"I believe so, but I look at you as usual."

As a matter of fact, from this moment she looked at me and talked to me as usual.

Sunday, she had the look of happy love; she had slept well, you could see happiness CONSCIOUS OF HER HAPPINESS on her slightly pallid face; she had a few attentions of love for me, especially as she gave me two little bouquets of balm. The time to leave was drawing near.

Mme. Nardot, who displayed perfect gaiety and kindness, had told me the previous evening that they had planned to urge me and Mme. Dubignon to stay until today, Monday, at eleven o'clock in order that we might all leave together. But I considered that Mme. Palfy didn't press me sufficiently. Moreover, I wasn't displeased to have her see Palfy without me. I rather hope that she found the evening long, and that this morning was less gay than usual.

When the time came to leave, I had a human failing: I keenly desired to stay, Mme. Dubignon did too, but didn't want to force me. Perhaps she was counting on my love to make me stay. Things were at this point when, at half-past six, they came in to say, "The horses are hitched to the calash." I said laughingly, "Well, that's that." I arranged everything. I had need of laughing, for I felt a violent desire to weep.

We got in, I waited for some time in front of the door, it seemed to me that I saw tears in her eyes, I kissed her tenderly. This kiss re-called that OF Wien.[1]

We started out briskly with Alexandre, who galloped to open the gates for us. The bilious Mme. Dubignon never got on my nerves so much; she set about talking ambition with me, the positions held by M. Z, his character. I was in a soft mood, those beautiful and very green woods were in harmony with my soul. I'd have gladly chucked her out the window as we were crossing the Saint-Denis plain. We arrived at a quarter past eleven, having left at twenty to seven. We stopped three quarters of an hour at Saint-Germain, and left there at nine o'clock. It was a quarter past eleven when I awoke Angéline.

Since my arrival, Paris has been ghastly boredom for me. I think I'm going to dine with her Wednesday.

June 5.—It seems to me that you become awkward if you think too much about proper behavior when you're about to enter a salon; you may reflect on it, if necessary, a long time in advance, but when the dance begins you should do what you please—think about it if your heart so desires; if not, read or start talking.

I wasn't exactly what you might call awkward yesterday. My entry into the salon might serve to give me an idea of that of a minister; everyone showed eagerness to speak to me, I didn't have time to listen to each person's politenesses, I smiled at everyone. The single person who interested me was the one to whom I spoke the least.

Dinner was announced as soon as I arrived, a quarter past five. Mme.

[1]See entry of November 20, 1809.

de Palfy was pretty and had very high colors. Was it the heat? Was it the presence OF HER LOVER?

I almost expected to be obliged to advise her to be careful. It so happened that her behavior was perfect, and that I was the one who sinned against this virtue.

My first mistake was as we left for a walk after dinner; she was gesticulating with her right arm while talking TO MISS Ka. [Mlle. de Camelin]. I passed my arm about hers, which was in the air. It was gay, it was good form, but it might have suggested too much familiarity, and it was very clumsy to anticipate the desire.

During the walk, I happened to say *we* once or twice. This misplaced *we* compromised her and me.

She didn't respond to my hand squeezes. We were forty paces ahead of the others during the walk, but Pulchérie [Le Brun] was with us, so this separation was only slightly imprudent and not at all advantageous. Instead of going at ten o'clock, I only left her at a quarter to twelve. HIS MOTHER kept us waiting and bored us beyond endurance; she's almost completely in her dotage, her soul is displayed in its nakedness, and what a petty soul it is! Not vile, but respectable, unfeeling, timorous and devoid of all generosity, AS THE SOUL OF Pacé in this last respect.[1]

June 6.—Dinner at the bilious lady's home (Saint-Gratien).

I got there at half-past five, at the same time as Mme. Palfy. I gave her my hand without uttering a word. We went in; instead of staying with her, I looked out the window. The husband being nothing more than a *Kafir,* the character of the mistress of the house was communicated to everyone. The dinner was excellent and too voluminous, and the company extremely dismal. I was the same.

Only, about nine o'clock, and as Mme. de Palfy got up to return (to Paris), I took her hand, which I squeezed several times. She didn't withdraw it; I even had the impression that she responded slightly. She was cool, gay, indifferent during the first hours; it seemed to me that her indifference vanished a bit when the time came to separate.

Did I behave well or badly? I've no idea. At least, I was perfectly natural. Will that proud coolness, opposed to her coolness, determine her to take a few steps or to abandon all? I'd forgotten her letters, she said with considerable bitterness:

"You think of me only when you see me."

I made some witless reply. I cursed a bit upon leaving her.

[1]How could anyone be so asinine? At bottom, reading this makes me impatient: to be so near happiness and not to obtain it! Poor woman, I feel sorry for her! April 29, 1819. [Note added by Beyle.]

June 7.—I haven't seen anybody. I worked for six hours at my office. I sent off her letters to her, together with this one:

"I don't know, madame, whether the two letters herewith enclosed say what they ought to say: this one will be more fortunate if you deign to see in it the expression of my respectful devotion.

"De B."

It seems to me that this letter is a little ill-natured.

June 10.—I arrived at Saint-Gratien[1] at half-past seven. They were at dinner. I waited, I saw *Maximus* [Napoleon] quite clearly. Her greeting when she saw me only briefly had the same eager and heedless appearance as before the battle. Her manner with me during our walk in the lovely solitary paths of the reserved park at Saint-Cloud was entirely new: a thoughtful and natural little look; the look, I might add, of a person who is enjoying his happiness. No attack on my part, outside some slight squeezes of the arm, to which she didn't respond. We composed some rebuses, I thought I saw her become more tender as the time to separate neared.

She said to the bilious lady, "We made up some rebuses with Palfy after you *were pleased* to leave us." As she pronounced the underlined words, she regarded me with a look that I didn't understand at first, but a minute later it appeared remarkable to me.

"Read this rebus in a low voice."

I whispered in her ear:

"I love you."

She resumed after a minute of silence:

"There's no 'I love you,' but 'I love.' "

I squeezed a bare arm above the elbow, she didn't withdraw her arm from the armchair on which it was leaning. To finish up the account of these microscopic adventures, I made up a rebus which said with pleasant and insincere asininity: "The earth is round and large, but I love only the spot that you're in."

June 11.—I DINE WITH HER.

I heard three or four persons say how do you do, and forty newcomers reply that their health was good. In all these compliments, not a single one stood out by its wit. An evening couldn't have been more inane. Love made me persevere until a quarter past eleven.

There was a difference between Maria AND HER HUSBAND. It was over a carriage arrangement, a bit of nonsense. Why on earth does that intelligent man cut the roots of his wife's affection because of things so stupid?

There was a noticeable tête-à-tête AT A WINDOW WITH F[lorian]. He

[1]Here, as in the entry of June 6, Saint-Gratien means Saint-Cloud.

doesn't cultivate her, and frequently lets twenty-five days go by without seeing her. Has he been her lover and does this coolness give him a new charm in LADY MARIA's eyes? Does she want to cloak her attachment for me, or does she want to whip up my blood? It's certain that she succeeded in the latter, not through her confidences to Florian, but through her coolness to me.

The morning [of June 14], as I got up, I was utterly transported by the thought of going to Montlignon [Saint-Cloud] and of seeing her. I reached there tired out and more in the mood to enjoy the pleasant languor of happy love than to act with firmness in order to procure some happiness from this love. I had a moment of marked bashfulness upon going into her salon, where she was. She only looked at me rarely and in moments when the most exacting prudence could not disapprove of these looks.

Yesterday, we returned at a quarter to nine. She got dressed, I went near the door to squeeze her hand a moment. The first part of this maneuver could be noticed. I squeezed her hand without reciprocity. She left for PAULINA's HOUSE at nine o'clock. I gave her my hand to help her down, which perhaps wasn't the height of prudence, it was clear that this gave me the only tête-à-tête that could have taken place during the day.

But alas, how did I employ it! I tried to take her hand, which she withdrew, I didn't have the *courage* to say an amiable phrase to her which she would have been sure to comment on during the tedious ride of three quarters of an hour. As she withdrew her hand, I said spiritedly, "What! Not even that?" As she didn't answer, I put her into her carriage silently.

June 16.—I clearly saw His Majesty pass on his return to the Tuileries from the Legislative Corps, on the Pont de la Révolution.

In the evening, MY LOVE tormented me and gave me a dull displeasure. I'm thinking of softening myself and reading some novels.

June 17.—This remedy succeeded. I wore out my sorrow at not having talked to her yesterday by paying eight visits. I then read *Mémoires d'un Homme de Qualité*. The style is a little too periodic, but there is genuine nobleness in this work, far above most novels. There are even some descriptions of manners and morals.

I said to myself this morning, "Lack of nobleness is not yet a source of success, quite the contrary—and it is a source of grief." I concluded from this that I ought not to go to Neuilly and that, as I'm going to Fontainebleau tomorrow, my absence will be a conspicuous one with the best effect. I found, however, that I would be sad during the voyage if I didn't see her. I went to Neuilly, she wasn't there. I went to Saint-Cloud, and, leaving Paris at half-past six, returned at half-past eight. I saw *George Dandin*. I think that perhaps I had more pleasure at her not being home than I would if I had found her. I don't have to reproach myself for BASHFULNESS. THE LITTLE K. [Mlle. Camelin] HAS RECEIVED ME WITH THE TENDER RESPECT THAT A WOMAN HAS FOR THE LOVER OF A SUPERIOR ONE.

It seems to me that all this whips up the blood; it's possible that I'll become really amorous. I think that success will be followed by at least a year of pleasure, since it took THE WANT OF IDEAS OF ANGELINA [Bereyter] AND HUNDRED and twenty NIGHTS EVER TOGETHER FOR EXPELLING LOVE. I was really satisfied with myself tonight as I drove back in my handsome cabriolet, AND THINKING TO MY SUCCESS IN THE HEART OF THE LITTLE K.

June 24, 1811.—. . . How many times have I thought of you in all the climes to which fortune has led me! Within the walls of Amasia, as beneath the tents of the Sudan, I dreamt of those enchanting eyes in whose smile my happiness dwells. I never look on you without being agitated for long after; when I at length recover my wits and venture to regard you, I see naught but that amiable politeness which wins you every heart and has made you celebrated in the Orient. It makes me ceaselessly repent my love. I repeat to myself that one must be lightheaded indeed to allow one's happiness to depend on the love of a woman who has no time to love and who moreover makes no distinction between me and all the others with whom she comes in contact. Often, full of self-disgust and humiliation, I return to Constantinople firmly resolved to flee you and to seek pleasure where I found it of yore. I bitterly reproach myself for being clumsy and ridiculous when I am with you. It seems to me that my spirit of enterprise makes your women friends laugh. I seek consolation in behaving less badly in the presence of other women, but I find a glacial chill in their presence, their love is valueless to me. My happiness lies in being loved by you; even without that, being loved by you would flatter my self-esteem in the most exquisite manner. You told me that you'd never been in love; since that moment, it has seemed to me that there is no glory in hearing it said that one is loved by lips that are used to saying it.

I realize all the difficulty of my enterprise, and I dare believe that, whatever bashfulness I may display, in spite of myself, in my love, you attribute enough steadfastness to me to go through with something in which all my happiness lies. I am aware that a word, an indiscreet glance, will lead me, as well as you, to certain death. I do not reproach you your idle amiability in public, I seek to imitate your indifference, and if Bostargi Bacha has my conduct spied upon, he will believe that I am occupied with something quite other than his favorite slave.

But are there not a thousand signals which are meaningless to all eyes except those of a faithful lover? I have won over by means of money the slave who will take this note to you. He says he will find the means of placing it in your hand without being seen, but he trembles with fear lest you let it slip. Deign to bear in mind that we are surrounded by dangers of all sorts, that all the eyes in the seraglio are turned toward you, that you should perhaps accord some indulgence to a rashness that would not be permitted were there any other way of conversing with you. I am assured of this slave's adroitness; but what would become of him should you let slip one of the letters which he will transmit to you? It is not merely indifference to its contents that you will be evincing, it is his head and your own that you will be placing beneath the sultan's sword. If there were ever to be the least misunderstanding, if ever you were to fear something from me, bear in mind that, before all else, I am prudent, I am convinced that, without the coldest presence of mind, I am lost, in fine I only quiver when the eyes I worship are cast on me.

It is possible that this note may pass before profane eyes, but first of all it is written in Arabic, and furthermore in it I have concealed all details that might make you suspected by the slaves of the seraglio. A thousand means are offered for the reply, the best one of all is the simplest. If a little pity for the torments I have been submitted to for so long does not give you the courage to employ it, drop this letter in the first rosebush in the direction of the sea as one leaves the harem, and, in order to indicate that it did not fall there by chance, sprinkle a few drops of ink on it at the moment of confiding it to the rosebush.

At any other time, I should not ask a reply to a first letter, but suffer me to repeat that we are in an extraordinary situation; are we to add obstacles coming from a few delicacies of self-esteem to the thousand obstacles that already separate us? I shall only begin to live again when I get this note back.

Ought I to speak to you of constancy, tenderness, eternal devotion? It seems to me that I would have no difficulty in speaking of them to another; but with you, Fatima, I know not how to lead up to the expression of the sentiments my heart has so long felt for you. I am unhappy indeed that you do not believe in them, but I venture to speak to your own heart; it may not share my sentiments, but I venture to think it believes in them and has seen their expression a hundred times.

I've toned down the outlines of this letter, there is more pride than love in it, I've put in it a little of that love I have for her when the perpetual plans I make to please her leave me some peace of mind.[1]

[1]This man ought to have been thrown out the window. 1819. [Note added by Beyle.]

June 25.—I don't know what it was that turned me against her. I didn't think she loved me, and my pride was wounded to pay my court all by myself. I've got a sure refuge, it's gaiety; when I take this road, I'm natural, my successes liven me up, and it seems to me that I ought to be pleasing to her. When I'm serious, I'm afraid of falling into the role of Orestes, that makes me awkward and gloomy.

The 24th she received me for five minutes with marked embarrassment. The reason was that we were almost alone, and a tête-à-tête frightens her more than it does me. That's quite natural.

The previous Tuesday at Saint-Gratien she greeted me with tenderness after an absence of seven days on my part, asking me at the end of my visit why I hadn't come the previous Tuesday.

Yesterday, the 25th, I had a mind not to go there. Mme. Bilious, to whom I said as much, cried, *"What childishness!"*

The word gave me some courage, I went. I was trembling as I went in. It was an official meal. She had the idle gaiety that is fitting at such a dinner.

I was dissatisfied and awkward during the first half hour. I finally recaptured my assurance, spoke judiciously and in a manner such as to be listened to with pleasure. During the dinner, I was dignified and distant with . . . , who was beside me. I had found coolness in her manners with me. She finally spoke to me, I replied. During the walk, that big ass of an L. gave her his arm, that consoled me and my gaiety finally took the upper hand. She came near me two or three times. Once while she was calling me I looked at the clock, which said eight. I don't know if she thought I was going to slip away, but from that moment the *official tone,* at which I noticed that I had the simplicity to be angered, appeared no longer. Maybe she put it aside out of sheer lassitude.

July 5.—Today, I went to Saint-Gratien AT HER MOTHER with the courage given by a little indifference and a few glasses of punch. I was gay and frivolous. I was well dressed (in striped trousers). She noticed that I was well dressed. That must have had an effect, since the majority of young men she sees dress badly purposely in the hope of being Prefects sooner.

At last, getting down from the step and enjoying perfect solitude, she began talking to me *ab hoc et ab hac,* fearing, I believe, the tête-à-tête as much as I. She had spoken to me two or three times about my book, I spoke to her about it in my turn:

"You've read the first chapter of my novel, I'll wager that you haven't read what's on the cover of the first volume?"

"What! What's there? Is there something out of the ordinary? I promise you that I'll read it when I go in, etc."

She evinced her astonishment with so much naturalness and so loudly that I feared THAT HER CHAMBERMAID, WHO WAS BY US, would hear her, which prevented me from adding, "What's on this cover interests me because it's by me."

I went up again, and I heard her calling from inside the carriage, "I hope you will come to see me one of these days."

Since her drive will be at night and alone with HER CHAMBERMAID, since I made a good impression tonight, since I rose above the rest of the company like a cedar of Lebanon, since she thinks I've gone to the country every day recently, it seems to me that tonight should add to the presumable impression I must have made UPON HER HEART.

SHE HAS REPEATED TO ME THAT HER HUSBAND HAS READ YESTERDAY THE LETTER WHICH I HAVE WRITTEN TO HER. "HE READS ALL MY LETTERS," SHE WAS SAYING TO ME, "I BELIEVE BY FEAR OF ANY compromising action AND NOT BY JEALOUSY."

My alleged tenderness results in my no longer being interested in any book.

July 6.—At five o'clock, I looked over the dismal town of Meudon. Seen from there, the Seine is ugly, Paris is ugly, the little flower bed beneath your eyes is execrable, the wood opposite is dreary, the road on the horizon to the right is unsightly without being rustic. Everything reminded me of the fat lord, the son of Louis XIV. The cage was quite worthy of the bird.

From there to M. D.'s house at Saint-Cloud. Walked with the poets.

From there I drove my horse at a gallop to Mme. de Palfy's.

I arrived there confident that she had read my book; she greeted me with the keen pleasure in her eyes and face that she showed for me at the end of 1810. She told me when I arrived, "Mlle. K. and I looked for something out of the ordinary in your book yesterday as soon as I got back; all we found was a page of verse in English."

Has she read it? Hasn't she read it? What would tend to indicate that she hasn't is the fact that she shared the secret with Mlle. . . . [de Camelin]. A lively and unmistakable pleasure to be with me. She spoke to me about my book in the middle *del passeggio* [of the walk]: "I don't like your book; it puts things too crudely." She already told me that yesterday.

I said to her during a moment when I was able to talk to her without being overheard, "I'm not going to tell you my secrets any more because you confide them to Mlle. . . . [de Camelin]."

I ought to have said, "Read what's printed on the inside of the cover of the first volume."

I'll say that to her tomorrow. I'll take along a copy of my work that I've just had bound, and I'll say to her, "If you'll promise me that you won't speak of it to anybody, I'll give you a copy of my works. But don't say anything about them before you have read them."

It would be better to make her understand the affair of the cover than to give her the printed work. The latter is bolder, it's a letter, but the ingenious part disappears.

At Saint-Cloud, a slight *disappointment* of ambition. The quarterly decree of the Council of State was signed; no one was put in ordinary service; a few Auditors, on the other hand, were put in extraordinary service. Here I am put off for three months. If I'd paid more court to the clerks, it might have passed; still, it's three months less of slavery.

July 7.—My faith, I didn't say anything to her. Not because of bashfulness, but because she appeared too distant with me. I don't say that it's the case in public: entering her house, I found her alone. She showed me a book she had in her hand, saying:

"This book is very nice."

"I'm sorry it isn't mine, I'll show you where my verse is, but on condition that you don't tell Mlle. K. about it."

During these words, she assumed a rather distant look, and went out on her terrace.

I confess that my pride kept me from persisting. I was gay with everyone, and slightly distant and respectful with her. Perhaps she's quite pleased at being loved, but doesn't want to run the risk of the peril. She said to me yesterday, "I've been told that you're going to get married." The idea came back in the conversation twice.

MEMOIRS OF MY LIFE DURING MY AMOUR FOR GRÄFFIN PALFY
FROM THE 18TH JULY 1811 TILL THE . . .[1]

July 18.—I arrived at an appropriate time, she was taking an after-dinner walk WITH HER CHILDREN AND Mme. Fanny beneath the fine trees of . . . She appeared to be very pleasantly surprised to see me again.

Leaving Mme. Fanny, she said to me shortly after:

"Give me your arm, I need a strong arm."

What a wonderful opportunity! But I had to retain my composure. She launched out on some badinage full of mimicry, and loud laughter, as when she's embarrassed. From time to time, however, she turned toward me and looked at me with eyes of love—and of happy love.

Heedless of her unrestrained badinage, I replied with forced laughter and a few words. Fanny was tactful enough to leave us twenty paces

[1] This is another title written by Beyle in English.

behind for a moment. Marie's pleasantries came more quickly, and soon she called HER ELDEST DAUGHTER Charlotte. I ought to have taken advantage of her joy at seeing me again to say to her, "What a pleasure it is to see you again!"—at any rate, the first simple words UPON MY LOVE. I didn't have the courage to interrupt the badinage.

Her whole manner spoke of love.

I was severely punished for not having the agility to attack; upon going in, we found some bores, who kept on arriving until eleven o'clock.

It's obvious that Machiavelli B. wouldn't have behaved as I did yesterday with Marie. But would he have had the pleasure that I was given by her glances and slightest actions? For characters of that kind, women are soon what the little Angel [Angéline] is for me at present. Consequently, I shouldn't envy them.

But that doesn't alter the fact that I ought to take action; I promise myself to speak of my love, well or badly, no matter how, tonight.

Tuesday, July.—This evening was ushered in BY A LETTER VERY AMIABLE (received from Saint-Gratien), in which there was neither a Monsieur nor a MY DEAR COUSIN—which shows at last that the absence caused by the trip to Mortefontaine was noticed.

THE COUNTESS PALFY SAID TO ME THAT AT MY MARRIAGE SHE SHOULD GIVE TO MY WIFE A COLLAR [necklace] LIKE THAT OF THE bilious lady.—"But is that becoming to brunettes?" "What naïveté!" SAID THE bilious lady.

I planned when I was leaving to say TO MY FAIR *what I was thinking at the moment,* but Corbeau left us only four or five seconds, which I employed IN SAYING, in regard to the cold, "The cold is in your heart, etc." This word wasn't bad, I squeezed her arm.

August 10.—DURING MY SILENCE ALL THE OCCASIONS [opportunities] had the same outcome. It was impossible to say four words to her without being overheard BY HER COURTIERS, and, when there was a possibility, bashfulness—resulting from *good breeding*—kept me from taking time by the scruff of the neck. I HAVE PROVED BY AN EVIDENT EXPERIENCE THE TRUTH OF MY PRINCIPLES ABOUT THE ART OF ROUSING LOVE IN THE HEART OF A WOMAN. THE 4TH AUGUST, I WAS READING THE EXCELLENT ESSAY OF HUME UPON THE FEODAL GOVERNMENT FROM TWO TILL HALF PAST $4\frac{1}{2}$; DURING THIS TIME, SHE WANTED MY PRESENCE; on the return, SHE CANNOT SAY A WORD WITHOUT SPEAKING OF ME OR TO ME. I made the mistake of not showing some enterprise. But, I repeat, I've got too much sensibility ever to be talented in the art of Lovelace.

During one of my trips (to Raincy), I found THE LITTLE π [Pulchérie Le Brun, niece of Pierre Daru]. I talked to her for want of something better to do. She hasn't much in the way of breasts and wit, TWO GREAT WANTS! Likewise for want of something better to do, I took a few liberties, there wasn't any resistance. So yesterday, not knowing what to do with myself, I got in my cabriolet and showed up at Villemomble. There were a lot of people there; I went out on the terrace, the little girl followed me, I took her arm and put mine around her a bit; later, in the salon, her knees and thighs. Her eyes thanked me by their look of love, outside that it was innocence itself. But, on the terrace, I became conscious of a great truth. Novelty is a great source of pleasure, you must give yourself up to it. I was sure of sleeping in the evening with the pretty Angéline, but I can only do anything with her now by making an effort, and by thinking of another woman. On the other hand, π, who is inferior in every respect, put me in a superb state.

But hasn't her mother noticed something? She didn't greet me as warmly as usual yesterday, but that may have been the result of fatigue.

As for myself, who am the sworn enemy of fatigue, I haven't been keeping up this diary because of the distaste for the physical action of writing. If I had a confidential secretary, I'd dictate four or five pages about myself every day, without any vanity.

Nosce te ipsum.—I believe, with Tracy and Greece, that therein lies the road to happiness. My means is this diary.

Faure's principles are becoming so different from my own, he's so *offensable,* that I can't ever talk to him with an open heart. He depresses me when I see him. He's still wildly in love, and here wildness is not the synonym of gaiety—quite the contrary, and very much the contrary. I am thus deprived of advice, a very useful thing: if I've begun a siege, it's because of a council of war held on the . . . with *Sagace* [Crozet].

I'd like to have Sagace here, he's the best adviser I could find; but nothing proves that he wouldn't have the weakness to be jealous of my apparent happiness.

You can't appear straight in a curved mirror. A great principle. For the Machiavellis and others of the same caliber, I'll always be open to slander. The means of avoiding annoyances which would deeply wound my pride and make me commit some asininity? I must remain unknown.

I've just read attentively the first two volumes of Hume. I no longer have anything more than an extremely vague idea of Henry II, Edward the Confessor and Egbert.

I retain only that which *portrays the human heart.* Outside of that, I'm a zero.

For the moment, I'm fed up with Paris. One thing alone would give me keen pleasure—TO WORK AT *Letellier,* and I haven't got the right kind of leisure for that. You don't slip out of deep attention, or, if you prefer, necessary enthusiasm, as you do out of a shirt. Eight or ten days in a row are needed. You encounter difficulties, and you work badly the first two days, finally you make progress. At present, that's out of the question for me. I have only a few minutes, a few days at the most, and when that happens I take some coffee, shut myself in and *am bored* because I haven't the objective that absorbs me. That's what happened to me today. Everything that takes me away from the knowledge of the human heart is without interest for me.

Tragedy, not being in my nature, irritates me; comedy interests me as a source of instruction.

August 11.—I COME THERE WITH almost no love; *ritornando diesen Abend io mi trovo riamante. Io sono stato* VERY MERRY AND *altomente* worthy, I refused OF DINING Tuesday AT MOTHER'S [returning tonight, I found myself in love anew. I was gay and genuinely worthy, I refused to dine at her mother's]. SHE ASKED ME WHY I didn't go there Friday.

π and Fanny paid me all sorts of attention. AT THE WALK, I could have had a tête-à-tête of an hour if I'd wished, but I didn't know what to do with it. I squeezed her hand twice (Mme. de Palfy's), absolutely impossible to do more.

(From there to Saint-Cloud).

"Would it be indiscreet to take a leave of absence this autumn?"—"Not at all, not at all. You'll have to wait until M. Lecoulteux gets back, and make your arrangements with him." The whole thing in the best-natured tone.

August 18.—Mme. de Palfy employed several arguments to dissuade me from taking MY TOUR.

1. That I ought to ask P. for it a second time. As I put forward the opposite opinion, she insisted, saying, "You certainly have a few little obligations to him!" The advice she gave me was very reasonable, and I'll follow it. It may hold up my voyage until September 20, when MY comrade returns. It seems to me unlikely that he'll return UPON THAT TOUR KNOWN BY EVERY ONE.

2. Lady Palfy said to me with the tone of a fond reproach, "If you give up your voyage, you'll be able to come to the vintage at Palfy with us. π will be there."

After our ten or twelve very tiring days—more than tiring for the soul because of the series of asininities—SHE HAS SAID TO ME COMING-OUT, more or less this:

"What's the matter with you?"—"This voyage is like a dagger in my heart."—"It would be easy for you to remove the dagger, give up your trip."—"It's the fear of not being allowed to take it that grieves me."

That appeared to make her feel the sting. (She's an adorable woman.)

From there to Mme. C. de C. . .'s,[1] to whom I said more or less the following, "It's absolutely necessary for me to make this trip. I love you passionately; for your part, you have no desire to love me. Moreover, YOUR HUSBAND looks on me with disfavor. I noticed it Sunday. I can no longer see you as frequently as in the past, that would cause me extreme pain. Perhaps my absence will arrange everything, and on my return he'll see me willingly."

[1]This paragraph is probably another disguised reference to Mme. Daru, but, as M. Martineau suggests, Mme. C. de C. . . may possibly be the married daughter of Mme. Beugnot, Clémentine Curial, who was to become Stendhal's mistress a decade later.

Return to Paradise

"THE object of my voyage," Beyle had written in his diary, ". . . is solely to acquaint myself with mankind." Never had he hinted that he might have more sentimental motives, yet all through the past decade the memory of Angelina Pietragrua had remained too vivid for it to be supposed that she had been entirely absent from his desire to revisit Italy. Indeed, upon his arrival, almost overcome with emotion in Milan, he had thoughts for little else. After "eleven years, not of faithfulness, but of a sort of constancy," the moment had come to realize his childhood dream of returning in a handsome uniform, like a storybook hero, to woo and win the woman with whom he had fallen in love as a young sublieutenant.

As usual, his imagination had surpassed the reality. Even with his illusions, he could not but remark that there was a certain reserve in Angelina's greeting. But it does not seem to have occurred to him at the time that she might have been getting along quite well before his unannounced arrival, that, indeed, his presence might prove downright embarrassing to her. And was he naïf enough to suppose that all those gentlemen who called on her were just so many innocent friends?

At least one of them, a captain of the Venetian Guards and roué of note by the name of Widmann, was certainly her lover—and the chances are that he was by no means alone. Of the other habitués, two of the most assiduous were Turenne—or Turcotti—a refined but mistrustful man of forty with whom Angelina had mysterious business dealings and whose jealousy she was extremely careful not to arouse, and one Migliorini, negligent in dress, deficient in ideas, but boasting an amatory prowess of an enviable sort.

Welcome or not, Beyle returned daily to chatter away in his bad Italian to Signora Pietragrua and her "distinguished" friends. He had grown slightly bolder with the years, and before the week was out he gathered up enough courage to make a timid "declaration." Angela, who was no novice in such situations, helped him along. When he awkwardly tried to steal a kiss, she coyly admonished him, "Receive and never take." This banal maxim struck him as almost oracular. Did it not go to the heart of his great problem? In his previous love affairs, he had always been panicked by the terrifying necessity of making the first move. But the words of the Italian woman now suggested the perfect alibi for his lack of aggressiveness: with him, "the courage necessary for the execution killed the sentiment." Neither Mélanie nor Mme. Daru—nor, for that matter, any of his previous sweethearts—had been well enough versed in lovelore to occasion the element of spontaneity that would have been needed to banish his self-consciousness. The voluptuous Angela, on the contrary, relieved him of the initiative, and, as soon as he realized that his "executive power" was no longer required, his tenderness came flooding back. The tête-à-tête that had started so coldly became, thanks to her tactful guidance, a debauch of kisses, tears and sentimental memories.

He progressed more rapidly with Signora Pietragrua in one week than he had with the inexperienced Mme. Daru in two years; and yet, for all his good fortune, he was forced to admit that he was bored.

Strange as it may seem, the chief discordant note was nothing less than Milan. For a decade, he had dreamed of this city as a terrestrial paradise, but for him, as already noted, a city consisted for the most part of the people who lived in it, and up to the present he had manifested very little interest in the conventional pastime of sight-seeing. It is true that Milan, almost alone of the cities he had visited, possessed an atmospheric charm, a charm evoked by a synthesis of memories, associations, sympathies: he loved, for instance, to walk along the Corso di Porta Orientale at nightfall because of the delightful mixture of gay society and mountain scenery; he loved to linger over an iced coffee on a café terrace while the church bells chimed the *Ave Maria;* he loved to return to the Scala, where the sensuous Italian music again released his romantic reveries; he loved late at night to be half awakened by the distant sound of a serenade in the street . . . But such pleasures began only at twilight; before tasting them, there was a whole day to be lived through, and, knowing no one in Milan, he soon found that the hours between rendezvous with Angelina were very long indeed.

Beyle, who had firmly believed since childhood that happiness without work—or study—was impossible, accordingly tried to find the answer to his problem in a few distracted efforts to practice *Mocenigo,* the name of an illustrious Venetian family which, for reasons best known to himself, he borrowed to designate his peculiar emotional reactions, intellectual occupations, outlook on life—all, in short, that composed the intimate expression of his character. During this trip, *Mocenigo*—forerunner of

"Beylism"—consisted roughly of observing the natural beauties of Italy and the influence of its climate, and Italian character, sculpture, painting, architecture and music.

Observing the character of the inhabitants—the avowed object of his trip—was an occupation that blended very agreeably with his pleasures, and from his two Milanese "observatories," Angelina's circle and the loge of Signora Lamberti, he culled his first notes on this land which he was later to know so thoroughly.

"I realize every day that my heart is Italian . . . ," he wrote his sister. "The wild love of gaiety and music, the freest moral standards, the art of serenely enjoying life . . . , all that is the character of the Milanese."

It was only to be expected that such a favored people should have given birth to great artistic achievement, and to occupy the long waits between rendezvous, he began casting a distracted eye on what Milan offered in the way of art. The resultant judgments could hardly have been more inept, for he was unaccustomed to the contemplation of inanimate objects, and his mind was entirely taken up with Angelina.

The latter, having several times urged him, with tact but with insistence, to get out of town, allowed him to make her conquest a few hours before he finally left. His thoughts no longer concentrated on what he would say the next time he saw Angelina, he employed the single day of his stop-over in Bologna in a whirlwind visit of palaces, churches and museums in tow of a guide. This venture in dilettantism so whetted his appetite for the novel occupation that, arrived in Florence, he set about sight-seeing with the voracity of a Cook's tourist.

During the forty-eight hours he spent in the Tuscan city, he accomplished, as his diary shows, an incredible amount of sight-seeing for a youth who had always professed contempt for everything in a city that was not human. True, he missed more than he saw, and his hasty art studies only led him to speak at length of a relatively obscure trio of painters, without even mentioning such celebrated Florentines as Cimabue, Giotto, Fra Angelico, Gozzoli, Filippo Lippi, Botticelli, Andrea del Sarto, Ghirlandajo, etc. For all that, he apparently considered his two-day inspection to be an adequate foundation for the writing of his own history of Florentine painting, since he did not return to the city until many years after the book was published!

But Beyle was not the man to let himself be troubled by the need of documentation. He might have looked at few paintings, but the years spent in psychological study had taught him to see what he looked at, to analyze it, to reflect on its interrelation and to generalize on it—a practice in which he was aided by the timidity of his character, for, as he says himself, the timid man is led to observe where the bold man sees nothing. His brief visits to the museums of Milan, Bologna and Florence, added to what he had learned from an eloquent art professor at school, proved to be sufficient for him to formulate a personal doctrine to which he was to adhere to his dying day. His taste might not be better than that of others, he admitted with befitting humility, but it had the merit of being *his own,* and his judgments, even if unorthodox, were worthy of respect.

For him and for "the happy few" who thought as he did, artistic expression was a special matter, "something very close to our mistress's thighs." Let the pedants worry about aesthetics and technique: the happy few knew that art was not an external phenomenon. "A passionate man who submits himself to the effect of the fine arts finds everything in his heart." That was the secret. To *feel* art, one must have a passionate heart, a tender soul; one must be capable of bursting into tears at the sight of the beautiful. Needless to say, Beyle felt himself pre-eminently qualified. His only standards were "expression, imagination and naturalness," or, as he later put it, "the exact expression of the soul's movements."

Art that came up to this requirement satisfied the psychologist in him by its truthful interpretation of the human heart, the dreamer in him by its communication of true and noble sentiments. For him, the finest painting, like the finest music, produced a sensation analogous to that of being in love.

This is the fundamental message to "the happy few" that is buried beneath the borrowings and the façade of false erudition in his own *Histoire de la Peinture en Italie,* which was the outgrowth of this trip. Few are the readers today of this fantastic history of Italian painting: it is a shame, for, sandwiched in between other men's ideas, is one of the most complete and delicately expressed expositions of Stendhal's method of venturing forth on "the pursuit of happiness": it is an exhaustive manual of *Mocenigo* turned "Beylism."

A few months earlier, it will be remembered, Beyle had hoped to be sent to Rome with his cousin Martial Daru. The latter was now Intendant of Rome and was living in the Quirinal, which was being altered in anticipation of Napoleon's arrival. When Beyle reached the capital, Martial and his wife greeted him hospitably, insisting that he stay at the royal palace. But sight-seeing was presenting unexpected charms, and Beyle had no desire to devote his limited stay to receptions and official dinners. So he did no more than take advantage of his cousin's influence to make the acquaintance of the Empire nobility in Rome and, what he considered more important, to meet Canova.

In those days, Canova was one of the high priests of the artistic world. All Europe regarded him as a great genius, and a visit to his studio was as much a tourist's duty as an inspection of St. Peter's. In this respect at least, Beyle was only too willing to do the conventional thing: he agreed with his age concerning Canova—he even ranked him above Michelangelo!

Just a fortnight after kissing Angelina good-by, he arrived in Naples, where he found Léon Lambert, his friend of the Marseille days, who was now working in the tax office of the newly created Kingdom of Naples, and the Vicomte Louis de Barral, who, according to *Souvenirs d'Egotisme*, owed his presence in the southern city to a sum of money Beyle had lent him the year before to flee the gambling dens of Paris.

On his return trip, he again stopped over in Rome, this time staying with the Darus at the Quirinal. During a couple of days in the Adriatic town of Ancona, he visited Livia Bialowiska, an Italian woman he had met at Brunswick after the death of her husband, a Polish colonel.

Livia, like Martial, Barral and Lambert, turned out to be a disappointment, and it was with a feeling of relief that he set out for Milan and Angelina. She alone had lived up to his conception of her.

Happily, he reviewed his rapid trip through Italy. The inns had been dirty and his companions boring, but he had found what he had always been seeking—sensations. Sensations of love, of natural beauty, of art, sensations such as only his beloved Italy could give him. "If a person possesses a heart and a shirt," he had written Pauline from Ancona, "he should sell his shirt in order to see the country around Lake Maggiore, Santa Croce in Florence, the Vatican in Rome and Vesuvius in Naples."

A month to a day after leaving Milan, he was again joyously walking through the streets of that city. Occupied with her own affairs, Angelina had gone to pass a few days in the mountains past Varese. Accordingly, Beyle went forth once more, this time through that fertile region of northern Lombardy which for him always represented the most beautiful portion of the most beautiful land in the world. His adventures here, as told in the following pages, were unsatisfactory but melodramatic enough to have done credit to the inventiveness of a writer of old-fashioned romances. Once back in Milan, however, Angelina gave him no cause for complaint: she was not a severe mistress—all she demanded was an element of the dramatic and a moderate number of complications.

And this time he discovered the answer to the problem presented by his previous visit: what was there to do when he was not with his Angela? He dropped into a bookstore to find out if there existed a work that would give him a background for the appreciation of Italian painting, and he left with an armful of volumes, notably Lanzi's *Storia Pittorica della Italia*.

The effect of this set of books was immediate and far-reaching. He started to read it, at once had the "extravagant idea" of making an abridged translation and, two days later, drafted a letter to a publisher announcing the format, the length and the date of publication of his completed work.

The last days of his leave fled by quickly with a few hours of intensive study, a secret tête-à-tête, a lovers' promenade through the streets at twilight, a few hours at the Scala in the evening.

On November 13, he left Angelina and Milan, crossing the Alps to visit his sister Pauline and her husband on their farm near Grenoble. As he continued his voyage to Paris, his heart was overflowing. Italy, with its natural beauty, its art and its love, had given him profound sensations, had completed the complex "real education" started nine years earlier in the garret room of the Rue d'Angivilliers, had given a new direction to his life. His restlessness of the preceding summer had evaporated, and he returned to his apartment in the Rue Neuve-de-Luxembourg fully determined to substitute the fruitful occupations of *Mocenigo* for the empty existence of a courtier.

1811   Paris—Milan—Bologna—Florence—Rome—
Naples—Rome—Ancona—Milan

Voyage in Italy

M. DE LÉRY [Beyle himself], captain and aide-de-camp, gave me permission before leaving to take whatever I wished in his manuscripts. I've had a copy made of a passage on style and of his excursions in Italy. In the account of the latter, there are several portions that are manifestly only intelligible to him.

PREFACE[1]

Non sum qualis eram. Unfortunately, I'm far from being the man I was in 1811. Accordingly, I won't correct anything in my 1811 diaries. They would lose in resemblance to my sensation whatever they might gain in clarity and charm. Upon my return from Moscow, I didn't recapture the passions that formerly animated my life. On the contrary, I thought during the retreat from Russia that the fine sensations of October 24, 1812, of the eighteen-day campaign, etc., would provide new nourishment for my soul.

[1] In 1813, thinking of writing a travel book on Italy, Beyle added this preface and divided his 1811 diary into chapters. He dictated some fill-ins and a copy of some entries, but, as he went no further with the project in its original form, the chapter divisions are not included here.

Boredom overtook me at Königsberg, and increased at Danzig. The listlessness in which I'm sunk at present wouldn't be disagreeable if I had the memory of the happiness I was given by the tastes that filled my life before my voyage to Russia, a voyage that, however, had the advantage of making me see things THAT NO *Mocenigo* FROM Cervantes, I BELIEVE, HAS EVER SEEN.

August 25.—AT PARIS I HAVE NO TIME FOR WORKING TO *Letellier.* I HAVE HERE NOTHING, BUT MY PASSION FOR C. PALFY; 'TIS A MONTH THAT I RE- PROACHED TO MYSELF THE MONEY WHICH I SPENT WITHOUT PLEASURE OF MIND, INTO THESE WALLS. I had the idea of asking for a leave to go to see Naples and Rome. I made my request to M. Daru, who received it with perfect benevolence. THERE ARE SOME FACTS WHICH BELONG TO Palfy's HISTORY. I renewed my request about the 20th of this month; it had the same success DURING OUR sojourn AT Compiègne.

Yesterday, August 25, 1811, I reserved a seat in the diligence which goes to Milan in ten days for 168 francs. I have the second seat for the departure of August 29 at eight o'clock in the morning. I went to Ver- sailles in an hour and a quarter.

There I saw the waters begin to play. A huge crowd was in the amphitheater facing the fountains of the Dragon. When they were playing in all their brilliancy, Their Majesties drove around the basin in a calash. I saw this spectacle very clearly, and it gave me the sensa- tion of grandeur. Everyone crowded forward to see Their Majesties and shout, "Long live the Emperor." I closely saw His Majesty, who was bareheaded.

It was the first time in my life that I saw the fountains play at Ver- sailles.

THESE ARE SOME HAPPY TIMES.

August 29.—I left at a quarter past eight with 2,800 francs, plus 40 francs, and 2 portuguese of 83 francs. Angéline and Faure accompanied me to the diligence. Angéline worships me. Her tears on the Pont des Arts the day before yesterday. The tears moistened the planks.

The previous evening at seven o'clock I was at Montmorency, where I stayed until half-past one helping Marie do up her packages. Kissing her (*eravamo soli* [we were alone]), I said to her:

"I hope to be more reasonable when I return."

A moment later she went into the salon again and complained, as she gathered up some handkerchiefs, that she was forgetting everything. I gave her THE LETTER TO LADY Leschenault unfolded but not open so she could see the handwriting, and said:

"You're forgetting this."

"Blank paper! It's quite possible, there are so many papers in this house."

That was spoken as Mlle. Mars says in *Les Fausses Confidences,* "Some money has been brought? It's quite possible."

She appeared to be moved, and I didn't have the presence of mind to open the letter and show her the side that was written on; certainly, in the state she was, she wouldn't have been able to resist the temptation to read it.

In the evening M. Debreuil [Faure] made a scene. I went to see Mme. de B. [Bézieux], at whose home I hadn't put in an appearance for two months. My visit didn't seem to put him out in the least. I spoke little in order not to shock him by being more amiable. He scarcely spoke except to Amélie, and said some things that were far too serious.

I was asked whether I was glad to be leaving Paris; I answered with gay gestures that I would be if I were sure of getting a daily letter to *the person in whose hands alone my destiny lies,* and of receiving one from that person. One of my motives for saying that was that I was thinking it. On the way out, Faure told me I'd done very badly to speak of the letters after what he'd told me. I didn't understand him at first, afterward I gently told him that he was going crazy. He answered energetically "that for a year he'd been weak, that I held him in contempt but that he'd get over it . . . , that he'd talked too much again, that he always talked too much but that he'd correct himself."

From which I concluded that it's to be feared he'll become insane as the result of a somber pride, wounded and turning everything into gloom. I reflected all evening long on this strange character. I went to see Mme. X., THE MOTHER, where I stayed too long in order that she'd be inclined to overlook the rareness of my previous visits.

I came back home, I reread an enormous signature. Angéline didn't come; Faure had told me he wasn't planning to come. She arrived at half-past twelve. I worked till a quarter to three.

August 29.—I was afraid of having as traveling companions some French military men covered with decorations rejoining their corps in Italy, stupid, insolent, swaggering and loudmouthed, in which case I'd have been obliged to joke with them. Luckily, I was spared this breed.

I found a gracious-mannered man whose face, it seemed to me, I'd seen before. He was an epicure and, like myself, in quest of happiness before all else. He was entirely natural, thirty-six years old, rather stout, but with perfect graciousness; in this respect, he was truly rare; making himself at home, moreover, and lifting the covers of the pots on the stove to see what we were going to have for dinner.

I took this man for a bourgeois of Milan, and the thought uppermost in my mind was the tremendous difference between a bourgeois of Milan and one of France. I wouldn't be doing an injustice to the former by taking as their representative M. Terasse, whose manners were almost elegant.

Tonnerre, August 31, half-past nine.—The second traveling companion is witless; he's here, lying beside the chest of drawers on which I'm scribbling.

He [Signor Scotti] is a native of Genoa; he left his native land six years ago; he was an ensign in the Navy of Naples. He was captured by the English, was a prisoner for four years, and escaped last August 14 by shaving off his beard; he's absolutely the picture of disappointment, with no vivacity. He looks like the engraving in the front of *Les Misères de la Vie Humaine* (a book translated by one H. Berton). He hasn't any wit at all, otherwise he might have some strange things to tell. But what's the good of putting a bottle adrift in the seas and rivers if its neck is plugged with a filter which keeps everything interesting from entering it?

We had a little woman who sells cotton, who blushingly essayed a few incorrect phrases on sentiment the first day; the second, she flattered herself, and last night, which we passed in the diligence, it seemed to me I heard "that's enough, that's enough," a couple of times, addressed to M. Scotti, her neighbor.

Besides her, we had a wealthy little bourgeois woman, bringing up her son well enough, but vulgar, greedy and huge.

In order not to sleep and to see the countryside, which was almost constantly level, I made two or three relays in the cabriolet, which, if it weren't for the night, would be the best place. The countryside appeared to me to be entirely level as far as Joigny. The bridge and the quays give a rather distinguished appearance to this burg.

We dined at Saint-Florentin, where we found some tavern girls who were almost shy. The girls were afraid we'd make fun of them. I saw some Spanish prisoners who were quite young. One of them spoke French and had the scabies. I gave them some money.

Between Saint-Florentin and Tonnerre the countryside became less level. The vineyards were in good shape, but the hillsides were barren and stony.

I nearly made two bad blunders: the first, yesterday at dinner, was to answer jokingly, saying yes to the driver, who asked Signor Scotti if he had escaped from the prisons of England. I'd have been doubly indiscreet, for, to my great astonishment, Signor Scotti denied that he had escaped and said—but you could see by his eyes that he was lying—that he had been exchanged. It appears that he's so honest that he's ashamed to admit he didn't keep his word.

The second blunder was that, while speaking to my companion from Milan of the pretty women who graced that city ten years ago, I named

Signora Gherardi. At the same time that I was deploring the death of such a beautiful woman, I nearly joked about her liaison with M. Petiet. When I asked for news of the Lechis OF Brescia, my companion smiled with mildness and a little melancholy, and said, speaking of the general, "He's my brother."

This encounter was all the more fortunate since I have always been in love with the eyes of this family. In Milan, I was enthusiastic about their faces. This one, whom I didn't ply with questions, was probably one of those young battalion chiefs whose manners were so gracious.

That name somewhat invalidated my comparison of M. Terasse, a typical French bourgeois, with one of Milan.

But Conte Lechi thoroughly realizes that naturalness is one of the qualities of his country. Tonight, we went to bathe in a little rustic bath, also full of naturalness, beyond a miserable prairie which lies below Tonnerre. On the way back, Signor Lechi spoke to me of the Conte di Castelbarco, who squandered twenty millions, ruined himself and no longer has more than 150,000 francs income. He told me that the persons who straightened out his affairs and paid the huge mass of debts made a fortune out of the business.

"He was a *great lord*," I said.—"Oh, not in the least! He always acted in the Milanese manner. Our kind doesn't assume such a manner." That was said superbly.

My Lechi is mildly voluptuous, always gracious in manner, even with a vulgar tradesman's assistant with whom we've just supped; but nothing of the French graciousness, in which is invariably to be seen the joy of well playing a brilliant role—if not even the pride in playing it. In his case, it's *gracious* grace, pure and simple. This man might equally well be a king or a well-to-do bourgeois.

I'm too bilious ever to have that graciousness of manner. I have a goal, toward which I'm proceeding steadfastly. Consequently, I'm lacking in that soft indolence which makes one confess, as he confessed yesterday, that one loves indolence more than all else. But I must remember this perfect model.

Sensibility is another symptom of the decided difference between such a man and M. Terasse. The latter, during our pleasant little bath this evening, extolled the rustic life, and outlined a little theory of happiness for me that was charming. Except for passion, with which I believe I'm animated, this theory seemed to be composed by me and for me.

Tonnerre lies against a hillside exposed on the north. The countryside has nothing remarkable about it.

But it seems to me that the inhabitants of a small town in France, built against the side of a hill, must be less petty and asinine than those of the same small town situated on a plain, and that a small town which is also a seaport, like Le Havre, is better than both. The sea imprints at least a dozen majestic ideas on the bourgeois: the immensity of the sea,—its dangers, voyages,—to see the landing of people coming from Canton,—the courage of people who brave the storm, of those who save vessels in danger,—the arrival of enemies, etc.

The object of my voyage, as may be seen, is solely to get acquainted with mankind; but I was wrong not to write last night.

Conte Lechi told me that ambition is in a state of ebullition in every city of Italy, and parties are formed to obtain the posts of Podestà (Mayor) and the other municipal offices; that when these people aren't given what they believe is their due, they are quite capable of avenging themselves. It would be necessary to observe that myself. The brevity of my trip won't give me the means to do that.

La Marini has taken to religion, one of the prettiest women I courted in 1801.

Saint-Seine, August 31.—I witnessed all the details of the rising *del gran pianeta*. We drove out of Tonnerre at three o'clock under a beautiful star-studded sky. I thought I made out a comet.

It formed a kind of pyramid; it was as far from the peak, which was the most luminous point, to the extremity of the rays as it is from the last star of the Great Bear's pole to the dipper formed by the four stars.

I watched this sight, and remarked that nothing made the East stand out. A few minutes later, I thought I saw a light which cut diagonally across the horizon; then the horizon stood out, and the sky was filled with a blue light; it reminded me of the dawn in *Les Bardes* (opera by Lesueur). I found that the opera's imitation was perfect.

This blue light grew more intense for a long time without its nature being changed. At length came the dawn's copper hue. The sky was all aflame with red; this light then faded and became radiant, not exactly at the horizon, but a little above it. On the horizon, a darker line was formed, I believe by fog.

The countryside began to stir, and we finally arrived at Montbard. We found Buffon's portrait at our hostess's. A girl led us to Buffon's old gardener. This thin little old man, all sinew and speaking distinctly, took us across seven or eight terraces, each thirty feet wide at the most.

We came to a trapeziform platform; from this platform, there was an extensive view, which unfortunately was only formed by sparsely wooded hills that had a barren appearance. Nothing in this view, as in the garden, inspired a voluptuous charm. I shared this reflection with Signor Lechi, who replied, "Consequently, there's nothing here that attracts except the desire to pay one's respects to the memory of a great man."

This shows how much, for an Italian, voluptuous charm forms an integral part of the notion of a beautiful garden. Buffon's doesn't cover enough ground; outside of that, it tends to inspire the notion of strength and magnificence. No voluptuous charm in all those walls and flights of steps; on the contrary, something unfeeling and dull. It's in the style of Versailles.

We went up a hundred and thirty-eight steps in the tower, a remnant of a château of the Dukes of Burgundy, given to Buffon by the king, and which used to occupy all the ground of the esplanade. The windows of this tower, set into walls five feet thick and with a bench beside the window, are unmistakably Gothic.

All these details come from the matter-of-fact sinewy gardener. He told us that in the family "we have deeds which prove that this tower was built more than nine hundred years ago." That would be the year 900. This man was with Buffon seventeen years. He saw *Jean-Jacques* kneel at the doorway of the study where Buffon used to work in the midst of silence.

He used to arrive at five o'clock or a quarter past five at the latest; at eleven, a roll and a decanter of water would be brought him. He would eat his lunch and come down at one o'clock sharp for dinner, say nothing to his guests, go back to work till five o'clock, at which time someone would come to get him, and he'd relax by chatting with his guests.

His gardeners were careful to sweep away the leaves before he passed. "There were six of us then," the old man said. "At five o'clock, the valet would go in and renew the candles." I asked several times in order to be quite sure that Buffon worked only by candlelight.

People avoided his garden house when they knew he was there. Buffon would come in May and leave in September. I was moved, I'd like to have stayed longer.

This austerity of work IS A LESSON FOR MYSELF. I'd like to have meditated and been sensitive to the *majesty* and *strength* exhaled by those gardens. My traveling companions were in such haste that I didn't have a chance to do so.

The plane trees didn't shade the pathways, although they were very tall. There were some foot and a half in diameter, and they were only planted forty-five years ago, the gardener assured us.

At the innkeeper's (M. Gauthier), I examined a portrait of Buffon painted by Drouais the younger; I saw physical strength in it, what's called beauty in France, but no thought, and especially no sensibility.

After Montbard, the mounting road goes over a plain that's arid, elevated and full of stones. There's only a foot of earth over the layers of yellow stone. Frequently, nothing can be seen from the door of the diligence but three trees. The road goes up hill and down dale a great deal. It passes near the source of the Seine, and arrives at Saint-Seine, where I'm writing this at a quarter past ten after a good supper served by some well-built girls to whom I devoted much attention, owing to my innate taste for tavern girls.

On the road, which was tedious, Signor Scotti sang. He sings well, and entirely in the Italian manner. I felt at once the ferocity *del mio maschio pensare* [of my male way of thinking] vanish and my heart grow tender. My sentiments embellish that part of a song which, according to the dominant passion, may provide my soul the most pleasure; I'm unable to embellish the verse of the best French play in this manner. That's perhaps whence comes my love of music, the boredom which I'm given by the French stage and my injustice toward bad music.

As soon as something is bad it no longer has any interest for my heart, the embellishing power ceases and boredom appears. Were I to lose all my imagination, I'd perhaps lose my taste for music at the same time. At the moment, this taste is far stronger than that for painting.

September 1, at ten minutes to four in the morning.—In the month of March this year, when I thought I was to be sent on a mission to Italy and going there with Crozet, I was simple-minded enough to read some travel books. They diminished Italy's attractions for me; old *Misson* alone appeared to me to have some naturalness. Now I am taking with me only the voyage of Arthur Young and that of Duclos, because they're themselves.

Dôle, September 1.—I witnessed the sunrise. I noticed that while the sky was still lit up by the blue light of dawn some of the cloud effects were sublime; that brought me back to this thought: what is truly great shouldn't affect anything: it should simply act, and the most trivial things that spring from it, when they are seen to be coming, will appear sublime and be admired for themselves.

We've seen three towns today: Dijon, Auxonne and Dôle. When you're familiar with two or three French towns, nothing is as insipid as those more or less shabby buildings thrown together in a haphazard way. Especially for me, who am only interested in things that portray man's manners and morals. At Dijon, I went to see Mme. Héliotte, who wasn't home. I wrote her a letter in an extravagant style. Naturalness would have appeared inane and without sentiment to a provincial.

Dijon is, in my words and in those of an inane expression, an overgrown village. Level situation, no river, a stream called the Ouche.

A common house well enough built, but a courtyard so cramped that I was conscious of nothing but shabbiness. A theater on a level with the ground.

A little bootblack who told me his life story.

Auxonne has a neat and well-populated appearance, balconies and perrons well built. It can be seen that capitals have been added to the houses.

Dôle, very agreeable situation. The promenade, or the Cours de Saint-Maurice, commands a fine view.

Of the three towns, I'd give my preference to this one. Its situation is picturesque. I'm overcome with sleep and am going to bed.

Written at Champagnole, September 2, at three o'clock, afternoon.—Before going to bed, I spent a long time watching the room of a woman across from whom I sat at supper and who looked quite possessable. Her door was ajar, and I had some hope of catching a glimpse of a thigh or breast.

A woman who'd have no effect on me if she were in my bed, gives me a delightful sensation when seen unexpectedly, then she's natural, *I'm not occupied with my role,* and I'm entirely given over to sensation.

My love affairs have always been a bit disturbed by my concern with being agreeable; in other words, being occupied with a role. In these circumstances you can't be thoroughly natural. It's not impossible to become bored in the presence of a mistress, you can't let her see your boredom; you'd lose her. But, for me, love would be a far keener pleasure if, like Signor Lechi for instance, when I'm with my mistress, I thought of nothing else.

Dôle was lit by a superb full moon. I took a few turns on the Cours Saint-Maurice, but I was a little concerned, during my day's excursion, with the effect produced by my appearance and especially my chari-vari,[1] on the women.

In the evening, I was also a little concerned with walking with an impassive and disdainful look beside some young Dragoon officers who were walking in an insolent fashion.

All this is sorry business, but, I'm only twenty-eight; I hope it will pass as I grow older.

The full moon was still lighting up the silent horizon when we left Dôle at three o'clock. The moon, appearing in its fullness in the middle of two corridors formed by hills and trees, formed, with the vast silence of the night, a sight comparable, in the opposite variety, to the sunrise.

We passed beside a bridge of five or six arches over the Doubs. The driver told me that, one Sunday two years ago, this bridge, being crowded with people, took it into its head to collapse. No one perished. A priest and two other persons remained on a pile; they went out in a punt to get them.

September 2.—My heart spoke today for the first time. Nothing is more

[1] Charms fastened on the watch chain.

insipid (producing boredom and gloom for me) than the sight of a town like Dijon. The flat plains around Paris also produce this effect. Today, as we came from Dôle to Poligny, I finally saw mountains and peasants which didn't remind me of Paris. I had pleasure in traveling. Character of the mountain fields.[1]

At one o'clock, between Poligny and Champagnole, where I'm writing this in a pine room that reminds me of the Chartreuse, I noticed, on the right as you go down, the first amphitheater of mountains which has struck my view since Melk, I believe.

The gorge of Poligny is very beautiful: the road, a good work of the Emperor, is of the same kind as that of Chailles.

I didn't pay much attention to all that; I was engaged with the amiable Lechi *in una discussione italiana intorno alla grandezza di Milan* [in a discussion in Italian on the greatness of Napoleon]. He reproached him for having deceived Italy by not leading it to liberty.

He afterward spoke of the art of being happy, ambition, the work of a Prefect and the gaiety of Venice, its government and morals. He spoke with such grace and comedy (without emerging from grace, a sublime thing *per uno che s'intende in questa arte* [for one who understands this art]) that I frequently wished I could take down what he was saying; I even tried to remember some of his phrases. But I no longer have anything but the sense of them, and I'd make it lose that charming grace.

He's certainly the man who's given me the most conversational pleasure in perhaps the past ten years; I don't recall another manner so amiable.

I'm writing as fast as my pen can go, otherwise it's obvious that I wouldn't have used the word *manner*. It's as far as anything can be from my man.

My amiable traveling companion confirmed my ideas, which I was beginning to fear were chimeric, on the happiness that's to be found in Italy.

There's but one obstacle, 'TIS THAT FOR MY TALENT, PERHAPS IT IS harmful *il vivere lontan dei miei stomachevoli modelli* [to live far from my disgusting models].

The sky is no farther from the earth, as Montesquieu says, than is the amiability of my Lechi from that of Z. The one is natural, jolly, frolicsome as a lass; the other is pedantic, affected, ponderous, boring.

I'm tired and can't keep myself from falling into the pine bed of the mistress of the Champagnole posthouse. It's a village traversed by the nascent Ain, which turns the sawmills.

There's a stony plain eighty feet above the level of the village

[1] I still recall it as I write this. October 22, 1817. [Note added by Beyle.]

houses. The square is ugly and unkempt; I have it beneath my window. But it recalls the Alps. The houses are shingle-roofed.

From Champagnole to Saint-Laurent, we followed a road that was a sort of terrace, now on the right, now on the left of a mountain torrent flowing far below between two rocky ridges.

During this time the moon rose. The hills around us looked like motionless waves. The moon, which lit them up, seemed close to us.

We arrived at Saint-Laurent, and landed in the midst of a meeting of traveling salesmen. I well observed the bourgeois absurdity. Nothing they did escaped from being the most overdone absurdity. They indulged in numerous gestures, scratched their heads, examined their forks, etc., in order to disguise their timidity. Their greatest feat was to have drunk eight bottles of wine while eating a beef salad at such-and-such an inn at Lyon with so-and-so. Beforehand, the company is acquainted at length with the inn and the comrade. After that comes the story, followed by forced laughter. One of them, ponderous, slow-witted and, I believe, a Grenoblois, cracked some jokes, based on mythology, which everybody admired. He uttered commonplaces which were repeated three or four times. This solemn wag had beside him a little fop of the Parisian variety who never took his eyes off him, repeated what he said, admired his sallies. The whole business was very strained. I said to Signor Lechi that the most natural and best-bred person at the table was our driver. Signor Lechi assured me that in Italy the same difference was to be remarked between the conversations of Milan and those of the provinces.

I took hold of the two backsides of a passable tavern girl; I heard a clarinet and a violin which were far from being the same, and yet which gave me pleasure.

La Vattay, September 3, eleven o'clock in the morning.—The character of the traveling salesmen's joking last night was *strained,* not comical, and launched with all the uneasiness of the most acute self-esteem. The amiable company took some time to see the point of the joke, and burst out into forced laughter which was absurd, especially toward the end, when some of the members started to laugh again and weren't followed by the others. The wag with the big nose, who was solemn, philosophic and disillusioned, afterward said quite simple things with affectation, as, in speaking of the wine, "Give me two fingers," and four seconds later, "or half an inch."

Then his admirer would look at him steadily with an expression of enjoyment and admiration; there would be laughter and they'd repeat the words two or three times, trying to imitate the drawl of the man with the big nose.

For them, he was a great man. Their sensation was the same as that which would have been produced by a genuine great man. Therefore, it was worth studying. I frequently make use of this observation, which facilitates the study of the passions. Would these salesmen, who were so ridiculous, have done better to keep quiet, like eight taciturn salesmen from Holland? No, it seems to me that they at least had the pleasure of an extreme mental activity; all their self-esteem was at stake. These petty souls, lacking the stuff to live by their own esteem unless it is propped up by that of others, have no pride and consequently far more vanity than I. In this great parade of wit, they have a life, a quantity of sentiment, a susceptibility of vanity unknown to me.

It's possible that tavern girls and music have given them pleasures of sentiment. They've certainly given some to me, who sleep with Angéline and go continually to the Opera Buffa and whose heart hasn't been moved by pleasures which should have entirely occupied it. It's an excellent preparation for pleasure, or rather an all-powerful antidote against boredom to have had one's heart *entirely occupied with something*.

Geneva, at the Ecu de Genève, September 3, at eight o'clock in the evening.—After writing my journal, I went up to Signor Scotti, who was smoking a cigar at the window, and remarked to him that the moon was lopsided; when I arrived, I'd seen it round. This morning, as we left, we saw it round again, and the tavern girl told us that there was a period when only a little portion of it could be seen. From which we concluded that we'd seen an eclipse without realizing it.

From Poligny to Gex, the road was full of up- and downgrades, and ran along the edge of the mountains. The countryside was very uninteresting, few trees, prairies with short grass studded with slabs of rock, pine enclosures, very sturdy houses; nothing majestic in the cliffs; it was wild without being beautiful.

At five o'clock in the morning, the diligence stopped at Morez, I believe, for the packages to be sealed with lead. This ceremony obviated similar inspections at all the bureaus scattered throughout the length of Switzerland. We were all asleep, and we woke up cold and surprised to be standing still.

Signor Lechi and I saw a hobnail factory; there were already eight or ten workingwomen present, most of them young. One, who looked like Mme. Héliotte, showed me the very simple process, which nevertheless requires two blows of their heavy hammer on the round-headed nails. They get two sous a thousand; they make ten or, at the most, twelve thousand of them. The hammer comes devilishly close to their nose.

After a slightly depressing and irritating political discussion, we arrived at La Vattay, where we were served meat balls like those at Grenoble, which I hadn't come across since Grenoble.

At half-past eleven, we had the view of the lake and Mt. Blanc. The lake very long and of a lovely blue; we could almost see the eastern end.

We were, so to speak, in the front row for Mt. Blanc. It seemed to grow considerably lower as we descended. A great spectacle which I'd have sketched at the time but which is now effaced by fatigue.

We reached Geneva at four o'clock. Near the bridge, we knocked off the overhanging portion of a shop roof. We were let out at the coach office and not at the Ecu de Genève. The ill nature and lack of care of the Geneva bankers who run the stagecoach business. Everything was dismal, rough and brutish, even the *facchino* who helped us carry our things to the inn. That's probably the result of the republican government: in this case, the absence of monarchical graciousness is very striking.[1]

Their city, through which I wandered with Signor Scotti, looks like a well-kept prison. It has a silence and gloominess the like of which I've never seen. The Place Saint-Pierre, overgrown with grass, crossed by a single listless blond young man who walked springily in order to give himself some gracefulness, offered us a striking sight.

I went to look again at the window which made such an impression on me five years ago, naturally after someone had recommended it to me, I forget who.

We admired the lake, exactly like the sea, from the Saint-Antoine bastion. We seated ourselves on La Treille, where no one came.

However, I saw five or six beautiful faces. Tall girls well built, pretty colors, full bosoms, pure eyes, but a cold look. These beauties charmed me five years ago. My experience with Angéline makes me prize them less now; I'm afraid of boredom with them.

Seeing this severity of Geneva, I thought that the character of the most illustrious man it has produced [Rousseau] might be explained by saying that this early education (viz, his promenades to Plainpalais, his reading, etc., etc.) was English, or *entirely devoted to passion*.

And his later education (the distinctions at the Comte de Gouvon's, his quarrels in Venice) was French, or *entirely devoted to vanity*.

The dismal young people who appear insipid in Paris ought to retire here. They'd perhaps be taken for agreeable nitwits. All the foregoing is badly expressed: the fault lies in my fatigue.

For fear of being read by someone indiscreet, I'm sending these forty pages to Paris.

At La Treille, Signor Scotti asked me where Piedmont was, as well as Savoy and the City of Savoy!

[1] I think I'll find the same thing in England. [Note by Beyle.]

At Charenton, he regretted not having embarked on the Seine to go to Marseille. He has very few ideas, and is a little shattered by his four years in prison.

I remarked the reasonable and polite manner the servants have between themselves in Geneva. That's far above the coarseness of this class in France, but it's not as gay.

Milan, Sunday, September 8.—My heart is full. Last night and today, I experienced emotions crammed with pleasure. I'm on the verge of tears. I arrived here about five o'clock yesterday; the details of the customs and the inn took us an hour, dinner as long again, and it was seven o'clock by the time that I at last came to the Corso of that Porta Orientale where, all rhetoric aside, the aurora of my life was passed.

As I was then so do I find myself now! No feeling of ambition enters into this reflection. I ascribe everything to Signora Pietragrua, and for the rest of my stay in Milan in the time of M. Petiet I see what brought about each result, I hold myself in tender pity. Not being able to be loved by Signora Pietragrua, who was loved by Louis [Joinville], in the millions of castles in Spain that I built for her, I pictured myself returning one day as a colonel or having some other situation superior to that of being an employee of M. Daru, of kissing her and bursting into tears.

It must be confessed that this plan wasn't an involved one, but it possessed what makes plans of this kind succeed, it was full of sentiment, I couldn't even think about it without shedding tears.

This plan came back to my mind yesterday as I realized that, after *eleven years,* I was in the position I desired so strongly at that time.

What a word, *eleven years!* My memories were not in the least blunted; they were given new life by an extreme love. I can't take a step in Milan without recognizing something, and eleven years ago I loved that something because it belonged to the city where she lived.

Dare I say what moved me the most upon arriving at Milan? It's obvious that this is written for no one but myself. It was a certain smell of manure peculiar to its streets. That, more than all the rest, seemed to prove to me that I was in Milan.

Last night, I experienced this overly strong and tender emotion which at the present moment pains me through the certainty, I believe, that it won't be shared. I was planning to go to see Signora Pietragrua today, but I was afraid of bursting into tears when I kissed her, and again appearing ridiculous to her; for I imagined that my unrequited love had made me appear ridiculous in the past. How pride enters into love! This thought made me feel my emotion painfully. I'd have burst into tears of pleasure if, possessing the ring of Angelique, I'd been able to go into her salon without being seen by her.

Yesterday, after leaving the Corso, which we saw only at night and at the time everybody had just left it, Signor Scotti and I went *alla* Scala.

This theater has had a great influence on my character. If ever I amuse myself by describing how my character was formed by the events of my youth, the Theater *della Scala* will be in the front rank. When I entered it, only a tiny bit more emotion would have been needed to make me lose my hold on myself and break down in tears.

I'm endeavoring to steer clear of exaggeration. I detest the *false* in everything as an enemy of happiness. But I believe that, were I in Milan as secretary of an embassy or anything else that didn't require too much work, I'd pass a happy year here.

The *arte di godere,* the art of enjoying life, appears to me here to be two centuries ahead of Paris. What adds to the merit of this circumstance is that the goodhearted, easygoing Milanese aren't indebted to reasoning for that, but to their climate and to the debilitating government which the House of Austria gave them; and happy people are necessary if you're going to be happy in even the smallest things, as I believe you can be in this land.

Beside the happiness of women and art, I feel that I'd find much happiness in having a circle of friends composed of people like Signor Lechi.

I must write down, lest I forget it, my condition in Milan during the months that followed the battle of Marengo. I'd never seen life, not the tiniest little bit of it, but I'd lived in all possible novels, including *Héloïse;* I believe that by this time I had read *Les Liaisons Dangereuses* and *sought emotions* in it. The lack of imagination and the pedantry of MY PARENTS for a long time spoiled the word *virtue* for me; I was incapable of imagining happiness, and, to tell the truth, I'm only capable of finding it even now far from what's called *virtue* in womanhood.

With the quality of being extremely sensitive, I therefore combined, in 1800, 1801 and 1803, that of desiring to be considered a *roué,* and it is obvious that I was the very opposite of this character.

No one took pity on me and came to my aid with charitable advice. I consequently went *without women* during the two or three years when my temperament was the most ardent. We don't remember pure (unalloyed) sensations. What I'm saying here of my temperament is consequently drawn from the little I know of natural history. They say that between the ages of nineteen and twenty-two we possess an ardor that abandons us soon afterward. Being born in 1783, I spent my seventeenth, eighteenth and nineteenth years in Milan and Lombardy.

I was consumed by sensibility, bashful, proud and unappreciated. The last word is put here without boasting and in order to indicate that, whenever my manner was bold enough to be noticed, everyone was astonished; people believed me to be the opposite of what I was. At the age of eighteen when I most adored Signora Pietragrua, I lacked money and had only a single suit of clothes, sometimes a bit frayed here and there.

Being nothing in Milan at the home of M. and Mme. Petiet and already having too much pride to make advances, I passed my days in extreme self-commiseration full of melancholy.

I saw Joinville, Mazeau, Derville-Maléchard and others succeed;[1] I saw them doing things which I felt that I could do better; they were happy, had mistresses. I didn't budge, I was waiting for some romantic hazard, as the breaking down of a carriage, etc., that fate might make my heart known to some sensitive soul.

If I'd had a friend, he'd have cast me into a woman's arms. Happy, I'd have been charming. Not assuredly by looks and manners, but by the heart, could I have been charming for a sensitive woman; she would have found a Roman soul in me for everything foreign to love; she would have had the pleasure of forming the manners of her lover, which have since been formed by dint of being knocked about by experience—and not too badly formed.

Undoubtedly, such a woman would have been loved by me as much as the most genuinely sensitive woman could wish to be loved. I shouldn't even have thought of anything other than a woman who would have loved me and whom I'd have possessed.

My sensibility wouldn't have given birth to lassitude; I believe that its various moods would have been capable of interesting every day and for many days a loving soul that was able to see my own.

Since then, I've been in love and deeply; but what a difference there is between what I experienced in the Rue Sainte [where he lived with Mélanie in Marseilles] and what I'd have experienced when I was staying in the Casa Bovara *sul* Corso di Porta Orientale!

Certainly, had I been loved in Milan, my character would be very different. I'd be much more of a ladies' man, and I wouldn't have that *residue* of sensibility *che puo servimi pell'arte* [which may be useful for art]. In Marseille, my head was too occupied for love to be the master of everything; I was beginning to observe. I was reading Tracy and Say.

The two years of sighs, of tears, of sentimental and melancholy effusions which I passed in Italy, without women, in that climate, at

[1]In 1817, I'm HAPPIER than all those people, especially the Petiets. [Note added by Beyle.]

that period of my life and without prejudices, are probably what gave me this inexhaustible source of sensibility which today, at the age of twenty-eight, makes me feel all, down to the slightest details, and makes me capable of dictating fifty pages of an artist's observations on the passage through the mountains this side of Isella, for instance.

I compare this present sensibility with a liquor which penetrates to the tiniest veins of the body into which it is injected. It suffices for everything, abounds everywhere.

With the exception of grace, I was therefore in Milan in 1800, I believe, in the same situation as Chérubin [of *The Marriage of Figaro*], but I probably was altogether lacking in grace.

Mazeau, having come to see me one day when I was sick in my room (Casa Bovara, above Mme. Petiet's dining room; behind my bed there was a picture of Ganymede, a picture forever sacred to me and which I shan't return to see)—Mazeau told Mme. Petiet that he'd come to see Beyle, who looked like a sick lion. My very curly black hair, the forceful look which I already had at that time and my pride lead me to think I had no grace with which I might be reproached.

As I was saying, at that time, so crowded with tender memories for me, Joinville, who was then M. Daru's assistant and who was goodhearted by nature, took me to see a tall, beautiful and superb woman he had. She was Signora Angelina Pietragrua.

This is the woman I've just seen again after a little less than nine years of absence.

I saw her another time about 1 Vendémiaire, Year X, on my way from Brescia to Savigliano, where my regiment was stationed. But my stay at Bergamo and Brescia had already separated me from her for a long time. I'm not sure but that, at Bergamo and Brescia, I even hated her.

I can thus say that it's ten years since I've seen her, ten years since I've seen what I loved the most in all the world.

I went to see her today at one o'clock. I went to her father's; a servant took me to her home. Luckily, I had to wait a quarter of an hour, and I had the time to compose myself a little.

I saw a tall and superb woman. There's always something majestic about her which comes from the manner in which her eyes, her forehead and her nose are placed. I found more wit, more majesty and less of that grace replete with voluptuousness. In my time, she was only majestic through the force of beauty, now she's also so through the force of her facial traits. She didn't recognize me. That gave me pleasure. I refreshed her memory by explaining that I was Beyle, Joinville's friend. "It's the Chinaman, *quegli è il Chinese!*" she said to her father, who was present.

My great love hadn't made me in the least ridiculous; it turned out that she recalled me only as a very gay person.

I joked about my love.—"Why didn't you tell me about it then?" she asked me twice. I joked on the balcony of her father's house, the same place where I told her, I believe, that I hoped soon to be a corpse on the Mantua plain. Obviously, I didn't remind her of this gracious manner of making love. There was a little embarrassment between us, during which I saw the action of her mind, above this sort of embarrassment. After ten years, she's a new acquaintance to make.

The suitor [Widmann] arrived shortly after; he's a Venetian lord, attached to the Viceroy with an honorary position here. I manifested an engaging politeness toward him.

That's the manner she had with me; she gracefully made me take off my hat, speaking to me of the Italian way.

It's five o'clock; I'll have to go to dinner. She invited me to go to her loge tonight. I'm also to be introduced to Signora Lamberti by Signor Lechi. The good Borrone invited me to his house and asked me if he might embrace me. That just about made the cup overflow; a little less majesty in Signora Pietragrua and I'd have thrown my arms around her and burst into tears.[1]

I went to drink a delicious cup of iced coffee and cream, superior in my opinion to anything to be found in Paris, and I returned to write this.

I've some idea of possessing Signora Pietragrua in passing; she told me that she had many things to tell me, that she'd indulged in many follies since the last time she saw me—all that loudly and distinctly in front of everybody.

I'm writing this after midnight. The play to which I've just been lasted from a quarter to eight until a quarter to twelve. We had the first act *dei Pretendenti* (translation of *Les Prétendus*), a bad ballet from *Phèdre,* the second act *dei Pretendenti,* a ballet that wasn't comical but was exaggerated.

Introduction to Signora Lamberti. Her kind of politeness.—Her uncle, the ninety-two-year-old abbot.—Remarkable morals.—A comedy, however good it may be, and precisely because it is good, cannot be common to several nations.—The scenes this evening were so indecent for a Frenchman that they'd seem unnatural to him.—I didn't find Signora Pietragrua, who probably wasn't at the theater. I'm dead with exhaustion.

September 9, Milan, Royal Inn.—I was planning today to write the

[1] I add six years afterward, in 1817, that, far from being exaggerated, this account comes far indeed from rendering what I experienced. [Note added by Beyle.]

Mocenigo part of yesterday. But I came back at midnight tired out, and I've only strength enough left to note the events of today.

I took a bath that was too hot and gave me a headache. I bought the comedies of Comte Giraud. Signor Lechi had mentioned one of them that aimed at producing laughter without stirring the emotions. I was obliged to spend an hour in bed. I purchased a cane before going to see Signora Pietragrua. I thought a cane would make me look four years younger. It worked very well; I discovered that I knew a dozen tricks with a cane which showed beyond a doubt that I was a man of the best society and a ladies' man. In this way I no longer had my hands behind my back *à la papa.*

I was at Signora Pietragrua's from two to five; from there to dinner at a caterer's near the Scala. I saw a pretty girl in this establishment; she looked to me like a whore; I'll try to find out about that tomorrow. I went to the Corso, from there I took a good-looking little fiacre which conducted me in a leisurely fashion to the theater *del Lentasio* at the Porta Romana. It was terrible, but I heard the charming music of Mayer's *Mélomane Italien.* That's one of the operas which contributed ten years ago toward giving me a taste for music.

After that there was a ballet with some grotesques and a pretty woman's thighs.

I'm in an unalloyed Italian mood; there's no similated good taste to alter its genuineness.

All that for twenty Milanese sous, from half-past eight till eleven o'clock. I went to take a sherbet on the Piazza del Duomo. I came home; I reserved a carriage for tomorrow. I read thirty pages of Comte Giraud, I wrote this, and I'm going to bed, very tired. Tomorrow I'll go back to the three hours spent at Signora Pietragrua's and the theater. It's possible that I may have Signora Pietragrua. With her here, Mme. Bialowiska at Ancona, Naples and Rome on top of that, I'll have nothing to desire. As I haven't any time to lose, I'll try to find out tomorrow whether, without following the thing up, she wants to spend a few happy moments with me. She looks at me a great deal. I'm a new acquaintance for her.

The streets of Milan are as commodious as ours are disgusting.

I didn't go to Signora Lamberti's *per fare almeno un poco di dignità. Andro quivi domani* [to show at least a little dignity. I'll go tomorrow].

A *vetturino,* who has the honest look of a German and whose father has forty mules in Rome, has just offered to drive me to Rome in a carriage which he assures me is very clean; that means it's passable; he'd drive me there in nine and a half days for six louis and a half; he told me I could go from Rome to Naples by diligence in twenty-four hours.

With the *vetturino*, I'd be able to sleep in a bed every night, but I'd proceed at a walking pace all day, which is annoying in this hot weather.

Another *vetturino* made me the same proposition. You'd have to be with a band of friends, it would be agreeable then.

Milan, September 10.—Details of yesterday, September 9.—I feel through every pore that this land is the home of the arts. I believe they hold the place in the hearts of this people that vanity holds in those of the French. Yesterday I looked for Appiani's frescoes; I went to San Fedele, I found the architecture magnificent; the whole church neatly covered with crimson damask, a cool and pure appearance. A Low Mass was being said and was being listened to by a score of the faithful scattered about on the benches of this vast church; suddenly, a charming little sonata began. It was a man at the organ with two women. He played a very gay and sprightly rondo. The beautiful, cool church heightened its effect.

Next to San Fedele is a large building of a noble architecture. I realize that I'm not overly sensitive to this art; it doesn't speak to my heart with enough clarity.

It ought to be shouted at those inhabitants of Paris who believe themselves so advanced in the things pertaining to good order and cleanliness, "You are barbarians, your streets exhale a foul stench, you can't take a step in them without being covered with a black mud which gives a disgusting appearance to the people who are obliged to go about on foot.

"That comes from the absurd idea of making a general sewer out of your streets. The sewers ought to be set underneath the streets. Look at the streets of Milan. Perfect cleanliness, an extremely smooth surface for the vehicles, smooth walking for the pedestrians, and yet in Milan they have nothing but stones, and the paving blocks of Versailles are unknown here."

This prosopoeia ran through my head all day; even if I'd wanted to splash mud on myself, I wouldn't have been able to do so.

About three o'clock, I went to the Contrada dei Meravigli. I had to wait a moment; she was coming back. She'd just asked a favor BY Méjan (MIRABEAU'S FRIEND). It seems that she has somewhat of a reputation for amiability or beauty in Milan, and that THE MIRABEAU'S FRIEND tried to pay court to her six years ago upon his arrival here, as he assumed a gallant manner with her yesterday.

Signora Pietragrua didn't greet me with gay and unrestrained eagerness, but with a thoughtful look and manner, albeit full of assurances of friendship, observing me a great deal, almost as one would a new acquaintance. It's a strange situation to see a friend again after having had no news of him for nine years.

I passed through Milan during the first days of Vendémiaire, Year X, on my way from Brescia to Savigliano to rejoin my regiment. Antonio [Angelina's son] played with my helmet and plume in the same apartment. She had me sit on the sofa beside her; I learned at the French Consul's that this was the place of honor. She'd promised to tell me the story of her rupture with Louis [Joinville].

This story is very involved. A year ago I shouldn't have understood that love. Louis is goodhearted and has good sense, but his manners are common, no wit; he's ugly, has a coarse face, but it appears that under the surface he's capable of being moved by the passions. I'd be almost inclined to believe that, outside the passions, he's like the Vicomte [Louis de Barral] when the latter isn't in a gaming room—everything seems inane to him. This state is probably often brought on by the lack of success in society. When we'd be talking of worldly success, Joinville often used to say things which amounted to this: "My kingdom isn't in that world." The fact is that he's ignorant of all the proprieties, and you can see at the first glance that he hasn't any wit at all; in short, he looks like a peasant introduced in society.

Milan, September 11.—Summary of the day of September 10.—Yesterday (September 10) I was so satisfied with myself that I was afraid some storm would blow up from Paris. My mind feared vaguely that such a time-absorbing pleasure would make me neglect some duty. In order to reassure myself, I recalled that many men have undoubtedly enjoyed the same pleasures but haven't said anything about it, that consequently my case wasn't an exceptional one and that I had nothing to fear.

There was undoubtedly much vanity in my pleasure, but vanity combined with a bit of sentiment; without this mixture, a pleasure of vanity is almost nothing for me after a few minutes.

Upon getting up yesterday, I went to see the French Consul (M. Flury, I believe). In his salon, I found some fine engravings of Constantinople and the portrait of a huge figure. I concluded that he'd lived in Pera and that this enormous being was his wife. He put in an appearance. He's a man with that kind of embonpoint which prevents one from thinking.

From there to the *Marino* to leave a note at the home of M. Saint-Romain, prosecutor general of the Imperial Court of Turin, with whom it appears that I'm going in a mail coach to Rome. I hoped I wouldn't find him in order that the negotiation might drag on, no engagement would be taken and I'd stay here a fortnight if I had Signora Pietragrua.

I had a carriage, a bit for convenience and a great deal out of vanity in respect to Signora Pietragrua. It mustn't be forgotten that, as far as general relations are concerned, I'm a new acquaintance for her. The influence of little things is extremely important in this case.

I arrived at one o'clock at Signora Pietragrua's. She'd been indisposed. Signor Widmann arrived soon after with the permit necessary to see the Brera. Signora Pietragrua decided to go. She left us to change her dress. While she was gone Signor Migliorini arrived; he's a handsome conscript with a benevolent look and a total absence of wit. It would be too boring to note down all the insipid things he said.

In an effort to be amiable, he talked a great deal. At first, he looked at me with a crusty seriousness, a manner in which asses always greet strangers. I reflected that the only thing worth winning over in a dolt is his affection; fortunately, my disgust didn't get the upper hand. Il Signor Migliorini gave me much pleasure by letting me make his conquest. I succeeded so well that, after leaving Signora Pietragrua, he accompanied me to the caterer Vieillard's and confided a secret method by which you can always have an erection, but only when you want to. He's busy at present putting this great secret to a test. You must have a tarantula, you reduce it to charcoal, with olive oil you make a paste out of this charcoal, you rub it on the big toe of the right foot, and as long as the drug is there you have an erection.

When you've had enough of this fine condition, you wash yourself in hot water.

Under the monarchies, this fine secret, giving the means of being pleasing to women, to the Mmes. Rebuffel, would be worth a fortune.

This reflection is obviously my own. During this entire recital, my man didn't show the least shadow of wit; the most favorable exclamation to which he was able to give birth was, *"That goes without saying."*

But he revealed manners and morals without being aware of it.
1. The Italian wariness: he was careful to assure me that he wouldn't think of trying out this great secret on himself.
2. It appears that he has plenty of women; he has a fairly handsome face, strength, health and gaiety, but no wit; that's what his person evinces.

Yesterday, he was in a frock coat and general négligé all day; it was in this costume that he made six or eight visits at the theater, and that he was in the loge of his general, the handsome Teodoro Lechi.

Signor Migliorini has been an officer attached to the Court. He explained to me that, by this means, he had some thirty women to whom he might demonstrate the effectiveness of his great remedy.

The Milanese dialect is full of sentiment (it's obvious that I'm not speaking of the sentiment of love), the ring of its words expresses sincerity and mild rationality.

This is the full-length portrait of one of the actors of our visit to the Brera. The most important was Signor Widmann, a gay man, loving music, scarcely given to thinking, loving indolence. I account for his lack of intelligence in a favorable manner. Those folks devote their youth to love-making, they enjoy themselves with ardor, they're all sensation, and consequently when their sensation fades all that's left is a handful of reflections which they've happened to make in the intervals between their pleasures.

Signor Widmann, who was something in the way of a Prince of the Empire, I believe, although allied to the Rezzonico family, whose name he's taken because of the 50,000 francs' income that a Rezzonico left him, has as much of high society's politeness as is permitted by the Italian naturalness.

This politeness, which would have disconcerted me ten years ago, put me at ease, and while with him I had the noblest, the politest and the most attentive manner.

In this respect, I'm entitled to be satisfied with myself; my friends may say what they wish, for they don't understand my manner.

It's justified by success. As we were taking leave, he waited for a carriage to pass, and then walked forty paces to say good-by to me and shake my hand.

We left Signora Pietragrua's. She motioned me to give her my hand, I declined, letting her see that it was because of Signor Widmann, who likewise declined, and finally as a stranger I accepted the honor of giving my arm *alla nostra dea*.

We saw the Brera (I'll put the description of it in elsewhere after seeing it again), as well as Rafaelli's studio, where Leonardo's *Il Cenacolo* [*The Last Supper*] is being made in mosaic and where Migliorini spouted some shocking asininities about the patience of the poor artists, who were present and accepted everything. I speak here only of the interests of gallantry and Mocenigo; that's already quite a bit at one time.

Milan, September 11.—As I was saying, we visited the rooms of the Brera; I was a man of the best society, a brilliant man and a man with personality. Signora Pietragrua had shown me the previous day that she liked this sort of man; she showed me that with a sagacity which made it evident to me that she understood delicate things quite well. I hit on some while speaking Italian, which isn't bad.

The arts carried the day, especially a handsome bas-relief (Hercules bringing back Alcestes). In the midst of the visit, I was obliged to reason with myself in order to return and be pleasing to Signora Pietragrua instead of admiring the portrait of Monti.

She put some shrewd questions to me in an effort to guess the nature of my work, which she knows only by my card. But, as my pride makes me exceedingly sensitive about this subject, I readily saw through her attack and got out of it naturally, even gracefully, in the meantime giving a touched-up notion of the thing.

I may mention that, for a character like my own, decorations are only good for something when traveling.

This visit to the Brera established my place in the opinion of Signora Pietragrua and Signor Widmann.

We went to the Casa Rafaelli. While there, I looked at her twice with extreme tenderness; each time our hands came in contact, they squeezed each other, as frequently did our arms. I paid her several brief and tender compliments.

She dismissed us at her door at half-past four; *al rivederci, questa sera al teatro* [good-by, until tonight at the theater] was the general parting word.

Signor Migliorini had shown us the portrait of his mistress, a married woman, stupid look; they joked about this intrigue with a naturalness and lack of constraint which would have made the hair of our poor impotents of France stand on end.

Signor Widmann's politeness, Signor Migliorini's tarantula.

I went in Vieillard's at five o'clock; my belle in curlpapers was still there. I was perfectly amiable with a table companion, to whom I gave some of my Burgundy wine.[1] It was very good and I did honor to my bottle (ten lire *di Milano*).

It was between four and half-past five that I enjoyed the perfect happiness of which I spoke. It began when I took Signora Pietragrua's arm. My companions' lack of ideas gave me a glimpse of boredom at Rafaelli's; it takes two to play tennis.

I went for a walk alone on the Corso; my happiness faded as fades that of some ambitious people.[2]

My memories were delightful, poignant; they were transformed into reality. I discovered that I was now in love with Signora Pietragrua. From that minute, a thousand little circumstances that had interested me in Milan paled. The chimes, the arts, music, etc., all the things which are charming for the heart when it's idle become colorless and without worth when love fills it.

At six o'clock, I found that I was in love with Signora Pietragrua;

[1] He was an extemporaneous poet and a parasite. [Note by Beyle.]
[2] Who, from the head of one class, put themselves at the foot of another. [Note by Beyle.]

bashfulness was born; from that moment a frightful gloom filled my soul.

This *gloom* came in large part from the fact that a thousand little springs of happiness through memories, little springs which made a river, at once dried up.

My carriage has been more bother than it's worth since I stopped comparing my present rank with that of an employee working with Inspector of Reviews Daru. The Scala no longer gives me the pleasure that I used to derive from the memory of the tender and melancholy sentiments I experienced in other days when I held a rank to which I was so superior.

I had tenderness and melancholy right at hand, I merely had to look up at the second loge in the second tier on the right.

I believe there's much vanity in my case, for I don't anticipate a great pleasure in being in Signora Pietragrua's arms. Really, Angéline [Bereyter] has disgusted me with the sight of bare thighs, a breast, etc.

It will be useful for Mocenigo if I remember how the charm of Milan suddenly disappeared when the memories grew intense enough to be transformed into reality; also my way of explaining this by the numerous sources of the *pleasure of memory* which dry up as soon as all I see in things is what might serve or harm my nascent love.

What would be the effect on me, going up to the second tier of loges, if I recognized the arrangement, the latticework on the lower part of the doors, for instance, while devoting all my thought to a graceful manner of entering Signora Pietragrua's loge and wondering what kind of a greeting I was going to receive?

That, if I'm not mistaken, is a precious observation.

I didn't make it at seven o'clock yesterday, when I was sitting in the pit, full of gloom and wrathful feelings toward my neighbors; I listened rather distractedly to the first act *dei Pretendenti Delusi,* and looked up from time to time at Signora Pietragrua, whose face I couldn't distinguish, but only her hat and arm.

I retained sufficient presence of mind to think of my dignity, and not to go to her loge right at the beginning. I had the patience to wait until the ballet began; but, on the other hand, I remained there throughout the ballet and half the second act. I was silent and rather serious while there.

She said right at the outset, "I don't know what's the matter with Widmann; his features seem to be all distorted." It was true.

She and I were alone a moment; I was embarrassed, but I covered it up by asking her the names of each person I'd just seen.

I saw that she was afraid I'd have a bad opinion of her because one or two of these persons took hold of her knees as a rhetorical gesture. I at once made that gesture. She explained to me that, in this city, she'd appear to be a prude if she took offense at that.

Signor Widmann returned, his features still distorted and solely filled with his emotion (a result of *naturalness,* a thing that wouldn't be found in France). I imagined he was jealous of me. At least, my presence bothered him; maybe he had some secret to tell Signora Pietragrua. It was pleasant to stay for the fine trio of the three suitors, but I had to trot along with Migliorini as soon as the end came. I stayed eight or ten minutes. I noticed that as soon as I left Signora Pietragrua and Signor Widmann began talking with interest.

I went down to the pit. I spent ten minutes with Signora Lamberti. Always an excessive politeness. She introduced me to the greatest doctor in Italy and his wife.

That didn't lift the gnawing *gloom.* I came back to my room furious; that is, I'd have taken pleasure in rending bleeding flesh if I'd been a lion, because I'd have been kept busy and consequently distracted, and besides that I'd have found consolation in doing something powerful. Not having anything to rend, I contented myself by reading the Royal Almanach, an interesting book which I looked through with extreme attention till after one o'clock.

While I was looking through it, the Venetian accent of the inn bootblack made me think that Signor Widmann was coming to demand satisfaction from me for having been pleasing to his mistress. That made my rage increase, but I recognized my error.

But *rage* at what?—At everything, but among other things, to have failed to maintain my dignity by staying too long in Signora Pietragrua's loge and making myself scorned by the woman I loved. I pictured her letting me see in five or six different ways that she could get along quite well without my love. The rage also came from bad humor at no longer having any pleasures of memory.

In a word, I was raging mad, in Alfieri's dismal way, I believe. During such moments, if ever I have a family, I'll make everybody wretched. Such moments come over me frequently when I've made visits that are too long. I'm very sure that the amiable Giacomo Lechi doesn't have any such moments, but it's also true that his mind doesn't form the numerous schemes that my rage required of mine, AND THE CHARACTER WANTS.

In speaking of my rage I still feel it a little. I've had a terrible aspect all day today (September 11); nothing has pleased me; but fortunately I haven't sent anybody packing off to the devil except my lackey, and even him not too harshly.

It's at times like this that I have need of a friend; but what would be required is the mildness of Signor Lechi and the sagacity of Crozet, and, above all, I'd have to have a talisman in my pocket to make myself liked by them, for at these times I'm hardly what you might call amiable.

The comical thing about my rage is that I see while writing this that Signora Pietragrua merits nothing but my praise. She regarded me several times with attention at the theater; I was overwhelmed with tokens of attention and complaisance; moreover, as a snuffbox was passed, I having lightly squeezed her hand, she sought and at once found an opportunity of squeezing mine in the most pronounced manner possible.

A strange result of much pride and sensibility, which I've gone into at length in order that the Beyle of 1821 may understand it.

But what is Signora Pietragrua after all? That's the thing that's essential.

Here will be found the modest assurance that I haven't enough facts. I beg that it be borne in mind that this is a two-month excursion in Italy, undertaken by a man who's slightly mad, as the foregoing proves. A year's experience would be required to purify my judgments. But anyway I'm noting the sound each thing produces as it strikes on my soul.

Character of Signora Pietragrua.—Signora Pietragrua, a tall and beautiful woman, is serious-minded. I no longer find anything romantic in her eyes. She finds that in Milan monotony kills pleasure; intrigues are marriages here. You have pleasure the first four months, and then you yawn together for a year or two out of respect for public opinion.

She finds that the Italians (of Milan) lack personality—she calls it wit—but she grants them talent; i.e., cunning and prudence in reaching any goal. She made that out the day before yesterday with perfect sagacity. I was about to applaud her, although she beat me. She finds that, when an Italian happens to get off an epigram, he says it in a ponderous way that kills its merit.

Mightn't I think that a little intrigue, quite unexpected and ardent, with me might be pleasing to her? That would break the monotony.

Yesterday, on the way to the Brera, I asked her with the laconic accent of mystery whether she loved her servant [*cavaliere*]; I told her that I had been under the impression that Signor Widmann was this servant.

I punished myself for the length of my visit yesterday by not going to see her today. It cost me dearly. But I must remember what Angéline told me about the effect the attentions and declarations of her lovers have on her. If I wish to please, it mustn't be so sure that I've been pleased.

I'm suppressing here a page of ridiculous and tender pathos, and, after having written twenty pages without interruption, I'm going to take a bath. Last night I was a bit mollified by a delightful serenade which half awoke me.

Today, I saw without pleasure the Ambrosiana, Leonardo's *The Last Supper,* San Celso, etc. The only thing I found that was any good for me was a caryatid (the one on the right as you go in San Celso). I'll go to see *The Last Supper* again and will write my entry in the refectory itself. I saw a sketch by Bossi (Ugolin). The children are placed with grace and are touching; the figure of the father is nothing more or less than that of a flayed man, instead of showing a happy man who's merely suffered misfortune for four days. The painter ought to suppress the *più lune* of Dante and assume that misfortune started only at the moment the door was sealed. It's nothing more than a cartoon.

I used to reproach myself for not having seen the Ambrosiana during my first stay in Milan. This remorse was overdone. This library offers not the slightest interest. There's a copy of *The Last Supper* painted, the guide told me, in 1596, a hundred years after the original, and the copyist complained even then that Leonardo's work was becoming effaced.

I experienced the *seccatura* [boredom] of guides. My servant butted in to praise Titian. A guide would keep me, I believe, from admiring *Il Matrimonio Segreto*. There ought to be dumb guides who'd lead you to a monument and simply point it out.

After these excursions, I went about on foot through the streets, but, as I've already said, I'm no longer touched by my memories of Milan. I returned to my room and wrote twenty pages in my journal. I went to take a bath. The bath gave me some thoughts, among others that of saying to Signora Pietragrua:

"When I left your loge, I was madly in love with you. I went to the pit in order to see you. I punished myself for this imprudence by not seeing you yesterday."

I see that I've forgotten what it was that gave a bit of graciousness to this idea.

I went to the Corso, which seemed to me boring. There was no one there but two women of the common people, on foot.

From there to the *Pretendenti*. Immediately after the first act, I went to *Capricciosa Pentita,* from which I came out at half-past eleven. Music full of grace, gaiety of the actors, but danger of picking up lice.

That's the only danger I've found thus far on my voyage.

The traveler who wants to amuse himself by writing everything he's read about the country of his rambles would be able to compose a journal of a hundred folio volumes. He who simply notes what he has felt is very limited.

Milan, September 12.—I plan to make my little declaration to Signora Pietragrua, and to find out whether I ought to stay in Milan or be on my way. Nothing retains me more than she does.

I've just been to the Royal Palace. There's nothing majestic about it except the ballroom and a concert room, which, however, seemed to me inferior to that of the palace in Vienna.

The room of the Council of State is shabby, but it's better than ours in this respect, that the light enters from above and the acoustics are good.

But it's in the same bad oblong form. They ought to be built in a semicircle.

The Milan palace looks poverty-stricken. The mirrors in it are small and divided into several parts, the clocks shameful, forty or fifty pieces of Jacobean furniture.

The clocks are from Paris, and there are a great many of those terrible old Gobelin tapestries.

The only fine things in this palace are the artificial marble floors and the paintings by Appiani.

The frescoes are very fine, but there's almost too much blue in them. This color lends freshness and majesty, but too much of it gives a cold and cadaverous effect.

I saw two or three portraits of the Viceroy's Lady which were shameful; the neck and hands were blue, the breast the same, formless, almost baggy.

The two portraits of the Emperor are majestic, of genuine stateliness, by means especially of the two victories in half-tone; but Appiani has made an inspired man of the Emperor. It would seem that painters only conceive genius in this way, and that the superior reasoning power which grasps the real relationships between things, as much as it's possible for man to do, and which dominates events by a cold prudence, is invisible to them.

LOVE. But this morning I was a very long way from this cold reason of which I speak. I counted the minutes. I intended to go to Signora Pietragrua's at one o'clock. Noon came around at last; I got dressed. I was tender and in a mood to make a fine declaration. I was all worked up; but it's precisely when I'm in that fine state that luck goes against me. I asked the woman at the door if she was at home. She said, "*Yes.*" I went up full of impatience; a pretty little chambermaid, lively and gay, told me with a sly little look, "*Servo suo, è sortita* [At your service, Signora has gone out]."

I went to the Brera, where, as I looked at the pictures, I attempted to reason with myself, to dull my soul and to take things gaily. After such efforts, you're dead as far as graciousness is concerned.

They turned us out of the Brera at two o'clock; I went to Signor Rafaelli's to see the work on *The Last Supper,* a Christ by Guido Reni, etc. I was attempting to kill time until three o'clock. Signor Rafaelli, I believe, a bilious little young man with the face of an artist, took me through his establishment; at length, I noticed that it was half-past three, and I escaped.

I went up to her apartment; but there was no longer any of that gentle emotion, no longer any tenderness. It was a couple of hours earlier that I should have been seen. She was alone; she would only have needed to be in a joking mood to make my declaration expire on my lips, and tonight I'd have been as surly as a bear. I told her with the tone of pure reason that I was in love with her, that it was in order not to run the risk of loving all alone that I didn't go to see her yesterday, etc., etc.

She said (more or less) that I was joking; and, as I sincerely assured her of the contrary, she said, "I'd like very much to believe that it was true."

Our whole colloquy was devilishly reasonable both in tone and character. But, since the French have much more vivacity in conversation than the Italians, this distant manner may have escaped her.

She told me right away that she'd also been in a bad humor yesterday when she saw at four o'clock that I wasn't coming, and that she'd gone out today in order to punish me.

Thereupon I said some things that were very good indeed, but said, in my opinion, in a way that was too cold. She addressed me in the second person singular, she wept, her tenderness redoubled when I recalled the traits of my former love.

It seems that this memory, which I've preserved for so long of a thousand little things, appeared remarkable to her—I don't dare say *touched her.*[1] When I tried to kiss her, she said, *"Receive and never take."* I find this maxim very suitable for my character, in which the force necessary for the execution kills the sentiment.

Consequently, I didn't steal any kisses, but I soon received some. Tenderness came back proportionately as I had no more need for executive power; I felt myself stimulated, and if the tête-à-tête had continued for long, I'd have gone through with things.

She wept, we kissed each other and spoke in the second person singular, continually on her part. We thoroughly discussed the question of my departure. She repeated several times in a voice tremulous with

[1] This is all very amusing for me to reread in 1817 (November 2, 1817) after what I've seen since then. [Note added by Beyle.]

emotion, "Leave, leave, I realize that you must leave for my peace of mind. Tomorrow I may no longer have the courage to say it."

When I told her I'd be too unhappy during the trip, "But you'll have the certainty of being loved."

She said with a look that was quite convinced, speaking of our relations together, "Why, it's like a novel!"

Does she feel what she says? Is it through coquetry?

That's a great question; but I want to try to make her really amorous, if she's not so already. I had a fine moment this morning, following which I smashed my watch crystal, after having her read, *"Angiolina t'ama in ogni momento* [Angelina loves thee every moment]."

Those are things that can't be resisted. She was afraid our blushes would compromise us. I assured her she needn't fear for me. Arrived a pupil of Pestalozzi and later the cavalier servant.[1] I was perfectly amiable with these gentlemen. As the result, I saw the keenest pleasure in her eyes, which, however, I didn't dare to regard too often for fear of not being able to keep up my role. I talked about Tracy to the savant, about the arts, granite and English to the servant.

This servant appeared to be possessed of intelligence, profoundity, tact and social experience, but he looked unhappy and suspicious; no fire, no nobleness, forty years old. She went to great pains to assure me that he wasn't at all her lover.

But she looks to me as though she had a very prudent behavior. It may be simply the Italian character which I'm seeing from near at hand.

This victory didn't give me an overwhelming pleasure. If she'd been home at one o'clock, things would have been entirely different.

I left her at five o'clock, after being perfectly amiable with the gentlemen.

I saw her again in her loge, where I was somewhat bored at being able to say and do only indifferent things. Still, we squeezed each other's arm, and for the first time I heard perfectly a Milanese conversation, full of quips, allusions and semi-indecencies—in a word, very difficult.

I remark that it's extremely difficult to judge a people whose language you don't know.

She gave me a rendezvous tomorrow at the Français in an illuminated loge, the tenth in the second tier; but I'll go to see her at one o'clock.

Milan, September 13.—I was wearing the same pair of trousers when I fought the battle of May 31 at Palfy[2] and that of September 12 at Milan.

[1] M. Turenne. [Note by Beyle.]

[2] See above, entry of June 3, 1811.

Mme. de Palfy's manner was replete with emotion; that of Signora Pietragrua seemed to me too replete with rationality.[1]

Besides, the Italian, being more profound and more susceptible to violent emotions and daring deeds, applies more rationality to the arrangements which concern his happiness, and consequently has a more unperturbed and indifferent appearance.

Signora Pietragrua, for example, who took a woman with her to serve as witness, and who was heedless of the consequences her act might have, left for Paris to justify herself before Joinville and then leave him; at whom, a few months earlier, an unsuccessful lover had fired a pistol and calmly denied the fact; who has since governed her conduct with the most consummate prudence—Signora Pietragrua, I was saying, couldn't be moved by an avowal she was able to foresee and had possibly planned to bring about.

Therefore, in spite of having too much rationality, it's possible that she loves me.

September 15, Sunday.—The Italian, being aware of the violent passions to which he may open the flood gates, is full of attention, and consequently appears to be unfeeling in moments when we French, who are sure of not losing our heads, give ourselves up completely to our emotion, which thus is weaker and appears to be stronger.

September 15.—I came away from her home full of admiration and almost of love. She'll make me shed tears when I leave Milan. That tender phrase, *to see her again after ten years,* when a thousand accidents during that time might have taken me away from her forever! To see her again and not to have her, to suffer the misfortune of being able to say, "Others have made more headway in her affection!"

She's just given me a half hour of the understanding of this sublime and tender character that made me so wild during the year of Marengo. She told me how she almost died during the year of the great plague, from which she was saved by the extraction of 400 ounces of blood; of the doubts about religion which came to her after this experience; she told me she'd read Dupuis (*Origine des Cultes*), but especially "her dear Elvezio" [Helvétius]; that she'd submitted her doubts to M. Turenne, and that she finally had them no longer.

After the affectionate way my declaration was received, there was a day (September 13, I believe) when I thought I was going to spend a month in Milan and be her lover.

At once Milan was displeasing to me. What was there to do when I wasn't with her? It seemed to me that I no longer loved Angiolina —at least I felt myself turned to ice.

[1] It's quite simple, lack of habit in Mme. de Palfy. She's the most and the least coquettish of women. [Note by Beyle.]

I cursed my pride quite sincerely. If she hadn't loved me, I'd have had some frightful moments, the thought of not being loved by this rare woman would have haunted me amidst all my pleasures.

She loves me, and boredom has come over me.

That means there's a source of unhappiness in me. How I'd like to have a friend who'd constantly prod this part of my soul with a red-hot iron!

I don't know whether it was yesterday or the day before that I went to see her. I might have her and stay, or leave and not have her.

When I arrived, she repeated several times, "Leave, Beyle, you must leave; leave, leave, you must leave."

I held out and appeared to be very hurt, but finally, amid the *più teneri baci* [the tenderest of kisses], I agreed to leave.

From that moment, everything changed and took on a moving complexion.

We spoke of the possibility of my settling down in Milan.

"How quickly I'd turn out all my friends and tell them, 'I'll see you at the theater if you wish.'"

She said that with the most genuine and richest ring in her voice, and her eyes akindle.

Yesterday, the 14th, in our little tête-à-tête of one o'clock that lasted twenty or twenty-five minutes, there were tears in her eyes several times, she abandoned herself in my arms; *ma nel mezzo dei più teneri baci* [but in the midst of the tenderest kisses], she wouldn't let me give her a kiss on the thigh. "What's to keep us from going farther? Is that the way to leave each other?" she repeated constantly, kissing me at the same time. "We're losing our heads more and more."

I felt myself in the presence of a superior mind.

I feel myself penetrated with an admiration for her that leads me to tenderness.

As I was saying, yesterday I went to hunt up M. de Saint-Romain. I only saw him this morning. Unfortunately, he's waiting for something, otherwise we'd have left tomorrow. I hope we'll be able to leave September 17.

But I'll see Angelina again on my way back to Paris, and at present my heart finds it impossible to go a year without seeing her.

I believe that, upon arriving in Paris, I'm going to become a miser and a flatterer in order to have the money and the leaves of absence to come to Milan.

Yet I'm very bored when I'm far from her.

Some importunate friends came in after our little tête-à-tête yesterday. I wanted to leave so as not to make them jealous; the void into which I'm plunged when I leave her made me stay on until four o'clock. We saw in succession Messrs. Widmann, Delfante, Turenne and the Comte d'Azas; I tried to be amiable, but that was perhaps one more reason for these gentlemen not liking me. The only feeling they can have for me is jealousy.

A week ago, after a long absence, I again saw Angelina, who didn't recognize me, and already my credit is equal to theirs, or, to be more accurate, superior.

If I had a couple of hours of privacy in a loge or on the promenade with Angelina, enough time to be natural, she'd fall in love with me.

Yesterday, she frequently had tears in her eyes.

This morning, we had a rendezvous at the bath. I had a hard time not to miss it. All turned out for the best. I told her all the errands I had done for her this morning. "Why, it's enough to make you giddy," she said with tears in her eyes.

We missed our rendezvous at her house. I found her sister and her handsome and stupid husband there. Then her mother, as well as the good Borrone, greeted me with friendliness of the German sort. Then Messrs. Tordorò, an abbot who looks as though he were a remarkable man, Widmann and Turenne.

She spoke to me from two o'clock till a quarter to three in front of the others, who were talking in low voices, of her illness, of how she was dying, of her doubts, etc. Why hasn't Mme. de Palfy a character like this? Great heavens, what happiness!

But, to come back to Angelina, I'd like to die in her arms. That mixture of majesty of soul and attachment for me would make me valiantly swallow the pill, which I'm sure to take as it should be anyway, thanks to my pride. But it would be so sweet for me to weep with Angelina.

Obviously, I'm far from Mocenigo. I no longer have the peace of mind that would make me find a piquant pleasure in things of this kind.

Her sister gave me a friendly greeting. This evening, after the *Ave Maria,* she's going to play some music for me with Signor Widmann at the Borrone home.

This morning at the bath she told me in an enigmatic fashion, because of the people listening, that she lived with her husband simply as a friend and, for the past two years, like a nun.

1. Therefore, I don't love her enough to live in Milan for her and not continually with her.

2. But I'd believe I had found happiness if I loved her in the Italian manner; i.e., being continually with her.

3. But she'll cause me to shed tears when I leave, and melancholy will be my traveling companion.

Here are the comets [*sic*] that I know: MATRIMONY, in the Year IV or V, before our time.[1]

M. Gros, ended in the Year VII;

M. Louis [Joinville].

ANOTHER FRENCH;

AND I MYSELF.

Milan, September 15 (written September 16).—All Milan was on the Corso and at the Porta Orientale to see the ascension [in a balloon] of Mme. Blanchard. She's the same one I saw very close up at Saint-Cloud on the occasion of the baptism of the King of Rome.

I WAS NOT DISPOSED TO SEE ALL THIS MOB AS MOCENIGO.

I was upset, but by emotions that were quite agreeable. I had the look of a madman and I sought Angelina in all the carriages. I didn't see her. I came back to dress, and at eight o'clock I was on Signora Borrone's balcony.

I'd planned to be a bit somber. I was quite as I should have been for the interests of the kind of love I have for Signora Pietragrua. I talked to her with ardor and naturalness; she told me not to be taciturn.

I joked with her sister, whom I saw again with pleasure. I talked about Court matters with Messrs. Turenne and Widmann.

Signor Widmann has the nobleness of a great lord; Italian nobleness, that is, naturalness, without bourgeois pride, as M. Sismondi remarks at the beginning of the fifth volume of his history.

M. Turenne hasn't any nobleness, but much good sense and sagacity.

If I weren't feeling tender and were traveling in the interests of Mocenigo, I'd owe it to myself to see as much as possible of Messrs. Turenne, Tordorò and Barizoni. They are, it seems to me, distinguished men. Another proof of Angelina's superiority.[2]

Signor Borrone greeted me as well as possible. They wanted to sing, but the piano was out of tune. We went to Signora Pietragrua's. I gave her my arm as we were going to her house. She seemed to be in love with me and promised *di lasciarmi dar un bacio sopra la coscia* [to let me kiss her on the thigh].

We sang. The choice of music was bad, but Peppina [Angelina's sister] has a beautiful contralto voice, thoroughly Italian, a *soave,* powerful voice, like the coffee *alla panera* of the Caffè Nuovo, Corsia dei Servi.

Angelina told me it pained her to see me so gay. When I was joking with her mother, she said, "Have you already forgotten what I told you?"

[1] Angelina was married about 1793 at the age of sixteen.

[2] And of my youth (1817). [Note added by Beyle.]

She said to me out of a clear sky, in the Italian manner, as though it were a result of her reflections, "Come tomorrow at half-past twelve."

That seemed to me to promise the denouement. I shouldn't want one if it were necessary to go on with my present life. If I sacrificed my Italian trip for her, I'd want to be with her all the time, on the shores of the Sesia, for instance, like a novel.

I smashed my cane when she told me she wouldn't permit *il bacio* [the kiss]. I said in a singsong voice, *"Van male e malissimo gli affari miei* [things are going badly, very badly, for me]."

Milan, September 16.—Magnificent weather, as warm as the month of June. I drove around Milan in a fiacre on the ramparts in an hour and three quarters. Superb vegetation. Fine effect of the Duomo seen from the Porta Romano.

Only my heart is Italian; if, in 1800, I'd mingled with society, as I'm doing now and as I'll do after a month's stay in Milan, I'd have acquired Milanese manners.

Good sense was in disgrace with me for a long time, and I must confess that I was in disgrace with it. If I'd been thoroughly familiar with the Italians, good sense and sagacity would have held the place of honor with me instead of being synonyms for indifference and weakness of feeling.

I'm writing this in Milan September 20, 1811. I was regretting the trip through Italy; consequently, I wasn't in love.

On September 18, I had a tête-à-tête of three quarters of an hour with her.[1] The previous day, we went walking together for an hour and a half, among other things we went to eat some grapes at a house she owns in an outlying district.

I had a burst of tender melancholy, and I recognized love.

If I don't write, I forget everything; but if I describe my feelings, I'm distressed. I'm convinced that what is pure feeling leaves no memory.

I was on the verge of growing tender; I wandered through the streets, not knowing what to do; I was only due to see her in the evening, at her mother's. I nearly had tears in my eyes, and my heart was heavy.

At seven o'clock, I saw her at her mother's. She was with M. Turcotti [Turenne], who'd told her he wouldn't leave for Venice until I'd gone. I barely had time to speak to her. She went out to buy something. Signor Chappuis, commercial traveler, had the courtesy to speak to me about my voyage. He recommended the mail coach to me. She came back, and I immediately left with Signor Chappuis to reserve a seat.

I believe that, if the courier which left two hours later, hadn't been

[1]No, it was another day. [Note by Beyle.]

taken, I'd have been crazy enough to leave. I was like a child, I wanted to rush things. I struck a bargain for 120 francs to Bologna. I could have had it for 100 francs, but I was in a rush.

My disappointment may be imagined when, returning to the good Signora Borrone's, I found that Angelina was no longer there. I loitered in the vicinity of the shop. I finally encountered her on the Piazza del Duomo. We went to see the comet on the Piazza Castello. It was superb and quite visible. She looked as though she were touched. I, who'd been so sad all day long, was angry not to be able to put on all my melancholy. Messrs. Turenne and Scagliotti were with her. I left her at her door.

September 19, she came to the Piazza Castello at a quarter past eleven. We got in a carriage and went to the Simonetta. I believe I'm really in love with her. She seems to love me too. Perhaps I'll have her Saturday, the day of my departure. I find her very incautious. It must be remembered that a false step in this land of sensibility doesn't have the same consequences as in Paris, the throne of vanity. Besides, I'm spoiling my love by talking about it. Adieu.

I saw her from three till a quarter to five. I bought Bossi. I heard with pleasure the trio of the second act of the *Pretendenti,* and have just read a comedy by Giraud in order to take my mind off her and to put myself to sleep. I'd drunk some coffee with woeful results.

September 20.—(I'm leaving at midnight tomorrow, the 21st, for Bologna at 120 francs.)

It rained this morning; I wrote Crozet a letter.

I have a somber happiness that seems to me Italian, far removed from the facile life of the sanguine man.

Italian character.—The joy of the Italians doesn't appear boisterous to me. It's expressed by a faint smile which is to be seen especially in the eyes, but there the smile is to be seen with an intensity rarely found on French physiognomies.

Signora Pietragrua told me there wasn't any *flash* in their wit. Everything has confirmed this observation.

I've been struck by their gross ignorance. The most intellectual of my Italians, Signor Turenne, placed Maupertius under Louis XIV. That trait isn't decisive, but I've noticed several that were striking. The most outstanding were those of Signor Scotti, who, although he has traveled, mistook two thatch-roofed cottages two leagues from Milan—and two isolated thatch-roofed cottages at that—for Milan.

In consideration of the little I have seen, I should readily grant the Italians unlimited sensibility and sagacity. In the knowledge of character, nearly all of them have a bit of Mocenigo.

3. Much naturalness.

4. No wit, strictly speaking, the wit of Duclos's kind.

5. Ignorance.

6. Little vanity.

7. Dirtiness.

Duclos's kind of thing would be entirely new to them. Nothing is farther from that silly kind of thing so common in Germany than the Italian manner, and in their writings they're almost silly.

What a fine encomium of this land was Signora Pietragrua describing the character of Signor Bossi (the artist) and ending by saying, "He's a genuinely dangerous man!"

It's in this land that Migliorini can be appreciated and not in Paris, where he'd be reproached for tying his cravat badly, for instance. Obviously, the only thing this land lacks in order to be the home of the arts is a large consumption of pictures.

September 21.—I'm leaving tonight. Yesterday, the 20th, I spent the evening at a piece of German nonsense by Iffland at the Patriotic Theater. The Italian audience laughed outright at the silly phrases dealt out in honor of the soldiers' bread.

I was waiting for it. I said to myself, "I'm caught," and I actually do believe it's love, but struggling against a strong character. I hope absence will permit me to get over it somewhat.

She was to have come, and she hasn't come. Can it be that she's nothing more than a coquette?

Yesterday I enjoyed a semi-favor.

When I returned to my room in the evening, my eyes were swollen shut and hurt me. I was a long time on the verge of crying.

I WAS, I BELIEVE, IN LOVE.

On September 21, AT half-past eleven, I won the victory I had so long desired.

It seems to me that perfectly pure pleasure can come only with intimacy; THE FIRST TIME, it's a victory; IN THE THREE following, you acquire intimacy. Afterward comes perfect happiness provided you have to do with an intelligent woman, lofty in character and whom you love.

But it's obvious that this *you* is myself at the age of twenty-eight years and eight months.

This victory was not easy. At a quarter to ten, I went into the little church on the corner of the Via dei Meravigli. I wasn't able to hear ten o'clock strike. I went by at five minutes after ten by my watch; no paper.

I went by again at twenty minutes after ten; she signaled to me. After a very serious moral conflict, in which I shammed unhappiness and almost despair, she was mine at half-past eleven.

I left Milan at half-past one, September 22, 1811.

Bologna, September 24.—The denouement of September 21 gave me back my sense of duty, and I'm consequently putting a half hour of freedom to good use by writing. This postface is an excuse for the lack of feeling in the said account, or rather, its lack of color.

I left Milan on the 22nd at a quarter to two in the morning. At midnight I read in the Caffè Mest. . . , next to the post office, of the Duc de Cadore's appointment.

I passed through Lodi, Pizzighettone, where the Adda appeared to me to be very wide, through Cremona, where I dined—a lonely and dismal look—and through Bozzolo. Finally Mantua at eleven o'clock. I took supper there. I wrote to Signora Pietragrua from there. I slept there a little, and was shamefully bitten by gnats. The whole day was a rest period, I slept constantly.

I left Mantua at two o'clock and passed over the Po at four. I was wide awake and appreciative. I was dying of hunger thanks to the bilious sobriety of my little courier who was unimpressionable, sagacious and silent. Afterward I dined at Modena, the cleanest and gayest Italian town I've visited.

September 23.—I reached Bologna at half-past six. Trouble getting lodgings and a bath. I reached the theater at a quarter past eight. I saw *Ser Marcantonio,* an opera by Pavesi which charmed all Milan last year, I believe. Signor Giacomo Lechi told me the story of this opera, and I saw Il Signor Marcantonio and talked with him in the loge *della* Gina *colla* [of Angelina with] Signora Crivelli, whom he serves.

The prima donna, Signora Marietta Marcolini, is a contralto of a perfect mildness of manner. I'd have liked more vigor. But that kind of mildness is admirable, and we could use some of it in France. I remained until the end because of Signora Marcolini. From time to time, I fell asleep.

I reached the Albergo Reale at half-past eleven. Tremendous racket made by my servant, and complete silence. After half an hour, the master of the house climbed over the door.

September 24.—This morning, I saw *Neptune,* by Giovanni di Bologna, San Petronius, the church of San Dominico, Guido's *Heaven,* the . . . gallery.[1]

A man unfamiliar with poetry experiences a greater amount of pleasure after reading La Harpe's *Lycée.* I could use a similar book on painting. And yet, for the arts, a sensibility uniquely applied to that sets me apart from the vulgar.

I invariably say to myself when somebody praises a picture by a

[1] I don't remember the name. [Note by Beyle.]

great master, "If I came across it on a street corner, would I pay any attention to it?"

I base my judgment solely on expression, imagination and naturalness.

In the ... gallery, a head that was nothing at all representing a countenance of the German variety (in the portrait room, the first) touched me.

A *Bathsheba* by Guerchino [Barbieri], in which David is too conspicuous and lacks genius, gave me pleasure. Some Guido Renis full of charm and devoid of color.

Two pictures of the Venetian school full of color: *Herodias Dancing* and *Marc Antony and Cleopatra.*

I came back to eat lunch and write, and I'm leaving.

The Palazzo Ercolani, built eleven years ago, already looks all dirty. The Italians go in for the grandiose. Statues of Hercules on the stairways, superb gallery, tables of hard stones, Chinese objects, and, amidst all that, cobwebs, dust, dirt in general and in particular. In Paris, we have cleanliness on the interior and shabbiness on the exterior.

In this palace, I didn't see a single room where I'd be able to work with pleasure. The dirtiness shocked me wherever I turned.

I haven't seen a single woman who struck me. We're in the country, my servant said. And anyway, the pretty women don't go abroad on foot in the morning in any land.

Great convenience of the colonnades, but dreariness of the view from the windows.

Bologna, September 24.—The Italians' variety of wit without flashes doesn't make them calculated to please their womenfolk. The victory of any Frenchman who desires to have wittiness, veiled by gracious manners, is assured. Even more so if he's noblified by elegant *dress.*

At the Marescalchi mansion, I found an Italian woman who had nothing to recommend her beyond those *Italian eyes* which I've had the pleasure of seeing praised by Arthur Young. I started talking, being gracious in order not to be shocking, and I'm convinced that in three quarters of an hour I was pleasing. My memory won't occasion any regrets, but I'm convinced that after that three quarters of an hour I stood as well with her as any other man. Her eyes reminded me of Livia's [Bialowiska]. Everything considered, I'll write her.

I've seen the Ercolani gallery. I've seen the university. Many gimcracks of natural history which were nothing to me, worse than nothing, boring.

From there to the museum (Sala della Nazione). A portrait of

Guido Reni painted by himself. The lankness of a sensitve man of sanguine temperament and some melancholy. The man who showed me the pictures appeared to have some intelligence. He told me it was true that Guido was *piuttosto malinconico* [inclined to be melancholy]. He quoted Vasari, Lanzi and a third one. There were many Carraccis. The brothers were poor, and painted on cheap canvas with common colors. A touching way of explaining their present blackness. I had little pleasure in seeing their pictures; now and then I felt some grandeur in them.

This afternoon, I was sensitive to painting.

Guido Reni's tender refinement pleased me.

I saw the apartments of the sons of the Tanari family. They live in a palace where there is a superb gallery. Their rooms are enough to make you sick: washstands like those of the inns; horrible beds whose heads touch the frames of magnificent pictures.

I'll say once again: grandeur and filth.

There are five Tanari brothers. Their father died two years ago. Their mother's spiritual director told her that the wrath of God would be unleashed on her house if she didn't have a Venus by Guido Reni burned. The poor Venus, for all the Italians' respect for the arts, was promptly burned up because she was nude.

This trait is worth checking. It's odd for 1809. Signor Aldini or Signor Marescalchi ought to know the truth about it.

I was impressed with the extreme simplicity and majestic appearance of the edifices in Bologna. At the home of Signor Marescalchi, who sends rather common furniture to his house from Paris, there's a room deserving of envy. It's full of choice pictures by Guido Reni, Guerchino and the Carraccis. Nothing common. It's estimated as being worth 500,000 francs.

There's a woman seen full face; it's by Guido Reni. It's absolutely the Mozart kind of sensibility, the Minette kind.

It was in this room that I found my Italian woman from Imola, to whom I made myself pleasing in three quarters of an hour. It's agreeable to come into contact with those sensitive souls and expressive eyes of Italy. You're able to follow the effect you produce. At the end of a half hour, the conversation had already become a private one between us. But the trouble is that the husbands and fathers, who also find you pleasing, monopolize you in order to have a conversation with you too.

The handsome Mercury leaping in the air is by Giovanni di Bologna.

They tried to make me admire a Virginius, a statue by a professor of Bologna: it seemed to me without genius; it's a mass of muscles and that's all. He was asinine enough to turn away the face of Virginius, who's grimacing at the angels.

This figure was executed through a subscription of Bolognese art lovers who contributed six francs a year for three consecutive years. The group once executed, it was found that there wasn't enough money to pay for it, and it was presented to the author.

Such a country deserves to have the arts.

Whether it was vanity or something else, my conversation with the Italian woman at the Marescalchi mansion made me feel that happiness might be found at Bologna.

And yet I have only thirty-six days more of freedom! Alackaday!

I've got to be in insipid Grenoble by October 24, a month from now. From Milan to Grenoble, four days; consequently, I'll have to leave Milan October 20. From Rome to Milan, five days; consequently, I'll have to leave Rome October 15. From Naples to Rome, two days; consequently, I'll have to leave Naples October 13.

And I shan't be there until the 30th of this month. It'll be necessary to divide my time between Naples and Rome, to be at Naples only four days, at Rome four days, and to leave Rome October 10 for Milan. And, back in Paris, I'll have so much leisure! If I don't take up my work with the Duc de Cadore, not being needed, I may be able to obtain some leaves of absence.

What a pleasure it would be to return to Italy in the month of March!

It would be better to be a Prefect only a couple of years later.

I've seen the Ercolani and Tanari galleries. There remain the Zambeccari gallery and the Madonna di San Luca for me to see.

The Italians are barbarians when it comes to convenience on the interior of the houses, but not in what concerns the exterior. My door at the Albergo Reale hasn't any latch. I'm either locked in or forced to leave the door open.

Bologna, September 25.—On the 25th, as M. de Saint-Romain hadn't arrived, I decided to leave alone for Florence by the mail coach. There are nine posts at nine francs each: that makes 81 fr.

The courier which leaves at midnight tonight would take me there for 48 francs, but it would mean losing a day. It takes fifteen hours to go from here to Florence; I'll consequently be there on the 26th at three or four o'clock in the morning. I can spend the day there and leave the same evening with the Rome courier.

At Bologna, all expenses paid, I still have 94 napoleons, or 25 doubles + 22 ditto. I'm pleased with the Albergo Reale and the servant. 94 x 20 = 1,880 francs. Everything's cheaper than in France.

September 25.—*Voyage from Bologna to Florence.*—I had a rendezvous with a M. de Saint-Romain, a mild-mannered man but one who, the Comte d'Azas told me, is a gambler. I believe, for a fact, that he must have gambled away his traveling money a second time, for he showed up at neither Bologna nor Florence.

Not having a carriage, I left Bologna the 25th at half-past eleven in a *legno di* post. It's the simplest kind of a vehicle, which is furnished about every two posts at the price of twenty or thirty sous a post.

I saw the countryside very well. There is nothing majestic about the Apennines, with the possible exceptions of the environs of Florence. In the vicinity of Bologna, it's a pile of little mounds separated by a multitude of irregular little gorges.

I felt the sun's heat intensely. It was the second time I'd been exposed to it; the first was at Sesto, on the shores of Lake Maggiore.

From Lojano to Pianoro, beautiful Lombardy spreads out like a sea beyond the nearby heights of the Apennines. It was a beautiful sight. Like the view of the real sea, it stimulates thought. In this one, you glimpse many houses lit up by the rays of the setting sun. My postilion told me that, when the sun rises, you can get a glimpse of the Adriatic Sea by the sun's reflections.

There's a Madonna of the Ants, to which all the winged ants go, according to what I'm told. But a thing of which I'm certain is that, five hundred paces to the left of the road, you ought to have a superb view. You'd have to go up to a house situated on a rather curious plateau midway between Pianoro and Lojano.

After Lojano, the road continues amidst a multitude of stunted chestnut trees. This tree produces a fine effect, its branches are boldly designed, as are its groups of foliage, and they mass up well.

I was keenly sensitive, I was happy. The rows of rock along the road at the right and seeming to extend toward Carrara produced the effect of opera scenery.

I applauded myself for traveling alone. Even Crozet would have detracted from the purpose of my voyage. I need a certain dose of conversation and the communication of my thoughts and feelings; not having a traveling companion who may serve for this purpose, I resort to the Italians. I'm thus forced to study them. The man who travels in order to enjoy the sound produced on his soul by mountains and foreign characters, and to know mankind, should beware of placing himself too far from nature.

Two Frenchmen, traveling in a comfortable carriage with an intelligent servant, would be able to transport the amiability of Paris and the pleasures of the salon to the midst of the Apennines, but they wouldn't appreciate the Apennines as I'm doing traveling alone in an entirely open carriage.

Florence, September 27.—I arrived at five o'clock in the morning of the 26th at the Albergo d'Ingleterra, run by Schneider, overcome by fatigue, wet, jolted, obliged to retain a hold on the front of the mail wagon and sleeping while seated in a cramped position. The terrific jolting caused by a road that was hard, but not kept in condition, and full of little holes, had reduced me to a state of utter distress. I was at the end of my endurance, to the full extent of the word, when I reached the city of Flore.[1]

I went to bed at six o'clock, leaving orders to be awakened at eight. I was hardly able to sleep, and didn't perspire at all; consequently, I had no rest.

Detail of the day of September 26.—I was awakened at eight o'clock. I dragged myself out to the posthouse, where I learned that all the seats were taken in the mail coach for the 26th and the 27th, and that I'd only be able to leave in that of Saturday, the 28th. I thought it over for two hours, and finally, not putting any stock in the words of a gambler, I reserved a seat for the 28th (81 francs for fifty leagues). I'm leaving tomorrow, Saturday the 28th, at six o'clock in the evening.

The Albergo d'Ingleterra is a splendid inn which would merit this title in France. Maybe it will turn out to be very dear, but, if the bill isn't exorbitant, it's a remarkable inn.

I took a nice clean bath there, and went out to see Florence in stormy weather. Terrific showers every quarter of an hour and some fine thunderclaps, the first ones I've heard this year.

This kind of weather, which would have been beautiful to contemplate from a castle in the midst of the Apennines, was not what was required to look at pictures in churches, which are naturally dark places.

The darkness made me see, to my astonishment, that the great masters didn't keep the tone of their pictures light and a bit more brilliant than nature, like Signor Bossi. His *Last Supper,* hung in a church, would produce a superb effect and be reduced to naturalness.

My first homage, as my first question, was for Alfieri. "Where is the house that Conte Alfieri lived in? Where is his tomb?"

"The house, there, to the left, beside the Arno; his tomb, in Santa Croce, far from here."

[1]It was one of the moments in my life when I was the weariest. I still remember it after two years. [Note by Beyle.] Yet, in his *Rome, Naples et Florence,* he gives the following version of his arrival: "The day before yesterday, my heart beat violently as I descended the Apennines to arrive in Florence. What childishness! Finally, at a turn in the road, my eye roved over the plain and I saw in the distance, like a dark mass, Santa Maria del Fiore and its famous cupola, the masterpiece of Brunelleschi. 'It's there that lived Dante, Michelangelo, Leonardo da Vinci!' I said to myself. 'There is that noble city, the queen of the Middle Ages!' . . . In fine, memories crowded into my heart, I felt myself incapable of reasoning, and I yielded to my folly as in the presence of a loved woman."

"Take me there."

I arrived there and at once saw the tomb of Michelangelo, that of Alfieri, that of Machiavelli and to the left as I returned, opposite that of Michelangelo, the tomb of Galileo.

It must be admitted that few churches are honored by such tombs. That almost gives you the desire to be buried.

Michelangelo's tomb. Three statues perched on the marble steps in such a way that they'd topple over if you weren't aware that they have iron supports in their backs.[1] Consequently, no effect.

The first tomb I ever saw that aimed at producing an effect was that of the Marshal de Saxe at Strasbourg. It's effective because the sculptor dared to be dramatic. There's action resulting in facial expression. The marshal is going down into a gaping tomb with a superb look of intrepidity. The sculptor lost part of his effect by making small steps which you feel couldn't support the weight of the illustrious dying man.

The second tomb, certainly not in merit but in the order in which I've seen them, is that of Maria Christina in Vienna. The dramatic action is perfect. The dark portal produces the greatest effect.

It's unquestionably and by far the leading tomb in existence. Thus, as long as Canova is alive, immortality may be purchased. Any man sensitive to the arts would go two hundred leagues with pleasure to see a tomb of the kind of that of Maria Christina.

The third tomb, as far as merit is concerned, is the one of Alfieri. The base, in the form of . . . , and the manner in which the inscription is placed are the noblest things I've seen.

The figure of weeping Italy seems to me to be a bit lacking in grace, at least when seen from the point where the spectator is placed. Maybe it's too large; the only thing that can be seen well is the thighs. The only way it can be seen, the whole bust is foreshortened. The tomb itself is well done; the base is sublime. That made it necessary to give this colossal majesty to the figure.

But perhaps what should have been done was to put the tomb four or five feet below the level of the church. The spectator's eye would have been about on the level of the figure of Italy.

Anyway, I'm going back in an hour to take another look at this fine monument which made me blush with sadness at the wretched plaster cases containing Racine, La Fontaine, Boileau and Molière, I believe, all together in a corner of the Musée des Monuments Français. We deprive ourselves of the pleasure we might have in seeing these great men represented in fine monuments at Saint-Roch or the Panthéon.

[1] I believe I exaggerated. [Note added by Beyle.]

But our degree of love for the arts AND THE FORM OF GOVERNMENT places us devilishly far from such an enterprise.

After Alfieri comes Machiavelli. They still had the bad taste for pompous inscriptions in 1787. The subscribers who erected this monument to Machiavelli two hundred and sixty-six years after his death consequently put on his tomb:

TANTO NOMINI, NULLUM PAR ELOGIUM
NICOLAUS MACHIAVELLI
obiit An. A. P. MDXXVII

It would have been so natural to put:

MACHIAVELLI
266 an. post obitum

And it would perhaps have been still better to put:

MACHIAVELLI

First names spoil inscriptions. Everybody knows perfectly well that there was only one Machiavelli.

Several common men are buried near these great men. The most ridiculous are those who've retained their huge wigs even on their tombs.

The violinist Nardini, who died in 1793, has a neat monument in good taste.

Machiavelli died on June 22, 1527.

Galileo's tomb is meaningless. He's been given a face out of Mathieu Lansberg.

But the things that will engrave the church of Santa Croce the deepest in my heart are two pictures that I saw there and that produced the most powerful impression I've ever received from painting. Here's my sensation of yesterday.

Mon Dieu, how beautiful it is! At each detail you make out, your soul becomes more enraptured. You're on the way to tears. Before other pictures, you're dissatisfied with yourself because of your lack of feeling, you attempt to arouse your soul, you finally force yourself to admire by explaining the beauties to yourself. That's what I've often felt in the Paris museum.

My admiration for St. Cecilia, the Madonna della Sediola and the Madonna in the Luxembourg has never gone as far as rapture.

I found this sensation yesterday in front of the four sibyls painted by Volerrano in the chapel of the Niccolini.

The ceiling of the same chapel is very effective, but my eyesight is not good enough to judge ceilings. It merely appeared to me to be very

effective. As for the four sibyls, anything I could say would be inadequate. It's majestic, it's living, it appears to be nature in relief; one of
them possesses that grace which, combined with the majestic, makes
me fall in love at once.

I believed I'd never find anything as beautiful as these sibyls, when
my servant stopped me, almost by force, to look at a painting of *Limbo.*

I was almost moved to tears. They start to my eyes as I write this. I've
never seen anything so beautiful. What I require is either expression or
beautiful female figures. All the figures are charming and sharply outlined, nothing is confused. Painting has never given me such pleasure.
I was dead tired, my feet swollen and pinched in new boots—a little
sensation which would prevent God from being admired in the midst
of His glory, but I overlooked it in front of the picture of *Limbo. Mon
Dieu,* how beautiful it is!

September 27.—I was all aflutter for two hours. I'd been told that this picture was by *Guerchino;* I worshiped this painter from the bottom of
my heart. Not at all; I was told two hours later that it was by Agnolo
Bronzino, a name unknown to me. This discovery annoyed me a great
deal. I was also told that the coloring was pale. At that, I thought of
my eyes.

My eyesight is tender, nervous, apt to become agitated, sensing the
slightest nuances, but shocked at the dark and harsh tones of the
Carrachis, for example. The pale manner of Guido Reni is almost in
harmony, not with my manner in judging the arts, but with my eyesight.

My whole admiration may be the result of the physical structure of
my eyes. At any rate, I'm going back to Santa Croce.

Tonight the *Cascine* and the play. A provincial theater in comparison with that of Milan. I'll write about that to Signora Pietragrua.
To change the tone: without any prejudice, I've seen nothing yet that
is comparable with the Scala, and yet I certainly ought to be allowed to
have a little prejudice.

My memories lose their style by waiting. Yesterday, to increase my
appreciation and for my own pleasure, I composed a dozen sentences
about what I'd seen. They were precise descriptions, forceful and
crammed with my sensations. I tasted pleasure a second time while
writing them. Today, the 27th, I've just written these fourteen pages
with cold reason. I'm going out at a quarter to ten. I almost don't feel
tired any more.

Florence, September 27.—I returned at half-past twelve from my morning's round. That's the routine that's best adapted for the repose of
the legs and eyes. My legs have been tired constantly since the beginning of my voyage.

What's required is this: coffee at eight o'clock, go out, lunch at noon, at six o'clock dinner, a walk, an hour during which I'm bored, and the opera.

During the idle hour this evening, I intended to put in an appearance at Mme. Adèle's.[1] Her presence in Florence detracts from the city's effect on me. I think of her, of what she made me suffer, of the pettiness of an unfeeling soul, of the unhappiness she gave me, or rather which I felt on her account, of the kiss on the staircase, etc.

Museum of Natural History.—What pleasure an anatomist must experience upon entering this museum! Nothing has ever appeared to me neater, more sharply defined, more instructive. The labels are so arranged as to give clear ideas without an effort. The lying-in room seems to me to be far superior to those of Bologna and Vienna.

I saw with the pleasure of profane eyes the muscles and the nerves, which are very clearly defined; the anatomy of the eye, with its camera obscura. The immense number of nerves distributed in a dog's nose; the anatomy of a calf's head, a goat's and a cat's. The anatomy of a silkworm, a bloodsucker.

I saw without pleasure a number of stones, minerals and birds. All that sort of thing means less than nothing to me. The collection seemed to be complete and well arranged. I paid more attention to the genuinely Florentine accent of the guardian who was talking to me than to the things he showed me. I saw an aquamarine, a very pretty stone.

He told me that bones of Hannibal's rhinoceros and elephants are to be found in the Arno Valley, that he sent some of them to M. Cuvier. Cuvier's genius is visible to me.

I saw the first skeleton that ever appeared handsome to me. You realize the type of beauty which a skeleton may attain—the majestic, and it actually has some of this quality. It's on the left as you go into the room of wax reproductions, in a handsome glass cage. The eye sockets, the nose, the jaws, the hipbones and the feet are nobly cast.

The weather is still stormy today.

When I got up this morning, I found a bright sun shining. I rejoiced, hoping to see the pictures distinctly. Two hours later, rain, wind, etc.

I went to the church dei Domenicani di Santa Maria Novella, which Michelangelo called *La Sposa*. I found nothing remarkable about this spouse.

A somewhat majestic altar. It's odd that they haven't got the talent to build an altar which would inspire the notion of respect. It would be so easy with an immense staircase, darkness and after the darkness an altar faintly illuminated from above.

[1] Adèle Rebuffel, now Mme. Alexandre Petiet.

I can't understand how the great geniuses failed to do that. Their altars must have cost enormous sums of money, or at least enormous labors. Everything is distorted. The marble is of the richest, and the effect is zero.

There's nothing but richness and patience, as a guide at the gallery said yesterday, speaking of those tables which are brilliant with mosaics in hard stones, common in Florence.

A finer luxury than our Gobelins would be a mosaic factory, like that of Rafaelli in Milan. But it would be necessary to have a manager who would forbid them to kill the colors. These people like only the blue and greenish; they smear them on everywhere.

The portrait of Benedict XIV, I believe, at the Institute of Bologna likewise has this defect.

The Gobelins have it thoroughly. I've seen them put green on the hand of the Emperor touching the pest victim at Jaffa. Anyone would have to be more than stupid not to reserve the green for the pest victims.

It's going to be necessary for me to attack painting. All the great painters of the three Italian schools have been lacking in expression. You see their characters doing the most extraordinary things with their faces stiff and composed. Their decapitations of St. John, so common, are all rose-water affairs.

A man named Hennequin, who painted *Orestes,* isn't a great artist, but if Domenichino, Albani and others had felt, like Hennequin, the need of expression, they'd have been far greater than they were. Expression is only a word in the voyager's lingo—for instance, the *delightful smile* and *divine languor* of Titian's *Venus* are to be found only in the descriptions of it.

He hasn't in the least brought out that unhappiness through the desire of a future happiness, the possibility of which is felt to be assured, and the beginning of pleasure which people who aren't artists call the languor of love.

Yet these great artists were capable of feeling; they were born in the most gesticulatory land in the world. What could have kept them from putting expression in their pictures?

Last night I read the gallery's notice. What makes all this kind of writing fall so flat is that it's written in a purely monarchical style: it condemns only by failing to praise.

Winckelmann also seems to me to have this defect; he doesn't regard nature first and the Greeks afterward, but the Greeks and then nature, which he finds admirable only in the points that are imitated, adopted, by the Greek statue makers. Yet the whole lot of them display a shocking lack of feeling. There's a head of Alexander at the gallery which expresses sorrow fairly well. They don't exhaust their superlatives in praising it.

I don't say these judgments are true for him who reads me, but they are so for me, H. B., born in 1783 and knocked around by eleven years of experience. They're what I think.

I believed for a long time that I was born insensitive to sculpture and even to painting.

But finally, near Isella, realizing the sort of cascade that would be befitting to place around the Palace of Poverty, I realized that I too understood the language of silent things. This morning, I saw a St. Lawrence who was utterly ridiculous because of his lack of expression. What a head for a Domenichino! The harrowing pain surmounted through hope and confidence in God.

Those heads existed among the thousands of ardent people put to death in all manners for the Christian religion, but the fact has never occurred to the artists.

Consequently, it's possible that in a few hundred years, there'll be a school of painting which, designing like present-day Frenchmen and seeing light like the Venetians, will at last succeed in expressing the nuances of passion. A virgin subject. At the gallery yesterday, I saw a Tancredi being cared for by Herminie; Tancredi is merely a conscript with a cartilaginous and ignoble nose; Herminie is a pretty girl who's playing the role of a pretty girl. But there isn't a shadow—I don't say of that divine nuance expressed by Tasso, of Herminie's heart torn between love and modesty—not a shadow of emotion.

It's a ceremony carried out with naturalness, and without affected dignity.

Raphael had expression in his heads of the Virgin, Michelangelo that of character and strength in his unfinished Brutus, which gave me the greatest pleasure yesterday in spite of the quibbling little inscription attached to it. Michelangelo hasn't at all sculptured the gentle soul and the touching conflict that Shakespeare shows.

All their Christs are wishy-washy. Not till yesterday did I see one who's putting up a struggle; but it was more of an athlete than the sublime character that may be attributed to Jesus Christ. But it must be admitted that the blend of the two natures (divine and human) offers genius the finest field for glory, but likewise the most difficult.

All the sculptured Christs I saw yesterday and today left me cold. The copy of Michelangelo's Christ on his mother's knees inspired nothing in me but reprobation for that great man.

I found naturalness in the inscriptions put by the husbands on the tombs of their wives. They praise them for never having quarreled in their households, and for having been good to their servants.

I find this naturalness praiseworthy, although the influence of the French dress coat I'm wearing at first gave me the affected smile of contempt.

I went out at two o'clock for my second excursion, I came back at six.

I've just been to Santa Croce, where I again saw my sibyl and the painting of *Limbo*. My sibyl has a German face of the Minette kind, very much noblified; but still she hasn't got the straight nose of Greek faces. She has a serene face, the eye alone is that of a lofty (or majestic) soul. Her posture is genuinely majestic.[1] She's talking to God with serene confidence.

This charming figure is something more than the others, but it's not all it might be. The color of the bare arm has changed a little and turned yellow. She's holding a marble tablet on which are these words:

AQUAE

ELEVA

VERUNT

ARCAM

The painting of *Limbo* still seemed charming to me, especially the side where the women are, to the spectator's right. While I was admiring it, a man of the people came over to explain it to me; I sent him packing, and walked away from the picture with dignity.

I realize that my critical reflections tend only to substitute my taste for that of others. If someone were to say to me, "What proof have you that your taste is worth more than that of President Dupaty?" I'd answer, "None." I can guarantee but one thing, and that is that I write what I think. There are perhaps eight or ten people in Europe who think as I do. I love these people without knowing them. I feel that they would be capable of giving me a lively pleasure. As for the others, in everything relating to art, I have the heartiest contempt for them, I desire nothing but to forget them. If I were known to them, I'd inspire the same sentiments in them. Thus, we can gain only by not knowing each other.

But I thoroughly realize that all this is but *il mio parere, forse senza verità* [my opinion, perhaps without truth].

Thus, I'm beginning to realize the reason for the red reflections which seemed to me so ridiculous in Rubens: they're for the purpose of aiding weak eyesights like mine.

Anyway, Rubens, because of the shamefulness of his women's breasts

[1] Majestic: a lofty soul engaged in a lofty action with a gesture which is natural. [Note by Beyle.]

and knees, and the Carraccis, because of their black tones and the common look of their faces, will never give me much pleasure.[1]

While waiting for the keys to the Niccolini Chapel at Santa Croce, I examined the picture of the martyrdom of St. Lawrence by Giacomo Ligozzi Veronese.

I wasn't able to see this picture yesterday because of a devil of a Mass. Masses have frequently been an obstacle for me; this morning at . . . [the Carmelites] a Mass prevented me from seeing the paintings of Masaccio. I make very clumsy genuflections as I pass in front of the high altars.

Assuming that the modest and true remark on the preceding page has been read, I'll say of Ligozzi's St. *Lawrence* that the figures are packed together like sardines, that the Roman magistrate would probably have been suffocated by the smoke from St. Lawrence's body. I don't know whether it's the result of my weak eyesight, but the majority of paintings seem to me lacking in space. I'd find them much more agreeable if the figures were spread over a canvas twice as large.

The lower extremities of St. Lawrence are pock-marked; outside of that, he's a handsome young man. His loins are beginning to sizzle; he's looking up at the sky all right, but he hasn't the quarter of the expression that the first monk you might burn would have. It might be said that he's a long way from having the sublime expression of which the subject is capable.

There are angels in the upper part of the picture. That's diminishing the effect gratuitously: as soon as the martyr sees angels, there's almost no more merit. What would be required is a vast serene sky, and the martyr looking up at the sky.

Another mistake is to have made the executioners nude like the saint. This destroys the effect. They ought to be clothed, the saint alone nude and placed in such a way that his facial features would be clearly visible.

Pitti.—I've seen the Emperor's palace, the former Palazzo Pitti.

Immense rows of rooms of great height, no furniture. The lack of mirrors is striking. By chance, I came across a little concierge who had absolutely the same Milanese haughtiness as I. He showed me everything in a hurry; it's agreed that I'm to return tomorrow, and that he'll shut me up in the palace.

There were some superb paintings. A marine by Salvator Rosa struck me.

A good German servant went through the gardens with me. With

[1]I've changed, not for Rubens, who still appears to me just as shameful, but for the Carraccis. [Note added by Beyle.]

the exception of the giant of the island and the posture of Eve, who is leaning on Adam, everything appeared to me to be mediocre. The garden is in tiers and has an agreeable view, especially toward the Via Romana.

Having nothing to do tonight at half-past seven, I went to Mme. Adèle's. If anything is capable of confirming my way of seeing French hearts, it's that visit. Politeness, calculation and indifference. Not even the interest that I'd call simple humanity. I didn't have the honor of her asking me when I arrived. What I said was all right, but, although I haven't had any feeling for her for three or four years now, I had a little warmth in my manner; less than I would have had with any other woman. I experienced a slight embarrassment, which could have been evident only through a bit too much activity. I found her in bed, about to have a baby. Such a degree of non-interest for a person with whom four or five years have been spent in seeing each other constantly! There's the heart of a coquette for you. Her eyes were flashing, pene-trating, clear and nice enough.

I didn't experience a shadow of bad humor or disappointment. My only sorrow was to observe one more imperfection in human nature. She invited me to dinner and, as I said I was leaving at five o'clock, to lunch. Her cook displayed more of the natural feeling of cordiality that one has, after four years, upon unexpectedly again seeing someone whom one used to see a lot.

I repeat that I have long considered this heart the most unfeeling in Paris, and that I wasn't in a bad humor.

I had a twinge of ambition when I saw what had been made of a position I held in contempt. And I'm expected not to love my dear Italians! I'm expected not to prefer a quarter of an hour's conversation with Signora Pietragrua to everything that Adèle could give me!

From her house I went to the Italian Comedy, and I found Alfieri's *Orestes*. Packed with speed, vengeance, eloquence; no interest. It seemed to me too sublimated. You're too little conscious of mankind in his characters; there isn't enough of the *human* for sympathy to be established.

A young actress whose forehead resembled that of Mélanie inter-ested me. She showed some fire, and was fifteen years old, I was told. She had the slenderness of early youth; I had mistaken it for that of the decline, and thought she was thirty-five years old. Her name is Car-lotta . . . ; I've forgotten her last name, which my neighbors told me. I'd won their friendliness by speaking with interest of Alfieri. "Are his tragedies given frequently?" "Very frequently; all of them are permitted here."

The audience drank in Alfieri. This manner of playing tragedy has much more naturalness and speed than our own.

Orestes and his sister wore their hair too long and tore it frequently. *September 28.*—I remember[1] that I left Florence with a one-eyed and miserly driver who, it seems to me, had been a handsome fellow, in his youth at least, to judge by his temper, which was exactly like that of my uncle, and by the wife he had in Rome, whom he had stolen from the architect Camporesi and who was far superior to him in all respects. Nevertheless, she'd thrown up everything in order to be his, and with a passion he didn't deserve. But he was a Frenchman, and the Frenchman abroad is like the duchess was for the bourgeois in other days.

The streets of Florence aren't at all gay. They're formed by a series of sturdy houses, so built that the owner could withstand a siege in them. As a matter of fact, that's the use to which several of these gentlemen put their houses; see *Sismondi* and *Machiavelli*. There was fighting in this city frequently when it was a stormy republic.

I left it by the Rome gate, which is at the end of the Boboli gardens. The road zigzags uphill. The horizon is spoiled in the direction of Prato by large barren hills. What's pretty in Florence is the little hills that immediately touch the city, like the one of the Chartreux, I believe.

From Florence to the environs of Rome, the countryside is mountainous, insignificant, like the environs of Namur, for example. My imagination had pictured it as more beautiful than my dear Lombardy, but there can be nothing more beautiful than that. Florence was the limit of my travels in Italy in early youth; I went there with General Michaud as his aide-de-camp.[2] A fine road from Pietramala. The novels of Anne Radcliffe. Real robbers. I used to read Ariosto on horseback as I escorted my general.

The most disagreeable mountain I've ever crossed in my life is that of Radicofani. I don't know what great sovereign made a fine road across it, Leopold, I believe. The posthouse built on the top of the mountain is a relic of his work; but the road, not having been kept up, is covered over with the big stones with which it was formerly paved. Besides, this Leopold didn't have any talent, not even any intelligence, I believe, but he sought well-being and was reasonable. That's more than is needed to be a good king of a little state, or a Prefect.

I stayed only a quarter of an hour at Siena, where the streets are narrow because of the heat, and the houses have something majestic about them.

[1] Written March 20, 1813. [Note by Beyle.]

[2] There is no record of a trip to Florence during Beyle's first stay in Italy, and it is difficult to see when such a visit could have been made.

As you approach Rome, the countryside takes on a little of the character of beautiful Italy again. The town of Viterbo is gay; the forest you traverse as you leave it offers thickly wooded hillsides that are an agreeable sight. They were afraid of robbers, and we were escorted by a gendarme. A little before we came to the desert which surrounds Rome, we had a beautiful view of a lake on the right.

I'd pictured this unhealthy desert as a swamp; not at all, it's a terrain containing much activity. The road rises and falls frequently. The hedges become borders of trees. The aspect of the countryside is very beautiful.

I saw Mount St. Orestes, which is Horace's Soracte. I next saw some large buildings at the foot of some hills. It was Rome. A moment later, I saw St. Peter's on our right. The postilion told us the story of a robbery that had been committed two days before on the road we were traveling over. The courier which preceded me and in which I hadn't reserved a seat in Florence because the seat was already reserved had been stopped (*saltato*). The robbers made the driver and the passengers lie face down on the ground, took 200 louis from the latter and beat them up. The robbery took place in a rather odd manner. One of the robbers pretended to be dead and lay across the middle of the road; the driver paid no attention to this dead man and kept right on going. A hundred paces farther on, some men asked him if he knew why this man had been killed. While he was answering, they threatened the postilion, stopped the horses, etc. They were robbers, whom the supposedly dead man soon rejoined.

The Porta del Popolo has nothing remarkable about it. The Milvio bridge is good-looking but small. The same thing applies to the fork in the roads inside the Porta del Popolo and the two churches on the right and left of the Corso. You can read on them in large letters the name of the cardinal who had them built. During the first days of my stay in Rome, I was shocked by this mania for inscriptions. At the Emperor's palace, some cheap painted wooden benches, which were worth perhaps ten or twelve francs each, bore the name and arms of the Pope who ordered them made.

But I thought then that nowhere have private individuals built so much for the public as at Rome. These private individuals were nearly all bachelors who left no family behind them to perpetuate their memory. The vanity of the inscriptions is therefore quite excusable, and we're only too happy to be indebted to it for such beautiful things.

My driver paid court to me in the hope of getting me to put up at an inn kept by his wife. I thought I was trapped, but, as I wanted to see the monuments in a hurry, I let him do as he wished with me. The inn appeared to me to be quite passable; I ordered a carriage at once. As it was a little delayed, I set out on foot to St. Peter's. I encountered my calash, got in, crossed the San Angelo bridge, the Via Transtevere, where I found myself among common people with superb faces. These physiognomies evinced the lofty character which the government hasn't held back.

I wasn't impressed very much by the façade of St. Peter's; what displeased me was the fact that the columns are engaged in the wall. On the other hand, the two fountains appeared to me superb.

The interior of St. Peter's pleased me greatly. I was especially impressed by the figure of Religion in the tomb of Benedict XIV [Clement XIII] by Canova. This figure, clad in a frock like that of a little girl, appeared to me very expressive. Mediocre people criticize it nowadays and say that Canova himself was dissatisfied with it— something that should be checked.

I returned to St. Peter's many times, and I believe it's the only monument I saw thoroughly during my stay in Rome.

I went to the Emperor's palace on Monte Cavallo. M. Pacé[1] insisted that I stay there. He and his wife made me a number of entreaties. I was possibly wrong to refuse, for they seemed a bit offended. I promised to visit them on my way back from Naples, and that's what I did. I saw the Duchesse Lante and Comte Miollis at M. Pacé's. I'd been acquainted with the latter previously, while he was in command at Mantua. He even honored me a little on a visit he made at Brescia to his friend General Michaud, whose aide-de-camp I was. I avoided being recognized; I didn't want to waste my time in Rome by attending official dinners. That's why I only went to see the authorities on the eve of my departure for Naples. I was invited to dinners everywhere, but I escaped by leaving town. M. Pacé introduced me to the Duchesse Lante, who showed natural and perfect politeness toward me. As she had been told that I was traveling for music, she asked me to select the pieces to be executed at her concert on Thursday, I believe. As a matter of fact, two or three pieces I had requested were sung at it. It's part of a voyager's politeness to have a goal in traveling. That relieves his new acquaintances of the embarrassment of not knowing what to say to him, and makes him a friend of all the enthusiasts of the art he has selected. I'm sufficiently interested in music always to be able to place myself under its auspices. In Milan, it immediately won me the friendship of Signora Lamberti's old uncle.

The concert was delightful, without any exaggeration. The duchess and her friends formed a troupe the like of which there are possibly not two in Italy. She has a theater in her palace, and it was for this theater

[1]Martial Daru, now Intendant of Crown Properties in Rome, was living at the Quirinal, where he was directing the work of beautifying Rome.

that Zingarelli composed *The Destruction of Jerusalem*. Signora Lante complained bitterly of the way this opera was pulled to pieces in Paris; and it's a fact that, as it was sung by her and her friends, it was unrecognizable. That interested me a great deal. SHE HAD, THEY SAY, SEVEN LOVERS, I SHOULD HAVE WISHED TO BE THE 8TH.

The Frenchmen had rather a heteroclite look at this concert. What could be farther from their manners and morals than a duchess singing with her friends through the love of music, and these friends playing the duet from *The Secret Marriage, "Se fiato in corpo avete,"* with the gayest kind of buffooneries! The poor Frenchmen were dumfounded at such a thing, notably a chief justice, who with his decorations and dark clothes, remained bolted down to his chair all evening, his legs tight together like an Egyptian statue.

M. Norvins appeared very spiteful and never stopped talking. His character inspired so much repugnance in me that I didn't go to see him. That's probably one of the reasons why I lost the battle of November 28, 1811.

M. Pacé took me to Canova's. I found this genuinely great man of a simplicity far indeed from all our petty niceties. In the five or six rooms which serve him as a studio, I followed the process of his work, from which he's removed all that's physically painful.

A mass of clay is prepared for him, and he makes the statue he has in mind. His assistants cover this clay with plaster, make a mold and reproduce the statue in plaster. Canova perfects it, his assistants make an exact copy of the plaster statue in marble. The marble is taken to Canova's private studio, and he puts the finishing touches on it. That's his only work in marble. It's reduced to a few strokes of the chisel.

It was in this studio, which is certainly the only place of its kind in the world, that I talked to him.

The people in Rome were badly frightened because of the robbery of which I spoke. They said there was a great commotion on the road to Naples. M. Pacé had the kindness to counsel me not to leave. He was quite in earnest about it, as was his wife. I told them I hadn't time to be cautious.

I left by a courier after spending four or five days in Rome, and I didn't find a shadow of danger on the road. I soaked myself in spirits while we were crossing the Pontine marshes. That's still another panicky terror which vanishes when you're on the spot. It reminded me of what I'd been told about the St. Bernard, Mont-Cenis and the road from Hanover to Wesel. I left Rome by the road which skirts the Colosseum.

I'm very displeased with myself for not having written at the time the impression made on me by the Colosseum. It was nothing more than a theater. It's more than half in ruins. It moved me to tears, and St. Peter's left me quite cold. What men those Romans were! Never anything but the useful, never anything without a reason.

Being alone in the center of the Colosseum and hearing the chirping of some birds nesting in the topmost arches, I was unable to hold back my tears.[1]

October 9.—In the environs of Gaeta I finally saw the sea at the end of the road. Charming view of Mola di Gaeta. Superb countryside all the way to Naples, the city of gaiety. Rome is a sublime tomb. You must be happy in Naples and in love in Milan.[2]

I'm writing this on October 9, 1811 in a fine large room facing Vesuvius at the Albergo Reale, Largo di Castello.

I wanted to take the other notebook to write an entry on Naples, but I couldn't find it. Up to now, I've noticed only the loss of a penknife and this notebook. It isn't worth getting mad about. In the notebook, there were some words on the Valais and Rome, the Duchesse Lante and pall of boredom cast over Rome BY THE TEDIOUS HOUSE OF Pacé.

I left Rome at half-past five on the afternoon of . . . The driver, who wanted to sell my seat, told me they were only leaving at six o'clock. I got there at half-past five; he'd left. I pursued him in my fiacre. As I'd resolved not to lose my temper while traveling, I didn't say anything. A rather uncomfortable voyage: I was a little afraid of robbers the first night. Dined at Mola di Gaeta. The inn's situation: superb view of the sea and Gaeta.

Crossing the Garigliano. My excessive delicacy suffered because the officer made all the soldiers get out of the ferry so I might identify the one to whom I had given some money.

I reached Naples on October 9 at half-past three in the morning. I saw at once that the panorama had given me an accurate idea of the city. At half-past three, there were seven or eight men still up at the door. Argument between two *lazzaroni* over which of them would carry my portmanteau. I took lodgings at the Albergo Reale, from which I saw Vesuvius perfectly, but not the sea. Lambert wanted me to put up on the fine Chiaja quay, but I'd have been roasted and blinded by the continual sunlight. At the Albergo Reale I have it only in the morning.

During the trip, I remarked that I was thinking tenderly of five women, that a rendezvous with one of these five women would afford

[1]This journal is devilishly cold in comparison with what I felt. I devoted only spare moments to writing it, and I wasn't able to make visible what I felt. (1813.) [Note by Beyle.] He speaks in four or five other places of the strong impression made on him by the birds in the Colosseum.

[2]End of what I wrote in 1813. [Note by Beyle.]

me a tender pleasure. These five women were Angela Pietragrua, Palfy, Mélanie, Livia B[ialowiska] and Angéline.

I believe I'm in love with the first. At least, since Bologna, I'd invariably have preferred to be with her than to be in the spot where I was. I surprise myself seven or eight times a day thinking of her tenderly, dreamily; my breathing quickens and I leave this sweet thought with regret.

In Naples, as in the rest of Italy, with the exception of Milan, I found bad music. That reconciles me with the Odéon. When I left Paris, I thought I'd return to it only with disgust after leaving divine Italy. The lack of company and friends that I feel in Italy and the less advanced state of civilization, which gives me little annoyances of detail, will make me return to Paris with pleasure if THE LOVE FOR THE Signora Pietragrua doesn't fill me with tender regrets. It seems to me that what I'm experiencing is love to the full extent of the word's meaning for me. I'm burning to return to Milan. Nothing has any effect on me. I'd be more sensitive to what I see if I'd skipped Milan. Maybe I won't go to Ancona.

The day after my arrival was a Sunday (October 6, 1811), and a review by the King on the Chiaja was announced. I walked under the trees of this promenade WITH Lambert, HIS WIFE AND THE VISCOUNT.[1] The King didn't come; the two or three hours passed there somewhat bored me.

The next day, we left at seven o'clock, passed the grotto of Posillipo, saw the baths of the Sibyl, lunched in the temple of Apollo, saw Lake Lucrin and the baths of Nero, where I got undressed but didn't go as far as Lambert and Barral.

We embarked and saw the thermae which have been misnamed the temples of Venus, Mercury, etc. We went in the direction of Pozzuoli, and saw the ruins of a fine temple of Serapis. We recrossed this town, where the *aria cattiva* also prevails, and went up to the Solfatara. I was tired. We finally got back to Naples and passed the evening chatting with Barral and Lambert.

Tuesday, October 8.—We went to Pompeii, which will be the point the farthest south of my trip. We roamed around the streets of Pompeii. We went down into the Herculaneum theater; impression of a mask. I yawned and dropped off to sleep at *The Vestal,* but I admired the San Carlo Theater. The ceiling is bad; the façade appeared to me agreeable to look at, and showed clearly that it was a theater and not a temple, as our own try to be.

---

[1]Louis de Barral. In his *Souvenirs d'Egotisme,* Stendhal says, "In 1810, it seems to me, M. de Barral having lost everything gambling, I lent him some money and forced him to leave for Naples."

Wednesday, October 9.—I remained in town, I saw the Studj, or museum. Poverty-stricken in pictures; but some portrait statues, beautiful for the most part through their naturalness. That of Balbus, founder of the Herculaneum theater, on horseback.

Absurdity of the Roman ladies, already advanced in years, having their portraits done as Venus. As Strombeck remarked, all Venuses take the posture of the Venus de Medici.

I admired the Via Toledo. It's the most beautiful I've ever seen, and certainly the most densely populated.

In Berlin, there's a street that's straighter and even wider. I believe it's the Friedrichgasse. But the houses aren't high enough, and you don't see a hundredth part of the population which swarms over the Via Toledo.

Toledo, Chiaja and the part of the city on the Portici side are the only things of their kind in the world.

This is no exaggeration; I saw Naples apart from its society. Everything in it was dead for me. Some good music would have brought me back to life; I heard nothing while there but bad; i.e., *The Vestal,* Fioravanti's *Raoul de Créqui* and Paer's *Camilla.* Had I had some company here like that of Signora Pietragrua in Milan or Signora Lamberti, for instance, the view of the places, mingled with observations on manners and morals, would have given me much more pleasure.

Thursday, October 10.—We left for Vesuvius at one o'clock in the morning.

We came out of the hermit's house at half-past four, we went a league farther on our donkeys and finally undertook the most painful climb I've ever made in my life. It would have been necessary to have been far less hurried and not to have eaten at the hermit's but to have had lunch at the crater instead. I was surprised not to see the infernal ebullition at the bottom of the crater.

The most beautiful view in the world is probably that which is to be enjoyed from the hermit's house. There was a book in which we found a platitude signed Bigot de Préameneu, Councilor of State in France. Not a single sensible thing, which is surprising. The names of Mme. de Staël and Schlegel.

The *lacrima christi* is undrinkable for me. It's like an ordinary Burgundy wine, in each bottle of which two pounds of sugar have been dissolved. The grapes are still on the vine today, October 10.

We were back in Naples at half-past one. I went to the posthouse: it was closed. I returned at five o'clock and reserved a seat in the courier of October 11. (It cost me 40 francs of Naples as far as Terracina; they cheated me out of 4 or 5 fr.)

In the evening, I went once again to the Chiaja. I was planning to go to the San Carlo, but my fatigue got the better of me and I went to bed at ten o'clock.

Friday, October 11.—This morning at six o'clock, a fine view of Vesuvius, whose outlines stood out against the sunrise beyond the two mountains. The lower one on the left is the former Vesuvius, where are found the stones that are worked. The Vesuvius that is now alive is a little higher and to the right of the other.

The people of Naples shout at the top of their voices, and are always asking for something. The fiacre horses here go very fast, and do so on a pavement which makes you tremble. The King's palace has a good appearance; they say the civil list is very rich.

It seems to me that no sovereign has country homes that can even be compared to those of the King of Naples—Portici, Castellamare, Caserte and Capo di Monte, where he's in the country with a view possibly unequaled in the world, and within fifteen minutes, I believe, of the San Carlo Theater. To be the Intendant of this civil list would be an agreeable position.

Return from Naples to Rome, second stay in Rome and en route to Ancona.—I left Naples on October 11, 1811, making a sacrifice to duty on the eruption predicted for the following day. It was the greatest sacrifice I could have made, and I was a fool to have made it. Stupidness is three quarters of zeal, said M. de Talleyrand. But in those days I was still all heart.[1]

October 19.—I'm writing these lines in Livia's room, on her table looking out on the sea which closes my horizon beyond all the chimneys of Ancona. The sea, that is its shore, isn't superb as at Naples.[2] It's nothing but arid rocks.

The streets in Ancona go continually up- and downhill, a circumstance which greatly restricts the use of carriages. The houses are of brick and very high. The streets are quite narrow.

Yesterday, the 18th, I went to San Cyriaque, but while I was there I didn't think of going to see the famous Virgin who opened her eyes after the arrival of the French, which meant that she wanted to see them driven out.

There aren't any trees in Ancona. The people go walking at the Porta di Francia, on the bare beach and in the direction of the new fortifications.

Livia took me to these two promenades October . . . , the day of my arrival.

I HAVE FIND HER MUCH BELOW MY IDEAS, BOTH FOR THE FIGURE [face]

[1] This paragraph was written March 20, 1813. The entries on the voyage and Beyle's second visit to Rome are missing.

[2] I wrote all this with boredom and lassitude. [Note by Beyle in 1813.]

AND FOR THE WIT. CONDUCING HER TO THE THEATER, THE VERY EVENING OF MY ARRIVAL, SHE HAD THE FIGURE hidden by a sort of hat, and, as she is about the same height of Signora Pietragrua, I had the pleasant illusion of being with the latter for a few steps.

Livia is bored in her little town of Ancona, where she doesn't see many people yet. Boredom makes her apathetic and even gives her a little bad humor. Her father lives with a family servant, which makes Livia unhappy. This father seems to me to have much of the character and wit of my cousin Rebuffel, and, like him, to be unappreciated. As soon as he saw me, he offered to put me up at his house. After a little hesitation, I finally accepted. I found Signora Livia free and plunged in boredom. Comparison of Mme. de Palfy, Mlle. Mimi de Bézieux and Bialowiska clearly shows me that one of the results of boredom is to cast a person into an apathetic inactivity which only augments the boredom, and that an almost certain way to avoid this terrible abyss is to devote oneself to an extreme activity, like LADY Palfy.

If you want to make a bored woman love you, you should conceal the theory, but little by little guide her to an increased activity; you'll soon be a source of pleasure to her.

To pay direct court to a woman you desire is the greatest of asininities. It can succeed only with a woman who hasn't any vanity—and women's vanity is a commonplace with all the philosophers. Given two sisters A and B: if you want to attract A, don't fail to start out by paying attention to B.[1]

Bialowiska was plunged in the apathy of boredom, and for no reason at all didn't want to take her lesson this morning; I persuaded her to take it by joking. She was certainly occupied by singing before me and by some things concerned with love. I wrote some of Mozart's music in the range of her voice and sent it to her.

From her master, I obtained entire confirmation of an idea of mine. *Bisogna novità pella musica* [novelty is necessary in music]. In Italy, that's a rule without an exception, and one which is quite in accord with the sensibility of a people born for the arts.

Were an opera by Cimarosa to be given, my maestro just told me, everyone would recognize it at the first measure, and the opera wouldn't be able to go on.

We agreed that possibly thirty years from now, Cimarosa's operas, being forgotten a bit, might again enjoy the greatest success.

October 19.—No sono colla Livia TAKE TO HER THE . . . [I'm at that point with Livia where I can take her by the . . .] without her getting mad. The first day, she gave me some kisses, but not like those of MISS

[1]This formula, already tried out with indifferent success on Adèle, Mélanie and Wilhelmina, is highly recommended in Stendhal's *De l'Amour*.

Angela Borrone. I could have her in TWO OR THREE DAYS, BUT I NOT DESIRE HER. What I desire is to see my Angela again. At eight o'clock this morning, I went to see my good Milanese, *il* Signor Casati, with whom I've been traveling since Foligno. He told me that we could leave tomorrow morning. Tomorrow's Sunday, October 20; we'll be in Milan on Wednesday, the 23rd.

I see the manners and morals much better at hazard like this than I should have done in my calash. With a calash and Crozet, I shouldn't have left the atmosphere of France. My Milanese told me not to be a dupe while traveling in Italy. It's difficult for me. The people are always asking for money and never seem to be satisfied. It's practically necessary to strike a bargain at each post. In this respect, as in all the others, civilization is less advanced than in France. But they have *sensibility* and the naturalness which is a result of it. This country is therefore eminently that of the arts.

I feel that I AM NOT ELOQUENT BUT [except] WHEN I AM natural, but at those times I AM PLEASING FOR WOMEN. Therefore, be perfectly natural with LADY Alexandrine.

I found less wit than I expected in all my friends of Italy. A few years ago, I was on their level; it would seem that I've progressed a few leagues on the river of KNOWING. Barral and Lambert appeared to me to be lacking in wit. The same thing applies to Bialowiska. Being somewhat bored yesterday, I read Cesarotti's *Juvenal*. In the preface, I found with pleasure the confirmation of my ideas on taste.

October 20.—The 19th, after dinner, her father spoke to me of my departure before her. Sadness, not somber and impassioned, but constant. It had no effect on me because it recalled that of Mlle. Mimi de Bézieux. A walk along the seashore beyond the Porta di Francia, of the same kind as the last walks with Mélanie.[1] We went to the theater, where the *Oro non Compra l'Amore* gave me pleasure.

Signor Casati came to tell me we were leaving at seven o'clock tomorrow if it was convenient for me. He came into the loge without knowing the ladies, and stayed there talking for ten minutes. That didn't appear strange to them. Less advanced civilization. I'm again writing this on her table on the 20th at twelve-twenty after having packed my portmanteaus. I'm leaving Ancona October 20 for Milan.

Written at Varese, Thursday, October 24.—I arrived in Milan on October 22, 1811 at nightfall, having taken less than a month to see the whole of Italy. I floated through the streets without touching the pavement. At last I saw the Porta Romana again.

As my trip becomes better, my journal becomes worse. Frequently

[1] Depressed, silent, ill humor: "Since you're leaving, there's nothing to say." [Note by Beyle in 1813.]

for me, to describe happiness is to diminish it. It's too delicate a plant, and mustn't be touched. Following are a few fragments describing moments of my second sojourn in Milan. But nothing can express the continual delight I experienced in those days and the wild vivacity that remained with me day and night.[1]

Yesterday, the 23rd, believing I was pursuing a wise policy, and filled with a transport of love which disturbed my soul and left me with the composure and glibness of a man determined to succeed in a difficult thing, I left Milan at half-past two for Varese.

I arrived at Varese at half-past eight. I hadn't ever read Ossian; I read *Fingal* for the first time in the carriage.

Today I had Ossianic weather and adventures.

I left on horseback at half-past six for Santa Maria del Monte. I reached this lofty and strange spot after going along hillocks as beautiful as those I imagined all through my childhood. The aspect of the village built around the church of the Madonna was strange. The mountains majestic. It's four miles from Varese to the village.

After two miles, you see the Lake of Varese, and, a mile higher, that of Arona (Lake Maggiore).

Vapor surrounded the rising sun. The lower hillocks appeared like islands amid a sea of white clouds.

It scarcely occurred to me to stop for all these beauties. I merely thought that, if I wished to live a few months in the midst of nature, I'd come and settle down at San Ambrogio, a mile past Varese, which is a small town, while San Ambrogio is a village.

Two thirds of the way there, I got down from my horse because he was missing his footing, and also because I wanted to arrive sooner.

I saw Signor . . . [Pietragrua], *il marito* [the husband], who was going down the hill. He greeted me in a friendly way. I went up the hill even more quickly; finally I was in the village. I was told to go up a staircase to reach the inn. I reached a very ornate church where a service was being chanted.

I went down again. I inquired as to the lodgings of Signora Pietragrua. I saw her at last. I haven't the time to describe what took place in my heart.

It suffices to recall that for her sake I left Naples and Rome with joy.

I didn't tell her the tender and charming things I had thought up while hastening from Rome to Foligno. I was all upset. I was about to kiss her; she reminded me that it wasn't the custom of the country.

She asked me if I knew all that had happened, that our rendezvous at the Alamanni baths was known, that her little hussy of a chamber-

[1]This sentence is one of those added in 1813.

maid, who was the noble object of Signor Turenne's flame, had given her away, etc., and if I'd received her letter.

She next had a quarrel to pick with me. She had opened, as I'd told her to, Faure's letters, and had thought she'd seen in them that I'd planned in advance to put her on my list when I passed through Milan. I've just read Faure's letters attentively; they reveal nothing but my love for Signora Pietragrua. There's only one sentence that might have appeared ambiguous to the amiable Angela. But I intend to have her read it again, and make her admit that this sentence does nothing more than show my love for her.

I hardly knew what I was doing. I had my chocolate with her, and we went for a walk together. Not a single grove on the mountain.

On the way from Rome to Foligno at night, I had composed the dialogue of our first meeting. I was going to say things so tender and gracious to her that tears started to my eyes.

Today, all upset, seeking to foresee everything and to reach an agreement on everything during the absence OF THE HUSBAND, I must have appeared to her stiff and pedantic. I was conscious of not appearing as tender as I really was. But the fear of seeing Signor Pietragrua come in at any moment kept me in continual agitation. What I wanted to do was to persuade her to return to Milan in the very near future. I was afraid all the time that I would forget something. In short, I wasn't amiable, and I'm afraid that this fact may have diminished her love.[1]

Written at Isola Bella, October 25, at nine o'clock in the evening.—
Yesterday, I wrote the foregoing with the intention of showing it to Angela.

Bothered yesterday by the presence of a handsome young man[2] and the fear of seeing the arrival of him whose presence would mean the end of my happiness, I was somewhat unintelligible and perhaps a little lacking in naturalness. I perhaps had a somewhat pedantic manner. Instead of showing my journal to Angela in order to beg her pardon for it, I've just written her with even more candor.

Perhaps it's the peculiar quality of a soul, which is the source of great things, not to be gracious at the moment of action, when it's seeking to muster all its strength. The adjective *great* applied to my actions of yesterday may be laughed at. The weight was small, but the lever was nothing.

I left Varese for Laveno at eight o'clock this morning, and arrived

---

[1] I believe that several times I was unintelligible for her. With a woman who's used to understanding those who speak to her at the first word, that must have produced chilliness. [Note by Beyle in 1813.]

[2] Antonio. [Note by Beyle.] The reference is to Angelina's sixteen-year-old son.

there at eleven o'clock. I passed through a countryside such that my imagination had nothing left to desire. It was the discovery of the land where one must go to enjoy nature—and it's only six hours from a large city. There's nothing left to desire.

I left by boat, still with the rain and intervals of fog, for the Borromean Isles. After a crossing which took an hour and a quarter, I came to Isola Madre, which I spent half an hour in seeing.

From there to Isola Bella, where I'm writing this. I saw the palace. Neglected paintings by Jordano (of Naples). I saw the garden which was *constructed* in 1670. Constructed is the word. Contemporary with Versailles. Larger for a private individual than Versailles is for a king, but just as barren for the heart as Versailles.

A delightful view from the terrace. To the left, Isola Madre and part of Pallanza; next, the branch of the lake which goes to Switzerland in the distance; opposite, Laveno; to the right, the branch of the lake which goes to Sesto.

Five or six shadowy outlines of mountains hidden by the clouds.

This view forms a pendant to that of the Bay of Naples, and is far more stirring. These isles seem to me to produce the sentiment of the beautiful in a greater quantity than St. Peter's.

At last my mind, invariably faultfinding through love of a too beautiful beauty, came across something with which no fault could be found—the countryside between Varese and Laveno, and probably all the Brianza mountains.

I believe that, even without the presence and memory of Signora Pietragrua, I'd prefer Milan to Naples and Rome.

I wrote an eight-page letter. Yesterday, my agitation somewhat prevented me from being amiable. My love was diminished,[1] it returned in its entirety today. I'm afraid I was a pedant yesterday. She remarked that we all had rueful faces. She showed me a letter from Cimbal [Widmann] with complaisance, but only a line of the one from Turenne.

Tonight I continued *Fingal* to the sound of rain and even thunder.

October 26.—Upon arising, I found, thanks to the sky, superb late autumn weather—heavy but very high clouds, snow on the mountain tops to the north of the lake, and a completely unobstructed view.

This journal is written for Henri, if he is still alive in 1821. I have no desire to give him the opportunity of having a laugh at the expense of the one who's alive today. The one of 1821 will have become reserved and fuller of hate.

[1] I thought so when I was writing. It was lucky for me that I left Milan in the middle of November. If I'd passed another month there, I'd have sent in my resignation and stayed. [Note by Beyle in 1813.]

Madonna del Monte, October 26, eight o'clock.—I've never seen an inn as comfortable as the one where I'm writing this. It's the Bellati Casa, adjoining the church. I wanted to be free to go out or come in during the night. I foresaw that this would be very difficult: everything was arranged naturally. I have an apartment looking out on the peristyle of the church, and here in my pocket I have the *benedetta chiave* [blessed key] which gives me my freedom. Signor Bellati, the curé's brother, entertained me for an hour and a half with all possible respect; for my part, I paid him court in order to come to the matter of the key, in the most friendly possible fashion. I had no need of committing that imprudence.

Angela committed one which well brought out the difference between Italian and French love. I'd come, in terrible weather, by what's called a *portantine* [sedan chair]. This unfortunate portantine wasn't in the least elegant; it was formed by several sticks, a cushion, a piece of canvas thrown over the sticks and an oilcloth umbrella stuck between the upper sticks with the handle against my cheek.

I thought Bellati's inn was at the other end of town from the one where Signora Pietragrua was staying. That was true as far as the inn was concerned; but they paid me the honor of taking me to the casa, my progress lit up by three torches and constituting an event, all this light passing before the door of . . . at half-past six, and beneath a narrow, dark passageway before the private door OF THE HUSBAND, a door which happened to be standing open.

I hunched myself up and drew my head in between my shoulders, and my ridiculous procedure was noticed by no one except Angela, who, a second later, IS GONE WITH HER SON AT MY CASA; SHE HAD GIVEN ME A LITTLE BILLET, AND SAID that at this very moment they were putting up two nuns in the room through which I'd have to enter; that nevertheless she'd do everything possible for me to come at midnight; that she'd be in Milan on Monday. She appeared to me charming as she said that. Here's the note she slipped into my hand:

A mezza notte. La gelosia del marito si è vivamente destata. Prudenza, e preparate tutto per ripartire domani mattina non più tardi delle 7 [At midnight. My husband's jealousy is thoroughly aroused. Be careful! Have everything in readiness to leave in the morning, not later than seven o'clock].

But it seems to me that this note was written previous to the arrival of the cursed nuns.

A minute ago, as I was writing the last line on the other page, someone came singing to my door, which I didn't think to reopen after closing it in the presence of Signor Bellati. Maybe it was the handsome Antonio; I went to open it at once; maybe he was bringing me the counterorder for the rendezvous for which I'd exposed myself to a wind like that of Mont-Cenis.

My Angela was right. It would be better for her to come here. I rejected this idea through general considerations: I thought of the inn at the other end of the village and of the frightful weather there would be at midnight tonight. It would have been better to make sure of the position of my quarters.

They are, moreover, the most picturesque and comfortable I know in which to compose a tragedy:

This morning, I went about Isola Bella from eight o'clock till nine. I went to lunch at Pallanza. I was at Laveno at noon; I left at once; arrived in Varese at half-past two.

Everything worked out well enough: I left in the kind of weather you find on Mont-Cenis. Halfway past San Ambrogio, I left the carriage and took the portantine. You know the rest. Here I am at half-past eight alone in my comfortable apartment, the storm and fog rapping on my windows and forming the only sound I hear outside my little fire. I'm going to read a volume of Ossian which makes up my entire baggage.

Madonna del Monte, October 27, ten minutes after seven.—Yesterday, at half-past nine, a second letter: *non è più speranza,* etc. [there's no longer any hope]. I consequently had nothing to do but to go to bed and read Ossian. I was dead tired; it hadn't occurred to me to sleep during the day. I mustn't forget that in the future; otherwise, I might drop off to sleep in the place of peril and not awaken until daybreak, or else, overcome with fatigue, I'd only have appreciated imperfectly the happiness of which two nuns, arriving yesterday *apposta* [at the place mentioned], deprived me.

Are these two nuns real persons or ghosts born of fear? Throughout the night, the heroes' souls wailed at the height of the tempest and these desolate souls are still wailing this morning. This morning, the daylight is depressing, fog surrounds us. If I'd been fortunate last night, I'd have proposed passing today here incognito and only leaving Monday. SHE WRITES TO ME THAT SHE WILL BE TO MORROW EVENING AT Milan. For my own part, I expect to be there at two o'clock today.

Milan, October 29.—I was planning to start this entry with a copy of an unhappy lover's letter which I've just written to Comtesse Simonetta [Angela]. But the copying would be even more tedious than the writing, and that's saying a great deal.

May Heaven be my witness that yesterday I wrote Angela an unhappy lover's letter, full of delicacy and in a firm style. This letter appeared detestable to Angela. "Would you write me like that if you were unhappy?" she asked me this morning in the STREET OF TWO WALLS [Contrada dei Due Muri].

It was there that I saw her freely for the first time. I tried not to think of this rendezvous before being at it in order not to lose my wits. I didn't have time to enjoy it. I barely had time to be natural and thus to enjoy myself. I informed her that my leave had been extended. She told me that HER HUSBAND had learned of my second trip to the Madonna del Monte from the very man who accompanied me. Our love is persecuted by every possible accident: the two nuns, that man who chanced to have a long conversation WITH THE HUSBAND.

She told me several times that, if one of his friends were to tell him all that took place between us, she'd scoff at it as she would at a novel. That thought seems to have struck her. She told me tonight that she'd write out our story at Novara.

This morning, she was really alarmed. It seems that there are some personal affairs between Turenne and her. I ought to tell myself that, as a result, it's all the more flattering for me to gain a victory.

This evening, BY HER MOTHER, AT half-past six, I saw her truly amorous and beautiful through love for half an hour. We talked on a bench in the shop while THE MOTHER was busy with the clerks. We were obliged to talk by means of jokes. This manner of being jokingly tender is the one in which I excel; I'm entirely natural and happy in it. I saw by her eyes and the flush that spread over her cheeks the sure effect of a lofty soul's naturalness on another heart of the same kind. She spoke of throwing up everything and following me to France. She told me she detested Italy.

It appears that she's overly sure of the effect she produces on everyone about her. She's so far above other women that none of her friends can think of neglecting her. You may be unaware of her merit, but, once you've appreciated it, since she appears to be the only one of her kind in Milan, you're compelled to remain at her feet.

That might flatter her self-esteem; I don't know whether she's capable of the reasoning necessary for that. But this certainty makes her listless.

This morning, thoroughly upset by all the ill fortunes that seem to be directed toward us, when I informed her of the miraculous extension of my leave of absence, she said, "You must go." She told me she was going to Novara.

The jealousy OF THE HUSBAND *s'è destata* [is aroused] like all the devils in hell. But I don't believe he can claim the honor of being jealous. He's the guardian of the interests of Turenne, whose presence is useful to his own interests.

I've got a rendezvous for ten o'clock. But that rogue of a wigmaker at whose home I've rented a room took it into his head to follow Angela as far as her new house.

Yesterday, the 28th, was a happy day. I was surprised to find myself saying, *"Mon Dieu,* but I'm happy!" And all that was because of Félix's letter informing me of my month's extension of leave. (I received 1,500 francs.)

If it weren't for my cursed love of the arts, which makes me too difficult on the subject of the beautiful in all descriptions, I thought that, because of my system and three or four lucky chances that have befallen me, I'd be one of the happiest of men.

THIS MORNING I HAVE MADE THAT A TIME, THIS NIGHT I SHOULD GO TO A VERY RESPECTABLE NUMBER. But in the first place the anxiety of waiting, and afterward what she told me, disturbed my mind too much for my body to be capable of being brilliant.

October 29.—I read in my room, in the Contrada dei Due WALLS, a hundred and fifty pages of Lanzi, who, in spite of all his critical, historical and timid gossip, has a real feeling for the arts because he's an Italian. He doesn't use as many superlatives as I feared.

He reproaches Leonardo for always setting out to paint masterpieces. In order not to fall into the error of that extraordinary man, I've just written four pages of inane sentences.

I've slept very little during the past month. My sensibility is stimulated by drinking coffee, traveling, nights spent in coaches and sensations. I'm growing a little thinner. My health is extremely good. Yesterday for the first time I slept for eight or nine hours, after a bath. I repeat that I'm enjoying the best of health. Only once did I have the slight fever which the first cold weather gives me.

I found cold weather at Parma returning from Ancona with Signor Felipo Casati. I found continual rain, fog, cold, etc. during my charming expedition to the Madonna del Monte.

October 30.—AT TWO O'CLOCK THE FAIR ANTONIO GIVES ME THE FOLLOWING LETTER:

> *"Mercoledi.*
> *"Une sol righa per ricordami a te, che amo più della mia vita, e per dirti che le più fatali combinazione mi hanno tenuta legata sino dopo le undici; che subito andai al noto sito, ma tu eri digia partito!*
> *" . . . Domani alle ore dieci spero d'essere più fortunata e poterti dire quanto ti amo e quanto soffro per te! . . .*
> *"P.-S. Alle ore sei di questa sera, io passerè davanti al Caffè del Sanquirico, in vicinanza della mia nuova casa, la bothega del quate fa angolo alla contrada del Bocchetto."*

[Wednesday. Just a line to remind you of me who love you more than my own life, and to tell you that the most inevitable circumstances detained me here until eleven o'clock; that I went to the appointed place as soon as I could, but you had already left.

[I hope to be more fortunate at ten o'clock tomorrow and to be able to tell you how much I love you and how much I suffer for you.

[P.S. At six o'clock this evening I'll pass in front of the Caffè del Sanquirico, near my new house; the café is on the corner of the Contrada del Bocchetto.]

Anyway, it was a natural mistake for her to make. I read Lanzi in my room until half-past eleven. But this misfortune is not without its advantages; it will increase her love.

Nothing would be lacking for me if she weren't going to Novara. I believe I'll have my freedom during the month of November.

October 30 or 31.—Yesterday, the last day of October, while waiting IN THE CHAMBER, I wrote the following letter:

Bologna, October 25, 1811

Gentlemen,

I have composed a two-volume history of painting in Italy from the Renaissance, about the end of the thirteenth century, to the present day. This work is the fruit of three years of travel and research. Signor Lanzi's history has been very useful to me.

I am sending my work to Paris to be published. I have been advised to ask you to announce it. It will appear in two octavo volumes at the end of 1812. If you do not find the following article suitable, I beg you, Gentlemen, to change it:

"At the end of 1812 there will appear a History of Painting in Italy from the Renaissance, at the end of the thirteenth century, to the present day. The author of this work, who has been traveling in Italy for the past three years, has been aided by the histories published by Signori Fiorillo and Lanzi. The one which is announced will be composed of two octavo volumes."

With the assurance of my deepest respect, I remain,

Yours faithfully,

Is. Ich. Charlier.

Angela spent an hour and a half with me. SHE SEEMED TO HAVE PLEASURE. FOR MY OWN ACCOUNT I MADE THAT TWO TIMES, AND FOR SHE THREE OR FOUR.

I WENT OUT AT 2½. I went to the Brera. I had to have my permit, and I returned to get it. I was interested in a painting by Giotto and a picture by Andrea Mantegna because of the wild idea that had come into my head. It has already cost me 104 fr., employed for:

Lanzi	22
Bossi	24
Vasari (11 vol.)	55
(There will be 5 more)	
Guida di Milano	
di Bianchoni	3
	104

This idea would make me lose my time AS *Mocenigo*. But, my self-esteem once established, I'd acquire some genuine knowledge of painting, AND PROBABLY MONEY SUFFICIENT FOR A SECOND TOUR THROUGH ITALY.

I saw her tonight for twenty-five minutes. She'd told me in the morning of the letter's success. I'll write out this story.

I'd have sufficient time to go to Venice and Genoa during her absence from November 2 to 15. But such trips don't give me any pleasure. Is it wise to utilize the time Venice might give me in seeing it when I haven't any desire to do so, just to be able to say, "I've seen everything"?

She'd like me to go to Venice out of prudence. You can go there in twenty-four or thirty hours.

Milan, Albergo della Città, November 2.—Undoubtedly the most beautiful woman I've ever possessed, and possibly ever seen, is Angela as she appeared to me tonight while I was walking with her through the streets by the light of the shops. I don't know how she came to tell me, with that naturalness that distinguishes her and without vanity, that some of her friends told her she frightened people. That's true. She was animated tonight. It appears that she loves me. YESTERDAY AND TODAY, SHE HAS HAD PLEASURE. She'd just had coffee with me in a solitary back shop; her eyes were brilliant; her half-lit face had a suave harmony and yet was terrible with supernatural beauty. It was as though she were a superior being who had chosen to be so beautiful because that disguise became her more than another, and whose penetrating eyes read your soul. That face would have made a sublime sibyl.

I met her at six o'clock in the Contrada del Bocchetto, near the Caffè Sanquirico, our usual meeting place; I went with her as far as her sister-in-law's, the wife of a famous chemist, at the Porta Ticinese, I believe, near San Lorenzo. I waited in a café; a quarter of an hour later, she came by again; we went to have coffee, and finally after a half hour's walk, I left her near the arcade on the Place des Marchands, still with the handsome Antonio.

November 6.—I went to see Bossi's *Last Supper* at Signor Rafaelli's. I was dissatisfied in respect to: 1. the coloring; 2. the expression.

1. The coloring is the opposite of that of da Vinci. The somber and majestic manner of da Vinci is especially appropriate for this scene. Bossi has used bright coloring in all parts of it. One thing is sure, his picture would produce much more effect in a church than that of Leonardo because it would be *noticed* and that of Leonardo would not be seen.

But in a gallery Bossi's picture will always be displeasing. A book composed by the author of a picture removes from the picture the grace that is necessary for it to be touching. If you want to demonstrate this, think of the opposite case: a picture, accidentally come across, by an unfortunate and modest author is at once interesting.

2. Expression.

As for the expression, I'll guarantee to show that Judas looks like Henri IV. The outthrust lower lip imbues him with kindness, and kindness that is all the greater because it isn't destroyed by the mind.

Judas is a goodhearted man who has the misfortune to be red-haired.

Without going beyond nature, the face of M. Norvins (of Rome) would at once make a better Judas.

The countryside glimpsed beyond the head of Christ gave me much pleasure, even before I noticed the genuine green.

A Christ's head by Guido Reni which I found in Rafaelli's studio was for me a terrible criticism of Signor Bossi.

The engraving by Morghen gave me far more pleasure. This isn't a decisive reason. I still need an interpretation of several painters. The Carraccis, for instance, whose blacks displease me.

November 7.—I saw the gallery of the Archbishop's Palace this morning. Handsome face of J. Caesar Procaccini. Copy of Correggio's Magdalen which seemed pretty to me. Fine portrait of a pope, said to be by Titian. Relief of a profile by Titian.

After that, I was too happy and occupied by the jealousy of those gents to have time to write. I left Milan November 13, and reached Paris November 27 at half-past five. GREAT.

The next day, a lost battle.

THE LAST PART OF A TOUR THROUGH ITALY, presented in all humility to M. H. de B., aged thirty-eight, who'll possibly be alive in 1821, by his very humble servant, gayer than he.

The H. B. of 1811.

Milan, October 29, 1811.

The Russian Campaign

WITH the exception of a few entries of minor importance, no diary exists for 1812, which happened to be one of the most eventful years of Beyle's life. He was too busy writing his art history during the first half of the year to keep a diary, and the notes he jotted down during the Russian campaign were lost in the disastrous retreat from Moscow. Most of the letters he wrote to Félix Faure and Mme. Daru, however, still exist and form a quite satisfactory substitute for the diary proper. Some of those given in the following pages have already appeared in English in *To the Happy Few,* Norman Cameron's translation of Stendhal's selected correspondence.

Upon returning, at the end of November 1811, to the gray skies and "bleached souls" of Paris, Beyle passed through some thoroughly unpleasant moments. Not only was he depressed by the realization that "the happy days of Italy" were over, but his three-month ramble had in some way resulted in his "disgrace," earning him Daru's displeasure, the hostility of his superiors and the insults of his equals.

Largely as a means of recapturing his Italian sentiments, he purchased a dozen fine apple-green notebooks and started to compose the history of Italian painting he had conceived during an idle moment in Milan a month earlier. Opening the first notebook, he affectionately printed in heavy block letters across the flyleaf: TO MILADY ANGELA G. The agreeable illusion that he was "speaking of love" to his mistress and the fair land of her birth was to spur him on as, with a totally unaccustomed perseverance, he labored week after week over the preliminary draft of his first sustained literary production.

On the practical side, he felt the need of a larger background of art and was convinced that a guide compiled by himself would be preferable to that of another, for, in the latter case, the author's ideas "might interfere with his own and lead him into discussions at the very moment that he ought to be experiencing sensations." Such a homemade handbook, too, would be very useful on his next trip to Italy—and besides, he rather hoped that its sale would pay the expenses of this next trip!

Translating, abridging and revising the ponderously learned and conveniently defunct Lanzi, he worked rapidly, sometimes completing as many as forty pages in a single day. By the middle of January, after six weeks of work, he had finished the history of Florentine art—actually more than he published five years later in his *Histoire de la Peinture en Italie*. All that was lacking were the politico-historical introduction and the capital chapters on the ancient and modern *beau idéal*. In a little more than six months of this congenial occupation, he had finished the first draft of his entire study—comprising the schools of Rome, Lombardy, Venice and Bologna, as well as that of Florence (the only one he was to publish)—dictated a copy of the whole, covered the copy with notes and begun the revision of the text.

Inevitably, his knowledge of the subject, almost negligible at the start, rapidly deepened as he progressed. As Inspector of the Emperor's Household Furnishings, he was commissioned to inventory the great collection of paintings and statues then in the Musée Napoleon, otherwise the Louvre. Furthermore, he soon began to read other books on Italian painting: to Lanzi, Vasari and Bossi, whose works he had bought in Milan, he added Ridolphi, Algarotti, Zanetti, Convivi, Mengs, Comolli, Baldinucci, Vasi, Belloni, Malvasia and many others. Each time a passage in one of these authors contained useful information or pertinent ideas, he unhesitatingly lifted it, remodeled it to suit his taste and squeezed it into his compilation.

After a bad start, the period from December 1811 to July 1812 turned out to be one of the pleasantest he had yet lived through. With no financial worries and little official work, he scribbled away in his pleasant apartment "in absolute solitude until six o'clock": his evenings were passed in amusing company or at the Opera Buffa. It was the kind of life he had always wanted: all that was now needed was to assure its permanence by coming into a title and a Prefecture.

He accordingly redoubled his entreaties to his father to give him a *majorat* and the financial aid necessary to obtain a barony. His resistance worn down, the elder Beyle at length agreed to establish the *majorat,* but, shrewd trader that he was, he found a way as original as it was ironic of "giving" the requisite property to his son, who in his eagerness to have a title had incautiously agreed "to sign anything." One of those solemn legal documents so beloved to old French families was drawn up stating that Chérubin, "wishing to establish a *majorat* of baron" for his son, turned over the Beyle home in the Rue de Bonne, Grenoble, to the latter

—who, however, was to pay for the gift by immediately mortgaging it for 45,000 francs! It was furthermore specified that the third floor was to be reserved for the use of Chérubin, while the second floor was to be occupied for life by its present tenant. As the house had only three floors, and the first was entirely taken up with stores, Beyle paid his father 45,000 francs for the "donation" of a house that was useless to him!

As a final touch of irony, the house did not even obtain a barony for him. Almost at the same minute the papers were being signed in Grenoble, Napoleon and his vast army were crossing the Niemen. The catastrophic Russian campaign was about to start, and, in the events of the coming months, barony, history of Italian painting, gay society, light operas and the rest passed by the board.

Napoleon's invasion of Russia was no sooner decided than Beyle began importuning the Duc de Cadore for permission to resume his duties with the Intendancy. After considerable difficulty and some delay, he was finally commissioned to carry a portfolio to the Emperor. His orders were given him July 23 by Marie-Louise in person, and the same evening he drove lightheartedly out of Paris in his little calash toward adventures that were to go from exciting to harrowing, to terminate several months later in a nightmare.

On September 14, he dragged into Moscow, exhausted, in the company of Victorine's brother Edouard and a trio of Angelina's "friends," Joinville, Widmann and Migliorini.

The French barely had time to look around the legendary Russian capital when their admiration turned to horror upon seeing the luxurious mansions and palaces one after another burst into flames. The last act of Count Feodor Vasilievich Rostopchin, Military Governor of Moscow, before evacuating the city had been to throw open the prisons and to give each of the freed convicts a firebrand with instructions to set Moscow on fire. While the remaining inhabitants fled, taking the fire pumps with them, the prisoners ran from building to building, touching off everything that was inflammable. Frantic efforts were made to stop the fire's progress, but the soldiers no sooner extinguished one blaze than a score of others started. Through four days and four nights, the city continued to burn, and Beyle's undramatized and rather disgusted description of the resultant disorder, pillaging and privation is probably as accurate an account as has been left by any witness of the historic event.

One thought caused him great anxiety throughout the confusion of these days. It was concerned with Mélanie Guilbert, whose memory had grown very precious since he gladly said farewell to her at Marseille six years earlier. In the interval, Mélanie had married a Russian general named Barcov and had come with her husband to live in Moscow. The day after his arrival Beyle had gone about town trying to locate Mme. Barcov, but all he found were a few of her friends, who were unable to give him any definite information. According to them, she had left for St. Petersburg a few days before the arrival of the French. She was pregnant, suffering from eye trouble, and had quarreled with her husband, who apparently was no longer with her. It seemed that Mélanie intended to set out for Paris but possessed barely enough money for the long, hazardous journey.

Worried by this news, Beyle wrote a mutual friend in Paris, requesting him, should he hear of Mélanie's return, to offer her lodgings in the closed apartment of the Rue Neuve-de-Luxembourg.

In the first weeks neither Beyle nor his companions suffered any very serious physical discomfort. But when they arose on the morning of October 12, they found the ground covered with a heavy frost. Soon it began to snow. Although a thaw had set in by the fifteenth, the weather remained foggy. It was an evil omen, and it meant that the cold northern winter had begun—several weeks earlier than usual. Napoleon, who had been marking time in the futile hope that Czar Alexander would finally decide to make peace overtures, heeded the sign and was alarmed by it. Within three weeks, he decided, the Army must be established in winter quarters.

Ordered to go to Smolensk, Mohilov and Vitebsk to make the necessary arrangements for assuring subsistence to the rear, Beyle started out on October 16 with 1,500 wounded and an escort of two or three hundred soldiers.

The trip was bad enough for Beyle's party, but for Napoleon and the army of 100,000 that marched with him, it was worse. Leaving Moscow three days later than Beyle, the troops found the roads continually barred by Cossack bands. At Maloyaroslavets on the twenty-third, there was a serious engagement with the Russians. After that, the march was constantly impeded by the Cossacks, who daily attacked isolated groups of French soldiers. Encumbered by the provisions and the artillery, the troops were soon exhausted: discipline grew slack, morale began to weaken. At Boragobuge matters grew rapidly worse. The provisions were running so low that the soldiers were willing to pay fantastic sums for moldy bread and cat meat. The thermometer suddenly dropped far below zero, and a heavy snowstorm made the advance all but impossible. The horses fell by the thousands, only to be eaten immediately by the undernourished soldiers. In the midst of all this, Napoleon was driven into a white fury by dispatches from Paris informing him that the French Empire had nearly been overthrown by the plot of the crackbrained Malet. Finally, on November 9, the Army began straggling into Smolensk, where it found that the troops who had arrived there a week earlier had exhausted the stores of food. This disastrous news completed the demoralization of the famished and frozen troops. All pretense of discipline vanished, and the soldiers went about the ruined town like wild beasts, ravenously falling on anything they could find.

Napoleon, who had already abandoned his original plan to stay in Russia until spring, seemed to have lost control of the situation. Scarcely arrived in Smolensk, where he had intended to take up winter quarters, he gave orders for the retreat to continue. Beginning November 12, detachments of soldiers were dispatched every twenty-four hours. New disasters awaited them in the Losmina Valley, where the Cossacks played havoc with the retreating forces. When at length the remnants of the Grande Armée were concentrated at Orsha, only 24,000 troops, plus 14,000 stragglers, remained of the half million who had crossed the Niemen five months earlier.

From Orsha to Borisov, the retreat became worse and worse. The temperature went as low as 40 degrees below zero Fahrenheit, and each morning when the soldiers started out they left hundreds of frozen corpses behind them. On November 26 and 27, they crossed the Berezina at Studianka, near Borisov. Most of the Army had already passed over the river in an orderly fashion when the stragglers, who had been loitering along the banks, were suddenly thrown into panic by rumors of another Cossack attack. They rushed wildly for the bridge, clogging the passage and trampling their comrades in scenes of indescribable horror. A week later the survivors arrived in Vilna, where Napoleon called his lieutenants into conference, told them of Malet's plot and announced that it was necessary for him to depart for Paris at once, leaving the Army in command of Murat.

Beyle, who had been prevented by the rapid development of events from continuing his mission to Mohilov and Vitebsk, left Smolensk on November 11, a day before the first detachments of regular soldiers. Still in charge of what few provisions remained, it was he who was responsible for the distribution of the only bread ration the Army received between Smolensk and Borisov. He later said that this service had been recognized by Daru in the name of the Emperor.

The ration of bread he distributed was a rare feast. Usually the men were happy to find anything to eat, and long afterward Beyle recalled with pleasure a piece of suet he bought for twenty francs in some village he passed through. He experienced considerable physical suffering: during the retreat, his ample waistline receded alarmingly, and he lost all his clothes except those he was wearing.

Alexandre Bergonié, one of Beyle's roommates at Moscow, told Prosper Mérimée many years later that he owed his life to his colleague. Arrived at the Berezina, Bergonié was so exhausted that he refused to go any farther until he had rested. Beyle, foreseeing the morrow's jam on the bridge, almost carried his friend across by force. "M. Bergonié used to praise endlessly Beyle's presence of mind, which he retained at a time when the most resolute were losing their heads," Mérimée says in his *H. B*. This testimony supports Stendhal's boast that, during the Russian campaign, he "distinguished himself by his sang-froid."

The Berezina crossed, the Army proceeded in disorder to Minsk. Beyle and his comrades were by now in a pitiful condition. It grew colder and colder. The supplies were exhausted, and he wrote that he kneeled in reverence at the sight of a few potatoes. It was only after arriving in Poland that they managed to find sufficient food in the towns they passed through. They were, however, still harried by bands of Cossacks, and many were the times when they were aroused in the middle of the night by a persistent cannonade. At Molodeczno, during one of these attacks, the culminating misfortune befell Beyle: he lost a large sum of money—possibly as much as 15,000 francs—part of his Brunswick diary, all the notes he had taken in Russia and, most tragic of all, the twelve precious notebooks containing the corrected and annotated copy of his *Histoire de la Peinture en Italie*.

Feeling his strength giving out, he left Molodeczno ahead of the Army with his other roommate, Antoine Busche. On December 7 he arrived at Vilna, "fed up with the pleasures of the snow" and revolted with the sordidness of human nature revealed by the retreat. There had been a few magnificent moments of solitude during the long march, but as soon as some companions joined him there was no longer "anything for the heart." His privations affected him far less than "the hideous spectacle of horrible suffering and lack of pity: at Vilna, the holes in the walls were plugged up with the frozen corpses of soldiers."

Some of his strength returned at Gumbinnen, where he arrived a few days later. After Königsberg he traveled with Commissary Balthazar Marchant in a mahogany sledge and nearly perished in the Frisches Haff when the ice gave way beneath the runners. He reached Danzig December 30 and remained there until January 8, when he set out for Berlin. On his thirtieth birthday, January 23, 1813, he left Berlin, and, following familiar roads, passed through Brunswick, Cassel, Frankfurt and Mainz, finally arriving back in Paris January 31.

In after years Beyle was wont to boast that he had taken the ten-week retreat "like a glass of lemonade," that he never believed there was "anything worth crying about" in its hardships, that it was only after he got back to Paris that he learned the retreat had been a terrible matter. There was unquestionably some braggadocio in this attitude, but for once he distorted the picture very little. If he had occasionally complained, he had nevertheless gone through the campaign courageously: he had got out of a dangerous situation as best he could; he had been dirty and hungry; he had lost clothes and money; he had been cold, exhausted and in poor health. But he was too intent on the problems of the moment to be conscious of the fact that he was playing a part in one of the most important events of modern history. It was only as the months and years passed and the memory of the disagreeable phases faded that the endless retreat was slowly transformed into the brilliant and heroic colors of an epic. The retreat from Moscow became celebrated; it was talked about in the salons, written about in books: to have participated in it was a title to glory, and Henri Beyle, like the others, was not reluctant to mention that he too had been one of Napoleon's Muscovites.

The right to that boast was at bottom his sole reward for the Russian experience. True, as he wrote in his quaint combination of French and English, "it had the advantage of making me see things THAT NO *Mocenigo* FROM Cervantes, I BELIEVE, HAS NEVER SEEN," and the eighteen-day trip from Moscow to Smolensk had provided him "new nurture for his soul." But he had not been in the mood to benefit from his experiences. "I had lost the habit of intense and extreme attention, because I was usually thinking only of things I held in contempt," he said after his return.

In brief, the inescapable company of swashbuckling vulgarians had made it impossible to appreciate the tragic grandeur of the spectacle.

1812 Russia

From letter to Pauline, Saint-Cloud, July 23, 1812.—I'm leaving at seven o'clock tonight for the banks of the Dvina; I came here to get my orders from Her Majesty the Empress. This princess has just honored me with a conversation of several minutes on the route I am to take, the duration of the voyage, etc., etc. Upon leaving Her Majesty, I went to the apartments of His Majesty the King of Rome, but he was sleeping; Madame the Comtesse de Montesquieu informed me that it would be impossible to see him before three o'clock; consequently, I have two hours to wait. That's uncomfortable in dress uniform and lace. Luckily, I recalled that my position of inspector might possibly give me some credit in the palace. I presented myself, and a room that was not being used at the moment was made available for me.

I'll go speedily as far as Königsberg, as I'm in the first courier. The Prince High Chancellor told me yesterday to try to fare better than one of my colleagues, who took twenty-eight days to go from Paris to

Vilna. It's hard to advance across those devastated deserts, especially with a wretched little Viennese calash loaded down with a thousand packages; there's not a single person who hasn't thought of sending one along with me.

From letter to Félix Faure and Mme. Pierre Daru, Smolensk, August 19.
—The fire appeared such a fine spectacle to us that, although it was seven o'clock, and in spite of the fear of missing dinner (a thing unheard of in such a town), and the fear of the shells which the Russians were firing through the flames at any Frenchmen who might be on the banks of the Borysthenes (Dnepr), we went down to the city gate which is next to a pretty chapel; a shell had just burst there, and everything was still smoking. We advanced a score of paces by running bravely; we crossed the river on a bridge that General Kirgener had ordered to be constructed in great haste. We went right to the edge of the fire, where we found a large number of dogs and a few horses that had been driven out of the city by the general conflagration.

We were about to drink in this rare spectacle when Marignier was approached by an infantry major whom he knew through having taken his place in a lodging at Rostock. This worthy fellow told us at length of his battles that morning and the day before, and then launched out in interminable praise of a dozen Rostock ladies whom he mentioned by name; but he praised one of them more than the others. Reluctance to interrupt a man so full of his subject, and the impulse to laugh, retained us till ten o'clock, when the bullets started raining down again.

We deplored the loss of our dinner, and I was arranging with Marignier that he should return the first to receive our deserved reprimand from M. Daru, when we saw an extraordinary light in the upper town.

We approached, we found all our calashes in the middle of the street, eight large houses near our own were belching flames sixty feet in the air and casting hot embers as big as fists on the house which had been ours for the past few hours; we had the roof pierced in five or six places, half a dozen grenadiers of the Guard were armed with long poles to beat off the sparks and make them fall; they handled their jobs very well. M. Daru took care of everything. Activity, fatigue, tumult till midnight.

Our house caught fire three times and we put it out. Our headquarters were in the courtyard, where, sitting on some straw, we kept watch on the roofs of the house and its dependencies, informing the grenadiers by our shouts where the falling embers were the thickest.

We were there, Messrs. Daru, Comte Dumas, Besnard, Jacqueminot, General Kirgener—all of us so exhausted that we dropped off to sleep as we talked; the master of the house (M. Daru) was the only one who resisted sleep.

The dinner we had looked forward to so much appeared at last; but, for all our appetite, since we hadn't eaten anything since ten o'clock in the morning, it was very amusing to see one of us after the other drop off to sleep in his chair, fork in hand.

From letter to Félix Faure, Smolensk, eighty leagues from Moscow, August 24.—How man changes! My former thirst for seeing things is completely quenched; after seeing Milan and Italy, everything repels me by its coarseness. Would you believe it, without anything that affects me more than anything else, without anything personal, I'm sometimes on the verge of tears? In this ocean of barbarity, there isn't a single sound that replies to my soul! Everything is coarse, filthy, stinking for the physical as for the mental. I've found but a mild pleasure in having some music played to me on a little out-of-tune piano by a creature who has about as much feeling for music as I have for the Mass. Ambition no longer means anything to me; the finest decoration wouldn't compensate for the mire into which I'm plunged. I picture to myself the heights on which my soul (composing literary works, listening to Cimarosa and loving Angela in a fine climate) dwells, like delightful hills; far from those hills, on the plain, are fetid swamps; I'm bogged down in them, and nothing in the world, with the exception of a map, recalls my hills.

Would you believe me if I said I have a lively pleasure in attending to official business that is concerned with Italy? I had three or four of these affairs, which, even when they were finished, occupied my imagination like a novel.

I had a slight annoyance in the region of Vilna, where I rejoined the Army at a time when this country wasn't yet organized. I suffered extreme physical pains. In order to arrive, I left my calash behind, and this calash hasn't rejoined me. It's possible that it's been pillaged. For me personally, that would be but a semi-misfortune, in the neighborhood of 4,000 fr. in lost possessions and inconvenience. What an asinine compliment to pay people!

Moscow, Oct. 4. (Diary of September 14-15).—I left my general supping at the Apraxin Palace. As we were coming out and were taking leave of M. Z in the courtyard, we noticed that, in addition to the fire in the Chinese village, which had been burning away for several hours, we had one near us; we went to it. The center of it was very intense. I got a toothache on this expedition. We were foolish enough to stop a soldier who'd just given a couple of whacks with his bayonet to a man who'd drunk too much beer; I went as far as to draw my sword, and I was even on the verge of stabbing the scoundrel. Bourgeois took him to the governor, who set him free.

We retired at one o'clock after spouting numerous commonplaces about fires—all of which didn't produce much effect, at least as far as we could see. Returning to the Casa Apraxin, we tested out a pump. I went to bed, plagued by my toothache. It appears that several of those gents were chickenhearted enough to let themselves be alarmed and to go running out at about two and five o'clock. As for myself, I awoke at seven o'clock, had my carriage loaded and had it driven to the rear of those belonging to M. Daru.

They were strung along the boulevard, opposite the club. There I found Mme. B., who was about to throw herself at my feet; that made a very ridiculous recognition. I noticed that there wasn't a shade of naturalness in what Mme. B. told me, a fact which naturally chilled me. Nevertheless, I did a lot for her by putting her fat sister-in-law in my calash, and inviting her to put her droshkies behind my carriage. She told me that Mme. Saint-Albe [Mélanie Guilbert] had often spoken of me.

The fire was rapidly approaching the house we'd left. Our carriages remained on the boulevard five or six hours. Weary of this inaction, I went to see the fire, and stopped an hour or two at Joinville's. I admired the voluptuousness inspired by the furnishings of his house; together with Billet and Busche, we drank three bottles of wine, which revived us.

I read a few lines of an English translation of *Virginie*, which, amid the general coarseness, revived me a bit morally.

I went with Louis [Joinville] to see the fire. We saw a drunken mounted cannoneer named Savoye strike an officer with the flat of his sword, and heap insults on him. He was in the wrong, and was obliged to end up by begging his pardon. One of his pillaging mates went forth through the flaming street, and was probably roasted alive. I saw a further demonstration of the general lack of character in the French. Louis found amusement in calming this man for the benefit of an officer of the Guard who'd have done him a bad turn at the first opportunity; instead of having the scorn for all this disorder that it deserved, he exposed himself to the risk of getting into trouble. For my part, I admired the patience of the officer of the Guard; I'd have given Savoye a saber blow on the nose—which might have led to trouble with the colonel. The officer acted more prudently.

At three o'clock, I returned to the line of our carriages and dismal colleagues. Stores of flour and oats had just been discovered in the neighboring frame houses; I told my servants to take some. They made a great show of being busy, put on the appearance of taking great quantities, and in the end their work amounted to very little. That's the way it is with everything everywhere in the Army, and it makes you irritated. It's all well and good to tell yourself it doesn't matter a damn anyway, but, as they're always bellyaching, you finish by getting out of patience, and I pass whole days of unhappiness. I'm far less impatient than another would be in my place, but I lose my temper. I envy certain of my colleagues to whom you could say, I believe, that they're the scum of the earth without their really getting mad; they raise their voices, and that's all. They wiggle their ears, as the Comtesse Palfy used to say. "A person would be unhappy indeed if he didn't do the same thing," she would add. She was right: but how are you going to display resignation like that if you have a sensitive soul?

About half-past three, Billet and I went to visit the home of Count Petr Soltykov; it appeared to us to be suitable for His Excellency. We went to the Kremlin to notify him; we stopped at General Dumas's quarters, which dominate the square.

General Kirgener said to Louis in front of me, "If they want to give me four thousand men, I'll guarantee to take care of the fire in six hours, and it will be put out." These words impressed me. (I doubt if he would succeed. Rostopchin continually had the fire spread to new places; if it were extinguished on the right, it would break out in a score of places on the left.)

We saw M. Daru and the amiable Marignier arrive from the Kremlin; we took them to the Soltykov mansion, which was inspected from cellar to roof; as M. Daru did not find all to his liking in the Soltykov house, he was requested to go to inspect some others in the direction of the club. We saw the club, decorated in the French manner, majestic and blackened by smoke. There is nothing of the kind in Paris that can be compared with it. After the club, we looked over a neighboring house, vast and superb; finally, a handsome square white house that they decided to occupy.

We were very tired, I more than the others. Ever since Smolensk, I've been completely without strength, and I was childish enough to interest myself and bustle around in this house-hunting. Interest is saying too much, but a great deal of bustle.

We finally moved into this house, which looked as though it had been lived in by a wealthy art lover. It was comfortably arranged, full of statuettes and pictures. There were some good books, notably Buffon, Voltaire—who's to be found everywhere here—and *La Galerie du Palais-Royal*.

A violent epidemic of diarrhea made everyone fear that the wine would give out. We heard the excellent news that we might help ourselves in the cellar of the fine club I have already mentioned. I persuaded Father Billet to go there. We entered it through a superb stable and a garden that would have been beautiful if the trees of this country did not have such a poverty-stricken aspect for me.

We sent our servants down into the cellar; they brought us up a large quantity of bad white wine, damask tablecloths and badly worn napkins of the same. We pillaged all these things to make sheets out of them.

A little M. J., from the Intendant General's office, who'd come over to do his bit of *pilfering* like us, set about making us presents of all we were taking. He said he was taking over the building for the Intendant General, and started in to moralize; I called him to order a little.

My servant was completely drunk; he heaped tablecloths, wine, a violin he had pillaged for himself and a thousand other things in the carriage. We had a little wine repast with two or three other colleagues.

The servants put the house in order, the fire was far from us and filled the air with copper-colored smoke; we had set ourselves in order, and were at last about to breathe freely when M. Daru came in and announced that we had to leave. I accepted the thing with courage, but it utterly disheartened me.

My carriage was crammed full, I put the poor pale-faced and boring de B., whom I pitied, in it. He's the most asinine and boring spoiled child I know.

Before leaving the house, I pillaged a volume of Voltaire, the one entitled *Facéties*.

My carriages that François was in charge of kept us waiting. We had barely got under way by seven o'clock. We encountered M. Daru, who was furious. We went directly toward the fire, following a part of the boulevard. Little by little, we advanced through the smoke, breathing became difficult; we finally went between blazing houses. None of our enterprises are ever perilous except through the utter lack of order and caution. Here was a long procession of wagons plunging into the midst of the flames in order to escape them. This maneuver would have had some sense to it only had the city been surrounded by a circle of fire. This wasn't the case in the least; the fire was limited to one side of the city, it was necessary to get out of it, but it wasn't necessary to go through the fire; what should have been done was to go around it.

The impossibility of the thing stopped us short; we turned back. As I was thinking of the great spectacle before me, I forgot for a moment that I'd turned my carriage around before the others. I was worn out, I was proceeding on foot because my carriage was full of the servant's plunder, and the paleface was perched on it. I thought my carriage was lost in the fire. François galloped headlong. The carriage wouldn't have been in any danger, but my servants, like those of everyone else, were drunk and quite capable of going to sleep in the middle of a blazing street.

On the boulevard as we returned, we found General Kirgener, with whom I was very satisfied that day. He restored our audacity—in other words, our good sense—and showed us that there were three or four roads by which we could get out of the city.

We followed one of them about eleven o'clock, we broke through the lines, arguing with some of the King of Naples' carters. I later noticed that we were following the Tverskoï, or Tver Street. We left the city, illuminated by the finest fire in the world, which formed an immense pyramid, which, like the prayers of the faithful, had its base on earth and its apex in heaven. The moon appeared above this atmosphere of flame and smoke. It was an imposing sight, but it would have been necessary to be alone, or else surrounded by intelligent people, in order to enjoy it. What has spoiled the Russian campaign for me is to have taken part in it with people who would have belittled the Colosseum or the Bay of Naples.

We went by a superb road toward a castle named Petrovski, where His Majesty had gone to take lodgings. Zowie! From my carriage, where I'd found a little room, I saw M. Daru's calash careen and finally fall into the ditch. The road was only eighty feet wide! Oaths, fury; it was extremely hard work to get the carriage up.

We finally reached a bivouac; it faced the city. We saw quite clearly the huge pyramid formed by the pianos and sofas of Moscow, which would have given us so much pleasure if it hadn't been for this incendiary mania. This Rostopchin will be either a scoundrel or a Roman; it remains to be seen how his act will be judged. Today, a notice was found in one of Rostopchin's castles; it said that there were furnishings worth a million, I believe, etc., etc., but that he was burning them so as not to leave the enjoyment of them to brigands. The fact of the matter is that his fine palace in Moscow was not set on fire.

Arrived at the bivouac, we supped on raw fish, figs and wine. Such was the end of this distressing day, during which we'd been kept on the jump from seven o'clock in the morning until eleven o'clock at night. The worst of it was that, at eleven o'clock, as I took a seat in my calash to go to sleep beside that boring de B., and sitting on top of bottles covered over with goods and blankets, I found that I was drunk from the effects of the bad white wine pillaged at the club.

From letter to Félix Faure, Moscow, October 2.—To complete the contrast between the autumn of 1811 and of 1812, extreme physical fatigue and food composed exclusively of meat have given me a fine bilious fever which promises to hold me fast. This illness was agreeable to me, as it gave me a week of solitude. I've had the time to see that, the circumstances being extremely boring, I had need of applying myself to something absorbing. Consequently, I again began to work on *Letellier*. What induced me to do this was the memory of the pure and often delightful pleasure I had for seven months last winter, starting December 4. This occupation interested me yesterday and the day before.

You should realize this truth, that happiness clarifies the judgment. On things relating to women, on the way to give them the sensations of amiability, etc., you had many opinions that seemed to be vitiated because, for weird reasons not existing in nature, like a large nose, a high forehead, etc., you persisted in always seeing yourself on one side of the scales. Happiness now places you on the other, and ought to lead you back naturally to the rules of pure *Beylism*.—I was reading Rousseau's *Confessions* a week ago. It was uniquely through the lack of two or three rules of *Beylism* that he was so unhappy. The mania of seeing duties and virtues everywhere put pedantry in his style and unhappiness in his life. He'd ally himself with a man for three weeks: boom, the *duties* of friendship, etc.! Two years later, this man no longer thinks of him; he looks for some somber explanation of that. *Beylism* would have said to him, "Two bodies come together; heat and fermentation are produced, but every state of this kind is temporary. It's a flower that must be enjoyed sensually, etc." Do you grasp my idea? The finest things in Rousseau stink of the empyreuma to me, and don't at all have the *Correggian* grace, which is destroyed by the slightest shade of pedantry.

It looks as though I'll spend the winter here; I hope there'll be some concerts. There will certainly be theatrical performances at the Court, but what kind of actors will be in them?

Nothing purifies me like music after association with asses; it's becoming dearer to me daily. But whence comes this pleasure? Music describes nature. Rousseau says it frequently abandons direct description, which is impossible, in order to cast our soul, through means of its own, into a position similar to that which would be given us by the object it seeks to describe. Instead of describing a quiet night, a thing which is impossible, it gives the soul the same sensation by producing in it the same sentiments as a quiet night would inspire.

Do you understand something of this? I'm writing you in a little room where two young asses from Paris are offering their opinion on what should be done in Moscow, and not leaving me the possibility of stringing two ideas together; I had a number of them to communicate to you, and here I am run dry.

As for music, it seems to me that my peculiar taste for good comic operas comes from the fact that they give me the sensation of the ideal perfection of comedy. The best comedy for me would be that which gives sensations similar to those I derive from *Il Matrimonio Segreto* and the *Pazzo per la Musica;* that seems to me clear in my heart.

From letter to Mme. Daru, Moscow, October 16.—. . . our conversations are the most boring in the world, we never talk about anything but solemn subjects, an enormous dose of self-importance, and a mortal hour is taken to explain something that might have been said in ten minutes. With this exception, everything is proceeding very well indeed, we haven't seen any women since the posthouse mistresses of Poland, but on the other hand we're great connoisseurs of fires. Our precipitous moves from one place to another during the first nights of our stay at Moscow were truly pleasant, but for you, madame, these things are commonplaces, they have been so well described to you that you know more about them than we do. You know that Moscow had 400 or 500 palaces decorated with a charming voluptuousness unknown in Paris, and which is to be seen only in lucky Italy. It's quite simple. The government was despotic. There were 800 or a thousand persons here who had from 5 to 15,000 livres income. What was to be done with this money? Go to Court? A sergeant of the Guard who enjoyed the Emperor's favor humiliated them, and furthermore exiled them to Siberia in order to have their fine horses and carriages. These unfortunates had no recourse other than pleasure, and they seem, judging by their houses, which we enjoyed for thirty-six hours, to have put this makeshift to good use.

From letters to Félix Faure, Smolensk, November 7 and 9.—Leaving Moscow on my mission October 16, I reached here November 2, after a highly interesting voyage which alone was worth coming to Russia for. Two fine attacks by Cossacks, the firm belief throughout one night that we'd be killed the next day . . .

Here I am again in this city which seems to me unique as far as picturesqueness is concerned. The snow heightens the effect of the tree-studded ravines amid which it's built. It's not very cold, two or three degrees, but, since we're in Russia, everyone thinks he's frozen. Our thoughts are entirely brought back to the physical: the great thing is to have or not to have boots or a coat. It's been impossible to write you for the past twenty days. There have been moments when I would have liked very much to preserve the memory of what I saw in my soul or round about me, but it was impossible to write. Today, all the sublimity of my soul is again neutralized by the forced society, I shan't say of any particular person, but of mankind. Deprived of a shield, my soul was exposed to all sorts of vexations, and became inane as the result; that's the state in which I have the honor of being after sleeping with two overgrown children on the floor of a little workroom next to the room where eight or ten colleagues were sleeping in the same fashion.

From letter to Mme. Daru, Smolensk, November 9.—I have just made a charming voyage; three or four times a day, I passed from extreme boredom to extreme pleasure. It must be confessed that the pleasures were not delicate; one of the liveliest of them, for instance, was one evening when we found some potatoes to eat without salt with some moldy munition bread. You can imagine our deep misery. This state of things lasted eighteen days; leaving Moscow October 16, I arrived here November 2. Comte Dumas had ordered me to leave with a convoy of 1,500 wounded, escorted by two or three hundred men. You can imagine the huge number of little wagons, the oaths, the continual quarreling; all these wagons bumping into each other, sinking deep in the mud. Regularly every day we spent two or three hours in a muddy ditch, and we lacked everything. It was then that I said, "To the devil with this crazy idea of coming to Russia." Arrived in the evening, after marching all day and covering three or four leagues, we bivouacked and went to sleep, freezing a bit.

On October 24, as we were building our fires, we were surrounded by a mob of men who began firing at us. Utter disorder, curses from the wounded; we had all the trouble in the world making them take up their rifles. We drove off the enemy, but believed we were in for some high adventures. We had a brave wounded general named Mourier with us, and he explained our situation. Being attacked at this hour of the evening by a great horde of infantry probably meant that we had 4,000 or 5,000 Russians ahead of us, partly troops of the line, and partly peasants in revolt. We were hemmed in, it was no more safe to retreat than to advance. We decided to stay up all night and at daybreak to form a hollow square with our wounded in the middle, and to attempt to break through the Russians; to abandon our wagons, if we were driven to it, and to form another little hollow square and to be killed to the last man rather than allow ourselves to be captured by the peasants, who would put us to death slowly by stabbing, or in some such pleasant manner.

After this fine resolution, we made an arrangement. Each of us put his least necessary possessions into a bundle, which was to be thrown out at the first attack so as to lighten the wagon. I was quartered with five or six wounded colonels whom I didn't know a week before and who have become intimate friends since the start of the journey.

They all agreed that our goose was cooked. We distributed our napoleons among the servants in an effort to safeguard a few. We had all become intimate friends. We drank what little wine remained. On the morrow, which was to have been such a great day, we started out on foot beside our calashes, armed from head to foot with pistols. There was such a dense fog that we couldn't see four paces in front of us. We continually came to a stop. I had a volume of Mme. de Deffand which I read almost to the end. Our enemies didn't consider us worthy of their wrath, we were only attacked in the evening by a few Cossacks, who stuck their spears into fifteen or twenty wounded.

From letter to Mme. Daru, Smolensk, November 10.—Getting into the carriage to leave Moscow, our excellent General Dumas complained of a pain in the side, a short time later he spat blood, the fact was that he had pneumonia in all its symptoms. What a sickness to have at his age, at this season and on this route! He's out of danger, but so thin, pale and weak that he asked His Majesty for a month's furlough, during which time M. Daru will be in charge of the Intendancy.

I didn't follow my chief during the march here from Moscow. He went to Maloyaroslavets to beat the Russians. It's too bad indeed that this victory has such a baroque name; they say that it was a superb engagement and that the Russians were never driven from their position in a manner more brilliant and honorable for the Army. I wasn't on hand when these fine things were happening, I left Moscow October 16, and arrived in Smolensk with a poor little convoy that had been mauled by the Cossacks, who, among other things, were rude enough to take my case of provisions, with the result that I lived for eighteen days on munition bread and water.

Our physical sufferings on the way from Moscow were diabolic. There isn't a porter at the markets who is as tired at the end of the day as we were every night after building our little hut of dry branches and lighting our fire. I'm still frozen as a result of it, as you are undoubtedly able to notice by my scrawl. You wouldn't recognize us. We're all enough to make anyone afraid. We look like our lackeys. That's literally true, the first one of us to reach Smolensk was mistaken for an insolent lackey because he stepped forward to shake hands with the master of the house. We're a long way indeed from the Parisian elegance. I'm considered the luckiest because, by dint of money and a mighty wrath at the vans that came close to my calash, I saved it—if you can call it "saved" to have but four shirts and a single coat. The worst of it is that everyone doesn't take it so gaily. A little gaiety would save the aspect of our hardship, but all those who haven't a rather forceful soul are full of bitterness.

From letter to Martial Daru, Smolensk, November 10.—I didn't follow headquarters in the march on St. Petersburg. They fought the Russians at Maloyaroslavets. Their Army was driven back toward Kaluga, which leaves us free to go to St. Petersburg via Vitebsk, Duneburg and Riga. I had the honor to be appointed Director General of Reserve Supplies.

I immediately had some letterheads printed, and left Moscow with a convoy of sick.

As we were far from the Army, we were attacked twice by Cossacks. These rascals put us on a diet of bread and water for eighteen days. M. Daru was good enough to be anxious about me. He arrived here the 8th, and since then we haven't had time to breathe.

Almost all of us lost our equipment, and were reduced to what we had on our person. All these little nuisances are for the wealthy ones of the Army, the common soldier is overflowing with napoleons, gold, diamonds, pearls, etc.; we think we are going to Vitebsk and Minsk.

My fingers are so cold that I don't know whether you'll be able to read what I've written.

From letter to Pauline and Comtesse Beugnot, Smolensk, November 20.— Decipher, if you have the courage, the rough draft I'm enclosing; it's a letter to Madame [Beugnot] and moreover it's the exact truth. I'm surrounded by asses who tire me out. Everything considered, it's the last time that I'll let myself be taken away from my goal, *la mia cara Italia*. We haven't got any ink; I've just manufactured seventy-five drops, which have been used up by my long letter. Therefore, adieu; don't show my letter to anyone.

Madame.

. . . We were driven out of five palaces in five days; finally, giving up, we went on the fifth day to camp outside the city [of Moscow]. On our way, we experienced the inconveniences that go with grandeur. We started out with our seventeen carriages along a street that wasn't yet burning very much; but the blaze traveled faster than our horses, and, when we were halfway along the street, our horses took fright from the flames of the houses on both sides; the sparks stung them, the smoke suffocated us, and we had a very hard time of it to turn around and get out.

I shan't speak to you, madame, of far more horrible horrors. One thing alone saddened me: it was on September 20, I believe, upon our return to Moscow; the sight of this delightful city, one of the finest temples of voluptuousness, transformed into charred and stinking ruins, in the midst of which wandered a few miserable dogs and a few women looking for something to eat.

This city was unknown in Europe: there were six or eight hundred palaces, the like of which not a single one is to be found in Paris. Everything in them was arranged for the purest voluptuousness. There were the most cheerful plasterwork and colors, the finest furniture from England, the most elegant cheval glasses, charming beds, sofas in a thousand ingenious forms. There wasn't a bedroom where you couldn't be seated in four or five different ways, and perfect comfort was blended with the most brilliant elegance.

It's all very simple: there were a thousand persons with incomes of five to fifteen thousand livres. In Vienna, people of that sort are solemn all their lives and dream of possessing the Order of St. Stephen. In Paris, they seek what they call an agreeable life, the kind of life that gives their vanity plenty of enjoyment; their hearts become shriveled, they are unable to be aware of others.

From letter to Pauline, Königsberg, December 28.—At Molodechno, I believe, thirty leagues from Vilna on the Minsk road, feeling that I was freezing and that my strength was giving out, I took the fine decision to go ahead of the Army. Together with M. Busche, I covered four leagues in three hours; we were lucky enough to find three horses still at the post. We departed and arrived at Vilna somewhat the worse for wear. We set out again the 7th or 8th, and arrived at Gumbinnen, where my physical strength came back a little, from there I arrived here, traveling a few leagues ahead of M. Daru.

Note to Pauline, Berlin, January 20, 1813.—I'm in very good health, my dear friend. I've entirely recovered. I'll leave about the 24th for Leipzig, where I'll await an order to go back to the Rue Neuve-de-Luxembourg if this agreeable order ever comes.

Note to Pauline, Berlin, January 23.—My dear friend, I'm leaving Berlin on my 30th birthday. Nevertheless, I'm experiencing the joy of a child. My first thought this morning was that Victorine was also thirty years old.[1] Let us hasten to enjoy life; time is fleeting.

[1] Victorine Mounier was born two days after Beyle.

Familiar Scenes

SOMETHING of the desolate chill of the Russian winter seemed to remain in Beyle during the weeks that followed his return to Paris. He was numb mentally and physically. The hardships of the past months had impaired his health: he suffered from pains in the left side and abdomen. "I'm tired out . . ." he wrote Pauline. "I'm cold inside. I drink two or three bottles of excellent wine. I take some punch, some coffee; nothing does any good; I'm still cold and hungry."

After the Russian adventures, the humdrum social life of his Parisian acquaintances seemed insipid. They were absorbed in the same old trivialities and but mildly interested in Cossack attacks, the burning of Moscow and the endless retreat through the snow.

Already a little forgotten, Beyle dreamed, for once in his life, of some bourgeois household where he might sit back and toast his feet on the fire. Add a pretty woman with an understanding soul, and life might again be worth living. But he knew of no cozy hearth corner, and loving souls à la Beyle were rare phenomena among the "dolls" of Paris. Of all the people he knew, the only one whose company gave him a little real comfort was Mélanie Guilbert-Barcov, who was now back in the city and whom, for lack of fresher conquests, he began taking for walks in the afternoon and to the theater in the evening.

A partial remedy for his "mental numbness" made its effect felt almost without his realizing it and took the form of a revival of his old ambition. He had worked conscientiously as an empire official; his efficiency in carrying out a difficult mission in Russia had pleased Napoleon. Seconded by the influential Comte Daru and even more so by Mme. Daru, he now considered the time ripe to reap a reward for his labors. He resumed his efforts to gain his father's aid in obtaining a barony; he entertained the hope of receiving some kind of decoration; the post of Master of Requests seemed within reach; but above all he aspired to the Intendancy of Rome or Florence, or a Prefecture in one of the Italian departments.

But luck was against him once again. When the Prefectures were given out, friends and acquaintances received appointments: for Beyle there was nothing. It was a severe blow to his ambition and pride, and as usual he hid his chagrin behind a mask of nonchalance. But the diary's insistence on his indifference betrays the bitterness of his disappointment. "After distinguishing myself more than anyone else, here I am at the end of the line," he wrote.

In order to occupy his mind with more pleasant things, he engaged a copyist and dictated a sketchy record of his visit to Rome in 1811 to replace the notebook lost on the road to Naples. Rereading the entire diary of his Italian trip jogged him out of the rut: he went over his notes and with zest started to work again on *Histoire de la Peinture en Italie,* attempting to replace in the original manuscript the numerous corrections contained in the twelve notebooks "eaten by the Cossacks" at Molodechno. Once again literature had supplied what life lacked.

But everything seemed to be against him. No sooner had he recaptured the joys of *Mocenigo* and complacently told himself that he would pass a quiet year in his favorite pursuits than Prussia made an alliance with Russia. A new conflict with France was the inevitable result, and Beyle was promptly ordered to rejoin the Army in Germany. Exasperated at the thought of being torn away from his studies to return to the coarse life of the Army, he wrote in desperation to Daru, begging him for employment in Rome or Florence. When his request went unheeded, he gradually resigned himself to his fate and took comfort in the illusion that perhaps, after all, the German campaign might in the end solve his problems by gaining him the Intendancy of Florence and a salary of 20,000 francs a year.

As he advanced through the awakening springtime countryside of the Rhineland, Hesse, Thuringia and Saxony, he again found the peculiar charm of Germany. Nearing the bivouac before Bautzen, he heard the sound of heavy firing nearby. The next day, from a safe distance, a band of youths from the Intendance staff witnessed the battle, possibly the only one that Beyle actually saw in his entire life, and undoubtedly the one that served him as a model for the famous description in *La Chartreuse de Parme* of the Battle of Waterloo—where the spectator *sees nothing*. His impression, written on the spot while the cannon fire was still booming, is a casual bit of realism and psychological speculation that forms a curious contrast to the conventional glorified and rhetorical battle scenes of the period.

Three days later the march was resumed. The headquarters convoy, consisting of eighty vehicles escorted by 110 soldiers of the 2nd Westphalian Light Infantry Battalion, had left Reichenbach early in the morning and had just passed through Niedermarkersdorf when a score of Cossacks attacked the rear guard. The Westphalians, all conscripts, were badly directed and loath to fight. Arriving at full gallop, the Cossacks wounded one of Daru's secretaries. There was a moment of confusion. Then a group of gendarmes, reinforced by infantrymen, made a vigorous charge and drove off the attackers. Although the entire skirmish lasted but a few minutes, it was the object of a severe inquiry, owing to the clumsiness of the defense: the commander was broken, and there were several arrests. As for Beyle, being at the head of the convoy, he saw practically nothing of the attack, as a contemporary report proves, and his sensational references to it in later years were merely flights of imagination.

At Görlitz he was questioned at length concerning the affair by Napoleon himself. It is to be regretted that no record exists of this interview, which was certainly the most intimate meeting that ever took place between the two. Beyle barely mentioned it in a letter to his sister early in June, in which he said, "I had a long conversation with His Majesty a week ago," but that the event impressed him is shown by the fact that he signed a draft dedication to the Emperor of his *Histoire de la Peinture en Italie,* "the soldier whom you buttonholed at Görlitz." "Beyle," said Mérimée, who was familiar with the affair, "was commissioned to give an account of the panic to the Emperor, who listened to him with concentrated fury."

In June he moved on as far as Glogau, then turned back to Sagan, where from June 10 until July 25 he filled the functions of Intendant under "the most honest and incapable of generals," the Marquis de Latour-Maubourg. His lethargy of Paris had by now completely disappeared. He was less bored than he expected to be with his army companions, and Germany contributed to reviving his interest in nature and humanity. "I haven't been bored since I left headquarters and the Court," he wrote Pauline. "Every day my billet takes me into a new comedy. I love to drop like this into the midst of seven or eight people. When I leave the next day, I'm already loved and hated, and I've seen two or three different characters."

Shortly after making another unsuccessful attempt to obtain an Italian appointment, he fell seriously ill with what he described as "a diabolical attack of a sort of pernicious fever," of which there was an epidemic in the town. On July 26, Daru released him from his duties, and, planning to use his illness as a pretext for revisiting Italy, Beyle went to rest for a fortnight in Dresden and then continued to Paris, where he arrived at the end of August, still in a weak condition.

Franz Josef Gall was practicing in the French capital at that time, and his phrenology was enjoying a popularity equal to that of psychoanalysis a century later. Interested in this new "science" as a possible key to the human mechanism, Beyle subjected himself to the treatment of its inventor. Whether Gall or other things were responsible, his fever abated somewhat, but his appearance was still haggard enough to impress the Duc de Cadore, who readily granted his request for a leave of absence in order to convalesce in the warm climate of Italy.

Back in Milan, he spent his first days much as he had two years earlier —in ecstatic happiness when he was with Angelina, in boredom when she was away on one of her frequent trips. Following her to Venice, he saw the city in a state of siege. The Austrian troops were advancing in the northeast. Venice was nervous; Milan feared an attack. The excitable Angelina was slightly hysterical, and nightly Beyle slept with his pistols at his side. He had half decided to return to France, flatter the Duc de Cadore and attempt to obtain a permanent appointment in Italy, when he received word from Paris that there was no need of his presence at the moment. Nothing loath, Beyle forgot his fears and, for another short period, settled down to a pleasant life of love, literary work and *dolce far niente*.

"Charming hours, a mellow tenderness, possibly the most charming of this trip," he wrote on November 10, after noting that he had spent an hour and a half with Angelina. Another note—like the first, written on the margin of his books—testifies as to his mood: "At the theater in the evening my sensibility prevented me from being amiable. On the other hand, I've never seen Gina so gay . . . As for my departure, it's not yet the moment to weep, for we'll see each other several times more." Together they went to hear the operas he loved at the Scala, to see his favorite pictures at the Brera, to witness the ballets of his future friend Viganò, then coming into popularity in Milan.

It was almost a repetition of those ideal days of 1805, when his ideological studies had mingled so harmoniously with his courtship of Mélanie. Paris had given way to Milan, Mélanie had been replaced by Angelina, but his ambition was at bottom the same as in 1805—to become a great "comic bard." For some three weeks he succeeded in achieving that magic Beylistic equation: love + work = happiness.

As the following pages show, his studies in Milan were highly fruitful for the future Stendhal; yet, pleased as he was with his work, the image of Angelina continued to intrude on his thoughts. Sometimes he broke off a sentence in the middle to indicate what was in his mind concerning his mistress, and once he suddenly interrupted his notes to announce the reported arrival via Switzerland of 60,000 Austrian troops. The time had not yet arrived when he might at last devote himself tranquilly to the joys of *Mocenigo*.

All Europe was astir, things were going badly in France, northern Italy was in terror of the threatened attack, and his vacation was approaching its end. He again resigned himself to his fate, and in the middle of November sadly left Italy, Angelina, his studies, and started back to his duties in Paris.

Italy, as always, had unleashed his reserves of sensibility, had given him the needed inspiration after a too long contact with the world of vulgarians. In 1811 he had gone to that "suave" southern land to study the human heart, and had left it with the determination to become an art historian. This time he had headed for Milan in the hope of recovering his health, and had departed with the resolution to lose no more time in establishing himself as the Molière of the nineteenth century.

1813 Paris—Germany—Milan

DIARY.—If you're discreet, read no farther. If you're not discreet but nevertheless an honorable man in the essential things, read on and make fun of the author, but don't repeat what you've read.

Coste, Infantry Commander.

Diary begun February 4, 1813, in Paris, Rue Neuve-du-Luxembourg, No. 3.

February 4.—I have no memory, none at all, and the result is that, whenever I've been discreet in the diaries OF MY LIFE which I've written up to now, I don't understand anything in them after a year or two.

While I was in Russia, I lost my Brunswick diary of 1806 and 1807, MY LOVES WITH Minette. It required an effort of imagination to recall what I had wanted to say. I was well pleased with myself in 1806, the essential was majestic, frequently eclipsed by asininities of affection and bashfulness.

I believe I am extremely sensitive, that's the outstanding trait. The sensibility is pushed to excesses that, if recounted, would be unintelligible to anyone but Félix, and even for him much talking is necessary.

This faculty produces charming thoughts, which vanish like a flash of lightning. I haven't yet been able to get into the habit of writing them on the wing, although I've bought notebooks for that purpose several times. I forget their subject matter frequently, and their style always. What ideas I had in my calash during my eighteen-day campaign from Moscow to Smolensk! I jotted down a few of them in a volume of Chesterfield that I pillaged in the country house of Rostop-chin; it was lost with the rest.

On the way here from Berlin, I had some other good ideas, I didn't write them down.

At present, I'm completely benumbed, I've lost all my passions. I haven't drunk up the pleasures of Paris with the avidity of the deer slaking its thirst in the . . . , the picture by Correggio. I had these pleasures yesterday, they slipped off me like water off a duck's back. They didn't penetrate to my heart.

I noticed on my way here from Mainz that I'd lost MY PASSION FOR MY HISTORY OF PAINTING. I was annoyed, but the fact was true. I limited myself to studying how the death of a passion may be recognized: the boredom inspired by boring things, the details of this passion's execution.

Will this passion come back? I'm not able to say. I feel numb at the moment; an old man of sixty is possibly no colder than I am.

The *nonum prematur in annum* is consequently worthless for me; I need to execute a thing while I'm still in love with it; without love, I'm worthless. That was confirmed for me by what happened OF MY COMEDY WHICH I WAS MAKING WHEN I WAS APPOINTED AUDITOR and which has remained where it was.

My genius (in the sense of *Génie du Christianisme*) is consequently fickle, that is not in love for long.

Mme. Palfy seemed to me even more lacking in soul and wit than at Di. . . , possibly because I found a veneer of haughtiness in her. That's a love that's quite dead. But what's left for me in the way of women? My faith, nothing. The thirst WHICH I HAD OF . . . was quenched in three days; she's no longer anything more than a con-venience, but one that I'm greatly indebted to.

But Prettechestinneka [Mélanie Guilbert] has unexpectedly appeared on the horizon. Embers can't be fanned into flames again, that's the theory.

But, knocked about by mankind, I have need of a bourgeois home where I could sit toasting my feet on the fire. Mme. de Perval might have given me that; she's goodhearted and unassuming, but the absence of intelligence is too evident, BY HER MOTHER SHE IS too bourgeois. Tinneka [Mélanie] hasn't this shortcoming; on the contrary, she lapses into the tragic, she has more OF WIT and experience, conversation with her is more possible, though not too much so.

I'm afraid of starting out and then going into bankruptcy, which would be unfair to Tinneka at a time when she is establishing her moral life here. My behavior with her is stationary while waiting to see which way the wind is blowing.

I find on returning that there are FOUR WOMEN to observe: Mmes. Palfy, de Perval, Tinneka, Doligny (*non parlo della mia* Angelina).

I'm experiencing some strange phenomena in my health. For the past three days, I've been eating three times as much as usual, and I'm always hungry, coffee doesn't stimulate my mind, wine drunk in the morning doesn't make me sleepy. I'm suffering a little from my chest. I have the tail end of a cold.

What would I do with them at the end of the third day? Consequently, no more of the bashfulness I used to have when I wanted to seduce them all, believed they all had the heart of Julie, and thought they would provide me with a life like the grove at Clarens.

Consequently, no more of the bashfulness of extreme expectations. My manners have been warped by these ridiculous ideas. All that lacks for me to be sure of success is to learn to let my indifference appear.

February 13.—Left Berlin January 23, at ten o'clock LESS a quarter.

The 24th, at 8 o'clock in the morning, at Brunswick.

The 25th, at 10 o'clock in the evening, at Kassel.

The 27th, at 2 o'clock in the morning, at Frankfurt (what an hour of sound sleep!).

At half-past 7 in the morning, crossed the Rhine in a sledge.

At half-past one, left for Paris.

The 31st, at half-past 9, arrived in Paris.

February 17.—I'm working on the comic.

Objection to Hobbes's definition of laughter.

In the trait of the fat Englishman talking to the trunk that has fallen on him in the overturned diligence at nightfall in America, told by M. Marchand at Königsberg, what superiority are we able to feel over the Englishman who made such a natural mistake?

Certainly, very little.

(He said in English, "Very good indeed, sir, as you wish; when you get tired of that position, perhaps you will change it.—WELL, VERY WELL, SIR, etc.")

Certainly, little: thus it's necessary for the Englishman's monologue to be drawn out in order to be sure to provoke laughter, which increases as the story goes along, the last words make you laugh more than the preceding ones. We find the Englishman stupid and inferior to us because he doesn't notice the hardness of the trunk and the fact that it doesn't answer him.

Two extremities are to be seen between which the comic fluctuates:

1. Either the person at whom we laugh seems extremely stupid, extremely inferior to us;

2. Or almost not at all, as in the majority of mistakes, for instance, that of the Englishman.

What difference does the diversity of the soil from which it springs introduce into laughter?

Pierrot, a source of laughter for the common people, produces laughter only through his blunders.

February 18.—I spent the morning in the reading room of the Rue de Grammont and later at the Jardin des Plantes WITH M.

At the reading room, I read: 1. Discourse XXXV [on the subject of laughter] in *The Spectator,* then Chamfort's *Eloge de Molière,* which made me think:

That we are interested only in ourselves; in laughter, our ego is only slightly involved, it's merely a question of knowing whether this ego is superior to such-and-such an individual.

February 25.—While waiting to be as impassioned and happy as I was from December 4, 1811, to May 5, 1812, I must study my ideas UPON THE COMIC and put them in order. Passion will come later.

March 6.—Ever since the 24th, when I drew up the outline of *Letellier,* I've been in a great mental chill, and passion is necessary if you are going to compose a scene. When I'm impassioned, I must write out the plan of study to be followed when I cool off. Possibly the reading of foreign plays. I've read a dozen French comedies with pleasure.

March 12.—I wrote the following truth to Félix:

Since my return, I've been plunged in deadly listlessness. For the past forty days, I've been vainly seeking my former passions: I no longer experience anything but the pleasures of reminiscence. I have no desire to go to the museum (the old pictures), I would have been more aware of my weakness there than elsewhere. From December 4, 1811, to May 15, 1812,[1] I reflected with extreme passion from eight in the morning till midnight on what is contained therein. I tried to find the way to get through my meals as quick as possible without making myself sick.

March 13.—The memory of my enjoyment during that period makes me find the pleasures of society flat and not worth the trouble. I see how much Fabio is bored, or rather how much I'd be bored if I were in his place, harnessed to those everlasting gaming tables. I'm able to go out in society as much as I wish through Z, Mme. Pallavicini, Mme. de Longueville, etc. I go only as much as is necessary, and even less. Last Sunday (after leaving Mme. Daru's), I went to Marie's. Her one-time

[1] At this period, several times mentioned by Beyle, he was engaged in writing his history of Italian painting.

fondness for me seemed to be revived, probably because my lack of fondness for her and my politeness makes me go through the motions of coquettish behavior. For me, my passion is ENTIRELY DEAD BY THE SEA'S SOUNDING SHORE. It's the same for Italy and Signora Pietragrua, for whom I no longer have anything more than a reminiscent fondness. Signora Pietragrua wrote me a couple of letters, to which I replied only reluctantly, thinking of the joy I'd have experienced at such an opportunity in other days.

Is this state of mental numbness a necessary result of a six-month struggle against disgust, unrest and danger? If, ten years hence, a dismal hazard were to make me embark with some bores on a return from Batavia to Europe, and if our ship were continually on the verge of sinking in the middle of the sea, would I experience the same results upon my return?

What is the quickest way of getting out of this premature old age?

I don't know the answer to all that. My laziness is such that it even prevents me from writing; if I had a copyist, I'd dictate. The Opera Buffa has little interest for me—enough to go to it, however. Wednesday, at the *Matrimonio*, I recaptured a bit of artistic sadness, which soon became dulled. I experienced a lively pleasure only during the duet, *"Voi ne credete,"* because I didn't know it by heart.

March 17.—On Sunday, March 6, I was astonished to realize that my fondness for Mme. Marie was reviving; the following Sunday, March 13, I went to see her; she lowered her eyes when she found herself alone in her salon. She seemed to be timid with me. She told me she regretted not being at the masked ball at the same time as I: she also said she knew a lot of things about me.

I think it's my liaison with Angéline, which has lasted only two short years. She must have heard about it from M. Bayle, the physician, who must have told Mme. Le Brun about it, or else from the Comtesse Doligny, who learned about it from my laundress, and who must have told her daughter, the Baronne Curial, about it. My behavior WITH LADY Palfy must be a great problem for Mme. Doligny AND FAIR ISLAND, the latter of whom showed decided signs of pettiness toward Mme. Gauthier in speaking of Mme. Doligny. Everything considered, he's a petty man, quite the son of his father and the brother of his brother.

Yesterday, the 14th, and the day before, the talk was of nothing but the fifteen Prefectures to be awarded, in which it appears that the Auditors will have a good share. The work was drafted last Wednesday and is being finished, they say, today; thus, at this minute, the Church is triumphing or collapsing.

That worried me a little, I'd be a little humiliated not to receive anything; on the other hand, to be a Prefect anywhere but in the fourteen Italian departments would run counter to my most cherished wishes.

The post of Master of Requests would suit me better, as it would bring me nearer that of Crown Intendant in Rome or Florence, which is the only thing I desire. To be a Prefect, even in Parma, wouldn't give me much pleasure.

They say there are two lists, one of M. de Montalivet and the other of M. Daru, that the latter has proposed all the Auditors of Russia, half or two thirds of whom would be ridiculous as Prefects.

Of those I know, the only ones I see as prefecturable are Bergognié, Busche, myself, Nicolaï, Pastoret and possibly Cochelet, if pretensions replace merit.

The three Auditors who stayed in the Medical School [at Moscow][1] would be three good choices.

As for myself, I'd have preferred that there weren't any appointments, that they were to give four decorations, four baronies, and that I were to receive a decoration, even though it were a blue one, as everything indicates it would be.

Busche gave me the first news of the Prefectures the 14th at the ball in Mme. . . . 's home, and the decree is dated the 12th.

Since the listless spell I've been experiencing, the first two hours of work I've done without looking at my watch ten times were today, from noon to two o'clock. I was correcting my trip to Italy in order to have it transcribed by M. Fougeol.

March 19.—Ambition.—I've just been to see Busche, who told me he was Prefect of the Deux-Sèvres, and who showed me the letter from M. de Montalivet. Bergognié is Prefect of the Jura. I'm the only one left of those who were at the Medical School. I wasn't overly jealous, probably through the hope of also having something, as I'm linked in public opinion with the two B.s; PERHAPS THE COLD OF YESTERDAY announces SOMEWHAT [something]. When we learn of an appointment, we promptly look to see if we're acquainted with the lucky ones, and we are jealous only in proportion to this acquaintance.

My morning was taken up with a never-ending visit from Fabio Pallavicini; I then went to see Mélanie, whom I found with all the symptoms of happiness, and a sensibility alert to all the little interests of the moment.

Sorrow of ambition.—Tonight my soul smarted a little from the sorrow of not being a Prefect when my two acolytes, Busche and Bergognié, are. Still, it's possible that I'd be even more grieved if I

[1]Bergognié, Busche and Beyle.

saw the necessity of shutting myself up for four or five years in some hole like Lons-le-Saunier.

But at the moment my soul is inactive, it would be busied by my appointment and the new interests of a Prefect's post. Besides, I'd thus have a political rank, and I'd be assured of seeing society from the upper side.

I've read almost a whole volume of Miss Bellamy's *Memoirs,* in which nature is well described by several touches. I had already read the book and entirely forgotten it. What was responsible for a large part of my dudgeon tonight was to have spent three hours of my morning with that bore of a Fabio, in whose opinion it's a great thing to be a Prefect.

If I haven't got anything, it's not through lack of merit or seniority, it's because somebody wanted to dominate my pride and see how I'd swallow the pill. I'll have to answer that by being gay with this person; when I have no further hopes of getting anything, my dudgeon will pass away in a couple of days.[1]

March 20.—I mustn't let myself believe a few years hence, on the strength of this diary, that the seventeen Prefectures which have just filed by without stopping meant overly much to me. I was less occupied with them than with a game of boston. I'd think about them in the evening when the theater wasn't interesting; yesterday, for instance, at *Romeo and Juliet* [Zingarelli's opera], which interested me sufficiently to keep me from leaving during the second act, like the first time.

Still, nothing could be more ridiculous than the roulades of the third act, which overloaded one of the finest and most ancient of tragic situations (Pyramus and Thisbe).

What a scene is that of Juliet rising from her grave! But a single lamp would have been required, and yesterday there were twenty of them; that made the tomb *pretty,* like those at Saint-Denis.

Ambition.—I thought yesterday that if, whereas Busche and Bergognié are Prefects, I had nothing at all, it would be extremely noticeable. Auditors six months before me, they had no mission in Moscow, or at least none that was important. Mine, on the contrary, was long, dangerous and essential, and His Majesty was pleased with it.

March 21.—This morning, the amiable Fabio Pallavicini lent me Chateaubriand's speech, which I read in the Café de Foy.

I wish public opinion admitted only men of this caliber among the number of men of letters. They know the colors of style. Such a speech is an admission ticket.

Once admitted, I find him mediocre, irrevocably mediocre, in that he's lacking in ratiocination; he's false.

[1]That's what happened (December 21, 1813). [Note added by Beyle.]

His speech develops the idea that the man of letters can no longer be content to weigh his diphthongs, that he should be occupied with the real interests of public life; but that's precisely what Chénier did.

Chateaubriand's commentary on Milton is even more palpably false. Historically false in the first place, and in the second place philosophically false. Supposing it were discovered tomorrow that Cervantes was the most odious of scoundrels, that wouldn't remove an iota of *Don Quixote's* merit.

Chateaubriand sins against good form by talking too much about himself. His praises are enigmas, in fine he doesn't think. This man SHALL NOT OUTLIVE HIS CENTURY. I'll wager that in 1913 people will no longer be concerned with his writings.

All the author says about the Frenchman, citizen by instinct and subject by choice, is very shabby. His history of France will at best be good only for women. There will be some *fine pages,* a form of praise that is a criticism in itself, in my opinion.

Yesterday, I dictated a few pages to fill the gaps in my tour of Italy. I believe a traveler who seeks amusement through writing all he's read on the country he's traveling through could write a diary of a hundred folio volumes. The one who limits himself to noting what he really has felt is very limited.

This morning, M. Bayle prescribed beer for my chest.

March 24.—My listlessness continues unabated. The absence of all passion irritated me today. I believe that my listlessness comes from my inability to conceive any boons more elevated than those I enjoy. That's the character of spleen. But I'll probably soon get over it. The uncertainty of my political status makes me think about it, and consequently prevents me from giving myself up to anything. I've just been to *Les Noces de Dorine,* which pleased me. Mme. Barilli, who had a cold, was graceful and charming. This morning, I went AT LADY PALFY'S, SHE WAS NOT AT HOME, BUT, SAYS HER SISTER, HAS SOMEWHAT TO SAY TO ME.

March 28.—*Bellamy.*—I've just finished Miss Bellamy's *Memoirs,* which touched me. I read them with more interest than four years ago, and, thanks to my memory, was able to extract new sap for the knowledge of mankind. It would be the same with Duclos's *Mémoires.* I can re-read books of this kind every four years, they are genuine mines FOR THE Mocenigo.

Miss Edgeworth, Carmontelle and memoirs written with truth are the sources of talent OF THE Mocenigo.

I AM LOVING MARIA because of a dream, I WAS WITH HER SPEAKING NATURALLY AND TENDERLY OF MY LOVE.

As soon as I have a slight pain in the mesentery, thought returns.

Ambition.—At a quarter to two, I lost my hopes OF BEING a Master of Requests.

I went to see the Duchesse de . . . , who told me that, at the time of the Prefectures, she had spoken about me to her husband, who said, "I have proposed him."

She said, "I believe he would rather have a decoration and be a baron than leave Paris."

"That will happen; as for being baron, the way the Emperor endows, that's more difficult. Has he spoken to you about it?"

"No, he hasn't said a word to me about it."

The duke's answer allows it to be understood that *all will happen* in good time.

This commentary is mine.

My soul is adrift. Why? From July 23 to January 31, 1813, not the slightest mental pleasure. Is that the reason?

March 27.—I read without any sorrow today, the 27th, in *Le Journal de Paris,* the decree naming the Prefects. It's dated the 12th and appeared not in the *Moniteur* but in the *Bulletin des Lois.*

The 14th, when they were talking so much about the Prefectures, they had already given them out the day before.

I dictated a few pages for my voyage in Italy, and spent the rest of the day WITH MELANIA AT Romeo.

My listlessness continues.

March 31.—I read the letters of Boileau and *Don Quixote* till one o'clock.

Yesterday, the sole topic of conversation was His Majesty's displeasure at the comedy, *L'Intrigante.*[1]

"Don't you see, messieurs, that you are being imposed upon?"

"This man must write no more plays!"

"How can a Minister of Police allow such things to get by?"

"But hasn't Etienne got some position in the police?"

Our institutions are too young to be exposed to the wind of jokes, which would uproot them. This is all right with me. But, in that case, there won't be any comedy left a hundred years from now. The absurdity of the reasoning of the people at Court is of a charming palpability.

I've just bought the last two copies of *L'Intrigante* at Barba's.

(I judge one passion by another, but it ought to be the same thing with ambition as with love, to which I apply the same terms.)

All I lacked AS Mocenigo was to have experienced and felt disgrace. Now, nothing is lacking.

---

[1] Etienne's comedy was badly received by the courtiers and was closed by Napoleon after the eleventh performance.

April 1.—Upon seeing in the *Journal de* . . . that the princes had formed a musical society in Vienna, it occurred to me that we have a nobility without fortune and without noble sentiments.

I've just had a very amusing conversation with Mélanie from seven to ten in the evening. I started out on the pursuit of ideas. She understood me, the pleasure of showing and demonstrating certain things to her made me see many things I already knew and discover several corollaries.

From there to the Café de Foy, and I came back to read *Don Quixote.* Wrote a second letter to Faure on my listlessness.

Sunday the 4th.—*Disgrace.*—There's no doubt about it, I haven't the time or the desire to cultivate society. Out of gratitude, I have to see M. and Mme. Daru, who have been good to me and to whom I am indebted for the tranquil position I am enjoying. They say that M. Daru is going to be a duke.

I've greatly neglected the Comtesse Doligny, a woman for whom I have unbounded esteem and even fondness, which would have degenerated into love if she hadn't praised me so much. She has just reproached me my negligence in a little note; I must be sure to tell her tonight that I don't go to see anyone else more than I do her.

April 6.—I stayed at Mme. Doligny's too long yesterday.

This morning, I was thinking distinctly about Mocenigo in bed. "I'll be lucky," I told myself, "if I'm not interrupted by a thousand little annoyances." It didn't fail. I only returned at half-past twelve, very distracted, after seeing M. Cardon and M. Labiche.

Ambition.—Yesterday, the *Moniteur* contained the declaration of war.[1]

Ought I to participate in the campaign?

I don't think so. I'm too bored by the applications and visits that have to be made every evening in silk stockings. Consequently, the only thing I'd have to recommend me is my service record. This year, my mission from Moscow to Borisov, and what M. Daru said to me at Bóbr seemed to promise me more advantages than the others. Quite the opposite.

Consequently, it would be better to spend a quiet year in Paris, with a little trip to Switzerland or Italy if I can, and not to spend six thousand francs uselessly to have a disagreeable time.

All this is true, possibly a little dudgeon makes me inclined to stay here. Were I to feel any taste for leaving, the excellent reason of doing what might be pleasing would make me leave.

April 7.—*Listlessness.*—The pain on the left side of my abdomen, mel-

[1] With Prussia.

ancholy and my blunt manner with anyone who interrupts me returned all together a bit today, and my listlessness disappeared.

I didn't permit this pleasant sadness to evaporate by going to see Mélanie, as I was tempted to do. I came home, where I wrote a note that was true and drawn from my personal observations on French *boredom* and Italian *melancholy*.

Perhaps my present calm comes from the diarrhea, more or less violent, which hasn't left me since I crossed the Berezina (about March 12, 1812) on the way to join His Majesty.

April 9.—Today, the 9th, summer heat. I enjoyed *Don Quixote*.

I haven't had any amorous inclination for the past ten days.

April 11.—In the evening, to M. Daru's, who told me, "M. Beyle IS IN ORDINARY SERVICE, I'm forewarning him."—"I THANK YOU, SIR." Said not with gaiety but AS reckoning WITH MY self-esteem, TWO self-esteems reckoning together.

I don't give a damn about my misfortunes of ambition. After distinguishing myself more than anyone else, here I am at the end of the line, like the captain of Louis XIV's turkey cocks.

April 15.—The 13th at eleven o'clock Miss Fanny said to me *amorevolmente* [amorously] AND WITH A MANNER TRULY Mocenigo, "YOU SHALL DEPART SOON, MILADY Daru is telling you in advance so that you can see IF THE GREAT FATHER[1] can't furnish you an excuse for not leaving."

Today, the 15th, I've just learned the details.

The marshal [Daru], the 13th at half-past ten in the evening, RETURNING FROM Saint-Cloud and arguing about the arrangements for the carriages with his niece, said during dinner:

"Messrs. So-and-so in such a carriage, I alone in my calash . . . I'm tempted to take Beyle with me."

"What! Beyle? Is he going? I believe he'll be very surprised . . ."

"Yes. He'll receive his order tomorrow."

" . . . Especially after the way he was rewarded."

"You have to do your duty."

At two o'clock today, I haven't yet received any order.

Never has an event so depressed me. I'm going to become barbarous and blunt for the arts. I believe that what so chilled me was the compulsory company of such coarse souls. I'm going to say when I get there that I can't mount a horse because of my bladder.

His Majesty left the 15th at one o'clock in the morning, the marshal the 14th at five o'clock in the morning. He's stopping for his meals, and will be overtaken by His Majesty.

[1]Dr. Henri Gagnon, Beyle's grandfather, who was in bad health and who died a few months later.

Yet I'd be unhappier if I had been appointed Sub-Prefect in any town other than Rome or Florence.

April 19.—I'm leaving with Biliotti April 19, 1813, for Mainz, furious. Félix's vain and petty COUNSEL.

I received from the government 700 + 2,222 fr. 50 = 2,922 fr. 50.[1]

From letter to Pauline, St. Avold, April 21.—I've never felt so depressed. I'm again going to see men and things of a kind with which I'm more than fed up. My departure appeared rather strange to everybody. Everybody was sorry for me—but will forget all about that in a couple of weeks. The result of my absence in Russia, which lasted 7 months, was that I was already a bit forgotten. This one, coming after a stay of 2½ months in Paris, will further increase my foreignness for my acquaintances. I've written to Z that I desire to be employed in Rome or Florence. I'm traveling with the most asinine and the coarsest of men. I read; he questions me incessantly in a loud voice, asking me the names of all the hovels we pass. For example, at St. Menehould he asked me who that house belonged to—pointing at a building in the town. That is the kind of animal I'm delivered up to for 6 or 8 months.

From letter to Pauline, Erfurt, April 29.—I've come here in spite of myself, but I'm less discontented than I would have thought. In order to derive a little memory and usefulness in the art of knowing mankind from my year 1813, my primary desire is still to retire to Italy, far from the dolts and the blunt-minded who people the world. France was a charming country from 1715 to 1789. Since then, there's been no more society; and naturalness, lively but without feeling, appears in all its insipidity. I'm counting (as much as you can count on the weakness of interest) on this campaign to win me the Intendance at Florence, which is worth 20,000 francs a year, and which I'd prefer from the standpoint of agreeableness to a Prefecture—to which, by all the proprieties, I'm entitled.

Diary written at Bautzen May 21, 1813, during cannon fire.—Coming out of Dresden at half-past two, I encountered the King face to face. Agreeable countryside along the Elbe, then a sandy forest, finally the most beautiful hills I have ever seen, to the right of the road.

At a quarter past ten in the evening of the 18th, we arrived at the bivouac. My dislike of coming in contact with petty souls made me prefer to remain alone in the marshal's calash rather than having to resort to scheming in order to get supper and a fire. I consequently supped on a piece of bread and a little wine. At a quarter past four,

[1] I've reread this diary, and have found it very good, only too badly written, described, December 21, 1813, after reading Shakespeare's *Timon of Athens*. [Note added by Beyle.]

I was sound asleep on the bed I'd had prepared for me; Marvolain woke me up very decently to give me an excellent bouillon. I discovered that there was an enchanting landscape in back of our bivouac, worthy of Claude Lorrain, formed by several plantations of trees in different shades of green growing on a hillside. The first plantation was formed of the most agreeable trees, distributed in irregular groups over a prairie.

We left at eleven o'clock the 19th, admiring the charming hills to the right of the road; reading some elegant extracts, I noted in pencil that it was a beautiful day of *Beylism,* such as I had pictured it, and accurately enough, in 1806.

I was comfortably installed and free from all care in an excellent calash, traveling in the midst of all the complicated movements of an army of a hundred and forty thousand men driving another army of a hundred and sixty thousand men, with the accompaniment of Cossacks at our rear. Unfortunately, I thought of what Beaumarchais so well said. "In every sort of property, possession is nothing, enjoyment is everything." I'm no longer enthusiastic about that kind of observation. I'm drunk on them, if I may be allowed the expression. It's the case of a man who has indulged in too much punch, and is obliged to throw up; he's disgusted with it for life. The insides of souls I saw during the retreat from Moscow disgusted me forever with observing coarse beings, the sword-wielders who make up an army.

We passed through Bischofswerda, a little town burned to the ground. The only thing I noticed was that in 1555 the insignia of the tailors was an open pair of shears, like today. Exactly everything was burned. The chimneys rising above the walls of the houses reminded me of Moscow. Here, the industriousness of the inhabitants had already been manifested: the poor devils had placed some bricks in such a way as to stop up the doors and windows of their houses, which had been completely destroyed by fire. I didn't see the purpose of this work, but it gave me a feeling of pity; that was likewise the feeling inspired in an old quartermaster of the gendarmerie in our escort, who said after a long silence, "It's too bad about this little town."

At seven o'clock May 19, we arrived at the bivouac before Bautzen. For two hours, I'd been hearing heavy firing on the left; it appears to have been one of General Bertrand's divisions, taken a bit by surprise by the enemy.

The 20th, at two in the morning, a false alarm. At eleven, we displayed a goodish amount of bravery by going three times to our sentry boxes under the fire from the town, which was a third of the cannon's range and might have blown us to bits.

We went as far as a little mound covered with blocks of granite;

to our right, we saw the sentry boxes quite near, and we were retiring after a quarter of an hour of conversation with our post, when we saw a great cavalry movement and His Majesty behind us on the left—and that the post was folding its cloaks. We returned; everything was being put in readiness for battle: the troops filed to the left, following the movements of the Emperor, and to the right toward the wooded hills.

I had a world of difficulty to persuade those petty souls to come to watch the battle. We could clearly distinguish Bautzen from the top of the slope opposite which it is situated. From noon until three o'clock, we had an excellent view of all that can be seen of a battle—i.e., nothing at all. The pleasure consists in being somewhat thrilled by the certainly that something is taking place before you that is known to be terrible. The majestic sound of the cannon fire is, in a large measure, responsible for this effect. It is in complete harmony with the impression. If the cannon produced the shrill sound of a whistle, I don't believe it would arouse so much emotion. I realize quite well that the sound of a whistle would become terrible, but it would never be as fine a one as that of the cannon.

At this battle, I found my companion of that of the Moskva, M. Edouard. This battle was for the passage of a river, the Spree, not very wide but with very steep banks. I imagine that the passage cost two thousand five hundred dead and four thousand five hundred wounded. We saw especially well the action between the town and the hills, where Marshals MacDonald and Oudinot were at the head of the Russians, who resisted with great perseverance. I distinguished especially well the rifle fire of the infantry skirmishers below the brickworks. We were taken by surprise by a volley, and driven into a cabin of branches and straw. During this time, a lively fusillade started up in a little village close to us.

We found all our carriages in movement; a fool of a baggagemaster made them go around in a *meandering* circuit.

Edouard's explanations of how to return opposite Bautzen: from there we had a good view of the battle. The spectators saw a whole lot with their imaginations. They recounted all the movements made by a battalion that had changed its position, form, etc. I let them go ahead and talk. A fourth arrival, to whom they talked about their battalion, asked them in all seriousness if it were not a hedge rather than a battalion. The only things that could be seen distinctly were the cannon shots; the more or less sustained fire of a fusillade could be heard. We were to the left of the town . . .

Fragment of the Diary of the 1813 Campaign
(in the original)
Intendancy at Sagan, June 7, 1813

June 6.—The day I was APPOINTED Intendant of Sagan started with a spill half an hour after midnight a rifleshot away from the Liegnitz gate through the stupidity of the postilion, for whom it seems to me that the word DULL was especially created. He made me understand the meaning of the DULL COLD EAR OF THE DEATH.

About two o'clock, while everyone was buzzing around M. Daru in the room where he was working, he said good-naturedly:

"Let's see now, who'd like to be Intendant?"

A circle was formed. I was reading behind the others purposely, having a vague hope of not being chosen and of going to spend ten or twelve days of the fifty that the armistice still has to run at Venice. As nobody answered, M. Daru added, "Come on now, who are the ones of the 1st class?"

They were designated by a buzzing of voices. He added, impatient at not receiving a reply and at seeing a group of fools spellbound at the sight of the decisions of their goddess, Ambition, "Who's the senior?"

They counted off slowly. M. Lafon said a few words.

"Ah, I know quite well that you're the senior. Well then, there's nothing else to do than to put M. Lafon at Glogau, M. Beyle at Sagan and M. Pastoret at Sprottau."

The count magistrate [perhaps Pastoret] started off from this point to indulge in a thousand pettinesses of soul; he said he wanted to write an epic poem; next he asked me if I had an English novel that he could translate. He smirked, became red as a lobster, ended up by writing M. Daru, who ended up by telling him with the politeness he considers due his father, "I have received your letter, but I haven't read it; what do you want?"

"To be employed in active service."

"But what could be more active than an Intendancy? I realize quite well that these aren't important ones, but they are the only ones open, and anyway they will last only through the armistice."

He started in again half an hour later, Daru sticking to his unanswerable argument; seeing the other's inadequate reasons, he was about to get mad when, thinking of his father, he ended up by saying to him, "See whether my letter to the prince has left, I'll change the name."

The count magistrate went to find out; a quarter of an hour later, "It's gone." I was observing this scene, which showed clearly enough the extreme pusillanimity and pettiness of soul which I believed myself entitled to attribute to the before-mentioned count magistrate, when the marshal inhumanly sent me to write a letter. Half an hour later, de Coëtlogon came in to tell me that he had the Intendancy of Sprottau. I asked Pastoret with a courtier's pretended innocence what he was trying to get anyway. He answered in an affected voice that La Moussaye was bringing him some packages with orders to give them to no one but him. Although he is a man with a sensibility taken from the novels of Mme. de Genlis, with badges, devices, a wisp of beard on his chin and other trivialities, I'm inclined to believe these packages are some work of the variety of *L'Esprit des Lois*. I believed I made out through his *singsong* phrases that he was seeking, by continuing to cohabitate with the marshal, to become his man, his favorite, his factotum, all that MYSELF might have been with a man of a different character.

I'm writing this at Lüben, worn out by thinking. Unfortunately, this day, which has been remarkable for the multitude of new thoughts, has been spent traveling in a calash. I believe it's the fruit of happiness, I left the Court to get my heart's enjoyment anew in my cherished liberty. Same effect at Moscow October 17. I stop writing, utterly worn out.

June 10.—Arrived at Sagan about four o'clock. I got out at the burgemeister's; from there to the Landrath's, where, having nothing to do, I skimmed through Sismondi—paying more attention, however, to my situation and to the nest I expected to build for myself than to the literature of the South.

Sagan, June 19.—This morning I recalled that fine phrase of Cimarosa, "*Scioltezza, amico, scioltezza, amico* [Flexibility, friend; flexibility, friend]." I wrote to M. Daru:

Monseigneur,
One of my colleagues assured me that, upon receiving a letter from Martial at Liegnitz, you said he was bored in Rome and would not remain there much longer. I am inclined to doubt the second part of the story. Would Your Excellency find it out of place if I were to remind him that I regard an Intendancy in Italy as the most suitable position I could obtain, as far as my happiness is concerned? I am practically certain of capably carrying out the duties of such a position;

at the same time, it is the least exorbitant request that I could make, and the logical promotion from my position as Inspector. Your Excellency is aware that any slight merits which are not rewarded immediately after a campaign are soon forgotten. In two years, it will be an obsolete honor to have taken part in the Moscow campaign. Consequently, it seems of capital importance for me to be proposed for the first vacancy in Rome or Florence. M. de Joly, of Paris, is arranging for me to be created a baron. I am thirty-one years old. Were I to be sent to Italy, I should desire nothing further, not even the Prefecture of Rouen.

> I am, with respect and gratitude, . . .
>
> Beyle.[1]

June 20.—Dinner at the general's, who, being sick, didn't come to table. I worked like a fool from nine to five, and didn't take advantage of the fine day, the promenade and the Sabbath. All the others have women (whores, it's true), I'm the only one to be alone. That irks me, but the delicacy which perhaps makes me sympathize *with my adverse party* prevents me TO HAVE PERHAPS THE SISTER OF MY . . .

June 21.—I've just borrowed a fine piano, which has been placed in my little bedroom, and a Monseiur . . . , piano teacher, has played the music of Mozart for an hour. Several of the pieces gave me a delightful pleasure, others bored me. Good executants are bad music priests; they spoil the music by, for instance, playing only fragments of sonatas.

The real German is a tall blond man with an indolent appearance. Events depicted by the imagination and capable of making a touching impression, with a blend of nobleness produced by the rank of the personalities involved, are his heart's real grazing ground, like this title which I've just come across: "Six Favorite Waltzes of the Empress of France Marie-Louise, played by the Imperial Guard upon her Entry into Strasbourg."

When music gives a German pleasure, the natural pantomime for him would be to become even more immobile. Instead of that, he tries to ape the Italian, I believe; his impulsive motions, made extremely quickly, look like an ordered exercise, and are very ridiculous. (He tries to be graceful, and what he does for that reason makes him displeasing, on the contrary.)

The German hasn't any modesty in his tender emotions.

[1]Following is Daru's reply, which Beyle copied in the manuscript of his diary: "*Letter of the colonel:* 'I have received, my dear Beyle, your long letters and your little note. I thank you for the one and the other. I should indeed like to see the person of whom you speak change his position, but it is not possible that I might have said that he is bored in his present position. However that may be, were there the occasion, I should with great pleasure place you as a candidate to be his successor.' "

June 28.—(Returning from sending off two detachments for the purpose of transporting some grain.)

The proprieties are, like the laws, drawn up by mediocre people for mediocre people. He who is an honest man only in that he abides by the law, just in order not to be hanged, is scarcely honest. He who does nothing but abide by the proprieties is scarcely distinguished.

But it's not forbidden to go farther than the law, and the public won't permit you to go farther than the proprieties. All the intercourse of Parisian men with incomes over 20,000 francs is imprisoned in this mediocre law of the proprieties, a law that's essentially inimical to all originality, to all talent. See Henri IV's letter on the first attempt to assassinate him. The civil law has been in the process of formation for a long time, a few thinkers have occasionally given it some pushes toward perfection. The law of the proprieties is of more recent date, and it's to be noted that society's narrowest minds are its arbiters. Any man who has a little wit is called an original, or eccentric, and this deprives him of all jurisdiction over the *proprieties*. Since this law has prevailed, the *originality* of a man has been able to manifest itself only in trifles that have not been foreseen by the *proprieties*.

Misson's *Voyage* is worth reading for several reasons, and I believe that, even for someone who's indifferent to the subject, it is agreeable. He's a man of good sense and a sagacity that makes him far superior to the mob of conceited asses who've written travel books on Italy.

Were I a great lord, I'd strike out half of Misson's text, and I'd publish a travel book in which, in the chapter on Naples, for instance, would be found: 1. what Misson has said about it; 2. the amiable de Brosses; 3. Duclos; 4. a few extracts from Swinburne and Lalande; 5. a few words from Arthur Young and Sismondi. In this way I'd have, at little expense, an excellent travel book. If I wanted to take the trouble to extract a hundred pages of Lanzi on the eight or ten great painters and their works in each city, the work would be nearly completed. This book should be undertaken by some compiler like Dentu or Guizot.[1] But intelligence is required for the choice of ideas. They'd eliminate, as going against the proprieties . . . (I've broken off here to give the order to remove eight missions from Eckersdorf, Petersdorf, etc.)

A travel diary should be full of sensations, a guidebook devoid of them. The latter should say: At St. Peter's *in Montorio,* see Guido Reni's *Assumption,* painted in 1553 and purchased for thirty-eight sous from the painter, who was then thirty-seven years old.

[1]Beyle, who had been contemplating a travel book on Italy since 1811, eventually wrote a book himself which somewhat resembles this description—*Rome, Naples et Florence.*

The mixture of sensation with information is detestable and greatly diminishes the pleasure of the voyager, who finds himself in the presence of what another man has felt, instead of being given over to his own feeling.

July 1.—Misson's Voyage.—If I wrote as they write today, I'd say that it's curious to observe the manners and morals in the midst of which the great artists of the sixteenth century made their appearance.

Misson shows that in 1688 the manners and morals regarding women's external conduct were far different from what they are today.

July 20.—I believe in 1813 at Sagan that we were too severe toward Cabanis.[1] What should have been seen in his book was observations and not assertions. Can you deny to an astronomer that a comet observed by him described such-and-such a movement? He says he's seen it. He doesn't know the cause of the movement. Cabanis doesn't prove that a man with a yellow complexion necessarily has what we call a bilious moral character, he simply says he's seen it. It's up to us to look at the thing if we wish.

Sagan, July 20, 1813, with a fever, reading Roland's letters on Italy and drinking an extract of aquatic herbs.

July 23.—Anniversary of my departure for Russia. I'm writing this at precisely a quarter past eight in the evening. First day of definite cessation of the fever. It's the second spell that lacks. They were very painful, with delirium. I began to feel sick July 6.

What a year the past one has been! The only things lacking were an Intendancy and an illness.

The count magistrate gives me some hope that His Excellency will allow me to go to Dresden. I've been replaced here, but only until I recover my health, by M. Bouquillard.

I arrived in Dresden July 28. In the evening, a hellish spell of fever. Two or three others like it. Afterward, M. Lherminier reduced them to ten hours, of which one was spent with a violent headache, the others in a very abundant sweat.

August 13, I had a mission for Frankfurt in regard to a letter written the 12th, after the denunciation of the armistice.

The 13th, at eleven o'clock at night, I was sweating profusely in bed when permission arrived for me to go to Paris. That kept me awake for two hours.

I have or am owed 6,000 francs, and my return trip will be paid.

Great feebleness, the fever persists; M. Lherminier says I must wait

[1] This passage, which is really a note for his future book, refers to Beyle's studies with Crozet in Paris two years earlier.

until I completely recover my strength, that if I could take six grains of quinine at intervals my fever would be cut.

Arrived in Paris August 20, 1813, with 1,000 francs in gold and thirty-one napoleons. Whipped up the horses from a little before Metz as far as Verdun, more or less.

Brief Outline of My Tour of Italy in 1813

September 7.—I finally arrived in Milan on September 7, 1813, which was this morning, at half-past ten. Our cabriolet, which was as brittle as glass, lost a shaft in the midst of a teeming rainstorm at eight o'clock last night, near Castellanza.

I believe the voyage has been good for me, but I'm still weak, especially when I'm excited. I was so much so at the Caffè Nuova that I spilled a cup of coffee *alla panera* on my fine new cashmere trousers!

At ten o'clock this morning, when we saw the Duomo of Milan, I reflected that my trips to Italy caused me to become more original, more *myself*. I'm learning to seek happiness with more intelligence.

All the characteristics of the Italians I meet are pleasing to me: 1. I believe, because I see the man who feels and not the man who calculates the interests of his vanity.

2. Because these people are different from the ones whom the interests of Mocenigo have forced me to dissect. For instance, the manner in which the woman selling bread at Isella requested the customs agent to take care of her little girl. Nothing flattering for the vanity of the customs agent, nothing noble, merely a benevolent smile and the ardor which the people of this land place in the things that are dictated by their heart.

That explains their indifference to everything foreign to the interests of their passion. The sincere good nature, far nobler than he suspected, of our host at Castellanza last night as he advised me about how to get our cabriolet repaired and to reach Milan.

I learned at M. Marchant's that FAIRISLAND [Louis Pépin de Belleisle] left eight days ago; through the same weakness that makes me lose time reading a collection of worthless anecdotes instead of working on something useful, I was annoyed at first by this news. I'd have had a good countenance going through the streets with that handsome young melancholy and noble Frenchman. But his conversation would have chilled me, and I'd certainly have been less *myself*.

I'm too weak to keep on chattering, I'm going to lie down on my couch.

September 8.—We made the rounds of all the theaters. I strained my eyes trying to discover who the people were in the loges of the Scala, especially in the 3rd in the 2nd tier on the right.[1]

September 9.—I've come back from the Brera and the Villa Bonaparte. I cast a lifeless eye[2] on the beautiful paintings in which I used to see so many things. I was extremely dejected. It was, I believe, a *touch of illness,* but it's all right because I've lost my sight before on days when I had a spell of fever.

Upon my return, the greatest joy at a quarter to two because of the attached note, when I was trembling for fear that I'd find her completely estranged from me.

I arrived at Monza the 9th. About half-past four, her window was open. I saw it from the portion of the avenue that passes near the Antonelli house, where she's staying. Happiness is spoiled by describing it.

I learned of THE DEATH OF Turcotti, OF HER BROTHER. I already suspected that of the amiable Widmann. I wrote to Félix about my feelings on learning of these deaths.

Grands Dieux, Ajax est mort et Thersite respire!

Widmann had the character that was the most after my own heart; such a man dies—a generous man, gaiety itself—while so many dull wretches still tread UPON THE STREETS OF Cularo [Grenoble]!

I returned to sleep at the posthouse, where I was comfortably put up; you dine quite passably there.

September 10.—I went to see her at half-past nine, which, in consideration of the proprieties, was a bit early. What would be required here are some Latin verses or some allusion to antiquity to draw a veil, in the manner of Montesquieu, over eight hours which sped away in sweet conversation.

I left for Milan. The ten miles in a few minutes less than an hour and a half (for 14 lir. *milanesi; ne dono quindici* [14 Milanese lire; I gave fifteen]). In the evening, I was upset a little by fever, the result of imprudence.

September 11.—*Sono felice* [I'm happy]. I stopped at No. 909. At three o'clock, she hadn't yet arrived. I changed my room at Marchant's. I

---

[1]This was Angelina Pietragrua's loge.

[2]September 23, I saw them again with my soul of other days. Domenichino's beautiful painting, which occupies the space where Guido Reni's St. Peter used to be hung, brought tears to my eyes, etc. I bought Mengs. [Note added by Beyle.]

read the bulletins of the battles of Dresden. I bought the comedies of Machiavelli and the life of Aretino. Comtesse Simonetta [Angelina Pietragrua] spoke to me a great deal about the Monbelli family; I hope to be able to see them with her. I believe that Signor Fossati is jealous: she talks too much about me and to me; but what excellent defects! They come from an excess of naturalness.

September 15.—I haven't written in the past four days because to describe happiness diminishes it. Yet, if I'm going to be truthful, I must say that I'm not experiencing the intoxication I had in 1811. My health, which is getting better, has been too weak, and besides novelty and ten years of absence are lacking. But I've reached, it seems to me, that second period OF LOVE where there is more intimacy, confidence and naturalness.

This evening, as I am due to go four days without seeing her, I realized that all I lacked to be happy was a little work.

I set about seeking some. I haven't got the green notebooks, so I won't work TO THE HISTORY OF P[AINTING]. Moreover, *bene dicendi sapere est fons.* That Latin ought to mean that, in order to write well, you should begin by knowing well. A fortnight's preparation would be necessary.[1] I'm not able to do any sustained work for so long. I'm not capable of sufficiently impassioned attention to take up *Letellier.* I ought to distrust the excuses I make to myself for not putting a hand to the trowel. Yet I believe I'm right this time. This winter in Paris, I'll work, I hope; but here it seems to me it would be difficult. I'm probably the opposite of J.-J. Rousseau in many things, and especially in that I can only work when I'm far from the sensation. It's not while strolling through a delightful forest that I'm able to describe this happiness; it's shut up in a bare room, where there's nothing to distract my attention, that I'm able to accomplish something.

But here I'm on the battlefield. I haven't had to fight any battles, but at bottom that changes nothing. So much the worse for me if I'm four days away from her; that's one disadvantage of the situation, but, since it doesn't change its nature, I'm unable to work.

Remains reading, as well as to write out my observations on Italian manners and morals, a thing entirely different from writing my life. No book makes me enthusiastic, and it's only in this happy state that I read with profit, with an increase of my store of ideas, or rather the rectification of my ideas, and draw ever nearer the truth. For me, the latter (in the knowledge of mankind) is like a painting covered by a coat of whitewash; some of the whitewash continually peels off and I draw nearer the desired truth.

[1] I was wrong; I should have worked on *L'Histoire de la Peinture.* A little work was all that I lacked for my happiness in 1813. [Note added by Beyle.]

September 14.—Seven or eight major facts confirm me in the opinion that this land is that of the arts. At Paris, the people are eunuchs who in several art varieties don't create or won't let others create, for instance, the ballet like that of Viganò.

September 16.—*Trip to Como.*—I can't see the Comtesse Simonetta again before Monday at five o'clock; to leave Milan solely in order to be at Monza would have been even more suspect. I considered that it was much more natural to come to spend four days at Como, and, on the return trip, passing near Monza, to stop off there as long as prudence, or rather love, permitted.

I therefore took a little *vetturino;* in the vehicle was a pretty grisette of Como, snub-nosed, nice little breast, sixteen years old, already a bit of bile and passion;—in short, a good Milanese;—but also a big lackey in the service of the *gran capitano* Pino. This latter individual made me a bit ashamed because of his livery, although I should have been glad, as it was a rare opportunity to study the Milanese lackey. Without once looking at him, I found in him naturalness, natural graciousness and boredom coming from not having anything to do during the five weeks the fat captain had been away, a circumstance with which he was overjoyed. *Lavoro a letto* [I work in bed], those were his words.

September 17.—This trip to Como, with boat rides on the lake all day and the little Monbellis in the evening, has been charming. That and my excursion to Monticello, for the pleasure given by the view of *beauty;* for sentiment, the walk at Monza in the huntsman's garden; for strangeness, the view of Venice from the top of the column of San Marco, the moonlight at the extremity of the gardens at the end of the Riva dei Schiavoni.

Monza, September 21.—Anniversary, at almost the same hour.[1] A little feverish sweating, which didn't put me in bad humor, announced the return of my soul.

Her tears in the cemetery as we walked around the little Pellegrini temple. Nothing is lacking in her.

I see on my suspenders[2] that it was September 21, 1811, at half-past eleven in the morning.

September 23.—Coming out of the Brera.—Is it your business to live or to describe your life?

You should keep a diary only to the extent that doing that might aid you to live *da grande* [nobly].

I've lost the habit of an attention that is strong and extreme, because

---

[1]On this date Angelina Pietragrua became his mistress. See entry of September 21, 1811.

[2]Characteristically, Beyle had written the date and hour on his suspenders.

I usually think only of the things that I hold in contempt, that I find unimportant.

September 24.—Nosce te ipsum.—The thing that will fail me the first when I get old will be my memory. The following passage from Cabanis is a strictly accurate description of what takes place in me. My attention is poured out over a subject and then flows off elsewhere. In Dresden, in spite of myself, my attention was too distraught to observe carefully the pictures of Correggio and Mengs. As my attention is again beginning to flood the soil of painting here, I now see what I lacked when I found myself in front of these great works.

To be all worked up over something and then to forget it completely, that's my history, *nel comporre* [when I'm composing]. I'm a stranger for THE HISTORY OF THE WAR OF THE SECESSION,[1] for which I was enthusiastic at Richmond, and in which I saw such great things.

The *nonum prematur in annum* has no meaning for me. After nine years, I'd hardly understand my work.

My lack of memory for what is history and isn't related to my subject is incredible, almost alarming. I can read the same book of history every two years with the same pleasure. Experienced at Liegnitz with Duclos's *Mémoires*. The only part I skipped as boring, because it was too well known, was the section on the speculation in the Rue Quincampoix.

These things being set down and deeply felt by me, here is the passage from Cabanis:

"It should be remarked that the sensibility behaves in the same manner as a fluid of which the total quantity is determined and which, whenever it is poured more abundantly into one channel, is proportionately diminished in the others."

(*Rapports du Physique,* etc. *Histoire des Sensations.* Quoted in No. 259 of the *Moniteur* of 1813.)

I left her at Monza on the evening of the 21st. I'm working because I'm far from her. I'm working on PAINTING, but I think I'll work a lot in Paris this winter, and, I hope, on *Letellier*.

Extreme concentration of attention on a subject shows only passion, and not genius. Look at Thomas, who, according to Hérault de Séchelles, used to ask his horse how it had passed the night.

On the plan of my voyage.—I would be surer of driving out the inane ideas OF THE ARMY and of kindling sufficient fire to work well in Paris this winter if I went to Rome or Naples. But these places will always be accessible, and will I always have a woman as superior and remarkable as the Comtesse Simonetta?

[1] A historical work that Beyle composed, or more properly copied, at Brunswick when he was hoping to be sent to Spain.

In the second place, will I find the sweetness of intimacy with a person who is at least my equal?

I speak of this intimacy only in relation to THE GRANDEUR.

Another reason: it's probable that I'll be APPOINTED IN Rome OR IN Florence. Another facility to SEE THESE COUNTRIES.

September 25.—All that is quite true, but the fact remains that I'm bored, and I shudder to think that it's already the 25th of September. I haven't enough time to find myself an occupation, a taste. I'm in the painful position of a man who is waiting for something. She promised me to write so I could go to see her about the middle of M. le Comte Simonetta's stay. He was due to arrive at Monza on the morning of the 22nd; consequently, I might have gone there the 25th. I've received nothing.

I've just spent an hour and a half at the Brera. The painting by Domenichino that comes from the Bolognesi church in Rome dominates all the others; it's Diana in the midst of her nymphs.

This excellent comparison, which is quite accurate, remained in my mind after hearing an *improvvisatore* last night at the Scala (Signor Gianini); a sonnet on the privations of poets wasn't at all bad. What a language this one is, in which verses can be composed that don't produce an execrable sensation as soon as they are declaimed!

Always naturalness and lack of *savoir vivre* in the spectators. The one whom, from his eyes and ardent appearance (a man of fifty), I had taken for a poet, who answered the *improvvisatore* by improvising himself. But it seems that he's getting too dull and common, and the audience disapproves of this.

This form of amusement has been spoiled by the police, who have forbidden a topic to be shouted out from the center of the *platea* [pit]. The *improvvisatore* now chooses from several topics suggested in writing at the entrance. It may be assumed that there's some preparation. Real improvision used to be practiced when, in the Piazza del Duomo, someone would wrap a 30-sou piece in a bit of paper on which I suppose were written these words: *La tomba d'Alfieri scolpita da Canova,* and the *improvvisatore* would sing.

Yesterday, rhymes were suggested from the sonnet on *fama* and the one on *la tomba d'Alfieri,* all the commonplaces of Italian rhymes, the abuse of a beautiful language, spoiled, profaned by asses. Thus, *rimbomba, tomba,* etc.

The sonnet was too inane. This extemporaneous poetry is like painting done in the manner of Luca Giordano. Besides, Signor Gianini is lacking in wit. His farewell to the City of Milan lacked it altogether; a few slightly pointed praises of some Milanese and their sojourn would have given extreme pleasure.

Rule.—The level of a passion mustn't be judged by the summits of a mountain.

One experiences a moment of ardor or tender emotion, and one consequently says to oneself, "I have such-and-such a passion." "No, monsieur, you must look at yourself in a moment of indifference, in the ordinary course of your life."

All this in connection with a few pleasant hours I spent in reading Mengs. It was quite otherwise in 1812. At that time, I shouldn't have been bored during the periods after dinner.

Base.—It's absolutely necessary for MY HAPPINESS that I be alone in the morning, and in company immediately after dinner, until ten o'clock at least.

I find nothing better to say about my liaison with the Comtesse Simonetta than this reflection of Duclos: "In the long run, only a mind serves to nourish a mind; left to itself, it does not produce for long." (Duclos, Vol. II, page 37.)

In the midst of my enthusiasm, I was stopped short by a disheartening sterility and listlessness, of which I didn't suspect the cause, which was this:

She had too much sensibility to be severe in the choice of the novels[1] that pleased her. It wasn't by their merit but by her own sensibility that she was moved. As for being jealous of them, in order to cure myself, I must consider that she would be entitled to be jealous of no one with more apparent justification than of Mme. de B., and yet how wrong she'd be!

No, love is a blissful fever. Nothing remains after it has passed. Ought I to have been unhappy not to have been for her what Louis was?

In every kind of property, possession is nothing, enjoyment is everything. As it happens, Louis saw an ordinary woman in her. All this shows that I'm as or more HAPPY THAN HE. But why couldn't I have been the first love of a woman so rare? There's the key to the problem. Only one bear was killed this year in the Sassenage mountains.

September 26.—Superb weather after a rainy week. I went to the Corso to see the places I've loved so much. On the way back, I stopped at her house, where I learned that her husband left only yesterday to rejoin her, and probably won't return to Milan before Wednesday.

Why didn't she write me between Wednesday and Saturday? Has she another lover?

I'd leave immediately for Venice. I'd have the pleasure of getting my revenge, whether she loves me or not. But, in either case, I'd weaken

---

[1] Louis AND I. [Note by Beyle.] The word "novels" undoubtedly should be read "lovers," among whom Beyle and Louis Joinville were two of many.

her confidence, a foreigner and a transient, naturally so open to suspicion. I'd kill her lover, if she had one; if not, I'd at least deprive myself of a charming illusion.

Last Sunday I was at Framezzina; the Sunday before that, with her in her garden. What should I do?

Milan is unbearable for me.

I've gone to Monza and Monticello. I'm sending the following twenty pages to Félix; I've written them solely for myself.

October.—Arriving from Venice at half-past six on the . . . , I received a letter from Signora Simonetta.

In my reply, I gave the following signals:

"The first window as you come from the Via dei 40 Martiri wide open at half-past eight, the hour when I'll pass by your door, will mean that you can come out at ten o'clock; half open, at eleven; half open with a cloth hanging from the window, at noon; wide open with a cloth will mean half-past nine; finally, wide open with two towels will mean one o'clock.

"Come at the indicated time to the Contrade dei Bigli. I'll come by at half-past eight. If there aren't any signals, I'll go at nine . . ."

Saw with her the first performance of the ballet, *Prometheus.* She was more beautiful than ever; we were alone with Antonio nearly all the time. Tomorrow at half-past twelve in the Via dei Bigli; she's afraid the Austrians will drive me out of here.

October 27.—The more I live, the more I see that in our business Molière is a classic. His coloring is unpleasant for me, but his comic vigor and good sense make me return to him.

In the other nations, society hasn't been sufficiently perfected to give birth to comedy. For example, *La Barone,* a comedy by Moratin translated by Signorelli, which I read this morning, gave me no pleasure because of the extreme vulgarity of the characters. Greek comedies—or, at the moment, merely the memory of them—make me crack my jaw yawning. My studies are therefore reduced to Molière, commented by twelve or fifteen pages of Collé, whose only lack was a little more mental vigor and the strong passions of a bilious man. If he'd had these, he would have come close to Molière. All his rules are excellent.

In fine, seeing that things are going badly in France, I'm leaving the . . . For the past month, I've been living in a fine room near the Piazza Belgiojoso. I had a good servant who was very bilious. I slept with my weapons all around me.

End of this brief rough sketch.

Milan, November 4.—Upon arriving in the public gardens from her house at four o'clock and seeing the mountains covered with snow, which produced such a romantic effect, I told myself that, with a couple of rules of conduct, I'd avoid the vexations that the effect I produce on my neighbors has been able to give me up to now.

In conversation, I must *restrain myself*. For instance, I shouldn't try to stand out the first time I'm presented to a Mme. Doligny. To be amiable, I need only not try to be so. What happened in the company of Mme. la Comtesse Simonetta is a striking example of this. My superiority is so certain that I'm the only one who can make it unappreciated, by laying myself open to accusations of having gone too far. I should talk, but not much during the first days, and by the end of the month the superiority, or what's worth more, a fine equality will be established.

Moreover, society is a coquette running after what seems to be held back from it, and disdaining what is offered. I must never be afraid of being accused, rightly or wrongly, of listlessness and sterility; I should consequently, on the first days, skirt these shortcomings without fear.

I believe I found out yesterday why the people of the South, who feel love so poignantly, have a liking for the Marini sort of thing— studied refinement in the expression of this sentiment, of which they are the best judges. It's because natural expression seems to them too easy; for them, it lacks that ingredient of pleasure which comes from the *feeling of a difficulty overcome*.

The Italians have sought the *feeling of a difficulty overcome* by giving an exaggerated refinement to the portrayal of love, overlooking the fact that, in the dramatic form *par excellence,* the impassioned man hasn't time to be witty. This bad taste has easily passed from the portrayal of love to that of other passions less commonly encountered. I had this idea a long time ago; it recurred to me when I read a worthless rhapsody in the *Moniteur*. Am I right in explaining this strange circumstance in such a way—that the people with the most feeling for love is the one which portrays it the worst?

November 8.—SHE IS GONE AT PAVIA, FOR HER SON. YESTERDAY TRUE PROOF OF LOVE. Her touching look as I was joking with Peppina. It's with that look that she ought to be portrayed. Excellent indecency of Italian joking: it's full of happiness. It shows that the person joking is capable of enjoyment even more than it does that his wit is refined. In that respect too, I AM thoroughly Italian.

November 8.—Everyone's clearing out. There's a sort of terror in the town. A couple of Cossacks would be all that is needed to make everyone flee. This disturbance that's brewing is very favorable to stir up the people. Were the latter cruel, the least quarrel would end in a massacre.

November 13.—The least distraction in the morning completely upsets me. My mind is a sluggard which asks nothing better than to lay hold of something less difficult than composing. Then, along about two or three o'clock, there comes disgust with this other occupation, and a fund of discontentment that lasts until I'm distracted by something else. Whereas three or four hours of work on my subject give me a fund of contentment for the whole day and redouble MY tenderness FOR the Comtesse Simonetta.

The comic poet's advantage in 1813. Not only have manners and morals changed, but they have become enormously perfected, there is more pleasure between indifferent people. The position of Mme. de Deffand compared with the salons of 1672.

After that, the manners and morals of the real pit at the comedy, people who are rich enough to be bored. They didn't have the fine arts, they came closer together in all nations, at the same time losing, it's true, some of their originality. Thus, the comedy of today may be more durable. It seems to me that Mme. de Deffand's salon was much nearer the perfection of monarchic manners than are those of comedy.

The End of an Epoch

BY MID-DECEMBER, Beyle had settled down in Paris and was making a determined effort to realize his lifelong ambition to become a "comic bard." A newly purchased season ticket took him several nights a week to the Théâtre Français, where, pencil in hand and an open copy of the play on his knee, he diligently scribbled commentaries opposite each place where the audience laughed. In his comfortable apartment he carefully went over the annotated texts, trying, as he had done a decade earlier, to track down the elusive laws of laughter and the comic. That magic "moment of genius" which was to enable him to dash off a masterpiece had not yet arrived, but, undiscouraged, he put the interval to use by drawing up a rough treatise on the art of writing comedies—composed largely of the notes he had been accumulating ever since 1803.

These studies led him to read the course in dramatic literature that Wilhelm von Schlegel had given in Vienna a few years earlier. Schlegel, although too "vague" to suit such a lover of precision as Beyle, undeniably had his merits: he spoke of a new thing called "romanticism" which distinguished Shakespeare, Calderon, Schiller and Goethe from the "classic" dramatists of Greece and France; he also in his cloudy way suggested a conception of comedy of which his reader highly approved—"that kind of gaiety which is detached from the world and its cares . . . something airy and fantastic . . . something which arouses sensations similar to those produced by music." This kinship between the appeal of music and the comedy was a phenomenon Beyle had always felt profoundly without being able to explain it to his own satisfaction. The expression *beau idéal moderne* (containing gaiety, grace, youth, etc.), which he had adopted in his art history, was an approach; Schlegel's neologism "romantic" was another: in fact, as Stendhal understood them, the two were fundamentally the same thing. But his thought along this line was to be developed completely only several years later in *Histoire de la Peinture en Italie,* and especially *Racine et Shakspeare.*

To ensure himself against being interrupted by further military campaigns, he wrote on December 15 to both the Duc de Cadore and Baron d'Hastrel, Director General of Military Conscription, requesting to be released from his army duties—incidentally giving each to understand that the other had already expressed willingness to grant his request. This little ruse worked: on Christmas Day a special decree was issued exempting "M. de Beyle" from further military service.

Unhappily for his "comic genius," he had chosen the worst possible time to return to his studies. On the day he wrote his letters, France was faced with the immediate invasion of the allied armies, with 225,000 troops waiting across the Rhine, 100,000 in reserve in Germany, 70,000 Austrians standing by in Italy and 100,000 English, Spanish and Portuguese under Wellington approaching over the Pyrenees.

The situation within the frontiers was no better: Napoleon's marshals were panic-stricken, and, if many of the common people were still loyal, the opposition of Talleyrand, the influential salons and the directing classes constituted a real danger for the Emperor. The newly formed Liberal party did not conceal its wish that the "Despot" were dead and out of the way. The majority of the Parisians were heartily tired of the arrogance shown by the Imperial functionaries and the endless warfare with the resultant conscription and excessive taxation, while in the provinces the public spirit had become so uncertain that Napoleon hastily decided to send out extraordinary commissioners chosen from the ranks of the loyal Senators.

This decision accounts for the fact that, just two days after being exempted from military service, Beyle received a letter from Comte Camille de Montalivet, Minister of the Interior, notifying him that he was to accompany the Comte de Saint-Vallier, Senator and newly appointed Extraordinary Commissioner of the 7th Military Division, to—of all places—Grenoble to aid in speeding up the conscription, supplying the troops with arms and clothing, completing the arrangements for provisions and raising and organizing the National Guard.

Dismayed at this sudden demolition of his plans, he hurried to consult Mme. Daru, but the days when she and her husband could help him were already over. "If it hadn't been for this wretched invasion," she told him, "you would have been appointed the Prefect of a large city" (the city in question was Toulouse or Le Mans, he believed). So he once again put aside his notebooks and, on New Year's Eve, set out for his native "mud-hole" on what was to be his last assignment for Napoleon.

The rebirth of Beyle's patriotism, his brave struggle against the appalling confusion, inefficiency and lack of co-operation in the 7th Military

Division, the return of his disgust and boredom—conveniently accompanied by that of his "intermittent fever"—and his trip back to Paris, with a detour through Orléans to avoid the invading Cossacks, all make an interesting story, but one that is told in his voluminous official correspondence of the period.

He rejoined Louis Crozet in the capital in time to see Marie-Louise and her son, the King of Rome, drive away from the Tuileries for the last time. On the morrow he witnessed the "fine battle" of Montmartre. The capitulation of Paris made Crozet ill, but Beyle, so he later said, "considered the thing more as a spectacle." The sight of the Cossacks at Orléans had made him realize that all was over. The Empire had eclipsed the country—and why weep at the passing of the cumbersome Imperial structure? He even assured posterity that he experienced a feeling of pleasure at the crash.

Paris, too, took its defeat lightly. While the fighting was still going on at the northern limits of the city, the Boulevards were gay and animated. The next day, when Czar Alexander drove along them, Napoleon's old supporters "waved white handkerchiefs from every window, and appeared to be drunk with joy." The holiday spirit persisted. "On the 31st, about nine o'clock in the morning," says Stendhal in his *Napoléon,* "the streets were as crowded as on the gayest promenade days . . . A group of men passed on horseback wearing white cockades and waving white handkerchiefs. They were shouting, 'Long Live the King!' 'What King?' I heard people asking all about me. We no more thought of the Bourbons than of Charlemagne."

Henri Beyle wrote many years later that, when he learned that the downfall of Napoleon was to be followed by a Bourbon restoration, he "had enough intelligence to realize that France no longer held anything but humiliation for a man who had been to Moscow," whereupon he unhesitatingly turned down a fine position under the new government and withdrew in disgust to Italy. The truth was not quite so simple.

While enjoying the unusual spectacle of a battle on the *butte* of Montmartre and mingling with the holiday crowds on the Boulevards, he apparently had not been fully conscious of the fact that he was about to lose everything, that the Council of State was to be dissolved, that the posts of deputy commissaries were to be abolished, that there would be no further need of an Inspector of the Emperor's Household Furnishings. It was a rude awakening on the morrow of the Restoration to find himself "cleaned out from cellar to garret" at the very moment when, at least so was his conviction, his situation was about to "become superb." On every side he saw former Republicans and Bonapartists join the Legitimists in a mad scramble for jobs under the new government. "Big ones and little ones followed their interests without ever a thought of *what people would say."* And Monsieur de Beyle, tyrant-hating son of the Revolution, did as the others did: he "eagerly adhered to the acts passed by the Senate since April 1, 1814"—in other words, swore allegiance to the Bourbons he professed to despise—and hurried forth, he too, to find himself "a little job."

What else was there for him to do? "I must either blow out my brains or seek to live as I can," he wrote his sister. His first thought upon suddenly finding himself without an income was characteristically to see how much money he could extract from his family. His uncle Romain Gagnon was in charge of a trust fund of 16,000 francs from his grandparents' inheritance; possibly Pauline and her husband could arrange their little fortune in such a way as to provide him with an annual income of 1,200 francs, while the "generous bastard" (Beyle still refused to believe that his father was a ruined man) must be prevailed upon to make over to him property yielding 2,400 francs a year. Repeating endlessly these and other details in the desperate letters he dispatched one after the other to Pauline, he devoted his time in Paris, despite a serious inflammation of the lungs, to making diplomatic calls, holding solemn conclaves with Bellisle and Crozet and covering reams of paper with mathematical calculations through which he hoped to extricate himself from his dilemma.

The situation was certainly a black one, for, instead of 9,000 or 10,000 francs a year in combined salaries and gratuities, all that now remained was 37,000 francs in debts!

The last hope of becoming a Prefect and repaying the money he had borrowed during the past four years had vanished. Some means had to be found to ensure himself of at least 6,000 francs annually—2,000 to pay the interest on part of his debts, 4,000 on which to struggle along "with many privations." He could sell his cabriolet and furniture for perhaps 6,000 francs, he had hopes of obtaining the 16,000 francs from his uncle, and, if worst came to worst, he could sell the house his father had "given" him as a *majorat* in 1812. This house would yield 75,000 francs, or 30,000 francs net when the mortgage of 45,000 francs had been deducted. Paying his debts from the total, he would have 15,000 francs left, which, sunk in an annuity, might provide 2,000 francs a year for "a poor devil accustomed to spending 10,000."

One thing was clear in his mind: should he really be doomed to lead a frugal existence, he would retire to Italy, where life was pleasant and living cheap. "Associated, as I am, almost entirely with wealthy people," he said, "it is impossible to live here in semi-poverty."

His single hope of salvation was represented by Comte, or rather Comtesse, "Doligny"—the Beylistic pseudonym for Comtesse Beugnot and her husband. Early in life Beyle had discovered the elementary truth that advancement comes much more quickly through "pull" than through drudgery, and he furthermore had never forgotten the words of wisdom he had heard as a child from his uncle Romain, "The only way to get ahead in the world is through women." He had practiced this theory very satisfactorily with the Darus. Since their influence had vanished with the passing of the Empire, he had promptly exchanged the salon of the Comtesse Daru for that of the Comtesse Beugnot, of whom he was sincerely fond, and whose husband gave promise of having nearly as much power under Louis XVIII as Daru had had under the Empire.

Jacques-Claude Beugnot, during the Empire, had been the Administrator of the Grand Duchy of Berg and Cleves, and, on the morrow of the Restoration, was appointed Minister of the Interior, to become six weeks later Minister of Police. As for Beyle, his attitude toward his new potential protector was much the same as it had been toward Daru: he respected Beugnot's position but had a contemptuous enough opinion of his character, considering him servile, lacking in personality, with a common mind and "the vanity of two Frenchmen."

But, as usual, luck was against Beyle: he had a rival, none other than his friend Louis Pépin de Bellisle, Mme. Beugnot's lover. As Beugnot hesitated to push two candidates simultaneously, things ended with Bellisle being appointed Master of Requests and Beyle getting nothing. And yet Beugnot seems to have done what he could for the latter. There was some question of a post in the Consulate of Naples and of a secretaryship in the Florence Embassy—and what was the glittering offer that Beyle later said he so haughtily turned down?

"I had asked for nothing," he wrote in *Souvenirs d'Egotisme.* "I was in an admirable position to accept. I replied in a manner not calculated to encourage M. Beugnot . . . The extreme contempt I had for the Bourbons—they were the scum of the earth for me—impelled me to leave Paris a few days after not having accepted M. Beugnot's kind proposition."

However all that may be, Beyle had by this time really resolved to leave Paris, perhaps forever, and settle down to a modest life in Italy. Reasoning things out, as was his wont, with pencil in hand, he scribbled the following note (quoted in Colomb's *Notice*):

"Fortunately, luxury means little to me, or rather it embarrasses me. I fully realize that it's possible to live in Paris in a fourth-floor room with one clean suit, a woman who comes in to brush it every morning and my entrées to the Français, or rather the Odéon, which I love. But vanity and self-respect are opposed to this kind of life. M. Doligny would no longer receive me in the same manner when he knew that I lived on 6,000 francs a year. That would be intolerable. Therefore, I must leave Paris. By a second stroke of luck, Paris has bored me for a long time and I love Italy, where with 6,000 francs and two dinners a month at the home of the Ambassador, I'll be respected."

He gave up his fine apartment in the Rue Neuve-du-Luxembourg, sold his furniture, carriage and horses, and moved into a cheap hotel room until he could make arrangements to go to Italy. All the projects he had been laboriously constructing since childhood had come tumbling down at his feet. The days of luxury were over: never again would he be entirely free from the specter of poverty.

It was the end of the Napoleonic era, which the curve of his own life had followed so closely; it was the end of his long and ardent "real education," of his youthful studies and ambitions and loves—and it was the end of his diaries. That is, of the diaries proper. For by now the habit of thinking with a pencil in his hand had become part of himself: until his dying day he kept a sort of shorthand diary on the margins of the books he read, but it was into the books he wrote that he poured the major part of his intellectual and emotional life. At bottom, the complete works of Stendhal are little more than a slightly disguised extension of the diaries he posted night after night throughout his youth.

1814 Paris—Grenoble—Paris

Chambéry, March 2, 1814.—Diary of my dismal sojourn at Grenoble.—On December 26, 1813, returning from dinner at Annette's, I received a letter from the Minister of the Interior notifying me that I was to go to *Cularo* [Grenoble] with M. le Comte de Saint-Vallier. I was deeply affected by the thought of leaving Paris and going far from the Opera Buffa and Angéline. This feeling was opposed by the joyous mood I've experienced every time there is a chance to go away and see new things.

I went to Mme. Daru's, where I made no attempt to conceal my dissatisfaction; I was a little too familiar with her. At eleven o'clock, I went to the home of M. de Saint-Vallier, whom I hadn't met at seven o'clock. I had the strongest prejudices against this amiable man, whom I'd never seen. I imagined that a Senator must be, generally speaking, either a man with one foot in the grave and an old imbecile, like Comte V..., or a crazy old fool, like Comte X. I was favorably impressed by M. de Saint-Vallier's welcome, which showed real kindness and wide social experience. I returned home, where I felt some emotion in announcing my departure to Annette. My sister, that sensible soul, didn't for one minute have any illusions, and she was sincerely sorry for me, well realizing the extent of the mudhole into which I was falling. That blackguard of an F. . . told D. . . that neither I nor my Senator would leave. From the 26th to the 31st of December, I stopped in twice a day at M. de Saint-Vallier's, not wanting to leave before him. I was beginning to have some hope that we wouldn't leave at all when, at eleven o'clock on December 31, his porter told me that he'd left that morning. I went back home to arrange my own departure, sent for my sister and her husband, and at three o'clock we left.

We slept two nights en route, and reached Lyon after sixty-one hours of driving, not counting fifteen or twenty hours of sleep and rest. We reached Lyon an hour after my Senator, and Grenoble on January 5, 1814, at three o'clock in the morning in beautiful moonlight and fine weather. On the way, I'd thought out all the means of defense which Grenoble gradually found through necessity.

How am I to describe, without renewing my apathy and boredom, the fifty-two days I spent in this headquarters of pettiness?

My reason tells me that they aren't any more *petty* and *stupid* in *Cularo* than in other towns of twenty-two thousand souls, but I'm infinitely more aware of the bad qualities of people whose past life I know only too well.

On my arrival, I went to lodge at my *bastard's*. On January 16, I believe, when we thought that Lyon had been taken, I went to lodge at the Prefecture, in an immense, bright, cold and damp room, in order to spare my Senator the annoyance of being awakened by the estafettes. Boredom gave me a fever. The Senator consented to take one of his relatives from Lyon with him; this young man arrived, I went back to stay at the *bastard's*. Two days later, in order to have more liberty, I rented, for forty francs a month, a room in the Rue Bayard from a M. L. . . , a genuine *Lovelace of the tavern,* as Mme. de Staël says of her son Albert. I never spoke to M. L. . . In this room, I had a few moments of solitude which were the least poisoned by boredom of all those I spent in Grenoble.

My poor sister, infinitely less sensitive than I, but with cold reasoning power, utterly and irrevocably undeceived concerning the bastard, was perishing from boredom; we thought of Mme. Derville [Sophie Boulon], of Vizille, whom I had never seen and who is a close friend of my sister. She came; I went with them to Claix,[1] to Vizille, and I

---

[1]Pauline's friend, with whom Beyle appears to have had a passing love affair, was the prototype of Mme. Derville, Mme. de Rênal's confidante, in *Le Rouge et le Noir.* The following passage from the novel describes an actual visit made by Beyle and the two young women to Claix:

"From the moment Mme. Derville arrived, it seemed to Julien that she was his

had the pleasure of putting a few truths about the arts and detailed truths about mankind into the heads of those pure-minded beings. The bastard sensed that he wasn't wanted, and that this conversation between respectable people was above him, and retired at ten o'clock. We kept on chatting until one o'clock in the morning.

On February 22, arrived a colleague attached to the commission, a young Auditor of the Council of State, the son of a man whose fortune made him influential. The same day, M. de Saint-Vallier wrote for me to return to Paris. A fortnight earlier, he had requested the blue cross (Order of the Reunion) for me. He renewed his request a few days later, but he hasn't spoken of it since I had him sign a letter for my recall, which seems quite natural to me, and I don't bear him the least ill will.

One of the sources of my annoyance in Grenoble was the witty little savant with the utterly petty soul and abject politeness of a dressed-up servant, named . . .[1]

This little . . . , with his everlasting chatter, held up everything, impeded everything; I was amazed to see that M. de Saint-Vallier didn't notice this general obstruction, and that he continually had words of praise for this gent. From that I drew unfavorable conclusions about my Senator's intelligence.

But he finally saw through this petty, and very petty, administrator who takes the *writing,* and not the *actions,* of which the writing is but the *note,* for the objective; and, during the closing days of my stay in Grenoble, he was fed up with him, and even said a few biting words to him, without ill humor or underhandedness.

March 29 Paris.—Departure of the Empress. Denon.[2]—We had breakfast at the Café de Foy at nine o'clock; we heard the mistress of the establishment say that the Empress's equipages were going to leave and that they had worked throughout the night loading the carriages. We went to the Tuileries, where we saw with a bit of stupefaction that the open

---

friend. He hastened to show her the view from the extremity of the new path beneath the great walnut trees; as a matter of fact, it was equal, if not superior, to the most admirable scenery that Switzerland or the Italian lakes can offer. If you climb the steep slope that starts a few paces from there, you soon arrive at lofty precipices bordered by oak groves that extend to the edge of the stream. It was to the summits of these perpendicular cliffs that Julien, happy, free and even something more, led the two friends, taking delight in their admiration of the sublime aspects."

[1] Baron Fourier, a geometrist of note, was at that time Prefect of the Isère. Many years later he was used by Stendhal as the model of the Prefect Boucaut de Séranville in *Lucien Leuwen.*

[2] This entry is in Louis Crozet's handwriting.

vans were being loaded beneath the windows of the King of Rome; we went nearer and saw a carriage with six horses standing before the perron. The pallor and sadness of the postilion who was driving the first two. At this moment, the crowd, which wasn't very large, appeared to us merely to be curious. We saw a lot of carriages arrive, one behind the other. That of the Empress came to a stop outside the door of her apartment nearest the Seine. We sauntered along on one side and then on the other, and finally took up places on the sidewalk at the entrance to the Pont Royal, uncertain whether the Empress would pass over the bridge or follow the Quai des Tuileries.

It was raining a little. Passing along the quay, we saw two red lancers who drank some brandy and were probably going as scouts on the road to Versailles. Finally, at thirty-two minutes after ten, we saw fifteen or twenty carriages coming out with an escort of fifty or sixty mounted grenadiers of the Guard. In the second carriage, which was drawn by eight horses, were the Empress and the King of Rome, the latter at the left, in a blue box coat and a round hat which permitted his fair hair to escape (exactly as we saw him the day before, bowing to the crowds on his return from the drive). The King of Rome hid the Empress from us. The crowd on the bridge showed no sign of emotion, it didn't have a clear idea of what was happening, it hadn't had the time to reflect like us. It wondered what this procession was, it suspected the truth, but it wasn't moved.

General Caffarelli, very pale, was on horseback a little ahead of the Empress.

We went back to the Tuileries by the Pont Royal gate; our attention redoubled, and we anticipated great events. We passed beneath the peristyle, where we saw some women and old men weeping. In the courtyard, the people of the lower class were unmoved, and the fairly well-dressed men were very solemn, but weren't terrified. The wealthy and well-bred people were solemn out of foresight.

The thing which occupied us the most was the fact that we found that this business matched the asininity which has governed everything done in Paris for some time past—to carry out such preparations in full daylight, whereas for the past fortnight the Empress has gone for a drive in the direction of Saint-Cloud every day, and it would have been such a simple matter one fine day not to return!

We heard it said in a group of people that the Empress was going to Rambouillet.

We went to the museum for a final view of the paintings. We'd already gone the day before with the same intention. Henri, having stopped in the courtyard a moment by chance, conceived the notion of saving at least the *Madonna della Seggiola;* he went into the office of the museum, where he found M. Joseph de La Vallée. La Vallée told Henri that M. Maret had written M. Denon two months before saying that he would receive no orders, but that what he considered should be done would be approved. M. Denon considered that he should do nothing before consulting King Joseph, who asked for two hours to think it over, and then ordered M. le Duc de Cadore to open the museum. They had taken down five hundred paintings in the space of a few hours and bought some gray paper, which Henri saw, to wrap them in.

Henri told M. de La Vallée that the Empress had just left, that consequently there were no precautions of policy to take, that, if there were no wagons, they ought to take some fiacres and *coucous*[1] and save the *Madonna* and the most valuable of the smaller paintings. M. de La Vallée said, "All right, I'll save my poor little Flemish paintings." He added that he would send for M. Denon. Henri said that he was going up to the museum and could be found there.

In the picture gallery, we found some artists, male and female, working as usual, merely a bit anxious and questioning the guardians, who played the role of braggarts, and maintained that there was nothing to fear. After looking at the *Madonna,* we left because Henri wanted to give fifty napoleons to Mme. Doligny, who was due to leave at noon. He went down to the office to say that he would be back in an hour. At the end of the Rue Impériale, we ran into M. Denon, dressed in blue and accompanied by . . . , his secretary. Denon wore an anxious look, he came up to Henri without bowing:

"Have you come officially?"

"No, I came to pay a final visit to the paintings, I went into the office and gave an art lover's counsel."

"In that case, I shan't listen to you."

"If that's so, I shan't say anything more."

"I like you and I hold you in high esteem, but I won't listen to you."

"I well realize . . ."

"If you had come with a message from the Duc de Cadore . . ."

Henri with heat: "No, no, I come at the request of no one. I merely offered some advice as an artist, as an art lover . . . If only the beautiful *Madonna della Seggiola* might be saved . . . The Empress has gone to Rambouillet. Well, the *Madonna* might be sent to her: the work involved amounts to nothing, and it would be that much gained."

"Yes, you are right, but I cannot act without official orders, and any-

[1] A type of two-wheeled fiacre.

way what's a little measure like that? Do you want me to risk doing something foolish? Send *one painting* to Rambouillet? After holding me back for two months, the Duc de Cadore comes to me at the last minute . . . And what's more, you haven't been sent by him . . . He hasn't said anything at all to you about the museum?"

"He told me to continue my inventory."

"Well then, I'm going to close the museum, and that's the end of it. I must be getting along. I wish you good day."

And his anxious look increased.

May 26.—I see with pleasure that I'm still capable of passion. I've just been to the Français, where I saw Mlle. Mars in *Le Barbier de Seville*. I was seated beside a young Russian officer, General Vaissikov's aide-de-camp (something like that). His general is the son of a famous favorite of Paul I. If I'd been a woman, this debonair officer would have inspired the most violent passion in me, a love in the manner of Hermione. I felt the nascent agitation; I'd already become bashful. I didn't dare look at him, so much should I have desired him. If I'd been a woman, I'd have followed him to the end of the world. What a difference between a Frenchman and my officer! What naturalness and tenderness in the latter![1]

Politeness and civilization elevate all men to mediocrity, but spoil and avenge those who might be excellent. There's nothing coarser and more disagreeable than an asinine, uncultured foreign officer. But at the same time, what officer in France could be compared with mine from the standpoint of naturalness united with majesty? If a woman had made such an impression on me I'd have spent the night trying to find where she lived. Alas, even the Comtesse Simonetta has made such an impression on me only a few times! I believe the uncertainty of my fate is increasing my sensibility.

June 3.—I've just been to the little comedy of *L'Hôtel Garni,* in the worst manner, badly constructed, but in which Mlle. Mars was nothing less than perfect. Baptiste the younger was very good. He believes that his hostesses are strumpets, and that the mother is handing over her daughter. His manner of becoming scandalized is comic here, and produces laughter a score of times at least. With a people having more imagination, with the Germans, for instance, the audience would be scandalized at the situation. That kind of comedy, I believe, can't be pleasing to souls susceptible to romantic comedy.

[1]This strange passage has been considered by some as evidence that Beyle had homosexual tendencies—although everything else in his diaries and private writings, as well as the testimony of his friends, indicates the contrary. For a full discussion of the question, see Henri Martineau: *Le Coeur de Stendhal,* Vol. I, pp. 322 ff.

IF I GO AT LONDON FOR A FORNIGHT [sic], TO SEND THE ESTAMP [print] OF MOSCOU TO FAIRISLAND WITH THIS MOTTO: Instead of the fires of Moscow, let me see those of Vesuvius.

When I don't immediately perfect an idea for its accuracy and style, I lose it forever.

June 30.—Realizing that I'm not to have the consulate at Naples, which the pretty Mme. Deafdo obtained FOR HER HUSBAND, I had an interview with M. Graculus on Rome. He told me, or rather I concluded from his personal chatter, that with six thousand francs I'd be well off there.

He's an ass. I remarked that he told me coffee was an *afattening* food. When those animals don't have a clear idea of something, they employ a new word; as I stared at him when he made this assertion, he repeated *afattening*. Graculus is a man who never talks about anything but himself, a genuine ass, and full of Grenoblois pettinesses to boot. Not a shadow of good breeding; he spoke badly of Martial—to me of all people! Colomb was with him, I went to see him yesterday, he repaid my visit this morning. With that kind of people, it's necessary to have a calling card filled with titles.

Since May 10, I've been working on *Haydn, Métastase et Mozart.* The end of this work gave me much pleasure and took away all my sensitiveness to the disappointment of not having M. Doligny APPOINT [me] SECRETARY TO [the] embassy OF Firenze.

July 1.—As soon as I make the tiniest little attempt to recall something, my talent diminishes. It diminishes in proportion as my memories disturb me; if it's necessary to combine two or three of them, I'm lost. If you want to take away all my feeling for a historical or biographical trait that has moved me, force me to read two or three authors in whom I have confidence. I can be good, if ever I am good, only in what I extract entirely from my heart.

IT IS FOR THAT that Mocenigo IS PERHAPS DONE FOR ME [sic].

July 4.—You know yourself and you don't change, but the thing that's necessary is to know yourself.

One of the things that perhaps casts the most light on my character is the joy I experienced last night in a very common room of a little hotel (Rue du Mail, No. 27) after leaving an apartment calculated in every way to be pleasing to a young man.

I've behaved well, and uncommonly well, toward everybody, and everybody has behaved badly toward me, and I'm too sensitive to those bits of nonsense. That sensibility applied to the blackguards who surround me, starting BY THE BASTARD, is the one and only cause of my griefs.

Being in the midst of unknowns, this superfluous and inconvenient sensibility won't have to be exercised.

It would be my pleasure to give my attention to my gold, and to be able to scorn completely my furniture, my linen and all such little things. That's what I'm going to find in a little hotel. When my too great kindness, or my too little concern with temporal things, leads the servants of a hotel to rob me and pay less attention to me than to the other guests, I'll change hotels. Painful experience has brought me back to this axiom: *Conceal thy life.*

I find that Mme. Doligny has become cool toward me. She has let a couple of weeks go by without inviting me to dinner, and yesterday when she asked me to come today she acted as though she were yielding to an old habit. I assume, but that would be BLACK indeed, THAT FAIRISLAND has shown her the letter in which I advised him to have Florentine (MISTRESS Deafdo). If that's the case, or if he's told her about it, it's a very large piece of villainy to produce very little result. He might have been afraid that I'd gain some influence at a time when a post of MASTER OF REQUESTS was being sought for him, or perhaps he simply WAS JEALOUS OF MY CHEERFULNESS. I found that he had a very slight shade of haughtiness TOWARDS ME, and I haven't gone up to his sixth-floor room in the past ten days.

I saw the charming lodgings of General Sébastiani this morning. They were ornamented with a score of paintings of the highest merit. Nothing could .be cooler and more rustic (Rue Saint-Honoré, Faubourg, No. 57). Well sir, I'd shudder if I were to be given such lodgings, I'd suffer mortally if their beauty were to be impaired. I prefer my little hotel by far.

I realize that I'm incapable of temporal affairs, apparently because I hold them in contempt.

I'm fed up with Paris, not in the least angry (I'm writing this for the Beyle of 1820). I was thoroughly disgusted with the profession of Auditor and the insolent stupidity of the powerful. Rome, Rome is my mother country, I'm burning to be on my way.

I've been sleeping for the past EIGHT DAYS WITH THE OLD PASSION; as MISS D.[1] is more natural, she pleases me more than all I'm leaving here. The face of Mme. la Comtesse Cl.[2] pleased me greatly yesterday. Her eyes are full of candor.

Here's the state of my finances: 200 francs at Longueville's, 600 at Turretin's, 800 at Oberkampf's.

I'm going to try to travel WITH THE SUM OF Longueville and to arrive IN *Italia* WITH THAT OF Turretin.

[1]Both "Miss D." and "the old passion" probably designate Mélanie Guilbert.
[2]Comtesse Curial, daughter of Mme. Beugnot, and Beyle's mistress a decade later.

I've found pleasure in working since May 10 on the Haydn affair, which is going to cost me 1,500 francs at Pierre's.[1]

[1]The printer Pierre Didot. Beyle's first book, which he signed by the pseudonym Louis-Alexandre-César Bombet, was published at his own expense, cost him 1,790 francs for an edition of 1,000 copies and had almost no sale. It appeared in January 1815 under the unwieldy title (shortened in later editions) of *Lettres écrites de Vienne en Autriche, sur le célèbre compositeur Haydn, suivies d'une vie de Mozart, et de considérations sur Métastase et l'état présent de la musique en France et en Italie.*

Index

THE NORTON LIBRARY